George III & Queen Charlotte

PATRONAGE, COLLECTING AND COURT TASTE

GEORGE III

QUEEN CHARLOTTE

PATRONAGE, COLLECTING
AND COURT TASTE

EDITED BY

Jane Roberts

ROYAL COLLECTION PUBLICATIONS

This publication has been generously
supported by Deutsche Bank AG.

Deutsche Bank ◩

Published by
Royal Collection Enterprises Ltd
St James's Palace, London SW1A 1JR

For a complete catalogue of current publications, please write to
the address above, or visit our website on www.royal.gov.uk

127423 (p/b)
127431 (h/b)

ISBN (p/b) 1 902163 87 7
ISBN (h/b) 1 902163 73 7

British Library Cataloguing in Publication Data:
A catalogue record for this book is available from the British Library.

Designed by Philip Lewis
Produced by Book Production Consultants plc, Cambridge
Printed and bound by Conti Tipocolor, Italy

All works reproduced are in the Royal Collection unless indicated
otherwise below. Royal Collection Enterprises are grateful for permission
to reproduce the following:

fig. 1 Guildhall Library, Corporation of London; fig. 13 photograph by
Harland Walshaw; fig. 14 Crown copyright: Historic Royal Palaces; fig. 17
By permission of the British Library; fig. 22 Science Museum/Science and
Society Picture Library; fig. 26 The City of Westminster Archives Centre;
fig. 27 By courtesy of the Trustees of Sir John Soane's Museum.

Every effort has been made to contact copyright holders of material
reproduced in this publication. Any omissions are inadvertent, and will
be corrected in future editions if notification of the amended credit is
sent to the publisher in writing.

FRONTISPIECE: P. Martini after P. Ramberg, *Portraits of their Majesty's . . .
[at] the Royal Academy, 1788* (detail; see fig. 20 on p. 158)
PAGE 6: Jean-Etienne Liotard, *George, Prince of Wales (later George III)*,
1754 (no. 1)

CONTENTS

CLARENCE HOUSE

More than thirty years ago I was invited to write the foreword for John Brooke's new biography of King George III, which set out to redress the prevailing and simplistic view of him as the 'Mad King' or the King who lost America. Ambitiously perhaps, Mr Brooke staked a claim for George III to be considered as 'the most cultured monarch ever to sit on the throne of Great Britain', and in doing so, opened many people's eyes to the extraordinarily diverse achievements of this much-maligned monarch.

Brought up as most people then were on the stereotyped view of George III, I myself only gradually came to appreciate the full extent of the King's achievements. In the sixty years of his reign he immersed himself in a tremendous range of practical, scientific and artistic interests including agriculture, astronomy, architecture, horology and the collecting of books, medals, paintings and drawings. His absorption with architecture and his skill as an architectural draughtsman I found particularly stimulating and appealing, while his creation of the King's Library and his wish to give encouragement to artists by founding the Royal Academy have been of lasting benefit to the cultural life of this country.

In 1974, shortly after the publication of Mr Brooke's biography, an exhibition devoted to the King's achievements as collector and patron was mounted in the original Queen's Gallery. This was the first exhibition of its kind and contributed significantly to the study of eighteenth-century decorative arts in the Royal Collection. In the intervening quarter century a great deal of new research has been carried out. The present exhibition, drawn entirely from the Royal Collection and shown in the new Queen's Gallery, sets out to cover fresh ground and to embrace not only the King's interests, but also those of Queen Charlotte, whose important contributions to the Royal Collection and to the encouragement of female accomplishments have not always been adequately recognised.

This new exhibition attempts to cover as wide a range of the King's and Queen's interests as possible and, in so doing, to bring before the public some of the most remarkable and beautiful treasures from the Royal Collection.

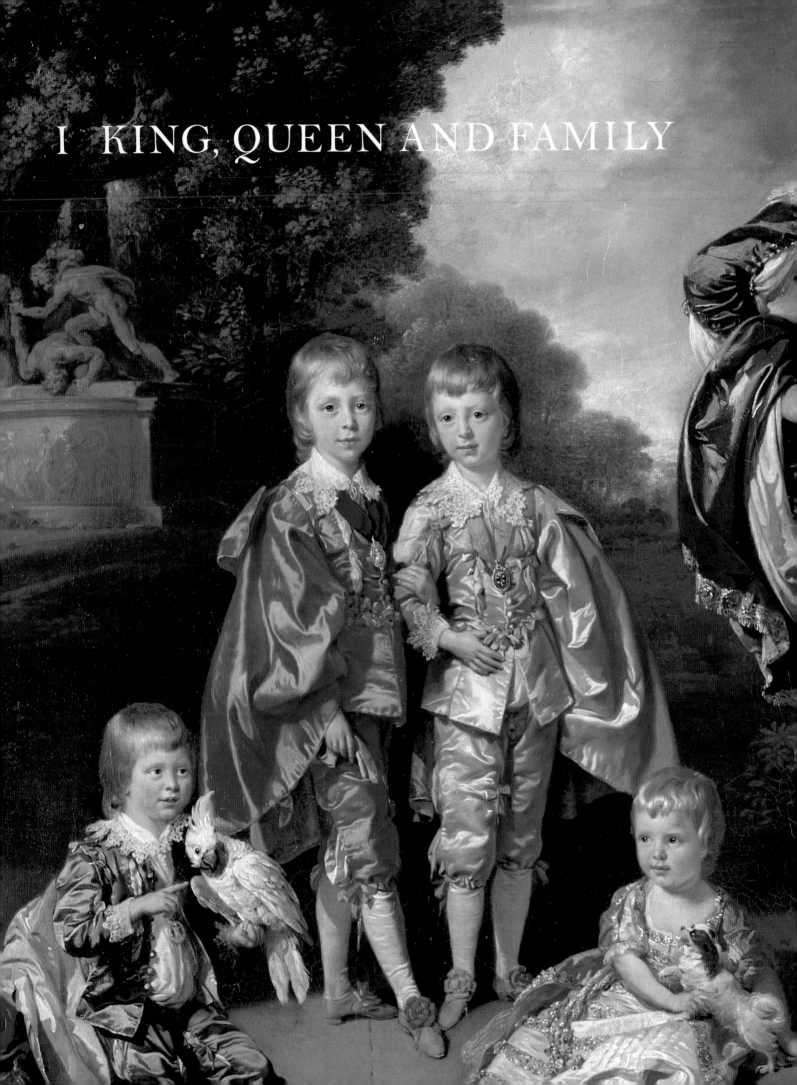

I

'No British monarch has ascended the throne with so many
advantages as George the Third.'

(HORACE WALPOLE, *Memoirs of the Reign of George III*)

THE REIGN OF GEORGE III was one of the longest in British history; it was
also one of the most significant, occurring at a time when the modern world
began to take shape. Acceding to the throne in 1760, aged 22, the King reigned
for nearly sixty years, dying in 1820 after an extensive period of debilitating illness.
Dogged at the outset by suspicion and often outright hostility, George III had by the
1780s gradually won the respect of his people and was the first of the Hanoverian
monarchs to achieve popularity.

George III presided over momentous events at home and abroad, extending from
the Seven Years War in the middle of the eighteenth century to the Napoleonic Wars
at the beginning of the nineteenth – a period that witnessed the War of American
Independence on the other side of the Atlantic, the establishment of the British Empire
in India, and the French Revolution across the English Channel. At the same time,
expansion of the economy, growth of radicalism, clamour for religious toleration,
spread of protest and stirrings of social reform coloured the domestic situation.

Amidst all this change, throughout his reign George III displayed an intellectual
integrity and a moral probity that were an example to the nation. These attributes,
when combined with his steadfastness of purpose and the sincerity of his patriotism,
eventually gained widespread recognition as admirable qualities for a time of such
upheaval, when many of the other European monarchies were under siege. Unfortunately,
many of George III's personal characteristics and aims were misunderstood when he was
a young man. Critics and caricaturists saw the King as priggish, hypocritical, tyrannical
and parsimonious. Yet, ultimately and paradoxically, it was his own personality, as well as
his longevity, that were seen to be advantages in the fluctuating circumstances of the
reign. By the end, therefore, it was the King himself who had become the prime symbol
of national identity and thus of national unity, in the same way as Elizabeth I had for the
Tudor dynasty.

The principal manifestation of this transformation in the public response to George III
was the Golden Jubilee of the reign celebrated on 25 October 1809.[1] This involved
numerous lusty renderings of the National Anthem and 'Rule Britannia' on formal occasions, as well as a host of parades, receptions, balls, fireworks and illuminations (fig. 1).
The Golden Jubilee of 1809 was the first event of its kind ever staged and it was marked
by a widespread outburst of joy, 'in outposts of the British Empire, throughout Scotland
and Wales and in well over 650 different locations in England'.[2] Public reaction was
expressed in quasi-religious tones. On 17 October 1809 a newspaper described 'The
whole nation like one great family . . . in solemn prayer and thanksgiving, for . . . the
Father of his People.'[3]

It is a supreme irony – indeed one of almost tragic proportions – that this apotheosis of George III should have occurred at a time when illness had again incapacitated him and was very soon to overwhelm him for the last time.[4] For the rest of his reign the King was to remain immured within Windsor Castle, attended only by members of his family and by doctors. The final images of George III, blind, deaf and frail, are painfully reminiscent of the central character of *King Lear* – a play with which he was all too familiar (fig. 2).

By contrast, the State Portrait (no. 3) painted by Allan Ramsay at the time of the coronation in 1761 – one of the most widely replicated royal portraits ever made – depicts an elegant young man full of optimism and brimful with idealism. Even so sceptical an observer of the Hanoverians as Horace Walpole was sympathetic, writing in the previous year, 'His person is tall, and full of dignity; his countenance florid and good-natured; his manner is graceful and obliging: he expresses no warmth, nor resentment against

anybody; at most, coldness.'[5] As heir to the throne – following the death of his father, Frederick, Prince of Wales, in 1751 – a great deal of effort had been expended on the King's education by a series of private tutors who had taught him languages (French and German), the classics, history and some science with mathematics. He was also introduced to the doctrines of the Anglican Church, as well as to the social accomplishments associated with court life. At the age of 17 George III's life had been given a firmer sense of purpose by John Stuart, 3rd Earl of Bute (1713–92), who was already advising his mother Augusta, Princess of Wales. Bute (fig. 3) had wide-ranging intellectual interests, as well as good looks and a well-turned leg for dancing, but he was not universally liked.[6] Guided by this 'Dearest Friend', George III adumbrated his principles of kingship whereby 'the interest of my country ever shall be my first care, my own inclinations shall ever submit to it. I am born for the happiness or misery of a great nation, and consequently must often act contrary to my passions.'[7] Such statements indicate to what extent the personality of George III was linked to his ideas. There was a determination that could all too easily turn into intransigence; there was a sense of duty that could be misconstrued as inflexibility; and there was a moral strength underpinned by strict religious principles that could be misinterpreted as self-righteousness. Yet, contemporaries were conscious that the King had a sense of responsibility and that his judgement would be based on his own exacting standards. As the reign advanced and the King was forced to react to events, it was seen that he had in fact redefined the role of monarchy.

That role could now be more easily fulfilled owing to the personal identification of George III with the nation as a whole. The claims of the Stuarts and the threat of Jacobitism had receded in favour of the Hanoverians and a newly formed sense of national identity was free to emerge. Success on the battlefield or in the war at sea encouraged such self-belief, but it can also be seen in the development of cultural institutions with royal support. The court was no longer the centre of patronage. It was regarded now more as a facilitator than as an instigator; it offered social cachet and served as one of several outlets as opposed to being a fountain-head; and at the same time it became more closely integrated with society.[8]

The relationship between the monarch, his ministers and Parliament during the second half of the eighteenth century has exercised some of the most distinguished historians in a debate that has lasted for many years.[9] Few monarchs have encountered so many political changes, or so wide a range of political personalities, as George III.

FIG. 3 William Wynne Ryland after Allan Ramsay, *John Stuart, 3rd Earl of Bute*, 1763. Engraving, published by W.W. Ryland (RCIN 662399)

Some fifteen ministries came and went during his reign. It was a golden age of parliamentary politics with the redefining of political parties and an increase in the powers of oratory exemplified by Edmund Burke, Charles James Fox and Richard Brinsley Sheridan.

What emerged was that, irrespective of his personal views, George III could not determine policy although he might still influence it. This he learnt painfully over such matters as the prosecution of the War of American Independence, when he was reluctant to accept defeat. Similarly, he had to learn to tolerate politicians whom he disliked. Although he enjoyed the company of Lord North and came to admire William Pitt the Younger, the radical Charles James Fox was a different proposition.

The King's conduct in public was dictated by the moral imperatives of his life in private. The example of his parents, Frederick, Prince of Wales (d. 1751) and Augusta, Princess of Wales (d. 1772), was an important formative influence, but so too was the nature of his upbringing alongside four sisters and four brothers (fig. 4). The interests

FIG. 4 George Knapton, *The Family of Frederick, Prince of Wales*, 1751. Oil on canvas (RCIN 405741)

pursued within this close-knit family circle were distinctly cosmopolitan. Significantly, his own marriage to Princess Charlotte of Mecklenburg-Strelitz in September 1761 was followed two weeks later by the coronation – events that symbolised the fusion of public and private responsibilities in a marital partnership. The marriage resulted in the birth of fifteen children over a period of twenty years and the family remained central to the King's life and outlook. Queen Charlotte's role was a difficult one and her appearance and manner invited comment from the moment of her arrival in England. Horace Walpole was not alone in hastening to report to his friends on these matters, but it was soon evident to all – not least the caricaturists – that by the standards of the time the marriage was a success.

Queen Charlotte (fig. 5) came from a small court and a tight-knit family in northern Germany where she had led a sheltered life, but she quickly adapted to the demands that were made on her in London. It was apparent from the start that both the King and the Queen would be assiduous in carrying out formal duties such as regular attendance on court days at St James's Palace with its investitures, Drawing Rooms, levees and private audiences. Correspondingly, both cared passionately about the upbringing of their children. Above all, they had a number of shared interests: philanthropy, music, books (including novels, poetry, history, philosophy and theology read in several languages), theatre and aspects of the sciences (the King liked agriculture, horology and astronomy, the Queen botany) – as well as the fine arts, which resulted among other things in a significant expansion of the Royal Collection. The variety in the furnishing and decoration of the royal residences during the reign is a reflection of this joint appreciation and it forms the background to their lives. As a court George III's was as enlightened as any in Europe, but it did not parade its interests in public; rather it indulged in the intelligent pursuit of private passions.

The everyday life of George III and Queen Charlotte was governed by regularity, frugality and religious observance. The King kept to a routine that involved early rising and few late nights. He preferred simplicity to excess, inclined more towards asceticism than preciousness, appreciated habit more than change, and was happy to offer his equerries barley water as opposed to fortifying them with beer or wine. Riding or hunting was the King's favourite recreation during the day; music, dancing and cards during the evening. He did not cosset himself, he kept fit, and he liked the open air whatever the weather. There was, in fact, very little difference between the way George III and Queen Charlotte behaved in public and in private (figs. 6 and 7). The King, in particular, was naturally inquisitive, polite and humorous. He was not afraid to engage people in conversation and would often arrive unannounced. Public appearances were frequent, particularly out of London at Windsor Castle, when – often accompanied by their children – the King and Queen walked on the terraces, or at Kew. Such openness had its

AFFABILITY.
"Well, Friend where a'you going, Hay?_ what's your Name, hay?_ where d'ye Live, hay?_hay?

FIG. 6 James Gillray, *'Affability' (Queen Charlotte and George III)*, 1795. Engraving, published by H. Humphrey (RCIN 814399)

FIG. 7 James Gillray, '*Temperance enjoying a Frugal Meal*'
(*George III and Queen Charlotte*), 1792. Engraving, published by
H. Humphrey (RCIN 809343, no. 382)

FIG. 8 James Gillray, '*A Voluptuary under the horrors of Digestion*'
(*The Prince of Wales*), 1792. Engraving, published by
H. Humphrey (RCIN 809343, no. 383)

attendant dangers and there were two assassination attempts on the King (1786 and 1800) – both by madmen, but with the country so often on the verge of political turmoil the King frequently put himself in danger when conducting formal business such as the State Opening of Parliament. Yet the ease with which the royal family mingled in public is a marked feature of the reign.

The amount known about the personalities and conduct of George III and Queen Charlotte sets them apart from previous courts. The evidence is direct and for the most part provided by women. They record intimacies shared with the King and Queen, the tensions within the family, the surprises, the disappointments, as well as the inconveniences, the longueurs, and sometimes the frustrations or physical hardships of being in attendance. For instance, Fanny Burney (later Madame d'Arblay), the daughter of the musicologist Dr Charles Burney, was appointed Second Keeper of the Robes to Queen Charlotte in 1786. She had not only a sharp eye for detail and an ear for dialogue, but also a degree of introspection and analysis that sets her memoirs of the court apart from any other. In her account the habits, idiosyncrasies, foibles, and speech rhythms of those around her bring the court to life.

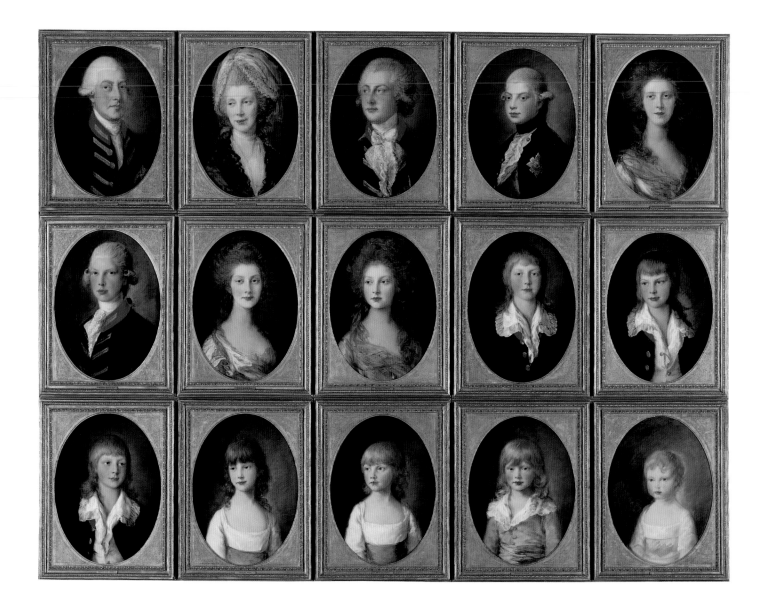

The King and the Queen each had their own separate households run by a Lord Chamberlain. The members of these households had specific duties, but they were in effect part of an extended family, particularly those involved in bringing up the children or serving as equerries and ladies-in-waiting. One, the scholarly Dr Richard Hurd, Bishop of Worcester (no. 164), whose manner appealed enormously to devout old ladies, was acknowledged as a friend after tutoring the older princes. His counterpart with respect to the princesses, Lady Charlotte Finch (no. 78), was equally loved and respected. Others, like the artistically gifted and twice-widowed Mary Delany (no. 165), benefited from the King's kindness; she was housed at his expense at Windsor where she was on hand as a universal aunt both to the royal family and to Fanny Burney. George III and Queen Charlotte, often with their children, stayed with friends when travelling – for instance, George Rose, Member of Parliament for Lymington in Hampshire, and the 2nd Earl Harcourt at Nuneham Courtenay by the River Thames near Oxford.

FIG. 9 Thomas Gainsborough, *The Royal Family*, 1782–3. Top row from left: George III, Queen Charlotte, Prince of Wales (later George IV), Prince William (later William IV), Princess Royal; middle row: Prince Edward (later Duke of Kent), Princess Augusta, Princess Elizabeth, Prince Ernest (later Duke of Cumberland), Prince Augustus (later Duke of Sussex); bottom row: Prince Adolphus (later Duke of Cambridge), Princess Mary, Princess Sophia, Prince Octavius, Prince Alfred. Oil on canvas (RCIN 401006–20)

As with all families, one of the chief causes of anxiety for George III and Queen Charlotte was the difference in outlook between the generations. From the start, the King's firm sense of morality set him apart and ran against the tenor of the times. He hoped that his standards were to be those of society in general and so it was important that members of his own family were seen to adhere to them.

George III evidently hoped that with proper management, quite apart from his personal example, his siblings – together with his own children – would comply with his wishes. This was not to be. Sexual misdemeanours were compounded by an intemperate attitude to the handling of money. Although he was fond of his children, as well as concerned for their futures, they caused him frustration and heartache; in the case of the Prince of Wales, the poor relationship between father and son had significant political repercussions. The lifestyle of George III's eldest son (fig. 8) was diametrically opposed to that of his parents and in some senses almost a reaction against it.

There were similar problems with the King's other sons, but they were less acute. Frederick, Duke of York (no. 37), allegedly the King's favourite son, pursued a rewarding career in the army; William, Duke of Clarence (no. 38), did the same in the navy for the first part of his life. Edward, Duke of Kent (no. 42), saw active service in the army in Canada and the West Indies and for a time was Governor of Gibraltar. The other three sons – Ernest, Duke of Cumberland (no. 45), Augustus, Duke of Sussex (no. 46) and Adolphus, Duke of Cambridge (no. 47) – were educated at Göttingen University. Of these, the Dukes of Cumberland and Cambridge pursued careers in the army; both were wounded on active service on the continent with the Hanoverian army. The Duke of Sussex had more intellectual pursuits.

George III's aim was to keep his sons occupied and thereby out of mischief. On the whole, it cannot be said that his plan succeeded. The King's daughters, on the other hand, were brought up on a different principle – namely that they should be kept at home and pursue interests that met with Queen Charlotte's approval. This must have been at least partly suggested by the unhappy marriages of the King's sisters. Therefore for his daughters all activities were carefully prescribed, all outings were elaborately planned, and they were chaperoned at all times. The pattern of this constricted life – based at Buckingham House, at Kew, or at Frogmore House close to Windsor Castle – was broken by occasional visits to friends (such as the Duchess of Portland, the Harcourts and Bishop Hurd) or to the West Country, usually Weymouth, for summer holidays. It is hardly surprising that the daughters themselves compared their existence to life in a nunnery. As the diarist Charles Greville wrote, 'There they were secluded from the world, mixing with few people, their passions boiling over, and ready to fall into the hands of the first man whom circumstances enabled to get at them.'[10] There were, however, advantages to such an upbringing and George III's daughters all developed skills in the arts.

The exacting standards of George III and Queen Charlotte as parents resulted in frustrations, misunderstandings and bewilderment, but theirs is a touching story – not least for the King's willingness to forgive his errant sons and unfulfilled daughters. Although George III and Queen Charlotte despaired over the Prince of Wales's weaknesses, they also in the end recognised his virtues, and for those of their children who died young – Princes Octavius and Alfred, and Princess Amelia – their sense of loss was profound.

FIG. 10 John Singleton
Copley, *The Three
Youngest Daughters
of George III (with
Windsor Castle in
the distance)*, 1785.
Oil on canvas
(RCIN 401405)

The reign of George III was a delicate balancing act between contrasting worlds: the public and the private, the official and the unofficial, and the formal and the informal. 'At one and the same time, Britons were being invited to see their monarch as unique and as typical, as ritually splendid and remorselessly prosaic, as glorious and *gemütlich* both.'[11] The dual nature of the reign is now recognised as a turning point in the history of monarchy. What emerged was a 'far more assertively nationalistic royal image, not a resurgence of royal power in political terms'.[12] Historians now argue that the innovation of George III's reign was not that he personified the country as Elizabeth I had, but rather that he identified himself with his people and they with him. This identification, which emboldened Mrs Arbuthnot on gate-crashing the King's funeral to refer to him once again as 'The Father of his people!',[13] created both a new sense of national identity and a new concept of monarchy. In short, George III was the first modern monarch.

1. George III's Golden Jubilee was celebrated after forty-nine – rather than fifty – years following ancient precedent. According to Jewish law, every seven years there was a general restitution (or jubilee), proclaimed by the sound of a trumpet. Every seventh jubilee (forty-ninth year) would be a particularly special occasion.
2. Colley 1992, p. 218.
3. Quotation from *The Day* (Colley 1984, p. 120).
4. The King's illness, a type of porphyria, has been fully discussed in Macalpine and Hunter 1969. Recent research by Professor Martin Warren (University of London) has suggested that arsenic poisoning may have precipitated the King's attacks of porphyria. Arsenic was widely used at the time both as hair powder and as a powerful medicine.
5. *Walpole Correspondence*, XXI, p. 449 (letter to Sir Horace Mann, Saturday 1 November 1760).
6. For Bute's character see Brooke 1972, pp. 46–7.
7. Quoted in Brooke 1972, p. 72.
8. See Brewer 1997, pp. 20–25.
9. Pares 1953; Butterfield 1957; Watson 1960; Brooke 1972. For a recent summary see G.M. Ditchfield, *George III: An Essay in Monarchy*, London 2002.
10. Greville 1938, I, p. 272.
11. Colley 1992, p. 232.
12. Colley 1992, p. 207.
13. *Arbuthnot Journal*, I, p. 5.

1. Portraits
Oils, pastels, drawings and prints (nos. 1–21)

1. Jean-Etienne Liotard (1702–1789)

George, Prince of Wales (later George III), 1754

Pastel on vellum. 40.6 × 29.8 cm (16″ × 11¾″)
RCIN 400897
PROVENANCE Commissioned by Augusta, Princess of Wales, 1754
LITERATURE Millar 1963, no. 581; Loche and Roethlisberger 1978, no. 177

2. Jean-Etienne Liotard (1702–1789)

Augusta, Princess of Wales, 1754

Pastel on paper. 64.8 × 51.4 cm (25½″ × 20¼″)
RCIN 400892
PROVENANCE Commissioned by Augusta, Princess of Wales, 1754
LITERATURE Millar 1963, no. 578; Loche and Roethlisberger 1978, no. 174

In 1754 Augusta, Princess of Wales, the mother of George III, commissioned a pair of portraits of herself and her late husband (Millar 1963, no. 579), and a series of portraits of herself and her nine children, from Jean-Etienne Liotard. Both sequences were to be in pastel; the portraits of the parents (including no. 2) were on paper, those of the children (including no. 1) were on vellum, and were slightly smaller in scale. In 1751 – the year of the death of Frederick, Prince of Wales (eldest son of George II) – George Knapton had completed a large family group portrait of the Princess's family (Millar 1963, no. 573). Liotard's work for the Princess was thus part of a sequence of portrait commissions placed by George III's parents.

Liotard, a portrait painter who specialised in pastels and miniatures, was a well-established and cosmopolitan figure by the time of Augusta's commission. He was born in Geneva and worked in Paris, Italy, Constantinople and Vienna. In the 1740s he had been commissioned to produce portraits of the Empress Maria-Theresa in Vienna, and then in 1749, having been introduced at the French court, portraits of Louis XV and his five daughters. The pastel portrait was extremely popular in the eighteenth century. Although it lacked the grandeur of oil painting, pastel was able to capture subtle tonal qualities, and an artist of Liotard's skill was able to exploit the capacity of this powdery medium to express the bloom of flesh.

These are surprisingly direct portraits – Liotard was known for his pared-down treatment and monochrome backgrounds which owed little to contemporary fashionable portraiture. Augusta's portrait has a particular liveliness, as though she had slipped out of a conventional, passive pose in order to make a remark. The resulting portrait gives a beguiling insight into her bearing and expression which more formal portraits rarely capture. The portrait hung as an overdoor in the King's Bed Chamber at Buckingham House, balanced by the (posthumous) companion portrait of Frederick, Prince of Wales (Millar 1963, no. 579; see Russell 1987, pp. 529–30). After Horace Walpole's visit in the early 1780s he commented on no. 2: 'extremely like, but the body very flat' (Walpole 1928, p. 79).

The portrait of the 16-year-old Prince of Wales has a similar subtlety. However, the exposure to light it has sustained over 250 years of continuously hanging, either in London or in Windsor, has caused fading of the fugitive pigment which Liotard used for the Prince's coat, which would have been a bright red; compare the colours in Bone's copy of Liotard's damaged enamel, made for the Prince Regent in 1815 (no. 22). In contrast the pigments used for the blue of the Garter sash, and for the face, remain strong. The same fugitive pigment, which was probably the cochineal-based substance carmine lake, seems also to have been used for the buttons on the Princess's dress, and for her jewelled tiara. According to Horace Walpole, George III had planned to hang the portraits of his brothers and sisters in the Dining Room at Buckingham House, but changed his mind on learning of the secret marriages of two of his brothers in the early 1770s (Walpole 1928, p. 79).

1

2

3. Allan Ramsay (1713–1784)

George III, 1761–2

Oil on canvas. 248.9 × 162.6 cm (8′ 1¹⁵⁄₁₆″ × 5′ 4¹⁄₁₆″)
RCIN 405307
PROVENANCE Commissioned by George III
LITERATURE Millar 1969, no. 996; Smart 1992, pp. 161–7;
Simon 1994, pp. 451–5; Smart and Ingamells 1999, pp. 111–21

This is one of the prime versions of Ramsay's State Portrait of George III in coronation robes. His coronation took place on 22 September 1761. The Scottish artist had already painted the sitter as Prince of Wales in 1758 for John Stuart, 3rd Earl of Bute, Ramsay's most important patron in London and George III's tutor and mentor. The success of that portrait and of a portrait of Bute (both Mount Stuart, Isle of Bute), led to this major commission. Ramsay wrote in 1766: 'I painted, from the life, a whole length picture of him for Hanover, a profile for the coinage, and another whole length which after the Coronation, I, by his Majesties orders dressed in Coronation robes. Soon after her Majesty's arrival, she likewise did me the honour to sit to me; and these two pictures in coronation robes are the originals from which all the copies ordered by the Lord Chamberlain are painted.' In December 1761 Ramsay reported to Lord Bute that he was

also working on a version in coronation robes for Hanover and one for Lord Bute (Mount Stuart, Isle of Bute). Walpole recorded seeing the painting (presumably no. 3) in March 1762, 'painted exactly from the very robes which the king wore at his coronation'.

Through an error John Shackleton (who died in 1767) was reappointed to the post of Principal Painter in Ordinary to George III on the King's accession. Ramsay, however, was given the title 'one of His Majesty's Principal Painters in Ordinary' and assumed the duties of the King's painter. His studio in Soho Square was described as being 'crowded with portraits of His Majesty in every stage of their operation'. The demand for versions of these official State Portraits was immense, from members of the royal family, sovereigns, heads of state, colonial governors, ambassadors, corporations, institutions and courtiers. Orders for 150 pairs, 26 of the King alone, 9 of the Queen alone, are listed. Ramsay resolved to 'give the last painting to all of them with my own hand' but employed several assistants, the best of whom were David Martin and Philip Reinagle.

Four pairs of Ramsay's full lengths are documented in the royal palaces at an early date. No. 3 and the companion portrait of the Queen (Millar 1969, no. 997) do not appear

3

in the set of *c*.1774 hanging plans of Buckingham House (see no. 115) and may previously have hung at either St James's Palace or Carlton House. One of the pairs was painted for Augusta, Princess of Wales, and framed in 1767–8 by the King's cabinet-makers John Bradburn and William France. For this exhibition no. 3 has been removed from its permanent frame (dating from the 1830s) set into the wall of the State Dining Room at Buckingham Palace; it has been placed temporarily in a frame supplied by Bradburn and France for another painting.

The elegant pose emphasises both the dignity and the reticence of the young King. Ramsay's debt to contemporary French art is evident, particularly to Jean-Marc Nattier and Louis-Michel van Loo. In the latter's contemporary portrait of Louis XV (version London, Wallace Collection), the King is in a similar magnificent setting with columns and drapery and a comparable range of delicate pastel colours: rose red, yellow and a purple-blue. In Ramsay's painting of George III the face is confidently created using grey underpainting, the flesh is enlivened by small touches of vermilion and the thickness and texture of the robes are brilliantly suggested, including the reflected light on the ermine. This successful combination of graceful and majestic was followed by other commissions from the royal family. The strength of Ramsay's position in the King's household is illustrated by George III's refusal of Lord Eglinton's request that he sit to Ramsay's younger rival Reynolds, with the words: 'Mr Ramsay is my painter, my Lord.'

4. Johan Zoffany (1733–1810)

Queen Charlotte with her two eldest sons, c.1765

Oil on canvas, 112.2 × 128.3 cm (3′ 8¹⁄₁₆″ × 4′ 2½″)
RCIN 400146
PROVENANCE Presumably commissioned by George III or Queen Charlotte, but first recorded in the possession of the Prince of Wales, 1794
LITERATURE Millar 1969, no. 1199; Webster 1976, no. 25, pp. 33–4

Queen Charlotte is seen here with the future George IV and Frederick, Duke of York, four years after her arrival in England and her marriage to George III. In September 1761 Horace Walpole had written of the 17-year-old Queen: 'She is not tall nor a beauty; pale and very thin, but looks sensible and is genteel. Her hair is darkish and fine: her forehead low,

her nose very well, except the nostrils spreading too wide; her mouth has the same fault, but her teeth are good. She talks a good deal, and French tolerably; possesses herself, is frank, but with great respect to the King' (*Walpole Correspondence*, XXI, p. 529). This description accords well with early miniatures of the Queen (for instance, nos. 28, 29) and also with her likeness in the present portrait. The start of work on this painting can be dated to shortly after September 1764 when the royal governess, Lady Charlotte Finch (probably seen reflected in the mirror in the further room; see no. 78), recorded the order and arrival of the fancy dresses of Telemachus for the 2-year-old Prince of Wales, the helmet decorated with his feathers, and a Turk's uniform for the 1-year-old Prince Frederick.

The setting is a ground-floor room on the garden (west) front of Buckingham House. The Queen's Apartments were in fact on the first floor (see nos. 112–16) rather than the ground floor, the site of the King's rooms. Zoffany shows the Queen surrounded by some of her finest possessions. The longcase clock with movement by Ferdinand Berthoud and case by Charles Cressent is still in the Royal Collection (no. 298); the table in the room beyond was also included in the portrait of the King (no. 8). The rich lace toilet-table cover was supplied in 1762 at a cost of £1,079 14s, on a table supplied by William Vile. The silver-gilt toilet service, almost certainly made in Augsburg, may have been brought to England by the Queen. (See also no. 382 and Walton 1975.) The pictures appear to be in the 'carved gilt frames in modern & elegant taste' associated with those recently acquired by the King from Consul Smith (see no. 148). The Queen's taste for the exotic can be seen in the chinoiserie figures (on the table behind her), the costumes of the princes, and the scene from the adventures of Odysseus or Aeneas in the painting above the door. The suggestion of a mythical world is wittily taken up by the play on the reflections in the mirrors. Telemachus, the son of Odysseus and Penelope, was renowned for being a dutiful son. The weapons with which the princes play may allude to their future duties in the outside world, but here, like the dog (a boar-hound), the princes concentrate on showing loyalty to their mother in this private world – which we can see only partly in reflections, like the faces of the Queen and Lady Charlotte.

The German artist Johan Zoffany arrived in London in 1760 and soon established a reputation for informal conversation

4

pieces in which accurate and lively portraits were set in surroundings showing the sitters' taste and circumstances. John Stuart, 3rd Earl of Bute, commissioned portraits of his children from Zoffany c.1763–4 and probably introduced the artist to the King and Queen. This was possibly the first of Zoffany's twenty-one royal commissions, seventeen of which are still in the Collection. The King nominated Zoffany to the new Royal Academy in 1769. He remained in favour for a further ten years, but after the unfavourable reception of *The Tribuna* (no. 161) was supplanted by other, younger artists.

5. Francis Cotes (1726–1770)

Queen Charlotte and the Princess Royal, 1767

Pastel on vellum. 97.5 × 84.4 cm (38⅜″ × 33¼″)
Signed and dated *F Cotes px.¹ / 1767*
RCIN 452805
PROVENANCE Presumably painted for Queen Charlotte or George III
LITERATURE Millar 1969, no. 717; Johnson 1976, no. 205

Charlotte, Princess Royal, the eldest daughter of George III and Queen Charlotte, was born in September 1766, following the births of Princes George, Frederick and William over the previous four years. The obvious pride of the young mother in her infant daughter is clear both from her pose and from

5

It is a measure of George III's fondness for this pastel that soon after its completion it hung in his bedchamber at Buckingham House; the Carracci painting hung in the adjoining Closet. In 1804 or 1805 Cotes's portrait was removed to Windsor, where in 1813 it hung in the King's Closet in the private apartments.

6. Francis Cotes (1726–1770)

Princess Louisa and Princess Caroline, 1767

Oil on canvas. 265.0 × 185.9 cm (8′ 8⅓″ × 6′ 1³⁄₁₆″)
Signed and dated *F Cotes. pxt 1767*
RCIN 404334
PROVENANCE Commissioned by Augusta, Princess of Wales
LITERATURE Millar 1969, no. 720; Johnson 1976, no. 220 and pp. 33–7

The affection between George III's two youngest sisters is reflected in this portrait, which was commissioned by their mother, Augusta, Princess of Wales. The painting shows the 17-year-old Princess Louisa, who was to die unmarried at the age of 19, seated beside a music stand. With her left hand she holds a guitern (an early form of the guitar); her right hand rests on a musical score. The younger Princess, 16-year-old Caroline, stands next to her sister with one hand resting on the back of the chair and the other holding a roll of music; a chamber organ is shown to her left. The portrait was commissioned shortly before Caroline's marriage to her first cousin, Christian VII, and her departure for Denmark in October 1766. She sat to Francis Cotes for two pastel portraits (Palace of Frederiksborg, Denmark, and collection of the Prince of Hanover) while she was still in England; these were to serve as the model for this image which was completed after her departure.

The bridegroom's father, Frederick V of Denmark (who in 1743 married George II's daughter, Princess Louisa; she died in 1751), had originally proposed that Christian should marry Princess Louisa; however her bad health prevented the match and the younger sister was instead chosen. The marriage took place in October (by proxy, in London) and November (in person, in Denmark) 1766, following Christian VII's accession to the throne (on his father's death) in January of the same year. Christian VII was entertained in state during his visit to England in September 1768. However, he was volatile and weak and Caroline eventually embarked on an affair which was to involve her in national

the fact that in 1767 two copies were commissioned: one in pastel for the Queen's Lady of the Bedchamber, the Countess (later Duchess) of Northumberland; and the second an enlargement in oil (Millar 1969, no. 718; Johnson 1976, nos. 206 and 215).

Francis Cotes made his name as a painter of pastel portraits, and was technically unsurpassed. In contrast to Liotard's pared-down approach (see nos. 1, 2) Cotes frequently resorted to classical allusion. In this portrait Cotes was probably influenced by Annibale Carracci's '*Il Silenzio*' (no. 156), which had been bought in Italy the previous year by the King's Librarian, Richard Dalton. The pose of the Madonna, who holds a protective arm around the Christ Child as she holds up a finger in order to silence the infant St John, is echoed by Queen Charlotte; however, as her gaze is directed out of the picture rather than towards the child, it is the spectator who is asked to be silent in order not to disturb the sleeping child. In his catalogue for the exhibition held at the Society of Artists in 1767, in which Cotes's pastel was included, Horace Walpole noted: 'The Queen, fine; the Child, incomparable. . . . The Sleeping Child is equal to Guido . . .'.

6

7

politics. The discovery of her relationship led to her downfall and divorce (in 1772), as well as the execution of her lover, the King's physician Johann Struensee. She was permitted to leave Denmark in 1772, although without her two children, and George III arranged for her to live at Celle in Lower Saxony, where she died two-and-a-half years later, at the age of 24. Christian VII's own mental derangement led to the establishment of a regency – under his and Caroline's only son, the future Frederick VI – in 1784.

A founder-member of the Royal Academy (see no. 159), Francis Cotes made extensive use of pastels, which may explain the delicacy of handling in his oil paintings. His style was closer to that of Allan Ramsay (see no. 3) than to that of Joshua Reynolds, and thus his paintings were more to the taste of the royal family. This is one of his finest oil paintings,

combining regal portraiture with bravura handling and psychological insight. It hangs in its original carved tabernacle frame, one of a pair supplied in 1768 by John Bradburn for £125 19s. The music table in the portrait may well be by the same maker.

7. Johan Zoffany (1733–1810)

George III, Queen Charlotte and their six eldest children, 1770

Oil on canvas. 104.9 × 127.4 cm (3′ 5⁵⁄₁₆″ × 4′ 2³⁄₁₆″)
RCIN 400501
PROVENANCE Presumably commissioned by George III or Queen Charlotte
LITERATURE Millar 1969, no. 1201 and pp. ix–xv; Webster 1976, no. 61; Ribeiro 1995, p. 208

In this family group, the costumes are based on those in paintings by Sir Anthony Van Dyck; such historicising dress had been fashionable since the 1740s. In the 1760s the King had brought many of his finest Van Dycks to Buckingham House and in 1765 he purchased the *Five eldest children of Charles I* (no. 155). Zoffany's portrait shows the King in a blue 'Van Dyke' suit trimmed with silver braid and bows, and the Queen in a white dress recalling those worn by Queen Henrietta Maria in Van Dyck's portraits. The poses and costumes of the two eldest Princes – George, Prince of Wales, wearing the riband of the Garter like his father; and Frederick, later Duke of York, wearing the riband of the Bath – are taken from Van Dyck's *George Villiers, 2nd Duke of Buckingham, and Lord Francis Villiers* (Millar 1963, no. 153). In Zoffany's earlier painting of the Princes (Millar 1969, no. 1200), they play in the Warm Room of the Queen's Apartments beneath this same Van Dyck painting. When no. 7 was exhibited at the Royal Academy in 1771, Horace Walpole's comment was 'in Vandyck dresses, ridiculous'.

This painting probably dates from early in 1770. Prince William, seated on the far left playing with a cockatoo, wears the riband of the Thistle; he was made a Knight of this Order on 5 April 1770 and the riband may have been added after the rest of the painting was completed. Prince Edward, later Duke of Kent, plays with a spaniel. The Princess Royal stands beside the Queen holding the hand of Princess Augusta, who has a teething coral in her other hand. The scene probably pre-dates the birth of Princess Elizabeth on 22 May 1770.

Pentimenti indicate that as Zoffany worked on the composition he replaced the liveliness and spontaneity of the figures, apparent in the preparatory sketch (Millar 1969, no. 1202), with the more static and formal figures seen in the finished work. Not only the costumes but the columns, the drapery, the way in which the Queen holds her child, and the inclusion of the crown, orb and sceptre on the table, are all reminiscent of Van Dyck's 'Great Piece' – *Charles I and Henrietta Maria with their two eldest children* (Millar 1963, no. 150). Zoffany has combined the eighteenth-century conversation piece with formal royal family portraiture in a way that can be traced back to *The family of Henry VIII* by a follower of Holbein (Millar 1963, no. 43). Here the Hanoverian dynasty is emphatically linked to its Stuart ancestry. The success of the portrait is indicated by the almost immediate production of small figure groups in biscuit porcelain (nos. 312, 313); these were closely based on those in the painting which would have been known to the modeller via Richard Earlom's engraving, issued in October 1770. The circumstances of the commission of this painting are unrecorded. It is listed in Princess Amelia's bedroom at Kew *c*.1800.

8. Johan Zoffany (1733–1810)
George III, 1771

Oil on canvas. 163.2 × 137.3 cm (5′ 4¼″ × 4′ 6¹/₁₆″)
RCIN 405072
PROVENANCE Presumably commissioned by George III or Queen Charlotte (with no. 9)
LITERATURE Millar 1969, no. 1195

This portrait, together with that of Queen Charlotte (no. 9), was painted in 1771 and exhibited at the Royal Academy in that year. Zoffany's ability to capture a likeness evidently appealed to the King's practical nature and preference for unpretentious art. (Horace Walpole's comment, on seeing the painting at the Royal Academy, was 'Very like, but most disagreeable and unmeaning figure.') Compared with that of Queen Charlotte, the portrait is uncluttered and the background remains unadorned.

These two portraits are Zoffany's most formal images of the royal family but even here the formality of dress – such as the General Officer's coat, the riband and star of the Garter and the Garter around the King's left leg – is combined with a surprisingly informal pose. Zoffany suggests that the King is alert and ready for action by the way in which his left hand is placed on his thigh in the same direction as his purposeful gaze. The King's right arm rests casually on the arm of the chair – implying that he is at ease – with the hat and sword laid aside on the table, which is also seen in no. 4. The chair was originally set at an angle to the picture plane: the first lines of brass studs are visible above the final version, which would have exaggerated the King's already complex stance. Mary Knowles embroidered a life-size copy of the painting and her embroidered self portrait (no. 457) shows her at work on a reduced copy of it.

8

9

9. Johan Zoffany (1733–1810)

Queen Charlotte, 1771

Oil on canvas. 162.9 × 137.2 cm (5′ 4⅛″ × 4′ 6″)

RCIN 405071

PROVENANCE Presumably commissioned by George III or Queen Charlotte (with no. 8)

LITERATURE Millar 1969, no. 1196

In contrast to the simplicity of costume and surroundings in the King's portrait (no. 8), Queen Charlotte is here shown wearing a fashionably laced silk dress under a black shawl, her pearl bracelets matched by a pearl necklace, earrings and the pearls that dress her hair. The pearl bracelets had been given to her by the King. The clasp of the bracelet on her right wrist is decorated with his miniature portrait by Jeremiah Meyer (see nos. 23, 442). Rich textiles surround her, the mauve drapery behind her head complementing the blue shades of her dress. The portrait was painted as a pendant to no. 8 and although it was not exhibited at the Royal Academy in 1771, both paintings were recorded on display in the Queen's Gallery at Kensington *c.*1785–90.

The flowers beside the Queen remind the viewer of her interest in botanic studies. Her pleasure in fresh flowers was recorded by Mrs Philip Lybbe Powys in 1767 after a visit to the Queen's Apartments at Buckingham House: 'tho' but in March, every room was full of roses, carnations hyacinths &c.' (*Lybbe Powys* 1899, p. 116). The jewellery in the Queen's wedding gift had been admired by Elizabeth Percy, Countess (later Duchess) of Northumberland, including 'amazing number of Pearls of a most beautiful Colour & prodigious Size' (Northumberland 1926, p. 28). Zoffany's skill at painting details and textures precisely is exemplified here by the still life of flowers and the sumptuousness of the Queen's dress with triple lace ruffs at the sleeves and lace on the dress meticulously depicted. Lace was one of the most expensive items in the royal wardrobe. The richly decorated (and carefully delineated) table and chair, probably of French manufacture, contrast markedly with the more sober and robust pieces in the King's portrait. In both cases it is likely that Zoffany has recorded actual pieces, but none of them appears to have survived.

10. Johan Zoffany (1733–1810)

Queen Charlotte with members of her family, 1771–2

Oil on canvas. 105.2 × 127.0 cm (3′ 5⁷⁄₁₆″ × 4′ 2″)

RCIN 401004

PROVENANCE Presumably painted for Queen Charlotte, possibly as a gift for her brother, Prince Ernest of Mecklenburg-Strelitz; first recorded in the Royal Collection, 1862

LITERATURE Millar 1969, no. 1207

This painting was probably commissioned by Queen Charlotte and must have been completed before Zoffany's departure for Florence in 1772 to paint *The Tribuna* (no. 161). Seated on a rustic bench, perhaps at Richmond or Kew, the Queen restrains Prince William, who wears the star of the Thistle. At the Queen's knees stands the Princess Royal holding a doll. The portraits of these children, particularly that of the Princess Royal, are very close to those in the slightly earlier *George III, Queen Charlotte and their six eldest children* (no. 7) and the same drawings may have been used for both paintings. Lady Charlotte Finch (see no. 78), Governess in Ordinary to the royal children until 1792, holds a baby who may be Princess Elizabeth (born 1770), or – possibly more likely (see below) – Prince Ernest (born 1771). The Queen's brother, Prince Charles of Mecklenburg-Strelitz, is on the far left, wearing the riband and star of St Andrew of Russia. He paid a rare visit to England in 1771 and was with the royal family at Richmond in August of that year. He was the Queen's favourite confidant, to whom she wrote throughout her life. He succeeded his elder brother, Adolphus Frederick IV, as Duke of Mecklenburg-Strelitz in 1794. Matching Prince Charles on the right is Queen Charlotte's third brother, Prince Ernest, wearing the riband and star of the White Eagle of Poland. He was in England for a longer period, leaving in spring 1772. Zoffany's three-quarter length of the Prince, painted in that year (Millar 1969, no. 1208), was exhibited at the Royal Academy in 1773 at the same time as no. 10. In July 1771 he had stood godfather in person to his namesake, the Queen's eighth child, Prince Ernest, later Duke of Cumberland and King of Hanover. Against the background of a country retreat she loved, the Queen is surrounded by the brothers for whom she felt such deep affection, her more immediate family, and Lady Charlotte Finch, who was her intimate friend. It is possible that the group was painted as a gift to Prince Ernest, as a memento of his godson and namesake and of his stay in England in 1771–2.

10

11. Thomas Gainsborough (1727–1788)

Queen Charlotte, 1781

Oil on canvas. 238.8 × 158.7 cm (7′ 10¹⁄₁₆″ × 5′ 2½″)
RCIN 401407
PROVENANCE Commissioned by George III
LITERATURE Millar 1969, no. 775; Lloyd (C.) 1994, no. 16

When this portrait was exhibited with that of the King
(Millar 1969, no. 13) at the Royal Academy in 1781, Sir
Henry Bate-Dudley praised it as 'the only happy likeness
we ever saw pourtrayed of her Majesty'. Gainsborough had
already received commissions from the King's brothers
but the exhibition of these major full lengths proved his
pre-eminence as unofficial court painter, 'the Apollo of the
Palace'. A portrait of Prince William, painted in the same
year, was followed by the set of fifteen ovals of the royal

11

family in 1782 (fig. 9). Queen Charlotte also owned the
famous portrait of Carl Friedrich Abel (San Marino,
Huntington Library and Art Gallery) and twenty-two
Gainsborough drawings which were all sold in 1819.

Reynolds commented on Gainsborough's practice of
'forming all the parts of the picture together'. Here all
the parts have a suggestive delicacy. The Queen's dress
of gold-spangled silk net over white silk, punctuated by
tasselled bunches of gold lace, dominates the painting. Its
intangible gauze-like effect is echoed by the flowers in the
Queen's powdered hair and in the foliage and sky in the
landscape beyond. Famous for capturing an exact likeness,
Gainsborough gives the Queen's unremarkable features
latent gaiety and animation as she moves into the light, her
dog in step with her. Her regal bearing is reinforced by the
height of her elaborately dressed hair, her easy control of
her hooped dress and train and the grandeur of the classical
temple behind her. James Northcote, Reynolds's pupil, also
praised the portrait: 'with what a graceful sweep she seems
to move through the picture! 'Tis actual motion, and done
with such a light airy facility . . . The drapery was done in
one night by Gainsborough and his nephew, Gainsborough
Dupont; they sat up all night, and painted it by lamplight.'
In the pendant portrait George III, in Windsor Uniform, is
in contrast more static, his figure set against two columns.
Although not State Portraits like those painted by Ramsay
in 1761 (no. 3), the two full lengths by Gainsborough have
been rightly described as 'portraits of grand informality';
they were much copied. George III hung the paintings in
the Dining Room at Buckingham House, although they
were briefly transferred to Windsor in 1804/5.

12. John Hoppner (1758?–1810)

Princess Sophia, 1785

Oil on canvas. 76.3 × 63.3 cm (30¹⁄₁₆″ × 24¹⁵⁄₁₆″)
RCIN 400168
PROVENANCE Presumably commissioned by George III and
Queen Charlotte
LITERATURE Millar 1969, no. 839; Wilson 1992, p. 135;
Neff 1995, pp. 156–7, 165, n. 5

This painting and the portrait of Princess Mary (no. 13),
together with the slightly larger portrait of Princess Amelia
(Millar 1969, no. 840), were exhibited at the Royal Academy
in 1785. The girls were respectively 8, 9 and 2 years old at

12

13

the time. The young Hoppner, whose German parents both probably held positions in the household of George III, had been recommended as 'a lad of genius' to the King, probably in the early 1770s (*Farington Diary*, II, p. 286: 2 January 1795). He was placed with John Chamberlaine, later Keeper of the King's drawings and medals (see no. 215), and also trained as a chorister at the Chapel Royal. He entered the Royal Academy Schools in 1775 and exhibited there from 1780 until 1809, showing mostly portraits and some 'fancy' pictures. The three portraits appear to have been the first of many royal commissions. Hoppner was particularly favoured by the Prince of Wales, who appointed him Principal Painter after the death of Reynolds in 1792.

The portraits of the Princesses Mary and Sophia were made as pendants and complement each other in terms of the sitters' dress and pose; they were hanging together in the King's Closet in the private apartments at Windsor in 1813, while the third of the group (of Princess Amelia) was at Kensington. According to a contemporary record, Hoppner travelled to Windsor to paint the Princesses. It has been suggested that the portrait of Sophia emulated the portrait of Miss Keppel (Oxford, Ashmolean Museum) painted in 1782 by Sir Joshua Reynolds, whom Hoppner greatly admired.

Although highly critical of his rivals' exhibits at the Royal Academy in 1785, Hoppner's own contribution did not escape unscathed. Horace Walpole described the portraits

as 'poor' in his copy of the exhibition catalogue, whilst an anonymous reviewer wrote, 'We cannot compliment the artist upon his success in portraying the lovely subjects. He has attempted a tenderness of colouring, and failed in giving that prominence to the features, which is requisite.'

Hoppner's historical reputation has suffered partly because of the supposed rivalry between him and Sir Thomas Lawrence. Both artists were made full Academicians on 4 April 1795 and two weeks later George III passed over Lawrence, his Principal Painter, to place a commission with Hoppner for a full-length portrait of the Princess of Wales in her wedding dress. However, after a quarrel with the King, Hoppner's commission was revoked and given to Gainsborough Dupont.

13. John Hoppner (1758?–1810)

Princess Mary, 1785

Oil on canvas. 76.2 × 63.3 cm (30″ × 24¹⁵⁄₁₆″)
RCIN 400167
PROVENANCE Presumably commissioned by George III and Queen Charlotte
LITERATURE Millar 1969, no. 838; Wilson 1992, pp. 41–3, 136–8

This painting belongs to the group of three portraits of George III's younger daughters painted in 1785 (see no. 12). It has been suggested that Hoppner's portrait of Princess

14

15

16

17

18

19

Mary was painted in homage to Rubens's famous painting of Susanna Fourment – *Le Chapeau de Paille* (London, National Gallery) – which enjoyed a great reputation during the later eighteenth century. The artist has deliberately portrayed the Princess – then aged 9 – as a young woman rather than a child, a distinction that he was careful to make from the beginning of his career. This would have been very apparent to visitors to the Royal Academy in 1785, where Hoppner's three portraits were exhibited with John Singleton Copley's large group portrait of the same Princesses playing in the grounds of Windsor Castle (Millar 1969, no. 712). Hoppner's anonymous criticisms of Copley's picture, printed in *The Morning Post*, appeared to be motivated by spite in the light of his own contribution, but his remarks about Copley's picture were echoed by other critics at the time. He was even more critical of Benjamin West's contribution to the Academy that year, which included two works from the series of paintings of the History of Revealed Religion, intended for the King's Chapel at Windsor. Hoppner's review criticised West for his 'particular patronage' despite the fact that he too had benefited from the King's benevolence.

14. Henry Edridge (1769–1821)

George III, 1803

Pencil and grey wash. 32.0 × 23.0 cm (12⅝″ × 9⅟₁₆″)
Signed and dated *H. Edridge, Jan.ʸ 1803*
RL 13864
PROVENANCE Commissioned by George III; acquired from Colnaghi by George IV, 5 September 1821 (16 gns.; RA GEO/28338)
LITERATURE Oppé 1950, no. 197; *Farington Diary*, V, pp. 1790, 1966

15. Henry Edridge (1769–1821)

Queen Charlotte, 1803

Pencil and grey wash. 32.1 × 22.6 cm (12⅝″ × 8⅞″)
Signed and dated *Edridge 1803*
RL 13865
PROVENANCE Commissioned by George III; probably acquired from Colnaghi by George IV, 5 September 1821 (16 gns.; RA GEO/28338)
LITERATURE Oppé 1950, no. 198

16. Henry Edridge (1769–1821)

Princess Augusta, 1802

Pencil and grey wash. 32.0 × 22.5 cm (12⅝″ × 8⅞″)

RL 13861
PROVENANCE Commissioned by George III; acquired by Queen Mary, possibly in 1924
LITERATURE Oppé 1950, no. 204

17. Henry Edridge (1769–1821)

Princess Elizabeth, 1804

Pencil and grey wash. 32.1 × 22.5 cm (12⅝″ × 8⅞″)
Signed and dated *Edridge 1804*
RL 14247
PROVENANCE Commissioned by George III; apparently presented to Lady Cathcart, 1804; bought at Robinson and Fisher, 14 November 1940, by Queen Mary
LITERATURE Oppé 1950, no. 210

18. Henry Edridge (1769–1821)

Prince Ernest, Duke of Cumberland, 1802

Pencil and grey wash. 32.3 × 22.8 cm (12¹¹⁄₁₆″ × 9″)
Signed and dated *Edridge 1802*
RL 13852
PROVENANCE Commissioned by George III
LITERATURE Oppé 1950, no. 214

19. Henry Edridge (1769–1821)

Prince Adolphus, Duke of Cambridge, 1802

Pencil and grey wash. 32.9 × 23.3 cm (12¹⁵⁄₁₆″ × 9⅛″)
Signed and dated *Edridge 1802*
RL 14246
PROVENANCE Commissioned by George III; acquired from Colnaghi by George IV, 26 November 1821 (16 gns.; RA GEO/28340)
LITERATURE Oppé 1950, no. 216

These six portraits have been selected from a large group of drawings in the Royal Collection by Henry Edridge, the prime versions of which were commissioned by George III. Several versions of the same portraits, with small variations, were made by Edridge, doubtless as a result of further royal commissions. There are six versions of portraits by Edridge of Princess Augusta and five of Princess Elizabeth in the Royal Collection.

As a young man Edridge was apprenticed to the portrait engraver William Pether (see no. 20). He later attended the Royal Academy Schools, and from 1786 he exhibited as a miniaturist at the Royal Academy (see no. 27). It is for small full-length portrait drawings that he is best known. These are as evocative of their period as are those by

Ingres of sitters in early nineteenth-century France or Rome.

In his diary the landscape painter and Royal Academician Joseph Farington records the two periods of sitting which George III, Queen Charlotte and their children granted Edridge, the first in summer 1802 and the second early in the following year. Farington records that on 20 June 1802 Edridge was at Windsor making drawings of the Princesses, 'but is obliged to wait their time & has them not to sit more than an hour in a day'. Of the later sitting, Farington noted on 25 January 1803: 'Edridge has been at Windsor 7 weeks making drawings of the Royal family. – The King sat to him on the 3 last days before His Majesty left Windsor. He had wished to sit no more, but consented on the Sunday sat on the Monday, Tuesday, & Wednesday & went to London on Thursday. – Edridge said a very strong impression of the goodness of his Majesty's disposition was made on his mind by what he saw of him.' The portraits of both the King and Queen were evidently made on the latter occasion.

The artist located the drawings of the Queen, and most of those of her daughters, at Frogmore House in the Home Park at Windsor (see nos. 136–42), where Queen Charlotte and the Princesses would spend their days, reading and drawing; Queen Charlotte described it to her brother as *mon petit Paradis Terrestre*. Frogmore House and lake are shown in the background of the Queen's portrait, whilst the Gothic Summer House, with its fretted castellations and terminal pinnacles, provides the setting for that of Princess Augusta. This sham ruin was designed by James Wyatt and the third daughter, Princess Elizabeth, for Queen Charlotte – the eighteenth century was the heyday of the construction of follies and hermitages of all kinds in the grounds of country houses. The faces of the Queen and Princesses are highly detailed and more strongly rendered than the background, creating focal points. Certain details are included to distinguish the sitters: Princess Augusta has a book within reach, as though she has just laid it aside, and wears a pendant in the form of an anchor, perhaps a naval allusion to her brother Prince William, to whom she was devoted. The portrait of Princess Elizabeth shows her with a pair of scissors in one hand and a piece of paper in another: she was evidently making her cut-out silhouettes (see nos. 79–82). Queen Charlotte wears a large portrait miniature around her neck and a smaller one on her wrist. In the undated miniature copy of the Queen's head in no. 15, by John Hopkins (Walker 1992, no. 833), the larger miniature is clearly based

on Beechey's portrait of the King, painted in 1799–1800 (see no. 26).

In contrast to these scenes of feminine leisure, George III and his sons Ernest, Duke of Cumberland, and Adolphus, Duke of Cambridge, are each depicted standing against the fortifications of Windsor Castle. The King and the Duke of Cumberland wear Windsor Uniform, a form of dress which was introduced by George III in 1779, comprising a tail coat of dark blue cloth with scarlet collar and cuffs; they also wear insignia of the Order of the Garter.

In the *Royal Residences* Pyne describes a group of these 'whole-length *portraits* in small' hanging in the Yellow Bed-Room at Frogmore: 'Upon the walls of this chamber are several drawings in that tasteful and light manner of uniting the brilliancy of coloured flesh with the freedom of the black-lead pencil, which distinguished the work of Edridge before he adapted his present rich and more elaborate manner' (Pyne 1819, I, *Frogmore*, p. 20).

20. William Pether (1738–1821) after Thomas Frye (1710–1762)

George III, 1762

Mezzotint with touches of drypoint. Platemark 62.0 × 43.0 cm (24⁷⁄₁₆″ × 16¹⁵⁄₁₆″)
RCIN 604349
PROVENANCE Probably George III
LITERATURE Chaloner Smith, III, p. 984; O'Connell 2003, no. 5.15

21. Thomas Frye (1710–1762)

Queen Charlotte, 1762

Mezzotint with drypoint. Platemark 61.4 × 43.0 cm (24³⁄₁₆″ × 16¹⁵⁄₁₆″)
RCIN 604595
PROVENANCE Probably George III
LITERATURE Chaloner Smith, II, p. 517; O'Connell 2003, no. 5.14

This fine pair of prints provides exceptional examples of the print-making industry in London in the mid-eighteenth century. The portrait of the Queen is particularly valuable for the detail with which her splendid and plentiful jewellery is depicted; Vile's jewel cabinet (no. 269) was made to house these magnificent jewels, also in 1762. Impressions of these prints, or derivations from them, circulated widely in England in the early years of the reign.

Thomas Frye was one of the most successful mezzotinters

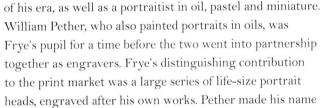

20

21

of his era, as well as a portraitist in oil, pastel and miniature. William Pether, who also painted portraits in oils, was Frye's pupil for a time before the two went into partnership together as engravers. Frye's distinguishing contribution to the print market was a large series of life-size portrait heads, engraved after his own works. Pether made his name with bravura mezzotints after paintings by Rembrandt and Joseph Wright of Derby which relied upon dramatic contrasts between areas of shadow and illumination.

Frye, who was born in Ireland, had in 1741 painted the portrait of Frederick, Prince of Wales (Millar 1963, no. 543). Over twenty years later his intention to make portraits of the young George III and Queen Charlotte took him to the theatre; this was presumably the only place where Frye could observe them and hope to secure their likenesses. It is said that the King and Queen, seeing the artist at work, obligingly turned their faces towards him, in effect granting

him an impromptu, informal sitting. The captions underneath the prints which Frye and Pether produced after these portraits attest to this immediacy, boasting that they were made *ad vivum*, from the life.

These two prints are remarkable for the delicacy with which the faces are represented. As well as the mezzotint technique, the tonal properties of which made it particularly suitable for portraiture, Frye and Pether have used drypoint for details in both portraits, a technique in which the surface of the plate is scratched directly with an etching needle in order to produce fine, delicate lines; this is particularly evident in the jewels around the Queen's neck. The velvety bloom of the ink shows that these are fine early impressions of the first state of the print, pulled before the printing surface of the copper plate became worn; it is highly probable that they were presented to the King and Queen by Frye in acknowledgement of their generosity in posing.

Miniatures (nos. 22–55)

22. Henry Bone (1755–1834) after
Jean-Etienne Liotard (1702–1789)
The Prince of Wales (later George III) in 1754, 1815

Enamel. Oval, 5.2 × 4.0 cm (2¹⁄₁₆″ × 1⁹⁄₁₆″)
Signed *HB* at right and inscribed on the back *His Majesty – Painted for the Prince / Regent by Hʸ Bone / R.A. Enamel painter / to His Majesty and / the Prince Regent / after an Enamel / by Leotard. / London Decʳ / 1815*
RCIN 421346
PROVENANCE Commissioned by the future George IV (35 gns.; Rundell, Bridge and Rundell's accounts for 14 December 1818; RA GEO/25944)
LITERATURE Walker 1992, no. 743

Bone's copy of Liotard's enamel is a valuable record of the damaged original, already described as 'badly broken' in 1877 (Walker 1992, no. 729). Another enamel version by Liotard, with differences only in dress, is in the Dutch Royal Collection (Schaffers-Bodenhausen and Tiethoff-Spliethoff 1993, no. 193); it is signed and dated 1754. Both of Liotard's enamels can be closely linked to the set of pastels commissioned by Augusta, Princess of Wales, from Liotard in 1754, which includes a similar image of the young George III (no. 1), but with differences in dress. The colour of the coat in the pastel portrait has faded from the original red to cream; it may once have been close to that seen here.

Bone was born in Truro in Cornwall, and began his career as a painter on hard paste china. In about 1779 he moved to London, where he established himself as the outstanding enamellist of his day, at the head of a family of miniaturists extending through his children to his grandchildren (Walker 1999, pp. 305–8). He was principally a copyist and his large-scale enamels were based on paintings by leading artists such as Reynolds, Lawrence, Hoppner and Opie, as well as some Old Masters and sets of historical portraits. Immensely prolific, Bone exhibited over 240 items at the Royal Academy between 1781 and 1832, when his eyes began to fail. Many of his enamels were elaborately framed, particularly those he made for the future George IV by whom he was appointed Enamel Painter in 1801, before holding the same position to George III (1809). Bone's preparatory drawing for the present enamel is in the National Portrait Gallery (Walker 1999, no. 215).

23. Jeremiah Meyer (1735–1789)
George III, 1767

Enamel. Oval, 5.2 × 4.4 cm (2¹⁄₁₆″ × 1¾″)
Signed and dated in monogram lower left *JM 67*
RCIN 421851
PROVENANCE Probably George III; certainly identifiable in the Royal Collection, 1877
LITERATURE Walker 1992, no. 251; Pointon 2001, pp. 58–9

Meyer was the miniaturist most closely associated with George III and Queen Charlotte. Born in Tübingen in Germany, he arrived in London *c.*1749, where he was trained (1757–8) by C.F. Zincke, the leading enamellist of the first half of the eighteenth century. Two years after becoming a British citizen, in 1764 Meyer was appointed both Miniature and Enamel Painter to the King and Miniature Painter to the Queen. He was a founder-member of the Royal Academy in 1768 and is included in Zoffany's group portrait (no. 159).

Meyer's association with the royal family dates from earlier than the appointment to his official posts suggests. Indeed, the present miniature is an enlarged and later variant of the one, set in an oval of diamonds within a pearl bracelet, sent by the King in 1761 as an engagement present to Princess Charlotte of Mecklenburg-Strelitz (see Walker 1992, pp. xv–xvi and fig. 20). Queen Charlotte is subsequently shown wearing this bracelet in several of her more important portraits – by Reynolds (Millar 1969, no. 1012), Zoffany (no. 9), West (Millar 1969, no. 1139), Lawrence (London, National Gallery) and Beechey (see no. 33). Queen Victoria inherited the bracelet and is shown wearing it in *The First of May* by F.X. Winterhalter (Millar 1992, no. 827).

A reduced version of the profile head was included in the ring given by the King to the Queen on their wedding day (no. 441).

Meyer's profile portraits of the King (see also no. 444) have been associated with the coinage, although none appears to have been used on coins produced by the London mint. Meyer's profile of the King, drawn from memory, was awarded a gold medal by the Society of Artists in 1761. The profile of George III used on a pistole of 1767 for the Electorate of Brunswick-Lüneburg was based on Meyer's portrait (see Forrer 1902–30, IV, p. 56; Eimer 1998, p. 67, no. 72).

Soon after the King's recovery from illness in 1789, Meyer died of a chill caught at Kew while waiting in a newly deco-rated damp room. Mrs Papendiek recorded that the artist's widow sent all his miniatures, both finished and unfinished, to the sitters without making a charge; the Queen was so delighted that 'she liberally rewarded Mrs Meyer for her honourable conduct' (Papendiek 1887, II, pp. 52–3). In addi-tion to these miniatures, a group of Meyer's enamels was recorded at Buckingham House by Horace Walpole in 1783. His description is sufficiently detailed to be worth quoting in full: 'Six large frames, in one room, glazed on red Damask, holding a vast quantity of enamelled pictures, miniatures & Cameos, amongst which six or eight at least of Charles I^st. There are also the best of those that belonged to the late Duke of Cumberland, & the Isaac Olivers bought of Dr Meade by the late Prince; but in general, the Miniatures are much faded, having been & being, exposed to the light & Sun. There are also some modern Enamels by Meyer, & miniatures by Humphreys' (Walpole 1928, p. 79).

24. Jeremiah Meyer (1735–1789)

George III, c.1775

Watercolour on ivory. Oval, 8.6 × 7.3 cm (3⅜″ × 2⅞″)
RCIN 420184
PROVENANCE Probably George III; Princess Mary, Duchess of Gloucester (d. 1857); by whom bequeathed to Queen Victoria
LITERATURE Walker 1992, no. 252; Lloyd (C.) and Remington 1996, no. 54

In contrast with Meyer's early portraits of George III (see no. 23), the present miniature depicts the King almost full face, which not only reveals more of his character but also allows Meyer to deploy his technical skills to greater effect. The drawing of the facial features is especially fine and the modelling is also remarkably deft around the nose, mouth

and chin. Meyer's skilful use of white – one of his trademarks – is evident in the highlights, and in the wig it is combined to remarkable effect with hatching. The miniature shows George III in his late 30s, a few years after Zoffany's three-quarters-length portrait (no. 8). Some related preparatory sketches are in the Meyer album in the Ashmolean Museum, Oxford (Brown (D.) 1982, no. 1361, ff. 2–3, nos. 1–3).

As far as technique is concerned, this miniature is com-parable in quality with Meyer's slightly earlier one of the Queen (no. 31). Although sometimes described as having faded (on the basis of the appearance of the coat of the military uniform), it is perhaps more correctly described as having been left unfinished.

25. George Engleheart (1753–1829)

George III, c.1783

Watercolour on ivory. Oval, 5.8 × 4.9 cm (2⁵⁄₁₆″ × 1¹⁵⁄₁₆″)
Signed lower left with the artist's initials *GE*
RCIN 421019
PROVENANCE George, 2nd Duke of Cambridge (d. 1904); his sale Christie's, London, 10 June 1904, lot 317; bought by 'Hodgkins'; acquired by Queen Mary, 1934 (*QMB*, III, no. 233)
LITERATURE Walker 1992, no. 218

Engleheart was the son of a German plaster-modeller who lived at Kew. He attended the Royal Academy Schools in 1769 and came under the direct influence of Sir Joshua Reynolds. He exhibited portrait miniatures at the Royal Academy between 1773 and 1822 and by 1775 he had estab-lished a flourishing practice in miniature painting with an extraordinarily prolific output. Following the death in 1789 of his friend Jeremiah Meyer (see no. 23), he was appointed Miniature Painter to George III. Beyond the world of minia-ture painting he moved in literary circles and was acquainted with William Hayley, William Blake and William Cowper.

The artist painted numerous portraits of George III even before his appointment as official Miniature Painter. His fee-book, which is still in family possession, includes a separate list of royal commissions, headed 'His Majesty' (Williamson and Engleheart 1902, pp. 36–45, 85–119). George III was painted no fewer than twenty-six times by Engleheart, very often from life; no doubt Engleheart also made copies in miniature after portraits of the King by Gainsborough and Beechey. The present example, however, is not derived from a particular painting, although the pose approximates to that of the King in Gainsborough's *Royal Family* painted in 1782

22

23

24

25

26

(Millar 1969, no. 778). Judging from the appearance of the King, the date is roughly the same and so the miniature would be the product of one of the six sittings given to the artist in October and November 1783. George III wears a General's scarlet uniform with the riband and star of the Order of the Garter. The drawing is extremely precise and the crumpling of the riband adds a realistic touch.

A similar, earlier, image is also in the Royal Collection (Walker 1992, no. 217).

26. William Grimaldi (1751–1830) after Sir William Beechey (1753–1839)

George III, 1800

Watercolour on ivory. Oval, 14.3 × 12.3 cm (5⅝″ × 4¹³⁄₁₆″)
Inscribed by the artist on the vellum backing *His Majesty George III / Painted by– / Mr. W : Grimaldi, enamel & / Miniature painter to their royal / Highnesses the Duke & Duchess of York / Albemarle Street / London. 1800 / For His Royal Highness / the Prince of Wales.*
RCIN 420656
PROVENANCE Commissioned by George IV when Prince of Wales (50 gns. for the image and 16 gns. for the framing; RA GEO/26807)
LITERATURE Walker 1992, no. 811

The miniature is a pendant to no. 33; both are derived from the full-length portraits painted by Sir William Beechey for George III, who hung them at Kew; the paintings are now displayed on the Grand Staircase in Buckingham Palace (Millar 1969, nos. 658–9). Beechey's portrait of the King was most probably undertaken in 1799–1800, immediately before exhibition in the Royal Academy. The image proved to be immensely popular with copyists and there are numerous examples in miniature in the Royal Collection alone (for example, Walker 1992, nos. 169, 205, 323–4, 744–5, 812, 814). Nearly all of these are limited to head and shoulders or half-length and give no indication of the military setting of Beechey's painting. The Queen was portrayed by Edridge in 1803 wearing an oval copy of the King's head in a locket surrounded by pearls (see Walker 1992, no. 833 and no. 15). The present likeness gained an even wider currency as a stipple engraving by R.M. Meadows published by Grimaldi himself in 1804. The King wears the uniform of a General Officer with the star of the Order of the Garter. The cocked hat is decorated with a cockade on a gold stem.

Grimaldi was the son of the 7th Marquess Grimaldi and succeeded to the title in 1800. As such he had a claim to the throne of Monaco. He was appointed Miniature Painter in turn to the Duke and Duchess of York (1791), and to George IV when Prince of Wales (1806) and then King (1824); he held no official position in George III's household but his position in the Duke of York's household was mentioned in the inscriptions on the backings of both nos. 26 and 33. He was trained by his uncle Thomas Worlidge and worked for several years in Paris (1777–83), although he exhibited regularly in London.

27. Henry Edridge (1769–1821)

George III, c.1803

Watercolour on ivory. 6.6 × 4.7 cm (2⅝″ × 1⅞″)
RCIN 420185
PROVENANCE First certainly identifiable in the Royal Collection, 1910
LITERATURE Walker 1992, no. 805

Edridge achieved fame as a prolific portrait draughtsman both on paper (see nos. 14–19) and in miniature; he made relatively few paintings. This miniature is a copy of the King's head in Edridge's drawing dated January 1803 (no. 14). It is a typical example of the artist's abilities in this medium:

27

a neat rectangular format, accurate drawing, and vigorous characterisation. The Royal Collection also includes a miniature by Edridge of Edward, Duke of Kent, painted in the 1790s (Walker 1992, no. 806). See also no. 78.

28. Unknown English artist

Queen Charlotte, c.1761

Watercolour on ivory. Oval, 5.8 × 4.7 cm (2⁵⁄₁₆″ × 1⅞″)
RCIN 420786
PROVENANCE Probably George III; Princess Mary, Duchess of Gloucester (d. 1857); by whom bequeathed to Queen Victoria
LITERATURE Walker 1992, no. 325

The crown on the chair (of English design) in which the young Queen sits demonstrates that this portrait post-dates the coronation in September 1761. However, it may have been made very shortly after that event for the Queen would appear to be slightly younger in no. 28 than in no. 29, dated 1762. For Horace Walpole's description of Queen Charlotte in September 1761 see no. 4. The gold cord with jewelled crucifix here worn by the Queen may be the 'necklace with diamond cross' described by Mrs Papendiek amongst the wedding gifts from George III to Queen Charlotte (Papendiek 1887, I, p. 12). It is therefore most unlikely that this is the portrait Colonel David Graeme was given at Mirow (near Mecklenburg) in June 1761 as a gift for George III shortly

28

29

30

31

after the Princess had been nominated as a suitable bride.

A small group of images of Queen Charlotte before her arrival in London is known, including no. 392. The portrait of the young Princess, made by the King's Librarian, Richard Dalton, in Mecklenburg in August 1761, does not seem to have survived (*Walpole Correspondence*, XXI, pp. 524–5).

The artist responsible for this striking miniature of the young Queen Charlotte has so far not been identified, although some suggestions have been made – for example Francis Sykes, Samuel Finney and a Miss Todhunter. Of these, Finney was appointed Enamel and Miniature Painter to Queen Charlotte in 1763 and the little-known Todhunter exhibited an unidentified miniature of the Queen at the Free Society in 1763. At present there is not enough evidence to make a positive attribution.

29. Monogrammist J.R.

Queen Charlotte, 1762

Watercolour on ivory in a surround and loop of half-pearls. Oval, 5.4 × 4.4 cm (2⅛″ × 1¾″)
Signed and dated on left *JR / 1762*. Engraved on the back with the sitter's monogram and dated *CR 1762* surmounted by a crown
RCIN 421016
PROVENANCE First certainly identifiable in the Royal Collection, 1851
LITERATURE Walker 1992, no. 296

The liveliness and immediacy of this image, combined with its considerable charm, suggest that it is a fairly accurate *ad vivum* portrait. It accords well with Horace Walpole's description of Queen Charlotte in September 1761, in particular 'the nostrils spreading too wide' (see no. 4). A notable feature is the elaborate bejewelled head-dress and parure. A number of prints of similar date also show the Queen in profile to left, particularly the mezzotints by J.J. Haid and J. McArdell. The identification of the monogram 'JR' has not been established.

30. Ozias Humphry (1742–1810)

Queen Charlotte, 1766

Watercolour on ivory. Oval, 9.1 × 7.4 cm (3⁹⁄₁₆″ × 2¹⁵⁄₁₆″)
Signed in monogram *OH* on left and signed and dated on the original backing card *Ozias Humphry pinxt. / 1766*
RCIN 420965
PROVENANCE Probably bought by George III from the exhibition at the Society of Arts, 1767; first certainly identifiable in the Royal Collection, 1851
LITERATURE Walker 1992, no. 231

The transformation of Queen Charlotte from a young German princess to consort of George III is here readily apparent. The attributes of a book and a rose-bush refer to the Queen's personal interests in literature and botany. Similarly, the playful gesture made with the sitter's left hand twisting her string of pearls may allude to her love of jewellery. The setting of a column and curtain creates the context of formal portraiture but, even so, the image painted by Humphry remains a straightforward portrait without any allegorical intention. As such, on this occasion it equates more with the work of Francis Cotes than with that of Sir Joshua Reynolds, as is clear from a comparison with the former's depiction of the Queen in the following year (no. 5).

The miniature may have been the one exhibited by the artist at the Society of Arts in 1767, when it was described as 'painted from the life'. Horace Walpole annotated his copy of the catalogue with the comment 'not very like', which implies that the face may have been somewhat idealised. There is some evidence to suggest that the miniature was later intended for use as the frontispiece for R.J. Thornton's book *A New Illustration of the Sexual System of Linnaeus* (1797–1807), but in the end an illustration by Beechey was preferred.

Although trained in London at the St Martin's Lane Academy, Humphry became apprenticed to Samuel Collins in Bath, where he established a flourishing practice and became acquainted with Gainsborough. He moved to London in 1764, where he was equally successful, allowing for visits to Italy (1773–7) and India (1785–7). Examples of miniatures by Humphry were seen by Horace Walpole when he visited Buckingham House in 1783 (see no. 23). Humphry was appointed Portrait Painter in Crayons to George III in 1792 but, owing to failing eyesight, he did not work during the last decade of his life. The artist's papers are preserved in the Library of the Royal Academy.

31. Jeremiah Meyer (1735–1789)

Queen Charlotte, c.1772

Watercolour on ivory. Oval, 8.7 × 7.0 cm (3⁷⁄₁₆″ × 2¾″)
RCIN 420000
PROVENANCE Probably George III (but see below); Princess Mary, Duchess of Gloucester (d. 1857); by whom bequeathed to Queen Victoria
LITERATURE Walker 1992, no. 255; Lloyd (C.) and Remington 1996, no. 55

This outstanding miniature demonstrates Meyer's finest qualities. The linear precision (most evident in the use of hatching in the hair), firm structure of the face, refined colouring and smooth modelling could not be improved upon on this scale. A particular feature of Meyer's more finished miniatures is the use of opaque white highlights, with the texture of small portions of whipped cream, seen here on the lace at the neckline. The best miniatures by this artist have been compared with porcelain produced at Meissen and Nymphenburg (Winter 1948, p. 132).

Meyer depicted Queen Charlotte in miniature on numerous occasions. An unfinished variant of the present example, slightly later in date, is in the Ashmolean Museum, Oxford (Walker 1997, no. 43), where there are also relevant sketches of the Queen in the Meyer album (Brown (D.) 1982, no. 1361, ff. 3–5, nos. 3–7). It has been suggested that the miniature in the Royal Collection was commissioned by Queen Charlotte in 1772 as a gift for her sister-in-law, Frederica, the wife of her brother, Prince Charles of Mecklenburg-Strelitz; that miniature later belonged to Ernest, Duke of Cumberland, King of Hanover. Alternatively, it might be identified with the miniature exhibited by Meyer at the Royal Academy in 1775.

The lace cap was much favoured by Queen Charlotte and she is shown wearing it in paintings by Zoffany (no. 10) and Gainsborough (Millar 1969, no. 779), as well as in a drawing by H.D. Hamilton (Oppé 1950, no. 288), and a miniature by J.H. von Hurter (Walker 1992, no. 237). The portrait by Gainsborough, one of a series of ovals of members of the royal family, was often replicated in miniature (see, for example, Walker 1992, nos. 170–71, attributed to Richard Collins).

32. Edward Miles (1752–1828)

Queen Charlotte, 1794

Watercolour on ivory. Oval, 7.3 × 5.8 cm (2⅞″ × 2⁵⁄₁₆″)
RCIN 420955
PROVENANCE Probably commissioned by Queen Charlotte; first certainly identifiable in the Royal Collection, 1870
LITERATURE Walker 1992, no. 270

A sitting with 'Mr Miles' – probably in connection with this miniature – is recorded in Queen Charlotte's diary on 4 April 1794; subsequent sittings were given, presumably to the same artist, on 9, 11, 16 and 17 April. Another version of this miniature was once in the Shelley-Rolls collection (sold Christie's, London, 13 February 1962, lot 17).

32

The depiction of the Queen has an informal air, which perhaps suited the artist's style. The eyes of his sitters tend to be set wide apart so that they have a look of surprise; the hair is blowsy and the clothes seem ill-fitting. The result is a sense of breadth in the technique (particularly in the white highlights) that applies equally well to the highly coloured flesh tones which suggest that the sitters are permanently blushing. The effect of the troubles of the last few years, including the King's illness 1788–9 and the French Revolution, seems clear from a comparison between this portrait and earlier images of the Queen. Ironically, the fashion for simple, untailored necklines, worn without fine ornamentation or jewels, originated in France.

Miles came from East Anglia and was trained at the Royal Academy Schools in 1772, afterwards exhibiting at the Academy between 1775 and 1797. Appointed Miniature Painter to Frederica, Duchess of York, in 1792, he described himself in the Royal Academy catalogue for 1794 – the year of his sittings with the Queen – as 'Miniature Painter to Her Majesty'. He was widely travelled, subsequently serving as Court Painter to Tsars Paul II and Alexander I at St Petersburg (1797–1806) and then living from 1807 in Philadelphia, where he taught drawing at the Academy and died. He does not seem to have painted miniatures while in the United States.

33

33. William Grimaldi (1751–1830) after
Sir William Beechey (1753–1839)

Queen Charlotte in 1796, 1801

Watercolour on ivory. Oval, 14.5 × 12.1 cm (5¹¹⁄₁₆″ × 4¾″)
Signed and dated on the stone pedestal lower right *Grimaldi / 1801.*
Inscribed on the vellum backing *Her Majesty the / Queen. / Painted
by – / Will: Grimaldi, Enamel & Miniature / Painter to their Royal
Highnesses / the Duke & Duchess of York. / Albemarle Street 1801*
RCIN 420657
PROVENANCE Probably commissioned by George IV; first
certainly identifiable in the Royal Collection, 1870
LITERATURE Walker 1992, no. 815

Like its pendant (no. 26), this miniature is derived from the
full-length portrait by Sir William Beechey, whose portrait of
the Queen (Millar 1969, no. 659) preceded that of the King; it
was painted in 1796 and was exhibited at the Royal Academy
in the following year. As with the portrait of the King, the
image proved to be popular with copyists although there are
fewer examples of the Queen in miniature in the Royal
Collection. An anonymous copy was given by the Queen to
Princess Augusta in July 1798 (Walker 1992, no. 328); a copy
by Bone was made in the following year, and was purchased
by the Prince of Wales in 1800 (Walker 1992, no. 748).
Grimaldi (see no. 26) has here taken greater liberties with
Beechey's original composition. Seen in half-length, the

Queen is similarly dressed and the Maltese lap-dog held in her arms is retained, but the classical urn on the right replaces the view of Frogmore House depicted in the background of the painting. The black mourning veil worn over the straw hat, decorated with yellow drapes, is probably a reference to the deaths of her brother Adolphus Frederick IV, Duke of Mecklenburg-Strelitz (see no. 443), and her sister Princess Christiane, both in 1794. The urn might also have the same funerary connotation. For the significance of the pearl bracelet with a miniature set with diamonds, see no. 23.

Beechey was for many years a popular painter with the royal family. He was appointed Portrait Painter to Queen Charlotte in 1793 and was subsequently frequently patronised by George IV when Prince of Wales and by Edward, Duke of Kent. Although his work was at first much appreciated by the King, Beechey fell from favour in 1806 when he caused a widely reported outburst of royal temper which resulted in the artist fainting onto a sofa in the room of a maid of honour (*Farington Diary*, VII, p. 2786).

34. J. Jacob Miltenberg (*fl.*1776–1790) after Thomas Gainsborough (1727–1788)

The Prince of Wales (later George IV) in 1782, 1784

Enamel. Oval, 7.5 × 6.2 cm (2 $^{15}/_{16}$″ × 2 $^{7}/_{16}$″)
Signed and dated on the reverse *J.J. Miltenberg. pinxit / Londini 1784*
RCIN 421947
PROVENANCE Dhainaut collection; bought by Queen Mary, 1952
LITERATURE Walker 1992, no. 285; Lloyd (C.) 1994, no. 44

The enamel is an accurate rendering in oval of the painting by Thomas Gainsborough now at Waddesdon Manor (The National Trust, The James A. de Rothschild Collection); the painting was commissioned by the sitter in 1782 for his boon companion John Hayes St Leger (1765–1800) – 'one of ye best fellows yt. ever lived'. At the same time, the future George IV commissioned a portrait from Gainsborough of St Leger himself (Millar 1969, no. 805). The paintings are outstanding examples of Gainsborough's late style. Both portraits were exhibited at the Royal Academy in 1782 and both were engraved – the portrait of the Prince of Wales by John Raphael Smith published in April 1783, and the portrait of St Leger by Gainsborough Dupont in May 1783. However, the close correspondence of the colours suggests that Miltenberg had seen the original portrait before making this copy in 1784.

The Prince of Wales wears a uniform of his own invention, since he was not commissioned into the army by his father until 1793. He wears the star of the Order of the Garter which is repeated on the shabracque (saddle-cloth). Significantly, a similarly decorated shabracque is a feature of the companion portrait, where its inclusion was specifically requested by the Prince of Wales, who had given it to St Leger.

Miltenberg is believed to have been of Swiss origin. Not many examples of his work are known. He exhibited twice at the Royal Academy, in 1776 and 1786. His style seems to have been derived from that of C.F. Zincke and is characterised in the present example by the intensity of colour that is not found, for instance, in the earlier and more sophisticated enamels of Jean-Etienne Liotard.

35. Richard Cosway (1742–1821)

The Prince of Wales (later George IV), c.1793

Watercolour on ivory. Oval, 8.5 × 6.9 cm (3 $^{3}/_{8}$″ × 2 $^{11}/_{16}$″)
RCIN 420004
PROVENANCE Presumably commissioned by George IV; first certainly identifiable in the Royal Collection, 1851
LITERATURE Walker 1992, no. 179; Lloyd (C.) and Remington 1996, no. 59

Just as Jeremiah Meyer is the miniaturist most closely associated with George III and Queen Charlotte, so Cosway stands in the same respect to their children. Indeed, it was Cosway's success in depicting George IV's (illegal) wife, Maria Fitzherbert, in miniature that led to his appointment as Principal Painter to the Prince of Wales in 1785 – a title that he characteristically recorded in Latin (*Primarius Pictor Serenissimi Walliae Principis*). Cosway is the artist who captured the essence of George IV's flamboyant years before he became King. To a certain extent, artist and sitter were similar in character and Cosway, like his patron, was relentlessly caricatured for his egotism as well as his extravagant and eccentric ways. The portrait of the artist, shown with exaggerated pose in the right foreground of no. 159 among his fellow Royal Academicians, is a vivid representation of the man who would have been perfectly cast as Osric in *Hamlet*. At the height of his fame Cosway lived for many years in Schomberg House in Pall Mall close to Carlton House, and not far from the court at St James's. In 1786 he was also appointed Miniature Painter to the future George IV, for whom he acted as artistic adviser until he fell from

34

35

36

37

favour in 1811. Cosway was a distinguished and prodigious collector in his own right, with a profound knowledge of European art.

The Prince of Wales is here shown wearing the uniform of the 10th Light Dragoons, a regiment of which he was immensely proud to be Colonel-Commandant, from 1793 until 1820. He found the uniform particularly attractive and was depicted wearing it in two paintings by Beechey (Millar 1969, nos. 660 and 664). A further picture by George Stubbs (Millar 1969, no. 1115) commemorates the future George IV's association with the regiment, but does not include his portrait. It is possible that this miniature was undertaken to mark the Prince's appointment as Colonel-Commandant. The riband and star of the Order of the Garter are worn over the uniform, together with a white cross belt decorated with Prince of Wales's feathers.

Several miniatures of this subject are recorded in the accounts submitted by Cosway to the sitter: five in the list for May 1795, at a charge of 30 guineas each (Millar 1986, p. 587), and further examples in a list for 1799–1800, at a charge of 25 guineas (RA GEO/26460). A slightly smaller version is in the Fitzwilliam Museum, Cambridge (Bayne-Powell 1985, p. 41; Lloyd (S.) 1995, no. 128), and a copy is in the Royal Collection (Walker 1992, no. 197). No. 35 is in Cosway's mature style. It is firmly drawn with a great deal of detail in the uniform, coiffure and facial features, with a fully realised sky background.

36. Jeremiah Meyer (1735–1789)

Prince Frederick (later Duke of York), 1767

Watercolour on ivory. Oval, 5.8 × 5.0 cm (2⁵⁄₁₆″ × 1¹⁵⁄₁₆″)
RCIN 420788
PROVENANCE Probably George III; first certainly identifiable in the Royal Collection, 1844
LITERATURE Walker 1992, no. 259

This is identifiable as the miniature of Prince Frederick exhibited by Meyer at the Society of Arts in 1767, on the basis of the attribute of the bishop's crozier recorded by Horace Walpole in his annotated copy of the catalogue. The crozier is a reference to the bishopric of Osnabrück in Germany to which the sitter was appointed as secular bishop in 1764 (27 February), at the age of 6 months. The diocese of Osnabrück, close to Hanover, lay within the Holy Roman Empire. It was part Catholic and part Protestant and

the nomination lay alternately with the Catholic chapter and the House of Hanover. A Protestant bishop had no ecclesiastical functions and need not even be in holy orders, acting instead as a head of state and receiver of revenues. From the time of his appointment to the bishopric, Prince Frederick, the King's second son, received an independent income of about £20,000 per annum, much to the chagrin of the Prince of Wales. The first payment to Prince Frederick as a lump sum was made when he came of age in 1784. He relinquished the bishopric in 1803.

There is a related drawing in the Meyer album in the Ashmolean Museum, Oxford (Brown (D.) 1982, no. 1361, f. 6, no. 8). An enamel by Meyer dated 1768 with a similar pose is also in the Royal Collection (Walker 1992, no. 260). A further related miniature by Meyer, showing the sitter slightly older, is in the Walters Art Gallery, Baltimore. The miniature was subsequently engraved as the frontispiece to *Hymns for the Amusement of Children* (1771) by Christopher Smart – a slightly incongruous juxtaposition given the subsequent career of the sitter (see no. 37).

37. Richard Cosway (1742–1821)

Prince Frederick, Duke of York, 1792

Watercolour on ivory. Oval, 8.1 × 6.6 cm (3³⁄₁₆″ × 2⁵⁄₈″)
At the back a braid of dark brown hair within a surround of blue glass.
Signed and dated on the original backing card *R^dus: Cosway / R.A. / Primarius Pictor / Serenissimi Walliae / Principis / Pinxit / 1792* (and *G.P.* in another hand)
RCIN 420649
PROVENANCE First certainly identifiable in the Royal Collection, 1910
LITERATURE Walker 1992, no. 181

The miniature is in its original locket frame, the back opening to reveal the inscription (see above) and a braid of dark brown hair within a surround of blue glass.

The sitter wears the uniform of Colonel of the Coldstream Guards with the star of the Order of the Garter, the visual effect of which is enhanced by the sky background. The head is based on a drawing made by Cosway around seven years earlier (engraved by L. Sailliar in 1787), showing the Prince full length in armour and holding a crozier. Prince Frederick was appointed Colonel of the Coldstream Guards on 27 October 1784, and in the same year he reached his majority and was created Duke of York. The drawing was therefore made at a turning point in his life; it is not surprising that the artist should have reused it.

In the year before the date of this miniature, the Duke had married Frederica, the eldest daughter of Frederick William II of Prussia. He successfully commanded the Allied troops against Napoleon in the 1790s and in 1798 was appointed Commander-in-Chief in Great Britain. After disgrace following the public outcry over the sale of commissions by his mistress, Mary Anne Clarke, he was eventually reinstated to his military responsibilities, which he continued to fulfil until the time of his death in 1827.

38. Jeremiah Meyer (1735–1789)

Prince William (later William IV), c.1780

Watercolour on ivory. Oval, 5.6 × 4.6 cm (2³⁄₁₆″ × 1¹³⁄₁₆″)
RCIN 420970
PROVENANCE Presumably George III; first certainly identifiable in the Royal Collection, 1870
LITERATURE Walker 1992, no. 263; Lloyd (C.) and Remington 1996, no. 56

Prince William, the third son of George III, is shown here at the age of around 14. The composition is appropriately replete with maritime allusions. The sitter wears a midshipman's uniform decorated with the riband of the Order of the Thistle and in the background is a mast with some rigging. The young Prince had joined the Royal Navy as a midshipman on 15 June 1779, aged 13. He sailed on board the *Prince George*, a battleship of 98 guns carrying the flag of Rear-Admiral Sir Robert Digby, and participated in the Battle of St Vincent (8 January 1780). He was then on active service on the North American station, where his potential abilities and undoubted shortcomings were noted by Nelson amongst others. There was a break in his career in 1783–5 when he was sent to Hanover, but he then resumed naval duties as a Lieutenant and post-Captain until concluding his career in the navy in 1790. By this time he had achieved the rank of Rear-Admiral and in 1789 he was created Duke of Clarence. He retained a close association with the sea for the rest of his life.

The present miniature is a brilliant characterisation and the hair is a bravura passage of drawing. Two other versions are recorded: one in the Royal Collection (Walker 1992, no. 264) and another in the Brunswick-Lüneburg collection (Williamson 1914, no. 13, p. 21). Meyer submitted a bill to

38

the future George IV on 30 August 1782 for 'a Copy of H.R.H. Prince William's Picture in a Circle large size for a Snuff Box'; this may be the version on the lid of a snuff box decorated with gold anchor and sextant, exhibited in London in 1986 (see Walker 1992, no. 263).

39. Ozias Humphry (1742–1810)

Charlotte, Princess Royal, 1769

Watercolour on ivory. Oval, 11.5 × 9.5 cm (4½″ × 3¾″)
Signed in monogram *OH* on the plinth and signed and dated on the original backing card *Ozias Humphry pixᵗ. / Jan. 1769 – / Princess Royal / of England / bo: Sep: 29ᵗʰ 1766.*
RCIN 420791
PROVENANCE Presumably commissioned by Queen Charlotte; first certainly identifiable in the Royal Collection, 1851
LITERATURE Walker 1992, no. 232; Lloyd (C.) and Remington 1996, no. 53

One of the main influences on Humphry's art following his arrival in London was Sir Joshua Reynolds, who had encouraged him in the first place to take up miniature painting instead of working in oil. Humphry, however, had an ambivalent attitude to the miniature, which he felt was a rather demeaning art form, and he was often discouraged by the failure of his fellow practitioners to do more to elevate its status. His own contribution was for the main part to follow Reynolds's example by giving his sitters an air of dignity by means of pose or characterisation.

The present miniature is a fine example of this ambition in the context of children, a subject in which Reynolds himself

39

was particularly well practised. The Princess's somewhat stiff pose captures the awkwardness of a child and this is underscored by the sense of vulnerability in the facial expression, but the setting of a marble step and a classical urn denotes the adult world. The flowers – a rosebud held in the hand and passion flowers and roses strewn on the ledge – are symbols for the blossoming of life often used in depictions of children. On completion, the miniature was exhibited at the Society of Arts in 1769. For a likeness of the Princess Royal in the following year, see no. 7.

The artist stated that at first he had been dissatisfied with the portrait, but that from an early stage he had been encouraged to finish it by Queen Charlotte (Royal Academy of Arts, Ozias Humphry papers, HU/1/139). At the same time, the Queen allowed him to begin a second miniature of the Princess Royal ('only the Head finished upon a very large thick square piece of Ivory'), the present location of which is unknown. An undated (and unassigned) invoice for either no. 39 or the second miniature is in the artist's account book in the British Library (Add. MS 22948). The charge was £42 – a considerable sum of money. The rich, dark tones of Humphry's miniatures are distinctive and may be described as Titianesque.

40

feeling about his miniatures in comparison with Cosway's confections.

Another version by Engleheart is in the Wallace Collection, London (Reynolds 1980, no. 152), and yet another remains in the possession of the Engleheart family (Williamson and Engleheart 1902, p. 22). The inscription on the backing of no. 40 accords with an entry for a miniature in the artist's account book: 'The Duchess of Wertemberg, for the Duke of Sussex, October 11, 1802', later annotated 'Never paid for' (Williamson and Engleheart 1902, p. 44).

Two years after the date of Cosway's portrait, the Princess Royal married Frederick, Duke of Württemberg (King from 1806). The marriage was the subject of a merciless caricature by James Gillray entitled *The Bridal Night.*

40. George Engleheart (1753–1829) after Richard Cosway (1742–1821)

Charlotte, Princess Royal (later Queen of Württemberg), in 1795, 1802

Watercolour on ivory. Oval, 8.8 × 7.1 cm (3⁷⁄₁₆″ × 2¹³⁄₁₆″)
Signed in monogram *E* lower right and inscribed on the backing card *G. Engleheart / Pinxit / 1802*
RCIN 420650
PROVENANCE Commissioned by Prince Augustus, Duke of Sussex; his sale, Christie's, London, 24 June 1843, lot 85; bought by George Anson for Queen Victoria (£21)
LITERATURE Walker 1992, no. 221; Lloyd (C.) and Remington 1996, no. 64

Although the image is copied from a work by Richard Cosway, painted for the Prince of Wales in 1795 and now in Plymouth City Museum and Art Gallery (see Millar 1986, p. 587 and Lloyd (S.) 1995, no. 129), the style is quintessentially Engleheart's. The placement of the figure in the oval and the sky background were pioneered by Cosway, but the firm drawing, the emphasis on the eyes and, above all, the use of greys and blacks for the shadows, are highly characteristic of Engleheart. There is in general a more workmanlike

41. Jeremiah Meyer (1735–1789)

*Prince Edward (later Duke of Kent), c.*1772

Watercolour on ivory. Oval, 6.2 × 5.3 cm (2⁷⁄₁₆″ × 2¹⁄₁₆″)
RCIN 420789
PROVENANCE Probably George III; presumably George IV; Mrs Maria Fitzherbert (d. 1837); by descent to her niece, Mrs Dawson Damer; by whom presented to Queen Victoria, 1838
LITERATURE Walker 1992, no. 265

There was some confusion in the past about the identification of the sitter in this miniature. The fact that it once belonged to Mrs Fitzherbert would indeed suggest a connection with George IV. However, Queen Victoria was in no doubt that it was a likeness of her father, Edward, Duke of Kent, and an engraved inscription on the reverse of the original locket reads: 'Miniature of My Father when a child, which belonged to the late Mrs Fitzherbert; given me by Mrs Dawson Damer, 1838. VR'. Its acquisition is also mentioned twice in Queen Victoria's journal (18 March and 5 November 1838). The association of Queen Victoria with Meyer's depiction of the children of George III and Queen Charlotte is of interest because of her important commission to Sir William Charles Ross for a set of miniatures of her own children.

Prince Edward, the fourth son of George III, appears to be a year or two older in this miniature than in Zoffany's group portrait of 1770 (no. 7). He was born in November 1767 so the miniature may have been painted in 1771 or 1772. Conceivably it was one of those seen by Horace Walpole when he visited Buckingham House in 1783 (see no. 23).

42. Unknown English artist after Richard Cosway (1742–1821)

Prince Edward (later Duke of Kent), 1790

Watercolour on ivory. Oval, 8.5 × 6.8 cm (3⅜″ × 2¹¹/₁₆″)
RCIN 420930
PROVENANCE Sir Frederick Lamb; by whom given to Queen Victoria, 1838
LITERATURE Walker 1992, no. 200

Prince Edward had a long but rather inglorious career in the army. Trained as a cadet in the Hanoverian Guard at Lüneburg, he was gazetted Brevet-Colonel in 1786. The uniform shown in this miniature is Hanoverian, for which the generous white turnback became regulation in 1787. After leaving Germany, Prince Edward was sent in fairly quick succession to Geneva, London, Gibraltar, Canada, the West Indies (where he distinguished himself on active service), and once more in 1802 to Gibraltar for a short stint as Governor. These movements have a bearing on the date of this miniature which, if painted in London, can only have been executed in January 1790. The quality falls below Cosway's normal fluency and it is in all probability a copy, perhaps by the artist's wife Maria. Other versions are known (for example, in the Dutch Royal Collection: Schaffers-Bodenhausen and Tiethoff-Spliethoff 1993, no. 196; and in the collection of the Duke of Württemberg at Schloss Altshausen), but none so far has been claimed as the prime version.

Prince Edward was created Duke of Kent in April 1799. In 1818 he married the Dowager Princess of Leiningen (*née* Princess Victoria of Saxe-Coburg-Saalfeld); their only child, the future Queen Victoria, was born in the following year, but the Duke died in January 1820, when the Princess was only 8 months old.

43. Unknown English artist after Sir William Beechey (1753–1839)

Princess Augusta, 1802

Watercolour on ivory. Oval, 9.0 × 7.3 cm (3⁹/₁₆″ × 2⅞″)
RCIN 420969
PROVENANCE First certainly identifiable in the Royal Collection, 1870
LITERATURE Walker 1992, no. 335

Princess Augusta, the second daughter of George III, is here shown at the age of around 30. A slightly earlier painting of Princess Augusta by Beechey (Millar 1969, no. 666) shows the Princess with an anchor pendant on her necklace (as in Edridge's drawing, no. 16) and an open sketchbook on her lap. Although she was a proficient artist (see no. 72), in no. 43 the Princess is seen acting out another role – as a spinner, suggestive of a wider iconographic tradition. Princess Augusta, who never married, was portrayed by Edridge in 1802 in the grounds of Frogmore House (see no. 16), which she inherited on her mother's death in 1818 and where she lived until her own death in 1840. Her collection of miniatures included works by Engleheart, Bone and others (Walker 1992, nos. 220, 745, 747).

The prototype for this miniature was a portrait painted by Sir William Beechey in 1802 and exhibited at the Royal Academy in that year. A version – presumably the original – was recorded in the Green Pavilion at Frogmore House and is visible in Wild's view published in 1817 (see no. 137). Following the deaths of both the Queen and Princess Augusta, Beechey's portrait passed into the possession of Mary, Duchess of Gloucester, by whom it was bequeathed to George, (2nd) Duke of Cambridge (sold Christie's, London, 11 June 1904, lot 74; see Williamson 1914, pl. XXIII).

The present miniature, with other copies after portraits by Beechey, may be by Lady Beechey, who painted under her maiden name, Anne Jessop. Several other miniature copies of Beechey's portrait are recorded: one is in the Brunswick-Lüneburg collection (Williamson 1914, no. 15) and another was sold from the Shelley-Rolls collection (Christie's, London, 13 February 1962, lot 17). Numerous engravings were also made.

44. Unknown English artist after Richard Cosway (1742–1821)

Princess Elizabeth, c.1790

Watercolour on ivory. Oval, 8.0 × 6.1 cm (3⅛″ × 2⅜″)
RCIN 420925
PROVENANCE First certainly identifiable in the Royal Collection, 1870
LITERATURE Walker 1992, no. 201

Princess Elizabeth, the third daughter of the King and Queen, is here shown in her early 20s. She was the most artistically gifted of the Princesses, working in a wide variety of different media, including miniature painting on ivory (see nos. 76, 78). In April 1818, seven months before Queen Charlotte's death, she married Frederick VI, Landgrave of Hesse-Homburg, and for much of the remainder of her life

41

42

43

44

she lived in Germany. Miniatures now in the Royal Collection, including nos. 54 and 78, may have returned to England following her death in 1840 (see Walker 1992, p. xxi).

This miniature is a copy after a lost work by Cosway, which is probably to be identified with that listed in an invoice submitted by the artist to the Prince of Wales in May 1795, at a charge of 30 guineas (Millar 1986, p. 587). It has been suggested that the style of the copyist here accords in its mannerisms with that of Anne Mee (see no. 50), who was influenced by Cosway. Other miniatures by Cosway of Princess Elizabeth, datable *c.*1800, include an oval set into a gold box from the Cumberland collection (Walker 1992, no. 183) and one given by the Princess to her friend Lady Dashwood (Christie's, London, 23 June 1981, lot 222).

45. Unknown English artist after Benjamin West (1738–1820)

Prince Ernest (later Duke of Cumberland), c.1776

Watercolour, silk and hair on card. Oval, 5.7 × 5.1 cm (2¼″ × 2″)
Mounted in a gold locket, with a lock of fair hair placed in the back, secured with a small gold true-love knot.
RCIN 421971
PROVENANCE Princess Elizabeth, Landgravine of Hesse-Homburg (d. 1840); by whom bequeathed to her sister-in-law Frederica, Queen of Hanover (d. 1841); by descent
LITERATURE Walker 1992, no. 339

45

This is not a conventional miniature. It is in effect a collage with the hair made of woven silk to which strands of real hair have also been applied. The silk has been stuck down onto card. The rest of the miniature has been painted in the normal manner.

The likeness is taken from the group portrait of six of the royal children, painted by Benjamin West in 1776 (Millar 1969, no. 1145). The painting was commissioned by George III and Queen Charlotte and was exhibited at the Royal Academy in 1777; it was hung first at St James's and then at Windsor.

Prince Ernest, created Duke of Cumberland and Teviotdale in 1799, was George III's fifth son; in 1815 he married his first cousin Frederica (daughter of Grand Duke Charles of Mecklenburg-Strelitz) and in 1837 he succeeded his brother William IV as King Ernest Augustus of Hanover.

46. Edward Miles (1752–1828)

Prince Augustus (later Duke of Sussex), c.1792

Watercolour on ivory. Oval, 7.5 × 6.1 cm (2¹⁵⁄₁₆″ × 2³⁄₈″)
RCIN 420651
PROVENANCE First certainly identifiable in the Royal Collection, 1870
LITERATURE Walker 1992, no. 274; Lloyd (C.) and Remington 1996, no. 65

The style of dress and hair, combined with the appearance of the sitter, suggests that this is a portrait of the King's sixth son at the age of 19, on the eve of his departure for the continent, or at the time of his brief return to London a year later. Owing to his asthmatic condition, Prince Augustus was forced to spend several years (1792–1800) in Switzerland and Italy. While abroad, in 1793 he married Lady Augusta Murray, a Catholic, in contravention of the Royal Marriages Act of 1772 and much to George III's displeasure. The marriage was declared null and void, as was his second marriage, *c.*1831, to Lady Cecilia Buggin. In 1801 Prince Augustus was created Duke of Sussex. In politics he was a liberal and championed reform, but his main interests were charitable and cultural. To those ends he became Grand Master of the United English Lodge of Freemasons in 1813, President of the Society of Arts in 1816, and President of the Royal Society in 1835. Prince Augustus declared in his will that he wished to be buried in the public cemetery at Kensal Green rather than in St George's Chapel, Windsor. A keen

46

47

bibliophile who specialised in collecting editions of the Bible, he also collected miniatures: no. 40 certainly, and no. 53 possibly, belonged to him. At the first of the sales of his collection (Christie's, London, 24 June 1843) over £200 was spent by Queen Victoria on miniatures to be added to the Royal Collection (Walker 1992, p. xxi).

Prince Augustus wears the star of the Order of the Garter, to which he had been appointed in 1786. In another autograph version of this miniature the sitter wears the Windsor Uniform (Walker 1992, no. 273); a third version, in Hanoverian uniform, is recorded in the Brunswick-Lüneburg collection (Williamson 1914, no. 19, p. 30).

47. Richard Cosway (1742–1821)

Prince Adolphus (later Duke of Cambridge), c.1793

Watercolour on ivory. Oval, 8.6 × 7.1 cm ($3\frac{3}{8}$″ × $2\frac{13}{16}$″)

RCIN 420785

PROVENANCE Probably commissioned by the future George IV (30 gns.); first certainly identifiable in the Royal Collection, 1870

LITERATURE Walker 1992, no. 184

The sitter wears the uniform of Colonel of the 1st Regiment of Hanoverian Guards with the star of the Order of the

Garter. He is therefore clearly identifiable as George III's seventh son, Prince Adolphus, appointed to the Order of the Garter in 1786 and raised to the rank of Colonel in the Hanoverian Guards in 1793. He had joined the Hanoverian Guards in 1790, aged 16, and was wounded three years later at Valenciennes in Flanders when fighting under the command of his brother, the Duke of York, with the Austrians and the Dutch against French revolutionary forces. He was created Duke of Cambridge in 1801 and in 1818 married Princess Augusta of Hesse-Cassel. Their second daughter, Princess Mary Adelaide, was the mother of the future Queen Mary, through whom a number of items from Prince Adolphus's collection re-entered the Royal Collection. (See also p. 389.)

This miniature is close in style to no. 35. A similar representation in miniature of the same sitter by Richard Livesay, who taught drawing to the royal family, is known from a coloured stipple engraving by Charles Knight published on 1 January 1794. No. 47 is almost certainly the miniature listed in the invoice submitted by Cosway to the Prince of Wales in May 1795, with a charge of 30 guineas (Millar 1986, p. 587).

48. Richard Cosway (1742–1821)

Princess Mary (later Duchess of Gloucester), c.1795

Watercolour on ivory. Oval, 7.9 × 6.4 cm (3⅛″ × 2½″)
RCIN 420647
PROVENANCE Probably commissioned by the future George IV
(30 gns.); first certainly identifiable in the Royal Collection, 1844
LITERATURE Walker 1992, no. 185; Lloyd (S.) 1995, no. 116;
Lloyd (C.) and Remington 1996, no. 61

48

Princess Mary, the fourth daughter of George III, is shown
here at the age of 19. Ten years earlier she had been painted
by Hoppner (see no. 13) and after a further ten years or so
there is Andrew Robertson's description of the beautiful,
fidgeting, laughing Princess (see no. 55). In 1816, at the age
of 40, she married her first cousin, Prince William, Duke of
Gloucester.

As with no. 49, only the head has been brought to a high
degree of finish. The body and the sky have been lightly
sketched in with the surface of the ivory much in evidence.
The soft texture of the hair, which is such a feature of
Cosway's miniatures, is a remarkable passage framing the
face and forming a contrast with the brightness of the
sparkling eyes. This miniature is an example of Cosway's
style at its most fluid and ebullient, produced when the artist
was working at the height of his considerable powers before
his eyesight began to fail. The handling is looser than in
no. 49 and this perhaps denotes a slight difference in date.
The invoice submitted by the artist to the Prince of Wales
in May 1795 includes a miniature of this subject, charged
at 30 guineas (Millar 1986, p. 587). A finished version by
Cosway, formerly in the collection of Adolphus, Duke of
Cambridge, was sold in London in 1961 (Sotheby's, London,
27 November 1961, lot 16) and a copy of it, painted for the
sitter, is in the Royal Collection (Walker 1992, no. 880:
attributed to Anne Mee). A group of family miniatures was
bequeathed by Princess Mary to her niece, Queen Victoria
(see nos. 24, 28, 31).

49

49. Richard Cosway (1742–1821)

Princess Sophia, 1792

Watercolour on ivory. Oval, 7.9 × 6.4 cm (3⅛" × 2½")
Signed and dated on the original backing card *R^dus Cosway. / R.A. / Primarius Pictor / Serenissimi Walliae / Principis / Pinxit / 1792* (and *G.P.* in another hand)
RCIN 420001
PROVENANCE Probably commissioned by the future George IV (30 gns.); first certainly identifiable in the Royal Collection, 1851
LITERATURE Walker 1992, no. 186; Lloyd (S.) 1995, no. 117; Lloyd (C.) and Remington 1996, no. 60

Princess Sophia, seen seven years earlier in Hoppner's charming oil (no. 12), was the King's fifth daughter. She is shown here at the age of 15, in a similarly fashionable dress to those worn by her sisters and mother at the same period (see nos. 32, 44, 48). The Princess was of a delicate and nervous disposition and never married.

Comparable with no. 48 in its lack of finish, the present miniature is a fine example of Cosway's rapid and free technique. The facial features have been worked up in some detail and the curls of the hair are depicted with a mass of individual strokes. On the other hand, parts of the costume and the sky in the background have been only sketchily laid in with the ivory left bare in several places (notably the dress). The predominance of white and blue, with the restricted use of colour for the features, results in a luminosity that is one of the principal characteristics of Cosway's style. The miniature is no doubt the one listed in Cosway's invoice submitted to the Prince of Wales in May 1795, charged at 30 guineas (Millar 1986, p. 587).

A number of versions of the artist's portraits of royal sitters were usually produced, often as gifts from the sitter to other members of the royal family. In this instance, versions are known to have belonged to Prince Adolphus, Duke of Cambridge (most recently sold Sotheby's, London, 8 June 1989, lot 148), and to Princess Mary, Duchess of Gloucester (inherited by Queen Mary, but not in the Royal Collection).

50

50. Henry Bone (1755–1834) after Anne Mee (c.1770–1851)

Princess Sophia in c.*1800*, 1806

Enamel. Oval, 6.7 × 5.6 cm (2⅝" × 2³⁄₁₆")
Signed lower right *H Bone* (initials in monogram) and inscribed on the back *Her Royal Highness / the Princess Sophia. / Painted by Henry Bone A.R.A. Enamel painter / to / His R.H. the Prince / of Wales / Jany 1806*
RCIN 421921
PROVENANCE Probably commissioned by the sitter; first certainly identifiable in the Royal Collection, 1877
LITERATURE Walker 1992, no. 771

This enamel is a copy made by Henry Bone (see no. 22) in 1806 from Mrs Mee's original of around six years earlier (Walker 1992, no. 853). Mee chose a rectangular format and shows Princess Sophia seated in half-length. Bone reduces the composition to head and shoulders in an oval. Another version is in the Dutch Royal Collection (Schaffers-Bodenhausen and Tiethoff-Spliethoff 1993, no. 199). Bone's preparatory drawing for this enamel is in the National Portrait Gallery (Walker 1999, no. 484).

Mrs Mee (*née* Foldstone) was described by Mrs Papendiek drawing the Queen and the Princesses at Windsor in 1790 (Papendiek 1887, II, p. 144), and paid frequent subsequent visits. For her portrait of Princess Amelia, see no. 54. She is best known for the series of 'Beauties' painted for the Prince Regent (Walker 1992, nos. 857–74).

51. Unknown English artist after Thomas Gainsborough (1727–1788)

*Prince Octavius in 1782, c.*1783

Oil on ivory. Oval, 4.6 × 3.6 cm (1¹³⁄₁₆″ × 1⁷⁄₁₆″)
RCIN 420648
PROVENANCE First certainly identifiable in the Royal Collection, 1910
LITERATURE Walker 1992, no. 340

The image is derived from the oval by Gainsborough forming part of the series of fifteen portraits known as *The Royal Family* (see fig. 9; Millar 1969, no. 791). These were painted at Windsor Castle in September and October 1782, probably for Queen Charlotte, and were exhibited at the Royal Academy in the summer of 1783. Although depicted by Gainsborough from life, by the time *The Royal Family* was shown at the Royal Academy Prince Octavius (the eighth son) had died, aged only 4, on 3 May 1783. When visiting the exhibition the sight of his portrait is said to have reduced the royal party to tears (Whitley 1928, I, p. 396). The King in particular was deeply distressed by the boy's sudden death – 'my mind is far from at ease; it has pleased the Allmighty to put an end very unexpectedly of the most amiable as well as attached child a parent could have,' he wrote on 14 June 1783 (Aspinall 1962–70, V, p. 698), adding 'There will be no Heaven for me if Octavius is not there' (Brooke 1972, p. 266). This miniature was probably painted soon after Prince Octavius's death. A version with the hair executed in collage (compare no. 45) is recorded in the Brunswick-Lüneburg collection (Williamson 1914, no. 22).

52. Unknown English artist after Thomas Gainsborough (1727–1788)

*Prince Alfred, c.*1782

Enamel. Oval, 4.4 × 3.6 cm (1¾″ × 1⁷⁄₁₆″)
RCIN 421024
PROVENANCE George, 2nd Duke of Cambridge; his sale, Christie's, London, 13 June 1904, lot 465c; bought by Queen Mary
LITERATURE Walker 1992, no. 345

Prince Alfred, the ninth and youngest son of George III and Queen Charlotte, was born in September 1780 and died in August 1782, just before his second birthday. An oval of Prince Alfred was included in the series of fifteen portraits comprising *The Royal Family*, painted by Gainsborough in September and October of 1782 (Millar 1969, no. 792), but the Prince had in fact died just before the artist arrived at Windsor Castle. Gainsborough therefore painted the portrait 'from remembrance', which accounts for its summary, almost ghost-like appearance. A number of painted copies, prints and miniatures were derived from the prototype, which was seen when *The Royal Family* was exhibited at the Royal Academy in 1783. A miniature by J.H. von Hurter in the Royal Collection, signed and dated 1782, has a lock of hair in the back and an engraved inscription *Vive nel mio Cuor* (Walker 1992, no. 240); another miniature was set into the lid of a circular tortoiseshell box given to the future King George V and Queen Mary in 1907 (Walker 1992, no. 344). It is possible that no. 52 and the other anonymous copy are the work of Mrs Mee.

51

52

53. Richard Cosway (1742–1821)

*Princess Amelia, c.*1790

Watercolour on ivory. Oval, 9.1 × 7.5 cm (3⁹⁄₁₆″ × 2¹⁵⁄₁₆″)
Inscribed, perhaps by the artist, on part of the card on which the
ivory was originally laid *H.R.H. Princess Amelia Rʳ Cosway*
RCIN 420003
PROVENANCE Probably commissioned by the future George IV
(30 gns.); possibly Duke of Sussex; (?)thence by descent to his son-
in-law Thomas Wilde, 1st Lord Truro; his sale, Christie's, London,
11 May 1893, lot 39; bought by Queen Victoria (250 gns.)
LITERATURE Walker 1992, no. 187; Lloyd (S.) 1995, no. 130

Princess Amelia, the sixth daughter and youngest child of
the King and Queen, was born in August 1783 and died in
November 1810. She was a particular favourite with all the
royal family: in December 1788, in the midst of his illness,
the King had asked to see the Queen and his 'Emily' (Hedley
1975, p. 162). This miniature shows the Princess a year or so
later. The pose is not dissimilar to that used by Sir Thomas
Lawrence in his portrait of Princess Amelia painted at
Windsor in September 1789 (Millar 1969, no. 881), on the
same occasion as the artist's famous representation of Queen
Charlotte (London, National Gallery). The sitter is aged 7
in the miniature, which may be identified with the portrait
listed in Cosway's invoice submitted to the Prince of Wales
in May 1795, charged at 30 guineas (Millar 1986, p. 587).
In 1802 Cosway painted another miniature of Princess Amelia,
which is in the Victoria and Albert Museum (Reynolds 1988,
p. 131, fig. 81).

Cosway's miniatures reveal great technical skill and
remarkable manual dexterity. The transparent watercolour
washes used in conjunction with the white of the ivory create
a sense of movement that helps to bring the sitter readily
to life. In this miniature only the head has been finished,
although the sitter's right hand has been briefly sketched in
and a locket is indicated around the neck. The figure was
clearly intended to be seen against a sky background, which
was another of Cosway's innovations in the art of the
miniature (see especially nos. 48, 49).

53

54. Charlotte Jones (1768–1847) after Anne Mee (*c.*1770–1851)

*Princess Amelia in c.*1800, 1812

Watercolour on ivory. Rectangle with sloping corners,
8.2 × 6.5 cm (3¼″ × 2⁹⁄₁₆″)
Inscribed on the original backing *The Princess Amelia / From an
original / Painted by / Miss Jones, / 1812*
RCIN 420220
PROVENANCE Probably commissioned by Princess Elizabeth;
first certainly identifiable in the Royal Collection, 1851
LITERATURE Walker 1992, no. 836

Charlotte Jones was a pupil of Richard Cosway, who had
painted Princess Amelia as a child (no. 53). Her appointment
as Miniature Painter to Princess Charlotte of Wales in 1808
culminated in a series of twelve portraits recording the
Princess's appearance at different stages of her life (Walker
1992, nos. 837–48 and fig. 18).

The present miniature of Princess Amelia is a variant of
one by Anne Mee painted *c.*1800, of which an autograph

54

55

copy is in the Royal Collection (Walker 1992, no. 855) and of which many other copies were made (for example, Walker 1992, nos. 885–91). The costume is probably inspired by depictions of Mary Queen of Scots. The miniature is likely to be one of two painted by Miss Jones for Princess Elizabeth, mentioned in a letter from her niece Princess Charlotte, in 1812. Princess Elizabeth was said to be 'pleased with both pictures' (Jones 1885, p. 10).

55. Andrew Robertson (1777–1845)

Princess Amelia in 1807, 1811

Watercolour on ivory. Oval, 8.7 × 7.0 cm (3⁷⁄₁₆″ × 2¾″)
Signed in monogram and dated on the right *AR 1811* and inscribed on the backing *painted, 1811, by A. Robertson 33 Gerrard street.*
RCIN 420652
PROVENANCE Commissioned by a member of the royal family; first certainly identifiable in the Royal Collection, 1870
LITERATURE Walker 1992, no. 902; Lloyd (C.) and Remington 1996, no. 71

The diary and correspondence of Andrew Robertson provide useful insights into the painting of miniatures of members of the royal family, during a series of sittings at Windsor Castle in 1807 (Robertson 1897, pp. 136–51). Having been appointed Miniature Painter to the Duke of Sussex two years previously, Robertson was commissioned to paint portraits of the Duke's sisters. During February and March he received numerous sittings from the Princesses Augusta ('so cheerful, so much conversation, such naiveté'), Elizabeth ('has fine countenance – sensible woman, knows a great deal of the art'), Mary ('beautiful creature – <u>most</u> difficult to paint, fidgets about, nor sits steady one moment – affable and laughs'), and Amelia ('lovely creature, fine features, melting eye, charming figure, elegant, dignified, finest hair imaginable'). Princess Amelia made a particularly strong impression on the artist, who recorded that she 'sits in hat, cap, etc., however, because the Duke of Sussex likes the dress – none of her fine hair seen. She is quite indifferent about her looks. She cannot be unconscious of her beauty, but no one ever thought less of it, or more careless of embellishment, further than her own comfort and respect for society requires.' He goes on to describe her as an 'angelic creature, modest, diffident, lovely' and records that she 'has a little hesitation in her speech when she is animated'. On the same occasion Robertson also painted the Duke of Sussex and he went on to paint the future George IV at Carlton House. He had hoped to paint George III and Queen Charlotte while at Windsor, but this does not seem to have happened.

The series of the Princesses was intended for exhibition and Robertson assessed them very highly – 'I have . . . outdone my best pictures'. Only two of the series – of Princesses Elizabeth and Sophia – are still in the Royal Collection (Walker 1992, nos. 899 and 900). By the autumn of 1807 Robertson reflected on his experience as follows:

> Pictures of that large size take such time to paint, that I should starve, were employment altogether in these. They are what have gained me reputation, but small miniatures are what we must live by. I now perceive my error, I have done more for reputation than emolument.

The success of the series, however, meant that there would be a demand for copies from members of the royal family, and Robertson noted that 'the Princesses pay better than the Dukes'.

Princess Amelia was George III's favourite daughter and when she lay dying of tuberculosis in 1810 Robertson was summoned by the King to Windsor Castle 'about 10 days before she died' to paint a replica of his portrait of 1807 (Robertson 1897, pp. 168–9). The rectangular copy made for the King remains in the Royal Collection (Walker 1992, no. 901) and no. 55 was painted a year later. A number of other versions are recorded, in the Brunswick-Lüneburg collection (Williamson 1914, no. 26), the Dutch Royal Collection (Schaffers-Bodenhausen and Tiethoff-Spliethoff 1993, no. 200) and elsewhere. Two enamel copies made by Bone for the Prince Regent are in the Royal Collection (Walker 1992, nos. 775, 776). Engravings of the image were also circulated. In a letter to Lady Harcourt dated 9 November 1810 – a week after Princess Amelia's death – Princess Elizabeth wrote: 'We have been, & are severely tried; yet I trust that God, who never has forsaken my beloved Father, will still stand by Him; yet the occasion of this sad illness is so different from every other, that I trust all who really love him will but give us time. Aggrivating subjects have been the causes of his former illnesses; this one is owing to the overflowing of his heart for his youngest & dearest Child; a child who had never caused him a pang, & who he literally doated upon' (*Harcourt Papers*, VI, p. 255).

Robertson was born in Aberdeen, where he studied under Alexander Nasmyth and Sir Henry Raeburn. Arriving in London in 1801, he entered the Royal Academy Schools and gradually built up a remarkably distinguished clientèle. Two of his brothers practised the art of miniature painting in New York and Sir William Charles Ross was his studio assistant in 1814. Robertson's miniatures are notable for their large format, vivid characterisation, rich colouring and strong highlights. His papers, edited by his daughter Emily in 1895, are an invaluable source. In many respects his work equates with portraits in oil by Raeburn.

2. Royal Art (nos. 56–84)

56. George III (1738–1820)

A ruined Corinthian temple in a landscape, c.1758

Pencil, pen and ink, black and white chalk on blue paper.
39.7 × 56.0 cm (15⅝″ × 22 1/16″)
RL K 206
PROVENANCE George III
LITERATURE Oppé 1950, no. 1; Sloan 2000, no. 68

This is one of a series of forty-five loose drawings, in black
and white chalk on blue-grey paper, originally housed
between the stiff blue card leaves of a volume labelled
'Landscapes drawn by H.M.'. The drawings are mostly
landscape compositions, containing architectural elements
in the foreground. The fact that the architecture is drawn
with the help of a ruler would appear to link these drawings
with the future King's lessons in perspectival drawing.
Joshua Kirby was the Prince's teacher of perspective drawing
from 1756 (see no. 209) but his lessons are likely to have
ceased by 1765 when he is described – in the past tense – as
having 'taught H.M. to draw' (Pennington 1809, III, p. 113).

All but two of the drawings are of imaginary, generically
classical landscapes; the two exceptions depict Windsor
Castle and Syon House. Others in the series feature classical
buildings derived from engraved sources – in the present
drawing the temple of Baal Shamin (of c.130 AD) at Palmyra,
as recorded in plate XXXI of Robert Wood's *Ruins of Palmyra*
(1753); in other drawings classical remains included in
publications such as Le Roy's *Monuments de la Grèce* (1758).
The recognisably English riverscape in no. 56 – and in
others of the series – was presumably the idea of the young
George III.

The competent handling of black and white chalk
throughout this series may also have resulted from lessons
with Kirby. The landscapes exhibited by Kirby at the Society
of Artists in 1767 and 1769 were said by Horace Walpole to
have been painted by George III. Kirby's official role at this
time was Clerk of the Works at Richmond and Kew.

57. George III (1738–1820)

*Perspective drawing of a classical building with
pavilion wings, 1760*

Pencil, pen and ink and grey wash. 34.8 × 47.0 cm
(13 11/16″ × 18½″)
Inscribed and dated *G.P.W. 1760*, with feathers below. Inscribed in
pen on the backing paper *This Drawing was Designed & Executed
for my Book on Perspective by His Majesty King George III*
RL K 93
PROVENANCE Joshua Kirby; returned to royal ownership at an
unspecified date (by 1950 kept with George III's other drawings
in the Royal Library)
LITERATURE Oppé 1950, no. 4; Roberts (J.) 1987, pp. 58–9;
Chambers 1996, p. 41

Like no. 56, this drawing was the result of Kirby's training in
the art of perspectival drawing. This skill was an important
accompaniment to the young King's architectural tuition
with William Chambers (see no. 85): while Chambers taught
the elements of architecture – and in particular the classical
orders – Kirby taught how to portray three-dimensional
forms on a flat, two-dimensional surface. The precise content
of Kirby's lessons is not known, but they are likely to have
included much of the information in his various published
texts (see no. 209).

An inscription on the backing paper, evidently in Kirby's
hand, indicates that the drawing was made by the King for
inclusion in Kirby's book on perspective. Plate LXIV of
Kirby's *Perspective of Architecture*, published in 1761, was
indeed a very precise reproduction of this design. In the
accompanying text Kirby explained that 'the Design was
made, and compleated for me, so as to come within the
compass of the plate: and I hope I may take the liberty of
saying, that This, and the last finished Print in the book
[plate LXXIII, also evidently drawn by the King – but
probably to Chambers's design], are esteemed by me as
the most valuable parts of it' (part 2, p. 55).

At an unknown date this drawing was added to others

56

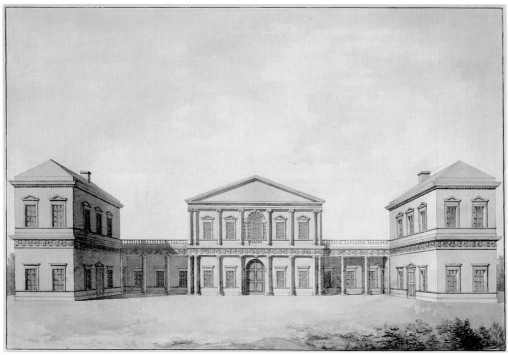

57

by the King that had been placed by Queen Charlotte in a
red morocco portfolio. The portfolio was kept in the Queen's
Library at Frogmore (see no. 140).

Kirby's plate was copied in an engraving, allegedly
designed by John Turner, published on 8 December 1761
(Cloake 1996, p. 71), with the following title: *A View of Their
Majesties Intended Palace at Richmond*. Although the façade has

general similarities with early schemes for Richmond Palace
– and indeed with Richmond Lodge (no. 120) and with the
end façades of Kent's model for a new Richmond Palace – it
seems inherently unlikely that this drawing is a design
rather than an exercise in perspective drawing, the subject
of Kirby's publication. The King's architectural designs are
discussed in the next section as nos. 92–4.

58

58. George III (1738–1820) and John Duval (*fl.*1748–1800) & Sons

*Snuff box, c.*1770

Gold, ivory. 2.0 × diameter 5.2 cm (³⁄₄″ × 2 ¹⁄₁₆″)
Inscribed inside the lid *The Ivory part / of this Box was turned by / H.M. KING GEORGE THE THIRD / and by him given to my Grandfather / JUNE 1774. / NB My Grandfather purchased the Lathe in Paris / and brought home with him a person / to instruct H.M. how to use it / Henry Duval*
RCIN 65779
PROVENANCE Gold box supplied by John Duval & Sons, 1769 (£50; RA GEO/16822), ivory turned by George III; by whom presented to John Duval, 1774; Lady Mount Stephen; by whom presented to Queen Mary, Christmas 1917 (Add. Cat., p. 27A, no. 21)
LITERATURE Roberts (J.) 1987, p. 213 (n. 19), pl. 14; *Royal Treasures* 2002, pp. 328–9, no. 293

George III was an enthusiastic amateur ivory-turner. In 1769 a French lathe ('*machine à guilloché*') and this gold box (without its ivory ornamentation) were supplied to the King by his Swiss-born jeweller John Duval. Virtuoso ivory turning was considered a suitable pastime for European kings and princes; both Louis XV and XVI also owned lathes and were skilled turners. In the 1730s and 1740s Lord Bute and Thomas Worsley, later key members of the young George III's household, discussed their activities as ivory-turners (*Chambers* 1996, p. 42).

No. 58 is one of a number of objects which incorporate ivory turned by George III. It was presented by the King to John Duval in 1774. Duval had also brought an instructor back with him from Paris in order to teach the King how to use his new lathe. A note, written on a scrap of paper inside the box, records that the instructor stayed for two months, after which the King paid him £100. In 1772 the King gave his sister Augusta, Duchess of Brunswick, a similar gold and ivory box (Brunswick, Herzog Anton Ulrich Museum, inv. 304). A watch with an ivory back turned by the King was recorded at Windsor in 1837 (Rundells 1837, f. 12).

59. Queen Charlotte (1744–1818)

Needlework pocket-book, 1781

Satin, coloured silks and enamelled gold.
Open 27.7 × 25.0 × 1.5 cm (10 ¹⁵⁄₁₆″ × 9 ¹³⁄₁₆″ × ⁹⁄₁₆″)
RCIN 45126
PROVENANCE Given by Queen Charlotte to Mrs Delany, 1781; George, 2nd Duke of Cambridge; Mrs FitzGeorge; Miss Rawley; H. Stretton (by whom sold 1927); Queen Mary, by 1931 (*QMB*, II, no. 432)
LITERATURE Hayden 1992, pp. 155–7

Queen Charlotte's skill as a needlewoman is well attested. The encouragement she gave to this female accomplishment is underlined by her financial support of Mrs Pawsey's school for 'embroidering females' and her patronage of the unusually gifted needlewoman Mary Knowles (see nos. 282, 457). No. 59, which was almost certainly worked by the Queen, was given to her friend Mrs Delany, who was also an accomplished artist and needlewoman (see nos. 165, 194), at Bulstrode, the home of the Queen's and Mrs Delany's close friend the Duchess of Portland. It came under cover of a letter, written at the Queen's Lodge, Windsor, on

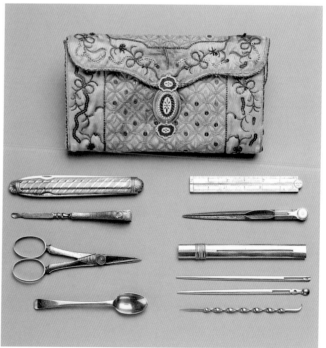

59

15 December 1781 (RA GEO/Add. 2/68), in which the Queen asks Mrs Delany to wear 'this little Pocket-Book in order to remember at times, when no dearer Person's are present, a very sincere well wisher, Friend, and affectionate Queen, Charlotte'. The 'Pocket-Book' was described by Mrs Delany's waiting-woman in some detail: 'Inside was a beautiful pocket case, the outside satin work'd with gold and ornaments with gold spangles, the inside lined with pink satin and contained a knife, sizsars, pencle, rule, compass, bodkin' (Hayden 1992, p. 155). The contents of the pocket-book still include the implements described (a composite set of gold, mother-of-pearl and steel), of which the bodkin is marked with the unidentifiable maker's initials *GC*.

In the previous month, at Bulstrode on 13 November, Mrs Delany had given Queen Charlotte a small notebook containing fragments of silhouettes, of ornament and figures rather than flowers (RA GEO/Add. 2/65). In the following year, Opie's portrait of Mrs Delany (no. 165) was painted for the King and Queen.

60. Queen Charlotte (1744–1818)

*Hygeia, c.*1806

Pen, ink and brown wash over pencil with wash borders.
35.4 × 40.5 cm (13 ${}^{15}\!/_{16}$" × 15 ${}^{15}\!/_{16}$")
RL K 299
PROVENANCE Among the '7 Drawings by Her Majesty Queen Charlotte' taken from the Library at Buckingham House by order of George IV, 1828 (see Oppé 1950, p. 19); Queen Charlotte's portfolio
LITERATURE Pyne 1819, I, *Frogmore*, p. 11; Oppé 1950, no. 6

Pyne records that Queen Charlotte drew throughout her life, although little of her work survives. She evidently passed on this enthusiasm to her daughters, for whom copying the works of Old Masters and contemporary artists, and designing schemes for interior decoration, was an absorbing pursuit for many years. In 1785 Mrs Delany recorded spending evenings at the Queen's Lodge in Windsor when the Queen and her daughters would 'sit around a large table, on which are books, work, pencils and paper . . . the youngest part of the family are drawing and working' (Hayden 1992, pp. 164–5).

This drawing was preserved within a paper wrapper inscribed in pen '7 drawings by Her Majesty', with 'Queen Charlotte' added in pencil. These seven works are among the few surviving drawings attributed to the Queen. They are all studies of the type which might have been set by a drawing master in order to instruct the pupil in composition; the figures are expressed by schematic ovoid and tubular forms, and lines show the process of constructing the illusion of perspective. This kind of instruction was fairly common in the latter part of the eighteenth century, when drawing books containing etched landscapes and figures in outline for the purpose of copying were sold to amateur artists. The drawings were formerly contained in a portfolio similar to, but larger than, that used to hold the King's drawings (see no. 57). They were evidently a late addition to the folder, which is lettered 'Drawings by the Princes & Princesses' and also contained nos. 74, 75 and 84. At Bad Homburg there is a series of drawings (with the addition of watercolour) by Princess Elizabeth, made at Windsor in 1806 in a style very similar to that in the Queen's series (*Elizabeth* 1990, no. 36). It is likely that Queen Charlotte's drawings resulted from lessons with the same – as yet unidentified – teacher. A folder of works by the Queen is noted in the posthumous inventory of Princess Elizabeth's collection at Darmstadt (Abt. D 11 Nr. 142/9 (ii)).

The subject represented here is an offering at the shrine of Hygeia, the goddess of health and the daughter of the physician Aesculapius, who was represented as a young woman holding a serpent in one hand and a cup in the other, out of which the serpent sometimes drinks. Other subjects in this group of Queen Charlotte's drawings include the Adoration of the Shepherds, Pygmalion and the Invention of Painting.

60

61

62

61. Charlotte, Princess Royal (1766–1828) after Benjamin West (1738–1820)

The Five Senses: Smell, 1784

Etching. Platemark 16.4 × 22.6 cm (6⁷⁄₁₆″ × 8⅞″)
Inscribed in the plate *CM 1784*
RCIN 816785

62. Charlotte, Princess Royal (1766–1828) after Benjamin West (1738–1820)

The Five Senses: Taste, 1784

Etching. Platemark 16.4 × 22.8 cm (6⁷⁄₁₆″ × 9″)
Inscribed in the plate *CM 1784*
RCIN 816786
PROVENANCE With no. 61, presented by Mr William Drummond, January 1988
LITERATURE Roberts (J.) 1987, p. 73

George III's commission in 1769 of the *Departure of Regulus* (no. 158) marked the beginning of a long period of royal patronage for Benjamin West. During his tenure as Historical Painter to the King, West had studios both in Buckingham House and in Windsor Castle, and from *c.*1780 to 1809 he rented a house in Park Street, Windsor. He painted many portraits of the royal family, and for a time also served as a drawing master to the princesses.

The Princess Royal made a group of five lively etchings, dated 1784, which allegorise the senses; two of these, *Smell* and *Taste*, are included in the present exhibition. These etchings were all copies of designs by West, whose drawing of *Taste*, signed and dated 1784, has recently surfaced, while his drawings for *Sound* and *Smell* were on the art market in 1968 and 1975 respectively (*Agnew's 130th Annual Exhibition*

of Watercolours and Drawings, March 2003, London, no. 8). Among the works by the Princess Royal in the Collection is a large watercolour drawing of an angel (RL K 1152) pasted into an album of prints and drawings included here as no. 64; this also reveals the influence of West and may date from around two years later than these etchings.

The Princesses were apparently taught to etch by Biagio Rebecca (1735–1808) and Peltro William Tomkins (1760–1840). The resulting prints were presumably distributed as gifts to family and friends, in the same way as Queen Victoria and Prince Albert distributed their drawings and etchings in the 1830s and 1840s (Roberts (J.) 1987, pp. 21–5, 95–7).

63. Charlotte, Princess Royal (1766–1828) after Giulio Clovio (1498–1578)

Head of Minerva, 1785

Etching, printed in red-brown ink. 28.3 × 20.4 cm (11⅛″ × 8¹⁄₁₆″)
RCIN 816795
LITERATURE Oppé 1950, p. 20 (under no. 7)

Like the etchings after West (nos. 61, 62), this print dates from the mid-1780s, when the Princess was receiving tuition from Biagio Rebecca or P.W. Tomkins. Etching was particularly suitable for amateurs because of its similarity to drawing. Very little pressure was required, and the etcher was able to sketch freely through the waxy ground upon the plate with the etching needle, as though with a pencil. It is not known where (nor by whom) the plates were 'bitten' and printed. By the end of the reign there was a small printing press at Frogmore, some elements of which – in an earlier location – could possibly have been used to print the Princesses' etchings.

63

64. Charlotte, Princess Royal (1766–1828) after John Miller (1715–1790)

A canna, 1783

Pen and ink over pencil. 46.9 × 33.4 cm (18⁷⁄₁₆″ × 13⅛″)
Inscribed above *Classis 1ˢᵗ· Ordo 1ˢᵗ / Monandria Monogynia / Canna*;
below *Windsor Decem[ber] / 1783*
RL K 1149 (f. 14 of volume RCIN 981149)
PROVENANCE Identified with the 'Princess Royal's Drawings and
Etchings' taken from the Library at Buckingham House by order
of George IV, 1828 (see Oppé 1950, p. 19)
LITERATURE Oppé 1950, no. 7

Like Queen Charlotte, the Princesses had a serious interest in
botany. The Princess Royal's drawing of the flowers and leaves
of a canna, pasted into a 37-page album of drawings and prints
inscribed with dates between 1780 and 1786, is an accurate
copy of a plate from one of the most important botanical
books of the eighteenth century, John Miller's illustrated
guide to the classification structure of the great botanist
Carl Linnaeus, subtitled *An Illustration of the Sexual System of*

This is a copy of a drawing in George III's collection
by the sixteenth-century Italian artist Giulio Clovio (see
Popham and Wilde 1984, no. 243). It represents the head of
Minerva, the goddess of wisdom, war and all the liberal arts,
who presided over sense, taste and reason. Rather than seeking
to emulate the smooth grey chalk of Clovio's drawing, the
Princess Royal has translated the complex forms of the
original into the idiom of a linear print. Some of Clovio's
details of the Gorgon's head on Minerva's cuirass, and a
battle between a horseman and foot soldiers on her plumed
helmet, have been simplified or elided. Just as the Princess
Royal later sought to disguise her drawings as etchings
(see nos. 67–9), so in this print she has etched her plate in a
hatched pattern in order to emulate the regular lines which
characterise engraving, the most laborious and skilled of
the print-making methods, and one which was thought to
require a great deal more intellectual strength and energy than
other forms. Another impression of this subject, printed in
black ink, is included in the Princess Royal's volume (see no. 64).

64

Linnaeus, published in 1777. It is a measure of the Princess Royal's intellectual curiosity that on the following page of Miller's volume is a more attractive, hand-coloured version of the same etching, without the lettering and the key, yet none the less the Princess Royal copied the diagrammatic version.

In this interest in botany the Princess Royal may also have been encouraged by Mrs Delany, who had become a great friend of Queen Charlotte after their first meeting in 1776 (see nos. 59, 165, 194). Mrs Delany was deeply concerned with botanical accuracy, always cutting the correct number of stamens and styles; likewise the Princess Royal's drawing faithfully records the details included in Miller's own plate. Queen Charlotte's copy of Miller's three-volume work was sold for 5 guineas at her posthumous library sale in 1819 (lot 1440). The catalogue of books belonging to Princess Elizabeth (Sotheby's, London, 7–11 April 1863) included not only Miller's *Sexual System of Linnaeus* but also James Sowerby's *Easy Introduction to Drawing Flowers* and his *Botanical Drawing Book*, both issued in 1788. However, all the flower subjects included in the Princess Royal's album pre-dated these didactic publications. Nine botanical subjects, all worked at Windsor and dated 1783, are included in this album. On the evidence of portraits of the Princess showing her painting flowers, her activity as a botanical artist continued to the end of her life (painting of 1826 by Stirnbrand, and miniature of 1827 attributed to J.G.P. Fischer; RCIN 402477, 420223).

65. Charlotte, Princess Royal (1766–1828)

A posy of flowers, 1784

Watercolour and bodycolour over pencil. 37.0 × 28.3 cm (14⁹⁄₁₆″ × 11⅛″)
Signed and dated *Charlotte Augusta Matilda May 1784*
RL K 303
PROVENANCE Princess Royal's volume (see no. 64)
LITERATURE Oppé 1950, p. 20 (under no. 7)

66. Charlotte, Princess Royal (1766–1828)

A vase of flowers, 1793

Pen and ink and wash. 72.0 × 63.9 cm (28⅜″ × 25³⁄₁₆″)
Signed and dated, on paper pasted onto the backboard,
Charlotte Augusta Matilda June 3ʳᵈ 1793
RL K 414
PROVENANCE Painted for Queen Charlotte; retained in the Collection after her death
LITERATURE Oppé 1950, p. 20 (under no. 7)

65

Both these flower pieces by the Princess Royal are in the style of works by Mary Moser (1744–1819), the leading professional flower-painter of her day. Moser was one of the only two female founder-members of the Royal Academy of Arts, established by George III in 1768 (see no. 159). According to Joseph Farington, she also served as drawing mistress to Queen Charlotte's daughters (*Farington Diary*, III, p. 919). In January 1790 it was reported that Princess Elizabeth was 'painting Miss Moser's flower piece most astonishingly well' (RA GEO/Add. 2/48) – presumably indicating a copy.

The Princess Royal's watercolour of a posy tied with a blue ribbon is probably a copy of a drawing by Moser, who made many similar watercolour studies of flowers, and it certainly anticipates the kinds of floral decorations with which the artist decorated the South Pavilion at Frogmore, a room newly built by Wyatt (see no. 137). Moser, having been commissioned by Queen Charlotte, decorated this room like a bower, with garlands of flowers on the walls and the ceiling

66

painted as though it were open to the sky, and with posies tied with fluttering blue ribbons. The Princess Royal has included such a ribbon here, as well as emulating the close observation and botanical accuracy which characterise Moser's work.

The monochrome drawing of a vase of flowers with an extravagantly drooping leaf, tulips and poppy heads in a neo-classical vase decorated with swags and masks, and resting upon a marble plinth, is very similar in style and execution to Moser's compositions, and was surely made under her tutelage. Twenty years later, the Princess painted a very similar subject on a pair of Ludwigsburg porcelain flower vases (no. 70). This drawing was mounted and framed so as to be consonant with the Princess Royal's other drawings (including nos. 67–9); particularly en masse, the grisaille tones of these works give the effect of engravings.

67. Charlotte, Princess Royal (1766–1828) after Abraham Bloemart (1566–1651)

Bearded hermit in contemplation, 1793

Pen and ink. 12.7 × 9.0 cm (5″ × 3⁹⁄₁₆″)
Signed and dated, on paper pasted onto the backboard,
Charlotte Augusta Matilda / September 30th 1793
RL K 384

68. Charlotte, Princess Royal (1766–1828) after Abraham Bloemart (1566–1651)

Bearded hermit praying, 1793

Pen and ink. 12.7 × 9.1 cm (5″ × 3⁹⁄₁₆″)
Signed and dated, on paper pasted onto the backboard,
Charlotte Augusta Matilda / November 24th 1793
RL K 380

69. Charlotte, Princess Royal (1766–1828)
after Abraham Bloemart (1566–1651)

Young hermit reading, 1793

Pen and ink. 12.6 × 9.1 cm ($4^{15}/_{16}$″ × $3^{9}/_{16}$″)
Signed and dated, on paper pasted onto the backboard,
Charlotte Augusta Matilda / December 1st 1793
RL K 388
PROVENANCE Drawn for Queen Charlotte; retained in the
Collection after her death

In a list made by Pyne of the prints which belonged to
Queen Charlotte, her taste for works by Netherlandish
artists working in the late sixteenth and early seventeenth
centuries is very apparent. These three drawings of hermits
by the Princess Royal are copied from a book of etchings,
presumably owned by Queen Charlotte, by Boetius Bolswert
(*c*.1580–1633) after designs by the Dutch painter and
draughtsman Abraham Bloemart (1566–1651). This book of
1610, *Sylva Anachoretica Aegypti et Palaestinae*, contains short
biographies of twenty-four desert saints alongside etched
portraits which depict them praying or reading in their cells,
with Bibles, bells, crucifixes and rosary beads. The Princess
Royal has copied the anchorites Arsenius (no. 67), Macarius
Aegyptius (no. 68) and Basilius Magnus (no. 69); this last
has a skull as a memento mori on his table.

The subject of the hermit was a very popular one in the
late eighteenth century, and hermitages – often complete with
picturesque hermits who would be hired on the condition
that they neither spoke nor cut their hair – sprang up in
secluded parts of many country estates. Princess Elizabeth
herself designed a hermitage, a small circular thatched building
with a porch, for the grounds of Frogmore. This was built by
September 1793, the same date as these drawings, suggesting
that its construction might have prompted the Princess Royal
to make copies from Bolswert's book. Inside the building was
a model of a hermit, amidst what is described in Ackerman's
Repository in 1823 as 'such accommodations as a recluse
may be supposed to want – wooden utensils, rude seats, and
a rough table, covered with excellent imitations of fruit' (see
Roberts (J.) 1997, pp. 225–6).

The Princess Royal made many copies of prints in
order to decorate Frogmore, where they still hang in their
original frames (some bearing the label of the carver Edward
Wyatt) and glazing with black and gold surrounds. Sixty
of her drawings were noted by Farington at Frogmore in
1797 (*Farington Diary*, III, p. 919) and a decade later the
Princess's Closet at Frogmore – containing the drawings –
was described by Pyne (Pyne 1819, I, *Frogmore*, p. 16).
Forty-five of the drawings survive, inscribed with dates
between August 1792 and May 1795; in 1990 these drawings
(which include nos. 66–9) were hung in a small room
overlooking the colonnade at Frogmore – probably the
same room as the Princess Royal's Closet. All the drawings
are executed with the same close, controlled pen strokes
in emulation of etched lines.

67

68

69

70. Charlotte, Princess Royal, Queen of Württemberg (1766–1828), decorator; Ludwigsburg Porcelain Factory

Pair of flower vases, 1812

Porcelain, painted in enamels and partly gilded.
Diameter 18.5 × 19.0 cm (7⁵⁄₁₆″ × 7⁷⁄₁₆″)
Each vase inscribed on the underside of the base with the monogram *C.A.M.* and *1812* painted in grey over the glaze.
RCIN 53333.1–2
PROVENANCE Probably given by the Princess Royal, Queen of Württemberg, to George III, *c.*1812
LITERATURE Roberts (J.) 1987, pp. 77–8, pl. 17

By the time of her marriage in 1797 to Frederick, Hereditary Prince, Duke and – from 1806 – King of Württemberg, the Princess Royal was an experienced artist. In Germany she found a new outlet for her talents in the productions of the porcelain factory at the palace of Ludwigsburg, near Stuttgart, which had been founded by Duke Carl Eugene of Württemberg in 1758, following the example of many other German rulers (including the Elector of Mainz, the Duke of Brunswick and the King of Prussia). The palace had been started in the 1700s with the aim of creating a German Versailles, and additions were made by successive Dukes, most notably Carl Eugene. The Princess Royal supervised the redecoration of the interiors (see Binney 1989).

The factory supplied the Princess with porcelain blanks, which she would decorate and inscribe on the base with the date and her initials C.A.M. (Charlotte Augusta Matilda). The decorated pieces would then be fired in her own kiln, in the grounds of the palace. These vases are in two sections. The upper part has a hole in the base while the lower acts as a saucer or reservoir, enabling small bulbs or other plants to be kept growing. On each, the Princess painted two panels of classical vases filled with roses, tulips and other flowers, all in grey on a pink ground; the painted decoration is very close to that found in the Princess's monochrome drawings of the 1790s (see no. 66). She also painted plates, and plaques to be mounted on furniture (see no. 71). In 1805 she had written to her father George III that she would 'venture to bespeak some flower pots after my design which I hope your Majesty will place in your palace' (Aspinall 1962–70, V, p. 341).

71. Charlotte, Princess Royal, Queen of Württemberg (1766–1828), decorator; attributed to Johannes Klinckerfuss (1770–1831)

*Travelling breakfast service, c.*1812–13

Mahogany, oak, porcelain, glass, gilt-metal. 20.6 × 33.3 × 26.2 cm (8⅛″ × 13⅛″ × 10⁵⁄₁₆″)
RCIN 54421

70

71

PROVENANCE Given to Princess Augusta (d. 1840); her nephew, George, 2nd Duke of Cambridge (d. 1904); his son, Rear-Admiral Sir Adolphus FitzGeorge (d. 1922); by whom bequeathed to Queen Mary
LITERATURE Roberts (J.) 1987, pp. 77–8 and pl. 18

The Ludwigsburg porcelain blanks supplied for the Princess Royal to decorate included useful wares (cups and saucers, plates, flower vases, etc.; see no. 70), many of which were given away to members of her family; and flat plaques, some of which were intended for the decoration of furniture. The Princess's repertoire of ornament, normally executed in monochrome, included vases of flowers and animals in land-scapes, many of the latter (as on no. 71) after prints published in 1738 by the German artist J.E. Ridinger (1698–1767); some of the models had been copied by the Princess for drawings framed and hung at Frogmore in the 1790s (see nos. 66–9). The court cabinet-maker at Württemberg, Johannes Klinckerfuss, regularly used plaques decorated by the Princess to adorn the plain Biedermeier-style furniture then in vogue (Wiese 1988, p. 273 and pl. 7) and was probably responsible for the manufacture of no. 71. It was evidently sent as a present to the Princess's sister, Princess Augusta, whose initials AS (Augusta Sophia) are engraved on the gilt-metal mounts of the cut-glass breakfast service.

72. Princess Augusta (1768–1840) after Giovanni Battista Piazzetta (1682–1754)

The Procuress, 1785

Black and white chalk on faded blue paper. 40.5 × 50.5 cm (15^{15}⁄₁₆″ × 19⅞″)
Inscribed *Augusta Sophia Decr. 1785*
RL K 515
PROVENANCE George III or Queen Charlotte
LITERATURE Sloan 2000, p. 234, no. 172

As well as copying prints and drawings by living artists, George III's daughters also used his unparalleled collection of drawings by Italian artists as models for their work (see also no. 63). Copying Old Master drawings was an estab-lished method of teaching, with its roots in Renaissance practice; in the seventeenth and eighteenth centuries it formed a central part of art academy instruction. By the late eighteenth century copying was also considered to be a suit-ably genteel recreation for ladies, revealing accomplishment and application at the same time as a modest deference to 'real' artists. Work by the Princesses provides a fascinating insight into amateur art practice of this period, although not a representative one – not only were they talented, they also received tuition from drawing masters who were amongst the best artists of the day, and they had the resources of

72

an extraordinarily rich collection from which to copy.

No. 72 is one of three copies (with Oppé 1950, nos. 13 and 14; see Roberts (J.) 1987, p. 76) made by Princess Augusta from George III's spectacular group of drawings by the Venetian artist Giovanni Battista Piazzetta. Piazzetta's drawings were acquired in 1762 with Consul Smith's collection; they were then framed and hung at Buckingham House. The originally blue paper of both Piazzetta's original (no. 177) and the Princess's copy has faded to buff in the course of two hundred years of exposure to light. The copy remains in its original eighteenth-century English frame. At Greiz there is a group of thirty-nine copies made by Princess Elizabeth after her father's Piazzetta drawings: in these the paper colour has remained unfaded as the copies were placed in an album in which they were protected from the light (*Elizabeth* 1990, no. 31).

Princess Augusta has taken pains to copy Piazzetta's drawing accurately, using the same medium and type of paper, keeping to the same scale, and attempting to reproduce some of the subtlety of Piazzetta's handling. Curiously, it seems that the moral ambiguity of the subject – prostitution is depicted without a framework of implied disapprobation – presented no impediment to the Princess.

Another group of copies after the Windsor Piazzetta drawings, including a copy of *The Procuress*, was sold in 1974 (Sotheby's, London, 11 December 1974, lots 16, 27, 47–50, 64). These copies, however, are more accomplished than those executed by Princess Augusta, and it is possible that they were made by one of the artists employed by George III as drawing masters.

73. Princess Elizabeth (1770–1840)

Fan commemorating the recovery of George III, 1789

Double chickenskin leaf painted in watercolour, bodycolour and gold; ivory, silver piqué, mother-of-pearl.
Guard length 26.0 cm (10¼″)
RCIN 25087
PROVENANCE Presented by Lady Holland to Queen Victoria, 1887
LITERATURE Roberts (J.) 1987, pp. 82–3

The recovery of George III from his first serious bout of illness early in 1789 was the occasion for widespread jubilation and festivities (see nos. 328, 451). In her record of one of these celebrations in April 1789, Fanny Burney (Second Keeper of the Robes, or dresser, to Queen Charlotte between July 1786 and July 1791) noted, 'The Queen graciously presented me with an extremely pretty medal . . . as well as a fan, ornamented with the words – *Health restored to one, and happiness to millions*' (*Burney Diary*, IV, p. 285). This is precisely the wording inscribed in the border of the present fan leaf.

A small group of painted fans associated with George III's recovery is known, including a number of almost identical examples, all of which are variants of the present fan (see Hart and Taylor 1998, pl. 39 and pp. 75–6). The box in which this fan was presented to Queen Victoria is inscribed more precisely: 'Painted by the Queen's Aunt Princess Elizabeth'. That Princess's artistic activities from the 1790s onwards are well documented (and see no. 288). Although there seems no reason to doubt her responsibility for the present fan, it would appear unlikely that the 19-year-old Princess painted quantities of similar fans unaided.

George III's recovery was also the subject of engraved fans, including one in the Royal Collection (RCIN 25062) and another published by T. Balster in March 1789 which incorporates a number of the same elements as are present in the painted examples (Cust 1893, p. 3, no. 9; Rhead 1910, p. 246). See also nos. 328 and 451.

74. Princess Elizabeth (1770–1840) after Marco Ricci (1676–1730)

Pastoral landscape with a youth climbing a tree, c.1790–95

Pencil, pen and ink and wash on tracing paper. 36.8 × 54.4 cm
(14½″ × 21⁷⁄₁₆″)
RL 17354
PROVENANCE Queen Charlotte's portfolio (see under Oppé 1950, no. 6)
LITERATURE Oppé 1950, no. 157; Sloan 2000, p. 211, no. 155

73

This drawing by Princess Elizabeth is a tracing of a pastoral scene by Marco Ricci (see no. 176), a large number of whose drawings were acquired by George III from Consul Smith in 1762. The brownish yellow appearance of Princess Elizabeth's drawing is due to discoloration of the thin tracing paper because of the oil used to render it translucent. Until the beginning of the nineteenth century tracing paper was known as 'transparent paper' or 'oyled paper'. Princess Elizabeth was a particularly accomplished draughtsman, and for many years it was assumed that this copy had been made by the English landscape painter Alexander Cozens (1717–86), who taught her brothers Princes William and Edward from 1778. A second traced copy by Princess Elizabeth of the same work is in the collection at Bad Homburg (Gotisches Haus, E 125), the Princess's home following her marriage in 1818 to Frederick VI, Landgrave of Hesse-Homburg. Other tracings by the Princess, at Greiz, were made between c.1790 and 1818 on the basis of watercolour views of Windsor Castle by Paul Sandby; the originals were at the time in the collection of Joseph Banks (Roberts (J.) 1995, p. 137).

75. Princess Elizabeth (1770–1840)
Woodcutters astride a log, c.1792

Grey wash over pencil. 15.8 × 20.2 cm (6¼" × 7¹⁵⁄₁₆")
RL K 341
PROVENANCE Queen Charlotte's portfolio (see under Oppé 1950, no. 6)
LITERATURE Oppé 1950, no. 15

The loose, rapid brushstrokes of this drawing show Princess Elizabeth working in the manner of Thomas Gainsborough, who was employed by George III from 1781 until his death in 1788 (see no. 11). Gainsborough may have owed his royal introduction to his longstanding friendship with Joshua Kirby, like him a native of Suffolk, who had been the King's drawing master (see no. 209). Gainsborough is recorded as having taught Queen Charlotte; according to one source, 'her majesty took some lessons of Gainsborough, during the then fashionable rage for that artist's eccentric style denominated Gainsborough's moppings' (Angelo 1828, I, p. 194). Queen Charlotte owned a number of landscape drawings by Gainsborough, amongst which were ten in coloured chalks; these were dispersed in the sale of the Queen's property after her death.

74

75

In addition to his tuition of Queen Charlotte, Gainsborough may have given lessons, or demonstrations of his methods, to the Princesses. A newspaper report in 1789 stated that the Princess Royal had successfully copied Gainsborough's drawings in the Queen's collection. A watercolour drawing by Princess Elizabeth, now at the Gotisches Haus, Bad Homburg (E 108), is a loose copy of a drawing by Gainsborough of a country track with a farm cart (Roberts (J.) 1987, pp. 70, 72), and a group of drawings and sketches, of landscapes and cattle, 'made [by Gainsborough] expressly for Princess Mary to copy', was exhibited some

years after the artist's death (Whitley 1928, II, p. 74).

This drawing of woodcutters is one of a uniform series of fifty-one grey wash landscape vignettes at Windsor by Princess Elizabeth. These served as patterns for the decoration on the pages of the bound manuscript catalogue of her collection of engravings after portraits by Joshua Reynolds, commenced in 1792; both the catalogue of the prints and the decoration were in Princess Elizabeth's hand. This particular design was used at the foot of the page listing some of the Reynolds portraits of sitters with names beginning with 'G' (see *Elizabeth* 1990, no. 50).

76. Princess Elizabeth (1770–1840) after Margaret Meen (*fl.*1775–1822)

Flower piece with bird's nest, 1792

Watercolour and bodycolour on vellum. 71.0 × 51.0 cm
(27¹⁵/₁₆″ × 20¹/₁₆″)
Signed and dated *Eliza fecit Nov 14ᵗʰ 1792*
RL K 613
PROVENANCE Painted for Queen Charlotte; retained in the
Collection after her death (at Buckingham Palace in 1866)
LITERATURE Roberts (J.) 1987, p. 74; Sloan 2000, p. 76, no. 51

Of all the royal children Princess Elizabeth was the most
prolific and certainly the most accomplished; her decorative
schemes for Frogmore were bold and extensive (see pp. 146–8).
She decorated the Cross Gallery at Frogmore House in the
mid-1790s with an ambitious mural scheme comprising
painted flower-garlands in swags, in the style of Mary Moser,
and panels of paper cut-outs, in the making of which she may
have been tutored by Mrs Delany (see nos. 17, 194). Princess
Elizabeth also decorated two other rooms at Frogmore in
the chinoiserie manner, and although her schemes no longer
exist they were illustrated by Pyne (see nos. 138, 141). Her
evident ambition and capability are clear from a contemporary diary description by Mrs Harcourt, the wife of General
– afterwards 3rd Earl – Harcourt, equerry to the King:
'Princess Elizth again is quite different from her two Elder
Sisters. She has great good humour – quick feelings – a great
deal of genius – an Imagination full of fire – much resolution –
much presence of mind – the same surprising Memory which
runs thro' the family – . . . She has a turn for conversation
& a peculiarity of Ideas which is just entitled to be called wit.
She writes as she speaks – often full of humorous conceits'
(*Mrs Harcourt's Diary*, pp. 49–50). In a diary entry of
February 1797 Farington notes that 'the Princess Elizabeth
has the most influence with the King & Queen. She has the
best understanding of any of the Princesses' (*Farington
Diary*, III, p. 775).

This accomplished work is a copy of a still life by the
flower painter Margaret Meen, now in the Victoria and Albert
Museum (520–1874), but which may once have belonged to
Queen Charlotte. The accounts for the royal nursery include
a payment, on 23 March 1792, to 'M. Meen' for Drawings
(£22 12s), which may have included that painting (RA GEO/
36940). Meen, who exhibited her work at the Royal Academy
between 1775 and 1785, founded and illustrated a periodical
in 1790, which in the event only ran to two issues, entitled

76

Exotic Plants from the Royal Gardens at Kew. In Queen
Charlotte's diary entry for 8 December 1789 she noted:
'I drew with Miss Mean from 10 till one' (RA). In 1822
Princess Elizabeth wrote affectionately to Margaret Meen
from her married home in Germany (Stuart 1939, p. 185).

77. Princess Elizabeth (1770–1840), decorator

*Side table, c.*1800

Satinwood, painted; watercolour on paper. 87.0 × 77.5 × 44.0 cm
(34¼″ × 30½″ × 17⁵/₁₆″)
RCIN 53107.1
PROVENANCE Made for Queen Charlotte

This table, which is one of a pair, was made for the Green
Pavilion at Frogmore House in the Home Park at Windsor
(see no. 137). This small square room, which lies at the north
end of the colonnade on the west front of the house, formed
part of James Wyatt's earliest additions made for Queen

77

The tables were made to stand either side of the door into the colonnade and are shown thus by Pyne. The tops, which are inset with a semicircle of paper painted with a broad border of flowers forming a continuous garland – with an outer border of acorns – were almost certainly executed by Princess Elizabeth. The Princess's artistic gifts, especially as a flower painter and decorator, were well recognised by her family and she was encouraged to collaborate with Wyatt on a number of architectural and decorative projects at Frogmore, recorded by Pyne and others (see no. 142). She contributed substantially to the character of Frogmore as a 'Temple of Flora', an effect which Queen Charlotte had deliberately encouraged by employing Mary Moser to decorate the walls and ceiling of the room balancing the Green Pavilion, at the south end of the colonnade.

78. Princess Elizabeth (1770–1840) after Henry Edridge (1769–1821)

Lady Charlotte Finch, *c.*1802

Watercolour on ivory. Oval, 10.0 × 8.0 cm ($3^{15}/_{16}'' \times 3^{1}/_{8}''$)
Signed on the backing *Eliza / The Picture of Lady Charlotte Finch*
RCIN 420972
PROVENANCE First certainly identifiable in the Royal Collection, 1870
LITERATURE Roberts (J.) 1987, pp. 79–80; Walker 1992, no. 809

Lady Charlotte Finch (1725–1813) was the second daughter of the 1st Earl of Pomfret. When Horace Walpole met her in Florence in 1740, he described her as 'the cleverest girl in the world; speaks the purest Tuscan, like any Florentine' (*Walpole Correspondence*, XXX, p. 15, no. 20). In 1746 she married as his second wife the Hon. William Finch, second son of the 7th Earl of Winchilsea and Vice-Chamberlain to the Household. Their son George, the 9th Earl of Winchilsea, is one of the figures in Zoffany's painting of the Tribuna Gallery in the Uffizi (no. 161): he stands in the right background, on the left of a group of four admiring the Venus de' Medici.

On 13 August 1762 Lady Charlotte was appointed Governess in Ordinary to the infant Prince of Wales; she remained governess to the royal children until 1792, in which capacity she retained their unbounded affection (see Shefrin 2003). She was also an intimate of Queen Charlotte and was included in Zoffany's family group (no. 10). Within the Royal Household Lady Charlotte organised standard

Charlotte in 1792–3. The furnishings chosen by the Queen for her 'little paradise' were simple and elegant, befitting a country retreat where she and her daughters were able to enjoy painting, drawing, needlework, music and botany away from the formality of the court. Most of the building and decoration at Frogmore was paid for privately by the Queen and the documentation is sparse. At this date she used the little-known cabinet-maker Thomas Soederberg fairly extensively at Buckingham House (*DOEFM* 1986, p. 838), chiefly for nursery furniture, and he may also have worked at Frogmore. Wyatt himself designed furniture and it is not impossible that he contributed designs for some of the furniture at Frogmore.

school lessons, as well as cultural pursuits such as music, dancing, drawing and needlework (see no. 4). The Princesses wrote to her on 18 October 1808, with stilted syntax: 'The Veneration, Attachment, and Respect which we <u>feel for</u> you Dearest Lady Cha . . . nor do we look back to the having been under your care as one of the least of the Mercies of Heaven' (RA GEO/Add. 15/448, quoted Millar 1969, no. 1207). She died at St James's Palace at the age of 88. At her funeral the coffin was 'followed by a long train of carriages, among which were five of the Royal Dukes' (quoted Walker 1992, no. 807).

Over one hundred miniatures, medallions and bibelots which formerly belonged to Lady Charlotte were bequeathed to her granddaughter Augusta Sophia Hicks and subsequently given to Queen Mary in 1933. The 'Finch Collection' includes a miniature of Princess Augusta after Beechey, given by the sitter in February 1801 (Walker 1992, no. 334/992), and the original miniature from which no. 78 was copied (Walker 1992, no. 807). That miniature was almost certainly painted by Henry Edridge at Windsor in 1802–3, when he was drawing the royal family (see nos. 14–19 etc.).

No. 78 is a further example of the varied and accomplished artistic activity of Princess Elizabeth, whose works included oil paintings, illustrations, silhouettes, prints, japanning and all aspects of interior design (see Roberts (J.) 1987, pp. 78–86). Interestingly, when depicted by others, it is normally with attributes of the arts in her hand: see, for example, her portraits by Edridge (no. 17), Beechey (Millar 1969, no. 667) and Stroehling (Millar 1969, no. 1096).

79. Princess Elizabeth (1770–1840)

Seven cut-out silhouettes of Cupid, c.1807

Cut paper, stained black. Various sizes: central figure maximum 7.5 × 6.0 cm (2^{15}⁄₁₆″ × 2⅜″)
RCIN 1047678.h, .k, .ag, .ai, .aj, .ak, .as
PROVENANCE Given by the artist to Miss Sarah Sophia Banks, 16 May 1807 and 13 June 1808 (nos. 1, 2, 3, 5, 10, 11, 13); Lady Dorothy Nevill; bought by Queen Mary, 1930

80. Princess Elizabeth (1770–1840)

Cut-out silhouette of a mother and children, c.1808

Cut paper, stained black. Maximum 12.2 × 9.8 cm (4^{13}⁄₁₆″ × 3⅞″)
RCIN 1047678.ap
PROVENANCE Given by the artist to Miss Sarah Sophia Banks, 13 June 1808 (no. 14); Lady Dorothy Nevill; bought by Queen Mary, 1930

81. Princess Elizabeth (1770–1840)

Four cut-out silhouettes and one monoprint of children, c.1809

Cut paper, stained black. Silhouettes various sizes: lower right group maximum 3.3 × 12.1 cm (1^5⁄₁₆″ × 4¾″); monoprint 9.0 × 10.8 cm (3^9⁄₁₆″ × 4¼″)
RCIN 1047678.f, .o, .w, .ad, .aq
PROVENANCE Given by the artist to Miss Sarah Sophia Banks, 11 July 1809 and 27 August 1811 (nos. 16, 20, 21, 22, 23); Lady Dorothy Nevill; bought by Queen Mary, 1930

82. Princess Elizabeth (1770–1840)

Cut-out silhouette of Diana the huntress, c.1811

Cut paper, stained black. Maximum 14.5 × 10.5 cm (5^{11}⁄₁₆″ × 4⅛″)
RCIN 1047678.ar
PROVENANCE Given by the artist to Miss Sarah Sophia Banks, 27 August 1811 (no. 19); Lady Dorothy Nevill; bought by Queen Mary, 1930
LITERATURE McKechnie 1978, pp. 214–15

These silhouettes were originally kept, with nos. 419, 420, in a dark green leather-bound album with a lockable silver clasp

78

79

80

81

82

bearing Princess Elizabeth's cipher. They have been framed for this exhibition. According to a note by Miss Banks, 'This delightfull Book . . . was a present from The Princess Elizabeth July 12. 1808. It contains some very beautifull and to me invaluable cuttings out by Her Royal Highness.' Twenty-six of the tiny items within were numbered by Miss Banks on the reverse, and the date of receipt was noted on a separate sheet kept at the front of the volume. The first cut-outs evidently arrived before the album itself; the last addition – a design for a garden seat – was presented on 9 September 1817, seven months before the Princess's marriage and departure for Germany and a year before Miss Banks's death. In addition to the twenty-six numbered items there are a few unnumbered monoprints clearly by Princess Elizabeth, and four portraits (including nos. 419, 420) of the King and Queen; these are not noted in Miss Banks's list and may not have been gifts from the Princess.

Princess Elizabeth was portrayed by Edridge in 1804 making cut-out silhouettes at Windsor (no. 17). She is said to have cut a profile portrait of the King in 1781, when she was only 10 (McKechnie 1978, p. 307, no. 404; see also RCIN 604515, 604516, 604435). Her eldest sister, the Princess Royal, also made cut-out silhouettes: her two groups of cupids and children are dated 1788 (Sloan 2000, no. 174b). Both Princesses may have been introduced to the technique of paper-cutting by Mrs Delany (see no. 194); after her death in 1788, the royal family's doctor at Windsor, James Lind, who was a prolific portrait silhouettist (see nos. 419, 420), may have been consulted for advice. The Princesses' silhouettes (some of which are on shiny paper, some matt) were mostly intended for a secondary, decorative function. Both Princess Elizabeth and the Princess Royal were closely involved in the preparation of garlands of flowers and foliage – entirely made of cut paper – for the ball at Frogmore in November 1793 (Kennedy Diary; see pp. 146–8). Small figurative silhouettes (both cut-outs and monoprints) form part of the mural scheme carried out by the Princess in the 1790s in the first-floor Cross Gallery at Frogmore House. At Bad Homburg there is a series of the Princess's cut-outs, painted on white paper and placed on a brown backing, with cupids and children as the main subject-matter (*Elizabeth* 1990, no. 38). Others were pasted onto firescreens or the covers of blotters. The different series of prints that were published on the basis of Princess Elizabeth's designs – *The Birth and Triumph of*

Cupid (1795), *Cupid as a British Volunteer* (1804) and *A Series of Etchings Representing the Power and Progress of Genius* (1806) – may all have been based on 'cuttings' such as those shown here.

Sarah Sophia Banks (1744–1818) was the only sister of Sir Joseph Banks and is well known as a passionate collector of trade cards and other ephemera; her collections are mostly in the Department of Prints and Drawings at the British Museum (Griffiths and Williams 1987, pp. 82–4). Her friendship with Princess Elizabeth arose from the close links between her brother and the King, whose honorary shepherd he was at Windsor and Richmond, in addition to having responsibility for the Botanic Gardens at Kew. The album also contains a dedicatory poem by the Princess: 'Sophia Zarah Banks – Genius, good sense, and Friendship kind, Must ever bring you, to my mind. Eliza'.

83. Berlin, Royal Porcelain Factory; decorations after Princess Elizabeth (1770–1840)

Pieces from a tea and coffee service, c.1810

Porcelain. Teapot 14.0 × 18.5 × 10.0 cm (5½″ × 7⁵⁄₁₆″ × 3¹⁵⁄₁₆″); coffee pot 18.8 × 19.5 × 10 cm (7⅜″ × 7¹¹⁄₁₆″ × 3¹⁵⁄₁₆″); milk jug 11.5 × 10.5 × 9.0 cm (4½″ × 4⅛″ × 3⁹⁄₁₆″); coffee cup 6.2 × diameter 6.8 cm (2⁷⁄₁₆″ × 2¹¹⁄₁₆″); saucer diameter 12.9 cm (5¹⁄₁₆″)
Each piece marked on the underside with the factory 'sceptre' mark (1803–13) in underglaze blue.
RCIN 35559, 35560, 35561, 35563.1, 35564.1
PROVENANCE Early history unknown; Miss Montgomery Campbell, by whom presented to King Edward VII, 1907
LITERATURE Roberts (J.) 1987, pp. 82–3

The circular reserves on this tea and coffee service are based on a set of twenty-six engravings from silhouettes by the Princess published in 1795 under the title *The Birth and Triumph of Cupid*, in which Cupid's progress is portrayed in a series of episodes denoted by the gilded captions. On one side of the coffee cup, for example, he fires his arrow and misses ('*Mistakes his mark*', pl. 8) while on the other ('*alighting on the World*', pl. 7) he appears to be floating in outer space. Cupid's triumph (pl. 26) is reserved for the panels on the teapot. According to the note which accompanied the gift of sixteen pieces of this service in 1907, Princess Elizabeth executed the paintings herself in collaboration with her sister, the Princess Royal. This seems unlikely however, and the mis-spelling of some of the gilded inscriptions suggests that the decoration was also done in the factory. Such a set, in the

83

rather austere *antique-glatt* pattern, would normally also have included an oval tray. Several of these sets were included in Queen Charlotte's posthumous sale, though none corresponds with no. 83. A similar Berlin service, with coloured reserves based on the same designs as here, is in the Johann Jacobs Museum, Zürich (*Elizabeth* 1990, no. 40).

The decoration of porcelain with designs by amateur lady artists had been pioneered by Wedgwood in the 1780s (see no. 288). Princess Elizabeth's published designs (for which see Roberts (J.) 1987, pp. 79–80) were particularly well suited to such use.

84. Prince Augustus (1773–1843)

A View of St Leonard's Hill, near Windsor, 1780

Bodycolour on thick board. 27.3 × 37.1 cm (10¾″ × 14⅝″)
Inscribed on verso *A View of St. Leonard's Hill near Windsor – His Royal Highness Prince Augustus Frederick aged 7 years and ¾*
RL K 369
PROVENANCE Queen Charlotte's portfolio (see under Oppé 1950, no. 6)
LITERATURE Oppé 1950, no. 16; Sloan 2000, pp. 140–41, no. 100

In the late eighteenth century instruction in drawing was considered to be an important part of a gentleman's – as well as a lady's – education, and as a result George III's sons were provided with a number of drawing masters, some of whom, like Alexander Cozens, were illustrious artists. One of the princes' longest serving tutors was John Alexander Gresse (1741–94), a painter likened in his day to Paul Sandby; Gresse taught the young princes between 1778 and 1793. According to the inscription on the verso, this view was painted when Prince Augustus, the King's sixth son, was not yet 8 years old. The Prince has probably coloured in an outline drawing of the contours of the landscape provided by his drawing master, much in the manner of a modern painting-by-numbers exercise. A very similar bodycolour landscape drawing of Windsor town and castle from the River Thames was made in the same year by Prince Ernest, the fifth son, and is inscribed on the back with the Prince's age '9 and a ½' (Oppé 1950, no. 16). Disbursements of £16 6s were made to Gresse in that year, according to an entry in the Queen's nursery accounts (RA GEO/36857). Paul Sandby, who in 1771 was described in the list of subscribers to Gandon's fourth edition of *Vitruvius Britannicus* as drawing master to the eldest son, the Prince of Wales, had made outline etchings of views of Windsor in 1777, 1780 and 1782 for the use of amateur artists.

St Leonard's Hill, south-west of Windsor, was the home from 1766 of Maria, Countess Waldegrave, who married the King's third brother, the Duke of Gloucester, at around the time of Maria's acquisition of the estate. The Duke failed to inform the King of his marriage until after the passing of the

Royal Marriage Act in 1772. The year of this view – 1780 – marked the reconciliation between the King and the Duke after an impasse of several years. In 1783 the house (which had been designed for the Gloucesters by Thomas Sandby) was bought by William (later 3rd Earl) Harcourt, a close intimate of the King and Queen.

Bodycolour – a popular medium for landscape artists in the second half of the eighteenth century – fell out of favour in the early nineteenth century because of the perceived crudeness of bright colour and opacity in comparison with the refined delicacy of watercolour.

84

II THE KING'S BUILDINGS

3. The King and his Architects (nos. 85–101)

85. Sir William Chambers (1723–1796)
Primitive buildings of conical and cubic form, c.1757

Pencil, pen and ink and watercolour. 49.0 × 33.2 cm
(19 ⁵⁄₁₆″ × 13 ¹⁄₁₆″)

RL 30311

PROVENANCE Drawn for George III

LITERATURE *Chambers* 1996, chapter 7, especially p. 70

The architect William Chambers was the key architectural influence on and adviser to the King for almost fifty years (fig. 11). He appears to have been introduced to the royal family in 1749, in connection with Frederick, Prince of Wales's new garden at Kew. Eight years later – after receiving a thorough professional training in both Paris and Italy – he was appointed Architect to the widowed Princess of Wales and at the same time he became architectural tutor to her eldest son, the future George III. The government department in charge of royal buildings was the Office of Works, where Chambers progressed from the position (from 1761) of one of the two Joint Architects (with Robert Adam) to Comptroller of the Works (from 1769); finally – from 1782 – he was the first holder of the new combined office of Surveyor-General and Comptroller. He was thus able to serve the King's interests very directly. Chambers was also a crucial figure in the early years of the Royal Academy, founded in 1768: he drafted the foundation document, was appointed the Academy's first Treasurer, and served as a crucial liaison between the Academy and the crown. Although Reynolds was President, he was aware that 'Sir William was Viceroy over him'. Chambers is shown between Reynolds and the Secretary, F.M. Newton, to left of centre in Zoffany's painting of the *Academicians* (no. 159). Throughout his life Chambers retained strong links with Sweden, where he was born. In 1770 he was made Knight of the Order of the Polar Star by Gustavus III of Sweden. After initial hesitation, he was permitted by George III to be addressed as 'Sir William' in England.

FIG. 11 Valentine Green after Sir Joshua Reynolds, *Sir William Chambers*, 1780. Mezzotint, published by V. Green (RCIN 640290)

This drawing was made in connection with Chambers's tuition of the future George III. In the late 1750s he was teaching the Prince on three mornings a week. His lessons covered both theory and practice. Meanwhile, Chambers's new buildings at Kew (see nos. 121, 122) served as full-scale models of architectural styles and of the different classical orders. The three figures here illustrate Chambers's manuscript essay 'The Origins of Buildings and Orders' (RL 30311A), made as part of his tuition of the future George III. The upper illustration represents the most basic construction, the 'conical' hut, 'composed of branches of trees spread wide at the bottom

◁ No. 94 (detail)
◁◁ No. 90 (detail)

85

86

and meeting in a point at the top, which were covered with Reeds, Leaves and Clay, to keep out the Rain, the Sun, and Cold winds'. Below is the cubic building, constructed of tree trunks placed upright, with wooden beams placed above the trunks along each side, and the flat roof supported by smaller pieces of timber laid across the building. The small drawing bottom right shows how a tree trunk evolved into the Tuscan order: the bark was removed, the trunk was raised on stones 'above the dirt and wet' and was covered with a slate to keep off the rain; finally, to prevent splitting, each end was firmly bound with osier (willow). Similar illustrations of primitive buildings were shown in Plate 1 of Chambers's published *Treatise* (see no. 87), for the introductory part of which the illustrated royal tuition manuscript effectively served as a first draft. In that publication Chambers acknowledged the work of 'Father Laugier', whose *Essai sur l'architecture* (published in 1753) likewise traced the evolution of the Doric order from primitive buildings.

For George III and his architectural interests, including his relationship with Sir William Chambers, see the forthcoming study by David Watkin: *The Architect King. George III and the Culture of the Enlightenment*, to be published by the Royal Collection in 2004.

86. Sir William Chambers (1723–1796)

*A primitive hut, c.*1759

Pencil, pen and ink and watercolour. 50.0 × 35.4 cm
($19^{11}/_{16}$″ × $13^{15}/_{16}$″)
RL 24812
PROVENANCE Drawn for George III
LITERATURE *Chambers* 1996, p. 71

The primitive building and elementary columnar structure were also discussed and illustrated in the diagrams accompanying Chambers's manuscript essay for the King (no. 85) and in Chambers's *Treatise* (no. 87). The freedom and delicacy of the handling of the wash and the depiction of the climbing foliage are reminders of the skills and techniques of draughtsmanship learnt by Chambers in Paris and Rome.

87. Sir William Chambers (1723–1796)

A Treatise on Civil Architecture, 1759

Open at p. 1 (*Of the origin of buildings*) and facing plate
(*The Primitive Buildings &c*)
London: William Chambers
[6,] iv, 86 pp., 50 pl. Printed. Bound in marbled brown calf with gold tooled edges, *GR.* monogram surmounted by small crown in centre; rebacked. 55.2 × 38.3 cm ($21^{7}/_{16}$″ × $15^{1}/_{16}$″)

RCIN 1150276
PROVENANCE George III (Windsor Library Catalogue 1780, f. 100)
LITERATURE Harris (E.) and Savage 1990, pp. 157–63; *Chambers*
1996, chapter 7

Chambers's *Treatise* is the first part of a projected architectural handbook. It covers the 'decorative part' of architecture, in particular the use of the classical orders; the text for the 'constructive part' was never written. According to the author, in the *Treatise* he set out 'to collect into one volume what is now dispersed in a great many, and to select, from mountains of promiscuous Materials, a Series of Sound Precepts and good Designs'. The *Treatise* quickly became the most popular practical work on architecture in the English language.

In a draft letter to the King, Chambers stated that the *Treatise* was 'originally written for Your Majesty's information' and added that 'Your Majesty's Gracious indulgence and encouragement first prompted me to render publick what at first was certainly not designed for publication'. Chambers's essay on 'The Origins of Buildings and Orders', written for the young King and still in the Royal Collection (RL 30311A), appears to have served as the first draft for the introductory part of the *Treatise*. The text and plate shown here demonstrate the progress from 'conic' to 'cubical' buildings, and the origin of the classical orders in the basic support structures of these buildings.

Although the *Treatise* was published by subscription, and 'His Royal Highness the Prince of Wales' heads the list of subscribers, it is likely that much of the expenditure involved in the book's publication was also borne by the future King. On the title page the author (correctly) describes himself as 'Architect to their Royal Highnesses The Prince of Wales and Princess Dowager of Wales'. Chambers published the book himself, and gives his home address (in Poland Street, Soho, London) as one of the locations from which it may be obtained. It is dedicated to the Earl of Bute, 'Groom of the Stole to the Prince', who may have introduced Chambers to the Prince and Princess of Wales. The third edition, published in 1791, was dedicated to the King.

Among those listed as subscribers to the publication are Joshua Kirby Esq., 'Draughtsman to his Royal Highness the Prince of Wales'; Mr Robert Adams [*sic*], Architect, and Mr G. Adams, 'Mathematical Instrument Maker to the Prince'. T. Sandby Esq., 'Architect to His Royal Highness the Duke', is noted as having subscribed for three copies.

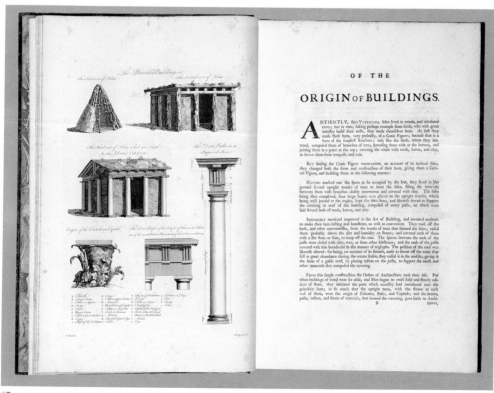

87

88. Sir William Chambers (1723–1796) and Giovanni Battista Cipriani (1727–1785)

Design for the State Coach, 1760

Pen and ink and watercolour over pencil. 34.1 × 60.8 cm
(13⁷⁄₁₆″ × 23¹⁵⁄₁₆″)
Inscribed *WC. The Kings State Coach figures JB Cipriani 1760.*
RL 17942
PROVENANCE Made for George III; bought from Colnaghi by the
Prince Regent (later George IV), 12 June 1811 (4 gns.; RA GEO/27638)
LITERATURE *Chambers* 1996, pp. 179–80; Marsden and Hardy 2001

According to the official journal of the Department of the
Master of the Horse for 1760, 'At the Commencement of this
Reign [25 October 1760] a very superb State Coach was
order'd to be built, after several Designs & Drawings, made
for that purpose and shewn to the Master of the Horse, were
examined & the approv'd parts thereof thrown into one by
Mr. Chambers.' The inscription on the present drawing
suggests that it was made at this early stage. The complexity
of the design and manufacturing process meant that the new
coach remained far from complete at the time of the King's
coronation in September 1761; indeed the final design was
still being discussed in June and July 1762. The new coach
was first used for the State Opening of Parliament on 25
November 1762; George III used it for subsequent state
openings and it has continued to be used – for state openings,
coronations and other important occasions – over the last
240 years. Adjustments have been made to increase the
passengers' comfort. When not in use it is on display in the
Royal Mews at Buckingham Palace (fig. 18).

The coach cost over £7,500, of which Samuel Butler (the
coachbuilder) received £1,673 15s, Joseph Wilton (the sculptor)
£2,500 and G.B. Cipriani (the painter) £315. Wilton's role
in the overall design was crucial and ensured the artistic
homogeneity of figures and architecture: the coach as actually
built differed in several respects (particularly concerning
the placing of figures) from its appearance in this initial
design by Chambers.

The coach was the most superb and expensive ever built
in England and its design and decoration are replete with
symbolism. Thus it serves as 'a triumphal peace-chariot',
and a 'rolling manifesto for the first Hanoverian monarch
to have been born in England' (Marsden and Hardy 2001).
When riding in the coach, the King would appear as Neptune,
monarch of the seas, and also Apollo, leader of the muses of
artistic innovation. This design shows the nearside of the
coach with paintings (on the door and panels) of Mars and
Minerva, with Mercury to symbolise peace. The antiquary
and patriot Thomas Hollis (1720–74) was a key figure in
the evolution of the decorative programme. In the course
of his travels in Italy in the early 1750s he had met each of
the artists involved. In late 1762 he paid repeated visits to
Wilton's studio to advise Cipriani on his decorative painting.
Among the unsuccessful competitors for the commission
were Samuel Butler and his nephew John Linnell, whose
design was engraved in 1761 (RCIN 504026), and Robert
Adam, whose design has not survived.

Chambers's role in the design of the coach presumably
arose from his position as the King's architectural tutor: he
was only appointed Joint Architect in November 1761. The
coach was one of a number of non-architectural projects in
which Chambers came to be involved. In the course of building
work at Buckingham House in the 1760s and 1770s there
were numerous occasions when his advice would be sought.
These included the design of the Pinchbeck Astronomical
Clock in 1768 (no. 302) and the garniture commissioned
from Matthew Boulton in 1770 (see no. 275).

89. Sir William Chambers (1723–1796)

Section of a domed building, c.1760

Pencil, pen and ink, pink and grey wash. 48.2 × 57.3 cm
(19″ × 22⁹⁄₁₆″)
RL 30364
PROVENANCE Made for George III

This is one of a very large number of designs – ground-plans,
sections and elevations – by Chambers and members of his
office which have remained in the Royal Collection since the
reign of George III. Only a few of them may be associated
with actual buildings. They are chiefly exercises in spatial
organisation and the articulation of façades through the
use of the classical orders, topics which naturally formed
part of Chambers's lessons to his royal pupil. The distinction
between these drawings and the more polished of those
normally attributed to the King (for instance, no. 94) can only
be guessed. The sophistication of the application of wash in the
present drawing would suggest a firm attribution to Chambers
himself. However, particularly from the later 1760s when the
architect's official and administrative responsibilities greatly
increased, the production of the finished drawings would
probably have been left to a member of his office.

88

89

The dramatic presentation style of this drawing – with the edges cut away (as if demolished) to right and left – indicates that we are to concentrate on the central domed feature, with circular rotunda below. Both the pictorial style and the centralised focus were doubtless inspired by the training which Chambers received in Paris and Rome. His (unexecuted) designs of 1751–2 for a mausoleum for George III's father, Frederick, Prince of Wales, had also incorporated a dome over a circular space below (*Chambers* 1996, p. 37). Other related projects include Chambers's (likewise unexecuted) design of 1759 for York House, the London residence of the King's brother, the Duke of York; and the 1770 designs for St Marylebone Church (*Chambers* 1996, pp. 127–8).

90. Sir William Chambers (1723–1796)

Design for Richmond Palace: elevation of the principal front, 1765

Pencil, pen and ink and wash. 45.0 × 62.9 cm (17¹¹⁄₁₆″ × 24¾″)
RL 29705
PROVENANCE Made for George III
LITERATURE *Chambers* 1996, pp. 43, 49–51; Cloake 1996, chapter XX

91. Sir William Chambers (1723–1796)

Design for Richmond Palace: plan of the basement, 1765

Pencil, pen and ink and wash. 45.4 × 62.8 cm (17⅞″ × 24¾″)
RL 30264
PROVENANCE Made for George III
LITERATURE See no. 90

Among the vast corpus of architectural designs by Chambers and his office which have survived in the Royal Collection, the folder containing '25 Elevations of a Villa, supposed to be that which was intended to have been built at Richmond' is the only group which was positively identified at the time, and which is approximately recognisable today. The drawings relate to the proposals, initiated soon after the King's accession, to replace the existing house at Richmond (Richmond Lodge: see no. 120) with a purpose-built royal residence. These were the latest in a series of proposals dating back to the late seventeenth century, to replace Henry VII's great palace at Richmond with a fitting royal residence. The site of the new building is recorded in 'Capability' Brown's plans for Richmond (e.g. RL 29670) and on a plan made for the King in the late 1780s (Cloake 1996, pp. 47–8, 76). It was a little way to the east of the Observatory, and immediately to the north of old Richmond Lodge.

Geometric Elevation of the Principal Front

90

Both of these designs relate to the second Richmond scheme, of 1765. This was also recorded in a wooden model formerly kept at Kew (*Chambers* 1996, p. 50, fig. 70). According to the scales on the drawings, the main façade was to be 328 feet (100 metres) long and the side façades were to be 225 feet (69 metres) long. Both the ground-plan and the articulation of the façade owe more than a little to Colen Campbell and James Paine, as well as to Kent's designs for Holkham Hall in Norfolk; all the relevant details could have been known to the King and his architect, Chambers, through engravings. There were to be two internal courtyards, separated by a chapel rising the full height of the building. A summary estimate of the cost of the proposed building amounted to nearly £90,000. The expense was doubtless the main reason that the project was not pursued. However, there was also a certain amount of local opposition. It proved impossible for the King to acquire some adjacent land which he considered essential for the project.

In spite of these problems, in 1770 construction work began on a smaller palace and reached ground-floor level before a further halt was called. The foundations were probably intended to be reused in Chambers's final Richmond designs

of *c.*1775, made following his visit to Paris in 1774 (*Chambers* 1996, p. 52, figs. 71 and 75). But in November 1775 Chambers was appointed to superintend the new works at Somerset House and the Richmond Palace project was abandoned. While many elements of the design and detailing of the 1775 scheme were reused by Chambers at Somerset House, the 1765 façade design was used by Quinlan Terry for the new block of offices in Whittaker Avenue, part of the Richmond Riverside development plan completed in 1988 (Cloake 1996, p. 74).

92. George III (1738–1820)
Details of the composite order, c.1759

Pencil, pen and ink and wash. Irregular, 57.5 × 40.6 cm
(22⅝″ × 16″)
R L K 447
LITERATURE *Chambers* 1996, p. 43

Three months after the King's accession, Horace Walpole noted that 'Building, I am told, is the King's favourite study'. And when the third edition of Chambers's *Treatise* was published in 1791, the royal dedication stated that 'The

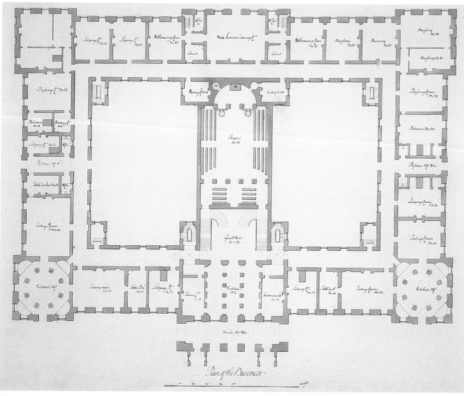

91

present publication treats of an Art, often the amusement of Your Majesty's leisure moments, and which, in all ages, great princes have delighted to encourage.' There was no doubt in the minds of George III's contemporaries that he was very keen on, and knowledgeable about, architecture.

As a result of Chambers's architectural tuition George III produced quantities of architectural drawings between the mid-1750s and the late 1780s. These included a set of drawings of the classical orders, once contained in a folder inscribed '22 Drawings of the Orders of Architecture'. It is likely that the drawings of orders – the basis of classical architecture – were made in the course of Chambers's lessons in the late 1750s. In order to produce these drawings the Prince of Wales would have had the assistance of his tutor in perspective – Joshua Kirby (see no. 209) – who had developed a drawing instrument (the workings of which had been explained in detail to the Prince) specifically for the correct delineation of the classical orders: the Architectonic Sector

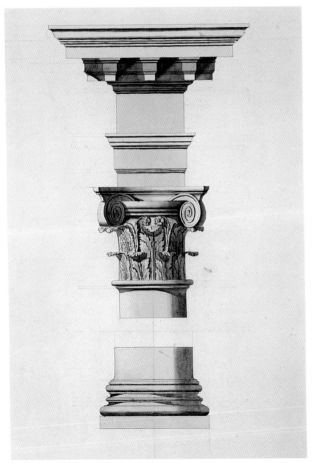

92

(see *Chambers* 1996, pp. 41–2). The details of the composite order shown in the King's drawing are indeed closer to those in Kirby's *Perspective of Architecture* (1761) than they are to those in Chambers's *Treatise* (1759).

One of the Prince's drawings was shown by Chambers to Robert and James Adam when they visited his London home in the spring of 1758. James thought it 'simple enough . . . however it shows his love for the art' (Fleming 1962, p. 249). The King's designs tend to follow Chambers's style at its most plain and unadorned; and by the same token, it is clear that the King's input into the designs produced for him by Chambers was very considerable. None of George III's drawings is dated. He was closely involved in the production of the hanging plans for Buckingham House in the early 1770s (see no. 115) and scribbled a ground-plan on the wrapper of military documents sent to him in 1774 (RL K 480). According to Greville, the King made numerous plans for the White House at Kew at the time of his convalescence there in 1788/9 (see no. 121), some of which have recently been identified in the British Library (Map Library, K. Top C/57a). As part of the King's farming activities at Windsor in the following decade – under the direction of the land agent Nathaniel Kent (see no. 219) – the King designed a farm labourer's cottage.

The King was also closely involved in the design of decorative features, either in his residences or in their furnishings. He designed the new neo-classical doorcases introduced to Buckingham House in the early 1760s (see no. 112) and made suggestions concerning the design of both the Pinchbeck Astronomical Clock in 1768 (no. 302) and Boulton's 'King's Clock' in 1770 (no. 277). His dexterity is demonstrated in the turned ivory box which he made at around the same time (no. 58).

93. George III (1738–1820)

Design for a Corinthian temple for Kew, c.1759

Pencil, pen and ink and wash. 57.7 × 40.0 cm (22 ¹¹⁄₁₆″ × 15¾″)
RL K 1419
LITERATURE Desmond 1995, p. 69; *Chambers* 1996, p. 45

This drawing provides the sole instance of a surviving design by the King which is specifically related to a documented – though unexecuted – building. It was engraved as one of the plates included at the end of Chambers's *Treatise* (1759); the explanatory text to the 1791 edition of the *Treatise* states

93

94

that it was 'made for Her late Royal Highness the Princess Dowager of Wales and proposed to be erected in the gardens at Kew'. The plate was dedicated to Thomas Worsley, Surveyor of the King's Works, but – uniquely in his publication – Chambers did not inscribe it as architect. An early impression of the plate, formerly in Worsley's collection, bears an inscription (possibly in Worsley's hand) stating that the design was due to the Prince of Wales: *Invenit Walliae Princeps Celsissimus & dedit*. The King's temple is close to a number of the garden buildings erected at Kew, to the designs of William Chambers. The reason that it was not built is unknown. It is intriguing that this temple design was published four years before the designs for the actual buildings were issued, in Chambers's *Kew* (1763).

The numerous compass points (down the centre, across the base of the temple, and in the column to left of centre) indicate the painstaking construction of the drawing.

94. George III (1738–1820)

A design for a domed Corinthian building, c.1760

Pencil, pen and ink and wash. 56.4 × 38.8 cm (22³⁄₁₆″ × 15¼″)

RL K 435

LITERATURE Roberts (J.) 1987, p. 60; *Chambers* 1996, p. 44

Among the King's designs are a number in which two or more elements are combined to form a more or less unified whole. In the case of the present design, a circular temple is placed on top of a square or rectangular building with a projecting portico. George III's interest in domed structures was clearly encouraged by Chambers, who made a number of designs with this combination (compare no. 89), most notably in his designs for St Marylebone Church in the 1770s. Unlike those designs, most of the King's architectural projects were made as exercises, without the intention that they would ever be built.

The King's drawings vary from the polished (as here) to the crude. The extent to which he was assisted in the drawing-up of his architectural designs will probably never be known. However, in March 1765 'the person who works about the king in all the designs in architecture which the king invents or directs himself' was identified – in a letter from the 6th Earl of Findlater to Mr Grant – as Mr Robinson (Fraser 1883, II, pp. 444–5). This useful individual was William Robinson (*c*.1720–75), a member of the Office of Works from the 1740s and Clerk of Works at St James's 1754–66; he appears to have been acquainted with Thomas Worsley. Robinson served unofficially as Chambers's clerk of works at Buckingham House from the start of the King's building activities there and was formally appointed to this position in 1769; he was appointed Secretary to the Board of Works in 1766. In spite of their close professional relationship, Chambers was frequently critical of Robinson, who was evidently more skilled as a draughtsman and administrator than he was as an architect. He supervised the alterations at Carlton House for the Dowager Princess of Wales in the 1760s, 'agreeable to HM's Instructions' and apparently to Robinson's designs, but without adequate budgetary regulation and much to the displeasure of Chambers (see BL Add. MS 41135, ff. 29–30). In June 1774, after seeing Robinson's designs for Somerset House, where Robinson was Clerk of Works from 1762, Chambers commented to Worsley that it was 'strange that such an undertaking should be trusted to a Clerk in our Office, ill-qualified as appears . . . while the King has six architects in his service ready and able to obey his commands. Methinks it should be otherwise in the reign of a vertuoso prince' (Harris (J.) 1970, p. 97). Robinson's sudden death in October 1775 left the way open for Chambers himself to take over the Somerset House project. While any designs produced by the King after 1775 were clearly not the work of Robinson, we can only guess at how many of his designs before that date were actually drawn by the King. In the same way, it is clear that Chambers would have had time to draw up only a fraction of the designs commissioned from him by the King.

95. Robert Adam (1728–1792)

Design for an illumination for the King's birthday, 1763

Pencil, pen and ink and watercolour. 48.0 × 125.0 cm
(18⅞″ × 4′ 1³/₁₆″)
Signed *Rob.ᵗ Adam Architect*. Inscribed *General Design of a Transparent Illumination, proposed to have been Executed in the Queens Garden In Honour of His Majestys Birth Day. The 4th June 1763.*
RL 17643a
PROVENANCE Made for Queen Charlotte; George III (Inventory A, p. 170)
LITERATURE Pyne 1819, II, *Buckingham House*, pp. 21–2; Oppé 1950, no.18; *Chambers* 1996, p. 46; Harris (E.) 2001, p. 67

In common with many of the other artists and craftsmen employed by the King immediately after his accession, Adam owed his introduction to his fellow Scotsman, the Earl of Bute. It may have been through Bute that both Adam and Chambers were appointed Joint Architects to the Board of Works in November 1761. In the event, however, Chambers proved to be an ideal royal servant while Adam worked more comfortably – and successfully – for private patrons. The chic and ornate style of Adam's decoration did not entirely please the King whose sixth son, Prince Augustus, reminded him (in 1791) of his previously stated views on Adam's work at Syon House: 'two [*sic*] much gilding, which puts me in mind of ginger-bread. Mere simplicity will always bear the preference' (Aspinall 1962–70, I, no. 674). Nine years later, Farington reported a telling remark by the King: 'I am a little of an Architect and think that the *Old* school (meaning that of Lord Burlingtons period which had more of magnificence)

95

is not enough attended to, – that the Adams's have introduced too much of neatness & prettiness' (*Farington Diary*,
IV, p. 1354).

This design is the more elaborate of two proposals
submitted by Adam for a temporary structure to be erected
in the garden of Buckingham House in June 1763, at the time
of the celebrations to mark the start of royal occupation of
the house, purchased in the previous year (see no. 108). In the
event Adam's other design (Oppé 1950, no. 19), for a much
simpler structure, was used. A detailed description of the
party, which took place at night and employed 4,000 lamps,
is included in the *Gentleman's Magazine* (XXXIII, pp. 300,
311). It was arranged by Queen Charlotte as a surprise for
the King, at the time of his twenty-fifth birthday. Adam
also made perspective views of both versions of the screen
(Sotheby's, London, 27–28 April 1988, lots 416–17), which
clarify the importance of the 'transparencies' (large back-lit
pictures, within the main architectural features) in the design.
The subject of the transparencies alluded to the King's role
as peace-maker – following the signing of the Treaty of
Paris and the end of the Seven Years War in the same year.
This style of decoration had been popular on the continent
for many years: in France, Rome and also in Mecklenburg,
where a small-scale 'illumination' had been staged to
celebrate the forthcoming marriage of the future Queen
Charlotte in 1761 (Hedley 1975, p. 34). It appears that some
of the materials used in Adam's 1763 screen were reused by
Chambers in 1768, for the pavilion erected in Richmond at
the time of the visit of the King's brother-in-law, Christian
VII of Denmark (*Chambers* 1996, p. 51).

Adam was involved to a limited extent in the remodelling
of Buckingham House. Three of his designs – none of which
was executed – remained with the descendants of Thomas
Worsley until their transfer to the Royal Institute of British
Architects in the 1960s: these designs concerned the main
façade, the doorcase in the Saloon, and a cornice for the
Queen's Dressing Room. However, Adam's 1761 design for
the chimneypiece in the Saloon was used, as was his ceiling
design for the Crimson Drawing Room (see nos. 111, 112);
these and a design for the illumination (mis-dated 1762) were
illustrated in Adam's *Works in Architecture* (1778). A magnifi-
cently bound copy of Adam's *Spalatro* book was presented to
the King in 1764, the year of its publication (no. 208). In 1766
a bracket designed by Adam (and made by Bradburn) was
supplied to support Eardley Norton's Astronomical Clock

(no. 300) in the King's Dressing Room at Buckingham
House, and in 1771 he supplied a design for a new sedan
chair for the Queen (see no. 274) – evidence that the
architect remained actively involved in the King's works
for over a decade.

A number of designs by Robert Adam for large royal
palaces have survived; these may all be connected with the
abortive Richmond Palace scheme. A single design, probably
from the 1760s, is similar in scale to Chambers's schemes of
a similar date (nos. 90, 91) and includes corner rooms labelled
'Queen's Cabinet' and 'King's Closet' (Tait 1993, p. 54). A series
of six drawings, the first of which is marked 'King's sketches'
with rooms labelled 'Queen's apartment' and 'Prince of Wales
apartment', may date from early in the following decade
(Soane Museum, Adam vol. 54/135–40; see Tait 1993,
pp. 52–3 and Rowan 2003, nos. 59–60).

96. John Yenn (1750–1821)

Design for the Music Room, Windsor Castle, 1794

Pen and ink and wash. 49.2 × 64.1 cm (19⅜″ × 25¼″)
Signed and dated *John Yenn Delint Anno 1794*
RL 18690
PROVENANCE Made for George III
LITERATURE *King's Works*, VI, p. 375; Roberts (H.) 1997;
Roberts (H.) 2001, pp. 3–5, 78–9

John Yenn was a pupil of Chambers from 1764 and five
years later was one of the first students to be admitted to the
Royal Academy Schools, where he was awarded a gold medal
in 1771. Drawings such as this well demonstrate his skill
as a draughtsman, working with the techniques learnt in
Chambers's studio to produce drawings of great beauty and
clarity. Yenn became one of the architect's chief assistants.
In 1774 Chambers described him as 'an ingenious faithful
intelligent servant' who 'for two or three years past has
managed a great part of my extensive business very much
to my satisfaction' (BL Add. MS 41135, f. 26). After the start
of work at Somerset House, Chambers depended on Yenn
increasingly, both in London and in the different projects
commissioned by the King elsewhere. In 1782 Yenn was
appointed by the Office of Works to the position of Clerk of
the Works at Buckingham House and Kensington Palace. He
was elected Royal Academician in 1791 and on Chambers's
death in 1796 he became Treasurer to the Royal Academy,
actively (occasionally acrimoniously) involving himself in
the politics of that institution.

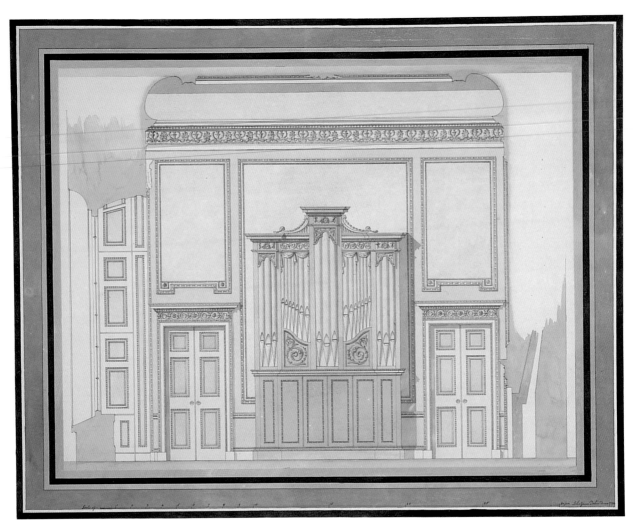

96

After completion of his work on the Queen's Lodge and Lower Lodge at Windsor, in 1781 Chambers was instructed to refurbish a set of apartments for the Prince of Wales in the eastern range of the Upper Ward. It is unlikely that the Prince used these rooms more than very occasionally, particularly after the start of work on Carlton House and Brighton Pavilion. In 1794 some of the Prince's apartments were re-allocated for the Queen's use, and a fine new Music Room and Drawing Room were established there. The decoration of these rooms was part of the 'Neo-classical Episode' before the King's decision to transform the castle into a Gothic palace with the help of James Wyatt (see Roberts (H.) 1997, and no. 129).

The Music Room was on the approximate site of the present Crimson Drawing Room, created by Wyatville thirty years later. Because of the awkward configuration of the castle, it provided the main access between the private apartments and the State Apartments. The decoration was in a restrained and – by now – rather old-fashioned style. The ornamentation was limited to friezes and panels of foliage. The Music Room was to be painted in a mixture of pale blue, pink and grey, and the Drawing Room was to be yellow, lilac and broken white. Although the decoration of these rooms was the responsibility of Yenn, they continued the spirit of William Chambers which had by now been a presence at Windsor for nearly twenty years. Yenn's designs, inscribed with dates between October 1794 and February 1796, are divided between the Royal Collection, the Royal Academy and the Victoria and Albert Museum.

The Music Room would have filled an important role in the lives of the royal family at Windsor. In 1788 the Princess Royal wrote that 'A love of music to distraction runs through our family' (Brooke 1972, p. 302). Music-making was part of their daily routine, from the earliest years of the reign. However, little is recorded of the furnishing and use of this room, apart from the fact that it contained a harpsichord (possibly Handel's own instrument), and that in 1804 the King intended to have Roubiliac's bust of Handel (possibly no. 252) placed on a bracket above the chimneypiece on the west wall.

At the same period Yenn was also involved in the refurbishment of the State Apartments at Windsor (see no. 129) and in the King's projects at Buckingham House, including the redecoration of the Saloon following the removal of the Raphael Cartoons in 1787 (see no. 111) and the provision of a new cold bath house for the King, erected in the garden to the south of the library wing (see *Chambers* 1996, p. 47). In addition, *c.*1800–1810 he worked on the Duke of Kent's apartments at Kensington Palace.

97. James Wyatt (1746–1813)

Frogmore House: design for the staircase hall (side elevation), 1794

Pencil, pen and ink and wash. 39.2 × 61.0 cm (15 7/16″ × 24″)
RL 26527

98. James Wyatt (1746–1813)

Frogmore House: design for the staircase hall (end elevations), 1794

Pencil, pen and ink and wash. 39.2 × 61.3 cm (15 7/16″ × 24 1/8″)
RL 26530
PROVENANCE Made for Queen Charlotte
LITERATURE Roberts (J.) 1997, pp. 216–19

Just as Chambers had been George III's favourite architect in the first part of his reign, so James Wyatt – some twenty-three years Chambers's junior – was the chief architect of the period between 1796 (the year in which Chambers died) and the start of the Regency in 1811. As with Chambers, the King was able to trust Wyatt to produce what he required. The first projects undertaken by the architect for the royal couple – at Frogmore (nos. 97, 98), and at Buckingham House (see no. 109) – were in an elegant neo-classical style which harmonised well with the work undertaken earlier in the reign by Chambers. However, his 1791 design for Little Frogmore had been in a decorative Gothic style (Roberts (J.) 1997, pl. 218) and this was the style which Wyatt was expected to follow for his later royal commissions, whether at Kew or Windsor (see nos. 124 and 126). As the King explained to the Princess Royal in September 1803: 'I have taken to the former [the Gothic] from thinking Wyatt perfect in that style' (see nos. 124, 127).

Wyatt's work in Frogmore House commenced soon after the purchase of the Great Frogmore estate in 1792 (see no. 136). It is clear that Wyatt was very closely involved in all the works at Frogmore, whether in the house or in the garden buildings. He was to modernise the house and convert it as a 'Trianon' where the royal ladies could retire. The start of work on Wyatt's staircase was noted by the Queen in her diary entry for 1 March 1794: 'To Day Mr Armstrong begun to put up the Scaffold of the Great Stairs at Frogmore'

97

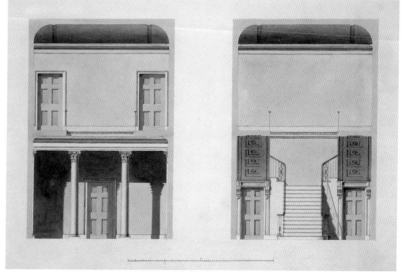

98

99

(RA GEO/Add. 43/3). In a curious parallel to his contemporary work at Buckingham House (1795: see no. 109), at Frogmore the original staircase, which rose around the four walls of the hallway, decorated with murals (uncovered in 1983) attributed to Louis Laguerre, was replaced with an 'imperial' stair. Wyatt had built a similar staircase at Heaton Hall, Manchester, as early as 1772.

Benjamin West told the diarist Joseph Farington that Wyatt owed his appointment as Surveyor-General to the intervention of Queen Charlotte and Princess Elizabeth, after 'building Frogmore &c &c for which it is believed He never recd. any pecuniary recompense' (*Farington Diary*, VIII, p. 2924).

99. Thomas Sandby (1721/3–1798)

A design for a road arch at Virginia Water, c.1765

Pencil, pen and ink and watercolour. 44.8 × 69.1 cm (17⅝″ × 27³⁄₁₆″)
RL 14649
LITERATURE Oppé 1947, no. 122; Roberts (J.) 1997, pl. 470

100. Thomas Sandby (1721/3–1798)

A design for a rustic summer house, c.1780

Pencil, pen and ink and watercolour. 22.2 × 23.7 cm (8¾″ × 9⁵⁄₁₆″)
RL 14715
LITERATURE Oppé 1947, no. 142; Roberts (J.) 1997, pl. 57

101. Thomas Sandby (1721/3–1798)

A design for a grotto and cascade at Virginia Water, c.1788

Pencil, pen and ink and watercolour. 26.5 × 45.7 cm (10⁷⁄₁₆″ × 18″)
RL 14666
LITERATURE Oppé 1947, no. 136; Roberts (J.) 1997, pl. 520

PROVENANCE Possibly George III; probably among the 'Various Sketches for Virginia Water' by Sandby noted by William Sandby in the Royal Library in 1892

Thomas Sandby occupies a unique position in artistic patronage during the reign of George III. He was a member, from 1746, of the household of the King's uncle, William, Duke of Cumberland, serving the Duke as Draughtsman – in Scotland, the Netherlands, and at Windsor – and, from 1764, as Steward of Windsor Great Park, of which the Duke had been appointed Ranger in July 1746; Sandby in effect acted as Deputy Ranger to both Prince William and his nephew (and successor as Ranger), the King's brother Prince Henry, Duke of Cumberland. He was therefore resident in the Great Park for much of his adult life. Two of the King's brothers were evidently very close indeed to Sandby, for the Duke of Cumberland and the Duchess of Gloucester stood sponsors to Sandby's two daughters Maria Frederica (born 1770) and Ann Sophia (born 1773) respectively.

100

101

However, Sandby also worked as an architect: in the list of subscribers to Chambers's *Treatise* of 1759 he was described as Architect to the Duke of Cumberland (see no. 87) and he designed an extension to the Duke's Windsor home, Cumberland Lodge, at around the same time. He also designed a new house at St Leonard's Hill for Lady Waldegrave, into which she moved – with the King's brother, the Duke of Gloucester – following their secret marriage in 1766 (see no. 84). In December 1768 Sandby was appointed first Professor of Architecture at the newly founded Royal Academy (see no. 159) and from 1770 he delivered a series of six lectures at the Royal Academy, which were repeated annually until his death. In 1777 he was appointed Architect of the King's Works, with James Adam (brother of Robert), and from 1780 to 1782 he was a member of the Board of Works as Master Carpenter, a titular office. His work in St George's Chapel in the 1780s (see no. 135) and his design for a picture gallery at the west end of the North Terrace (Roberts (J.) 1997, pl. 54) were probably associated with these appointments. The fact that a number of Sandby's topographical views were engraved as illustrations in Chambers's publications (including *Kew*), and that he provided (with his younger brother, Paul) crucial records of both Richmond Lodge and the Dutch House at Kew, *c*.1770–2 (nos. 120, 123), further indicates his multifarious skills and roles. Sandby's work as a military draughtsman and topographer is represented here by his panoramic watercolour of the military camp on Warley Common in 1778, which was part of the King's military map collection (no. 193).

It is likely that each of these designs – and the many others of the same type in the Royal Collection – was intended for Windsor Great Park. No. 99 may have been made for Prince William, Duke of Cumberland, who created the great artificial lake – Virginia Water – by building a pondhead at the south-eastern corner of the park in 1749. The Duke had purchased the masonry and decorative carvings of the Holbein Gate, Whitehall, after its demolition in 1759. An early proposal to re-erect the gateway as a screen at the southern end of the Long Walk was abandoned prior to Sandby's proposal (seen in no. 99) for the erection of the gateway as a road bridge at the Blacknest end of Virginia Water (see Roberts (J.) 1995, no. 46).

The design for the rustic summer house (no. 100) was probably made for the King's brother, Prince Henry, Duke of Cumberland, who continued Prince William's work at Windsor but showed less interest in architecture than either his uncle or his brother. The original pondhead at Virginia Water and many of Prince William's landscape features there were destroyed by torrential rainfall in September 1768. The cost of repairing the lake would be considerable, especially because it would involve the diversion of the main road (the present A30) in order to secure the new pondhead. There is little evidence that Prince Henry attempted any reparations. However, in August 1781 the King himself announced that 'the water in the Great Park and Windsor should be restored with considerable Improvements (which Improvements his Majesty has approved of . . .)'. Sandby was closely involved in the designs for these works. When the new pondhead collapsed soon after completion, he was nicknamed 'Tommy Sandbank'. A stronger pondhead was then constructed, which incorporated a waterfall and grotto – similar to the original 1750s arrangement – as shown in no. 101. Work on the new pondhead and cascade was completed by the time of the King's recovery and return to Windsor in March 1789. On Prince Henry's death in the following year, the King was finally able to take over the running of the Great Park for himself (see nos. 218, 219). The Duke was not replaced as Ranger, but Sandby appears to have continued in his role as Deputy Ranger – under the King.

4. The Royal Residences (nos. 102–142)

George III was the first English king to have a family of grown-up sons and daughters since Edward III in the fourteenth century. Since the seventeenth century the principal royal residences had been concentrated in the south-east of England. On his accession the King inherited St James's Palace (built by Henry VIII) and Kensington Palace (acquired by William III and Mary II). In addition to the ancient stronghold of Windsor, there were two other royal residences outside London: Hampton Court Palace (acquired by Henry VIII) and Richmond Lodge (acquired by George II). In the early years of the reign Richmond was the principal royal retreat: as well as Richmond Lodge, the royal family used the Dutch House and – after the death of the Dowager Princess of Wales, in 1772 – the White House. The use – and periodic adaptation – of so many different residences was necessitated by the rapidly increasing size of the royal family (fig. 12). The favourite residences of the King and Queen tended to be those that they had personally acquired and furnished: Buckingham House in London, and Frogmore House close to Windsor Castle, which came into royal possession respectively in 1762 and 1792. A combination of circumstances led to the Dutch House (today's Kew Palace) becoming a favourite residence in the first decades of the nineteenth century; it was there that Queen Charlotte died, in 1818.

The most significant visual records of these houses in George III's reign are the plates in W.H. Pyne's *History of the Royal Residences*, issued in parts but finally published in three volumes in 1819. The advertisement for Pyne's publication, placed in Ackermann's *Repository* in October 1815, indicated that some of the views were already complete; the project had therefore presumably been instigated some time before. Jutsham recorded the arrival of the first and second issues at Carlton House in August 1816 'from Mr Pyne' – 'in Colours, with their Letter Press' (Jutsham II). For consistency, the individual views are here dated to the year of publication inscribed on the associated print.

One quarter of Pyne's hundred plates were devoted to Windsor Castle; twenty-four to the Prince Regent's town palace at Carlton House; thirteen each to Kensington Palace and Hampton Court Palace; eleven to Buckingham House, eight to St James's Palace and six to the Queen's residence at Frogmore. Kew – in other words, the Dutch House – was named in the 1815 advertisement, but did not feature in the final work.

FIG. 12 Anonymous, *'The Royal Dozen or the King and Queen of Great Britain with the Ten Royal Children'*, c.1774. Engraving (RCIN 604695)

Pyne's plates show the appearance of George III's residences in the last years of his life, when the King was confined at Windsor. When studying them it is perhaps worth remembering the striking account of the uncarpeted 'cold and hard-rubbed' floors at Buckingham House in 1802, and the King's opinion 'that carpets and other means of great warmth are injurious to health' (*Gentleman's Magazine*, LXXII, p. 1184; see also p. 124 below). After the declaration of the Regency in February 1811, many of the furnishings (and in particular the curtains and upholstery) were replaced. However, the architectural context had remained largely unchanged from the time when the King and Queen had been actively engaged in the furnishing of their residences.

The three volumes of Pyne's publication were dedicated to Queen Charlotte, to the Prince Regent, and to the Duke of York. In addition to several copies of the published work, the Royal Collection also contains what appear to be the finished watercolours for the engraved plates; it is these – rather than the published plates – which are included here. They were formerly contained in a single album, which was probably acquired by George IV (see Oppé 1950, under no. 657).

KENSINGTON PALACE (nos. 102–104)

102. William Westall (1781–1850)

Kensington Palace: The south and east fronts, 1819

Watercolour and bodycolour over pencil. 20.5 × 28.3 cm (8⅟₁₆″ × 11⅛″)

RL 22148

LITERATURE Pyne 1819, II, *Kensington Palace*, opposite title page; Watkin 1984, pp. 61–2

Kensington Palace was much used by sovereigns from William III to George II, and the majority of the miniatures, drawings and historical jewels in the Collection appear to have been at Kensington at the time of George III's accession. However, they were soon transferred – with many of the finer paintings – to Buckingham House and by 1795 Kensington was described as 'entirely forsaken' (Lysons 1792–6, III, p. 185). Pyne considered that 'as Kensington Palace is so rarely visited, it would be well to select the best remaining graphic works, particularly the portraits, to add to the interest of the other royal collections' (Pyne 1819, II,

Kensington Palace, p. 78). His text conceals the fact that Kensington was the home of the Prince Regent's estranged wife, Caroline of Brunswick, between 1808 and 1813, and of two of George III's sons – Prince Edward, Duke of Kent, from 1804, and Prince Augustus, Duke of Sussex, from 1810. It was at Kensington that the Duke of Kent's only child, the future Queen Victoria, was born in May 1819, the month in which this view was published. (At this period the Kents occupied rooms on the first floor in the south-east portion of the palace, shown here.)

The core of Kensington Palace is the early seventeenth-century villa purchased by William III from the Earl of Nottingham in 1689. Over the following thirty years the villa was converted to the palace that has survived largely unchanged to this day. Sir Christopher Wren was initially in charge of the work but his assistant Nicholas Hawksmoor gradually assumed responsibility. The first phase of work, from 1689, included the Stone Gallery (to the left in this view). In the 1690s the main eleven-bay palace block was added, with the principal rooms at second-floor level; in this view all but the two most easterly (corner) windows on the second floor light the King's Gallery (see no. 103). At the same period a series of apartments was added to the north for Mary II, who died in her newly completed Bedchamber at Kensington in 1694. On the east front, the pediment marks the suite of three rooms (including the Cupola Room) built for George I, *c.*1718.

103. Charles Wild (1781–1835)

Kensington Palace: The King's Gallery, 1816

Watercolour with touches of bodycolour over etched outlines. 19.8 × 25.0 cm (7¹³⁄₁₆″ × 9¹³⁄₁₆″)

RL 22158

LITERATURE Pyne 1819, II, *Kensington Palace*, opposite p. 78; Watkin 1984, pp. 72–3; Waterfield 1991, no. A2; *Royal Treasures* 2002, no. 435

The King's Gallery is the principal room on the second floor of the south-facing block built at Kensington in 1695–6 as part of the first wave of William and Mary's works (see no. 102). It was approached via Wren's great staircase to the north-west (the King's Stair), and runs east–west, lit by a line of windows on the south wall. Doors at the far end lead into closets and thence into the remainder of the King's Apartments.

102

103

104

The Gallery is still used today as originally intended (and as shown here) – for the display of paintings. Wild's view records the appearance of the Gallery following redecoration by William Kent for George I in 1725–7: the chimneypiece (surmounted by William III's wind-dial), doorcases, ceiling (painted with scenes from the Odyssey), and crimson damask used for the wall-hangings and curtains, all date from that period.

However, by the time of Wild's view the original picture hang – with matching Palladian frames – had been replaced by a miscellaneous assemblage. The painting on the end wall – Sebastiano Ricci's *Adoration* (no. 143) – was acquired by George III with Smith's collection and was later moved to Hampton Court. In 1993–4 the crimson silk was reintroduced, the woodwork was repainted, and some of the paintings which hung in the King's Gallery at the time of Kent's changes were returned, in their uniform architectural frames.

104. James Stephanoff (1789–1874)

Kensington Palace: The Queen's Gallery, 1819

Watercolour over pencil. 19.9 × 25.3 cm (7¹³⁄₁₆″ × 9¹⁵⁄₁₆″)
RL 22155
LITERATURE Pyne 1819, II, *Kensington Palace*, opposite p. 67; Watkin 1984, pp. 71–2; Roberts (H.) 1995

This room is the largest in the apartments added for Mary II to the north of Kensington Palace in the years around 1690. In this watercolour the east-facing windows light the line of royal portraits along the west wall. Zoffany's portraits of the King and Queen (nos. 8, 9) were recorded in the Queen's Gallery c.1785–90. Thereafter a number of changes were made in the furnishing of the gallery, including the introduction of the organ cabinet (no. 264), shown here at the far end. This appears to have resulted from a royal commission in the 1740s; it was altered for George III and Queen Charlotte, probably in 1763; the six tall cabinets between the windows (see no. 265) would have been introduced to Kensington with the organ cabinet.

ST JAMES'S PALACE (no. 105)

105. Charles Wild (1781–1835)

St James's Palace: The north front, 1819

Watercolour with touches of bodycolour over pencil.
19.7 × 28.8 cm (7¾″ × 11⁵⁄₁₆″)

RL 22161

LITERATURE Pyne 1819, III, *St James's Palace*, opposite title page; Watkin 1984, pp. 49–50

In George III's reign St James's Palace was the ceremonial centre of court life. The main part of the palace – with the great gatehouse shown to left of centre in this view – was built by Henry VIII, on the site of a leper hospital. Additional buildings, including those that continue in use as the State Apartments, were introduced by Christopher Wren for Queen Anne in the early eighteenth century. These apartments culminated in the great Drawing Room and Council Chamber (now the Entrée Room and the Throne Room) overlooking the south front of the palace. It was in these rooms that the formal levées, Drawing Rooms and audiences took place throughout the eighteenth century.

The royal cabinet-maker William Vile supplied much new furniture for the Queen's rooms at St James's in the early 1760s (see nos. 266–9). However, in 1767 Mrs Lybbe Powys commented that 'tis Impossible as it now is' for the King to reside there in comfort as well as in state: hence the royal family's increasing use of Buckingham House. There are descriptions of weekly concerts in the palace at this period, on which occasions the King and Queen performed alongside professional musicians. Levées took place on Wednesday and Friday mornings and were attended by men only; until the King's illness in 1788, they also took place on Monday when Parliament was sitting. Drawing Rooms (which were open to both sexes) took place on Thursdays and Sundays and were attended by both the King and the Queen. These were the occasions at which new infant princes and princesses were first displayed to the public.

In January 1809 a fire destroyed a large portion of the buildings in the south-eastern part of the palace. According to Pyne, this included 'the most interesting and picturesque part of the ancient structure, and comprehending the king's and the queen's private apartments . . . [and] some of the old state apartments . . . Since which event the palace has not been visited by their Majesties but on a few public occasions; the courts of late having been held at her Majesty's palace of Buckingham-House, or at Carlton-House, the palace of his Royal Highness the Prince Regent' (Pyne 1819, III, *St James's Palace*, pp. 79–80).

105

HAMPTON COURT PALACE
(nos. 106–107)

106. William Westall (1781–1850)
Hampton Court Palace: The east (garden) front, 1819
Watercolour with touches of bodycolour over pencil.
19.5 × 28.8 cm (7¹¹⁄₁₆″ × 11⁵⁄₁₆″)
RL 22124
LITERATURE Pyne 1819, II, *Hampton Court,* opposite title page

Like Kensington Palace, Hampton Court Palace – on the River Thames to the south-west of London – has not been occupied by the sovereign since the reign of George II. George III seldom visited it, preferring the other rural residences at Richmond and Kew – or Windsor.

The earliest buildings at Hampton Court date from the start of the sixteenth century, when Cardinal Wolsey erected for himself a residence of royal proportions and grandeur. It was confiscated by Henry VIII in the 1530s and was further enlarged and enhanced. Soon after the accession of William and Mary in 1689, Christopher Wren was commissioned to create a new royal palace at Hampton Court – set within an up-to-date formal garden. Work on this magnificent project continued into the early eighteenth century and resulted in two separate apartments – for the King, and for the Queen –

arranged around a new courtyard (Fountain Court) and looking east and south over splendid gardens. The brick and stone façade shown here, in front of the east-facing rooms of the Queen's Apartments, was the chief external face of this new work. The three windows beneath the pediment at first-floor level light the Queen's Drawing Room.

107. Richard Cattermole (?1795–1868)
Hampton Court Palace: The Queen's Guard Chamber, 1819
Watercolour with touches of bodycolour over pencil.
20.2 × 26.8 cm (7¹⁵⁄₁₆″ × 10⁹⁄₁₆″)
RL 22126
LITERATURE Pyne 1819, II, *Hampton Court,* opposite p. 19

The appearance of this room – called the 'Banqueting Hall' by Pyne – well demonstrates the state of Hampton Court by the end of George III's reign. Since the death of Queen Caroline in 1737 no sovereign or consort had lived there and many of the paintings and furnishings were transferred to other royal residences. The main rooms remained maintained and furnished, for the benefit of the visitors who made appointments to view the royal apartments. But other rooms – as here – were no more than store rooms.

The Queen's Guard Chamber was the first room in the suite of Queen's Apartments on the first floor of the palace,

106

107

commenced by Sir Christopher Wren for Mary II in the 1690s. The Queen's rooms were arranged around the north and east sides of Fountain Court, in the eastern area of the palace. The behatted figures either side of the chimneypiece are intended to represent Yeomen of the Guard, who would have stood in the Guard Chamber when the court was in residence. The chimneypiece was probably designed by Sir John Vanbrugh in the reign of George I. At the time, this room was used by the Prince of Wales (the future George II).

BUCKINGHAM HOUSE (nos. 108–118)

108. William Westall (1781–1850)

Buckingham House: The east (entrance) front, 1819

Watercolour and bodycolour over pencil. 21.8 × 27.0 cm (8⁹⁄₁₆″ × 10⅝″)

RL 22137

LITERATURE Pyne 1819, II, *Buckingham House,* opposite p. 1; Watkin 1984, pp. 75–7; Harris (J.) 1993, p. 30

Buckingham House was the principal London home of George III and Queen Charlotte and was purchased by the King in 1762. The house had been built in 1702–5 by John Sheffield, Duke of Buckingham and Normanby (1648–1721), probably to the designs of William Talman. The principal façade shown here is essentially that of the original house;

however, in the 1760s the King removed many of the more ornate baroque features (including the row of statues on the skyline, angle pilasters and forecourt fountain) and added a pediment over the front door – to ensure that it complied with his rather more sober taste. The assemblage of subsidiary buildings in the background to right and left of the main house were also George III's additions, of the 1760s and 1770s. These contained (at right) the Prince of Wales's apartments and (at left) the suite of library rooms. The mast is associated with the weather vane over the chimneypiece in the East Library rooms (no. 118).

George III had bought the property from Sir Charles Sheffield (d. 1774), the illegitimate son of the Duke of Buckingham, for £28,000. The purchase was concluded early in 1762, a few months after the King's marriage and coronation, and shortly before the birth of his first child. Buckingham House was intended principally for the use of Queen Charlotte, and was habitually referred to as 'The Queen's House'. In the year of the house's purchase, the King explained to Lord Bute that it was 'not meant for a Palace, but a retreat' (Hedley 1975, p. 71). Buckingham House soon became the chief home of the King and Queen while St James's Palace, a short distance along the Mall to the east, was the official seat of the court. All but the eldest of the King and Queen's fifteen children were born at Buckingham House.

In July 1762 the Office of Works assumed responsibility for superintending the works involved in making Buckingham

108

House fit for the King's occupation; this involved a certain amount of new building, and a considerable amount of adjustment of the existing building, including full redecoration. By 1774 £73,000 had been spent on the project. The work was managed by a combination of the King's friend and Surveyor of the Board of Works, Thomas Worsley, and the King's architect, William Chambers. George III's birthday celebrations in June 1763 (see no. 95) marked the initial completion of works at Buckingham House, and the occupation of the building by the King and his family. In 1775 the house was transferred to Queen Charlotte by Act of Parliament, in exchange for Somerset House in the Strand, which had formerly served as the Queen's dower house but which was now to be rebuilt for governmental and institutional purposes.

The front door led directly into the Entrance Hall (no. 109). In the main block, reading from the left, the first three windows at first- and second-floor level lit the great staircase hall (nos. 109, 110), while the central three lit the Saloon (no. 111). By the date of this view Buckingham House had been largely abandoned by the royal family: the Queen had died, the King was confined to Windsor, and the Prince Regent held court at Carlton House along the Mall to the east. In the following reign George IV decided to combine the domestic, official and ceremonial activities of the monarch

on a single site and Buckingham House was rebuilt as Buckingham Palace. Although the core of the building shown here survives in the heart of Nash's palace, it is today scarcely recognisable. The principal survivor of George III's building work at Buckingham House is the Riding House, erected 1762–6 and now part of the Royal Mews.

109. Richard Cattermole (?1795–1868)

Buckingham House: The staircase from the Entrance Hall, 1817

Watercolour and bodycolour over pencil. 20.8 × 26.1 cm (8³⁄₁₆″ × 10¼″)

RL 22139

LITERATURE Pyne 1819, II, *Buckingham House*, opposite p. 7; Watkin 1984, p. 80; Harris (J.) 1993, p. 31; Jackson-Stops 1993, pp. 44–5

The staircase was one of the principal features of the original Buckingham House. It was approached directly from the southern end of the Entrance Hall and rose through two storeys; it was the subject of two plates in Pyne's publication – the present one, drawn by Cattermole, and no. 110 drawn by James Stephanoff. The walls were decorated with murals by Louis Laguerre recounting the story of Dido and Aeneas. The original arrangement of the stair and hall is shown in early

109

eighteenth-century plans and in a ground-plan of 1776 (Russell 1987, fig. 46): the stair rose in three flights around the west, south and east walls of the hall from which it was separated by a screen, with two freestanding columns. Vile supplied eight mahogany lanterns for the hall in 1763 (see no. 271).

In 1795 (following a scheme proposed by Chambers in 1776) the staircase was changed to the 'imperial' stair shown here, in which a central initial flight divides into two at a half landing before returning in two final flights. The architect responsible for this work was James Wyatt, who introduced a similar change at Frogmore at around the same time (see nos. 97, 98). The new staircase would have involved a major adjustment of the architecture in the south-west corner of the staircase hall (the right half of this view); Wyatt's magnificent Corinthian order and arches blend so harmoniously with Laguerre's painted architecture – and with Chambers's building work of the 1760s – that it is difficult to differentiate one from the other. Other changes made in the 1790s would have included the addition of further freestanding columns in the Entrance Hall (seen clearly in no. 110), supporting the Saloon above.

Cattermole's view shows – at right – two of the large Venetian paintings which George III hung in the Entrance Hall: Canaletto's view of the Pantheon (no. 146) and the *Landscape with Triumphal Arch to George II* (Levey 1991, no. 672). Other paintings in the latter series, including nos. 152 and 153, are also recorded in the hall in the 1819 Buckingham House inventory.

110. James Stephanoff (1789–1874)

Buckingham House: The staircase, 1818

Watercolour and bodycolour over pencil. 25.1 × 20.0 cm (9⅞″ × 7⅞″)
RL 22138
LITERATURE Pyne 1819, II, *Buckingham House*, opposite p. 5; Watkin 1984, pp. 80–81; Harris (J.) 1993, p. 31; Jackson-Stops 1993, pp. 44–5

Stephanoff's view of the magnificent staircase hall complements Cattermole's view of the initial flight of stairs (no. 109), giving a fine indication of the bold fictive architectural setting provided by Laguerre, and of the size and appearance of the ceiling painting. In addition, it shows how – as part of the alterations made for George III (see no. 109) – the north wall (facing us in this view) was repainted with *trompe-l'oeil* architectural recesses, particularly the central one surrounding the door to the Saloon. The door itself had been introduced by Chambers in the 1760s; its insertion must have involved the destruction of some of Laguerre's murals. The new fictive architecture provided a suggestion of architectural relief and grandeur in this area which was previously absent. Responsibility for the painting may have lain with William Oram, an employee of the Office of Works who restored Verrio's King's Stair at Hampton Court at around the same time (see *King's Works*, V, p. 136).

The door at left on the first-floor landing led to the Queen's Breakfast Room (no. 113). At the foot of the stairs a small

110

part of the Entrance Hall is shown, with its freestanding columnar supports and paintings by Canaletto and other Venetian masters adorning the walls.

111. James Stephanoff (1789–1874)

Buckingham House: The Saloon, 1818

Watercolour and bodycolour over pencil. 20.1 × 25.1 cm
(7¹⁵⁄₁₆″ × 9⅞″)

RL 22141

LITERATURE Pyne 1819, II, *Buckingham House*, opposite p. 13;
Watkin 1984, pp. 82–3; Jackson-Stops 1993, pp. 45–7; Worsley
1993, pp. 101–2

The Saloon was the largest room in Buckingham House and occupied the first and second floor in the centre of the entrance front of the house, immediately above the Entrance Hall. George III's works in the 1760s may have involved a complete reconstruction of this room: as shown in this view, it is the work of a combination of the King's architects – Robert Adam, William Chambers, John Yenn and probably also James 'Athenian' Stuart.

The room was evidently in a fit state to receive the seven vast Raphael Cartoons from Hampton Court in 1763. They were described in the Saloon by Horace Walpole in 1783, hanging edge to edge on all except the window wall, with

'light green Damask' below. Cipriani's finely detailed ceiling, possibly designed by James Stuart, was presumably in place by 1763; it replaced one painted by Laguerre. The chimney-piece on the north wall was designed by Robert Adam; it was included in his *Works in Architecture* with the date 1761. Adam's design for a massive doorway, flanked by Ionic columns, may have been intended for the opening on the left leading to the Crimson Drawing Room (Colvin 1968, pl. 28).

After the Raphael Cartoons were removed in 1787 (to be taken first to Windsor, then back to Hampton Court), the walls of the Saloon were decorated in the manner shown here. Elevations for the new decorative scheme were supplied by John Yenn (see Jackson-Stops 1993, pl. IV).

Stephanoff's view also records the furnishings supplied in 1799 by the carver and gilder William Adair: six large sofas and three small ones (for the window bays; see Smith 1931, p. 92). These were originally covered with white cotton velvet, painted with flowers by Princess Elizabeth. Further changes were made after the fire at St James's Palace in 1809, the declaration of the Regency in 1811 and Parliament's decision in 1812 to grant Queen Charlotte her own establishment, including income for the upkeep of Buckingham House. A number of the formal receptions previously held at St James's were now transferred to Buckingham House, hence the presence of the fine canopied throne in the Saloon. New upholstery (in red) was introduced at the same time.

The site of George III's Saloon is now occupied by Nash's Green Drawing Room. The chimneypiece, still surmounted by the same white marble clock – with figures of Vigilance and Patience, carved by John Bacon the elder in 1789 – is now in the Queen's Presence Chamber at Windsor Castle.

112. James Stephanoff (1789–1874)

Buckingham House: The Crimson Drawing Room, 1817

Watercolour and bodycolour over pencil. 20.3 × 25.3 cm
(8″ × 9¹⁵⁄₁₆″)

RL 22142

LITERATURE Pyne 1819, II, *Buckingham House*, opposite p. 14;
Jackson-Stops 1993, pp. 50–51; *Royal Treasures* 2002, no. 414

This room – entitled the 'Drawing Room' in Pyne's publica-tion – was in the centre of the Queen's Apartments on the west or garden front of Buckingham House, where it lay between the Queen's Breakfast Room (no. 113) and the Second Drawing Room (no. 114). Through the central door

111

112

in this view can be seen the canopied throne in the Saloon next door (no. 111).

At the time of the King's purchase of Buckingham House, the room was called the 'Japanned Room' owing to the black and gold panelling which adorned the walls. In 1763 the panelling was transferred to the room immediately to the south – the Queen's Breakfast Room – where it is shown by Pyne (see no. 113). The painted ceiling, new doorcases, dado rail and frieze, and the marble chimneypiece, were introduced at the same time. While the ceiling was designed by Robert Adam, the doorcases followed the King's own design, as recorded in a drawing presented to Thomas Worsley. The drawing – inscribed by Worsley *Invenit, designavit dedit Georgius III* – was noted in Worsley's inventory as 'A drawing of a door etc. done by the King and given me to execute at the Queen's House' (*Chambers* 1996, pp. 48–9, fig. 69). The chimneypiece garniture, including Matthew Boulton's sphinx vases and clock (nos. 276, 277), was made for the King and Queen in the 1770s. They had been particularly anxious to garnish the chimneypiece of the Queen's bedroom with Boulton's wares; the bedroom is not among the rooms shown by Pyne and it is likely that its furnishings had been removed and redeployed amongst the other rooms on the first floor by the time of Pyne's publication.

Pyne's views of the Queen's Apartments at Buckingham House show them after they had been rehung in the opening years of the nineteenth century with paintings from the King's rooms on the floor below. The two large pictures either side of the central door – Van Dyck's *St Martin* and the Rubensian *Philip II of Spain* – hung in the King's Drawing Room until *c.*1804. The other paintings shown by Stephanoff include Rubens's *Balthasar Gerbier and his family* on the left wall, and Domenichino's *St Agnes* to the left of the chimneypiece.

At the time of Horace Walpole's visit in 1783 the room was hung with red damask; this had been replaced by crimson satin by the time of this view. The change was part of the alterations made *c.*1812, the date of the suite of new giltwood seat furniture, and of the torchères attributed to Tatham, Bailey and Saunders (no. 292), shown here at either side of the main doorway.

113. James Stephanoff (1789–1874)

Buckingham House: The Queen's Breakfast Room, 1817

Watercolour and bodycolour over pencil. 20.2 × 25.3 cm (7¹⁵⁄₁₆″ × 9¹⁵⁄₁₆″)

RL 22145

LITERATURE Pyne 1819, II, *Buckingham House*, opposite p. 20; Watkin 1984, p. 86; Jackson-Stops 1993, pp. 48–50

This west-facing room was immediately to the south of the Crimson Drawing Room on the first floor. The door at the left led directly into the staircase hall (see no. 110) while that to the right of the chimneypiece led into a closet adjoining a small private staircase leading to the King's Closet and Bedroom on the ground floor below.

The black and gold painted panelling was transferred from the Crimson Drawing Room in 1763. It had been part of the furnishings of the original Buckingham House and was acquired with the house by George III in 1762. The King's cabinet-maker William Vile repaired and reassembled the panelling for its new setting. Evidently it was not thought appropriate to add a painted ceiling of the type introduced into the two rooms to the north. The mahogany organ to the left of the chimneypiece is probably that supplied by John Bradburn in 1766/7; it is now in The Queen's Chapel, St James's Palace. In the 1770s and 1780s a number of paintings were recorded hanging in this room, including two large canvases by Van Dyck: *Charles I and M. de St Antoine* and *The 'Great Piece'*. These were among the pictures transferred in 1804 to Windsor, where they are shown by Pyne in the Queen's Presence Chamber (no. 130).

A notable feature of the decoration is the porcelain displayed on the chimneypiece and on the ledge above, and over the doors. Queen Charlotte is known to have assembled a fine group of porcelain from a wide variety of different sources. In 1783 Horace Walpole described the impression created by these pieces: 'Some modern jars of Chinese porcelaine, many of Chelsea porcelaine, & a few of Seve' (Walpole 1928, p. 78). Among the recognisable pieces shown in this view are the pair of King's vases (see no. 275) on the chimneypiece.

The arrangement of the drapery on the window wall – and the seat furniture – shown here was introduced in January 1810 by Elliot Son and Francis, upholsterers. Eight years earlier an anonymous account in the *Gentleman's Magazine* recorded that the velvet curtains had been 'painted by Princess Elizabeth, in shades of brown and maroon, in

113

114

imitation of cut velvet' (LXXII, p. 1184). The carpet recorded in Stephanoff's view may also date from 1810; in 1802 there was no carpet.

114. James Stephanoff (1789–1874)

Buckingham House: The Second Drawing Room, 1818

Watercolour and bodycolour over pencil. 19.8 × 24.9 cm (7¹³⁄₁₆″ × 9¹³⁄₁₆″)

RL 22143

LITERATURE Pyne 1819, II, *Buckingham House*, opposite p. 16; Watkin 1984, p. 83; Jackson-Stops 1993, pp. 50–52

The Second Drawing Room (also known as the 'Warm Room': in 1802 it was one of only four rooms at Buckingham House to be carpeted) was located immediately to the north of the Crimson Drawing Room in the Queen's Apartments. It was the setting for Zoffany's painting of the Prince of Wales and Prince Frederick (Millar 1969, no. 1200), painted *c*.1765 soon after the completion of the King's building works. That painting already shows the marble chimneypiece and (in reflection) the new doorcases designed by the King. However, the rococo overmantel mirror and seat furniture had been replaced by the time of Stephanoff's view.

Zoffany's painting does not include the ceiling, which may have been completed shortly before. It was painted by Cipriani to a surviving design by William Chambers (*Chambers* 1996, no. 87, fig. 190). Notes on the design record that Cipriani was paid £225 for '17 pictures & 4 Genii', while Charles Cotton received £120 for 'painting in Gold and colour all the ornaments', and the upholsterer Samuel Norman received 12 guineas 'for pasting up the work'.

The paintings recorded by Stephanoff include portraits by Van Dyck also shown by Zoffany in the room over fifty years before. Other paintings shown here were already in this room in *c*.1774 (see Russell 1987, pp. 530–31; RL 26333): these include two Holy Families by Andrea del Sarto; and (to left and right of the chimneypiece) Maratta's *Virgin and Child with St Francis* and Cagnacci's *Jacob, Rachel and Leah*. The lacquer cabinets on stands survive in the Collection (RCIN 21627). The chimneypiece was transferred to the Queen's Presence Chamber at Windsor by William IV.

115. Anonymous English

Buckingham House: The Queen's Dressing Room (later the Blue Velvet Room) – hanging plan, c.1774

Pencil, pen and ink, pink and grey wash. 37.5 × 52.7 cm (14¾″ × 20¾″)

RL 26331

PROVENANCE Made for George III

LITERATURE Russell 1987, pp. 530–31, fig. 57

This is one of a series of hanging plans for the King's and Queen's rooms at Buckingham House, made *c*.1774, after the completion of the first wave of building work on the house. Many of the plans are annotated by the King, who was closely involved in fixing the appearance of the principal rooms of his new home (see Russell 1987). This design was preceded by a draft (RL 26330) and by large outline plans for five of the six miniatures cases (RL 26325–9). It is possible that these drawings were made by William Robinson of the Office of Works, who drew up many of the King's designs at this period (see no. 94). The bows and ribbons shown here are unusual in the Buckingham House hanging plans but were clearly appropriate for one of the Queen's rooms.

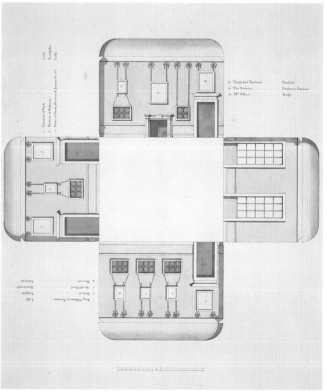

115

The room shown here was located at the north-west corner of Buckingham House. It was originally the Queen's Bedchamber. Vile's bookcase (no. 267) was almost certainly made for the east wall of this room (the left wall in this view). However, after the creation of a new bedroom for the Queen in 1766/7, the room served as her dressing room; by 1817 it had been renamed the Blue Velvet Room (see no. 116).

The appearance of the room was recorded by Mrs Lybbe Powys in March 1767: 'Round the dressing-room, let into the crimson damask hangings in a manner uncommonly elegant, are frames of fine impressions, miniatures &c., &c.' (*Lybbe Powys* 1899, p. 116). The frames (with small hexagonal panes) for miniatures, suspended below the paintings, are clearly indicated on this design. The arrangement was also noted by Horace Walpole in 1783: 'a vast quantity of enamelled pictures, miniatures and cameos, amongst which six or eight at least of Charles 1st'. The miniatures were still there in 1796; the new hang shown in no. 116 was probably introduced *c.*1812. The paintings noted in the *c.*1774 hang include – on the north wall – portraits by Rembrandt (White 1982,

no. 167) and Van Dyck (Millar 1963, no. 114); on the east wall Rubens's self portrait (RCIN 400156) hangs between portraits of the Duke and Duchess of York (Millar 1963, nos. 274 and 240); Barocci's painting of the Nativity (Shearman 1983, no. 12) hangs over the chimneypiece.

116. Charles Wild (1781–1835)

Buckingham House: The Blue Velvet Room, 1817

Watercolour and bodycolour over pencil. 19.6 × 24.9 cm (7 11/16″ × 9 13/16″)

RL 22144

LITERATURE Pyne 1819, II, *Buckingham House*, opposite p. 18; Watkin 1984, p. 87; Jackson-Stops 1993, pp. 52–3; *Royal Treasures* 2002, no. 413

This room, at the north-west corner of Buckingham House, had originally been used as the Queen's bedroom, but in the late 1760s it became her dressing room (see no. 115). It is shown by Wild soon after the completion of redecoration and refurnishing carried out from *c.*1812; this work involved

116

brighter and richer colours, new curtains, carpets and upholstery, and bolder gilding. The carpet is particularly magnificent; it was probably a product of the Wilton or Kidderminster manufactories. This is one of the few carpeted rooms shown by Pyne: the King considered that carpets were potentially injurious to health (see p. 110), and his own apartments (on the ground floor of Buckingham House) were therefore uncarpeted.

In the new decorative scheme the walls were hung with light blue silk, and a deeper blue velvet was used for the curtains and upholstery. The arrangement of the furniture – including a set of new giltwood chairs – suggests that the room may no longer have been used as a dressing room; the 'dressing table' – lit by a pair of King's vases (see no. 275) on torchères – between the windows is unusually high.

Some of the paintings included in the earlier hanging plan (no. 115) survived in this room: for instance, the portraits of the Duke and Duchess of York (the future James II and his first wife), used as overdoors on the east wall. However, all the landscapes shown here were recent introductions from the King's rooms on the floor below; they included paintings by Poussin, Claude and Rubens.

117. James Stephanoff (1789–1874)

Buckingham House: The Octagon Library, 1818

Watercolour and bodycolour over pencil. 21.2 × 24.9 cm (8⅜″ × 9¹³⁄₁₆″)

RL 22147

LITERATURE Pyne 1819, II, *Buckingham House*, opposite p. 26; Watkin 1984, pp. 84–5; *Royal Miscellany* 1990, no. 13; Jackson-Stops 1993, p. 54

This view of one of the King's four library rooms – entitled by Pyne 'The King's Library (II)' – shows the fine octagonal room added at the south-eastern extent of Buckingham House. These rooms occupied a wing added by Chambers to the southern end of the original building soon after the arrival of Consul Smith's books in London in 1763. After the Great (or West) Library of 1762–4 came the South and the Octagon Libraries in 1766–7, and finally the East Library (see no. 118) in 1772–3. Pyne only included views of the Octagon Library and the East Library in his publication; however, an engraving of the Great Library, entitled 'Library No. III', was issued in June 1818 (fig. 26). Another view of that room was used to illustrate the catalogue of the King's Library (Barnard (F.) 1820, I, p. i).

The principal access to the library rooms at ground-floor level was via a door from the King's bedroom, which led immediately into the Great Library. A staircase in the heart of this wing allowed access by staff and visitors from the basement floor, which contained the offices and rooms for the bookbinders (see p. 222). George III was keen to ensure that his library was as comprehensive as possible and scholars were encouraged to use it. An early visitor was Mrs Philip Lybbe Powys who in March 1767 described the three library rooms then extant (see p. 126). Samuel Johnson's famous interview with George III took place in these rooms in the same year.

In the Octagon Library, which was 42 feet (nearly 13 metres) wide, books filled all the available shelf space. The arrangement of books is largely undocumented. In this view the shelves between the door and the chimneypiece appear to have the added protection of cupboard doors, which may have been glazed; the remaining books were apparently on open shelves. The octagonal desk in the centre of the room was supplied for this position, probably by Bradburn, and survives – in altered form – in the Royal Library at Windsor Castle (see Roberts (H.) 1990b). Above the desk is the astronomical clock supplied by Eardley Norton in 1765 at the cost of £1,042 (no. 300). The room was lit by large lunette windows at high level; through one of these openings can be seen part of the first-floor room above the East Library.

The Octagon Library was the most spatially adventurous of these new rooms. Its form was almost certainly inspired by the library wing designed by Robert Adam in 1762–3 for Lord Bute's London residence, Bute (later Lansdowne) House (Harris (E.) 2001, pp. 130–31, pl. 192).

118. James Stephanoff (1789–1874)

Buckingham House: The East Library, 1817

Watercolour and bodycolour over pencil. 21.2 × 25.4 cm (8⅜″ × 10″)

RL 22140

LITERATURE Pyne 1819, II, *Buckingham House*, opposite p. 9; *Royal Miscellany* 1990, no. 12

Although this view (entitled 'The King's Library (I)' by Pyne) has previously been identified with the first of the library rooms – the Great or West Library (see fig. 26) – contemporary plans demonstrate that the room shown here can only be the East Library, added in 1772–3 parallel to the Great Library. In 1774 its roof was raised to accommodate

117

118

the new Marine Gallery for the display of the King's models of ships and seaports, described by a German visitor in 1786 (*Sophie in London 1786*, pp. 145–6). The operation of the wind-dial over the chimneypiece was described to the same German visitor by François-Justin Vulliamy, father of the maker (see no. 307). This view indicates something of both the quantity of books and the potential for disorganisation which prevailed in the library by the end of George III's reign. The portfolio labelled 'Hollar', propped up against the side of a desk, suggests that part of the collection of prints and drawings may have been kept in this area.

The Great, Octagon and East Libraries were the only rooms in the King's Apartments for which interior views are known. In 1766 Mrs Lybbe Powys described the King's rooms as 'fitted up rather neatly elegant than profusely ornamental' (*Lybbe Powys* 1899, p. 116). Pyne commented that 'although sufficiently spacious to admit of splendid decoration, [they] are remarkable for their plainness, being in character with those habits of simplicity which some great men have affected, but which in his Majesty George III were the offspring of a genuine love of domestic quiet in the bosom of his family. They are not without decoration, however; but the ornaments selected by this virtuous sovereign are such as change not with the fashions of the times.'

RICHMOND AND KEW (nos. 119–124)

119. Thomas Richardson (*fl.*1762–1802?)
Plan of the Royal Manor of Richmond, 1771

Pen and ink and grey wash and watercolour on vellum.
50.2 × 60.5 cm (19¾″ × 23¹³⁄₁₆″)
RCIN 503056
PROVENANCE Made for George III
LITERATURE Desmond 1995, pp. 65, 76–7; Cloake 1996, II, *passim*

This fine and decorative plan records the adjacent estates of Richmond and Kew, to the west of London, in the year before the death of the King's mother, the Dowager Princess of Wales. Thereafter the two estates were jointly occupied by the King; however, they were only physically united in 1802.

The plan is oriented with north at top right; the town of Richmond (with its ferry crossing over the River Thames) is shown at centre left. The plan was made at the time of the

King's proposals to build a new palace at Richmond (see nos. 90, 91), and to set it within a new landscape garden. The central strip of land within the curve of the river represents the remains of the village of West Sheen, purchased by George III in the 1760s as part of this scheme. Lancelot ('Capability') Brown was engaged to redesign the landscape at the same time. His work involved the destruction of the park buildings and formal planting that had been introduced to Queen Caroline's pleasure grounds at Richmond by William Kent and Charles Bridgeman in the 1730s. According to Arthur Young, writing at around the time that this plan was made, 'Richmond Gardens have been lately altered: the terrass and the grounds about it are now converted into waving lawn that hangs to the river in a most beautiful manner' (Young 1771, II, p. 247).

Within the area of the Old Deer Park at top left on this plan (just above the Lodge) is the King's Observatory (fig. 13), built by Chambers (as a gift from the Dowager Princess of Wales to her son) to enable the King to view the transit of Venus in 1769. The Observatory was erected close to the site of the temporary pavilion designed by Chambers to entertain the King's brother-in-law, Christian VII of Denmark, who had visited Richmond in September 1768. To the right of Richmond Lodge are Queen Charlotte's pleasure grounds and the clearing containing her 'New Menagerie' where exotic birds and animals (among them kangaroos sent from Australia) were kept. Soon after the date of this plan, the menagerie building was converted into a thatched tea house (Queen Charlotte's Cottage; fig. 14). Immediately below this is the broad band representing the Kew estate with (from left to right) the Pagoda – in a circular clearing – at the left end of the two lawns, the lake, a further area of lawn and the White House with adjacent buildings. The Dutch House is indicated between the White House and the river. At far right is Kew Green and Kew Bridge. The title plaque includes views of two of Chambers's pleasure buildings on the Kew estate – the Pagoda and the Mosque (see no. 122). The King's farms, where some of his Merino sheep were kept, occupied part of the area left white along the bottom of the plan.

A number of versions of Richardson's plan are known. The King's detailed plan of the main upper central area remains in its original ornately tooled red leather case (*Enlightenment* 2003, fig. 147). All of these plans were 'Taken under the Direction of Peter Burrell Esq. His Majesty's Surveyor

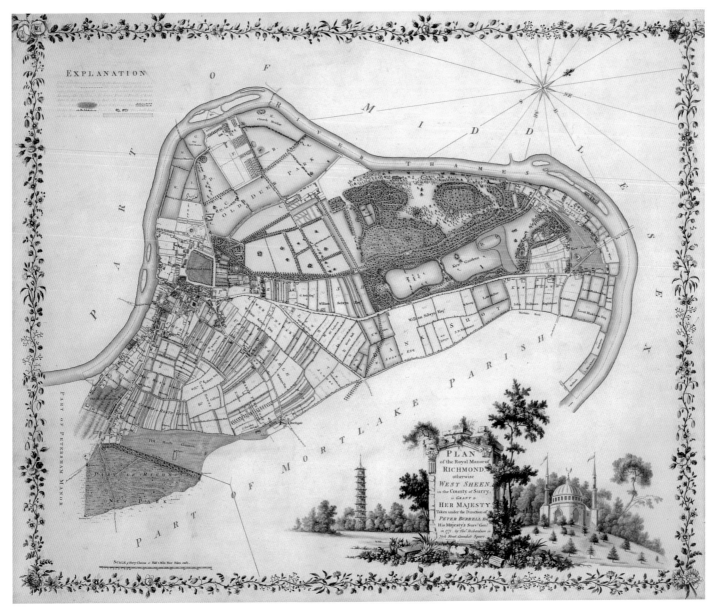

119

FIG. 13 Richmond Observatory, designed by William Chambers, 1769

FIG. 14 Queen Charlotte's Cottage, Kew, erected *c*.1772

General' in 1771, to record 'the Royal Manor of Richmond . . . in grant to Her Majesty'. The manor of Richmond had been formally granted to Queen Charlotte in October 1770.

120. Thomas Sandby (1721/3–1798) and Paul Sandby (1730–1809)

Richmond Lodge, c.1770

Pencil, pen and ink and watercolour. 38.8 × 62.0 cm (15¼″ × 24⁷⁄₁₆″)
RL 14711
LITERATURE Oppé 1947, no. 159; *King's Works*, V, pp. 224–7; Cloake 1996, II, chapter XVIII

Richmond Lodge was the King's first country residence. The earliest building on the site – around 200 yards (180 metres) to the east of the Observatory – was the home of the Keeper of the Old Deer Park at Richmond. In 1704 it was rebuilt by the Duke of Ormonde, who held the crown lease. Ormonde was involved in a plot to prevent the accession of George I and following his disgrace in 1715 Richmond Lodge became a residence of the Prince of Wales. On the accession of George II in 1727 the Lodge was granted to Queen Caroline, who made significant changes in the surrounding landscape, with the help of William Kent and Charles Bridgeman. In 1760 Richmond Lodge and its pleasure grounds became the property of George III. Although in 1761 a guidebook stated that the Lodge was 'unsuitable to the dignity of a King of England' (quoted Desmond 1995, p. 67), part of the royal couple's honeymoon was spent there and for seven years from 1764 Richmond was the royal family's chief country retreat, where they would stay from June to late October (Hedley 1975, pp. 47–8, 93). Small adjustments were made to the house for its new occupants. Among the furniture transferred to Richmond in the 1760s for the Queen's use were the pair of cabinets and stands (no. 272) and the Vile secretaire cabinet (no. 268); these were both refurbished by Bradburn for their new setting.

In the 1760s and early 1770s there were recurring proposals – all of which were ultimately abortive – to replace

120

Richmond Lodge with an entirely new building, Richmond Palace (see nos. 90, 91). Some of the pressure on space was eased when the two eldest Princes moved to the Dutch House in May 1771, where their education was to continue in the charge of governors. After the death of the King's mother early in the following year, the Queen announced to her brother Charles, 'We are going to move this summer to Kew, it will be better and more private' (Hedley 1975, p. 111). In late April they visited Richmond Lodge for the last time. The house was demolished following the drawing up of an estimate in July 1772 of the expenses involved (RA GEO/15981). The date of this watercolour of the south front may be guessed from the age of the boys – the Prince of Wales and Prince Frederick – who appear to be a year or two younger than in no. 123.

121. William Woollett (1735–1785)
after Joshua Kirby (1716–1774)
The White House at Kew, 1763

Etching and engraving. Platemark 31.3 × 46.8 cm (12⁵⁄₁₆″ × 18⁷⁄₁₆″)
RCIN 702947.a

122. Edward Rooker (?1724–1774)
after William Marlow (1740–1813)
A View of the Wilderness, with the Alhambra, the Pagoda and the Mosque, c.1763

Etching and engraving. Platemark 31.6 × 47.3 cm (12⁷⁄₁₆″ × 18⁵⁄₈″)
RCIN 702947.s
LITERATURE Chambers 1763; *Chambers* 1996, chapter 6; Cloake 1996, chapter XXI

Kew was the country home of the Prince and Princess of Wales, the parents of George III. The royal residence there was named Kew Palace on the engraved plate, but is here described as the White House to distinguish it from the other houses called Kew Palace at the same period or subsequently. The original building had been owned by a succession of private individuals until around 1730, when Frederick, Prince of Wales – who had arrived in England from Hanover in 1729 – took the lease. William Kent soon remodelled the house in the latest Palladian style. The Portland stone facing applied to the garden front gave rise to the house's new name: the White House.

After the death of the Prince of Wales in 1751 his widow and children continued to use the White House as one of their chief residences. On the death of the Dowager Princess in February 1772 the King and Queen resolved to move their summer residence from Richmond Lodge to Kew, of which the freehold was finally acquired in 1799. As at Buckingham House, at Kew the Queen's rooms were upstairs and the King's rooms – including the library – were downstairs. Fanny Burney describes the house as 'small, dark and old-fashioned', adding that 'there is no form of ceremony here of any sort . . . The Royal Family are here always in so very retired a way that they live as the simplest country gentlefolks' (*Burney Diary*, II, pp. 402, 406).

It was from Kew House that the Queen wrote, in July 1784, to thank Lord Bute for his *Botanical tables* (see no. 286). There was a greater possibility of privacy at Kew than in London or at Windsor. It was therefore to Kew that the King was taken in late November 1788, after the onset of his first serious illness. The plight of the royal family at this time was not eased by the fact that the house was 'in a state of cold and discomfort past all imagination': it had rarely been occupied in winter. Greville reported that in the course of the King's enforced stay at Kew, he 'resorted to an occupation not uninteresting to Him in settled days. He drew Plans of The House, & contrived & sketched alterations to it – & this He did with tolerable accuracy', adding – some weeks later – that 'In his more sedate moments He amused Himself with Drawing Plans' (Greville 1930, pp. 119, 152). When the illness recurred in 1801, the King was again sent to the White House, by now in the process of being dismantled prior to demolition (in 1803): he had decided to replace it with a new building – the Castellated Palace (no. 124) – and the contents of the White House were to be temporarily transferred to the Dutch House.

The site of the White House now lies within the grounds of the Royal Botanic Gardens, which owe their ultimate origins to Frederick, Prince of Wales. From the late 1740s there are references to the development of a botanic garden on a 9-acre (3.6 hectare) plot to the south of the Orangery close to the White House. The Earl of Bute was closely involved in the evolution of the garden from 1747, and particularly from 1760 (the stated commencement of the physic or exotic garden). He continued to be associated with Kew until the death of the Dowager Princess of Wales in 1772, when his role as unofficial superintendent of the Royal Gardens was taken over by Sir Joseph Banks.

A View of the PALACE from the Lawn, in the Royal Gardens at KEW. Vüe du PALAIS pris de la Plaine, aux Jardins Royales de KEW.

121

A View of the Wilderness, with the Alhambra, the Pagoda and the Mosque.

122

Bute was also closely involved in the buildings erected in the grounds of Kew Palace, to the designs of Chambers, from the 1750s. When the architect presented the Earl with a volume of drawings of Kew (now in the Metropolitan Museum, New York), he stated that the buildings had been 'Plan'd by his Lordship, and executed under his Inspection' (*Chambers* 1996, p. 42). The park buildings shown here – all located at the southern end of the Kew estate – include the Pagoda (1761–2) with the Alhambra (1758) to its left and the Mosque (1761) in the right distance. While the Pagoda has survived, with a few of Chambers's smaller park buildings (the Orangery and Temples of Aeolus and Bellona), the Alhambra and Mosque have not.

Both plates were engraved for William Chambers's *Plans, Elevations, Sections and Perspective Views of the Gardens and Buildings at Kew*, published in 1763 and dedicated to the Dowager Princess of Wales. The publication was 'undertaken by Royal Command' and entirely funded 'by Royal Bounty' – from the King. Kirby, who provided three designs for the plates, was the King's perspective teacher from 1756 and in 1761 was appointed Joint Clerk of the Works at Richmond and Kew (see no. 209). The impression of the White House (no. 121) is a later state of the print, with the lettering altered to appeal to a continental market.

123. Thomas Sandby (1721/3–1798) and Paul Sandby (1730–1809)

The Dutch House, Kew, c.1771/2

Pencil, pen and ink and watercolour. 36.1 × 69.0 cm
(14 3/16″ × 27 3/16″)

RL 14712

PROVENANCE Colnaghi; from whom purchased by the Prince of
Wales (later George IV), 26 June 1804 (7 gns.; RA GEO/27267)

LITERATURE Oppé 1947, no. 160; *Sandby* 1985, no. 24; Cloake
1996, chapter XIX; *Princes as Patrons* 1998, no. 83

The Dutch House – which survives today as Kew Palace –
was a subsidiary royal residence immediately next to the
White House. This view is from the paddock to the north-
east; the tree-lined riverside walk runs across the centre of
the composition.

The red brick house had been built in 1631 by Samuel
Fortrey, a merchant. In 1728 the property was leased to
George II's wife, Queen Caroline. George III – who occasionally used the house in the 1750s – inherited the lease in
1760 and finally purchased the house and grounds in 1781.
With increasing numbers in the royal nursery it provided
supplementary accommodation, particularly for younger
members of the royal family. In May 1771 the two eldest

boys – the Prince of Wales and Prince Frederick, aged
respectively 9 and 8 – were promoted from the royal nursery
to be put in the charge of governors. While in London they
occupied the new north wing at Buckingham House and
when at Richmond they were based in the Dutch House,
which was soon transformed into a 'miniature academy' and
became known as the Princes House (Hedley 1975, p. 106).
In this watercolour the Prince of Wales, identifiable by his
Garter sash, is seated in the carriage at left. The other
children in the group are presumably his younger brothers:
Princes Frederick (born 1763), William (born 1765), Edward
(born 1767) and (in reins) Ernest (born 1771). Early in
1773 the Duchess of Northumberland described how, when
in London, the three elder Princes and the three young
Princesses 'all go once a day round the Garden at the Queens
House' (Northumberland 1926, p. 197). Their routine was
evidently similar when they were in the country.

The house was close to the site of the Castellated Palace
(see no. 124). When building work commenced on that project
in 1801, the White House was demolished and its contents –
including the Zoffany family group (no. 7) and paintings by
Canaletto, Sebastiano Ricci and Zuccarelli (nos. 150, 151) –
were transferred (temporarily, it was thought) to the Dutch

123

House. Following the recurrence of the King's illness in 1804, in the absence of any other suitable residence the Dutch House was used as his convalescent home. It became gradually clear that the Castellated Palace would never be completed, and that the royal family's use of the Dutch House would continue. While the increasingly blind and sick King moved back to Windsor (after a final visit to Kew in January 1806), the Queen divided her time between Buckingham House, Windsor and the Dutch House. There, on 11 July 1818, she witnessed the marriages of two of her sons: the Duke of Clarence (later William IV) to Princess Adelaide, and the Duke of Kent to the Dowager Princess of Leiningen; and four months later, on 17 November, she died in her bedroom at Kew. Although the Prince Regent ordered the demolition of the 'Old Red House . . . in wch the Queen died', as being 'unworthy of Repair', the order was not carried out (Hedley 1975, p. 306).

Michelangelo Rooker's engraving after this watercolour, published in 1776, is inscribed *P. Sandby delin*. As with so much of the work of the Sandby brothers, it is likely to have been a collaborative effort, with the architecture and landscape setting by Thomas and the figures by Paul. The watercolour does not appear to have been a royal commission for it was purchased by the Prince of Wales in 1804. Unusually for the watercolours in the Prince's collection, it was already housed in a 'burnished gold frame' at the time of acquisition and remained framed until it was transferred from St James's Palace to the Windsor Print Room in December 1940. The original frame has not survived.

124. William Innes Pocock (1783–1836)
The Castellated Palace, Kew, c.1817

Pencil and wash. 12.9 × 41.1 cm (5¹⁄₁₆″ × 16³⁄₁₆″)
Inscribed on verso *The Castle, by King G III at Kew Green / W.I Pocock c1816*
RL 17948
PROVENANCE Bought from Martyn Gregory by HM The Queen, 1977
LITERATURE Desmond 1995, pp. 81–2; Cloake 1996, pp. 142–6

The Castellated Palace was built on the site of a number of old buildings on the riverside at Kew, a few hundred yards up river from the Dutch House and overlooking the village of Brentford. After finally abandoning Chambers's plans for Richmond Palace twenty-five years earlier (see nos. 90, 91), the King intended this new building to be the main royal residence at Richmond and Kew.

Although work did not begin until 1801, already in January 1794 Farington recorded that 'Wyatt lately shewed Hodges a set of designs for a Palace to be built at Kew, which the King has a serious intention of doing' (*Farington Diary*, I, p. 141). The project was a topic for discussion in the correspondence between the King and the Princess Royal, by now living in Württemberg. In March 1800 the Princess Royal wrote: 'I am very glad to hear from my sisters that your Majesty intends building at Kew, being convinced that it will amuse you very much.' And in a letter of September 1803 the King remarked to the Princess: 'the villa I am building at Richmond . . . advances but slowly, [due] partly to a certain lack of diligence in Wyatt and partly to the present lack of

124

workmen . . . I never thought I should have adopted Gothic instead of Grecian architecture, but the bad taste of the last forty years has so entirely corrupted the professors of the latter, I have taken to the former from thinking Wyatt perfect in that style, of which my house will I trust be a good example. The body of the house is now compleated, and now the floors and windows are preparing' (Aspinall 1962–70, III, p. 328; IV, p. 135).

The vast building, made up of a number of different elements as shown here, used various technical innovations such as cast-iron supports. The £40,000 allocated in 1800 had risen to £100,000 by 1806, at which point the increasingly blind King appears to have lost interest in the project. By 1811 the building was almost completely roofed and some estimates suggested that the cost had risen to £500,000. The Prince Regent abandoned the project and left the building in the state in which it is shown here. Demolition was finally ordered in 1827. Where appropriate, materials were reused in Buckingham Palace and Windsor Castle, both of which were then being rebuilt. Like some of the King's later architectural projects at Windsor, the Castellated Palace was the victim of both the King's 'building mania' and the gradual decline of his health. As Princess Augusta reported in July 1804: 'The ideas of building continue as extravagant as ever, altering every House, unroofing without end to add stories; in short, had He his own way at present, this, nor all the Countries in the World, could stand the expense' (*Harcourt Papers*, VI, pp. 188–90).

Before entering the Royal Collection this watercolour was part of a small sketchbook of English views by Pocock; it was originally folded down the middle. Some pages of the sketchbook were dated 1816 in the watermark; one of the drawings was inscribed 1818.

WINDSOR CASTLE (nos. 125–135)

Although the royal residences at Richmond and Kew were initially favoured by George III, from the mid-1770s he came to use Windsor increasingly. During his first serious illness (1788–9), the King was removed from Windsor to Kew, but was comforted by reminders of Windsor – 'the place I love best in the world' (Greville 1930, p. 111). The castle had been continuously occupied since the eleventh century; its

surrounding parkland provided ample opportunities for the King's sporting interests, in addition to his agricultural and architectural pursuits (see nos. 125, 219).

When – in 1776 – the King first decided to return to Windsor, Chambers advised that the royal apartments in the castle could not be made habitable, even for the King's occasional use, without considerable expenditure: they were cold, old-fashioned, and were anyway occupied by a number of Grace and Favour tenants. The State Apartments – occupying the north range of the Upper Ward – were likewise unsuitable for domestic use: they had been open to the public intermittently since the seventeenth century. Queen Anne's 'Garden House' on the south side of the castle was therefore gradually enlarged and upgraded for royal use. This building (renamed the Queen's Lodge) was later supplemented by Burford House to the south-east (Lower Lodge, purchased in 1779) so that the whole family could be accommodated at Windsor in some comfort (see figs. 15, 16). Sir William Chambers was closely involved in the execution of these works, at a total expense of around £50,000, but it is likely that some of the designs – particularly for the exterior elevations – were provided by the King himself (*Chambers* 1996,

FIG. 15 Benjamin West, *Queen Charlotte and her children at Windsor*, 1779: detail, with the Queen's Lodge and the south front of Windsor Castle. Oil on canvas (RCIN 405405)

pp. 52–3). Few descriptions, and no visual records, of the interiors of these buildings have survived.

While work on the Queen's Lodge was under way, the royal family may have (temporarily) used the south-east tower of the castle. Meanwhile, work began on transforming the State Apartments on the north side of the Quadrangle; the resulting changes, commenced in the late 1770s and continuing for two decades, were recorded in Pyne's views, of which a selection is shown here. In 1781 the Prince of Wales was allocated the majority of the rooms in the east range of the Upper Ward, for which elegant japanned furniture was supplied by John Russell, with richly carved cabinet pieces by William Gates (see no. 284). In 1794–6 part of this range was again refurbished – to Yenn's designs – for the Queen's use (see no. 96), and the south-east tower was refitted for the Prince's occasional use (Roberts (H.) 2001, pp. 3–5). In the late 1780s the King was also closely involved in the refurbishment of St George's Chapel (see no. 135).

From the last years of the eighteenth century until his death in 1813 James Wyatt was engaged to carry out some major changes to both the exterior and the interior of the castle, which may be seen as the start of its transformation – completed under Wyatt's nephew, Jeffry Wyatville – from

medieval fortress to Gothic palace. In 1804, after the initial works had been finished, the royal family moved from the Queen's Lodge into their new apartments in the castle. The resulting room use is shown in plans published by Lysons in 1806 (Lysons 1806; see Roberts (H.) 2001, figs. 8 and 9). It was reported that although 'Mr Wyat, ye architect, has ye Sole Direction [of the building work at Windsor]... His Majesty plans all the alterations himself; it is his great amusement' (Kennedy Diary, January 1804).

In addition to the Queen's existing rooms on the east front, new rooms were prepared for her use (as bedroom, dressing room and closet) in the south-east tower. Initially the Queen was not pleased with this change and reported to Lady Harcourt, on 6 November 1804 – two days after the move: 'I have changed from a very comfortable & Warm habitation, to the Coldest House, Rooms & Passages that ever existed, & that all Idea of Comfort is vanished with it' (Hedley 1975, p. 221). The apartments allocated to the princesses were divided between the east range (Elizabeth and Amelia) and the south range (Mary, Augusta and Sophia). Their rooms were decorated in the latest fashion, with hints of Grecian style, honeysuckle arbours and so on. Apart from the Prince of Wales, now displaced to the

Queen's Lodge, the princes now occupied the south-west range.

The King's Apartments were quite separate from those of the Queen and their children. They were located on the ground floor below the State Apartments, in the north range of the Upper Ward, overlooking the North Terrace. According to Lysons's plan, the King occupied a suite of twelve rooms, ranging from his bedroom (below the King's Presence Chamber) to his library (below Queen Elizabeth's Gallery). These were refurbished in (for him, surprisingly) fashionable taste, with Grecian couches – and even thick pile rugs. Five rooms were shelved as library rooms. Windsor was the King's final home: he was confined to these rooms for nine years until his death in 1820.

125. Matthew Dubourg (*fl*.1809–1838) after James Pollard (1797 – after 1859)

George III returning from hunting, 1820

Etching with aquatint, hand-coloured. Platemark 34.8 × 46.8 cm (13¹¹⁄₁₆″ × 18⅞₁₆″)
RCIN 604491
LITERATURE Roberts (J.) 1997, pp. 62–4

This print and its pair were published in the year of the King's death but record scenes at Windsor over ten years earlier. They both show the King and his family enjoying the sport of hunting, in this case to the south-west of the castle. Initially both the Home Park and the Great Park at Windsor were stocked with deer for the royal sport; from the 1780s the deer were concentrated in the Great Park, to enable the King's farming activities to proceed in the Home Park. The King was an active participant in the activities of the Royal Buckhounds, which were based at Swinley before transferring to new buildings close to Ascot Heath *c*.1790. In the course of a good day's hunting, the hunt would cover vast areas of the countryside: from Bagshot to Maidenhead to Wallingford. According to a contemporary account, 'H.M. and T.R.H.'s [the Prince of Wales and Duke of York] for the first time hunted in black velvet caps' at Windsor in October 1780.

Pollard's preparatory studies for these prints are also in the Royal Collection (RL 17180–81).

126. Charles Wild (1781–1835)

Windsor Castle: The Upper Ward, 1819

Watercolour and touches of bodycolour over pencil.
19.6 × 25.1 cm (7¹¹⁄₁₆″ × 9⅞″)
RL 22096
LITERATURE Pyne 1819, I, *Windsor Castle*, opposite p. 83; Watkin 1984, pp. 8–10

This view of the Upper Ward shows the Quadrangle with the Round Tower to the west, in their original form, before

HIS MAJESTY KING GEO. III. RETURNING from HUNTING.

125

126

127

Wyatville's transformations in the following decade. As part of those changes the equestrian monument to Charles II was moved to the foot of the Round Tower mound, and turned around to face east, into the courtyard. To the right is the south façade of the northern range, containing the State Apartments, the entrance to which was through the archway at right. To the left is the west end of the southern range, including the archway of the 'Rubbish Gate', the chief entrance to the Quadrangle from the south at this time.

The view records a number of the changes made for George III to the exterior of this part of the castle and in particular the replacement of the round-headed doors and windows – a hallmark of Hugh May's work of the 1670s – with pointed openings and Gothic tracery. These features, introduced by James Wyatt in the early years of the nineteenth century, can be seen on the square tower at left (which contained apartments for the King's sons) and along the whole of the right-hand façade; elsewhere, May's windows were allowed to remain. The whole quadrangle was again transformed in the course of Wyatville's work in the 1820s – particularly by the addition of the Grand Corridor around the eastern and southern ranges – but many of James Wyatt's windows survived his nephew's changes (see Roberts (H.) 2001, fig. 6).

127. Charles Wild (1781–1835)

Windsor Castle: The Staircase, 1818

Watercolour and touches of bodycolour over pencil.
20.2 × 25.2 cm (7^{15}/$_{16}$" × 9^{15}/$_{16}$")
RL 22097
LITERATURE Pyne 1819, I, *Windsor Castle*, opposite p. 87; Watkin 1984, pp. 14–15

The staircase led the visitor from the State Entrance in the northern range of the Quadrangle (see no. 126) to the State Apartments on the floor above. Following May's work in the 1670s, there were two principal staircases, one leading to the King's Apartments, and one to the Queen's Apartments. Among the projects undertaken by James Wyatt at Windsor *c.*1800 was the introduction of the new staircase shown here. The old King's Stairs, opening from the east end of Horn Court to the north-east of the State Entrance, were demolished and the old Queen's Stair immediately to the north of the entrance was replaced by Wyatt's new stair, which occupied

the same space and now gave access to both the King's and the Queen's Apartments.

Wyatt's bold architectural scheme, oriented north–south, involved a single flight of stairs, with a landing at mid-way, rising from the Entrance Hall to a landing outside the King's Drawing Room on the floor above. Above the new stair was a high octagonal lantern, nearly 100 feet (30 metres) above floor level, ornamented with Bernasconi's Gothic plasterwork, to match the Gothic vaulting of the Entrance Hall below.

128. Charles Wild (1781–1835)

Windsor Castle: The King's Audience Chamber, 1818

Watercolour and bodycolour over pencil. 20.6 × 25.2 cm (8^{1}/$_{8}$" × 9^{15}/$_{16}$")
RL 22109
LITERATURE Pyne 1819, I, *Windsor Castle*, opposite p. 166; Watkin 1984, pp. 29–30; Roberts (H.) 1997, p. 177

The King's Apartments at Windsor, which date from the reign of Charles II, all overlook the North Terrace. The Audience Chamber was the third of the sequence of King's Rooms; in the 1830s it was remodelled by Wyatville as the Ante-Throne Room. From the late 1770s George III began to refurbish these rooms, with the assistance of his architect William Chambers. The resulting changes are recorded in the plates of Pyne's *Royal Residences* for the Audience Chamber (no. 128), the Drawing Room, the Bedchamber, the Dressing Room (no. 129), and the Closet.

The Audience Chamber received particularly lavish attention at this time. According to Pyne, the changes were carried out 'under the direction of his Majesty . . . with great elegance'. Although many of the seventeenth-century elements were retained – including Verrio's fine ceiling painting, and the richly carved cornice – up-to-date colours, finishes and furnishings were introduced. The walls were relined with Garter blue flower-bordered silk, and a new marble chimneypiece was introduced in 1786. George III's veneration of the Order of the Garter, seen throughout his work at Windsor, was reflected in the series of paintings executed by Benjamin West for this room in 1787–9 (see Millar 1969, nos. 1158–64). They record the exploits of Edward III and the Black Prince, culminating in the foundation of the Order in 1348.

A striking element of this view is the throne canopy 'and its appendages': according to Pyne, Robert Campbell

128

129

was responsible for the splendid new throne, the canopy was produced by Mrs Pawsey to designs by Mary Moser, and the pilasters were painted by Biagio Rebecca under the direction of Benjamin West. In the almost complete absence of bills for furnishings at this period, Pyne's illustration, together with his summary of the designers and craftsmen involved at Windsor in the 1780s, has led to the attribution of several pieces of furniture in the Collection (see nos. 282, 289). Pyne's canopy, but not its hangings, cresting and back-cloth, may have survived in the Garter Throne Room (Roberts (H.) 1997, fig. 3).

129. Charles Wild (1781–1835)

Windsor Castle: The King's Dressing Room, 1816

Watercolour and bodycolour over pencil. 20.2 × 25.3 cm (7¹⁵⁄₁₆″ × 9¹⁵⁄₁₆″)
RL 22105
LITERATURE Pyne 1819, I, *Windsor Castle*, opposite p. 147; Watkin 1984, pp. 25–6

The King's Dressing Room overlooks the North Terrace, between the King's Bedchamber (to the east) and the King's Closet (to the west). The room benefited from a considerable programme of refurbishment from the late 1790s. John Yenn's design for four large oval giltwood mirrors – two for the Dressing Room and two for the Closet, shown by Pyne on the window wall in both cases – is in the Royal Collection (RL 18728; Roberts (H.) 1997, fig. 8). Three of these mirrors have also survived (RCIN 53003; Roberts (H.) 1997, figs. 7, 8). According to instructions on Yenn's drawing, which is undated, the frames were to be carved by Richard Lawrence, and the mirror plates were to be supplied by Robert Campbell. The furniture includes a fine French *bureau-plat*, probably dating from the 1740s. The table – which may have been acquired by George III – was used by Queen Victoria when she signed the Royal Assent to the Australian Commonwealth Bill in July 1900 and was subsequently sent by her, as a permanent memento, to Australia; it is now in Parliament House, Canberra (Roberts (H.) 2002, fig. 13).

Among the paintings are (over the chimneypiece) Guido Reni's *Cleopatra*, acquired by Frederick, Prince of Wales, Carracci's *'Il Silenzio'* (no. 156) and a *Virgin and Child* attributed to Guido Reni, both acquired by George III himself. All these had been transferred to Windsor from Buckingham House shortly before Pyne's views.

Curiously, Wild has recorded Verrio's ceiling painting of Jupiter and Danae *in situ*. However, between 1807 and 1811 Matthew Cotes Wyatt (James Wyatt's son) had replaced this with a scene from the story of St George – one of a series of paintings executed at that time in the King's Closet, King's Dressing Room and Queen's Dressing Room (*King's Works*, VI, p. 379).

130. Charles Wild (1781–1835)

Windsor Castle: The Queen's Presence Chamber, 1817

Watercolour with touches of bodycolour over pencil.
20.4 × 25.1 cm (8¹⁄₁₆″ × 9⁷⁄₈″)
RL 22099
LITERATURE Pyne 1819, I, *Windsor Castle*, opposite p. 90; Watkin 1984, p. 20; *Royal Treasures* 2002, no. 401

This room was the second in the sequence of the Queen's Apartments; these apartments faced south into the Quadrangle, and then west into Engine Court. The first room in the Queen's Apartments (as in the King's) was the Guard Room, just visible in this view through the open doorway. After the introduction of Wyatt's great new staircase – which rose towards the King's rooms on the north side – it was accessible from a balustraded landing around the top of the stairs (see no. 127).

Although the room as shown here retains most of its original late seventeenth-century features – Verrio's ceiling painting of Catharine of Braganza (consort of Charles II) attended by the Virtues, and carvings by Grinling Gibbons and Henry Phillips – some elements of the furnishings are more recent introductions. In front of the chimneypiece the French royal flag, given annually as a 'rent banner' by the Duke of Marlborough, is shown draped over a small Boulle writing table which may have been acquired by George III (see no. 260). The two large paintings by Van Dyck on the north wall – *Charles I and M. de St Antoine* and *The 'Great Piece'* – were recorded in the 1770s and 1780s in the Queen's Breakfast Room at Buckingham House, but were transferred to Windsor in 1804.

In the 1830s a marble chimneypiece, recorded for Pyne in the Second Drawing Room at Buckingham House (no. 114), was transferred to this room. The Queen's Presence Chamber is one of only three rooms at Windsor that still retain their late seventeenth-century ceilings and decoration.

130

131

132

133

131. Charles Wild (1781–1835)

Windsor Castle: The Queen's Audience Chamber, 1818

Watercolour and touches of bodycolour over pencil.
21.0 × 25.3 cm (8¼″ × 9¹⁵/₁₆″)
RL 22100
LITERATURE Pyne 1819, I, *Windsor Castle*, opposite p. 9

The Audience Chamber is at the south-west corner of the Queen's Apartments, between the Presence Chamber (no. 130) and the Ballroom (no. 132). The decoration is very similar to that in the Presence Chamber. However, in 1807 the original overmantel was replaced with Edward Wyatt's remarkable carved panel (no. 291), intended at once to blend with and to emulate the seventeenth-century work. Edward Wyatt was a cousin of the King's architect, James Wyatt, through whose influence he was in 1798 appointed carver and gilder to the Office of Works.

The two large paintings by Zuccarelli (Levey 1991, nos. 689–90) were acquired by George III with Consul Smith's collection. They hung at Hampton Court before being transferred to Windsor, before 1813.

132. Charles Wild (1781–1835)

Windsor Castle: The Queen's Ballroom, 1817

Watercolour with touches of bodycolour over pencil.
19.8 × 25.2 cm (7¹³/₁₆″ × 9¹⁵/₁₆″)
RL 22101
LITERATURE Pyne 1819, I, *Windsor Castle*, opposite p. 99;
Watkin 1984, pp. 22–3; *Royal Treasures* 2002, no. 40

The next room in the Queen's Apartments – after the Audience Chamber (no. 131) – was the west-facing Ballroom, looking onto Engine Court and leading (to its north) into the Drawing Room (no. 133). At this date the late seventeenth-century panelling, carving and ceiling (painted by Verrio with Charles II giving freedom to Europe) survived relatively unaltered. The room was the largest in the Queen's Apartments and served the combined function of gallery and ballroom. Elements of two of the four sets of silver furniture shown here survive in the Royal Collection (see nos. 257, 258). The other two sets – the central ones in this view – were acquired in 1732 for George II's palace at Herrenhausen, near Hanover. With the three silver chandeliers in this room, and the two in the Queen's Drawing Room, they were housed at Windsor during the Napoleonic upheavals but were returned to Hanover shortly afterwards.

The paintings include (on the far wall) Ramsay's portrait of Queen Charlotte and her two eldest sons in 1764, and facing it (out of view) Copley's painting of three of the princesses in 1785 (fig. 10; see Millar 1969, nos. 998, 712). Both pictures had been transferred to Windsor from Kensington in 1804/5.

In the 1830s the Queen's Ballroom was altered to its present appearance by Wyatville for William IV. At that time most of the seventeenth-century decoration was removed and the marble chimneypiece recorded by Pyne in the Queen's State Bedchamber (no. 134) was transferred to the centre of the east wall of the Ballroom, to replace the two chimneypieces shown here.

133. Charles Wild (1781–1835)

Windsor Castle: The Queen's Drawing Room, 1816

Watercolour with touches of bodycolour over pencil.
20.0 × 25.3 cm (7⅞″ × 9¹⁵/₁₆″)
RL 22102
LITERATURE Pyne 1819, I, *Windsor Castle*, opposite p. 106;
Watkin 1984, pp. 18–19

The Queen's Drawing Room is at the northern extremity of the Queen's Apartments and is bounded to the east by the King's Closet and to the west by the Queen's State Bedchamber (no. 134). Verrio's ceiling (replaced by Wyatville) depicts the Assembly of the Gods.

The paintings include six upright landscapes by Zuccarelli, purchased by George III with Smith's collection in 1762 (Levey 1991, nos. 693–8). They seem to have hung at Windsor from an early date, but were first recorded in the Bedchamber before being transferred to this room. They are hung against a series of Mortlake tapestries of the Seasons.

The furnishings include two of the five silver chandeliers from Hanover, temporarily housed at Windsor during the Napoleonic upheavals (see no. 132). The set of painted seat furniture was part of the late eighteenth-century refurbishment of the State Apartments. The ship models in glazed cases may have been transferred from the library at Buckingham House, where some were described earlier in the reign (see no. 118).

134

134. James Stephanoff (1789–1874)

Windsor Castle: The Queen's State Bedchamber, 1818

Watercolour with touches of bodycolour over pencil.
20.2 × 25.4 cm ($7^{15}/_{16}$" × 10")
RL 22103
LITERATURE Pyne 1819, I, *Windsor Castle*, opposite p. 116;
Watkin 1984, pp. 20–21; *Royal Treasures* 2002, no. 403

The State Bedchamber lay immediately to the west of the
Drawing Room; apart from small closet rooms to the west
(accessible through the central door in the right wall), it was
the last room in the Queen's Apartments. It is unlikely that
Queen Charlotte ever slept in this room: her private apartments were on the east front of the castle. However, in 1778
a magnificent new canopied bed was delivered for her State
Bedchamber at Windsor, decorated with similar fine floral
needlework to that seen on the King's throne canopy in no.
128. The bed, and the two armchairs and ten stools supplied
at the same time, remain in the Collection (see no. 282).

The room as shown in this view was created by James
Wyatt as part of his work in the State Apartments in the
early years of the nineteenth century. Before 1804 the space
was occupied by the Bedchamber to the north and by an ante
room and service staircase to the south. To complete the
decoration, Verrio's ceiling, depicting Diana and Endymion,
was joined by a new area of ceiling, painted in a very similar
style by John Rigaud – showing Jupiter presenting Diana
with her bow and arrows. In the 1830s the room was substantially changed when the Royal Library was transferred to
this room and the rooms to the west. As part of these changes
a new plasterwork ceiling was introduced and the marble
chimneypiece was moved to the Queen's Ballroom (no. 132).

Queen Charlotte's embroidered bed and suite of seat
furniture were removed at the time of Wyatt's changes.
Among the contents of the room recorded for Pyne are
Lely's 'Windsor Beauties' on the right wall, and – at the
far end – the painted chest-of-drawers (no. 280), almost
certainly acquired by Queen Charlotte.

135

135. Charles Wild (1781–1835)

Windsor Castle: The Quire of St George's Chapel, 1818

Watercolour and bodycolour over pencil. 25.0 × 21.1 cm
(9 ¹³⁄₁₆″ × 8 ⁵⁄₁₆″)
RL 22115
LITERATURE Pyne 1819, I, *Windsor Castle*, opposite p. 182;
Watkin 1984, pp. 34–5

During his periods of residence at Windsor, George III
worshipped regularly at St George's Chapel in the Lower
Ward of the castle. The chapel is the religious seat of the
Order of the Garter; the banners of the Garter Knights are
here shown suspended over their stalls. Services were also
occasionally held in the chapel in the State Apartments in
the Upper Ward, splendidly decorated as part of Charles II's
work at Windsor. And among the King's unexecuted
schemes for Windsor was a 'Chapel of Revealed Religion'
which would have replaced the seventeenth-century chapel.

This view of the east end of St George's Chapel records
many of the changes introduced there, at the King's expense,
between 1785 and 1791. These included additional choir
stalls – brilliantly executed facsimiles of the fifteenth-
century originals – and the virtual rebuilding of the altar wall,
including a reredos designed by Thomas Sandby and a great
stained-glass window of the Resurrection of Christ, painted
by Benjamin West. Overall responsibility for the work was
entrusted to Henry Emlyn (*c.*1729–1815), who was employed –
as carpenter, builder and architect in the castle – by both the
Office of Works and the Dean and Chapter; he retired from
these positions in 1792, by which time the work was virtually
complete (see no. 287 and Roberts (J.) 1976–7). The King's
patronage of stained-glass painting – particularly at St
George's – was on a lavish scale, but few examples have
survived (see Baylis 1998).

FROGMORE HOUSE, WINDSOR
(nos. 136–142)

136. Charles Wild (1781–1835)
Frogmore House: The garden front, 1819

Watercolour and bodycolour over pencil. 18.4 × 24.9 cm
(7¼″ × 9 ¹³⁄₁₆″)

RL 22118

LITERATURE Pyne 1819, I, *Frogmore*, opposite p. 1; Watkin 1984, pp. 89–90; Cornforth 1990; Roberts (J.) 1997, chapter 16

Frogmore House occupies its own small estate less than a mile to the south of Windsor Castle. It was not part of the medieval parkland surrounding the castle and until 1848 it was not part of the royal domain, but was held by private individuals via a series of crown leases. However, its proximity to the castle – and its seclusion – meant that it held an obvious attraction for the royal family and in 1792 the lease was acquired for the Queen by her friend General (later 3rd Earl) Harcourt. Two years earlier the lease of the smaller estate to the north – Little Frogmore – had also been acquired for the Queen. The two were now thrown together and work soon began on landscaping the grounds. The garden was always one of the chief attractions of Frogmore and much time was spent by the royal ladies 'botanising' there.

The core of the building is the seven-bay house built *c*.1680, probably to the designs of Hugh May. The entrance front faced north-east and the garden front (shown here) south-west. Work on the house was entrusted to James Wyatt but his name does not appear in any of the surviving accounts,

136

and it was claimed that he received no payment for his services (see p. 106). In July 1793 Queen Charlotte wrote from Frogmore ('my sweet temple') to inform her Treasurer that 'Mr Wyatt is just returned . . . with many pretty tantalizing proposals about my little paradise, of which many must be rejected, but not all . . . now the finishing of the rooms is to be settled, and some must be adopted for particular purposes, some alterations must take place, and as I am not at all eager to finish at once but can wait with patience' (Roberts (J.) 1997, p. 217).

Most of the building work was carried out between June 1793 and late 1795, with further work in 1801 and 1804. By May 1795 single-storey pavilions linked by an open colonnade had been added to the garden front. Further additions were made, to left and right, in 1804 when a pair of two-storeyed bowed extensions and matching single-storey rooms were added to the garden front. Inside the house doorcases, window frames and chimneypieces were replaced with crisp neo-classical models, and the staircase was rebuilt (see nos. 97, 98).

In 1793 Queen Charlotte had written, 'I mean this place to furnish me with fresh amusements every day'. Although the Queen and her daughters passed long periods at Frogmore – painting, botanising, music-making or reading – they never passed a night there. Numerous guests were entertained at Frogmore, particularly at the fêtes held in the garden (see no. 142).

On 23 December 1818, five weeks after her death, the Queen's most intimate possessions were laid out at Frogmore so that her four youngest daughters could reserve what they wished prior to the auction (see Appendix). The house itself was bequeathed to Princess Augusta, who moved in after her father's death in 1820.

The publication dates of Pyne's views of Frogmore (all of which are included here) range from June 1817 (no. 137) to August 1819 (no. 136) – by which time the Queen had been dead for nine months, and the contents had been sold at auction. The views were clearly prepared some time before their publication.

137. Charles Wild (1781–1835)

Frogmore House: The Green Pavilion, 1817

Watercolour and bodycolour over pencil. 20.0 × 27.4 cm (7⅞″ × 10¹³⁄₁₆″)

RL 22121

LITERATURE Pyne 1819, I, *Frogmore*, opposite p. 13; Watkin 1984, p. 96; *Royal Treasures* 2002, no. 429

The Queen's earliest additions to the late seventeenth-century house at Frogmore, completed by mid-1795, were the two single-storey pavilions linked by a colonnade stretching across the garden front (see no. 136). The Green Pavilion was at the northern end of the colonnade; the room decorated with flower paintings by Mary Moser was at the southern end. In this view, the French windows leading into the Mary Moser room are visible at the end of the colonnade. The windows at right are wide open, to reveal the new landscape garden.

Many of the family portraits shown here are no longer in the Royal Collection: this applies to Beechey's charming painting of Princess Augusta – later the owner of Frogmore – holding a spindle (at left; for a miniature copy see no. 43). Other items recorded by Pyne in this room include Wright's painting of the Queen's sea passage to England in 1762 (no. 157), and the pair of side tables shown at either side of the door into the colonnade, their tops decorated with flowers by Princess Elizabeth (no. 77).

138. Charles Wild (1781–1835)

Frogmore House: The Japan Room, 1819

Watercolour and bodycolour over pencil. 20.3 × 25.2 cm (8″ × 9¹⁵⁄₁₆″)

RL 22122

LITERATURE Pyne 1819, I, *Frogmore*, opposite p. 17; Watkin 1984, pp. 96–7; Roberts (J.) 1987, pp. 82–4; Hagedorn 2001 (and unpublished thesis by I. Reepen cited therein)

The Japan Room – now the Yellow Drawing Room – is in the centre of the garden front of the ground floor of Frogmore House, looking onto the garden through the colonnade. A drawing by Henry Wigstead, inscribed 'Frogmore Hall at the Fete 1797', almost certainly shows this room decorated – with garlands, medallions, urns and trellis-work – for the fête at Frogmore to celebrate the marriage of the Princess Royal to the Hereditary Prince of Württemberg in May 1797 (see fig. 17; the paper garlands cut by the princesses and their Windsor friends, and assembled by Princess Elizabeth, had first been used in 1793: see Hedley 1975, p. 186).

The lacquer panels shown here, which gave the room its name, were painted by Princess Elizabeth. They – or the panels in the Black Japan Room, discussed but not illustrated by Pyne – appear to have been a relatively late addition to the décor for on 19 September 1807 the Princess informed her

137

138

FIG. 17 Attributed to Henry Wigstead, *Frogmore Hall at the Fete 1797*. Watercolour with pen and ink (London, British Library, Add. MS 18674, f. 2)

friend Lady Cathcart: 'I am busy putting up my Japan room at Frogmore which place is as dear to me as ever' (RA GEO/Add. 21/254/9). Some of these lacquer panels are almost certainly identifiable with those in Princess Elizabeth's married home, the Schloss at Bad Homburg. One of those panels is signed *Eliza*.

Other decorative work undertaken by the Princess included – at Buckingham House – the seat furniture in the Saloon, upholstered in white cotton velvet and painted with flowers; and the brown and maroon curtains painted in imitation of cut velvet, described in the Queen's Breakfast Room in 1802. At Frogmore the Princess's artistic activity could be found in most rooms of the house, and also in the grounds where she designed the Gothic Ruins, with the assistance of James Wyatt (see no. 17). In 1797 the diarist Farington described a 'long narrow room' (the Cross Gallery on the first floor) decorated by Princess Elizabeth 'with painted flowers, & subjects of Children &c cut in paper, & finished by Tomkins'; the connection with the Princess's silhouettes is clear (no. 79).

139. Charles Wild (1781–1835)

Frogmore House: The Dining Room, 1819

Watercolour and bodycolour over pencil. 20.1 × 25.1 cm (7¹⁵/₁₆″ × 9⅞″)

RL 22119

LITERATURE Pyne 1819, I, *Frogmore*, opposite p. 3; Watkin 1984, p. 94

Queen Charlotte's Dining Room occupied the southern bow added to the garden front of Frogmore in 1804. According to Pyne, it was 'fitted up in a style of elegant simplicity in conformity with the notions of Her Majesty'. The room was hung with portraits of the Queen's family, most of which left the Collection after her death.

The marble chimneypiece, carved with masks and vines, was purchased in Rome in 1795 by Prince Augustus from the eccentric English sculptor John Deare; the frieze was carved by Deare and the chimneypiece had been designed by George Hadfield, another English artist working in Rome. Two other chimneypieces acquired at the same time were intended for Carlton House. Although the latter were confiscated by the French, the sale of this surviving chimneypiece – completed by Vincenzo Pacetti – was finalised in February 1800. The route by which it reached Frogmore is not known (Fusco, Fogelman and Stock 2000, p. 104).

140. Charles Wild (1781–1835)

Frogmore House: The Queen's Library, 1817

Watercolour and bodycolour over pencil. 20.0 × 26.1 cm (7⅞″ × 10¼″)

RL 22120

LITERATURE Pyne 1819, I, *Frogmore*, opposite p. 8; Hedley 1975, pp. 102–3; Watkin 1984, p. 95; *Royal Miscellany* 1990, no. 15

The Queen's Library occupied the pavilion at the southern end of the house, immediately next door to the Dining Room. The open door at back right led directly through into the open door at back left of the view of the Dining Room (no. 139). It was here that Queen Charlotte kept her botanical collections, her printing press and a large part of her library; these were all dispersed at auction in June 1819 (but see

139

140

141

nos. 248, 286). Among the items included in this sale was the herbarium of the Revd John Lightfoot, which had been purchased after Lightfoot's death in 1788 as a gift from the King to the Queen; it was housed in twenty-four mahogany cabinets at Frogmore (see p. 387). Some of the more personal items in the Queen's library were retained by her family after her death. These included the red morocco portfolios containing drawings by the King and their children (see nos. 57, 60, 74, 75, 84).

141. Charles Wild (1781–1835)

Frogmore House: The Green Closet, 1819

Watercolour and bodycolour over pencil. 25.1 × 20.0 cm (9⅞″ × 7⅞″)

RL 22123

LITERATURE Pyne 1819, I, *Frogmore*, opposite p. 21; Watkin 1984, pp. 92–3

The Green Closet was located on the first floor at the north-western corner of the house, overlooking the garden. According to Pyne, the lacquer panelling here was 'original japan' rather than an imitation produced by Princess Elizabeth (compare no. 138). The cabinet and chairs were made of Indian cane and the porcelain vases on the top of the cupboards and cabinet are probably all of Far Eastern origin. This room may have housed some of the imperial gifts presented to George III by the Emperor Qianlong in 1793. These included porcelain, jade, red lacquer caskets, carved lacquer panels and silk. In the course of his visit to Frogmore in 1797, Joseph Farington noted 'some presents from the Emperor of China' (see nos. 479–84).

142. J. Merigot (*fl*.1772–1816) after Matthew Cotes Wyatt (1777–1862)

A Jubilee at Frogmore, 1809

Etching and aquatint. Cut within platemark 37.3 × 56.3 cm (14 11/16″ × 22 3/16″)

RCIN 700895

LITERATURE Hedley 1975, pp. 233–4; Roberts (J.) 1997, pp. 220–31

One of the chief attractions of Frogmore for the royal family was the 35-acre (14.2-hectare) garden, in which they could walk, read and entertain. This view is from the garden front of the house and shows the artificial lake created by 1796, and some of the newly planted shrubs and trees. However, the main part of the Frogmore grounds was to the right of this view, in the area later occupied by the mausolea of the Duchess of Kent, and of Prince Albert and Queen Victoria. The guiding spirit behind the landscaping undertaken for Queen Charlotte appears to have been Major William Price, the younger brother of Uvedale Price, the pioneer of the picturesque theory of gardening. The lake was the setting for many of the garden buildings erected – to the designs of James Wyatt, and of Princess Elizabeth – in the 1790s and 1800s (see no. 16).

Numerous fêtes or entertainments were held in the new gardens. The Jubilee fête in 1809, the subject of this print, was attended by nearly 1,200 people. There were fireworks and illuminations, an 'elegant supper' was offered to the guests, and an elaborate water pageant was staged on the lake, celebrating the triumph of Britannia. The temple on the island was a temporary structure, designed by Princess Elizabeth and executed by James Wyatt; it contained a portrait of the King, who was unable to attend the festivities owing to his increasing blindness and ill-health. In several respects the temple looks back to Robert Adam's designs for the illuminated screen in the garden of Buckingham House in 1763 (no. 95).

The water pageant was recorded by James Wyatt's son, Matthew Cotes Wyatt. He was employed in various projects at Windsor, including the painting of new ceilings in the State Apartments (*King's Works*, VI, p. 379).

A Jubilee at Frogmore

142

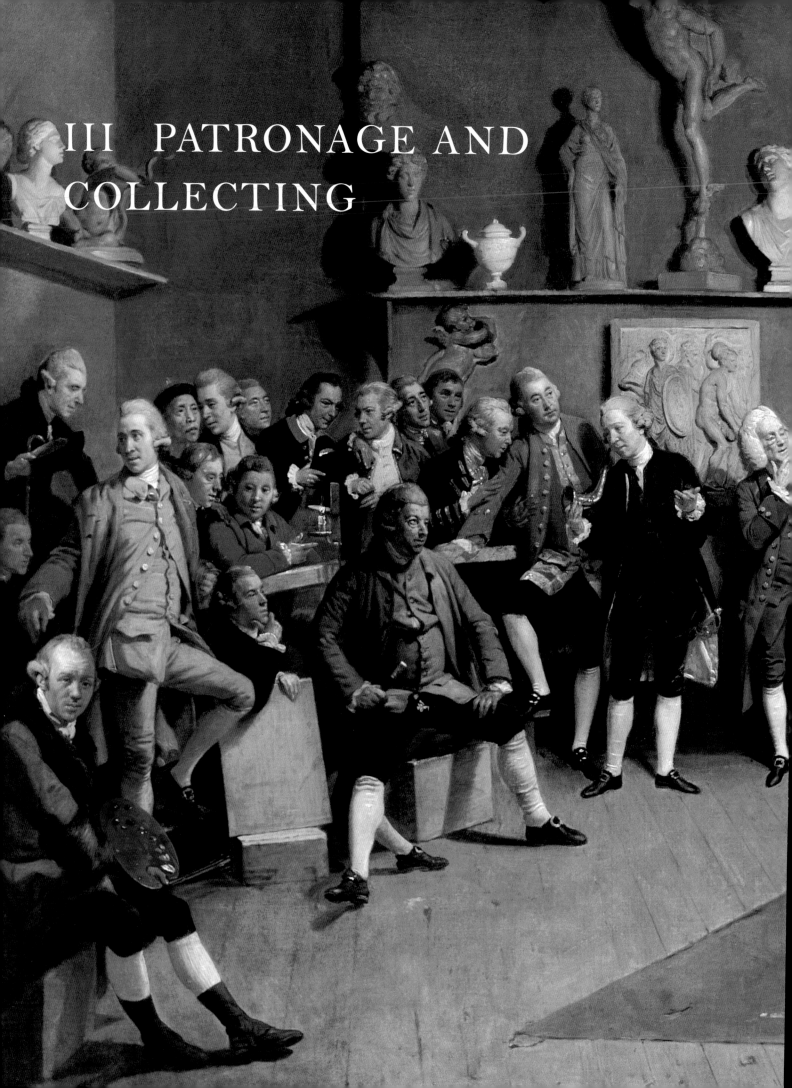

III PATRONAGE AND COLLECTING

III

'We are patronized by a Monarch, who, knowing the value of science and of elegance, thinks every Art worthy of his notice, that tends to soften and humanise the mind.'

(SIR JOSHUA REYNOLDS, *Discourses*)

CONSIDERATION OF GEORGE III as a collector and patron of the arts has always been a secondary concern for the historian and biographer. By contrast, his father Frederick, Prince of Wales, and his son George, Prince of Wales – later Prince Regent and George IV – are perhaps remembered first of all for the contributions they made to the Royal Collection. This may be explained at its simplest by the fact that Frederick never ascended the throne, and George IV spent only his final ten years as King. George III's reign was the last in which the monarch would be deeply engaged in politics and foreign affairs, and it was a time of almost unparalleled economic, scientific and political upheaval. The loss of the American colonies, the growth of industrialisation and its social consequences, and the impact of revolution and war in Europe, have all overshadowed the King's achievements in the field of the arts. But it is important for an understanding of the King's approach to collecting to appreciate that he too had a sense of the proper degree to which it should be pursued.[1] George III inherited his father's love of the arts but not his extravagance. He was not the sort of collector for whom money was no object. His father left debts of £92,968, much of which was owed to artists and craftsmen,[2] and George IV was capable of exceeding his income by such a sum in a single year's expenditure on art and building.[3]

Well over half of the works of art in this catalogue were acquired before 1780. As early as 1770 the King wrote to the British Ambassador in Paris, Earl Harcourt, that he had, 'at least for the present, given up collecting paintings'.[4] Having filled his modest residences with pictures, and having a sufficiency of furniture, plate and porcelain, this most reasonable of collectors concluded that 'enough was enough'. The self-denying ordinance was not absolute, however; one area in which acquisition never abated, proceeding at a steady annual rate for sixty years, was the library.

George III's accession was greeted with enthusiasm and optimism, particularly in artistic circles. Within a week of the event, Horace Walpole wrote to Horace Mann, British Consul at Florence, that the new King seemed to like medals, adding 'I imagine his taste goes to antiques too perhaps to pictures'.[5] This was disingenuous, for the future King had already been collecting for some years, and there is every indication that in the crucial decade since the death of his father in 1751, artists, architects and those surrounding the heir to the throne had been laying down plans to be effected immediately after his accession.[6] The key figure was John Stuart, 3rd Earl of Bute (1713–92; fig. 3), who had served in the household of George III's parents, and took on the role of mentor to the Prince, supervising his education in history, architecture, music and 'natural philosophy'.[7] Appointments of official artists and architects were swiftly made, and a new state coach was ordered in 1760 by the Master of the Horse,

Lord Huntingdon, to designs by William Chambers, Joseph Wilton and Giovanni Battista Cipriani (see fig. 18 and no. 88). The iconography of the coach, a collective work of art of extraordinary symbolic potency, was prescribed by the Whig *virtuoso* Thomas Hollis (1720–74), and its elaborate themes must surely have been developed when Hollis, Huntingdon, Wilton, Chambers and Cipriani had all met in Florence in the mid-1750s.[8] The Royal Academy of Arts, for whose foundation in 1768 the King was personally responsible, had been devised in outline more than ten years earlier. The onset of George III's reign was therefore a beginning in one sense only. A more correct impression is of an artistic juggernaut having built up a full head of steam before the wheels were finally engaged on the Accession Day, 25 October 1760.

But such was the nature of George III's education that for him, and for many of his contemporaries, the arts were part of a broad spectrum of complementary spheres of interest which we now consider quite separate, such as astronomy, meteorology, botany, geography, agriculture and music. As well as forming his own outstanding art collection, Lord Bute assembled one of the most impressive private scientific 'cabinets' in Europe,[9] and printed his own treatise on botanical classification (see nos. 250, 286). The

FIG. 18 The Gold State Coach in the Royal Mews, Buckingham Palace.

botanist Joseph Banks (1743–1820) can be found in lengthy correspondence with the industrialist and entrepreneur Matthew Boulton (1728–1809) about the best material for tagging the ears of sheep,[10] while the ingenious potter Josiah Wedgwood (1730–95) was elected to fellowships of both the Society of Antiquaries and the Royal Society.

For the King, all these interests came together in the library which he assembled at Buckingham House over the best part of sixty years. In his preface to the handsome printed catalogues published from 1820, the librarian Frederick Augusta Barnard declared that 'The present Royal Library . . . has been collected upon such a comprehensive and liberal design of embracing every species of knowledge, that the Possessor of it can call to his aid, upon any subject, all the Learning and Wisdom which the mind of man has hitherto communicated to the world.'[11] By that time it comprised 65,000 volumes and 19,000 unbound pamphlets. Besides these there were maps of all kinds, globes and architectural and topographical models, notably of the harbours of the English coast and of the principal trading colonies, by reference to which (and to the wind-dial over the chimneypiece of the East Library: see no. 307) the King could judge whether conditions were favourable for the fleet to put to sea.[12] The library rooms at Buckingham House were open for the use of scholars on application to the librarian, and it seems always to have been the King's intention that his collection of books should serve as a national library.[13] When he came to the throne there was nothing of the kind. The old royal library, accumulated since the reign of Edward IV, had been presented to the British Museum in 1757 – having spent decades in store in a dormitory of Westminster School – and while the Bodleian at Oxford had already been in existence for nearly two hundred years, it was the preserve of members of the University.[14] The King's librarians – on the advice of Samuel Johnson, among others – set out to acquire not simply rare items of bibliophilic interest, such as incunabula and illuminated manuscripts, but also modern historical, topographical and academic texts and runs of learned journals.

It was whilst in pursuit of books that George III's agents made the most notable purchases of pictures and drawings for their royal master.[15] In these, the King's interests were initially represented by Lord Bute. In 1755 Bute appointed as the Prince's Librarian Richard Dalton (?1713–91; fig. 19), who had trained as a coach-painter in London before pursuing his artistic studies in Bologna and Rome in the early 1740s. By the time of his appointment he had travelled further in Italy, Greece and Asia Minor, returning in 1750 to publish a series of engravings after his landscapes of the Levant.

When Dalton returned to Italy in 1758–9 it was specifically to acquire books, medals, and Old Master drawings for the Prince of Wales and for Bute himself. There is no doubt that he was well chosen for the task, having an extensive knowledge of old Italian family collections and a remarkable skill in extracting choice works from them, but reports of his character are not favourable. Horace Mann wrote to Horace Walpole in 1761 that Dalton seemed 'very ill-qualified for the post of a librarian, being totally illiterate'.[16] By November 1758 a group of 700 drawings was ready to be dispatched for the Prince of Wales (the consignment left Livorno three months later), and in 1763 he acquired for the King the large – and unequalled – collection of drawings by Guercino from the Gennari family (see nos. 186, 187); his visits to Italy in 1768–9 and 1774–5 resulted in fresh purchases for the King, both of drawings and of works of art of other kinds.

FIG. 19 Thomas Patch, *Richard Dalton*, 1769. Engraving (RCIN 502799)

Although heir to the throne between 1751 and 1760, and with a separate household from 1756, George III was not entitled to the income from the Duchy of Cornwall that his father had enjoyed and which was to be at the disposal of his son, the future George IV, from 1783, because this privilege had since its establishment in the fourteenth century been reserved for the *filius regis* (king's son). His budget for purchases before 1760, made through Lord Bute's 'separate account' at Coutts, was therefore limited, and the results are all the more impressive in the light of this.[17] His two greatest acquisitions from Italian collections, both of which were orchestrated by Bute, post-date his accession. In May 1762 the Scottish architect James Adam — brother of the King's Architect, Robert Adam — secured for the King the cabinet of drawings of Cardinal Alessandro Albani, which incorporated the collections of the painter Carlo Maratti and of Cassiano dal Pozzo,[18] and in the same year Bute's younger brother, James Stuart Mackenzie, acquired the library, engraved gems, coins, drawings and pictures of Joseph Smith, British Consul at Venice. This was undoubtedly George III's single greatest purchase, adding to the Royal Collection at one stroke some 50 canvases and 143 drawings by Canaletto as well as paintings and drawings by Visentini, Sebastiano and Marco Ricci and Zuccarelli, and what was later recognised as a masterpiece by Vermeer.[19]

The Smith collection arrived in London soon after the King and Queen had taken up residence at Buckingham House, and the finest of the Canalettos, notably the early series of views of the Piazza di San Marco, were hung in the Entrance Hall with the larger canvases by Zuccarelli. A valuable series of drawings in the Royal Library (including no. 115) gives a clear idea of the arrangement of pictures in the house by around 1774.[20] They show that in addition to the King's purchases, the house was hung with paintings garnered from other palaces, notably Hampton Court and Kensington, and from the annotations in the King's hand it is clear that he directed the arrangements. The 'imports' included both of Van Dyck's colossal portraits of Charles I from the early 1630s, and some of Prince Frederick's best pictures, including the *Family of Sir Balthazar Gerbier* by Rubens and his studio.[21] Most importantly, and as it turned out most controversially, the Queen's Saloon on the first floor of the east front of the house was hung with the tapestry cartoons of the *Acts of the Apostles* by Raphael, which were removed from the gallery at Hampton Court designed in 1699 by Wren for their display.[22]

At this date (*c*.1774), apart from isolated portraits by Nathaniel Dance and Francis Cotes, the only contemporary artist represented in Buckingham House was Benjamin West, for seven of whose paintings the King reserved one of his ground-floor apartments known as the Warm Room. Richard Dalton had met the Philadelphian painter in Venice in 1762, and seems to have given him a commission on behalf of George III and encouraged him to come and work in London.[23] These plans misfired and it was not until he was settled in London some years later that West was introduced to the King by one of his first British patrons, Robert Hay Drummond, Archbishop of York. In 1768 the King commissioned the first of the historical subjects that were to be hung in the Warm Room, *The Departure of Regulus* (no. 158). Its appeal for the King lay in the highly moral subject-matter (like that of *Timon of Athens*, commissioned from Nathaniel Dance in 1765) and the reminiscence of the art of Poussin, whom George III admired so much.[24] With *Regulus*, the King initiated the most durable of any of his relationships with painters.

PORTRAITS OF THEIR MAJESTY'S AND THE ROYAL FAMILY
Viewing the Exibition of the Royal Academy. 1788.

When in 1761 the commission was awarded for a State Portrait of the new King, the Scottish painter Allan Ramsay was the obvious choice. Lord Bute had earlier commissioned from his fellow Scot a luminous full length of the Prince of Wales, and at the accession Ramsay was appointed as the King's Principal Painter. His State Portrait (no. 3) has been called the most distinguished since Van Dyck's of Charles I (1636),[25] and much of the artist's remaining career was devoted to the production of replicas for official or diplomatic use. The King had also sat to Joshua Reynolds before the accession, but there was no meeting of minds between the two men and although George III was pleased to appoint Reynolds as first President of the Royal Academy in 1768 and to award him a knighthood the following year, it was only on Ramsay's death in 1784 that Reynolds succeeded to the post he had long coveted, of Principal Painter.[26] With Thomas Gainsborough things were quite different. Charming and amusing rather than lofty and intellectual, with many friends and interests – notably musical ones – in common with the King, Gainsborough was able to get on such terms with the royal family as would lead to a succession of dazzling portraits, most notably the full lengths of 1781 (see no. 11).[27] In the German painter Johan Zoffany Queen Charlotte found the perfect recorder of the domestic family life that preoccupied her for the first two decades of her marriage. It was probably through Bute that Zoffany began in 1764 to

FIG. 20 P. Martini after P. Ramberg, *Portraits of their Majesty's* [sic] *and the Royal Family viewing the Exhibition of the Royal Academy, 1788*. Engraving (RCIN 750535.a)

portray the royal family in a series of pictures that have proved as valuable a record of the royal residences at this early stage in the reign as they have of their inhabitants. Zoffany was one of the King's personal nominees for the Royal Academy on its foundation in 1768, and his ingenious group of the Academicians (no. 159) is a precious record of its early history. The King's attitude to the later generation of painters, favoured by the Prince of Wales, is exemplified by his response to Thomas Lawrence's portrait of Master William Linley (Dulwich Picture Gallery): 'Why doesn't the blockhead get his hair cut?'[28]

The foundation of the Royal Academy (see fig. 20) was no sudden impulse on anyone's part. In 1755 a group of artists including Reynolds and Louis-François Roubiliac had advanced a plan for such an institution, and both the Society of Dilettanti and the Society for the Promotion of Arts, Manufactures and Commerce had offered endowments. In 1768 a memorandum containing a 'useful plan' for establishing a 'Society for promoting the Arts of Design' was presented to the King by his former architectural tutor William Chambers; the memorandum was also signed by other artists with whom the King had already had dealings, including Nathaniel Dance, G.B. Cipriani, Zuccarelli, Angelica Kauffmann, Joseph Wilton, Thomas and Paul Sandby and Charles Catton. The King gave the plan his unequivocal approval and, with Chambers strategically placed as Treasurer, substantial financial assistance.[29]

Wilton and Chambers, who must share the credit for the design of the King's magnificent new state coach, had earlier collaborated in the creation of a 'Gallery of Antiques' for George III's mother Princess Augusta in the garden at Kew in the 1750s, where Wilton's statues of Muses were arranged in an arcaded setting intended to evoke Mount Helicon. Despite his appointment as Sculptor in Ordinary to the King in 1760, Wilton received no direct commissions from the King. Wilton's disappointment was shared by the many agents and dealers who were ready in Italy to supply antique marbles. For George III, sculpture had its proper place in Westminster Abbey. He was content to sit to Wilton, to Agostino Carlini (the only other sculptor-member of the Royal Academy) and to Joseph Nollekens for portrait busts, but these were commissioned by others. He does seem to have warmed to John Bacon, assuring him that his not having travelled abroad would not hinder his career. All that needs to be said of the King's lack of regard for 'Old Master' sculpture can be understood from his having given away Giambologna's colossal marble *Samson and a Philistine*, which he had acquired with Buckingham House in 1762, to his friend the Surveyor of the Office of Works, Thomas Worsley.[30]

In the furnishing and decoration of the Queen's House, as it was first called in 1762, distinctions have correctly been drawn between the comparative plainness of the ground floor, which contained the King's Apartments, and the richness of the Queen's rooms on the principal floor.[31] As was the case with pictures, the King introduced furniture from the other palaces. Of the newly commissioned furniture, the most imposing pieces were library-related. In 1761 William Vile supplied four mahogany 'paper cases' for the library, and extended a 'Grand Medal Case',[32] and in 1766–7 Vile's former assistant John Bradburn supplied library furniture costing a total of £577 8s which probably included the large octagonal desk visible in the centre of Pyne's view of the Octagon Library (no. 117) and the two colossal mahogany presses shown by Pyne in the

East Library (no. 118). Bradburn's succession to Vile's position in the royal service came about abruptly in June 1764, possibly as the result of a disputed bill,[33] and thereafter he was often employed in altering his master's work, including the glazed bookcase with a strongly architectural design which Vile had made for Queen Charlotte's apartments in 1762 (no. 268). This piece forms a striking contrast with the painted chest-of-drawers and corner cupboards (no. 280) which were probably supplied for the Queen in around 1770, and indeed with Vile's own jewel cabinet (no. 269), whose general form and engraved ivory inlays suggest a taste formed in continental Europe, if not in fact a European craftsman's hand. The Queen's liking for rococo furniture is suggested by the inclusion of Cressent's longcase clock (no. 298) in Zoffany's portrait of the Queen with her eldest sons (no. 4).

There was a watershed in the supply of furniture for the royal palaces in 1782 with the abolition of the Office of the Great Wardrobe, whose preserve this had been since the Middle Ages. This was part of a more general reduction and restructuring of the Royal Household intended to eradicate sinecures and to bring the whole administration under the authority of the three Great Officers of State: the Lord Steward, the Lord Chamberlain and the Master of the Horse. From 1782 it was through the Lord Chamberlain, rather than the Master of the Great Wardrobe, that commissions relating to the official functions of the Royal Household were placed. During the early 1790s considerable sums were spent by the Lord Chamberlain's Department on the refurnishing of the state rooms at St James's, where the King's levées and official business were still conducted. With the continuing architectural modification of the Queen's House later in the decade – in particular the Queen's Saloon – suites of giltwood furniture were ordered from Samuel Beckwith, William France and John Russell, who supplied three pairs of sofas – the largest pair being 4.6 metres (15 feet) long – for the Saloon in April 1799.[34] The chair frames were carved and gilt by William Adair, and the stuffed seats covered in white cotton velvet, painted with floral designs by Princess Elizabeth.[35] Towards the end of the century, by which time the principal apartments at Buckingham House, Windsor and St James's had been provided for, the emphasis passed to the private apartments of the enlarged royal family and their households, and there was a distinct move from mahogany into the lighter woods, and towards 'japanned' or painted furniture, sometimes in 'advanced' colour schemes. In 1804, for example, John Russell supplied a set of twelve 'antique' chairs for the Queen's Apartments at Windsor which were 'painted and japanned in Party Colours brown and white Strokes and yellow', and he rejapanned another set for the Queen's Lodge in white, green and purple.[36]

The King and Queen seem to have acquired almost no continental furniture, although they were ready to use what already existed within the Collection.[37] It is easy enough to point to a contrast in this respect with their son George IV, but his taste for French furniture in particular was encouraged by its sudden and abundant availability following the end of the *ancien régime*. Earlier acquisitions in this area included the Florentine cabinet (no. 261) purchased for the King and Queen in Italy by Dalton, who at the same time obtained in Rome 'A Harpsichord Case, ornamented with Paintings in the Stile of Polidoro'.[38]

The supply of musical instruments, particularly harpsichords and organs, is another constant feature of the accounts of George III and Queen Charlotte.[39] For both

FIG. 21 Inigo Barlow after Isaac
Cruikshank, *Representation of a
Royal Concert, at Buckingham House,*
1792. Engraving (RCIN 750554)

Representation of a Royal Concert, at Buckingham House

of them, music was of the greatest importance (fig. 21). The Queen is said to have played
the harpsichord in her cabin during the rough voyage across the North Sea on her first
journey to England (see no. 157), and certainly did so at St James's Palace on the evening
of her arrival. Her singing teacher, Johann Christian Bach, son of Johann Sebastian and
Master of the Queen's Band, arrived in London from Strelitz in the summer of 1762
and was in attendance at St James's three times a week in the 1760s; among his many
dedications to his pupil is an organ concerto of which the finale comprises variations on
'God Save the King'. The Queen's Band employed some of the leading instrumentalists
of the day, including the viola da gamba player and composer C.F. Abel (1723–87) and
the oboist J.C. Fischer (1733–1800). Under the Queen's patronage Bach and Abel staged
public concerts in London between 1765 and 1781 that provided a platform not only
for their own compositions but also for the best foreign musicians visiting London. The
8-year-old Mozart played before the King and Queen at Buckingham House on three
occasions in 1764, and dedicated six sonatas to the Queen in 1765.[40]

The King's musical tastes were both passionate and conservative. During the 1770s
and 1780s he made numerous purchases of scores and part-books of composers such as
Palestrina, Scarlatti and Lully. Payments for copies and arrangements of the scores of
Handel's oratorios feature throughout the royal accounts for the 1760s, such was the
appeal of their uncompromising Old Testament themes and use of the English language.
But the King's analysis of the scores themselves, and of Handel's mastery of dramatic
colour in his orchestrations, reveal a deep understanding of the composer's greatness.
The entire corpus of the composer's manuscripts, together with his harpsichord and
bust by Roubiliac (no. 252), were presented to the King in around 1772–4.[41]

George III's financial support of the Royal Academy of Arts was not an isolated
case. In 1760 he contributed £1,600 to the Royal Society (founded in the reign of

Charles II) for two expeditions to observe the transit of Venus, a rare phenomenon that occurred twice in the 1760s.[42] The King's scientific interests were, like so much else, greatly encouraged by Lord Bute, and informed by the demonstrations conducted by the itinerant lecturer Stephen Demainbray (1710–82), the most successful member of the new profession engaged in public instruction in geometry, mechanics, astronomy and mathematics that grew up in the 1740s and 1750s. His lectures, which the Princes George and Edward (Duke of York) attended in 1755, were illustrated by models and apparatus which explained scientific principles and their applications, for watermills, pile drivers, inclined planes and the like. Demainbray became the first Keeper of the new observatory at Richmond, built for the King to Chambers's designs for the observation of the 1769 transit of Venus, and his collection of instruments remained there after his death in 1782.[43] Demainbray was succeeded as Observatory Keeper by the Hanoverian William Herschel (1738–1822), who had settled in England in 1757. In 1781 he had discovered the planet Uranus, and his proposal to name it *Georgium sidus*[44] cannot have hindered his appointment. The King purchased five substantial telescopes from Herschel in 1785,[45] and from George Adams, who had been appointed Mathematical Instrument-Maker to the King in 1760, he ordered a large collection of apparatus for pneumatic, mechanical and geometrical experiments, including two exceptionally ornate silver microscopes (fig. 22).[46] The King's collection of scientific instruments was presented to King's College, London, for teaching purposes, but in 1927 it was transferred to the Science Museum, where it has recently been re-displayed.

FIG. 22 George Adams the Elder, *Silver microscope, c.*1763. (Science Museum, London, inv. no. 1949–116)

FIG. 23 Thomas Burke after Angelica Kauffmann, *Her Majesty Queen Charlotte raising the Genius of the Fine Arts*, 1772. Mezzotint, published by W. W. Ryland (RCIN 604622)

In view of these interests it is not surprising that the King should have engaged the leading horologists in the creation of some of the most sophisticated and expensive clocks, barometers and watches in existence. The King's involvement in the creation of Christopher Pinchbeck's magnificent four-dialled astronomical clock (no. 302) extended to the design of its case, a role he also undertook for Matthew Boulton's case for the mantel clock by Thomas Wright (no. 277). Further evidence of such activity comes in John Bradburn's account for a glass case for one of the King's clocks in 1766, which included an extra charge of £1 10s for 'extraordinary trouble and attention in blowing the glass according to His Majesty's direction'.[47]

In accounts of the King's character, his retiring disposition and aversion to grandiloquent displays are so often mentioned that his acquisitions of gold and silver plate might be expected to be modest. In fact, the Coronation Service by Thomas Heming (see p. 319) was one of the largest orders for new plate received by the Jewel House during the entire century. Undoubtedly the service lacks the truly eye-catching qualities and *jeu d'esprit* of the Marine Service made for George III's father Prince Frederick, with its *rocaille* fantasies by Nicolas Sprimont,[48] but it does include pieces of the highest quality whose designs were derived from fashionable French models. During the 1770s, probably through the British Ambassador Lord Harcourt, the King's Hanoverian Lord Chamberlain placed an order with the leading French goldsmith Robert-Joseph Auguste for a large and extremely fashionable neo-classical service for the palace of Herrenhausen.[49] That the King understood the occasional role of a grand display of plate can be judged from his re-employment of the baroque suites of silver furniture in the newly restored State Apartments at Windsor in 1804 (see nos. 257, 258). In February 1805 the King gave 'a Splendid Ball' at the castle at which was also displayed the silver furniture and buffet plate which had been rescued by the Duke of Cambridge from the palace of Herrenhausen in the face of the French invasion.[50]

George III seems to have shown no desire to emulate either his German cousins or the French King in the foundation or ownership of porcelain factories. His interest in ceramics was part of his all-embracing enthusiasm for natural philosophy and for the encouragement of British 'manufactures'. In July 1786 Wedgwood presented the King with a pyrometer which he had devised to measure the diminution of porcelain bodies at very high temperatures,[51] and two years later the Worcester manufacturer John Flight expressed the hope that the King 'being of a Curious Mechanical Turn and fond of seeing manufactories of all sorts . . . might visit Ours'.[52] John and Joseph Flight were awarded a royal warrant in 1789, but this was not followed by significant orders. By this date the King had received as gifts both the Fürstenberg and the Neapolitan Services (nos. 325, 329), and in 1772 he had inherited from his mother Augusta, Princess of Wales, a Meissen service that had belonged to his father Prince Frederick.[53] Josiah Wedgwood had high hopes of a commission from the King, believing that royal patronage would encourage wider sales, or as he put it: 'begin with the *Head* first, and then proceed to the inferior members'.[54] Wedgwood did succeed with the Queen, and from 1766 had been allowed to style himself 'Potter to Her Majesty'.[55] His reappellation of his creamwares as 'Queen's Ware' undoubtedly brought him commercial advantages.[56] It was also from Queen Charlotte that royal favours were chiefly bestowed on other factories (see fig. 23). The Mistress of the Robes, the Duchess of Ancaster, introduced the Queen to the Derby factory's London warehouse in 1776, and their sales books record her orders for three dessert services in 1781 and 1784.[57]

The Queen's Sèvres vases caught the eye of Horace Walpole on his visit to Buckingham House in 1783. He also noticed oriental porcelain, and her enthusiasm for the oriental is one of the strands of Queen Charlotte's taste that distinguishes it from the King's. It manifested itself soon after her arrival in England, since she had some model pagodas and ivory furniture by 1762 and a pair of 'mandarin' figures can be seen in the background of Zoffany's painting of *c.*1765 (no. 4). It may have been the Japan Room which the King and Queen 'inherited' at Buckingham House that inspired the creation at Frogmore in the 1790s of the Black and Red Japan Rooms, whose decoration was carried out by Princess Elizabeth, and which can be seen in Pyne's illustrations filled with oriental objects including porcelain, lacquer and cloisonné enamels (nos. 138, 141). All of these materials – along with the Indian ivory furniture and quantities of Chinese silk, fans and costumes – feature heavily in the catalogues of Queen Charlotte's posthumous sales.

If the Queen's oriental inclinations show her apart from the King, so do her botanical interests, or at least the extent of them. It seems that in this one area the influence of Lord

FIG. 24 C. Grignion after William Hogarth, *Frontispiece to the Catalogue of Pictures exhibited in Spring Gardens, May 1761*. Britannia's watering can is filled from George III's fountain. The water nourishes the tree stems symbolising the arts of Painting, Sculpture and Architecture. Engraving (RCIN 812005)

Bute over George III was not complete. 'I wish the King had any taste in flowers or plants,' wrote the botanist Peter Collinson, in a letter of 1768, 'but he has none, there are no hopes of encouragement from him, for his talent is architecture.'[58] The King purchased a herbarium for Queen Charlotte and her name is perpetuated by perhaps the most spectacular plant introduction of the reign, the 'Bird of Paradise' or *Strelitzia reginae*.[59]

To what extent did George III and his Queen fulfil the expectations of those who declared their hope for a general artistic renaissance in 1760 (fig. 24)? The difficult part of this question concerns the degree to which the careers of individual artists and craftsmen, and the increasingly industrialised makers of luxury decorative wares, were significantly affected, and the artistic life of the nation as a whole improved, by royal patronage. It is difficult because the economic and social change that characterised late eighteenth-century Britain was itself the main engine of more widespread patronage, and the court was no longer so crucial.[60] There can be no doubt of George III's personal responsibility for Britain's national library and Royal Academy, and from the narrower perspective of the Royal Collection, he left it very greatly richer than he found it. Indeed, there have been few significant additions since 1820 to the collection of Old Master drawings for which the Royal Collection is particularly well known.[61]

Writing of George III's declaration of 1770 to Lord Harcourt that he would not purchase Van Dyck's great portrait of Charles I in the hunting field which was then on offer in Paris, Sir Oliver Millar is surely right in remarking that 'only a collector whose emotions were rarely involved in his picture-buying can have rejected such a piece'.[62] It is this restraint, the refusal to abandon himself to excess in any field of activity, coupled with the highest sense of duty, that characterised everything that the King did.

1. John Brooke's biography of George III, published in 1972, was the first in modern times to give his artistic achievements their proper place. For assessments of George III as a collector see Millar 1969, pp. xi–xxiii, and *George III* 1974. I am grateful to my colleagues Christopher Lloyd, Martin Clayton and Emma Stuart, and especially to Jane Roberts, who has made available her unpublished lecture on George III as a collector.

2. These are itemised in BL North (Sheffield Park) Papers 61860, I, ff. 75–6. See also Rorschach 1990.

3. In 1784 the 22-year-old Prince of Wales spent £147,293 on Carlton House, against a parliamentary allocation of £30,000.

4. *Harcourt Papers*, III, p. 102.

5. *Walpole Correspondence*, XXI, p. 449. For visual expressions of these aspirations see William Hogarth's engraved frontispiece to the catalogue of the Society of Artists exhibition of 1761 (fig. 24) and Thomas Pingo's medal *The Arts Protected by King George III* of 1760 (Brown (L.) 1980, no. 6).

6. The 16-year-old Prince George made his first significant purchase, two volumes of water-colours by Maria Sibylla Merian, in 1755 (see nos. 166, 167).

7. The eighteenth-century term for what is today called 'science'.

8. For the coach see Marsden and Hardy 2001.

9. See Turner 1967.

10. *Banks Letters*, pp. 132–3.

11. Barnard (F.) 1820, I, pp. viii–ix. On the formation of the library see Brooke 1977, and p. 221 below.

12. The collection of topographical maps and naval charts comprised approximately 50,000 images. For a detailed study of these collections see Barber 2000 and *Enlightenment* 2003, pp. 158–65.

13. George III's books, topographical maps, naval charts, globes, coins and medals, were presented to the British Museum by George IV in 1823. George III's future intentions for his library are suggested by his having purchased and presented to the museum in 1762 the vast collection of pamphlets relating to the Civil War known as the Thomason Tracts (see Paintin 1989).

14. National libraries had been established in European cities much earlier than even the Bodleian, which was founded in 1595, sixty years after the purpose-built Bibliothèque Nationale in Paris.

15. It should be borne in mind that the Old Master drawings acquired in Italy by George III were mounted in volumes and kept on library shelves.

16. *Walpole Correspondence*, XXI, p. 478. For Dalton's activities in Italy see Mahon and Turner 1989, pp. xxii–xxxiv, and Ingamells 1997, pp. 267–70. Lord Bute's role in the acquisition of works of art from Italy for George III, and his correspondence with Dalton, are extensively discussed in Russell (forthcoming), chapters 3–4.

17. For the mechanism of the 'separate account' see Russell (forthcoming). Although the King did not make the Grand Tour, his Italian acquisitions were a great deal more impressive than those of his brother Edward, Duke of York, or indeed of his sixth son Augustus, Duke of Sussex, who lived for many years in Italy.

18. See p. 208.

19. For Smith see p. 196 and Vivian 1971. For the purchase of his collection by George III see Levey 1991, pp. xxxvii–xlvi; Vivian 1989, pp. 17–36, and *King's Purchase* 1993. The sale was agreed in the spring of 1762, and the final payment towards the total purchase price (including interest and the cost of transport) of £20,805 was paid in June 1764.

20. This date appears in some unrelated jottings on the reverse of one of the drawings, which are otherwise undated. See Russell 1987.

21. Millar 1963, nos. 143, 144 and RCIN 405415.

22. Shearman 1972, pp. 152–5.

23. Ingamells 1997, pp. 990–92 and Von Erffa and Staley 1986, pp. 264–5, no. 195.

24. As, for example, when he was shown the set of *Seven Sacraments* which Sir Joshua Reynolds had acquired for the Duke of Rutland (Millar 1969, p. xvii).

25. Millar 1969, p. xiii.

26. By which time the embittered Reynolds dismissed the position as of 'near equal dignity with his Majesty's rat catcher'. See Lloyd (C.) 1994.

27. Gainsborough's opinion of George III's taste in pictures is quoted by Henry Angelo (1828, I, p. 354): 'The King is a good connoisseur, and conversant in the works of the Old Masters; much more so, indeed, than many of his courtiers, who hold their heads so high upon the advantage of foreign travel.'

28. As recounted by S.P. Denning, Keeper of the Dulwich collection, 1821–64 (see *Linley Sisters* 1988, p. 100). The portrait was exhibited in 1789.

29. The King provided £5,000 from his Privy Purse (see *Chambers* 1996, p. 54).

30. The gift was made some time between 1762 and 1778, together with two unspecified Egyptian statues. The Giambologna group had been acquired in Spain by Charles I when Prince of Wales, and given by him to the Duke of Buckingham. It later belonged to John Sheffield, also Duke of Buckingham but unrelated to the former owner, who placed it in Buckingham House. It is now in the Victoria and Albert Museum (see Pope-Hennessy 1964, II, pp. 460–65, no. 486).

31. See Jackson-Stops 1993.

32. PRO LC9/306, no. 29. See Roberts (H.) 1990b. Two tall carved mahogany cabinets in the Victoria and Albert Museum and the Metropolitan Museum of Art, New York, may be the end-sections of the 'Grand Medal Case'. See Shrub 1965.

33. *DOEFM* 1986, p. 924.

34. PRO LC11/7, Quarter ending 5 April.

35. *ibid.* The work entailed several journeys to Windsor by the upholsterer William France to discuss the coverings with the Princess. The

36. coverings had been replaced in crimson by the time Pyne's view of the Saloon was published in 1819 (see no. 111).

36. PRO LC11/9, Quarter ending 5 January 1805.

37. See Roberts (H.) 2002.

38. RA GEO/15602–3.

39. Kirkman, Zumpe and Snetzler are among the names that feature in the surviving accounts. In addition, there are four elaborate drawings by Robert Adam for a pianoforte case for Queen Charlotte (Soane Museum, vol. 49, nos. 2–5).

40. *Mozart Letters* 1986, pp. 46–7, and O.E. Deutsch, *Mozart, a documentary biography*, Stanford 1974, pp. 38–9.

41. See Lansdale 1965, pp. 331–2, 337–8. The manuscripts were presented to the British Museum by Her Majesty The Queen in 1957.

42. *The Record of the Royal Society*, 4th edn, London, 1940, p. 139. For the second occurrence of the transit of Venus in 1769, the King donated £4,000 to the Society of Arts. It proved more than sufficient for the expedition, and the balance was spent on a commission to Joseph Nollekens for a bust of the King. George III made a further contribution of £3,000 in 1784 to enable the Society to carry out a triangulation to determine the difference in longitude between the Greenwich and Paris observatories. For the significance of the transit of Venus and for George III's scientific interests in general, see Morton and Wess 1993.

43. They are now in the Science Museum in London along with George III's personal collection of instruments (Morton and Wess 1993).

44. *sidus* is the Latin term for a heavenly body.

45. One of these, which was presented by the King to the Duke of Marlborough, survives in the Whipple Museum of the History of Science at Cambridge.

46. See Morton and Wess 1993, pp. 243–72. The King's own microscope is now in the Museum of the History of Science in Oxford while the second, which subsequently belonged to George IV, is in the Science Museum in London.

47. *DOEFM* 1986, p. 95.

48. *Royal Treasures* 2002, nos. 178–80.

49. Much of the Hanoverian service was recently acquired by a Rothschild family trust and placed on public display at Waddesdon Manor, Buckinghamshire (see Glanville 2003, p. 29).

50. Kennedy Diary.

51. The device, consisting of about eighty pieces of clay and calibrated gauges, is in the King George III Collection at the Science Museum (Morton and Wess 1993, p. 479, no. E149).

52. Worcester, Dyson Perrins Museum, MS Diary of John Flight, 1785–91, entry for 14 September 1788. For this and other extracts see Sandon 1978, pp. 217–32. George III's inspection of Flight's porcelain factory is often mentioned by ceramic historians, but it created less interest at the time than his visit to the woollen manufacturers at Stroud in Gloucestershire in the same month.

53. This is mentioned in an undated memorandum in the King's hand, perhaps written in December 1772, concerning his late mother and father's possessions. BL North (Sheffield Park) Papers, 61860, f. 55.

54. Josiah Wedgwood to his partner Bentley, 7 September 1771 (*Wedgwood Letters* 1965, p. 114).

55. In an undated letter to Bentley probably from the mid-1760s, Wedgwood offered congratulations on Bentley's having obtained an order from Queen Charlotte and hoped to repeat them 'one of these days . . . upon his receiving the like honor from his Majesty!' (quoted in Dawson 1985, p. 639).

56. Wedgwood wrote to Bentley on 31 May 1767 about the public display of new services as being 'absolutely necessary to be shown, in order to do the needful with the Ladys in the neatest, genteelest and best method'. Quoted by M. Baker in *Wedgwood* 1995, p. 231, n. 28. Without evidence it would be wrong to assume that Wedgwood was frustrated in his failure to win a large order from the King because of his well-known sympathy with the American rebels' cause.

57. Bemrose 1898, pp. 89–92. A smaller number of purchases by the King, including a dinner service with green borders and roses at the centre, is also recorded. The Queen's purchases were generally made by Henry Compton, her Page of the Backstairs.

58. Peter Collinson to W. Bartram, 16 February 1768, quoted in Desmond 1995, p. 69.

59. For a recent assessment of the Queen's interests see Orr 2001.

60. The King's awareness of the importance of manufacturing was confirmed by Wedgwood's partner, Thomas Bentley, following a private audience with the King in 1770: 'The King is well acquainted with business, and with the characters of the principal manufacturers, merchants, and artists, and seems to have the success of our manufacturers much at heart, and to understand the importance of them' (quoted Brooke 1972, p. 304).

61. The changing importance of royal patronage is discussed in Lloyd (C.) 1998.

62. Millar 1969, p. xv.

5. Paintings (nos. 143–165)

The following entries are ordered by date of acquisition by the King and Queen.

PAINTINGS FROM THE COLLECTION OF CONSUL JOSEPH SMITH (nos. 143–153)

George III acquired around five hundred paintings from Smith. Of these, two thirds were by Italian artists and one third by northern artists; among the latter was Vermeer's *Lady at the virginal* (RCIN 405346). The paintings were mostly contained in 'neat Italian frames', many of which survive today. Although a number of important earlier Italian paintings were included in this purchase, the core of Smith's collection was formed by works by his Venetian contemporaries, from which the following selection has been made.

143. Sebastiano Ricci (1659–1734)
The Adoration of the Magi, 1726

Oil on canvas. 325.5 × 291.5 cm (10′ 8⅛″ × 9′ 6¾″)
Dated on the steps *MDCCXXVI*
RCIN 405743
PROVENANCE Joseph Smith; from whom bought by George III, 1762
LITERATURE Daniels 1976, p. xv and no. 159; Levey 1991, no. 640; Knox 1994

The Venetian artist Sebastiano Ricci travelled extensively in Europe, working all over Italy and in Vienna and London. His style developed from the late baroque of Luca Giordano to the delicacy and elegance of the rococo. On his return to Venice from England in 1716 Sebastiano, with his nephew Marco, produced the series of seven large paintings of New Testament subjects to which this picture belongs (Knox 1994). Marco contributed the architectural backgrounds. In 1742 Joseph Smith had the paintings engraved by J.M. Liotard as in his collection and they were described in 1749 in a volume published by Smith's protégé Giambattista Pasquali; the volume was issued anonymously but the author was Abate Pietr'Ercole Gherardi of Modena.

Six of the series are still in the Royal Collection; two are now on loan to the National Trust at Osterley Park, and one is lost. The large scale and subject-matter of the paintings have prompted the suggestion that the series was commissioned by a member of the royal house of Savoy in Turin, for whom Sebastiano and Marco Ricci undertook many commissions in the 1720s; it is further suggested that the paintings were only acquired by Smith when the commission fell through. It is more likely, however, that Smith commissioned the series himself. The 1742 and 1749 publications indicate his pride of ownership, as part of his large collection of Ricci paintings and drawings. His ownership of sixteen preparatory drawings for the *Adoration of the Magi* (including no. 172) may indicate that he was involved with the project from the outset. Another painting in the series is dated 1724 so that 1726, the date painted on the steps, could mark the completion of the group. George Knox has outlined the way in which the series might have been hung in a single room in Smith's house in Venice, before the house was altered in the 1740s, when the series could have been displayed in two rooms.

The sixteenth-century Venetian artist Veronese was the key influence on Ricci's work. This composition is based, in reverse, on Veronese's *Adoration of the Magi* (London, National Gallery) which was painted for the church of San Silvestro, Venice, in 1573. Ricci translates the grandeur of Veronese's scene, with its composition built around imposing architecture seen from a low viewpoint, into eighteenth-century elegance. The squarer format allows concentration on the finery of the retinue. Sebastiano Ricci was the forerunner of the great master of the rococo, Tiepolo, who looked back at both these paintings when he painted his altarpiece of the same subject for the monastery of Schwarzach in Franconia (now Munich, Alte Pinakothek).

A view published by Pyne in October 1816 showed Sebastiano Ricci's *Adoration* hanging at the far end of the King's Gallery, Kensington Palace (see no. 103); however, by that date the painting had already been transferred to Hampton Court.

143

144

145

144. Giovanni Antonio Canal, called Canaletto (1697–1768)

Venice: The Piazzetta towards S. Giorgio Maggiore, c.1724

Oil on canvas. 173.0 × 134.3 cm (5′ 8⅛″ × 4′ 4⅞″)
RCIN 401036
PROVENANCE Commissioned by Joseph Smith; from whom bought by George III, 1762
LITERATURE *Canaletto* 1980, pp. 31–8; Constable and Links 1989, no. 55; Levey 1991, no. 382; Kowalczyk 2001, pp. 22–4, 64–8

This painting and its pendant (no. 145) are part of a set of six large views of the Piazza San Marco and the Piazzetta in the heart of Venice. The series may have been Canaletto's earliest commission from Joseph Smith, who sold his pre-eminent collection of paintings, prints and drawings by the artist to George III in 1762. Each view in the set, comprising four of upright and two of horizontal format, has been carefully composed so that architecture dominates either the left of the view, as here, or the right as in no. 145. Sharp diagonals are emphasised by the deep shadows cast by evening light. The paintings were probably arranged symmetrically in a room in Smith's residence on the Grand Canal, the Palazzo Balbi (now Palazzo Mangilli-Valmarana). A closely related preparatory drawing for each view (also in the Royal Collection) may have been the basis for discussion between artist and patron. The care taken over the composition of the architecture and the changes made during the course of painting suggest that the balance and effect of the whole was important to both of them.

The left corner of the Palazzo Ducale and the column of San Marco frame the church and campanile of San Giorgio Maggiore. The set of paintings must date before 1726–8 when the crowning element of the campanile (in the centre of the present view) was altered from conical to onion shape; in 1774 it was replaced by the one seen today. The fluid, broad strokes, particularly those defining the figures, the strong diagonals and contrasts of light, can be found in Canaletto's view of *The Stonemason's Yard* (London, National Gallery) which has been dated 1725. It is generally agreed that the set precedes both that painting and the series of four paintings commissioned by Stefano Conti (private collection), datable 1725–6.

Canaletto combines several viewpoints and distorts topography for dramatic effect. For example, San Giorgio is heightened, noticeable in comparison with the drawing (Parker 1990, no. 4); and from this viewpoint there should be one upper window in the Palazzo Ducale, not two. Mathematical instruments were used to establish the architecture: a straight edge ruled out the right side of the column and perspective lines on the Palazzo Ducale. In the preparatory drawings a beam and pulley project from the loggia of the Palazzo, discernible as a pentimento in the final painting. The paintings appear to have arrived in London unframed; if so, this would strengthen the suggestion that they had been set into a room in one of Smith's houses in Italy. George III framed them in English 'Maratta' frames when he hung them in the Entrance Hall of Buckingham House (see nos. 109, 110).

145. Giovanni Antonio Canal, called Canaletto (1697–1768)

Venice: The Piazzetta towards S. Maria della Salute, c.1724

Oil on canvas. 172.0 × 136.5 cm (5' 7¹¹⁄₁₆" × 4' 5¾")
RCIN 405073
PROVENANCE Commissioned by Joseph Smith; from whom bought by George III, 1762
LITERATURE *Canaletto* 1980, pp. 31–8; Constable and Links 1989, no. 146; Levey 1991, no. 383; Kowalczyk 2001, pp. 22–4, 64–8

This painting and its pendant (no. 144) are part of a set of six large-scale views of Venice commissioned by Joseph Smith. As in no. 144 viewpoints are combined and architecture moved and distorted, here giving weight to the right side of the painting. If the view of the Biblioteca Marciana is accurate, the column of San Marco (seen on the right in no. 144) should intervene between the Biblioteca and the distant Santa Maria della Salute, and the column of San Teodoro would be higher. In the preparatory drawing (Parker 1990, no. 3) the column of San Teodoro is not included and the column of San Marco dominates the left side of the view. In the painting Canaletto included the column of San Marco and then painted it out, framing the left side of the painting instead with a mast and sail. The steps of the bridge, the Ponte della Pescaria, have been brought forward, the Dogana (Customs House) and the Salute are too close together and both bulk larger in the middle distance. There is visible evidence of Canaletto's use of ruling instruments to lay in his design and outline architecture. Dividers outlined the dome of the Salute.

Offsetting the grandeur of the architecture in sombre browns are the figures, their bright clothes caught dramatically in the late afternoon light, the artist brilliantly turning the thick paint with each stroke to assume the shape of the forms described. When Horace Walpole saw Canaletto's

paintings in the Entrance Hall of Buckingham House, he described them as 'bolder, stronger & far superior to his common Works' (Walpole 1928, p. 79).

146. Giovanni Antonio Canal, called Canaletto (1697–1768)

Rome: The Pantheon, 1742

Oil on canvas. 183.5 × 105.7 cm (6' 0¼" × 3' 5⅝")
Signed and dated *ANT.CANAL FECIT / ANNO MDCCXLII*
RCIN 400524
PROVENANCE Commissioned by Joseph Smith; from whom bought by George III, 1762
LITERATURE *Canaletto* 1980, pp. 60–67; Constable and Links 1989, no. 390; Levey 1991, no. 371

In 1742 Canaletto painted five upright views of Rome for Joseph Smith. Like the earlier set of Venetian views (see nos. 144, 145), these were probably designed for a particular room. They too may have arrived in London unframed, after their acquisition by George III in 1762, since they were hung in English frames in the Entrance Hall of Buckingham House – alongside the Venetian views (see nos. 109, 110). The Roman set includes the major sights of ancient Rome with three triumphal arches and nos. 146 and 147. The Pantheon, dedicated to all the gods, was the best preserved monument of ancient Rome and the greatest symbol of the Empire. The glory of an imperial age now long past is suggested by the heaviness of the architecture, which emerges from deep shadows and shows the ravages of time. The vertical format, the low viewpoint and the admiring group of visitors on the Grand Tour emphasise this sense of a monumental past, the brightly clad figures contrasting with the browns of the stonework.

The prominent signatures are the first in Canaletto's work and are unusual. It has been suggested that artist and patron wanted to promote a new subject at a time when the War of the Austrian Succession had greatly reduced the number of visitors to Venice. There is no record of Canaletto visiting Rome again after his youthful visit in 1719–20. For these paintings he may have relied on prints or the drawings he made in Rome in his youth. It has also been suggested that Canaletto's nephew, Bernardo Bellotto, with whom he was closely associated, may have supplied material to his uncle. Bellotto was in Rome in 1742, returning to Venice in that year or in 1743.

146

147

The first temple on the site of the Pantheon was built
in 27 BC by Agrippa, but the existing building with its
dedicatory inscription was erected by Hadrian in the second
century AD. It was one of the few monuments of pagan
antiquity to be converted into a church in the seventeenth
century. Its thirteenth-century campanile was replaced by
bell towers in the seventeenth century. The fountain is shown
without the obelisk bearing the arms of Pope Clement XI
installed in 1711. Canaletto set out the architecture by ruling
and incising. The figures are less integral to the scene than
in the earlier set of views. The prosaic cart in the right
foreground contrasts with the ebullience of the coach and
horses arriving behind. The influence of Bellotto and of
Gian Paolo Panini's contemporary views of Rome has been
traced in such details.

147. Giovanni Antonio Canal, called Canaletto (1697–1768)

*Rome: The ruins of the Forum looking towards
the Capitol*, 1742

Oil on canvas. 190.0 × 106.2 cm (6′ 2¹³⁄₁₆″ × 3′ 5¹³⁄₁₆″)
Signed and dated *ANT.CANAL FECIT / ANNO MCCXLII* (D
omitted from date)
RCIN 400714
PROVENANCE Commissioned by Joseph Smith; from whom
bought by George III, 1762
LITERATURE Kozakiewicz 1972, I, pp. 39–40, 222, II, pp. 50–51,
464–5; *Canaletto* 1980, pp. 60–67; Constable and Links 1989, no. 387;
Levey 1991, no. 372; *Bellotto* 2001, no. 18; Kowalczyk 2001, no. 4

This painting and no. 146 are from the set of five views of
Rome, commissioned by Joseph Smith and prominently
signed and dated 1742. When painting these views Canaletto

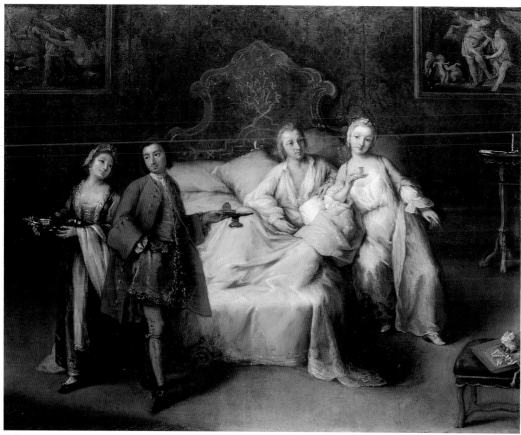

148

149

probably referred to studies made when he visited Rome in 1719–20. A drawing of the same view as that recorded here, but with a wider format (British Museum, 1858-6-26-224), is closely associated with Canaletto, and may be an early work by him. The drawing also served as the basis for paintings with the same format by Canaletto and his studio and by his nephew, Bernardo Bellotto; these are all also usually dated to the early 1740s.

The main features, lit from the right, occur in both painting and drawing, but Canaletto uses the narrower format of the painting to dramatise the view, realigning the ruins to suit his purposes. From the low viewpoint the temple of Castor and Pollux in the foreground is higher than the towers of the Palazzo Senatorio on the Capitoline Hill behind and all are neatly linked together by the angle of the temple of Saturn in the middle distance. The many chimneys, often Venetian in character, accentuate the painting's vertical accent.

As the market place and then the political, religious and civic centre of Rome, the Forum was the heart of the ancient city. The temple of Castor and Pollux, built in honour of the twin heroes in 484 BC, was rebuilt many times, the last in 6 AD. The temple of Saturn was one of the most ancient sanctuaries in the Forum, perhaps inaugurated as early as 498 BC. It was restored in the third and fifth centuries AD, as recorded by the inscription. It is seen against the rear façade of the Palazzo Senatorio, the seat of Roman government, which was rebuilt during the sixteenth century by Michelangelo. The group of admiring visitors and the local Romans such as the knife-grinder seem to be dwarfed and insignificant beside the heavy stone of the architecture associated with an ancient past and the government of a lost empire.

148. Pietro Longhi (1702–1785)

The Married Couple's Breakfast, 1744

Oil on panel. 48.9 × 60.3 cm (19¼″ × 23¾″)
Signed and dated *Petrus Longhi / 1744*
RCIN 403029
PROVENANCE Possibly commissioned by Joseph Smith; from whom bought by George III, 1762
LITERATURE Spike 1986, p. 196; Levey 1991, no. 537

George III bought two pairs of paintings by Longhi from Joseph Smith, of which this work and its companion (no. 149) remain in the Royal Collection. Both paintings were recorded at St James's Palace in 1819. The frames are good examples of the 'carved gilt frames in modern & elegant taste' in which

Smith's paintings were described in the 'Italian List', drawn up in George III's reign; they are refined products of a Venetian workshop (see *King's Purchase* 1993, pp. 58–62).

The subject of this painting is not clear – it was described as a 'Bride sitting by her bridegroom in bed' in the Italian List. The familiar look that the man directs towards the younger woman, who may be his bride, might be an allusion to their recent union, which is happily less turbulent than that of Venus and Adonis in the two pictures hanging on either side of their bed. Those paintings appear to depict the goddess trying to prevent her mortal lover from going to the chase and they may have been deliberately included by Longhi as an ironic comment upon the fleeting nature of love. This would support the possibility that this painting shows the couple's first breakfast after their marriage.

This pair of paintings, probably commissioned by Consul Smith, seem to have been an important commission for Longhi. They are among his few paintings on panel and both are signed and dated, which was unusual for the artist. There are five preparatory drawings for this painting and one for its pair (no. 149) in the Museo Correr, Venice.

149. Pietro Longhi (1702–1785)

Blind-man's Buff, 1744 (?)

Oil on panel. 48.7 × 60.5 cm (19⁹⁄₁₆″ × 23¹³⁄₁₆″)
Signed and dated *Petrus Longhi F 174[4?]*
RCIN 403030
PROVENANCE Possibly commissioned by Joseph Smith; from whom bought by George III, 1762
LITERATURE Levey 1991, no. 538

This is a companion piece to no. 148. Longhi's particular talent for small interior scenes, carefully observed and charmingly peopled, was quickly appreciated in his native Venice, where he became a successful painter after training in Bologna with Giuseppe Maria Crespi. The careful characterisation of the figures in Longhi's pictures, some of which appear to be portraits, and the great care with which he observed everyday objects – for instance the footstool in this picture – elevate his work from being merely decorative. His stylistic sources appear to have been French and his pastel tones and rococo lightness of handling have more in common with the work of artists such as Lancret or Pater than with his Italian contemporaries.

The game of blind-man's buff (see also no. 458) was a popular subject in French art and it is possible that Longhi based this painting on a French engraving. Here, the game is being played by a fashionably dressed group in a contemporary interior. The picture in the background appears to depict the suicide of the Numidian queen, Sophonisba, a popular subject in seventeenth-century Italian painting. However, it is not clear why Longhi chose to include such a tragic subject within a scene of mirth.

150. Francesco Zuccarelli (1702–1788)

*Landscape with Diana reposing from the chase, c.*1740

Oil on copper. 53.0 × 38.8 cm (20⅞″ × 15¼″)

RCIN 401275

PROVENANCE Possibly commissioned by Joseph Smith; from whom bought by George III, 1762

LITERATURE Levey 1991, no. 678

The Consul Smith collection included a large group of paintings by Zuccarelli of which this highly finished small

work on copper and its pair (no. 151) are possibly the finest examples. The feminine subject-matter and sensuous treatment of these two pictures suggest that they might have been commissioned by Smith as decoration for his wife's apartments in the Palazzo Balbi (now Mangilli-Valmarana) on the Grand Canal. Smith was to have an important influence upon the young Zuccarelli's career, also commissioning him to paint eleven overdoors in collaboration with Antonio Visentini (nos. 152, 153).

Zuccarelli arrived in Venice from his native Florence in about 1730 and by the end of the decade his landscape paintings were reaching England – possibly via the Consul. In 1752 the artist visited England, where he was to remain for a decade, returning again from *c.*1764 until *c.*1771. In 1768 he was one of the founder-members of the Royal Academy (see no. 159) and in 1771 he received a direct commission from George III for two large paintings (costing £428 8s). Twenty-seven paintings by Zuccarelli, together with eight

150

151

152

works made in collaboration with Visentini, survive in the Royal Collection.

Diana, identified by the crescent moon in her hair, is shown resting after hunting with hounds, with her quiver of arrows laid by her side and her maids in attendance. Unlike most of Zuccarelli's landscape paintings, a great deal of prominence has been given to the figures (and dogs) in this picture and its pair. The idyllic landscape and sensuous semi-clad women evoke the work of French rococo artists such as Boucher, which Zuccarelli may have known through engravings. However, the rich palette relates more closely to the work of northern Italian landscape artists such as Marco Ricci (nos. 174, 175).

151. Francesco Zuccarelli (1702–1788)
Landscape with Europa and the Bull, c.1740

Oil on copper. 53.4 × 39.1 cm (21″ × 15⅜″)
RCIN 401274
PROVENANCE Possibly commissioned by Joseph Smith; from whom bought by George III, 1762
LITERATURE Levey 1991, no. 677

The Rape of Europa was a popular subject in painting from the sixteenth century onwards. As recounted in Ovid's *Metamorphoses*, Book II, Jupiter falls in love with Europa and abducts her in the form of a bull. Zuccarelli's painting concentrates on the earlier part of the tale in which Europa's handmaidens decorate the beautiful white bull with garlands of flowers – here aided by Cupid. In the distance Europa can be seen being carried off by the bull, which is led by Cupid. However, the drama of the tale as told by Ovid is ignored in

Zuccarelli's painting, which concentrates on the gentle pastoral nature of the scene. The artist painted many versions of the story throughout his career.

Both this painting and its pair (no. 150) hung in Princess Amelia's bedroom at Kew *c.*1800. In the same room were a number of other pictures purchased from Joseph Smith, such as Sebastiano Ricci's *Sacrifice of Polyxena* (Levey 1991, no. 645) and Canaletto's *Caprice view of Rome with ruins based on the Forum* (Levey 1991, no. 367). Apart from these paintings and a group of four landscapes, the room also contained Zoffany's portrait of the Princess's family in Van Dyck costume (no. 7).

152. Antonio Visentini (1688–1782) and Francesco Zuccarelli (1702–1788)
Capriccio with a view of Burlington House, London, 1746

Oil on canvas. 79.5 × 130.7 cm (31⁵⁄₁₆″ × 51⁷⁄₁₆″)
Signed and dated *Visentini et Zuccarelli / Fecerunt Venetiis 1746*
RCIN 400685
PROVENANCE Commissioned by Joseph Smith; from whom bought by George III, 1762
LITERATURE Levey 1991, no. 671; Knox 1996

Trained as a painter, Antonio Visentini had an association with Consul Smith which began around 1717, and led to his production in 1735 of a set of engravings after Canaletto's series of views of the Grand Canal in Smith's collection. Visentini was also to act as an architect and general artistic factotum for Smith until the latter's death in 1770.

Smith and Visentini shared a great interest in the designs and theories of the sixteenth-century Venetian architect Andrea Palladio, whose work they considered superior to

153

that of later baroque architects. Smith published a reprint of Palladio's architectural treatise, *I quattro libri*, in 1768 (no. 238). In 1743–4 he had commissioned from Canaletto a series of pictures depicting Venetian monuments, including the principal buildings of Palladio in imaginary settings. It was perhaps the combination of their interest in Palladio and the commission to Canaletto that prompted Smith to commission a series of eleven overdoor *capricci* of English neo-Palladian buildings. Visentini painted the buildings using volumes of British architectural engravings for reference, whilst Zuccarelli (see no. 150) painted most of the figures and all of the landscape settings. They date from 1746 and were possibly intended as overdoors for the Consul's villa at Mogliano on the Venetian mainland near Treviso. Eight of the views were hung in the Entrance Hall at Buckingham House by 1819 (see no. 109). They were moved to the Grand Corridor at Windsor Castle in 1828.

Visentini's view of Burlington House was based upon plates 23–4 in the third volume of Colen Campbell's *Vitruvius Britannicus*, published in 1725. Burlington House was the London home of Richard Boyle, 3rd Earl of Burlington, the amateur architect who did so much to promote the neo-Palladian style in England. The new façade for Burlington House, built in 1718–19 probably to the designs of Campbell and of Burlington himself, was inspired both by Palladio's Palazzo Porto-Colleoni at Vicenza and by the Jacobean architect Inigo Jones, whose work was in turn indebted to Palladio. In the nineteenth century Burlington House became the home of the Royal Academy and the façade was drastically remodelled.

153. Antonio Visentini (1688–1782) and Francesco Zuccarelli (1702–1788)

Capriccio with a view of Mereworth Castle, Kent, 1746

Oil on canvas. 82.7 × 131.5 cm (32⁹⁄₁₆″ × 51¾″)
Signed and dated *Visentini et Zuccarelli / Fecerunt Venetiis 1746*
RCIN 400687
PROVENANCE Commissioned by Joseph Smith; from whom bought by George III, 1762
LITERATURE Levey 1991, no. 675; Knox 1996

Visentini and Zuccarelli were able to collaborate with perfect harmony in this commission. Zuccarelli – who painted the landscape settings and most of the figures – had the easier task since he could work freely from his imagination, and the landscapes in which he sets his English buildings are in no way different from those he was used to painting for his pastoral scenes (see nos. 150, 151), while the figures are those of his contemporaries in Venice. Meanwhile Visentini – who painted the buildings – had to provide accurate renditions of buildings that he had never seen and of which he only had plans and elevations. The Palladian prototypes for these English buildings, most of which were in the Veneto, could have assisted Visentini in his work to ensure that he gave them a convincing, three-dimensional quality. This would certainly have been the case with the present view of Mereworth Castle in Kent, which was a direct copy of Andrea Palladio's Villa Rotonda near Vicenza. Mereworth was designed by Colen Campbell for John Fane, later 7th Earl of Westmorland, and was complete by 1723.

154. Giovanni Francesco Barbieri, called Guercino (1591–1666)

The Libyan Sibyl, 1651

Oil on canvas. 116.2 × 96.6 cm (45¾″ × 38¹⁄₁₆″)
RCIN 405340
PROVENANCE Ippolito Cattani, 1651; probably bought for George III by Richard Dalton in Italy, early 1760s
LITERATURE *Guercino in Britain* 1991, no. 31; *Il Guercino* 1991, no. 136; Levey 1991, no. 521

The Libyan Sibyl was one of the twelve women of antiquity with the gift of prophecy. Traditionally Sibyls had foretold the coming of Christ in the Sibylline Books and had been adopted by the Christian Church as pagan counterparts to the Old Testament prophets. The Libyan Sibyl had prophesied the manifestation of Christ to the Gentiles. Guercino has not included her usual attribute of a lighted taper or torch and instead identifies her by the inscription on the book on which she rests her right elbow, while she remains deeply immersed in her reading. The depiction of Sibyls was popular in the seventeenth century. Although Guercino painted the subject throughout his career, he produced the largest number in the 1640s and 1650s.

154

This is a late work by the Bolognese artist, in which the strong chiaroscuro of his early works has lightened and his style is refined and classical. The painting has been identified as one of two half-length Sibyls painted for Ippolito Cattani (or Cattanio) of Bologna, for which Guercino received 120 ducatoni (or 150 scudi) on 4 December 1651. The pendant is the *Samian Sibyl* (private collection); a workshop replica, sold to the Grand Duke of Tuscany in 1777, appears in the foreground of Zoffany's *Tribuna* (no. 161), which was still being completed at the time; its inclusion in the painting may have been intended as a compliment to the King on his excellent purchase of the *Libyan Sibyl*. The *Samian Sibyl* looks heavenwards whereas the *Libyan Sibyl* remains absorbed in her reading. She has a noble grandeur despite the size of the painting. The few colours are subtly modulated and are simply counterbalanced by the white of her turban and the knotted sash at her waist.

Guercino was immensely popular in eighteenth-century England. No payment is recorded for the painting but it was probably acquired in Bologna in 1763 by Richard Dalton, the King's Librarian, with the help of the engraver Francesco Bartolozzi. Dalton was buying extensively for the King in Rome and Bologna at this period. He had already bought a large number of Guercino drawings (including nos. 186, 187) from the Gennari family in Bologna, descendants of Guercino's nephews. Bartolozzi produced an engraved version of the painting, as he did of the Carracci *'Il Silenzio'* (no. 156). The King hung the painting in the Warm Room in the Queen's Apartments in Buckingham House in a carefully planned hang of Flemish and Italian seventeenth-century paintings (see no. 114).

155. Sir Anthony Van Dyck (1599–1641)

The five eldest children of Charles I, 1637

Oil on canvas. 163.2 × 198.8 cm (5′ 4¼″ × 6′ 6¼″)
Signed and dated *Antony van dyck Eques Fecit, / 1637*.
RCIN 404405
PROVENANCE Commissioned by Charles I (£100); sold by the Commissioners of the Late King's Goods to Captain Geere, 14 May 1650 (£120); purchased by Francis Trion, 17 May 1653; recovered by Charles II, by 12 May 1660; possibly given by James II to the Countess of Dorchester (later 1st Countess of Portmore); her son, 2nd Earl of Portmore; from whom bought by 'Mr Pinchbeck'; from whom bought by George III, 6 February 1765 (£525; RA GEO/17131)
LITERATURE Millar 1963, no. 152; Millar 1969, pp. xiv–xv

155

Van Dyck's masterful painting acknowledges both the youth and the status of its royal subjects, breaking with the earlier tradition of presenting royal children as miniature adults. The picture was commissioned by Charles I but left the Royal Collection twice, during the Commonwealth and under James II, before being repurchased by George III in 1765 and hung (by 1774) in the King's Apartments at Buckingham House (Russell 1987, p. 529). The synthesis that Van Dyck achieved in the portrait was described by the nineteenth-century artist Sir David Wilkie: 'the simplicity of inexperience shows them in most engaging contrast with the power of their rank and station, and like the infantas of Velasquez, unite all the demure stateliness of the court, with the perfect artlessness of childhood' (Millar 1972, p. 76).

George III's admiration for the early Stuarts and the aesthetic of Charles I's court was reflected in this purchase as well as in Zoffany's fashionable family portrait in Stuart costume (no. 7). The King hung many of his finest Van Dycks in Buckingham House and two of them can be clearly seen in Zoffany's portrait of the Prince of Wales and Prince Frederick, painted c.1765 (Millar 1969, no. 1200). However, eighteenth-century attitudes towards childhood, which was increasingly regarded as a distinct, innocent phase of life, are reflected in many of the portraits of George III's children (see nos. 12, 13). In fact, John Singleton Copley's painting of the *Three youngest daughters of George III* (Millar 1969, no. 712) was criticised for being over-ebullient and unbefitting of royalty (Neff 1995, pp. 155–8).

George III's taste for Van Dyck might have been sparked by that of his father, Frederick, Prince of Wales, who had a high regard for the collection of Charles I and had purchased Van Dyck's double portrait of Thomas Killigrew and William,

Lord Crofts, in 1748 (*Princes as Patrons* 1998, no. 29). Similarly, George IV's interest in the later Stuarts, and his attempts to reclaim items associated with the exiled dynasty, may equally have been inspired by his father. However, in 1770 the King decided not to purchase Van Dyck's portrait of Charles I *à la chasse* (Paris, Musée du Louvre) as he had 'at least for the present, given up collecting pictures' (Millar 1969, p. xv).

156. Annibale Carracci (1560–1609)

The Madonna and sleeping Child with the Infant St John the Baptist ('Il Silenzio'), 1599–1600

Oil on canvas. 51.2 × 68.4 cm (20³⁄₁₆″ × 26¹⁵⁄₁₆″)
RCIN 404762
PROVENANCE Farnese Collection (Palazzo del Giardino, Parma), by 1678; Duke of Parma, by 1708; acquired in Italy by Richard Dalton; from whom bought by George III, 27 May 1766 (£262; RA GEO/17153)
LITERATURE Levey 1991, no. 432

This small devotional painting dates from the period when Annibale Carracci was completing his greatest work, the vault of the gallery of the Palazzo Farnese, Rome, which merged Roman classicism with a renewed study of nature and initiated seventeenth-century baroque art. An understanding of the human form is here combined with ideas derived from the High Renaissance. The image of the infant Christ asleep, prefiguring his death, is found in Raphael's composition *The Madonna of the Veil* (Paris, Musée du Louvre). Annibale's painting may also have been dependent on one of Sebastiano del Piombo's versions of the subject from the 1530s (e.g. Naples, Galleria Nazionale di Capodimonte; Hirst 1981, pp. 137–9) which was in Cardinal Alessandro Farnese's collection at this time. Carracci probably derived the gesture of enjoining silence from Michelangelo, but in Michelangelo's presentation drawing it is St John rather than the Madonna who puts his finger to his lips (De Tolnay 1960, no. 196, pl. 158). Carracci makes the gesture the fulcrum of the composition. The Baptist is cautioned not to wake the Infant Jesus before his time. His future sacrifice is alluded to by the resemblance of the table to an altar or tomb, and by the shroud-like cloth on which

156

he sleeps. The gesture of St John touching Christ is similar to that of the putto touching a spine of the crown of thorns in Annibale's *Pietà* (Naples, Galleria Nazionale di Capodimonte), which dates from the same period.

Such a considered use of sources in a carefully balanced pyramid composition bestows considerable grandeur on this small painting. Each form is clearly delineated with the classical restraint typical of Carracci's style at this time. In the subdued atmosphere the figures emerge from deep shadows. The Christ Child has the weight of natural sleep but his pale flesh alludes to his future death. The painting was much copied, most notably by Domenichino (Paris, Musée du Louvre).

The acquisition of no. 156 was a major success for Richard Dalton, probably assisted by the engraver Francesco Bartolozzi, who produced a print of it in England in 1768. By *c.*1774 the painting was hanging prominently in the King's Closet in Buckingham House with other sixteenth- and seventeenth-century Italian paintings. The poses of the figures in Cotes's portrait of the Queen and the Princess Royal (no. 5) – completed in 1767 and hung in the next room, the King's Bed Chamber – were clearly influenced by Carracci's painting.

PAINTINGS COMMISSIONED BY OR PRESENTED TO THE KING AND QUEEN (nos. 157–165)

157. Richard Wright (1735–1775)

Queen Charlotte's passage to England, 1762

Oil on canvas. 89.8 × 128.6 cm (35⅜″ × 50⅝″)
Signed and dated *R: Wright Pinx*
RCIN 403525
PROVENANCE Presumably painted for Queen Charlotte
LITERATURE Millar 1969, no. 1194

This is almost certainly the first painting exhibited by the Liverpool-born marine artist Richard Wright at the Society of Artists in 1762, as *A View of the Storm when the Queen was on her passage to England, painted from a sketch drawn on board the Fubbes yacht.* The vessel carrying Princess Charlotte of Mecklenburg-Strelitz can be seen in the middle of the fleet with the Royal Standard flying at the main. Originally named the *Royal Caroline*, after George II's wife, the yacht was renamed the *Royal Charlotte* before it set forth to collect the Princess from the north German town of Stade on 28 August

157

158

1761. It was accompanied by a flotilla under the command of
Admiral Lord Anson, consisting of four other royal yachts
escorted by six ships-of-war.

The fleet weathered three severe storms before arriving
in England on 6 September, and it was reported that the
Princess, whose first sea journey it was, described the ocean
as an 'Element terrible'. The journey had been so rough that
it was decided that the yacht should land at Harwich rather
than travelling up the Thames to Greenwich as planned.
The Princess, who was 'much fatigued', spent the night near
Colchester and embarked upon the final stage of her journey to
London by coach the following morning. Increasing numbers
of eager crowds had gathered to witness the royal procession
which reached St James's Palace at a quarter past three. It was
reported that the Princess threw herself at the King's feet upon
meeting him, but that he raised her up, embraced her and led
her into the palace, where the royal couple were to be married
by the Archbishop of Canterbury that evening (see Hedley
1975, pp. 37–41). The painting was described by Pyne in the
Green Pavilion at Frogmore in 1819 (see no. 137).

158. Benjamin West (1738–1820)

The Departure of Regulus, 1769

Oil on canvas. 225.4 × 307.2 cm (7′ 4¾″ × 10′ 0¹⁵⁄₁₆″)
Originally signed and dated *Benj. West / pinxit / Londini 1769*
RCIN 405416
PROVENANCE Painted for George III
LITERATURE Millar 1969, no. 1152; Von Erffa and Staley 1986,
no. 10 and pp. 46–55

George III's commission to the American artist Benjamin
West for a series of six neo-classical paintings, for the Warm
Room in his apartments at Buckingham House, was placed
in February 1768 when West showed the King his picture
of *Agrippina with the ashes of Germanicus* which he had just
completed for Robert Hay Drummond, Archbishop of York.
The King commented upon the rarity of the subject and
proposed 'another noble Roman subject . . . I mean the final
departure of Regulus from Rome'; he then commenced to
read Livy's account of the story to the artist. Regulus,
the Roman consul and general, was taken prisoner by the
Carthaginians in 255 BC. He was sent back to Rome to discuss

peace terms and an exchange of prisoners. However, Regulus distrusted the peace negotiations and insisted on returning to certain torture and death in Carthage. West's painting is set within a neo-classical composition that reflects – amongst other things – the Raphael Cartoons in the King's collection, which West greatly admired. From 1763 to 1787 the Cartoons hung in the Saloon at Buckingham House (no. 111) where West – and other artists – could have seen them.

West's arrival in England from Italy in 1763 occurred at a time when artists were seeking to create a distinguished national school of history painting. George III was eager to support such a goal and Benjamin West was able to fulfil such aspirations remarkably well. The King was also a keen supporter of the proposal to found a national academy for the teaching and display of arts. His patronage of West and the foundation of the Royal Academy in 1768 were closely inter-twined. At the King's instruction, *The Departure of Regulus* was shown at the first Royal Academy exhibition in 1769, and of the 136 works included, it most completely represented the high-minded art that the Academy had been founded to encourage. However, only West was really able to produce a great body of history painting as only he enjoyed sustained royal patronage, while other distinguished artists continued to fulfil the demand for portraiture. He succeeded Sir Joshua Reynolds as President of the Royal Academy in 1792.

West painted around sixty pictures for George III between 1768 and 1801. From 1772 he was described in Royal Academy catalogues as 'Historical Painter to the King' and from 1780 he received an annual stipend from the King of £100. In the 1780s he gave drawing lessons to the Princesses (see nos. 61, 62) and in 1791 he succeeded Richard Dalton as Surveyor of the King's Pictures. During these years West effectively monopolised all royal patronage except for portraiture, although he did paint many royal portraits as well. His main subject-matter was history painting – a category which included classical and medieval as well as recent historical events, such as his famous image of the death of General Wolfe at Quebec in 1759 (Millar 1969, no. 1167; see also nos. 128, 135).

159. Johan Zoffany (1733–1810)

The Royal Academicians, 1771–2

Oil on canvas. 101.1 × 147.5 cm (3′ 3 ¹³/₁₆″ × 4′ 10¹/₁₆″)
RCIN 400747
PROVENANCE Presumably commissioned by George III
LITERATURE Millar 1969, no. 1210; Webster 1976, no. 74

In December 1768 George III had approved the Instrument of Foundation of the Royal Academy, the principal aims of which were to teach students 'the Arts of Design' and to mount annual exhibitions. The forty Academicians were to be distinguished painters, sculptors or architects. Initially the Royal Academy had no permanent home, but in 1771 the King made available rooms in Somerset House, originally a royal dower house (see p. 116). In the same year he probably commissioned Zoffany, whom he had personally nominated a member in 1769, to record the Academicians. The resulting painting is thus set in a room in the house originally built for the Duke of Somerset *c.*1550, but added to (by Inigo Jones and others) in the seventeenth century. In 1774 it was reported that parts of the building were in a state of collapse. The following year Buckingham House assumed the role of the Queen's official dower house and in 1776–96 the present Somerset House was built to the designs of Sir William Chambers, on the site of the old building.

Zoffany here refers to two of the Academy's teaching methods: drawing plaster casts of famous statues, and drawing living models. Both were studied by lamplight to accentuate the shadows and relief of forms. The Royal Academicians (RAs) – here shown in place of the students – are gathered to watch the Keeper of the Academy, George Moser, arrange a male nude. Francesco Zuccarelli, one hand on his knee, checks the positioning, as does Richard Yeo, the medallist, who stands directly under the lamplight. To left of centre, hand on chin, is Dr William Hunter, Professor of Anatomy at the Academy and obstetrician to the Queen. Listening to the President, Sir Joshua Reynolds, who holds an ear trumpet, is Sir William Chambers, the Treasurer, and next to him is Francis Milner Newton, the Secretary. Seated far left is Zoffany himself, with his palette and brushes. Behind him leans Benjamin West, who was to succeed Reynolds as President in 1792, and Tan-che-qua, a Chinese modeller, who was a visitor to the Schools of the Royal Academy in 1771. To the right of him are the miniaturist Jeremiah Meyer, Dominic Serres, and – in conversation with each other – Paul and Thomas Sandby. Three Royal

159

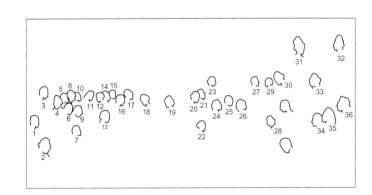

1 John Gwynn (1713–86), architect; RA 1768

2 Johan Zoffany (1733–1810), painter; RA 1769

3 Giovanni Battista Cipriani (1727–85), painter; RA 1768

4 Benjamin West (1738–1820), painter; RA 1768, President 1792–1820

5 Tan-che-qua, a Chinese artist who came to England in 1769

6 George Barret (1728/32–84), painter; RA 1768

7 Mason Chamberlin (1727–87), painter; RA 1768

8 Jeremiah Meyer (1735–89), miniaturist; RA 1768

9 Joseph Wilton (1722–1803), sculptor; RA 1768, Keeper 1790

10 Dominic Serres (1719–93), painter; RA 1768, Librarian 1792

11 Paul Sandby (1730–1809), watercolour painter; RA 1768

12 Thomas Sandby (1721/3–98), draughtsman and architect; RA 1768, Professor of Architecture

13 Francis Hayman (1708–76), painter; RA 1768, Librarian 1770

14 William Tyler (d. 1801), sculptor and architect; RA 1768

15 John Inigo Richards (fl .1753–1810), painter; RA 1768, Secretary 1788

16 Francis Milner Newton (1720–94), painter; RA 1768, Secretary

17 Sir William Chambers (1723–96), architect; RA 1768, Treasurer

18 Sir Joshua Reynolds (1723–92), painter; PRA 1768–92

19 William Hunter (1718–83); RA Professor of Anatomy, 1768

20 Francesco Bartolozzi (1727–1815), engraver; RA 1768

21 Agostino Carlini (d. 1790), sculptor and painter; RA 1768, Keeper 1783

22 Charles Catton (c.1729–98), painter; RA 1768

23 Richard Wilson (1713/14–82), painter; RA 1768, Librarian 1776

24 Richard Yeo (c.1720–79), medallist; RA 1768

25 Samuel Wale (1721–86), painter; RA Professor of Perspective 1768, and Librarian 1782

26 Francesco Zuccarelli (1702–88), painter; RA 1768

27 Edward Penny (1714–91), painter; RA 1768, Professor of Painting

28 Edward Burch (1730–1814), miniaturist; RA 1771, Librarian 1794

29 Peter Toms (c.1728–77), painter; RA 1768

30 George Michael Moser (1706–83), enamellist; RA 1768, Keeper

31 Angelica Kauffmann (1741–1807), painter; RA 1768

32 Mrs Mary Moser (1744–1819), painter; RA 1768

33 Nathaniel Hone (1718–84), painter; RA 1768

34 Joseph Nollekens (1737–1823), sculptor; RA 1772

35 Richard Cosway (1742–1821), painter; RA 1771

36 William Hoare (1706–99), painter; RA 1768

Academicians were not included in the painting: Thomas Gainsborough and George and Nathaniel Dance. Nude models precluded the physical presence of the two female Academicians, Mary Moser and Angelica Kauffmann, who are represented by painted portraits on the wall on the right, behind one of the most recently elected Academicians, the fashion-conscious Richard Cosway, cane in hand.

When the painting was exhibited in 1772, it drew 'the densest crowd about it' and Walpole praised its strong likenesses. Its success may have encouraged the King and Queen to commission *The Tribuna* (no. 161) from the artist in the same year.

160. Johan Zoffany (1733–1810)
John Cuff and his assistant, 1772

Oil on canvas. 89.8 × 70.0 cm (35⅜″ × 27⁹⁄₁₆″)
Signed and dated *Zoffanÿ pinx / 1772*
RCIN 404434
PROVENANCE Presumably commissioned by George III
LITERATURE Millar 1969, no. 1209

160

John Cuff (1708–72), Master of the Spectacle Makers Company 1748–9, designed a microscope with a single vertical pillar in 1743, a design which continued to be made well into the nineteenth century and examples of which he sold to the King and Queen. From the size of the lens he is polishing, and the contents of the workshop shown here, Cuff seems to be producing lenses and mirrors for telescopes rather than microscopes. He is known to have sold a wide variety of scientific instruments including barometers, telescopes, hygrometers, circumferentors and thermometers as well as microscopes, 'at the sign of the Reflecting Microscope, against Serjeants' Inn Gate in Fleet Street' 1737–57, and at another location in Fleet Street the following year. A note in the inventory of pictures at Kew *c.*1800–1805 (when the painting hung in Princess Augusta's bedroom), and the painting's entry in the British Institution exhibition catalogue in 1814, identify the sitter as John Cuff. Although the identification has been disputed, payments were made to Cuff on behalf of the King in 1770 and 1771, just before the date of this portrait. The idea of showing the sitter surrounded not by his inventions, but informally, in working clothes at his bench, is unusual for this date and suggests that it may have been commissioned by George III.

Horace Walpole criticised the painting: 'Extremely natural, but the characters too common nature and the chiaroscuro destroyed by his servility in imitating the reflexions of the glasses.' It is precisely the meticulous recording of the scene, as in a Netherlandish painting, and the vivid portraits of working men, which make the painting so extraordinary. As in his conversation pieces, in which Zoffany gathered together and recorded sitters' treasured possessions, here Zoffany has carefully constructed this setting to give the illusion of reality, extending the canvas at the lower edge to give more space around the sitters. Light from the window focuses attention on the figures, as if they were on a stage in one of the theatrical pictures produced by Zoffany for David Garrick in the 1760s. The artificial structure is combined with apparent objectivity in the high finish and precise painting of each detail. With the immediacy of theatre Zoffany makes Cuff, in contrast to his serious assistant, pause in his work to glance up with a slight smile, his spectacles – the mark of his profession – balanced precariously on his forehead.

161

161. Johan Zoffany (1733–1810)

*The Tribuna of the Uffizi, c.*1772–8

Oil on canvas. 123.5 × 155.0 cm (4′ 0⅝″ × 5′ 1″)
RCIN 406983
PROVENANCE Commissioned by Queen Charlotte
LITERATURE Millar 1967; Millar 1969, no. 1211; Paulson 1975,
pp. 138–48; Webster 1976, no. 76; Moore 1985, no. 109; *Royal
Treasures* 2002, no. 24

In the summer of 1772 Zoffany left London for Florence
with a commission from the Queen to paint 'the Florence
Gallery'. He was still working on *The Tribuna* late in 1777
and did not return to England until 1779.

The Tribuna, an octagonal room in the Uffizi designed
by Bernardo Buontalenti for Francesco de' Medici in the
late 1580s, housed the most important antiquities and High
Renaissance and Bolognese paintings in the grand-ducal
collection. In 1737 the collection was ceded to the Tuscan

government by the Grand Duchess Anna Maria Luisa. The
Uffizi, and in particular the Tribuna, became the focal point
for visitors to Florence. By the 1770s it was arguably the
most famous room in the world. Zoffany has portrayed the
north-east section but has varied the arrangement and introduced other works from the grand-ducal collection to create
his own Tribuna. Assisted by George, 3rd Earl Cowper
(1738–80), and by Sir Horace Mann (1706–86), the artist
was granted special privileges: for example, seven paintings,
including Raphael's *Madonna della Sedia*, were temporarily
transferred from the Pitti for Zoffany to paint.

Admiring the works of art are connoisseurs, diplomats
and visitors to Florence, all identifiable, so that the predomi-
nantly Flemish seventeenth-century tradition of gallery
views is combined with the British eighteenth-century
conversation piece or informal group portrait. One of several
changes made by the artist was to show Lord Cowper

162

admiring his own Raphael, the *Niccolini-Cowper Madonna* (Washington, National Gallery of Art). This is held by Zoffany himself: Lord Cowper hoped to sell it to George III. The King had recently bought Guercino's *Libyan Sibyl* (no. 154). The unframed *Samian Sibyl* on the floor, a workshop copy of its pendant acquired for the grand-ducal collection in 1777, may have been intended as a reference to this purchase and as a compliment to the King.

The King and Queen – neither of whom visited Italy – were critical of the inclusion of so many recognisable portraits, described by Horace Walpole as 'a flock of travelling boys, and one does not know nor care whom'. Even so, *The Tribuna* is an outstanding example of Zoffany's technique and the consummate portrayal of the Grand Tour and eighteenth-century taste.

162. Dominic Serres (1719–1793)

The royal visit to the fleet, 1774

Oil on canvas. 154.3 × 245.6 cm (5′ 0¾″ × 8′ 0¹¹⁄₁₆″)
Signed and dated *[D] Serres / 1774* [on buoy]
RCIN 404558
PROVENANCE Presumably painted for George III
LITERATURE Millar 1969, no. 1072–5; Russett 2001, pp. 97–102

This is the first of four paintings by Serres recording George III's visit to inspect the British fleet, from 22 to 26 June 1773. Like the King's visits to army encampments at the same period (see no. 163), fleet reviews provided opportunities for the display and inspection of the armed forces. The picture records the moment when the King arrived by barge from Portsmouth to meet the fleet at Spithead, and came on board the *Barfleur*, a ship of 90 guns, which can be seen in the centre of the composition. The flags of the Lord High Admiral, the Royal Standard and the Union flag were hoisted on the *Barfleur* when the King boarded, on the sight of which the surrounding warships, their yards manned by sailors, fired a 21-gun salute. The ships' names are legible on their sterns and the accuracy of Serres's record is apparent when the painting is compared to his drawings made over the four days (RL 27977–9, 27988).

The description of the visit in the *Annual Register* includes mention of 'a very great number of yachts, and other sailing vessels and boats, many of them full of nobility and gentry', in attendance. Presumably Serres was on one of these small craft, which are included in his painting. A high viewpoint was the convention in marine painting at this date, and it was not until the later work of Romantic artists, such as

163

de Loutherbourg (see no. 163) and Turner, that the viewpoint was lowered. The *Annual Register* reported that at the time of the visit the King expressed 'the highest approbation of the good order and discipline of his fleet, the excellent condition of the dock-yard, arsenals, and garrison, . . . and showed the utmost satisfaction at the demonstrations of loyalty and affection with which he was received by all ranks of people'.

Dominic Serres, a native of Gascony, arrived in England in around 1745. His good manners and naval experience may account for his successful artistic career, as his training was minimal. He was a founder-member of the Royal Academy (see no. 159). His son John Thomas Serres (1759–1825) succeeded him as Marine Painter to George III. Details of the commission for the four paintings of the 1773 review are not recorded.

163. Philippe Jacques de Loutherbourg
(1740–1812)

Warley Camp, 1778: The Mock Attack, 1779

Oil on canvas. 122.9 × 184.0 cm (4' 0⅜" × 6' 0⁷⁄₁₆")
Signed and dated *P.J. De Loutherbourg 1779*
RCIN 406348

PROVENANCE Commissioned by Lieutenant-General Pierson; by whom presented to George III, 1779/80
LITERATURE Millar 1969, no. 932; Joopien 1973, no. 59

George III's visit to the military camp at Warley near Brentwood in Essex took place on 20 October 1778; the King and Queen stayed for the nights of 19 and 20 October at Thorndon Hall, the seat of the Catholic peer Lord Petre. The day began with a review of the troops, the subject of de Loutherbourg's pendant painting (Millar 1969, no. 933). The Light Infantry and Grenadiers then 'marched with the artillery through the woods towards Little Warley (followed by the whole line in two columns), where, as well as in the adjacent woods, several batteries were placed, and many manoeuvres of attack and defence were performed, with the continued firing of musquetry and cannon, to which the situation and variety of the ground were very favourable and afforded much pleasure to the numerous spectators'. The manoeuvres are shown on Daniel Paterson's plan of Warley Camp (no. 211). The King and Queen 'beheld the whole from a stand erected by Lord Petre in the centre of the scene', seen here (amidst smoke) in the centre middle distance. After the mock attack, which took place on the slopes of Childerditch and Little Warley Commons, the King was introduced to several officers who had taken part. He expressed his 'great satisfaction at the appearance, discipline, and good order of the several regiments, and the royal artillery; and likewise his approbation of the manoeuvres which were performed' (*Annual Chronicle*, 1778, Appendix, p. 237).

The attack was led by Lieutenant-General Pierson, who commissioned this painting and its pendant from de Loutherbourg and presented them – presumably in their magnificent frames – to the King. Both pictures were exhibited at the Royal Academy in 1779. De Loutherbourg's obvious care in recording the scene is very much in contrast with the broad treatment of the landscape in the large canvas of *Banditti in a Landscape* (Millar 1969, no. 934) which he painted for the Prince of Wales in 1804. The artist's career was both illustrious and prolific, ranging from stage design for the theatrical impresario David Garrick to landscapes and history paintings, and achieving the title of 'Historical Painter to HRH the Duke of Gloucester' in 1807. By that date the Warley Camp paintings were hanging in the Music Room in the Dutch House at Kew (Kew House Inventory).

164

164. Thomas Gainsborough (1727–1788)
Richard Hurd, Bishop of Worcester, 1781

Oil on canvas. 76.0 × 63.0 cm (29^{15}⁄$_{16}$″ × 24^{13}⁄$_{16}$″)
RCIN 400750
PROVENANCE Probably painted for Queen Charlotte
LITERATURE Millar 1969, no. 801; Lloyd (C.) 1994, no. 19

This portrait was probably commissioned by Queen Charlotte. It was praised as 'finely executed' when it was exhibited at the Royal Academy in 1781, at the same time as Gainsborough's full-length portraits of the King and Queen (including no. 11). Richard Hurd (1720–1808) was a scholar, a critic praised by Gibbon, and an author whose publications included many sermons, pamphlets and editions of Horace's work. His *Letters on Chivalry and Romance* (1762) stand at the start of the Romantic movement in England. Hurd was made Archdeacon of Gloucester in 1767 and Bishop of Lichfield and Coventry in 1774. He was a favourite with the royal family and an ally of the King on the episcopal bench. In 1776 he was appointed Preceptor, responsible for the education of the King's two eldest sons (the Prince of Wales and Duke of York). Following his appointment as Bishop of Worcester and Clerk of the Closet in 1781, the royal family visited him at

Hartlebury Castle and at the Bishop's Palace, Worcester, in August 1788. Hurd turned down the King's offer of the Archbishopric of Canterbury in 1790 as 'a charge not suited to his temper and talents'. In the event of a French invasion after war broke out again in 1803, it was to the Bishop's Palace that the King planned to send his family.

In the 1780s Hurd assisted in drawing up the programme for Benjamin West's series of paintings illustrating the history of revealed religion for the King's new private chapel at Windsor, a project never realised. According to Horace Walpole, Hurd was 'a gentle, plausible man affecting a singular decorum that endeared him highly to devout old ladies'. In Gainsborough's portrait the ground is left visible in the surround and in the loosely painted white rochet but the confident gaze is from a well-defined face.

Inventories confuse this portrait with a very similar one, also by Gainsborough and of the same dimensions (Millar 1969, no. 802), but it is likely that this is the one mentioned by Fanny Burney in 1786: 'He is, and justly, most high in [the Queen's] favour. In town she has his picture in her bedroom, and its companion is Mrs Delany [no. 165]. How worthily paired! What honour to herself, such honour to them! There is no other portrait there but of royal houses' (*Burney Diary*, III, p. 138).

165. John Opie (1761–1807)

Mary Granville, Mrs Delany, 1782

Oil on canvas. 76.4 × 63.9 cm (30¹⁄₁₆″ × 25³⁄₁₆″)
RCIN 400965
PROVENANCE Commissioned by George III and Queen Charlotte
LITERATURE Millar 1969, no. 975; Hayden 1992, p. 170

Mrs Delany (1700–1788) is best described in the words (written by Dr Hurd) of her memorial plaque, in St James's, Piccadilly: 'She was a lady of singular ingenuity and politeness and an unaffected piety. These qualities endeared her through life to many noble and excellent persons and made the close of it illustrious by procuring for her many signal marks of grace and favour from their Majesties.' Mary Delany, *née* Granville, was first married at the age of 16 to Alexander Pendarves, a wealthy land-owner more than forty years her senior, and then, more happily, to Patrick Delany, Dean of Down. She was widowed for the second time at the age of 68 and went to live for six months of each year with her friend the dowager Duchess of Portland at Bulstrode Park, Buckinghamshire. The two women shared a great passion for botany, the Duchess patronising artists such as the famous illustrator Ehret (no. 192). It was at Bulstrode that Mrs Delany, in her seventy-third year, began to make her famous cut-paper flowers (no. 194). In his *Anecdotes*, Horace Walpole commented that Mrs Delany was 'a lady of excellent sense and taste, who painted in oil, and who invented the art of paper mosaic'.

Mrs Delany first met the King and Queen in 1776 at Bulstrode, which is 30 minutes' carriage drive to the north of Windsor. The royal visits to Bulstrode were followed by return visits (from the Duchess and Mrs Delany) to Windsor. Mrs Delany became much loved by the King, Queen and princesses. For the pocket-book given by Queen Charlotte to Mrs Delany in December 1781, see no. 59. After the Duchess of Portland's death in July 1785, Mrs Delany's small personal income proved insufficient. The King therefore arranged for her to receive an annuity of £300 and a house in St Albans Street, Windsor, into which she moved on 30 September 1785, and where she lived for the rest of her life. It was in

165

this house that the King and Queen first met the novelist Fanny Burney, who served the Queen as Second Keeper of the Robes for five years from July 1786 to July 1791.

This portrait by the Cornish artist John Opie was commissioned by George III and was described in February 1782 in a letter from Horace Walpole to Horace Mann: 'it is pronounced like Rembrandt, but as I told her, it does not look older than she is, but older than she does'. The portrait was soon placed in the Queen's Bedchamber at Buckingham House. Mrs Delany wears a locket with the letters *CR* – a reference to Queen Charlotte, who had almost certainly given the locket to her as a token of her friendship.

6. Drawings, watercolours and gouaches (nos. 166–194)

THE EARLIEST FULL INVENTORY of the Royal Collection of drawings is the so-called Inventory A, compiled (mainly from earlier lists) in the second decade of the nineteenth century, towards the end of George III's life. The collection of Old Master drawings has grown little since that date. Inventory A describes, in varying degrees of detail, the contents of the many albums of drawings that were then kept in the library of Buckingham House, a number of which survive almost intact to this day. Many of these survivals – notably those from the collections of Cassiano dal Pozzo, Consul Joseph Smith and Carlo Fontana – preserve the bindings in which George III acquired them. But those volumes were the exception within the King's library, for the drawings had usually been remounted with characteristic wash borders, rearranged by artist and school, and placed within new albums (see no. 170), presumably by the King's bindery after its creation around 1770. Most of the albums bound for George III were broken up in the late nineteenth and early twentieth centuries, though many of the drawings from those albums retain their eighteenth-century mount sheets.

The process of assembling these albums for George III often destroyed all physical trace of earlier ownership, and consequently the provenance of many of the Old Master drawings now in the Royal Collection has been lost. However, it is known that on his accession in 1760 George III had inherited the splendid collection of drawings by Leonardo da Vinci and Holbein, and current research suggests that many of the other fifteenth- and sixteenth-century Italian drawings were also already in the Collection at this time.

George III's earliest purchases were made before he acceded to the throne. Ninety-five coloured drawings and etchings by Maria Sibylla Merian (nos. 166, 167) were acquired at auction in 1755, when the Prince was aged 16. In the same year Richard Dalton was engaged as the Prince's Librarian, under the eye of Lord Bute, who seems to have been almost entirely responsible for the formation of the Prince's taste in Old Master drawings. In May 1758 Dalton set out for Italy to buy works of art for the Prince; he stayed there for just over a year. His first consignment was dispatched from Livorno in late February 1759: 'a fine collection of Drawings are sent to Leghorn carefully packt for HRH to the Number of near 700, one Rafaele amongst them, about 40 fine ones of Guercino and several of the Carracci & other eminent Masters'. Dalton was again in Italy in 1762–3, 1768–9 and 1774–5 (Ingamells 1997, pp. 267–70). Although few of the drawings acquired for the King on these trips can be identified, the 1762–3 visit presumably saw Dalton acquire much of the remainder of the 836 drawings from Guercino's studio now at Windsor (nos. 186, 187).

Dalton was, however, not the only agent acting for the King in Italy, and he was not responsible for the two most spectacular acquisitions of George III's reign. Bute's brother, James Stuart Mackenzie, conducted the negotiations for the purchase of Consul Joseph Smith's collection in 1762, described below. And it was James Adam, brother of the King's Architect Robert Adam, who with great tact secured the collection of Cardinal Alessandro Albani in the same year. Though the Albani collection did not include, as Smith's did, paintings, gems or a library, the drawings were perhaps even more spectacular and certainly more numerous (see p. 208 below). But there are no detailed inventories of either the Smith or the Albani collection and there is no firm evidence for the provenance of several important groups of drawings. Were it not for a single line in a list of disbursements by Dalton, for example, it would probably be assumed that the drawings by Sassoferrato (no. 188) had come with the Albani collection.

The years around 1760 also saw the purchase of individual drawings or groups of drawings at auction. Around sixty Dutch and Flemish drawings still in the Royal Collection (including nos. 189, 190) were acquired following the sale of the collection of Abraham van Broyel in Amsterdam in 1759. In the same year a part of the renowned collection of the painter Benedetto Luti, reputed to contain around 15,000 sheets, was acquired from his heirs in Rome by the dealer William Kent, who brought them to London where he sold them at two auctions in December 1760 and December 1762. A sketchbook compiled by Luti's pupil Bartolomeo Altomonte contains a number of free copies of drawings in Luti's collection, and the originals of many of these copies can be identified today at Windsor (see Heinzl 1966). Many more drawings may have been purchased at auction in these years, for it is only by chance – the exceptional detail of the descriptions in the Van Broyel sale catalogue, or the existence of Altomonte's sketchbook – that it is possible to identify drawings from those two sources.

Bute's resignation in 1763 and his subsequent withdrawal from a position of influence over the King brought an end to the heroic period of George III's acquisition of Old Master drawings. Dalton continued to glean works of art when he could, but the King's developing tastes led him to pursue works closer to his personal interests, such as the 263 watercolours for Mark Catesby's *Natural History of Carolina, Florida and the Bahama Islands*, acquired in 1768 (see nos. 191, 192), and the formation of the Military, Maritime and Topographical Collections (see no. 193).

The drawings and watercolours are here discussed and ordered by approximate date of royal purchase.

166. Maria Sibylla Merian (1647–1717)

*Pineapple with cockroaches, c.*1700–1702

Watercolour and bodycolour over etched outlines, on vellum.
48.4 × 34.7 cm (19¹⁄₁₆″ × 13¹¹⁄₁₆″)
RL 21156
PROVENANCE Dr Richard Mead; his sale, Langford's, London,
28 January 1755, lot 66; bought by the Prince of Wales (later
George III; £158 11s)
LITERATURE Rücker and Stearn 1982, p. 87

167. Maria Sibylla Merian (1647–1717)

*Passion flower with insects, c.*1700–1702

Watercolour and bodycolour on vellum.
37.8 × 28.8 cm (14⁷⁄₈″ × 11⁵⁄₁₆″)
RL 21175
PROVENANCE As for no. 166
LITERATURE Rücker and Stearn 1982, p. 104

Maria Sibylla Merian was one of the most extraordinary artist-naturalists of her time. Her father was the painter Matthäus Merian, and after he died her mother married the flower still-life painter Jacob Marell. With Marell as a teacher, Merian began to specialise in depicting flowers, fruit, and also insects, spiders, butterflies and moths. In 1675 she published a set of her own engravings of flower motifs, which was followed in 1677 and 1680 by two further series. Her first scientific work, *Der Raupen wunderbare Verwandelung und sonderbare Blumennahrung* (The Wondrous Transformation of Caterpillars and their Remarkable Diet of Flowers), was published in 1679. In 1699, after seeing insects which had been brought to Holland from the Dutch colony of Surinam in South America, Merian made a pioneering expedition there in order to study and record the indigenous butterflies and moths. She returned to Amsterdam in 1701, where she worked on the plates and text to the *Metamorphosis Insectorum Surinamensium*, published in 1705.

166

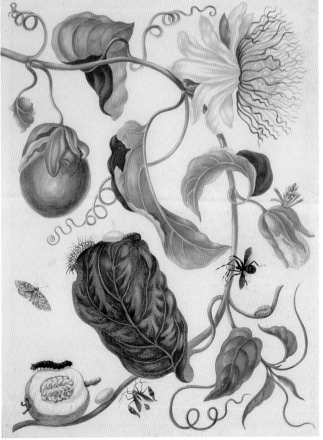

167

Of the ninety-five watercolours by Merian at Windsor, sixty correspond with the plates in the *Metamorphosis*. These are painted over etched outlines on vellum and must have been intended as a 'deluxe' edition before the plates were fully etched. Properly prepared, vellum has a far smoother surface than paper; this allows very precise marks to be made with the tip of a fine brush. The way in which Merian builds up the colour gives a startlingly three-dimensional – at times virtually *trompe-l'oeil* – quality to her drawings. The watercolours were acquired in two volumes (which survive at Windsor) at the sale of the collection of Dr Richard Mead (1673–1754). These were among the future George III's earliest acquisitions.

Alongside each print in the *Metamorphosis* are Merian's detailed observations, which often describe the interdependence of the insects and plants or fruits in her pictures. She remarks on the 'delicacy and beauty' of the pineapple, and notes that cockroaches 'are the most infamous of all insects in America on account of the great damage they cause to all the inhabitants by spoiling their wool, linen, food and drinks; sweet things are their usual nourishment, for which reason they are extremely partial to fruit'. The text also records how the caterpillars which are depicted with the passion flower metamorphosed as Merian was making her drawing.

DRAWINGS FROM THE COLLECTION OF CONSUL JOSEPH SMITH (nos. 168–180)

The best documented of all George III's purchases of Old Master drawings was that of the collection of Consul Joseph Smith. After an abortive attempt by the Consul to sell his library to the then Prince of Wales for £10,000 in the late 1750s, the sale of Smith's entire collection to the King, for £20,000, was agreed in spring 1762. Dalton signed a copy of Smith's library catalogue (the *Bibliotheca Smithiana*, 1755) as his receipt for the books contained therein – including his albums of prints and drawings – in Venice on 28 January 1763. Six albums of drawings from Smith's collection survive virtually intact in the Royal Library. Two contain drawings and prints by Antonio Visentini; a further two contain drawings by Sebastiano Ricci (see nos. 172, 173) and Giovanni Ambrogio Figino respectively; one consists of a set of outline copies of the reliefs on Trajan's Column, by an artist believed by Smith to be Giulio Campi (though the style does not support this attribution); and the sixth consists of caricatures, mostly by Marco Ricci and Anton Maria Zanetti, but also including a few by earlier draughtsmen. A further three albums of architectural drawings by Visentini were transferred to the British Museum with the King's Library in 1823.

The majority of Smith's albums of drawings were, however, broken up after their entry into the Royal Collection. These included works by Smith's contemporaries Canaletto (nos. 178, 179) and Marco Ricci (no. 176), and the albums of Old Master drawings that Smith had bought from the Sagredo family in the early 1750s, among which were four volumes of drawings by Giovanni Benedetto Castiglione (no. 171) and 'three large Volumes, formerly collected in the time of the Carracci, by the family of Bonfiglioli of Bologna', specified in Smith's 1761 will (see Vivian 1989, p. 24). The volumes of Old Master drawings had been bought by Zaccaria Sagredo (1653–1729) from the Bonfiglioli family in 1728, along with a number of framed drawings. While the contents of the 'three large Volumes' remain largely unidentified, we know from Inventory A that they included three studies of the *Madonna and Child* by Raphael. Several other drawings (including nos. 168, 169) can be identified either from an inventory of the Bonfiglioli collection in 1696, or from Jonathan Richardson's description of his visit to the Bonfiglioli palace in 1719. It is now clear that Sagredo's collection – and subsequently Smith's – also included a number of drawings by Netherlandish artists such as Crispin van de Passe (see no. 170 and Rutgers 2002).

168. Raphael (1483–1520)

*Christ's Charge to Peter, c.*1514

Red chalk (offset). 25.7 × 37.5 cm (10⅛″ × 14¾″)
RL 12751
PROVENANCE Bonfiglioli family, by 1696; from whom bought by
Zaccaria Sagredo, 1728; from whose heirs bought by Joseph Smith,
1752; from whom bought by George III, 1762
LITERATURE Popham and Wilde 1984, no. 802; Vivian 1989, no. 47

Shortly after Giovanni de' Medici was elected as Pope Leo X
in 1513, he commissioned Raphael to produce a series of
large cartoons of the *Acts of the Apostles*, to be transported
to Brussels and woven as tapestries for the Sistine Chapel.
Seven of the cartoons survive, now in the Victoria and Albert
Museum on loan from Her Majesty The Queen. The present
sheet is an offset from a preparatory drawing for the cartoon
of *Christ's Charge to Peter*. It was made by laying a blank,
slightly dampened sheet of paper (which became no. 168) over

a chalk drawing, and pressing or rubbing the two to produce a
reversed impression. Offsets could be used during the preparatory process to monitor the final effect of a composition when
the end product also reversed the design, as with mosaics,
prints and tapestries, which are woven from the back.

This is one of nine autograph drawings by Raphael that
can be shown to have been acquired by George III. It was seen
hanging in the Palazzo Bonfiglioli by Jonathan Richardson
when he visited Bologna in 1719, though – unlike many
drawings framed for display – the sheet has suffered little
from the effects of light, damp or insects. After entering
the Royal Collection, however, the drawing was dismissed as
a derivation after the master and separated from the other
works by Raphael: 'The Heads are noble Ideas, but the Christ
and St Peter are very disagreeable, being half Studys only
of the naked Body. The thought stolen from Raphael's design
in the Cartoon' (Inventory A, p. 48).

168

169. Guido Reni (1575–1642)

A falling giant, c.1638

Red chalk. 28.2 × 23.1 cm (11⅛″ × 9⅛″)
RL 3461
PROVENANCE As for no. 168
LITERATURE Kurz 1988, no. 364; Vivian 1989, no. 51

The drawing is probably to be identified with that listed in the 1696 Bonfiglioli inventory as 'a drawing of a giant by Guido, in a frame and gilt case with glass'; according to Inventory A, eighteen drawings of Madonnas by Reni and his studio also came to the Royal Collection from the Bonfiglioli, though this may not be accurate. The present study corresponds closely, but not exactly, with the central figure in a large chiaroscuro woodcut of the *Fall of the Giants*, executed by Bartolomeo Coriolano to the design of Guido Reni; sketched to the lower right of the sheet are the head and arm of a second giant for the print. The figure in the drawing is about 8 per cent larger than that in the print, and even when it is scaled down the contours do not match, demonstrating that the route from drawing to print was freehand rather than mechanical. Coriolano had produced his first woodcut after Reni in 1627, and towards the end of his life Reni provided Coriolano with several designs for chiaroscuros. Reni was plagued by gambling debts, and this collaboration must have been seen by the master as an easy way to earn some money. This woodcut was first published in 1638; three years later Coriolano produced a second version, with small variations. Why he should have gone to the trouble of cutting a second set of blocks is unknown, and it can only be assumed that he had somehow been deprived of the first set.

170. Crispin van de Passe the Elder (1564–1637)

Ovid's Metamorphoses, I, *c*.1600

41 ff. Bound in brown calf with gold tooling and George III's large crown finishing tool (no. 195) in the centre.
27.1 × 35.3 cm (10¹¹⁄₁₆″ × 13⅞″)
RCIN 970323
PROVENANCE Possibly Zaccaria Sagredo (d. 1729); from whose heirs bought by Joseph Smith, 1752; from whom bought by George III, 1762
LITERATURE White and Crawley 1994, p. 46

The two volumes of Van de Passe's studies for the *Metamorphoses* formed part of George III's collection of prints and drawings, which was kept in the library rooms at Buckingham House. The early history of the drawings is not known, but the inclusion of 141 drawings by Crispin van de Passe in volume 7 of Sagredo's drawing collection is intriguing (see Rutgers 2002, p. 321, n. 42). The *Metamorphoses* drawings were probably remounted after their arrival in the King's collection. The stiff card to which they are now applied, and the calf binding, are similar to that found on a number of volumes made up for George III. The gold tooled border on the front and back boards, including a roll consisting of repeating floral, celestial and stylised motifs, is similar to the style of tool used on the Burnet binding (no. 206). The large crown (no. 195) indicates George III's ownership and was a finishing tool much used for larger volumes in the King's collection. (See illustration on p. 224.)

Crispin van de Passe began his artistic career in Antwerp in the early 1580s, and was primarily an engraver and print publisher. His prints, engraved from his own or from others' designs, covered a wide range of subjects: portraits, historical, allegorical and mythical scenes, book illustrations and so forth. The small drawings in the present volume were executed – in pen and ink with touches of wash – as preparatory studies

169

FIG. 25 Crispin van de Passe, *Actaeon transformed into a stag, c.1600.* Pen and brown ink with grey wash (RL 14921)

for a publication issued in book form in Cologne in 1602, consisting of prints of scenes from Ovid's *Metamorphoses.*

Ovid, a leading figure in the social and literary world at the court of the Emperor Augustus (63 BC – AD 14), wrote the *Metamorphoses* – a collection of mythological tales of transformation – from about AD 2 onwards; the stories were extremely popular with later writers in the Middle Ages and Renaissance. This series of colourful and dramatic stories

made excellent subjects for the artist, and Van de Passe's published series of prints derived from these drawings went into a second edition in 1607, with an increased number of plates.

171. Giovanni Benedetto Castiglione (1609–1664)

Christ on the cross with lamenting figures, c.1660

Oil paint on paper. 26.2 × 39.0 cm (10⁵⁄₁₆″ × 15³⁄₈″)
RL 3894
PROVENANCE Probably Zaccaria Sagredo; belonged to Joseph Smith by 1755; from whom bought by George III, 1762
LITERATURE Blunt 1954, no. 192; Vivian 1989, no. 59

Giovanni Benedetto Castiglione was born and trained in Genoa, and may have picked up the technique of drawing in oil paint on paper from Van Dyck, who was in that city intermittently between 1621 and 1627. The rich, flowing strokes of the brush that this technique allowed were ideally suited to Castiglione's verve as a draughtsman; he produced many such drawings throughout his itinerant career, mostly as independent works of art rather than studies for paintings. The present sheet relates in its extremes of emotion to a number of other oil

171

drawings of the Crucifixion, saints in ecstasy and so on, which probably date from the final phase of Castiglione's career.

George III acquired his magnificent group of around 260 drawings, oil sketches and monotypes by Castiglione from Consul Smith in 1762. They were listed in Smith's will of 1761 as 'four Volumes containing original drawings by Gio. Benedetto Castiglione great part whereof are the most capital of his Performance, these likewise belong'd to the said Nobleman Sagredo'. Smith bought the drawings from the heirs of Zaccaria Sagredo at some point between 1743 and 1755, though he also apparently acquired a number of drawings by Castiglione from Francesco Algarotti. The earlier history of the Castiglione drawings is unknown, but it is inherently probable, given their number, quality and condition, that they had mostly been together as a group since the artist's lifetime.

172. Sebastiano Ricci (1659–1734)
The Adoration of the Magi, c.1726

Pen and ink with grey wash over black chalk.
33.0 × 31.2 cm (13″ × 12⅕₁₆″)
Inscribed on the verso *No. 2. / JS.*
RL 7098
PROVENANCE Joseph Smith; from whom bought by George III, 1762
LITERATURE Blunt and Croft-Murray 1957, no. 238; Vivian 1989, no. 3

This drawing and the following one (no. 173) come from an album of 211 drawings by Sebastiano Ricci, acquired by George III with the collection of Joseph Smith. After travelling widely in Europe, for most of Sebastiano's last two decades he was based in Venice, during which time he became a friend of Smith. The majority of the drawings in

172

Smith's album thus date from the latter part of Ricci's career, and include forty-one drawings for paintings also in Smith's collection – the present drawing is one of sixteen for no. 143. According to the Latin inscription on the title page of the volume, Smith considered that Sebastiano Ricci was the greatest painter of his time (Blunt and Croft-Murray 1957, no. 532; repr. *King's Purchase* 1993, p. 25).

The composition of the drawing agrees in its broad outlines with that of the painting, though there are many differences of detail. The poses of only the Madonna and Child, St Joseph and the kneeling magus correspond closely with those as painted, and the background architecture (painted by Sebastiano's nephew Marco) was to be lowered in height, suggesting an open-air scene rather than the enclosed ruins seen here.

The drawings by Sebastiano in Smith's album (and those by the sixteenth-century painter Giovanni Ambrogio Figino in another album from Smith's collection, also preserved intact in the Royal Library) are mounted with wash-and-line borders in the style more commonly associated with Smith's friend, the collector Anton Maria Zanetti the Elder (1680–1767), as can be seen for example in a second album of drawings by Sebastiano, now in the Accademia in Venice, from Zanetti's collection (see Morassi 1926). Further, many of the finishing tools used to decorate the bindings are common to the Zanetti and the Smith volumes, and it must be concluded that both collectors had their albums made up by the same bindery in Venice.

173. Sebastiano Ricci (1659–1734)

Study for the head of a Pharisee, c.1728–30

Black, red and white chalks, partly washed over, on pale buff paper. 31.1 × 24.2 cm (12¼″ × 9½″)
RL 7134
PROVENANCE As for no. 172
LITERATURE Blunt and Croft-Murray 1957, no. 269; Vivian 1989, no. 7

The drawing is a final study for the head of the Pharisee seated at the far right of the table in Ricci's huge painting of the *Magdalen anointing Christ's feet* (Levey 1991, no. 639). The painting, over 6 metres (20 feet) wide, was the largest of the series of seven New Testament subjects (including no. 143) owned by Joseph Smith. Like the drawings, these paintings were acquired by George III in 1762; the *Magdalen* now

173

hangs at Hampton Court. There is no documentary evidence for the date of the painting. Marco Ricci probably collaborated in the background architecture, which would date much of that portion to no later than his death in January 1730; but the notable inclusion of a portrait of Marco amongst the attendant figures may have been intended as some sort of memorial, suggesting that Sebastiano was still at work on the painting when his nephew died.

The drawing is unusually elaborate for a working study, in a three-chalks technique (with strokes of a brush dipped in water to blend and soften the chalks) more commonly associated with French than with Italian draughtsmen. On his journey back from London in 1716, Sebastiano had visited Paris where he met Antoine Watteau, copying a number of his drawings in this technique. Four of these copies are also to be found in the Smith album.

174

175

174. Marco Ricci (1676–1730)

A winter landscape, c.1720

Tempera on leather. 31.1 × 46.4 cm (12¼″ × 18³⁄₁₆″)
RCIN 400582
PROVENANCE As for no. 172
LITERATURE Levey 1991, no. 611; Scarpa Sonino 1991, no. T113

175. Marco Ricci (1676–1730)

Landscape with peasant women and animals at a trough, c.1725–30

Tempera on leather. 29.8 × 43.8 cm (11¾″ × 17¼″)
RCIN 400555
PROVENANCE As for no. 172
LITERATURE Levey 1991, no. 603; Scarpa Sonino 1991, no. T105

Marco Ricci was the nephew and probably the pupil of Sebastiano Ricci. From an early age he concentrated on landscape, and he also developed a specialism in theatrical scenery design. Marco often collaborated with his uncle, painting the architectural or landscape backgrounds for Sebastiano's large canvases, or enlisting Sebastiano to paint the figures in his own small landscapes. Marco's most distinctive paintings are small idealised landscapes in tempera on leather, of which thirty-two remain in the Royal Collection. Seven of these (though not including nos. 174, 175) were among twenty-four from the collections of Joseph Smith and Anton Maria Zanetti reproduced in etchings by Davide Fossati in 1743. All are similar in size and format, and all remain in their early eighteenth-century Venetian carved and gilt frames. Only one is dated, with the year 1728 (Levey 1991, no. 616). It seems that they were executed over a period of several years, perhaps throughout the 1720s and maybe even before then. Levey thought that no. 174 was one of the earlier of the series, from around 1720, and no. 175 rather later, on the grounds of its apparently more accomplished handling, but a firm internal chronology for the whole series is impossible to establish.

No. 175 is an arcadian landscape of the type that had been painted by Italian artists for over a century, though here with an unusually mountainous background that may owe something to Ricci's upbringing in Belluno, fifty miles north of Venice in the foothills of the Dolomites. Winter landscapes such as no. 174 were a much less common subject in Italian art, and Ricci may have been inspired by Netherlandish paintings that he had seen on his journeys to England between 1708 and 1716 or in Venice – Joseph Smith himself owned a copy of a winter landscape by Adriaen van Ostade that remains in the Royal Collection (White 1982, no. 140).

176. Marco Ricci (1676–1730)

A pastoral scene with a youth climbing a tree, c.1720

Pen and brown wash (faded). 36.7 × 52.7 cm (14⁷⁄₁₆″ × 20¾″)
RL 01155
PROVENANCE As for no. 172
LITERATURE Blunt and Croft-Murray 1957, no. 144

Joseph Smith's will mentioned that he owned 'whole volumes' of drawings by Sebastiano and Marco Ricci, without mentioning their number. While the drawings by Sebastiano are mostly still contained within their original Venetian binding (see nos. 172, 173), those by Marco were remounted for George III with his typical wash borders in two volumes, listed in Inventory A as *Paesi* (landscapes) and *Architettura* (architecture, but chiefly theatrical scenery). Those two volumes contained a total of 106 drawings; in addition there was a portfolio of 27 large landscapes, and 13 drawings framed and hanging at Buckingham House (including the present sheet, thus accounting for its faded condition). All but one of these drawings remain in the Royal Collection.

Few of Marco Ricci's drawings can be dated with any certainty, though it is probable that, as with those by Sebastiano, the majority of Smith's group date from the latter part of Ricci's career. The drawing was traced by George III's third daughter Princess Elizabeth (no. 74), though from an early date there was a confusion about the authorship of both original and tracing, with the present drawing ascribed in an early inventory to 'one of the Royal princesses', and the copy catalogued as by their teacher Alexander Cozens.

177. Giovanni Battista Piazzetta (1682–1754)

The Procuress, c.1730

Black and white chalks on faded blue paper.
41.2 × 55.5 cm (16¼″ × 21⅞″)
RL 01251
PROVENANCE Presumably Joseph Smith, and thus bought by George III, 1762
LITERATURE Blunt and Croft-Murray 1957, no. 32

Piazzetta's paintings and drawings, sombre in tone and of an insistent largeness of form, stand in stark contrast to the high-keyed and airy work of Sebastiano Ricci (no. 143) and

176

177

Giambattista Tiepolo in early eighteenth-century Venice. He was renowned for his drawings of heads; these were drawn in black and white chalks on a dull blue paper that has in almost every case faded to buff, for they were finished works intended to be framed and hung. The Royal Collection holds thirty-six of Piazzetta's drawings of this type, the largest group in existence, and though undocumented they were most probably acquired by George III with Joseph Smith's collection. Until the middle of the twentieth century

the drawings hung at Buckingham Palace, where they are recorded in 1877 and where they had presumably been since they were acquired.

Few of Piazzetta's heads are portraits. They are instead character heads, of priests, philosophers, Moors, children and Venetian youths, and belong to a tradition of such heads that had periods of popularity throughout European art, particularly in seventeenth-century Holland. The present sheet is one of a pair in horizontal format, each

178

showing three figures in a lascivious interaction. Here an old procuress takes a coy girl by the hand, as a bravo stands behind dangling a bag of coins. Nearly all of Piazzetta's drawings in George III's collection, including the present one (see no. 72), were copied by the King's daughters.

178. Giovanni Antonio Canal, called Canaletto (1697–1768)

Venice: The Piazzetta, looking north, c.1732

Pen and ink over pencil. 27.0 × 37.5 cm (10⅝″ × 14¾″)
RL 7437
PROVENANCE As for no. 172
LITERATURE Constable and Links 1989, no. 550; Vivian 1989, no. 32; Parker 1990, no. 25

Canaletto's reputation as the greatest Venetian view-painter of the eighteenth century is much stronger in the Anglo-Saxon world than in his native Italy, where few of his paintings and drawings are to be found. Most of Canaletto's patrons were young English gentlemen on the Grand Tour,

and his dealings with the *milordi* were often facilitated by Joseph Smith, whose palazzo on the Grand Canal was a meeting place for tourists. Smith himself was Canaletto's greatest patron: between the mid-1720s and 1762 he assembled a collection of 50 paintings, 143 drawings and 23 etchings that was purchased by George III with the rest of Smith's collection in 1762.

For the fifteen years or so before Canaletto left for England in 1746, Joseph Smith was himself the principal customer for Canaletto's drawings, and it seems likely that he actively encouraged the artist to produce drawings for his collection. Though many of the motifs replicate those seen in Canaletto's paintings, the drawings are independent works of art, and many fall into distinct groups, uniform in size and style. Smith mounted his drawings by Canaletto on the pages of an album, together with the etchings and two prints after paintings of London by the artist. This album was broken up early in the twentieth century and the binding does not survive, though it presumably matched Smith's four surviving albums of 'artistic' (rather than architectural) drawings.

179

The present drawing shows the Piazzetta in Venice, looking north towards San Marco. To the right is the Palazzo Ducale, beyond which is the south flank of the narthex of San Marco and, in the distance, the Torre dell'Orologio; to the left are the Campanile and the façade of the Libreria. (The reverse of this view, looking out over the Bacino, is shown by Canaletto in no. 144.) The drawing has been related to one in outline in Darmstadt that bears the date 1732, a study for a painting commissioned the previous year by Lord John Russell, the future 4th Duke of Bedford, and still at Woburn Abbey. While the views all show the Piazzetta from the same standpoint, the perspectives of the Darmstadt drawing and Woburn painting are exaggerated, the Libreria is reduced in height, and the sunlight is shown falling from the east, rather than from the west as here. It is therefore doubtful that the present drawing is truly preparatory for the Woburn painting. None the less, its style does appear to be of the early 1730s, and the drawing may have been an independent development from that project.

179. Giovanni Antonio Canal, called Canaletto (1697–1768)

The Benavides garden, Padua, with a classical arch and a statue of Hercules, c.1760

Pen and brown ink with grey wash over pencil.
34.2 × 54.2 cm (13⁷⁄₁₆″ × 21⁵⁄₁₆″), in two pieces
RL 7563, 7539
PROVENANCE As for no. 172
LITERATURE Constable and Links 1989, no. 827; Parker 1990, nos. 142–3

The garden was identified by Corboz (1985, p. 119) as that constructed during the sixteenth century in the Palazzo Mantova Benavides in Padua, built by Bartolomeo Ammanati in 1544–6, featuring a triumphal arch and a colossal statue of Hercules. Canaletto has taken some liberties with the form of the arch, and the staircase to the left and pavilion to the right are inventions, but the general disposition of the main features is accurate.

The drawing is now composed of two pieces of paper, which came to George III on the pages of different Smith albums. While the left-hand portion was mounted in the Canaletto album, the right-hand portion was mounted at the end of an album of prints and drawings by Antonio Visentini.

The preceding two folios of that album bore two further drawings that were catalogued by Parker as by Canaletto (Parker 1990, nos. 120 and 123), though it has recently been claimed with good reason that they are in fact the work of Canaletto's nephew and pupil Bernardo Bellotto (1721–80; see *Bellotto* 1991, nos. 39 and 41). No such suspicion can attach to either portion of the present drawing, whose execution carries all the habitual marks of Canaletto. It is probable that the right portion was cut off, possibly by Canaletto himself, to salvage a moderately successful composition – the left portion with the arch – from a sheet which was somewhat lopsided, and which also revealed Canaletto's discomfiture in drawing a figure larger than his accustomed inch-high shorthand. A small area of foliage was scratched out either side of the join, to the left of Hercules's neck. Perhaps wishing to keep his Canaletto album 'pure', Smith mounted the discarded fragment with the two Bellotto sheets at the end of the Visentini album for want of anywhere else to put them. Like Canaletto's magnificent drawing of a *Capriccio with a terrace and loggia* (Parker 1990, no. 141; *Royal Treasures* 2002, no. 384), which has very similar dimensions, this must have been one of the last to have been drawn for Smith before the sale of his collection to George III. The two parts of the present drawing were reunited in 1979.

180. Francesco Zuccarelli (1702–1788)

A hunting scene, c.1750

Black and white chalks on blue paper (faded to brown), laid on linen, on a strainer. 65.2 × 48.8 cm (25^{11}/$_{16}$″ × 19^{3}/$_{16}$″)

RL 23785

PROVENANCE Probably Joseph Smith, and thus bought by George III, 1762

LITERATURE Blunt and Croft-Murray 1957, no. 581

There are five large chalk drawings by Zuccarelli in the Royal Collection, uniform in height and drawn in black and white chalks on a blue paper that has discoloured to a dull brown through exposure to light over the last 250 years. Such large chalk drawings are highly unusual, perhaps unique, in Zuccarelli's *oeuvre* – his independent landscape drawings are generally small, and executed in light pen and wash – but the composition and figure types leave little doubt that the drawings are his. All five drawings are romantic landscapes of a type common in Italian art from the seventeenth century onwards, with no specific subject but featuring peasants,

180

travellers and huntsmen arranged before towns, trees and picturesque vistas.

There is no evidence of how these drawings entered the Royal Collection. The paintings by Zuccarelli in the Collection were acquired both from Joseph Smith (see nos. 150, 151) and directly from the artist when he was in England between *c.*1764 and *c.*1771; but the unaccustomed nature of the drawings suggests that they were executed for Smith, who likewise seems to have induced Canaletto to produce drawings of a type unusual for the artist.

DRAWINGS FROM THE COLLECTION OF CARDINAL ALESSANDRO ALBANI (nos. 181–185)

George III's greatest single purchase of drawings and prints was that of the collection of Cardinal Alessandro Albani (1692–1779). Albani's drawings incorporated the earlier collections of Cassiano dal Pozzo and Carlo Maratti, including unrivalled groups of drawings by Poussin, Domenichino and the Carracci, and fourteen volumes of drawings by Carlo Fontana that had been bound by the architect for presentation to Albani's uncle, Pope Clement XI. Richard Dalton may have made overtures to the Cardinal in the late 1750s, though he described the collection as 'rather beneath my expectations not so many capital ones as expected', and it may be wondered if he had been shown the entire holdings. The attempt to acquire the Albani collection was probably revived by Robert Adam (see no. 95), at around the time of his appointment as Joint Architect of the King's Works in November 1761. Adam had come to know the collection while studying in Rome between 1755 and 1757, and his younger brother James (1732–94), who had arrived in Rome in February 1761, took on the role of agent and managed to enlist the support of Albani's mistress, the Contessa Cheroffini, as a dowry was reportedly needed for their daughter. Negotiations were conducted in secret – even Albani's librarian, Johann Joachim Winckelmann, was kept in the dark – and in May 1762, James Adam received authorisation from London to proceed with the purchase for the asking price of 14,000 *scudi* (£3,500), plus 500 *scudi* to the Contessa as a 'tip' (for details about these negotiations see Fleming 1958). Although the purchase was an undoubted coup, Adam was primarily pleased that it raised his profile, no doubt for future, more lucrative deals in antiquities: 'I am highly satisfied that the King is pleased with this affair which really was a trouble-some one though worthwhile both because of its making me more known to H.M. and of more consequence among my countrymen here.' The collection, 'containing betwixt drawings and prints, 200 volumes in folio', was transported to Livorno in July 1762, from where it was shipped to London together with the Smith collection, arriving in July 1763.

181. Annibale Carracci (1560–1609)

A study for two Apostles, c.1605

Black and white chalks on blue paper.
44.8 × 30.3 cm (17⅝″ × 11¹⁵⁄₁₆″)
RL 1798
PROVENANCE Probably Domenichino (d. 1641); by whom bequeathed to Francesco Raspantino; by whom sold to Carlo Maratti; by whom sold to Clement XI, 1703; by whom bequeathed to Cardinal Alessandro Albani, 1721; from whom bought by George III, 1762
LITERATURE Wittkower 1952, no. 332

The drawing is a first study for two Apostles in the *Assumption of the Virgin*, one of a series of frescos executed by Annibale's pupils to his designs in the Herrera chapel of San Giacomo degli Spagnoli (now Nostra Signora del Sacro Cuore) in the Piazza Navona, Rome. The frescos were detached in the nineteenth century and the *Assumption* is

181

182

now in the Museu Nacional d'Art de Catalunya, Barcelona.
The figures are drawn as if seen from below, as the *Assumption*
was to be painted over the entrance arch to the chapel, but
this effect was much diluted in the painting where only the
right arm of the principal figure and the cloth held by him
appear in the form drawn here.

Unlike most of the other large groups of drawings now at
Windsor, those by the Carracci entered the Royal Collection
from several sources. A few were in England by the seventeenth century; others can be identified in the Bonfiglioli and
Sagredo collections, and were thus purchased by George III
from Joseph Smith; but the majority, some 550 sheets, came
to the King with the Albani collection. They had originally
belonged to Domenichino, who trained with Ludovico Carracci
in Bologna and who was, between 1602 and 1609, one of
Annibale's main assistants in Rome. Domenichino was thus
in a position to assemble a fine group of sheets by the Carracci,
which he occasionally consulted for motifs during his mature
career. On Domenichino's death his collection of Carraccis
passed with his own drawings to Francesco Raspantino,
and from then on the two groups shared a common history.

182. Domenichino (1581–1641)

*St John the Baptist revealing the Saviour to Saints
Peter and Andrew, c.1625*

Red chalk, squared in black chalk.
25.1 × 38.6 cm (9⅞″ × 15³/₁₆″)
RL 357
PROVENANCE Bequeathed to Francesco Raspantino; then as for no. 181
LITERATURE Pope-Hennessy 1948, no. 756; *Domenichino* 1996, no. 75

The drawing is a final study, though with some differences,
for one of the frescos in Domenichino's greatest Roman
project, the *Evangelists* and *Scenes from the life of St Andrew*
painted in the church of Sant'Andrea della Valle. The corresponding fresco is in the crown of the vault over the choir,
and serves as an introduction to the whole cycle. It depicts
the apocryphal moment at which St John the Baptist points
out Christ to the first Disciples to be called, Saints Peter
and Andrew (ill. *Domenichino* 1996, p. 286).

Domenichino trained with the Carracci (see no. 181) and
was like them a tireless draughtsman. On his death he left
the contents of his studio, including over 1,700 of his own
drawings, to his pupil Francesco Raspantino. An inventory
of 1664 lists the works then in Raspantino's collection;

some time afterwards, the bulk of the collection was acquired by Carlo Maratti, and from Maratti the drawings passed through the Albani collection to George III, for whom they were remounted in thirty-four albums. The present sheet was the first in volume eight, one of three containing a total of 157 drawings thought to be for the Sant'Andrea project.

Francesco Bartolozzi made an etched copy of this drawing shortly after its acquisition by George III, the only one of Domenichino's drawings to be reproduced in this way. Bartolozzi's print was subsequently published by John and Josiah Boydell in *Seventy-Three Prints Engraved by F. Bartolozzi &c. from the Original Pictures and Drawings . . . in the Collection of His Majesty &c.* (London, n.d.).

George III's library, and only recently have a few intact volumes of prints been identified, mostly among the King's Library in the British Library (see Griffiths 1989).

The present drawing is one of the finest of the antiquarian sheets from Cassiano's collection. It shows the front of the so-called *Trophy of Marius*, one of a pair known in Rome since the Middle Ages and moved in 1590 to the Capitoline Hill, where they still stand. The attribution of the drawing remains controversial, though the facial type of the central figure and the technique support an attribution to Pietro da Cortona during the later 1620s, when he was emerging as one of the leading painters in Rome under the patronage of the Sacchetti and of Cassiano's employers, the Barberini.

183. Attributed to Pietro da Cortona (1596–1669)
The trophy of Marius: front view, c.1625–30

Pen and ink with wash and white bodycolour, on blue paper.
52.2 × 34.3 cm (20⁹⁄₁₆″ × 13½″)
RL 8249

PROVENANCE Cassiano dal Pozzo; his brother Carlo Antonio dal Pozzo; sold by his grandson to Clement XI, 1703; Cardinal Alessandro Albani, by 1714; from whom bought by George III, 1762

LITERATURE *Cassiano* 1993, no. 2; *CDP* (forthcoming)

The drawing comes from the 'paper museum' of Cassiano dal Pozzo (1588–1657), one of the great collectors of seventeenth-century Rome, not so much for the magnificence of his collection (though he was Poussin's most important patron) but for its range. He commissioned and collected many thousands of drawings and prints to form a visual encyclopedia, principally of antiquities and natural history. After Cassiano's death his younger brother Carlo Antonio (1606–89) continued to add to the 'paper museum', but the dal Pozzo library, including the volumes of drawings, was sold by Carlo Antonio's grandson to Clement XI in 1703. As the Vatican library was unable to find the necessary funds, the Pope's nephew – Cardinal Alessandro Albani – took over the purchase by 1714. George III acquired the bulk of the dal Pozzo library with the rest of the Albani collection in 1762, but it suffered depredations both before and after this time, and only about half of the dal Pozzo drawings now remain together in the Royal Collection. The equally extensive collection of prints in the 'paper museum' suffered even more. Many of the albums were broken up and dispersed within

183

184. Nicolas Poussin (1594–1665)

Scipio Africanus and the pirates, 1642

Pen and ink with wash over black chalk.
32.7 × 46.6 cm (12⅞″ × 18⅜″)
RL 0698

PROVENANCE Probably drawn for Cardinal Francesco Barberini
but passed to Cassiano dal Pozzo; his brother Carlo Antonio
dal Pozzo; by whose grandson sold to Clement XI, 1703;
Cardinal Alessandro Albani, by 1714; from whom bought by
George III, 1762

LITERATURE Blunt 1945, no. 251; Rosenberg and Prat 1994,
no. 273; Clayton 1995, no. 52

George III, who greatly admired Poussin's paintings (see
p. 157), owned two volumes of drawings by the artist. The
first, assembled in the artist's lifetime by his friend and
patron Cardinal Camillo Massimi, was inherited by the King
from his father, who had bought it from Dr Richard Mead.
The second was apparently identical with that described
in the Albani library by Winckelmann in 1759, and was
purchased by George III with the Albani collection three
years later. The origins of this second album are not certain,
but it was probably put together by Cassiano dal Pozzo (see
no. 183), one of Poussin's closest associates over many years.
The album was arranged broadly thematically (Old Testament,
New Testament, ancient history, mythology) in a manner
similar to Cassiano dal Pozzo's 'paper museum', and
contained two antiquarian drawings bearing inscribed
numbers of a type found on most of the drawings in the
'paper museum'.

Several sheets from the album date from Poussin's period
in Paris in the early 1640s, and we know from surviving
letters that he was at that time sending drawings back to
Cassiano in Rome. On 27 June 1642, Poussin wrote to thank
Cassiano for giving him the opportunity to make a drawing
on the subject of the Roman general Scipio Africanus for
Cassiano's employer, Cardinal Francesco Barberini. No. 184
appears to be that drawing, large and carefully executed,
though how Cassiano secured it for his own collection
rather than Barberini's is unknown. The episode shown by
Poussin was taken from the Roman author Valerius Maximus:

184

Scipio was in retirement at his coastal villa when pirates landed, apparently planning to attack. But their intention was merely to pay homage to the general, and they were allowed by Scipio's companions to proceed unmolested.

185. Carlo Maratti (1625–1713)

An allegorical design in honour of Pietro da Cortona, c.1675

Black chalk. 41.4 × 29.9 cm (16⁵/₁₆″ × 11¾″)
RL 4091
PROVENANCE Probably Clement XI and/or Cardinal Alessandro Albani; from whom bought by George III, 1762
LITERATURE Blunt and Cooke 1960, no. 317

Carlo Maratti was the leading artist in Rome after Bernini's death in 1680. He saw himself as the inheritor of the classical tradition beginning with Raphael and passing through the Carracci, Domenichino and his master Andrea Sacchi, and like these precursors he was a prolific draughtsman. The group of some 280 sheets by Maratti and his pupils now in the Royal Collection is assumed to have been bought by George III with the Albani collection, although this is not certain. While Maratti had sold his collection of drawings by earlier masters to Clement XI in 1703, it is unlikely that he would have disposed of his own drawings while he was still active as a painter. These drawings were probably acquired by the Pope or Cardinal Alessandro after Maratti's death ten years later (though they are not mentioned in the late inventories of Maratti's collection).

This drawing depicts winged Time trampling Envy while holding aloft a plaque with a portrait of the painter Pietro da Cortona, who had died in 1669 (see no. 183 and Honour 1961). The likeness was based on a posthumous medallion by François Chéron, which in turn derived from a portrait by Pietro's pupil Ciro Ferri. Sculpted tombs like this may be found in Roman churches (and Maratti did provide designs for sculpture), but the pictorial nature of the background suggests a two-dimensional project, most likely a commemorative engraving. However, no engraving from the design is known before it was reproduced by Francesco Bartolozzi over a century later, after the drawing had passed into George III's collection.

185

OTHER DRAWINGS ACQUIRED BY GEORGE III (nos. 186–193)

186. Giovanni Francesco Barbieri, called Guercino (1591–1666)

Four youths singing, watched by an old man, c.1625

Pen and ink with wash. 26.6 × 38.1 cm (10½″ × 15″)

RL 2515

PROVENANCE Bequeathed to Benedetto and Cesare Gennari, and by descent; purchased by Richard Dalton for George III, *c.*1758–64

LITERATURE Mahon and Turner 1989, no. 280

On Guercino's death the thousands of drawings in his studio (including his collection of drawings by other artists) passed to his nephews, Benedetto and Cesare Gennari, and by the mid-eighteenth century most had descended to Cesare's grandson Carlo Gennari. Many were framed, a number were kept loose in portfolios, but the majority were mounted in albums, explaining the remarkably fine state of preservation of many of Guercino's drawings today. From the 1740s this inheritance began to be dispersed. Groups of drawings were sold to John Bouverie, to William Kent, and to Richard Dalton, Librarian to George, Prince of Wales, who purchased about forty drawings in 1758. This first tranche was followed by much larger (though undocumented) acquisitions by Dalton, presumably on one or both of his return visits to Bologna in 1759 and 1763. George III eventually owned more than eight hundred drawings by Guercino and his studio, mounted in sixteen albums. Possibly while the drawings were still in Italy, a number of them – including no. 186 – were etched by Francesco Bartolozzi (see no. 215 and Mahon and Turner 1989, pp. xxviii–xxxi).

While many of Guercino's figure studies can be related to his paintings (including no. 154), a few must be regarded as independent drawings, alongside his landscapes (no. 187), caricatures and grotesques, and the careful handling of the wash here suggests that the pictorial effect of the drawing was important to the artist. The subject of an informal concert occurs occasionally in the sixteenth century, and was given fresh impetus by artists in the circle of Caravaggio; the dandified cast of youths demonstrates Guercino's knowledge of paintings by the *caravaggisti*, which he would have seen during his stay in Rome between 1621 and 1623.

186

187. Giovanni Francesco Barbieri, called Guercino (1591–1666)

Landscape with a winding road leading up to the gate of a town, c.1635(?)

Pen and ink. 28.6 × 21.2 cm (11¼″ × 8⅜″)
Verso inscribed *1635 / Sono in tutti Carti numero 32 / che fanno 32 disegni / Opera del Sig: Gio: Francesco Barbieri / da Cento*, followed by a paraph
RL 2762
PROVENANCE Possibly bequeathed to Benedetto and Cesare Gennari, and by descent; in which case purchased by Richard Dalton for George III, *c.*1758–64 (but see entry)
LITERATURE Mahon and Turner 1989, no. 247

Guercino's landscape drawings belong to a tradition of Bolognese romanticism quite distinct from the classically composed landscapes of the Roman school. The Carracci were largely responsible for spawning both schools, but the way in which their followers interpreted their example diverged dramatically. Guercino was one of the most prolific of the succeeding generation of Bolognese landscape draughtsmen, and the Royal Collection possesses more than forty of his highly individual compositions.

The reverse of this sheet is inscribed in a manner unique among the hundreds of Guercino drawings at Windsor (though most remain pasted to their solid early twentieth-century mounts, and other similar inscriptions may be revealed in the future). The inscription – '1635. There are in total 32 sheets which make 32 drawings, the work of Signor Giovanni Francesco Barbieri of Cento', followed by what appears to be an elaborate paraph (a calligraphic mark of ownership) – is in the hand neither of Guercino himself nor of his brother Paolo Antonio, and must date from a later arrangement of Guercino's drawings. Consequently the date apparently ascribed to the drawing must be regarded with caution, and if the paraph is indeed a mark of ownership, the sheet (and perhaps another thirty-one by Guercino) may have reached the Royal Collection separately from the Gennari group acquired in instalments by Dalton.

187

188. Giovanni Battista Salvi, called Sassoferrato (1605–1685)

The Mystic Marriage of St Catherine, c.1650(?)

Black and white chalk on buff paper.
42.2 × 27.4 cm (16⅝″ × 10¹³⁄₁₆″)
RL 6084
PROVENANCE Purchased in Rome by Richard Dalton for George III, 1769 (RA GEO/15602)
LITERATURE Blunt and Cooke 1960, no. 879

Sassoferrato was one of the most fascinating artists of the seventeenth century, painting not only copies of Raphael, Perugino and other 'Old Masters' but also his own composi-tions, in a deliberately archaising style completely at odds with the prevailing baroque and more elegantly restrained even than the works of Poussin and Sacchi. The Royal Collection holds the largest surviving group of drawings by Sassoferrato, sixty sheets that were bought in Rome by Richard Dalton for George III in 1769, for the modest sum of twenty Roman crowns (£5). They presumably came *en bloc* from the artist's studio, but their earlier history is unknown; the present sheet is heavily fly-spotted down the right edge, and must have lain in a portfolio with that edge exposed at some time. It is a final study for the life-size *Mystic Marriage of St Catherine* in the Wallace Collection,

188

London (P.646), the finest of Sassoferrato's paintings to be found in Britain. Given his limited development over a long career and the paucity of his dated works it is almost impossible to date undocumented paintings such as this on stylistic grounds.

189. Hendrick Avercamp (1585–1634)

A game of kolf *on the ice, c.*1620

Pen and ink with brown wash, watercolour, red chalk and bodycolour. 17.5 × 23.5 cm (6⅞″ × 9¼″)
RL 6470
PROVENANCE Abraham van Broyel sale, Amsterdam, 30 October 1759, lot D216; bought by Pieter Yver; George III (Inventory A, p. 118)
LITERATURE Welcker 1979, no. T140; White and Crawley 1994, no. 244

The deaf-mute Hendrick Avercamp, based in the provincial Dutch town of Kampen, was the first Netherlandish artist to specialise in paintings (and drawings) of winter scenes. Here he has drawn a game of *kolf op het ijs*, the winter version of *kolf* in which players hit a ball towards a pole; the fashionable costumes of the onlookers suggest a date of around 1620. The Royal Collection holds roughly one-third of Avercamp's

189

surviving drawings, many attractively finished in water-colour and probably made to be sold rather than as studies for paintings. That was no doubt the immediate purpose of the present drawing, although the figure of the man playing *kolf* and the sleigh in the background are to be found in a circular painting by Avercamp of a winter landscape in the Kunsthalle, Hamburg (Welcker 1979, no. 551).

Michiel Plomp has identified in the Royal Collection around sixty drawings that were included in the auction of Abraham van Broyel's collection, held in Amsterdam on 30 October 1759 and succeeding days (see Plomp (forthcoming)). These were among over a hundred Dutch and Flemish drawings acquired at the sale by the dealer Pieter Yver (1712–87), who, if not acting directly for the Prince of Wales, presumably sold the group of sixty to the Prince (or King) shortly thereafter. The present drawing was probably one of a pair by Avercamp in the Van Broyel sale. Each was described as 'A Winter scene with many figures, drawn with washes, height 5¼, width 8 inches'; the second drawing depicts *Two ladies and a gentleman on a horse-drawn sleigh* (White and Crawley 1994, no. 243), the measurements of which correspond closely with those given in the sale catalogue.

190. Gerrit van Battem (*c.*1636–1684)

*Winter scene outside a town, c.*1670

Watercolour and bodycolour. 27.7 × 40.8 cm (10 $^{15}\!/_{16}$″ × 16 $^1\!/_{16}$″)
Signed at lower left *Battem*
RL 12922
PROVENANCE Abraham van Broyel sale, Amsterdam, 30 October 1759, lot D178; bought by Pieter Yver; presumably George III
LITERATURE White and Crawley 1994, no. 293

Gerrit van Battem specialised in imaginary landscapes executed in watercolour and bodycolour, intended to be framed and hung; the present composition was one of his favourites, and several other versions are known. Like the drawing by Avercamp (no. 189), it was purchased by Pieter Yver at the Van Broyel sale, one of a pair of gouaches by Van Battem that fetched the large sum of 132 guilders. It was described as 'A rare and pleasant landscape of Winter, with a view of a town with a castle, with very many figures, not inferior to the preceding, in watercolour and of the same size [height 11, width 16 inches].' The other gouache of the pair, of a river landscape with travellers, also remains in the Royal Collection (White and Crawley 1994, no. 296). Together with three further watercolours by the artist, and thirty by other Dutch and Flemish artists (RL 12898–933), these hung in Buckingham Palace until 1950, presumably since their acquisition in the eighteenth century.

190

191. Mark Catesby (1682–1749)

The ivory-billed woodpecker and willow oak, 1723–9

Watercolour and bodycolour with gum arabic, over pen and brown ink and traces of graphite. 37.5 × 27.1 cm (14¾″ × 10¹¹⁄₁₆″)
RL 24829
PROVENANCE Thomas Cadell; from whom bought by
George III, 1768
LITERATURE McBurney 1997, no. 5

192. Georg Dionysius Ehret (1708–1770)

*Magnolia, c.*1736–47

Watercolour and bodycolour with gum arabic, over graphite.
40.5 × 29.3 cm (15¹⁵⁄₁₆″ × 11⁹⁄₁₆″)
RL 26084
PROVENANCE As for no. 191
LITERATURE McBurney 1997, no. 51

191

192

Beginning in 1712, the English naturalist and amateur artist Mark Catesby made a series of expeditions to the British colonies in North America for the purpose of documenting the indigenous flora and fauna which, as he put it, 'were Strangers to *England*'. His resulting book, the first on its subject, was *The Natural History of Carolina, Florida and the Bahama Islands*, issued in parts between 1729 and 1747. The book is an extraordinary visual record of the plants, mammals, lizards, snakes, insects, corals, fish and birds which he found on his travels. These are original watercolour drawings for the illustrations.

One of Catesby's aims was to depict animals and birds in their natural habitat. The willow oak (*Quercus phellos*), one of nine species of oak he describes and illustrates in a later work (the *Hortus Britanno-Americanus; or a Curious Collection of Trees and Shrubs, the Produce of the British Colonies in North America; adapted to the Soil and Climate of England*, published posthumously in 1763), is depicted as accurately as the woodpecker (*Campephilus principalis*). Catesby discovered eight different species of woodpecker. He collected live (or shot) specimens which he preserved (by one means or another – dried, or in jars), so he could send them back to England; he tried to draw animals from life wherever possible.

The celebrated German botanical illustrator Georg Dionysius Ehret was invited to contribute illustrations to Catesby's *Natural History*. No. 192 actually depicts two different species of magnolia – the leaf of the cucumber tree (*Magnolia acuminata*) with the flower of the sweet bay (*Magnolia virginiana*) – suggesting that specimens had become separated *en route* from Virginia to England and were then incorrectly matched up. Unlike Catesby, Ehret did not visit North America. In the etched plate Catesby added a velvet ant to the image, borrowed from a page of his own insect studies.

Catesby dedicated the first volume of his work to Queen Caroline, consort of George II, and the second to Augusta, Princess of Wales, the mother of George III. Both were keen

193

amateur botanists, and the Princess of Wales may be seen as the founder of Kew Gardens. When George III acquired a unique three-volume set of Catesby's *Natural History* from a London dealer, Thomas Cadell, in 1768 he may already have known the published work. In this set the engraved plates were replaced by the preparatory watercolours on which Catesby based his plates. The colours in the 263 watercolours – protected from the light – have remained extraordinarily fresh. Following an extensive conservation campaign in the 1990s, involving both watercolours and bindings, the watercolours have now been separately mounted, and their places in Catesby's volumes have been taken by facsimile reproductions, made by Alecto Historical Editions.

193. Thomas Sandby (1721/3–1798) and Paul Sandby (1730–1809)

The camp on Warley Common, 1778

Pen and ink and watercolour. 49.1 × 147.3 cm (19⅝″ × 58″)
RL 14729
PROVENANCE Presumably painted for George III (Military Maps Catalogue, f. 46)
LITERATURE Oppé 1947, no. 158; Hodson (forthcoming)

Although George III's reign coincided with the flowering of the particularly English art of watercolour painting, the King was little concerned with this; nor was he much interested in the contemporary development of landscape painting. However, his role in the gathering of topographical and historical records was considerable. He formed three vast collections of drawings, watercolours and prints – a Geographical, a Maritime, and a Military Collection. The larger items in these collections were kept rolled; the smaller items were kept flat or folded, in large boxes with decorated spines. Other pieces were individually bound (see no. 211). The collections were housed in the King's library rooms at Buckingham House, where they were stored in the special library tables (see fig. 26). The old pressmark of this water-colour (*5 Tab. 2*) indicates that it was kept rolled in the library. Whereas the Geographical Collection was presented to the British Museum with the King's Library by George IV, and is now in the Map Library of the British Library at St Pancras, the Military Collection remains in the Royal Library at Windsor Castle; the Maritime Collection passed to the Admiralty but is now mostly in the British Library (see Barber 2000).

This magnificent watercolour was included in the early list of George III's collection of military maps and plans as 'The Camp on Cox Heath, 1778'. However, the cataloguer of that collection (Dr Yolande Hodson) has recently established that it is instead a record of the camp at Warley, Essex. The camps at both Warley and Cox Heath (near Maidstone, Kent) took place between 28 May and 11 November 1778 and each was visited by the King; this coincidence may have contributed to the mis-identification of this view. The rich foliage suggests that it is a record of the camp during the summer, some time before the King's visit on 20 October; the review and 'mock attack' staged for the King were recorded in Daniel Paterson's plan of the camp (no. 211 – also part of the King's military map collection) – and in two paintings by de Loutherbourg (see no. 163). The large house just below the horizon at far left is Thorndon Hall, the seat of Lord Petre, with whom the King and Queen stayed during their visit; it had been completed in 1770 to the design of James Paine.

Thomas Sandby (see no. 99) was first trained as a surveyor. In the early 1740s he moved from Nottingham to London where he received further – specifically military – training in the Ordnance Office. This watercolour is the product of his continued attachment to the Ordnance Office, which lasted until his death. Sandby's meticulous panoramic records of the landscape in the Netherlands and in Windsor

Great Park in the 1740s and 1750s (see Roberts (J.) 1995, no. 42) are landmarks in the history of English watercolour painting and are the context in which the present view should be seen. He was also active as an architect (see nos. 99–101) and was noted for his skill in perspective: the depiction of the windmill – of a model typically found in Essex – is particularly striking. For the figures which 'people' his views, Thomas frequently sought the assistance of his younger brother, Paul, a skilled artist in both oils and watercolours. Paul was doubtless responsible for the figures in the left foreground in this view; his study for the foot soldier is also in the Royal Collection (Oppé 1947, no. 378).

194

194. Mary Delany (1700–1788)

A stem of stock, 1781

Watercolour and gouache on paper, cut and pasted onto backing paper painted black. Oval, 25.0 × 17.0 cm (9^{13}⁄₁₆″ × 6^{11}⁄₁₆″)
Inscribed by the artist on the verso of the backing paper
Bulstrode Oct.ʳ 1781
RL 27999
PROVENANCE The artist's nephew, Bernard Dewes (d. 1822); by whom given to his niece, Fanny Ram (*née* Port); by descent to her great-grandson, Sir Granville Ram; by whom presented to King George VI, July 1942

Mrs Delany (seen in Opie's portrait of 1782: no. 165), an extraordinarily proficient needlewoman and artist, had been interested in botany since her youth. After the death of her second husband in 1768 she was invited to spend a large part of each year with the widowed Duchess of Portland at Bulstrode, Buckinghamshire, where gardeners and plant collectors – such as John Lightfoot, Philip Miller, Joseph Banks and Daniel Solander – were frequent visitors. In 1772, while artists such as G.D. Ehret made painted records of plants and the Duchess continued to add to her collection of dried flowers, Mrs Delany began work on her own florilegium or *Hortus siccus* (dry garden). She wrote: 'I have invented a new way of imitating flowers', using scissors, paints and paper – often cut into many hundreds of tiny pieces – to depict a single plant. The surface or finish of the paper was carefully chosen to ensure that the correct impression was given. Typically in this late specimen (made when Mrs Delany was in her early 80s), the matt, almost furry, texture of the stock leaves is carefully imitated, and the plant is shown at life size.

The florilegium project occupied Mrs Delany for much of the following decade. The major surviving records of her activity are the ten volumes in the British Museum, containing nearly one thousand separate flower studies or silhouettes. The King and Queen took a keen interest in Mrs Delany's work, visiting Bulstrode to see the *Hortus siccus* for the first time in 1776. Soon after this visit plant specimens began to arrive at Bulstrode from Kew. After a visit to Bulstrode in December 1781, the Queen sent Mrs Delany a pocket-book containing tiny tools and bodkins (no. 59), to assist her in her work. However, by this time the artist's eyesight was failing. The later flower mosaics, including no. 194, are less complex and include much less fine detail than those of the 1770s. In the twelfth codicil to her will (first made in 1778), Mrs Delany bequeathed to the Queen a selection of twenty of her flowers in paper mosaic. These may have been contained in the volume – described as containing ninety-three of Mrs Delany's sketches – included in the posthumous sale of Queen Charlotte's collection in 1819; their present location is not known.

The backboard of the oval fruitwood frame bears the label of 'Dodds, No. 51 St Martin's Lane', presumably identifiable with William Dodds, active at this address at the end of the eighteenth century and documented as supplying frames to the Dowager Duchess of Bedford (*DOEFM* 1986, p. 249). The fact that the backboard is also inscribed by Mrs Delany's nephew Bernard Dewes, at the time that he presented the piece to his niece, indicates that it has been framed – and exposed to light – for around two hundred years. The faded colouring in comparison with the brightly preserved colours of the British Museum florilegium is particularly marked.

7. Books and binding (nos. 195–251)

GEORGE III'S LIBRARIES

THE FIRST AREA in which George III demonstrated a keen and acquisitive personal interest was books. With the encouragement of the Earl of Bute he was purchasing printed books and volumes of drawings (see nos. 166, 167) in the 1750s, before his accession to the throne. In January 1761 – before his marriage, coronation and acquisition of Buckingham House – it was reported that a range of rooms at St James's Palace was being prepared to receive the new King's library. George III is best known in the bibliographical world for his accumulation of the King's Library, which was presented by George IV to the British Museum and is now part of the British Library. That book collection, which was originally housed in a suite of rooms added to his new London residence, Buckingham House (see fig. 26 and nos. 117, 118), was intended for use primarily by scholars: Dr Johnson's 'private conversation' with George III took place in one of the new library rooms in February 1767.

The King's Library collection was listed in the five-volume *Bibliothecae Regiae Catalogus* compiled by George III's Librarian F.A. Barnard and published in 1820–29. It consisted of around 65,000 titles and was designed as a 'universal' library to cater for a broad range of subject interests. An important core was provided by the extraordinary collection of manuscripts and printed books acquired from Consul Smith in 1762 (see Morrison 1993/4). But the King also possessed other, private, libraries at Richmond and Kew (see no. 217), at his summer retreat at Weymouth, at Windsor Castle, and at Cumberland Lodge in Windsor Great Park. The last-named collection, which originated in the library inherited by George III from his uncle, William, Duke of Cumberland, in 1765, was known as the Windsor Library; in the 1830s it was amalgamated with the other library collections in the rooms in Windsor Castle which continue to be occupied by the Royal Library, along with copies of its catalogue (compiled 1780–1812, by F.A. Barnard). It contained over 2,500 titles and closely reflected the King's personal interests. The collection was divided into five main subject areas: Theology, History, Jurisprudence, Science and Arts, and Classical literature, from which the present selection – covering subjects such as music, architecture, medals, agriculture, ancient and modern literature, history, natural history, travel literature and militaria – has been made (nos. 206–47). Among these are books which were part of the King's Library collection, but which were excluded from the gift to the British Museum as subjects of particular interest: for instance, incunables (nos. 213, 214) and military affairs (nos. 210, 211).

It is not known precisely either when or how George III acquired his books: his library was paid for entirely from his own resources but the accounts of his Privy Purse

are incomplete and inadequately itemised. His Librarians – Richard Dalton from 1755 to 1773, and Frederick Augusta Barnard from 1774 (who continued *en poste* until his death in 1830) – were active in purchasing books for the King at home and overseas. Barnard travelled on the continent between 1768 and 1771, acquiring books for the King; he had received a lengthy letter of advice from Dr Johnson before his departure. In addition, George Nicol (the King's Bookseller) made purchases for the King, particularly at London sales. It is known that George III spent a sizeable proportion of his private income on books, and had agents at book sales both in Britain and on the continent. The King's copy of the Mainz Psalter of 1457 (RCIN 1071478) was purchased from the University of Göttingen in 1800.

Books were frequently presented to the King by authors or publishers (see nos. 207, 209, 215), or by fellow book collectors such as Jacob Bryant (nos. 212–14). An exceptional gift of six oriental manuscripts (including no. 473 and the Padshahnama) was sent to the King by the Nawab of Oudh in 1799.

LITERATURE Barnard (F.) 1820; Brooke 1977; Paintin 1989; Patterson 1996

THE ROYAL BINDERY

George III's love of books extended beyond their contents. Thomas de Quincey noted that 'his care extended even to the dressing of the books in appropriate bindings, and . . . to their *health*'. The King's visits to Buckingham House were punctuated by visits to the bindery there. The binders were instructed to have clean aprons for these occasions, but to continue working as if no one were present, unless directly addressed by the King. George III was one of the first employers to 'give the hour' (a reduction in working hours demanded by the binders' trade union), and a poem published in 1796 indicates the value that he placed on the outward appearance of his books:

And yet our Monarch has a world of books,
And daily on their backs so gorgeous looks;
So neatly bound, so richly gilt, so fine,
He fears to open them to read a line!

. . .

But here's the dev'l – I fear too many know it –
Some kings prefer the *Binder* to the *Poet*

A rather different view had been expressed by Mrs Lybbe Powys following her visit to Buckingham House in March 1767: 'the Books are said to be ye best Collection anywhere to be met with, and one is more apt to believe so, as their outsides are not so gilded and letter'd as one generally sees in rooms of this kind, where many are lovers only I believe, to give one an ostentatious idea of the owners learning' (BL Add. MS 42160, f. 20).

George III is known to have employed binders before his accession; Andreas Linde was Binder to George III's father, Frederick, Prince of Wales, and served the Prince's son in the same capacity. Following the accession, George III's first official binder was Walter Shropshire who was appointed Binder in Ordinary in December 1760 and continued *en poste* until his death in 1785. Shropshire is better known as a bookseller than as a binder. His role may therefore have been more as a co-ordinator of binding activities – assigning work elsewhere – than as an actual binder. The range and scale of work required of the royal position is well beyond what we know of Shropshire's activities. The King also spent considerable sums on bindings supplied by James Campbell, working in the Strand, who is listed as his Bookbinder in the Royal Kalendar, from 1767 to 1769 or 1770. It was Campbell who recommended John Polwarth to George III; although Polwarth was nominally only Chief Finisher (that is, applier of decoration at the end of the binding process), he appears to have been in charge of the Royal Bindery *c.*1786–93. Thomas Lowndes held the post of Binder to the King between 1793 and 1799, and then William Armstrong between 1800 and 1820.

George III's bindery was located in the basement rooms below the Octagon Library at Buckingham House (see no. 117), added in 1766–7. Five rooms were allocated to 'Bookbinders' in a plan sent to the King in March 1776 (Westminster Public Library, Box 39/31/1–2). Although it is normally stated that the Royal Bindery was established between 1780 and 1786, it is therefore likely that it was in existence from the 1770s, if not the late 1760s. The changed appearance of the King's books as a result of the Bindery's establishment may be the reason for the difference of opinion about the King's books, in the descriptions of 1767 and 1796 noted above. When, in 1828, the King's Library and its staff were transferred (with Armstrong as clerk) to the British Museum, the binding tools appear to have been retained in royal ownership. The Royal Bindery was re-established at Windsor when the Royal Library was transferred there under William IV.

Many of the finishing tools supplied for George III's bindery have survived, and a number remain in use to this day. In 1940, at the suggestion of the binding historian G.D. Hobson, the Royal Librarian (Owen Morshead) had copies made of ink impressions of the tools, rolls, pallets and panels belonging to the bindery. Over seven hundred items are listed, including most of those discussed here; it is likely that the majority of these tools date from the reigns of George III and George IV, although a small number are of a later date.

It is not known, for the most part, who made finishing tools for George III's bindery, though a few are signed by R. Brook (Richard Brook, Seal Engraver to the Royal Family, *c.*1802–17). He was succeeded by Robert Scott (*fl.*1817–31), Engraver of Brass Ornaments to His Majesty's Library. Of the tools shown here, which date from between *c.*1770 and *c.*1820, the striking royal crown may be seen on the board of no. 170 and on several other volumes of prints and drawings; it is likely that the identifying letters 'G' and 'R' and the figure 'III' above were provided by three separate tools. Other finishing tools, including some of the smaller ones shown here, were used on the front board and spine of Seneca's *Tragoediae* (no. 213; see illustration on p. 225). The reproduction binding of Claude's *Liber veritatis* (no. 205) was made in the Royal Bindery to demonstrate the continuing existence and use of tools from George III's bindery. The original volumes are displayed in the bookcase by William Vile (no. 267). The first two volumes (published in 1777) with George III's arms, were early products of the Royal Bindery, using tools most of which survive today (nos. 199–204). The third volume, published in 1819, was not bound until well after George III's death in 1820. It was probably passed to an outside binder who used very similar tools to achieve a good match with the first two volumes, and replaced George III's arms with the cipher of William IV.

LITERATURE De Quincey 1863, pp. 167–8; Ramsden 1958; Nixon and Foot 1992, pp. 96–7; Foot 1993, pp. 229–31, 317–18; Conroy 2002, pp. 9–10, 48

Nos. 170 and 195.

195. *George III's large crown finishing tool*

Brass mounted on laminated board. 7.8 × 10.0 × 3.4 cm (3¹⁄₁₆″ × 3¹⁵⁄₁₆″ × 1⁵⁄₁₆″)
RCIN 96001
Used on the boards of no. 170; RB Impressions E

196. *Centre finishing tool*

Brass. Printing face 1.3 × 1.0 cm (½″ × ⅜″)
RCIN 96002
Used on the boards of no. 213; smaller version of RB Impressions 536

197. *Corner finishing tools*

Brass. Printing face 1.9 × 1.0 cm (¾″ × ⅜″)
RCIN 96003–4
Used on the boards of no. 213; RB Impressions 305

198. *Finishing tool in the shape of a Tudor rose*

Brass. Printing face diameter 0.5 cm (³⁄₁₆″)
RCIN 96005
Used on the boards of no. 213; RB Impressions 615

199. *Finishing tool in the shape of a five-pointed star*

Brass. Printing face diameter 0.3 cm (⅛″)
RCIN 96006
Used on the spine of no. 205; RB Impressions 635

200. *Pallet tool*

Brass. Printing face 0.5 × 6.9 cm (³⁄₁₆″ × 2¹¹⁄₁₆″)
RCIN 96007
Used on the spine of no. 205; pallet tool of pattern on RB Impressions 707 (a roll tool)

201. *Lozenge centre tool*

Brass. Printing face 2.1 × 1.2 cm (¹³⁄₁₆″ × ½″)
RCIN 96008
Used on the spine of no. 205; RB Impressions 162A

202. *Floret tool*

Brass. Printing face 0.6 × 0.8 cm (¼″ × ⁵⁄₁₆″)
RCIN 96009
Used on the spine of no. 205; RB Impressions 402

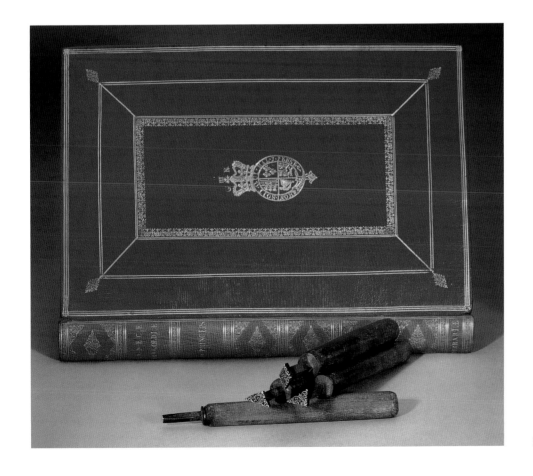

No. 213 with nos. 196–8.

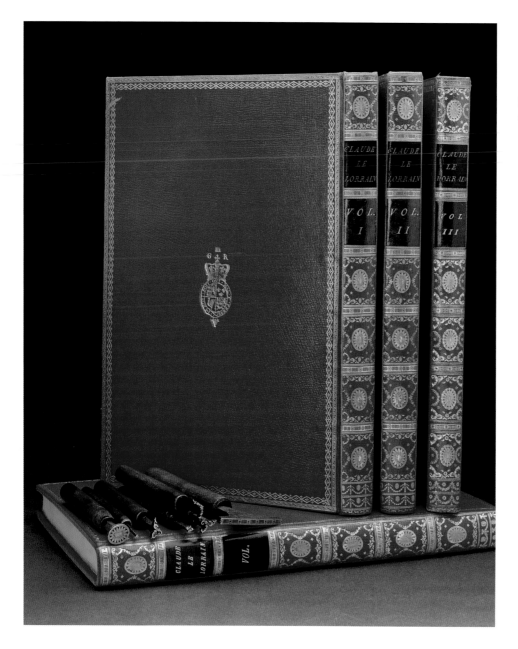

Nos. 205 and 243, with nos. 199–204.

203. *Floret tool*

Brass. Printing face 1.2 × 0.9 cm (½″ × ⅜″)
RCIN 96010
Used on the spine of no. 205; RB Impressions 124

204. *Corner finishing tools*

Brass. Printing face 1.9 × 1.1 cm (¾″ × 7/16″)
RCIN 96011–12
Used on the spine of no. 205; RB Impressions 294
PROVENANCE Supplied for use in George III's bindery

205. Royal Bindery, Windsor

Reproduction of volume 2 of Claude's Liber veritatis, 2003

Red sheepskin with green leather labels and gold tooling.
42.0 × 29.2 cm (16 9/16″ × 11¾″)
RCIN 1101143
PROVENANCE Made for display in The Queen's Gallery

THE KING'S BOOKS (NOS. 206–247)

206. Gilbert Burnet, Bishop of Salisbury

(1643–1715)

*Bishop Burnet's History of his own Time. Volume I,
from the restoration of Charles II*, 1724

London: Thomas Ward
[16,] 836 pp. Printed. Bound in red goatskin, gold tooled, with
the arms of George II as Prince of Wales on boards. 47.2 × 31.0 cm
(18⁹⁄₁₆″ × 12³⁄₁₆″)
RCIN 1027878
PROVENANCE George II as Prince of Wales; George III
(Windsor Library Catalogue 1780, f. 31)

Although George II presented the old Royal Library to the
newly founded British Museum in 1757, a small number of
books appear to have been kept back from this gift. In 1760
these passed into the possession of George II's grandson and
successor, George III; they remain in their original bindings.

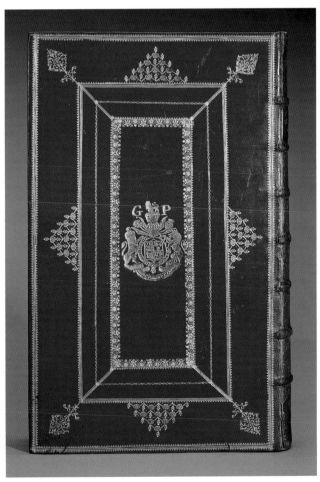

206

Burnet, the son of an Aberdeen lawyer, was a popular preacher
and at one time chaplain to Charles II. His opposition to
Catholicism, in the last years of Charles II's reign when both
the King and his brother (later James II) were supporters of
'popery', led to his final dismissal and retirement to the
continent. Burnet wrote several biographical works and
a history of the Reformation, but his best-known publication
was his *History of his own Time*. This copy of volume I appears
to have been bound for George II when Prince of Wales
(1714–27), as may be seen by the label of difference on the
coat of arms, by the initials *GP* (*Georgius Princeps*; Prince
George) and the Prince of Wales's motto *Ich Dien* (I serve),
incorrectly spelt. This is an example of a panel binding, the
frames produced by the use of roll tools. The three main
frames use the same tool, a series of longer 'hyphens' topped
with a shorter one, used back to back on the outer frame
and on the outer edge of the two inner frames. The floral
roll used on the inner frame has as recurring features a sun
(with a face), an anthemion and a daisy; a similar roll tool
was used on bindings done for the library of Robert (1661–
1724) and Edward (1689–1741) Harley, Earls of Oxford
(Nixon 1978, pp. 138–41). This binding also shows another,
earlier example of the pyramid-shaped decorations that occur
on the Desaguliers binding (no. 210) on the sides of the
middle frame, which have been built up using only three
different tools. The floral lozenges on the corners of the
middle frame were also a popular mode of decoration.

207. Edward Hyde, 1st Earl of Clarendon

(1609–1674)

The Life of Edward Earl of Clarendon, 1759

Oxford: Clarendon Press
[10,] 534 pp. Printed. Bound in red sheepskin, gold tooled,
with the arms of the University of Oxford on boards.
47.7 × 30.7 cm (18¾″ × 12¹⁄₁₆″)
RCIN 1023375
PROVENANCE Presented by the University of Oxford to the
future George III, May 1760; George III (Windsor Library
Catalogue 1780, f. 30)

Edward Hyde began his career as a lawyer and an MP, and
became one of the closest advisers of both Charles I, during
the period 1641–5, and then of Charles II during his exile
before the restoration of the monarchy in 1660. In that year
Hyde's daughter Anne married the King's brother, the future

James II; Hyde's granddaughters succeeded to the throne as Mary II and Queen Anne. He was created Earl of Clarendon in 1661, but became unpopular as Lord Chancellor and was exiled for life in 1667. During his exile he composed his autobiography, *The Life of Edward Earl of Clarendon*, which was also later incorporated into his revised version of his *History of the Rebellion*, an account of events during the Civil War, down to 1660. A more successful part of his life after 1660 was his chancellorship of Oxford University, which he was keen to restore to its old reputation. His manuscripts were left to the university on his death, and the profits from the *History of the Rebellion* were used to build a home for the University Press. The autobiography of one of its chief benefactors, printed at the Clarendon Press, was therefore an appropriate gift from Oxford University to the future King. (For the 1767–86 edition of Clarendon's *State Papers*, also from George III's library, see no. 237.)

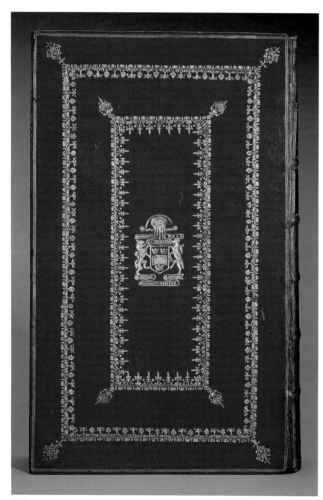

207

The fine panel binding was probably done in Oxford, the frames built up with a series of one- and three-line, and floral roll tools; the outer edge of the two decorated frames uses the same tool. The inner edge of the innermost frame is formed of a delicate dentelle tool; the corners of the frames carry ornaments featuring crowns and sceptres. The arms of the University of Oxford appear in the middle, with supporters and the university's mottoes: *Dominus Illuminatio Mea* (the Lord is my light), and *Bonitas Liberabit, Regnabit Veritas* (Goodness shall liberate, truth shall rule).

208. Robert Adam (1728–1792)

Ruins of the palace of the Emperor Diocletian at Spalatro, 1764

[s.l.]: Robert Adam
xii, 34 pp., 61 pl. Printed. Bound in red goatskin, gold tooled.
53.7 × 39.2 cm (21⅛″ × 15⁷⁄₁₆″)
RCIN 1071086
PROVENANCE Presented by the author to George III, 1764; George III (Windsor Library Catalogue 1780, f. 66)
LITERATURE Nixon 1978, pp. 160–61; Brown (I.G.) 1992; Brown (I.G.) 1993

Robert Adam is today known as one of the foremost practitioners of the neo-classical style of architecture (see no. 95). The son of the architect, builder and entrepreneur William Adam, he undertook the Grand Tour (1754–8) after his university education, though with more constructive ambitions towards the antique than most of his contemporaries. He became acquainted with archaeologists and architects, and designed fantasy buildings based upon what he saw in Rome. The climax of his tour was Dalmatia, which he visited in 1757 in the company of the French architect Charles-Louis Clérisseau (1721–1820) and two other draughtsmen. Clérisseau's speciality was in fantasy buildings or actual buildings set in imagined, romantic landscapes, and he was to provide the picturesque views and romanticised images of the palace at Spalato (formerly Spalatro; now Split) for Adam's *magnum opus*. The publication of large folio volumes of illustrations of the antique was in its heyday, and offered a perfect opportunity for Adam to make his name and challenge his rivals with a magnificent production. Adam took seven years to produce his volume after the visit to Dalmatia, finally publishing it in 1764. The engravings were supplied by Francesco Bartolozzi among others and the publication may be seen as part of Adam's single-minded ambition to

208

establish himself as the leading architect in England as well as Scotland.

In his presentation copies of this magnificent book, Adam appears to have used a hierarchy of binding colour and ornamentation, appropriate to the importance of the recipients. Royal recipients, and institutions with royal patronage, received red goatskin bindings; friends and lesser patrons received mottled brown calf bindings; and it has been suggested (based on two surviving copies) that members of the Orders of the Garter or of the Thistle received, respectively, blue and green coloured bindings. The present binding is clearly one of the royal presentation copies, in red goatskin, with the Royal Arms in the central ornament, shaped like a Roman shield. The anthemion border, in neo-classical style, is common to all copies, but where this and other high-status copies really stand out is in the dentelle (lace-like) work, featuring a marvellous jumble of figures such as mermaids, trophies, tridents, rosettes and garlands. The style is part neo-classical, part rococo. The volume was dedicated to George III and at least two copies were presented to him: the present one, and an almost identical copy now in the British Library. The binder is not known.

209. Joshua Kirby (1716–1774)

Dr Brook Taylor's method of perspective made easy, 1765

Open at part II, p. 40, pl. XIV B.II
London: Joshua Kirby
2 pts in 1: x, 70 pp., 14 pl.; viii, 66 pp., 21 pl. Printed. Bound in red calf, gold tooled, rebacked, with George III's large crown finishing tool (no. 195) in centre. 55.0 × 38.0 cm (21⅝″ × 14¹⁵⁄₁₆″)
RCIN 1150780
PROVENANCE Presumably presented by the author to George III (Windsor Library Catalogue 1780, f. 97)
LITERATURE Harris (E.) and Savage 1990, pp. 254–8; Owen 1995; *Chambers* 1996, pp. 41–2

Kirby was born in Suffolk and initially worked there as a painter and topographer. With the encouragement of William Hogarth he became a specialist in perspective – particularly for architecture – and in 1754 published (by subscription) his first manual on the art of perspective, based on the work of the mathematician Brook Taylor (1685–1731). Shortly before the book's publication Kirby was made an honorary member of the St Martin's Lane Academy, where he lectured on perspective. Through Bute's influence, in 1756 he was appointed 'Drawing Master' to the future George III, in which capacity he gave lessons in both landscape and architectural perspective (see nos. 56, 57). Following his accession, the King continued to support Kirby and his son, William. As Joint Clerks of the Works at Richmond and Kew Palaces from 1761 they were close both to the King and to Chambers, for whose publication on Kew the elder Kirby supplied three designs (see no. 121). Later in the same decade the King funded William's extensive architectural studies in Italy (see Oppé 1950, p. 70).

This is the second edition of Kirby's *The Perspective of Architecture*. When it was first issued in 1761 it was made clear that the publication had been 'Begun by command of His Present Majesty, when Prince of Wales, by Joshua Kirby, Designer in Perspective to His Majesty'. The 1761 edition was dedicated to the King, who had evidently funded the publication. In addition to a celebrated frontispiece by Hogarth, it included two plates made on the basis of designs supplied by the King himself (see no. 57). George III's close involvement with the publication is further indicated by the text of his 'Architectural Treatise' (RA GEO/Add. 32/1742-60), which is the equivalent of a first draft of Kirby's 'Description and Use of a New Instrument called the Architectonic Sector', incorporated into the 1761 publication.

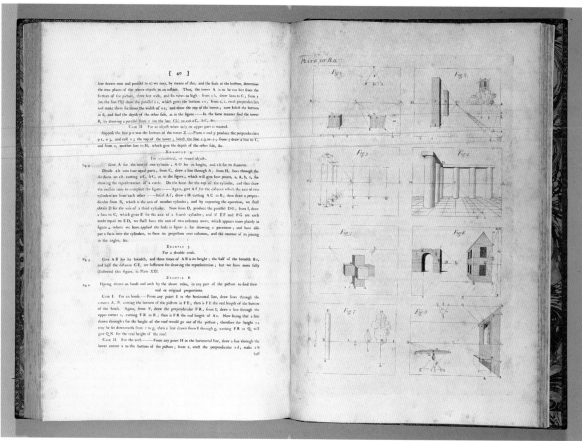

209

The 1765 edition (shown here) indicates that the author was by now 'Designer in perspective to their Majesties': Queen Charlotte had evidently also begun to take lessons with Kirby – her 'architectural protractor', inscribed by Kirby and dated 1765, is in the Museum of the History of Science, Oxford (see Turner 1992). However, 'this more perfect Edition of my Book' was dedicated to the Earl of Bute. Kirby divided his work into two parts, bound in a single volume, containing an introduction to the use of perspective and an explanation of the practice of perspective. The displayed opening falls within chapter III of part II, concerning the rules of perspective 'more particularly applied to Common Practice'. The diagrams and figures provide explanations for the text. Of the eight figures shown here, explanations of figures 4 (cylindrical or round objects) and 5 (a double cross), with parts of 3 (adjustments of perspective scale) and 6 (placement of a house in a picture) can be found on the facing page.

In general, Kirby's publications were well received. However, they were later dismissed by Thomas Malton as 'puerile in a degree beyond belief'.

210. Thomas Desaguliers (1725?–1780)

An account of the state and service of the artillery, 1765

[8,] 107 ff., 27 pl. Manuscript on paper. Bound in red goatskin with blue onlay, gold tooled, with George III's arms. 52.6 × 38.3 cm (20 11/16″ × 15 1/16″)
RCIN 1087907
PROVENANCE Presented by the author to George III, 1765; excluded from George IV's gift of the King's Library to the British Museum (noted in vol. II of the manuscript catalogue, RCIN 1028961, f. 10)

Thomas Desaguliers was a member of the Royal Artillery and, with the rank of Captain, was made Chief Firemaster at the Woolwich Arsenal in 1748, a post he held until his death, as Lieutenant-General, in 1780; his father, J.T. Desaguliers, was chaplain to Frederick, Prince of Wales. He brought a new scientific approach to the art of gunnery and the making of cannon. Active service at the Siege of Belleisle, off the west coast of France, in 1761, where he took command of the artillery force, enabled him to put his experimental ideas on artillery to practical use, and contributed strongly to the success of the British engagement. On his return to Woolwich he was made Colonel-Commandant of the Royal Regiment of Artillery, and spent the rest of his life on his experiments, particularly with rockets; he also created instruments, still in use a hundred years later, for examining the bores of cannon. In 1763 he was elected a Fellow of the Royal Society. When the King and Queen visited the Royal Artillery at Woolwich Warren in 1770, they were given a guided tour of the Royal Laboratory by Desaguliers. Later they attended a demonstration of a heavy 12-pounder gun fired twenty-three times with shot in a minute. According to newspaper reports of the day, this 'surpassed any quick firing ever yet practiced [*sic*]. The method is entirely new and supposed to be the invention of Colonel Desaguliers' (Hogg 1963, I, pp. 436–7).

This manuscript is a report of the state of the artillery in the British army; a second copy was made for George III's brothers, Edward, Duke of York, and William Henry, Duke of Gloucester (RCIN 1085816). The present copy was prepared for George III and was given a splendid mosaic binding, with blue and cream onlay (patches of leather laid over the base leather), and blue and gold painting on the fore edges. A variety

of single tools – including birds, palm leaves and several floral designs – was used to build up the elaborate pattern. For example, the pyramids on the edges of the inner frame were built up from at least ten individual tools; compare the simplicity of a similar decorative scheme on the Burnet binding (no. 206). Simpler roll tools were used to create straight edges for the frames. Within a sunburst in the middle are the Royal Arms, and the initials *GR* (*Georgius Rex*; King George).

211. Daniel Paterson (1739–1825)

Plan of Warley Common (1778), in 'Encampments in South Britain, 1778–82', 1784

120 pp. Watercolour and ink. Bound in red goatskin, gold tooled, blue label on front board. 37.5 × 54.5 cm (14¾″ × 21⁷⁄₁₆″)
RCIN 734032 (p. 53)
PROVENANCE Presented by Major-General George Morrison to George III, *c.*1784 (Military Maps Catalogue, f. 97)
LITERATURE Hodson (forthcoming)

The encampments recorded in this volume were part of the national effort to produce a well-trained professional army, following British defeats in America and in the light of a possible war with France. The King frequently visited the camps to inform himself of the state of the army, and also to boost the morale of his troops. The camp at Warley Common, south of Brentwood, Essex, from 28 May to 11 November 1778, was also recorded in watercolour by Thomas Sandby (no. 193). It consisted of four battalions of 'Regulars' and eight of militia, in addition to '2 corps with the Artillery', amounting to around 10,000 soldiers in all, under the command of Lieutenant-General Pierson. With the exactly contemporary camp at Cox Heath, it was one of the two largest encampments of the period.

The main events of the royal visit to Warley camp, on 20 October 1778, were recorded in a pair of paintings by P.J. de Loutherbourg (see no. 163). According to contemporary reports, the royal couple remained among the military exercises between 10 a.m. and 4 p.m., and revisited the camp after dinner. Their residence for the nights of 19 and 20 October – Thorndon Hall, the seat of Lord Petre – is shown at upper right on the plan, which also includes an explanation of 'the manoeuvres performed before His Majesty'.

This volume is part of George III's collection of military maps and plans, which was retained in royal ownership when the King's Library was presented to the British Museum in

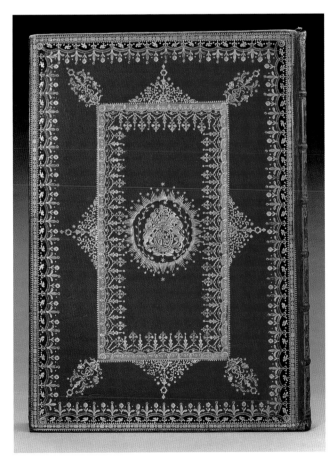

210

the 1820s (see Hodson 1988). A companion volume concerns encampments in southern Britain between 1756 and 1762 (RCIN 731068). Both volumes were dedicated to the King by George Morrison (1704?–99), Quarter-Master-General of the army, and remain in their original ornately decorated bindings. The Royal Collection contains a number of other plans by both Morrison and Paterson, chiefly dating from the period 1746–8 when they were serving under William, Duke of Cumberland, in the Netherlands. Morrison, an accomplished military engineer, surveyor and draughtsman, had a long association with the King and his family. Daniel Paterson, assistant to the Quarter-Master-General, was one of the most accomplished cartographers active in England in the later eighteenth century. He became Lieutenant-Governor of Quebec in 1812 but is best known for his Road Books, the first edition of which (*A New & Accurate Description of all the Direct & Principal Cross Roads in Great Britain*, 1771) was dedicated to Morrison.

212. Jacob Bryant (1715–1804)

A List of Books Given to the King by Mr Bryant October 1st, 1782

Open at f. 3
28 ff. Manuscript in pen and ink. Bound in marbled paper cover.
23.0 × 18.8 cm (9^1⁄$_{16}$″ × 7^3⁄$_8$″)
RCIN 1145267.a
PROVENANCE Presented by Jacob Bryant to George III, 1782
(King's College Archives, ff. 1–5)
LITERATURE Attar 2002

By the 1780s, George III's library at Buckingham House was at the peak of its development. John Adams, the first American minister to Great Britain (subsequently second President of the United States), who visited it in 1783, was struck with admiration. The King had been acquiring books, not merely by purchase but also by gift. The 1782 gift from Jacob Bryant was, however, exceptional in both its scale and its bibliographical importance. Bryant was an antiquary, educated at Eton and King's College, Cambridge. He became

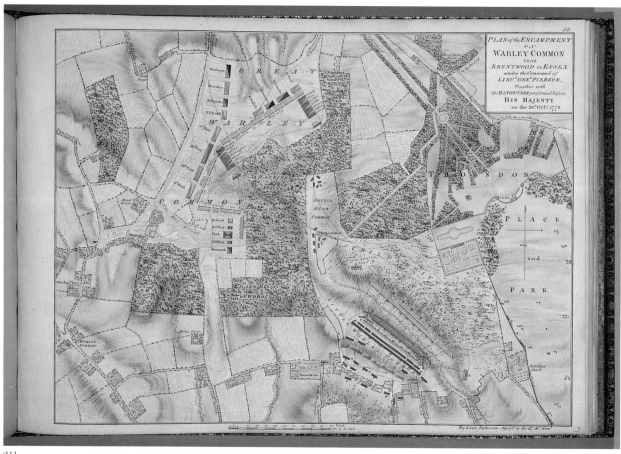

211

a Fellow of King's and private tutor to the Marquis of Blandford, later 4th Duke of Marlborough (and George III's Lord Chamberlain), from whom he received considerable patronage, including the run of the library at Blenheim Palace and an annual pension of £1,000. By 1786 Bryant was living in Cippenham near Windsor, and became well acquainted with the court of George III. The novelist Fanny Burney, then Second Keeper of the Robes to Queen Charlotte, mentioned him frequently in her diaries as a highly engaging man of great intelligence and dry humour. In 1782 he listed ninety-two incunables (books from the infancy or cradle of printing, 1450–1500) to be presented to George III; twenty-seven of these finally came to the King and are included in Bryant's list. (At least thirty-eight of the remainder are in King's College, Cambridge.) This manuscript catalogue, in Bryant's own hand, describes the gift and to some extent reveals his selection criteria. His chief concerns were the rarity of the item, the quality of the printing and the edition. Item 9 (Seneca's *Tragoediae*, no. 213) and item 11 (Sidonius Apollinaris) for example were the first printed editions, while items 8 and 10 were described as 'very ancient'. Other rarities that Bryant presented were a Sarum

Missal, printed entirely on vellum (item 27 in Bryant's list, no. 214) and two works printed by William Caxton, the first English printer. All these books were excluded from George IV's gift to the British Museum.

213. Seneca (*c*.4 BC–AD 65)

Tragoediae, 1478

Ferrara: Andreas Belfortis
348 pp. Printed. Bound in red sheepskin, gold tooled, with George III's arms on the boards.
31.3 × 21.8 cm (12 5/16″ × 8 9/16″)
RCIN 1057904
PROVENANCE Charles Spencer, 3rd Duke of Marlborough (1706–58); by whom given to Jacob Bryant, by 1755; by whom presented to George III, 1782 (item 9 of Bryant's list, no. 212)
LITERATURE ISTC is00433000

Seneca the Younger, or the Philosopher, is well known to history both as tutor to the Emperor Nero and as a writer of prose and poetry. The most important of his poetical works to survive were his nine Tragedies adapted from Greek originals. This is the first printed Latin edition, produced in Ferrara, the domain of the Este family, and a centre for artists and writers from all over Europe. Its first printing press was established in 1471, but Ferrara never achieved great success as a printing centre. The Frenchman André Beaufort (Andreas Belfortis) was the most prolific printer in Ferrara during the incunable period (1450–1500).

The inclusion of this volume in Bryant's gift to George III may be attributed to its status as *editio princeps* (first printed edition) of an important classical work, and to Bryant's perception of its rarity. The comment 'not mentioned by De Buré' (Guillaume François de Bure, author of a seven-volume bibliography on rare books, published 1763–8) occurs frequently in Bryant's manuscript catalogue (no. 212) as an indication of assumed rarity, and he saw this edition of Seneca as no exception. An inscription at the back of the book (*dono mihi datum ab Honorabiss. C:S – D.M*) suggests that it was given to Bryant by Charles Spencer, 3rd Duke of Marlborough.

Like the majority of books included in Bryant's gift of incunables to George III, this volume was rebound in the Buckingham House bindery. The simple panel design (see illustration on p. 225) uses a variety of three- and two-line roll tools, with floral lozenges at the corners of the centre frame and a decorated roll inside the inner frame. The Royal

212

Arms appear in the centre. The spine is tooled with other floral devices, a lozenge, corner tools and roll tools. Some of these finishing tools still survive and are displayed alongside (nos. 196–8).

214. *Sarum Missal*, 1497

Open at f. CVI (the Resurrection)
Rouen: Martin Morin
574 pp. Printed on vellum with hand-coloured woodcut illustrations. Bound in brown calf with onlaid black calf central panels, with George III's arms, rebacked.
38.9 × 27.5 cm (15 ⁵⁄₁₆″ × 10¹³⁄₁₆″)
RCIN 1057923
PROVENANCE Jacob Bryant; by whom presented to George III, 1782 (item 27 of Bryant's list, no. 212)
LITERATURE ISTC im00721000

This Missal, or service book for the Mass, is one of the rarest items presented to George III by Jacob Bryant (see no. 212). It is one of seven extant copies (of which four are incomplete) and the only surviving copy printed entirely on vellum. It was produced in Rouen, the third-ranking printing centre in France after Paris and Lyons, for the English market. The Use of Sarum (the form of the Mass used in Salisbury and its neighbouring dioceses) was not common outside England, but was the most widely accepted Use within England until the Reformation. Its most striking deviation from the Roman rite was its elaborate ceremonial, particularly in the rituals leading up to and during Easter, when several imposing and colourful processions were staged.

The volume is open at the page for the celebration of Easter Day. In the large woodcut illustration the resurrected Christ is shown emerging from a coffin, with the marks of the nails in his hands and feet (the Stigmata). Saints Peter (bearded) and John stand to the left of Christ and the Three Maries stand to the right, each holding their cask of ointment, which they had brought to anoint the dead body of Christ. The soldiers set to guard the tomb lie sleeping at the foot of the picture, and Jerusalem appears in the background. The image was originally printed in black and then somewhat clumsily over-painted. The two angels in the lower border hold an empty shield, which could have been used by an owner of the book to fill in his own coat of arms.

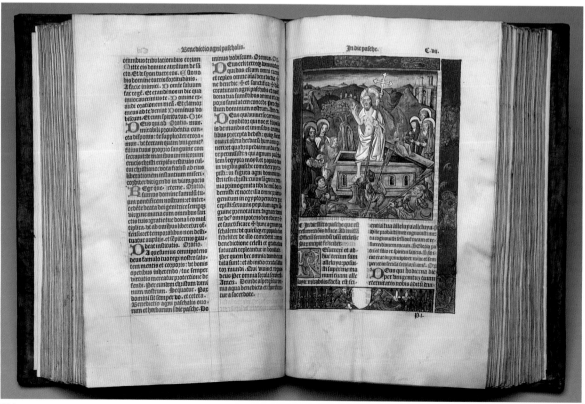

214

215. John Chamberlaine (1745–1812); Francesco Bartolozzi (1727–1815), engraver

Imitations of original drawings by Hans Holbein, in the collection of His Majesty, I, 1800

Open at Queen Jane Seymour
London: John Chamberlaine
86 pp., 42 pl. Printed. Bound in brown calf, gold tooled, rebacked in red goatskin. 55.0 × 43.2 cm (21⅝″ × 17″)
RCIN 809364.a
PROVENANCE Presumably presented by John Chamberlaine to George III, *c.*1800
LITERATURE Parker 1983, pp. 20–22; Roberts (J.) 1993, p. 23

The appearance of Chamberlaine's *Imitations* of Holbein's portrait drawings in the Royal Collection was an important landmark in making public the contents of that great collection. Holbein's drawings – originally housed in a 'great book' – had passed in and out of royal ownership since the mid-sixteenth century, finally returning there before 1675 (see Parker 1983). They were 'rediscovered' in a bureau in Kensington Palace in 1727 by George II's wife, Caroline of Ansbach, who framed and hung them at her favourite residence, Richmond Lodge (see no. 120); by the 1740s they had been returned to Kensington; under George III they were unframed and remounted in two volumes. During these years several unsuccessful attempts were made (particularly by George Vertue) to publish the drawings. Between 1774 and his death in 1791, Richard Dalton – George III's first Librarian – had engraved copies of thirty-five of Holbein's drawings. Thirty-three of these plates were published by W. Richardson in 1792 as *The Court of Henry the Eighth*; there are loose impressions of a number of subjects in the Royal Collection and the British Museum. The quality of Dalton's reproductive prints was uniformly poor.

John Chamberlaine is first named in George III's Privy Purse accounts in 1772 when he was paid 'for Modelling various Fortifications' and 'for Drawing Plans &c' (RA GEO/17272). On Dalton's death in February 1791 he was appointed Keeper of Drawings and Medals to the King, working alongside the Librarian, Frederick Augusta Barnard (who assumed the additional responsibility of the drawings and medals on Chamberlaine's death). The eighty-four plates included in Chamberlaine's *Imitations* of Holbein's drawings were

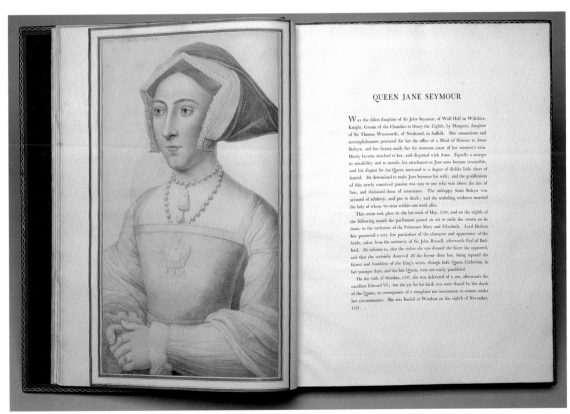

215

published serially between March 1792 and February 1800; Chamberlaine's Introduction is dated 4 June 1800, which is the date of the publication of the complete series. The publication appeared in fourteen parts; each part included six plates, with accompanying text by Edmund Lodge, Lancaster Herald. All but four of the plates were engraved by Francesco Bartolozzi, the Florentine engraver transported to England by Dalton in 1764 and 'bound' to work for Dalton for the following three years. In 1768 Bartolozzi was appointed engraver to the King; he signed most of his Holbein plates as 'Historical Engraver to his Majesty'.

The first important series of reproductive prints relating to drawings in the Royal Collection was Bartolozzi's engraving after drawings by Guercino; these were probably partly produced in Italy, shortly before the King's purchase of the original drawings, which included no. 186. After the *Imitations* of Holbein's drawings, Chamberlaine published a selection of the King's other Old Master drawings as *Original Designs of the Most Celebrated Masters of the Bolognese, Roman . . . Schools*, issued serially between 1795 and 1807. He acted as publisher, editor and general co-ordinator of both these publications.

The opening shows Bartolozzi's reproduction (issued in March 1795) of Holbein's study of 1536/7 for his portrait of Jane Seymour, third consort of Henry VIII and mother of Edward VI. She was originally lady-in-waiting to Henry's previous Queens, Catherine of Aragon and Anne Boleyn, and married the King in 1536. She died shortly after giving birth to the King's son and was Henry VIII's favourite wife.

Although the advertisement for Chamberlaine's publication stressed its importance for connoisseurs and artists – many of whom 'have never heard that such a collection is extant, and very few indeed have ever seen the originals' – the text accompanying the individual plates provides historical and genealogical information concerning the sitters. In the circumstances, it was not surprising that Holbein's drawings were 'completed', and the colouring enhanced, by Bartolozzi. The folio publication was reissued in 1823. At the Prince Regent's suggestion, a quarto edition was issued in 1812 (see Dyson 1983).

AGRICULTURE AND HORTICULTURE (nos. 216–219)

216. George III (1738–1820)
Essay on agriculture

Open at pp. 2–3
Manuscript. 2ff. 35.5 × 22.7 cm (14″ × 8¹⁵⁄₁₆″)
RA GEO/Add. 32/2020–21
PROVENANCE Presumed to be part of the papers of George III and George IV taken by the 1st Duke of Wellington (executor to George IV) to Apsley House where they were rediscovered in 1912 and returned to Windsor Castle (see De Bellaigue (S.) 1998)
LITERATURE Roberts (J.) 1997, pp. 71–5

George III's papers at Windsor include a number of 'essays' or 'treatises', most of which are thought to date from the late 1750s. However some – such as the essay on the loss of the American colonies (RA GEO/Add. 32/2010) – are clearly later. In this essay the King points out that an industry such as agriculture, which uses home-produced materials, is more profitable to the nation than one which uses imports. He advocates the improvement of pasture lands so that they can be converted to arable crops, and the introduction of crop rotation. He opens his account by stating: 'Agriculture is beyond all doubt the foundation of every other art, business

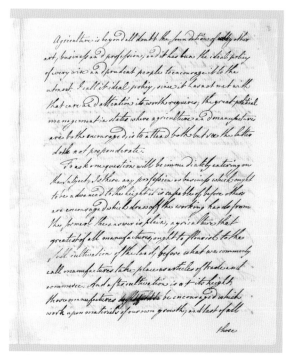

216 (p. 1)

and profession; and it has been the ideal policy of every wise and prudent people to encourage it to the utmost' (p. 1).

In April 1787 the King's 'Further remarks on Duckett's mode of Cultivation' was published in Arthur Young's *Annals of Agriculture*, under the pseudonym of Ralph Robinson, the King's shepherd at Windsor. Similar topics were discussed and elaborated upon in Nathaniel Kent's publications, and in his journals (see no. 219) concerning the Windsor farming ventures in the 1790s, the period of the King's greatest agricultural activity and the time of the publication of Gillray's caricature of 'Farmer George' (fig. 6).

217. John Hill (1716?–1775)

The Vegetable System, plates, I, 1759

Open at plate 48 (Asters)
London: John Hill
108 ff. Printed, hand-coloured illustrations. Bound in brown calf, gold tooled, with George III's arms.
45.5 × 29.0 cm (17^{15}⁄$_{16}$″ × 11^{7}⁄$_{16}$″)
RCIN 1050566
PROVENANCE Presumably presented by the author to George III (Kew Library Catalogue 1780, f. 38; Kew Library Catalogue 1785, f. 38)
LITERATURE Desmond 1995, pp. 36–40, 63

John Hill was a controversial figure, an apothecary and botanist – who also at various times was an actor, a playwright, and a gossip writer – and indulged in pamphlet campaigns against bodies such as the Royal Society which did not, in his opinion, give him his due recognition. Notwithstanding his somewhat dubious record, by the end of the 1750s he had come under the patronage of John Stuart, 3rd Earl of Bute who, as a fellow botanist, encouraged him in his project to publish his massive work, *The Vegetable System*, a contribution to systematic botany on Linnaean lines. It ran to 26 folio volumes of text, with 1,600 copperplate engravings, published between 1759 and 1775. The dedication in the first volume is to George III, then still Prince of Wales. The work won Hill the Swedish Order of the Vasa from the King of Sweden in 1774, and in the last two volumes of text he is named as Sir John Hill, on the strength of this honour. George III's copy is bound as nine volumes of text and nine of hand-coloured plates, and is listed in both the 1780 and the 1785 catalogues of his Kew Library, as are several of Hill's other books on botany.

In 1758 Hill had produced a pamphlet proposing the creation of a botanical garden at Kensington Palace (George II's residence), and early in 1761 his patron, Lord Bute, secured the post of gardener there for him. Under the same aegis,

216 (pp. 2–3)

217

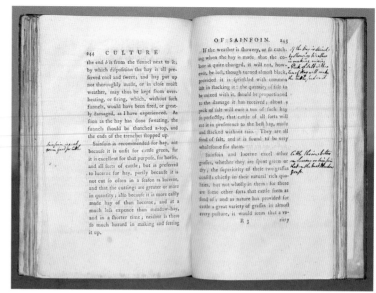

218

Hill also seems to have occupied some role in the royal botanical gardens at Kew. He is referred to by some sources as Superintendent, but there is no evidence that any such appointment was made. Whatever his status there, his *Hortus Kewensis* (1768), listing the plants grown in Kew Gardens according to their botanical classification, certainly shows familiarity with the gardens, and is dedicated to Augusta, Princess of Wales.

218. *The improved culture of three principal grasses*, 1775

Open at pp. 244–5
London: G. Robinson
[16,] 320 pp. Printed, with manuscript annotations.
Bound in brown calf, rebacked.
21.9 × 14.8 cm (8⅝″ × 5¹³⁄₁₆″)
RCIN 1057372
PROVENANCE George III (Kew Library Catalogue 1780, f. 35; Windsor Library Catalogue 1780, f. 90)
LITERATURE Cloake 1996, pp. 117–21, 125–6, 148; Roberts (J.) 1997, pp. 59, 71–5, 544

George III was keenly interested in improving crops and stock-breeding, an interest almost certainly aroused by Lord

Bute, whose own early adulthood was spent 'amusing himself with the study of agriculture, botany and architecture'. From the 1760s George III was improving the estates he had inherited at Richmond and Kew, which included two farms, and by the mid-1780s he was also farming in the Little Park in Windsor. His experiments in breeding Merino sheep to improve wool quality, under the supervision of Sir Joseph Banks, included public auctions of surplus stock. Until 1790, however, the King had no direct input in the running of Richmond and Windsor Great Parks. On the deaths in 1790 and 1792 respectively of the Duke of Cumberland and Lord Bute, George III took both Rangerships himself, and employed Nathaniel Kent (see no. 219) as Land Agent. For the next decade he was assiduous in his frequent inspections of improvements to parkland and farms in Windsor Great Park.

In his 1791 proposals for Windsor, Kent states that 'any judicious and well applied Experiments made by His Majesty in the present Instance, would stand so conspicuously pre-eminent, that Noblemen, and Gentlemen, would follow so striking an Example' (Kent 1791, ff. 4–5). The King's substantial collection of books on agricultural improvement, listed in the Kew Library catalogues of 1780 and 1785, was transferred to Windsor in the 1790s, necessitating the insertion of an extra leaf in the Windsor catalogue. Many of these books were given in 1927 to the library of the School of Agriculture in Cambridge (since 1974 in Cambridge University Library). This volume on improvement of pasture, and several of Young's publications, remain in the Royal Library.

The marginal annotations in the present publication are in the King's hand: 'Sainfoin is good green food for Cattle'; 'If the Hay is stained by Showery Weather in making, mixing a Peck of Salt with a Ton of Hay will make the Cattle feed on it'; 'Cattle thrive better on Lucerne or Sainfoin that [*sic*] on the best Meadow Grass.' Each provides an *aide-mémoire* of the salient point of a paragraph, presumably to speed up reference to the volume by a practising farmer.

219. Nathaniel Kent (1737–1810)

Journal of the progressive improvements in Windsor Great Park, II, 1793–4

Open at f. 47 with fold-out plan of Norfolk Farm 195 ff.
Manuscript, watercolour and ink diagrams. Bound in red goatskin, gold tooled. 25.5 × 20.4 cm (10 1/16″ × 8 1/16″)
RCIN 1047478
PROVENANCE Written for George III
LITERATURE Kent 1791, ff. 15–17; Cloake 1996, pp. 117–18; Roberts (J.) 1997, pp. 67, 73–5

Nathaniel Kent became an agricultural consultant after studying Flemish methods of cultivation, then considered the most efficient in Europe, while a diplomat in Brussels. Much of his work was based in Norfolk, a county well suited to the Flemish methods, and renowned for its agricultural innovation, with such land-owners as Thomas Coke of Holkham. As the senior land agent of a partnership that included his nephew, William Pearce, and John Claridge, he was asked in 1791 to submit proposals for managing Windsor Great Park for George III (see no. 218).

Kent's proposals were approved, and his agency was engaged to manage the park; in 1792 they took on Richmond Park as well, and managed both for a decade. He kept a journal of all their visits to Windsor, of decisions made, instructions given and work carried out. This, the second volume of the journal, covering 1793 and 1794, includes a plan of Norfolk Farm, the 400-hectare (1,000-acre) farm established by George III to the south-west of Cumberland Lodge. In 1791 Kent had proposed that: 'This Farm from its congeniality of Soil to that of many parts of Norfolk, might be called the Norfolk Farm . . . The Turnip System should be adopted upon it and Cooke's drilling and hoeing Machine may be used with great Advantage' (Kent 1791, ff. 21–2). On later pages of Kent's journal, he illustrated the King's own design for a dwelling for a farm labourer (pp. 98–100; see Roberts (J.) 1997, p. 68).

Kent's suggestions for improving the parkland include planting copses to vary the view, and removing dead trees and some of those in straight lines. These echo the recommenda-tions of the landscape-gardener Humphry Repton (1752–1818), whose *Sketches and Hints on Landscape Gardening* (1794) the King claimed to be impatient to read. Both that volume and Kent's own *Hints to Gentlemen of Landed Property* (3rd edn, 1793) appear in his Windsor Library Catalogue.

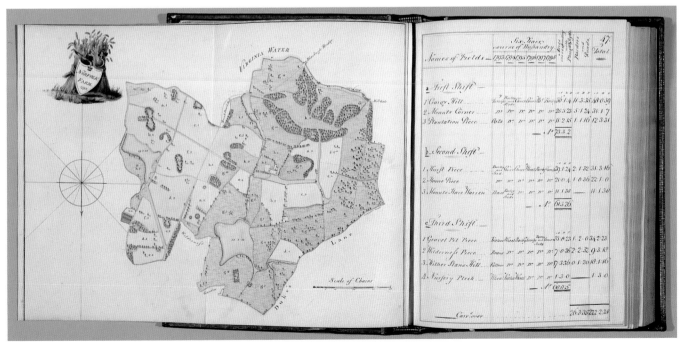

219

THE KING'S BOOKS, DISPLAYED IN THE VILE BOOKCASES (nos. 220–247)

The following books from George III's library, listed in chronological order of publication, are displayed on the shelves of Vile's bookcases, nos. 267 and 268. (See also illustration on p. 220.)

220. Fulvio Orsini (1529–1600)

Familiae Romanae quae reperiuntur in antiquis numismatibus ab urbe condita ad tempora Divi Augusti ex bibliotheca Fulvi Ursini, 1577

Rome: Giuseppe degli Angeli
Printed. Vellum binding. 36.0 × 25.0 cm (14 3/16″ × 9 13/16″)
RCIN 1076269

221. Aelian (*c.*170–235)

Sophistae varia historia, 1701. 2 vols.

Leiden: Johannes du Vivie and Isaac Severinus
Printed. Red goatskin binding, gold tooled spine.
20.3 × 12.6 cm (8″ × 4 15/16″)
RCIN 1058715–16

222. *Degl' istorici delle cose Veneziane*, 1718–22. 10 vols. in 11

Venice: il Lovisa
Printed. Red goatskin binding, gold tooled spine.
28.2 × 20.5 cm (11 1/8″ × 8 1/16″)
RCIN 1029395–405

223. William Holder (1616–1698)

A Treatise of the Natural Grounds, and Principles of Harmony, 1731

London: J. Wilcox and T. Osborne
Printed. Brown calf binding, gold tooled spine.
20.5 × 13.0 cm (8 1/16″ × 5 1/8″)
RCIN 1073037

224. Jacque-Auguste de Thou (1553–1617)

Histoire universelle, 1734. 16 vols.

London: [s.n.]
Printed. Red goatskin binding, gold tooled spine.
29.1 × 22.5 cm (11 7/16″ × 8 7/8″)
RCIN 1047769–84

225. Robert Estienne (1503–1559)

Thesaurus linguae latinae, new edn, 1734–5. 4 vols.

London: Samuel Harding
Printed. Vellum binding. 43.0 × 29.3 cm (16 15/16″ × 11 9/16″)
RCIN 1055396–9

226. Giovanni Battista Passeri (1694–1780); Vincenzo Franceschini (1680–*c.*1744), engraver

Lucernae fictiles musei passerii, 1739–51. 3 vols.

Pisa: Gavelli
Printed. Vellum binding. 36.6 × 25.8 cm (14 7/16″ × 10 3/16″)
RCIN 1079266–8

227. Alessandro Tassoni (1565–1635)

La Secchia rapita: poema eroicomico, 1744

Modena: Bartolommeo Soliani
Printed. Vellum binding. 27.5 × 21.8 cm (10 13/16″ × 8 9/16″)
RCIN 1121304

228. Johann Ludolf Walther (d. 1752)

Lexicon diplomaticum, 1745

Göttingen: Johann Peter and Johann Wilhelm Schmidt
Printed. Vellum binding. 45.7 × 30.5 cm (18″ × 12″)
RCIN 1055395

229. Colluthus of Lycopolis (5th century)

Raptus Helenae, 1747

Leeuwarden: Willem Coulon
Printed. Red goatskin binding, George III floral monogram on boards. 20.8 × 13.0 cm (8 3/16″ × 5 1/8″)
RCIN 1058010

230. Jean de Ferreras (1652–1735)

Histoire generale d'Espagne, traduit . . . par M. D'Hermilly, 1751. 10 vols.

Paris: Gissey [*et al.*]
Printed. Brown calf binding, gold tooled spine.
27.5 × 21.6 cm (10 13/16″ × 8 1/2″)
RCIN 1028731–40

231. William Gibson (1680?–1750)

A New Treatise on the Diseases of Horses, 2nd edn, 1754. 2 vols.

London: A. Millar
Printed. Brown calf binding, gold tooled spine.
20.9 × 10.5 cm (8 1/4″ × 4 1/8″)
RCIN 1055305–6

232. Charles Guischardt (1724–1775)

Memoires militaires, sur les Grecs et les Romains, 1758. 2 vols.

Hague: Pierre de Hondt
Printed. Red goatskin binding, gold tooled spine.
28.5 × 24.0 cm (11 1/4″ × 9 7/16″)
RCIN 1082188–9

233. Antonio Francesco Gori (1691–1757)

Thesaurus veterum diptychorum consularium et ecclesiasticorum, 1759. 3 vols.

Florence: Gaetano Albizzini
Printed. Vellum binding, gold tooled spine.
39.8 × 27.5 cm (15¹¹⁄₁₆″ × 10¹³⁄₁₆″)
RCIN 1079936–8

234. *The Book of Common Prayer, and administration of the sacraments*, 1760

Cambridge: Joseph Bentham
Printed. Black sheepskin binding, gold tooled spine.
42.2 × 27.5 cm (16⁹⁄₁₆″ × 10¹³⁄₁₆″)
RCIN 1052122

235. Callimachus (*c.*310/305–*c.*240 BC)

Hymni, epigrammata et fragmenta, new edn, 1761. 2 vols.

Leiden: Samuel and Joannes Luchtmans
Printed. Red goatskin binding, gold tooled spine.
21.0 × 13.5 cm (8¼″ × 5⁵⁄₁₆″)
RCIN 1058008–9

236. José Quer y Martinez (1695–1764)

Flora espanola o historia de las plantas, que se crian en Espana, 1762–4. 4 vols.

Madrid: Joachin Ibarra
Printed. Brown calf binding, gold tooled spine.
27.2 × 21.8 cm (10¹¹⁄₁₆″ × 8⁹⁄₁₆″)
RCIN 1057400–403

237. Edward Hyde, 1st Earl of Clarendon (1609–1674)

State papers . . . commencing in the year MDCXXI, 1767–86. 3 vols.

Oxford: Clarendon Press
Printed. Red morocco binding, gold tooled spine.
47.6 × 31.0 cm (18¾″ × 12³⁄₁₆″)
RCIN 1023360–62

238. Andrea Palladio (1508–1580)

I quattro libri dell' architettura, 1768

Venice: G.B. Pasquali (facsimile edition of the 1570 original)
Printed. Red sheepskin binding, gold tooled spine.
35.1 × 26.3 cm (13¹³⁄₁₆″ × 10³⁄₈″)
RCIN 1079104

239. Bulstrode Whitelocke (1605–1675/6)

A journal of the Swedish ambassy in the years M.DC.LIII and M.DC.LIV, 1772. 2 vols.

London: T. Becket and P.A. de Hondt
Printed. Brown calf binding, gold tooled spine.
27.0 × 23.0 cm (10⁵⁄₈″ × 9¹⁄₁₆″)
RCIN 1027838–9

240. Molière [Jean-Baptiste Poquelin] (1622–1673)

Oeuvres, 1773. 6 vols.

Paris: Compagnie des Libraires Associés
Printed. Red goatskin binding, gold tooled spine.
20.3 × 13.4 cm (8″ × 5¼″)
RCIN 1121797–802

241. Edward Ives (d. 1786)

A Voyage from England to India, in the Year MDCCLIV, 1773

London: Edward and Charles Dilly
Printed. Brown calf binding, gold tooled spine.
27.8 × 21.9 cm (10¹⁵⁄₁₆″ × 8⁵⁄₈″)
RCIN 1141308

242. Johann Carl Hedlinger (1691–1771)

Oeuvre du Chevalier Hedlinger, ou, Recueil des medailles, 1776–8

Basel: Chretien de Mechel
Printed. Red goatskin binding, gold tooled spine.
35.7 × 27.0 cm (14¹⁄₁₆″ × 10⁵⁄₈″)
RCIN 1076267

243. Claude le Lorrain (1600–1682)

Liber veritatis, 1777–1819. 3 vols.

London: John Boydell
Printed. Red goatskin binding, gold tooled spine.
42.9 × 29.2 cm (16⅞″ × 11½″)
RCIN 808991.a–c
See pp. 224 and 226.

244. Alberto Fortis (1743–1803)

Travels into Dalmatia . . . in a series of letters from Abbé Alberto Fortis to the Earl of Bute, 1778

London: J. Robson
Printed. Brown tree calf marble binding, gold tooled spine.
27.2 × 22.0 cm (10¹¹⁄₁₆″ × 8¹¹⁄₁₆″)
RCIN 1141306

245. Johann Caspar Fuessli (1743–1786)

Des Ritters Johann Carl Hedlingers Medaillen-Werk, 1781

Augsburg: Johann Jakob Haid *und Sohn*
Printed. Red goatskin binding, gold tooled spine.
38.3 × 28.0 cm (15¹⁄₁₆″ × 11″)
RCIN 1076265

246. Johann Caspar Fuessli (1743–1786) and Johann Elias Haid (1739–1809)

Collection complette de toutes les médailles du Chévalier Jean Charles Hedlinguer, 1782

Augsburg: Jean Jacques Haid *et fils*
Printed. Red goatskin binding, gold tooled spine.
38.7 × 27.5 cm (15¼″ × 10¹³⁄₁₆″)
RCIN 1076266

247. George Margetts (*fl.c.*1780–1790)

Longitude tables for correcting the effect of parallax and refraction, 1790

London: George Margetts
Printed. Red goatskin binding, gold tooled spine.
30.0 × 24.9 cm (11¹³⁄₁₆″ × 9¹³⁄₁₆″)
RCIN 1081256

QUEEN CHARLOTTE'S LIBRARY

Like the King, Queen Charlotte was a book-lover and a keen book-collector. Madame de Genlis, who visited Windsor in 1782, provides telling information on the Queen's love of books: 'It is well-known that in general the title of reader to a prince is merely an honorary title; but the Queen of England really loved reading, and at Windsor, where the princess lived in complete privacy, M. DeLuc [Jean André DeLuc, 1727–1817, Reader to the Queen from 1774] was daily summoned to read for three or four hours' (quoted in Orr 2001, pp. 199–200).

After her death her library – of more than 4,500 titles – was sold by Christie's (9 June – 16 July 1819) for just over £2,700. A few books, bearing the Queen's writing, were excluded from the sale (see p. 386). The Queen's library was first concentrated in rooms to the north of the Queen's Apartments, in 'the new wing' of Buckingham House (see no. 267) but the core was later transferred to a room added to the ground floor of Frogmore House (Windsor) in 1804 (see no. 140). The Queen's books closely reflected her range of interests. Some of her earlier acquisitions were appropriate to her position as young mother – she owned several books on the diseases and education of children. She also collected in the fields of natural sciences (a speciality that would last her lifetime), theology, history and geography, and had a considerable music library. She read widely in modern literature: by the

time of her establishment at Frogmore she had acquired works by Jane Austen and by the fashionable Gothic novelists such as Anne Radcliffe, and Cook's 74-volume series of Popular Novels. Several works on natural history were dedicated to her, for example Lord Bute's *Botanical tables* (no. 250), presented to her in a fine painted box (no. 286). Botany was one of her chief interests, superbly demonstrated by her 'little paradise' at Frogmore, whose grounds and garden owe much of their present beauty to her knowledge and enthusiasm. She maintained a library there, including her collection of novels, and her Librarian, Edward Harding, set up a small printing press, known as the Frogmore Press. (It produced only two titles, and some history cards for the use of children.) Since the sale in 1819 a few items from the Queen's library have returned to Windsor. Some of these are displayed here in the two bookcases by William Vile (nos. 267, 268).

LITERATURE Pyne 1819, I, *Frogmore*, pp. 8–9; II, *Buckingham House*, p. 17; *George III* 1974, pp. 10–11; Hedley 1975, pp. 102–3, 135, 260–61.

THE QUEEN'S BOOKS (nos. 248–251)

248. Andrew Coltee Ducarel (1713–1785)

An account of the Collegiate Church or Free Chapel and Hospital of St Catharine, 1763

[5], 55 ff., 5 pl. Manuscript. Bound in red goatskin, gold tooled.
33.0 × 21.5 cm (13″ × 8⁷⁄₁₆″)
RCIN 1140706
PROVENANCE Presented by the author to Queen Charlotte; presented by Queen Charlotte's daughters to Sir Herbert Taylor (1775–1839, Master 1819–39), January 1829; bequeathed by Lady Taylor to her niece Miss Disbrowe; by whom presented to Hon. William Ashly (1803–77, Master 1839–77), October 1859; given by Mrs Ashly to Revd J.H.S. St John Blunt (d. 1889, Master 1879–89); given by Lady Florence Blunt to Revd Arthur L.B. Peile (1830–1912, Master 1889–1912); given by his executors to Revd Severne Majendie (d. *c.*1927, Acting Master 1914–*c.*1927); passed to Queen Mary; placed in the Royal Library by HM Queen Elizabeth, May 1952
LITERATURE Jamison 1952; Hedley 1975, p. 89

George III and Queen Charlotte shared a strong sense of social responsibility (see Prochaska 1995, chapter 1). Queen Charlotte's charitable causes, where known (she frequently gave alms through intermediaries), reflected her own position as wife and mother; nor was she over-moralistic in her attitudes. One of her most visible charitable acts was to patronise Thomas Coram's Magdalen Hospital for penitent prostitutes (George III patronised the companion Foundling Hospital). Queen Charlotte's patronage of the Free Chapel and Hospital of St Catharine was traditionally associated with queens consort and therefore commenced when she became Queen. The foundation had been set up in the twelfth century by Matilda, consort of King Stephen, and was confirmed in all its possessions and privileges by Eleanor, consort of Henry III. Its privileged position, as the only ecclesiastical foundation belonging to queens of England, enabled it to survive the Reformation, when other similar foundations were dissolved. It aimed originally to support a small staff of about twenty individuals, and to distribute daily charity to the poor. The post of Master was in the Queen's gift.

This manuscript history of the foundation was executed for Queen Charlotte by Dr Ducarel, the Commissary of St Catharine's and antiquary and Librarian at Lambeth Palace.

The book was illustrated with the coats of arms of all the queen patronesses before Queen Charlotte, to emphasise the historical importance and context of the foundation. It has also been continued up to the present era; the last patroness to be added before the book was placed in the Royal Library was Queen Elizabeth, consort of King George VI. The book was bound for presentation by Ducarel, the finishing using floral motifs of carnations and tulips for the border. The inner central lozenge was built up with individual tools, with a royal crown in the centre. The crown was also used on the spine, with the other royal emblems of the thistle and the rose.

Following Queen Charlotte's death, the volume was apparently presented by her daughters to Sir Herbert Taylor, Private Secretary to George III from 1805 to 1811 and from 1811 to the Queen, whose executor he was (see p. 386). Sir Herbert became Master of St Catharine's in 1819; the volume belonged to a number of subsequent Masters before being returned to royal ownership under Queen Mary.

249. Stéphanie-Félicité du Crest, Madame de Genlis (1746–1830)

Les veillées du château, 1784. 4 vols. (lacks v. 4)

Paris: Lambert and Baudouin
Printed. Grey sheepskin binding, gold tooled spine.
20.2 × 13.5 cm (7¹⁵⁄₁₆″ × 5⁵⁄₁₆″)
RCIN 1120175–7

250. John Stuart, 3rd Earl of Bute (1713–1792)

Botanical tables, containing the different familys of British plants, 1784. 9 vols.

[s.l.]: privately printed
Printed. Red goatskin binding.
30.2 × 24.5 cm (11⅞″ × 9⅝″)
RCIN 1123772–80

See no. 286.

251. Daniel Bellamy (d. 1788)

The truth and safety of the Christian religion, 1789

London: J. Deighton
Printed. Red goatskin binding, gold tooled spine.
27.9 × 23.2 cm (11″ × 9⅛″)
RCIN 1051976

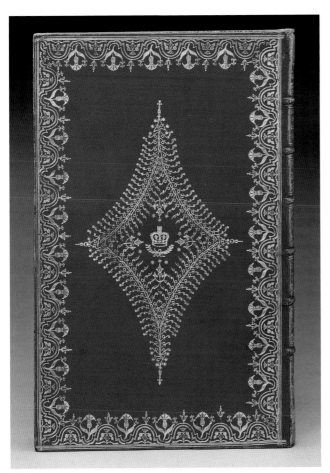

248

8. Sculpture (nos. 252–256)

252. Louis-François Roubiliac (1702–1762)

George Frederick Handel, 1739

Marble. Height 71.0 cm (27 ¹⁵⁄₁₆″)
Inscribed on the back *HANDEL / AETATIS SUAE 54 / MDCCXXXIX* and signed on the side of the support *ROUBILIAC.F.*
RCIN 35255
PROVENANCE Apparently given by the sitter to John Christopher Smith (1683–1763); his son, John Christopher Smith; by whom given to George III, *c.*1772–4
LITERATURE Esdaile 1924, p. 51; *George III* 1974, no. 48

George III admired the music of Handel (1685–1759) above that of all other composers. Although there were long-standing links between Handel and the King's family – he was appointed *Kapellmeister* to the Elector of Hanover (the future George I) in 1710, and Composer to the Chapel Royal in London in 1723 – George III's fervour was no mere endorsement of these existing associations. When Prince of Wales he had often met the great composer, and Handel himself is said to have remarked of the young Prince: 'While that boy lives, my music will never want a protector' (*Burney Diary*, IV, p. 248).

The King was a prime mover in the Handel Commemoration at Westminster Abbey in 1784, and his enthusiasm ensured that Handel became in some sense the 'court composer in perpetuity' of the British monarchy; portraits, reliefs or busts of him (though apparently not no. 252) were placed on brackets above organs and harpsichords at Buckingham House, Windsor and Brighton until well into the nineteenth century (see nos. 96, 113).

Roubiliac was born in Lyons in 1702. Little is known of his early life, but his artistic training may have been partly undertaken at Dresden. He won the second prize for sculpture at the Académie Royale in Paris in 1730, and had settled in London by the end of that year. He made at least four portraits of Handel. The earliest was the sculptor's first great success, the life-size statue commissioned for Vauxhall Gardens in 1738 (London, Victoria and Albert Museum), and

the last was the composer's monument in Westminster Abbey, unveiled in 1762. The present bust belongs to a group of contemporary portraits by Roubiliac in which male sitters are shown in the style known as *en negligé*. The tasselled cap and heavy cloak with tasselled buttonholes may not have been Handel's, since they also appear – similarly disarranged – on Roubiliac's bust of Isaac Ware dated 1741 (Detroit Institute of Arts; version London, National Portrait Gallery). The bust was given to George III – together with a harpsichord and the majority of the composer's manuscripts – by J.C. Smith the Younger (1712–95), the composer, organist and conductor, who had been Handel's pupil and his amanuensis

252

◁ No. 254 (detail)

245

253

during the years of his blindness from 1752 (Coxe 1799, pp. 54–5). It is probably this bust that was seen by Horace Walpole in the King's Apartments at Buckingham House in 1783 (Walpole 1928, p. 79). Handel's manuscripts were presented to the British Museum (now British Library) by Her Majesty The Queen in 1957.

253. Louis-François Roubiliac (1702–1762)

George II, (?)*c*.1761

Marble. Height 77.8 cm (30⅝″)
Signed on the back *L F / Roubiliac / inv*^t.
RCIN 31614
PROVENANCE Commissioned by Field-Marshal Lord Ligonier; by descent to his granddaughter, Mrs Francis Lloyd; by whom presented to the Prince Regent, 1817
LITERATURE Esdaile 1928, pp. 80, 91–2

This bust of George III's ageing grandfather and its companion (RCIN 35256), a portrait of the veteran Field-Marshal Lord Ligonier (1680–1770) who commissioned the pair, reveal the extent by which Roubiliac surpassed all his contemporaries in the carving of marble. The distinct character of each material, whether steel, silk, hair or ageing skin, is conveyed to an almost miraculous degree, while the extravagant knot in the end of the King's mantle stands on its own as a masterpiece of *trompe-l'oeil*. It was Roubiliac's practice to arrange or 'model' real drapery before applying starch to fix it in the form in which he wanted to carve it in marble.

A payment of £153 11s to Roubiliac in February 1763, referred to in Ligonier's regimental accounts (archives of Lloyds Bank), probably applies to this commission, although since this is far more than the sculptor normally charged for two busts it may also have included the preparatory terracottas. (The terracotta of Ligonier is now in the National Portrait Gallery; see Kerslake 1977, I, pp. 168–9.) George II disliked having his portrait taken, and no sittings are recorded for this bust. Since that of Ligonier is additionally inscribed *ad* [*vivum*] it seems likely that the King's bust was produced after his death (aged 76) in October 1760, and that the likeness was based on a portrait made in his last years.

254. John Bacon (1740–1799)

George III, 1775

Marble. Height 79.0 cm (31⅛″)
RCIN 31610
PROVENANCE Commissioned by the sitter as a gift for the Prince of Wales (later George IV)
LITERATURE *Royal Treasures* 2002, no. 68

There has never been a sculptural equivalent of the State Portrait, an approved likeness made at the time of accession and repeated for use in official settings, but John Bacon's bust of George III, with its concentration on the robes of state and insignia, was widely reproduced. The prime original was commissioned in 1770 by Dr William Markham, Dean of Christ Church, Oxford, who was appointed Preceptor to the Prince of Wales in the following year. In addition to the present bust (dated 1775 on the inserted disc), copies commissioned by the King survive in the University of

254

Göttingen (1773) and the Society of Antiquaries (1780). There is another copy at Eton College (undated), and a further one was made by Francis Chantrey for William IV in 1827, for the Temple of Military Fame at Kew (RCIN 2034). After Queen Charlotte's death in 1818 a 'Bust of His Majesty, by Bacon', which had been in her possession, was sent to the King's Library at Buckingham House, and casts were taken for each of her heirs, the four youngest princesses (RA GEO/50387–8). One of these plaster casts survives at Frogmore (RCIN 53349). An engraving of the bust by S.W. Reynolds was published as the frontispiece to the *Bibliothecae Regiae Catalogus* (the catalogue of the King's Library) in 1820.

Bacon entered the Royal Academy Schools in the foundation year of 1768, and was awarded the Academy's first gold medal for sculpture in 1769. Following the Christ Church commission he found favour with the King, who recommended him for the execution of monuments in Westminster Abbey. Bacon represented George III in a quite different guise in 1789, at full length accompanied by naval attributes and a reclining figure of the River Thames, in the bronze group for the courtyard of Somerset House. In the same year he supplied a superb marble clock surround with figures of Vigilance and Patience, to stand on the chimneypiece he had earlier carved for Queen Charlotte's Saloon at Buckingham House (see no. 111).

255

255. Sir Richard Westmacott (1775–1856)

Samuel Johnson, c.1791–2

Marble. Height 86.7 cm (34⅛″)
RCIN 33445

256. Sir Richard Westmacott (1775–1856)

David Garrick, c.1791–2

Marble. Height 83.0 cm (32¹¹⁄₁₆″)
RCIN 1391
PROVENANCE Nos. 255 and 256 first noted when sent from Carlton House to Windsor Castle, by order of George IV, November 1828

The greatest literary critic and lexicographer and the greatest actor of the eighteenth century are portrayed in Roman garb befitting the heroic status they had achieved in their own time. They are further united by their lifelong friendship and common origin in the city of Lichfield,

Staffordshire, and by the equal esteem in which they were held by George III. After they moved to London together in 1737 their careers proceeded at very different rates with the younger man, Garrick (1717–79) scoring early successes and rapidly achieving wealth and widespread fame, while Johnson (1709–84) struggled as a journalist until the completion of his great *Dictionary* in 1755. His fortunes subsequently improved and in 1762 he was granted a pension by George III. Johnson was often admitted to the library rooms at Buckingham House; on one celebrated occasion he conversed with the King about the literary scene and the merits of contemporary journalists, writers and thinkers (Boswell 1826, II, pp. 33–9). In the year after Johnson's death, the King received (from Johnson's friend, Bennet

256

Langton) an early manuscript list of possible literary projects – Johnson's 'Designs' (RCIN 1047020).

Such was the King's admiration for Garrick that in September 1761 he took Queen Charlotte to his performance in *The Rehearsal* at Drury Lane, two days after her marriage, which itself had taken place on the very day of her arrival in London for the first time.

These two portraits are versions of Westmacott's busts – on the adjacent monuments in Lichfield Cathedral – by which Garrick and Johnson were commemorated in the city of their birth (Harwood 1806, p. 85). Their remains lie side by side in Westminster Abbey. On Garrick's Lichfield monument are inscribed Johnson's words: 'His death eclipsed the gaiety of nations, and impoverished the public stock of harmless pleasure.' In April 1791 it was reported that James Wyatt was making designs for the Lichfield monument and would put them in the hands of 'a statuary' for immediate execution (letter of Edmund Hector to James Boswell, 8 April, MS Yale [C1528]). Westmacott must indeed have lost no time, since he departed for Italy in the autumn of 1792, not returning until 1796. The monuments were set up in 1793. In his long and prolific career Westmacott made very few portrait busts, but his first two exhibits at the Royal Academy in 1797 were in this form, and nos. 255 and 256 closely resemble one of them, a posthumous portrait of the architect Sir William Chambers (marble; London, Sir John Soane's Museum). All three share a crudeness that might be expected in such early works.

9. Furniture (nos. 257–292)

257. (?)Dutch

Silver stands, c.1670

Silver. 101.0 × 45.0 × 39.5 cm (39¾″ × 17¹¹⁄₁₆″ × 15⁹⁄₁₆″)
One stand marked with an assay scrape; one tripod base an
electrotype replacement
RCIN 35298.1–2
PROVENANCE Part of a suite of silver furniture probably
acquired by Charles II, *c.*1670

258. Andrew Moore (1640–1706)

Silver table, 1699

Silver and oak. 85.0 × 122.0 × 75.5 cm
(33⁷⁄₁₆″ × 48¹⁄₁₆″ × 29¾″)
Struck with the maker's mark of Andrew Moore; the top
engraved *HR. Sculp.*
RCIN 35301
PROVENANCE Part of a suite commissioned by William III for
Kensington Palace in 1698 (PRO LC5/109, f. 279) and delivered
in 1699 (PRO LC9/46, 3 October and 23 November)
LITERATURE *Royal Treasures* 2002, no. 78; Winterbottom 2002

On his accession in 1760 George III inherited three late
seventeenth-century suites of silver tables, mirrors and
stands. These had been displayed in the State rooms in
Windsor Castle since the reign of Queen Anne and in the
early years of the King's reign they were regularly cleaned
and repaired. A further set was in the collection of Frederick,
Prince of Wales, at Leicester House in the 1740s. These were
the remnants of far larger suites of silver furnishings, which
had been displayed throughout the royal palaces during the
reigns of the later Stuarts. The popularity of silver furnishings
had however diminished in the first half of the eighteenth
century and in February 1764 'three silver tables and six
stands', together with numerous old sconces, chandeliers and
firedogs 'which are not English Standard', were 'Delivered to
be melted . . . to be reduced into English Sterling to complete
his Majesty's Gift of 8000oz of old Plate to the Duke of

Gloucester' (PRO LC9/45, f. 218) – part of a generous gift for
the King's brother, Prince William, Duke of Gloucester.

Thereafter the three sets disappear from the Jewel House
records. However in February 1805 an account of 'their
Majesties' Fete at Windsor Castle' noted 'the novel and grand
appearance of four silver tables, between each window [in the
Queen's Ballroom]. Two of them came from Hanover, and had
been repaired and beautified for this occasion . . . One of the

257

other tables was presented by the Corporation of London to King William, and the other by the same body to Queen Anne. The magnificent effect of the tables was considerably heightened by four most elegant pier glasses over each with silver frames' (*Gentleman's Magazine*, 25 February 1805, pp. 262–3). In addition five silver chandeliers, also from Hanover, were hung in the Ballroom and the Queen's Drawing Room next door (see no. 133).

This magnificent arrangement was recorded in a view of the Queen's Ballroom in 1817 (no. 132). It would therefore appear that elements of at least two of the sets of silver tables, mirrors and stands were spared the melting pot in 1764. One composite surviving set includes two stands, a table and a mirror decorated with the cipher of Charles II (RCIN 35299–300). The stands (no. 257) are marked with an assay scrape, which might indicate a continental, perhaps Dutch origin; the design, however, is of markedly French inspiration and reflects the influence of Parisian silversmiths such as Claude I Ballin and Nicolas de Launay, who supplied silver furniture for Louis XIV at Versailles in the early 1680s. The second table (no. 258) belongs to a set including mirror and stands (the latter now missing) made for William III in 1699. It would therefore appear that by 1805 George III had had a change of heart, and that these examples of high baroque furnishings were now deemed suitable for his newly refurbished apartments at Windsor Castle. The silver furnishings from Hanover (noted above) had originally been acquired by George II in 1732 for his palace of Herrenhausen near Hanover. They had been brought to the safety of England during the Napoleonic Wars and were returned shortly afterwards. The two tables, mirrors and four stands survive in the collection of the princes of Hanover at Marienburg.

259. South German

Casket, c.1680

Tortoiseshell, oak, crystal, silver, enamel, pietra dura, gilt bronze.
44.0 × 74.5 × 57.0 cm (17⁵⁄₁₆″ × 29⁵⁄₁₆″ × 22⁷⁄₁₆″)
RCIN 35474
PROVENANCE Possibly acquired by Queen Charlotte; first certainly identifiable in the Royal Collection, 1826

Elaborately decorated caskets of this type were made in a number of European cabinet-making centres but the tradition seems to have been strongest in southern Germany, especially Augsburg. Among the leading Augsburg makers of the

259

second half of the seventeenth century, Melchior Baumgartner is known to have utilised the full range of silversmith's, glass engraver's, stone-cutter's and enameller's techniques to create cabinets and caskets of the highest quality: the casket in the Royal Collection signed by Baumgartner and dated 1664, which forms part of Charles Clay's organ clock, is an outstanding example (RCIN 30037; see *Princes as Patrons* 1998, no. 51).

No. 259 is also decorated with rich materials including engraved crystal panels, cabochon crystals in enamelled silver frames and (on the base of the interior) an exceptional panel of Florentine pietra dura geometrically inlaid with agate, lapis and other stones in gold *cloisons*, perhaps of late sixteenth-century date. The casket may have been acquired by Queen Charlotte, whose liking for the decorative and ornamental contrasted with the King's more austere taste. Not surprisingly, it appealed to her son George IV, who took it to Carlton House. When stored there in 1826, its Buckingham House provenance was carefully noted but with no further indication of its former location (Carlton House Inventories, vol. J, p. 270).

260. Attributed to André-Charles Boulle (1642–1732)

Writing table, c.1680

Oak, ebony, tortoiseshell, pewter, brass, gilt bronze.
79.7 × 41.8 × 35.5 cm (31³⁄₈″ × 16⁷⁄₁₆″ × 14″)
RCIN 35489
PROVENANCE First certainly identifiable in the Royal Collection, 1817
LITERATURE Harris (J.) 1997, under no. 39; Roberts (H.) 2002, p. 5 and fig. 4

No. 260 with the
top open and closed.

Although it is not known when this elegant little table
entered the Royal Collection, it is reasonably certain that it
was not one of George IV's numerous acquisitions of French
furniture. In George III's reign it was selected, perhaps on
account of its nationality and the fact that it is inlaid with
fleurs-de-lis and dolphins, as a stand on which to display
the French royal flag, tendered every year by the Dukes of
Marlborough on the anniversary of the Battle of Blenheim
(13 August), as 'rent' for the royal manor of Woodstock,
bestowed on the 1st Duke of Marlborough following his
reverence for tradition, George III had intended placing the
flag in a new building, to be known as the Blenheim Tower,
which was to be added to the north front of the castle, to the
designs of James Wyatt. This project, begun in 1806, was
soon abandoned and the flag was then displayed on the table,
as seen in the view of the Queen's Presence Chamber (see
no. 130) drawn by Charles Wild in 1817 for Pyne's *Royal*

Residences. In the previous year the table had appeared in
another room recorded for Pyne's publication, standing on
the steps of the throne at the east end of St George's Hall
supporting the French Republican tricolor (Pyne 1819, I,
Windsor Castle, opposite p. 176). The flag has been presented
annually by the Dukes of Wellington on the anniversary
of the Battle of Waterloo (18 June 1815) as 'rent' for the
estate of Stratfield Saye; the first presentation took place
in 1816, the year of publication of Pyne's St George's
Hall view.

A second, almost identical, table is in the Getty Museum
and it has been suggested, partly on account of the decoration,
that both were made for Louis, the Grand Dauphin (1661–
1711). They have been attributed to the royal cabinet-maker
Pierre Gole (c.1620–84). However, an attribution to Boulle
may be more sustainable, for Gole seems rarely to have used
metal marquetry and then not in combination with tortoiseshell, as found on these tables (Pradère 1989, p. 49).

261. Italian

Table cabinet, c.1680

Ebony, oak, pietra dura, gilt bronze. 66.0 × 80.5 × 43.5 cm
(26″ × 31¹¹⁄₁₆″ × 17⅛″)
RCIN 11894
PROVENANCE Acquired by Richard Dalton in Rome for George III
and Queen Charlotte, late 1760s (220 crowns; RA GEO/15602);
Queen Charlotte's sale, Christie's, London, 7 May 1819, lot 111;
bought by the Prince Regent (later George IV; £367 17s)

It is likely that this cabinet was among the substantial
purchases made for the King and Queen in Rome in the late
1760s by Richard Dalton, the King's Librarian. A long list
of Dalton's acquisitions – including paintings, drawings,
watercolours, books, cameos and casts – amounting to 5,808
Roman crowns, notes 'A Curious Cabinet with Drawers,
enrich'd with hard Stones in Rilievo represent⁵. Fruit',
priced at 220 crowns. While there is no certainty about this
identification, the probability that it is the same is increased
by the fact that no. 261 was included in the sale of Queen
Charlotte's possessions. It was repurchased by the Prince
Regent, who seems to have inherited from his mother a
fondness for pietra dura. When the cabinet was acquired by
Dalton, it was without a stand. By 1819 it was on a stand
(which no longer survives) 'with 9 Mosaic Pannels representing Landscape &c' (Jutsham II, p. 71). This stand may have
been made to Queen Charlotte's order to take the 'Nine
small Pannels, as above' [i.e. of pietra dura], purchased for
100 crowns by Dalton at the same time as the cabinet.

261

The pietra dura panels – nine on the front carved in medium
and high relief with fruit, four on the sides and top, inlaid
with birds and fruit – are characteristic of Florentine work
of the last quarter of the seventeenth century and the cabinet
itself, which is little more than a vehicle for the display of the
panels, was probably constructed at about the same date.

262. Burkat Shudi (1702–1773)

Two-manual harpsichord, 1740

Oak, pine, walnut, brass, steel. 96.0 × 95.0 × 246.0 cm
(3′ 1¹³⁄₁₆″ × 3′ 1⅜″ × 8′ 0⅞″)
Signed in pen on the upper name batten *Burkat Shudi fecit Londini.*
Inscribed in pencil on the upper surface of the lever of the lowest
note of the lower manual *94 f 1740.*
RCIN 11896
PROVENANCE (?)Commissioned or purchased by Frederick, Prince
of Wales; by descent to his son, George III; (?)Buckingham Palace
by 1825 (BP Inv. 1825, p. 2)
LITERATURE Dale 1913, p. 40; Boalch 1995, p. 614

Both George III and Queen Charlotte were regular and
competent players of the harpsichord. The King purchased
three instruments in February 1764: one from 'Capt. Shadwell'
and two from Jacob Kirkman (1710–92), who was also paid
a quarterly retainer for tuning the Queen's harpsichord
during the 1760s and early 1770s (RA GEO/17115 *et seq.*).
The newly married couple held private concerts every
week at St James's, at which 'The Queen and Lady Augusta
play on the Harpsichord & sing, the Duke of York plays
on the Violoncello, & P. William on the German Flute'
(Northumberland 1926, p. 41).

The Swiss-born keyboard-instrument-maker Burkat
Tschudi came to London in 1718, after which he began to
use an anglicised form of his name. He was employed by
Frederick, Prince of Wales as a tuner and supplied two
spinets in 1751, for the young Prince George and for his
sister Augusta (RA GEO/55296). No. 262 is one of the earliest
of his harpsichords to survive, from a considerable output
spanning the years from 1729 to 1793, by which time Shudi's
son-in-law John Broadwood had taken over the firm. Recent
conservation work has revealed that this instrument was
originally made as the harpsichord component of a claviorgan,
superimposed on a chamber organ of the same outline shape.
Shudi is known to have made such instruments with the
organ-builder John Snetzler (1710–85), and Handel is thought
to have used one in performing his oratorio *Saul* in 1738. The

262

choruses were accompanied on the organ and the recitatives and arias on the harpsichord, played from the same keyboard. Claviorgans (see also no. 264) seem to have proved difficult to maintain, and at some point later in the eighteenth century no. 262 was separated from its organ. This is conceivably the instrument that was listed in the 1825 inventory of Buckingham Palace as 'A Harpsichord by Handell [*sic*] in a Walnuttree Case' (King's Sitting Room). No maker of that name is recorded, and any association with the composer might have suggested an identification with the instrument by Jan Ruckers dated 1612 (RCIN 27934; on loan to the Benton Fletcher Collection, Fenton House, London), presented to George III (see no. 252); however, that instrument has a black-painted (rather than walnut) case.

263. Attributed to Pierre Langlois (*fl*.1759–67)

*Two commodes, c.*1763

Rosewood, pine, oak, gilt bronze.
RCIN 21235.3: 84.6 × 152.5 × 67.5 cm (2′ 9⁵⁄₁₆″ × 5′ 0½″ × 2′ 2⁹⁄₁₆″);
RCIN 21235.4: 84.5 × 154.0 × 67.4 cm (2′ 9¼″ × 5′ 0⅝″ × 2′ 2⁹⁄₁₆″)
RCIN 21235.3 and .4
PROVENANCE Probably made for Princess Amelia (d. 1786); (?)Prince Charles or Prince Frederick of Hesse; anonymous sale Squibb's, 23 April 1818, lot 86, and 25 April 1818, lot 83; bought by Bailey and Sanders for George IV when Prince Regent (£243 12s; PRO LC 11/26, qtr to October 1818)

LITERATURE Harris, De Bellaigue and Millar 1968, pp. 212–13; Thornton and Rieder 1972, p. 185, figs. 19 and 20; Roberts (H.) 2001, p. 332 and fig. 419

These two commodes, which form part of a unique set of four in the Royal Collection, are of a model which is now generally attributed to the French émigré cabinet-maker Pierre Langlois. The speciality of this highly individual craftsman as a manufacturer of 'Commodes . . . inlaid in the Politest manner with Brass & Tortoiseshell . . . touttes Sortes de Commodes . . . Inscrutez de fleurs en Bois et Marqueteries, garnies des Bronzes doreez' is made clear in the text and decorative border of his trade card; and it is on his work in this category of furniture, mostly executed in an idiosyncratic 'Louis XV' manner, that his reputation rests. The lavish use of engraved brass inlay on the tops of these commodes, consisting of a finely drawn basket of summer flowers and detached sprays of narcissi, distinguishes them from others of this model and may provide an unexplored link with the circle of John Channon or Frederick Hintz, both known for their use of engraved brass (Gilbert and Murdoch 1993). Intriguingly, all four commodes are inscribed on the tops: the brass inlay of one of the two not exhibited is clearly dated 1763 and of those exhibited one (RCIN 21235.3) is signed *J M Dutton* and the other (RCIN 21235.4) *F M La Cave*

(in reverse). Dutton remains unidentified; François Morellon La Cave (*fl*.1723–65), evidently of Huguenot origin, is recorded as an etcher and engraver who collaborated with William Hogarth and is presumed to have joined Langlois for this apparently unprecedented commission. Among the émigrés working for Langlois was his son-in-law, the bronze founder and mount-maker Dominique Jean, who may have made the exceptional mounts on these commodes.

Viewed individually – and even more so as a group – the elaborate decoration and ponderous architectural form of these commodes represent a style markedly different from that favoured by George III and quite unlike the type of light-hearted French or French-inspired furniture (e.g. no. 280) admired by Queen Charlotte. Langlois never became an official supplier to the court but it seems that he may have attracted the patronage of the King's unmarried aunt, Princess Amelia (1711–86), the second daughter of George II. This independent-minded Princess, who was close to both George III and her great-nephew, the Prince of Wales, owned a substantial house in Cavendish Square and in 1761 acquired Gunnersbury Park, Ealing. It seems likely that these commodes were made to stand under a set of four large gilt pier glasses in the Saloon at Gunnersbury and that they are referred to in the advertisement for the sale of the house and contents following her death as 'FRENCH COMMODES of exquisite Workmanship, most elegantly decorated with chased and engraved Or Molu'. The sale of the contents (Skinner & Co., 7 May 1787) was cancelled when the house failed to reach its reserve and the principal furniture, including the commodes, may then have been retained by Princess Amelia's heirs, her nephews Prince Charles and Prince Frederick of Hesse. A sale of the residual contents of Gunnersbury (Christie's, 16 June 1792), which was by then owned by Gilbert Ironsides, included the pier glasses (Saloon, lots 12–15) but not the commodes. The link with Princess Amelia was noted only after they had been acquired at auction (without any stated provenance) in 1818 for the Prince Regent's use (Carlton House Inventories, vol. E, pp. 17 and 62).

264. Attributed to Benjamin Goodison (*c*.1700–1767); alterations attributed to William Vile (*c*.1705–1767)

Organ cabinet, c.1745 and (?)1763

Mahogany. 346.0 × 259.0 × 107.0 cm
(11′ 4½″ × 8′ 5¹⁵⁄₁₆″ × 3′ 6⅛″)
RCIN 1366
PROVENANCE Probably made for Frederick, Prince of Wales; altered for George III, 1763
LITERATURE Smith 1931, pp. 78–9 and pl. 69

The strongly Palladian form of this cabinet lends support to the generally held theory that it may originally have been made in the 1740s, either for George II or (perhaps more likely) for Frederick, Prince of Wales. If this was the case, Benjamin Goodison, as principal cabinet-maker to the Great Wardrobe and to the Prince and Princess of Wales, was highly likely to have been involved in its manufacture. Its large and unusual form reflects its purpose, which was to house an upright harpsichord and organ (claviorgan). The Prince and Princess of Wales, who were passionately fond of music, had a number of organs at Leicester House and Carlton House, including at least two 'machine' or mechanical organs. (See also the chamber organ shown in Cotes's portrait, no. 6.) Organ cases there were regularly cleaned and polished by Goodison; and payments for mechanical work are recorded to John Pyke in the 1740s and to George Pyke and John Snetzler in the 1760s. In 1763 Christopher Pinchbeck was paid for substantial alterations to the 'Great Organ' (evidently a 'machine organ') at Carlton House. This included the preparation of '23 Large Barrels' (RA GEO/55510).

There is, however, nothing in the Great Wardrobe or Duchy of Cornwall accounts which can with any certainty be identified with this object, in either its original or its adapted form. Furthermore, William Vile's bill for 'Altering the Organ and upright Harpsichord' for the Japan Room in the Queen's House (PRO LC9/310, qtr to Christmas 1763), often cited in connection with no. 264, can only with some difficulty be made to match the cabinet as it exists today. The removal (at some point in the nineteenth century) of all trace of the original machinery from the interior has further complicated the picture, although cuts and old fixings in the framework indicate where keyboard, pedals and stops were once located.

Vile's bill of 1763 describes the substantial reconstruction for Queen Charlotte of the cabinet of an existing organ and upright harpsichord (or claviorgan) – conceivably from

Carlton House – and the addition of considerable quantities of new carving. The latter included 'Ovals of laurel' and 'Vinetree Ornaments', which are among the few elements on no. 264 that match this bill (although with no trace of the gilding mentioned therein) and which, together with the vigorously carved drops of flowers and foliage, compare in style and technique with the carving on the bookcase (no. 267), made by Vile for Queen Charlotte in the 1760s. In 1763 the organ cabinet which Vile had modified was replaced in the Japan Room at Buckingham House with a 'very grand' new organ cabinet, supplied by his successor John Bradburn at a cost of £392 12s (PRO LC9/314, qtr to Christmas 1766); Bradburn's organ is probably that shown in Stephanoff's view of 1817 (no. 113). No. 264 was presumably then moved to the Queen's Gallery at Kensington Palace where it is shown with some of the matching set of cabinets (see no. 265) in a view of that room, also by Stephanoff (no. 104), published in 1819. A year later the organ and cabinets were refurbished at the Prince Regent's request by France and Banting (PRO LC11/28, qtr to 5 January 1820) and in June 1820 the 'Large Organ belonging to the King' was noted at Kensington Palace in a list of the late King's property (RA GEO/32622).

265

265. Attributed to William Vile (c.1705–1767)

Cabinet, c.1763(?)

Mahogany, oak, pine. 179.0 × 101.0 × 51.5 cm
(5' 10¾" × 3' 3¾" × 1' 8¼")
RCIN 148.7
PROVENANCE Probably made for George III and Queen Charlotte
LITERATURE Laking 1905, p. 47 and fig. 20; Smith 1931, pp. 78–9 and pl. 68; Edwards and Jourdain 1955, p. 53 and pl. 67

This and the nine matching cabinets (one of which is no longer in the Royal Collection) are usually said to have been made to house organ rolls associated with the organ cabinet which William Vile altered in 1763 for Queen Charlotte, tentatively identified with no. 264. Notwithstanding the complete lack of documentation, the absence of any mechanical part of the organ and the fact that the cabinets themselves are entirely devoid of any fittings (or any sign of fittings), stylistic and circumstantial evidence appear to support this traditional identification and attribution.

The crisp and lively carving on the door fronts is entirely consistent with Vile's work at this date and moreover matches in certain respects the carving which he is thought

to have added to the organ cabinet (no. 264). It is also of some significance that the cabinets have been associated with this organ from at least the early nineteenth century. If the supposition that the cabinets were made to hold organ rolls is correct (and if not, it is difficult to conceive what other purpose they served), then the alterations to the organ cabinet which Vile undertook in 1763 presumably coincided with substantial (but apparently undocumented) mechanical changes to the upright harpsichord and organ (claviorgan), since both instruments were always intended to be played manually. Claviorgans, giving the player an unusual range of solo colours, were comparatively rare and were always at a disadvantage in being difficult to keep in tune (Williams 1971, pp. 77–87). They enjoyed a vogue in England from the 1730s to the end of the century and were considered especially suitable for such works as Handel's theatre oratorios where the harpsichord (for recitatives) alternated with the organ (for choruses).

266. Attributed to William Vile (c.1705–1767)

Commode, c.1761–4

Padouk, rosewood, oak, pine, gilt brass. 88.0 × 166.5 × 68.5 cm
(2′ 10⁵⁄₈″ × 5′ 5⁹⁄₁₆″ × 2′ 2¹⁵⁄₁₆″)
RCIN 39228
PROVENANCE Probably made for Queen Charlotte
LITERATURE Laking 1905, p. 76 and fig. 14; Gilbert 1978, I, no. 223

This elaborately shaped commode, veneered with lustrous and richly figured golden padouk (and dark rosewood on the interior drawers), inlaid on the top with finely engraved brass and fitted with lavish mounts of chased gilt brass, expresses very clearly the manner in which French rococo design of the 1740s and 1750s was adapted to suit English taste. Furniture pattern-books such as Thomas Chippendale's *Director*, published in three editions between 1754 and 1762, were extremely influential in promoting this taste: the third edition includes (as pl. LXX) a 'Commode Table' of markedly similar design to no. 266.

The probability is that no. 266 was made by William Vile in the relatively brief period in the early 1760s when he held the royal warrant and supplied a great deal of expensive new furniture for the young King and Queen at St James's Palace and the Queen's House. Vile's workshop, while not generally considered innovatory in matters of design, evidently mastered this fashion very quickly, especially when supplying Queen Charlotte, whose personal taste seems to have been more adventurous than the King's (see no. 268). Although no clearly recognisable documentation has come to light, Vile's first bill for furnishing Queen Charlotte's apartments at St James's included two pieces of furniture (one for the Bedroom, the other for the Wardrobe) which were evidently of similar design to no. 266. Each was described as 'a fine Large Comode Chest of Drawers . . . Neat Wrot Brass feet and Ornaments up the Corners finished with Gold Lacquer' and cost £25 (PRO LC9/306, Bill 75, qtr to Michaelmas 1761).

The only direct parallel to no. 266 is a pair of undocumented commodes of very similar form, said to have belonged to George III's Prime Minister, Lord Grenville (1759–1834) – or perhaps more likely to his father George

266

267

Grenville (1712–70), who was also Prime Minister. These, which are now divided between the Victoria and Albert Museum and Temple Newsam House, Leeds (Gilbert 1978, I, no. 223), have the same highly distinctive pierced angle mounts and very similar foot mounts. Comparable features are also found on the Cumming barograph (no. 305).

267. William Vile (c.1705–1767) and (?) John Bradburn (fl.1760–d. 1781)

Bookcase, 1762 and (?)1767

Mahogany. 265.5 × 261.6 × 71.8 cm (8' 8½" × 8' 7" × 2' 4¼")
RCIN 252
PROVENANCE Made for Queen Charlotte (£107 4s; PRO LC9/308, no. 8, qtr to Christmas 1762); her son, George IV; by whom given to his sister-in-law, Augusta, Duchess of Cambridge; her son George, 2nd Duke of Cambridge (d. 1904); acquired by his niece, Victoria Mary, Princess of Wales (later Queen Mary), 1904
LITERATURE Smith 1931, p. 78 and pl. 66; Edwards and Jourdain 1955, p. 53; Harris, De Bellaigue and Millar 1968, p. 114; Roberts (H.) 1990b, pp. 383–4 and pl. IV

The wording of William Vile's bill for the bookcase traditionally identified with no. 267 – 'a very handsome Mohogany Bookcase . . . the whole very handsomely Carv'd . . . £107 4s' – implies that it was made for Queen Charlotte (rather than the King) at Buckingham House. First, there is a reference to the fact that the carving on the bookcase was to match another piece of the Queen's furniture, in her 'Buro Closet' at St James's – perhaps the unidentified 'Exceeding neat Mahogany Glass Case . . . Carved Exceeding Rich and neat & Exquisite fine Wood', charged at £100 (PRO LC9/306, no. 75, qtr to Michaelmas 1761). Second, the bill mentions that the bookcase was constructed so as to conceal a door into an adjacent water closet – a configuration that only fits Queen Charlotte's Bedroom, which lay in the north-west corner of the first floor of Buckingham House overlooking the garden. That there is now no sign of such a door is probably due to an alteration executed five years later at a cost of £31 by John Bradburn, Vile's successor, at which point 'the Whole Front' was 'made into one Press' (PRO LC9/314, no. 8, qtr to Midsummer 1767). This work was carried out to coincide with the creation of a new bedroom for the Queen, overlooking the east front of Buckingham House, and the addition of a new wing which included a library for the Queen. The bookcase was probably the one recorded in the Queen's Blue Closet in the 1825 inventory of Buckingham House among the considerable quantity of old-fashioned furniture considered not worth keeping (RCIN 1114747, p. 128). In Wild's view of the room a few years earlier (no. 116) the space formerly occupied by both bed and bookcase is shown as the right wall; the arrangement of doors was clearly altered as part of the c.1767 work.

The strong architectural character of the bookcase – suggestive of the influence of Sir William Chambers and on the face of it perhaps more likely to appeal to the King's taste than the Queen's – is considerably tempered by the lavish carved decoration, which includes vividly and minutely rendered flower-swags and drops, oval laurel wreaths and rococo scrollwork and clasps. These embellishments may have been carried out by the specialist carver Sefferin Alken (fl.1744–83), who is known to have worked for Vile (and Chambers) on other occasions.

The bookcase is shown with a selection of books from the King's and Queen's libraries, as listed above (within the sequence nos. 195–251).

268. William Vile (c.1705–1767) and (?) John Bradburn (fl.1760–d. 1781)

Secretaire cabinet, 1762 and (?)1767

Mahogany, thuya, oak, gilt bronze. 213.4 × 94.0 × 45.7 cm (7' × 3' 1" × 1' 6")
RCIN 2571
PROVENANCE Made for Queen Charlotte (£72; PRO LC9/307, no. 21, qtr to Lady Day)
LITERATURE Smith 1931, pp. 73–4 and pls. 62–3; Edwards and Jourdain 1955, p. 53 and pl. 60; Harris, De Bellaigue and Millar 1968, pp. 112–13, 218

This highly distinctive piece of furniture has traditionally been identified with an entry in William Vile's bill of 1762 for 'an Exceeding fine Mohogany Secretary . . . a Sett of Shelves at Top with a Crown Carv.d at Top', supplied in 1762 for Queen Charlotte's Dressing Room at St James's Palace for the considerable sum of £72. Assuming the identification to be correct, no. 268 was originally differently configured, with open shelves in the upper section: the present cupboards, with Chinese fretwork doors and sides backed with panels of glass, were added by John Bradburn five years later, by which time the secretaire had been moved to the Queen's apartments at Richmond Lodge. Bradburn's bill, which includes the cost of making a drawing of the new element to show to the Queen at Richmond for her approval, as well as the manufacture of the 'Neat Mahogany Glass Case ... with Neat frett Work Doors in front, and Ends, and 8 Squares of plate Glass to Ditto', cost £22 (PRO LC9/314, no. 61, qtr to Midsummer 1767). Although no mention is made of it, Bradburn evidently reused the carved upper section of Vile's cabinet with the crown finial. This transformation, which was carried out extremely neatly, is just perceptible from the back of the cabinet.

268

With this piece, notably in the most unusual commode-shaped base, Vile departed some way from the conventional form of a 'Lady's Secretary' of the kind popularised by leading makers of the period, for example Mayhew and Ince in their pattern-book of 1762, the *Universal System* (pl. XVIII). Other features, such as the choice of glamorously flared mahogany veneers, exotic thuya-wood decoration for the interior of the writing drawer and elaborately scrolling crowned cornice, all suggest an attempt by the cabinet-maker to develop a distinctive vocabulary for the Queen's furniture. Bradburn's skilful alteration, in which Queen Charlotte evidently played a decisive role, added a further exotic strand to the rich vocabulary already present, while also providing two lockable glazed cabinets to contain and protect valuable books.

The secretaire cabinet is shown with a selection of books from the King's and Queen's libraries, within the sequence nos. 195–251.

269. William Vile (*c*.1705–1767)

Jewel cabinet, 1762

Mahogany, amboyna, rosewood, holly, olive, padouk, oak, ivory.
108.0 × 81.3 × 55.9 cm (42½″ × 32″ × 22″)
RCIN 35487
PROVENANCE Made for Queen Charlotte (£138 10s; PRO LC9/308, no. 8, qtr to Christmas 1762); her daughter, Princess Mary, Duchess of Gloucester (d. 1857); (?) George, 2nd Duke of Cambridge; (?) by whom given to his sister, Princess Mary Adelaide, Duchess of Teck (d. 1897); by descent to her grandson, George, 2nd Marquess of Cambridge; from whom bought by his aunt, Queen Mary, 1951 (£5,000)
LITERATURE Edwards and Jourdain 1955, p. 53 and pls. 62–3; *QG Treasures* 1988, no. 107

This sumptuous object, often seen as William Vile's masterpiece, was the single most costly piece of furniture Vile made for either the King or Queen. Placed in the Queen's private apartments in the south-east angle of St James's Palace, the jewel cabinet was part of the expensive refurnishing of St James's undertaken by Vile (with his partner John Cobb) following the King's marriage in 1761. Two years later, by which time the focus of royal interest had shifted to Buckingham House, the cabinet had been moved to the Queen's new bedchamber there and Vile then supplied a marbled leather cover for it at a cost of 9s 6d (PRO LC9/309, no. 54, qtr to Michaelmas 1763).

Vile's bill for the cabinet describes it as 'very handsome ... made of many different kinds of fine Woods', and alludes to the most distinctive feature as follows: 'all the Front, Ends

269

and Top inlaid with Ivory in Compartments and neatly Engraved'. The use of engraved ivory decoration, which includes Queen Charlotte's coat of arms on the hinged top and trophies emblematic of Fame or Victory and Plenty on the doors, is virtually without parallel in English furniture at this (or any) date, and suggests some familiarity with continental practice – Italian or German – within Vile's workshop. The tradition of ivory inlay was certainly well established in northern Germany and is seen in the contemporary work of Abraham Roentgen. Roentgen was in England in the 1730s and maintained connections with the German community in London in the following decades.

The 'fine Locks', also referred to in Vile's bill, were supplied by Mrs E. Gascoigne, a specialist metalsmith used by several leading cabinet-makers at this date, and were constructed with great precision to safeguard the Queen's magnificent jewellery. These jewels were much remarked on by contemporaries and included pieces inherited by George III from his grandfather George II, as well as the share which the King had bought from his uncle, the Duke of Cumberland (see Appendix, p. 385). Among the highlights were a diamond stomacher valued at £70,000, two diamond necklaces, drop earrings, rings and flower-sprays as well as a great quantity of large pearls. Some of these are seen in Thomas Frye's portrait of the Queen, published in 1762 (see no. 21).

270. William Vile (c.1705–1767)

Work table, 1763

Mahogany, oak. 79.4 × 97.2 × 70.5 cm (31¼″ × 38¼″ × 27¾″)
RCIN 11109
PROVENANCE Made for Queen Charlotte (£9 15s; PRO LC9/310, no. 8, qtr to Christmas 1763)
LITERATURE Smith 1931, p. 78 and pl. 64; Edwards and Jourdain 1955, pl. 65; Harris, De Bellaigue and Millar 1968, p. 113

In the design of this table, the extravagant rococo forms and chinoiserie decoration of the kind popularised in Thomas Chippendale's *Director* (first published in 1754) and Mayhew and Ince's *Universal System* (published in 1762) have been carefully modified by Vile to suit a patron with more restrained tastes. The controlled curvilinear outline is discreetly enriched with gadroons, beading, scrolls, foliage and blind fretwork, crisply executed in the finest and most lustrous mahogany to create a fashionable yet practical piece of furniture for the Queen's use. The bill indicates that this 'neat mohogony Work Table' was supplied for Queen Charlotte's Dressing Room at Buckingham House at a cost of £9 15s and that originally the hinged top, for use as a reading stand when raised, enclosed a lockable well (the lock made to fit the Queen's key) with twelve compartments on one side. These compartments, which were perhaps intended to contain materials for needlework or drawing, have since been removed and the surface leathered.

270

271

London art market (Sotheby's, London, 19 November 1993, lot 16). The design of these lanterns may have been influenced by Thomas Chippendale's more extravagantly rococo formula, first published in 1761 and issued as plate CLIII (right half) in the 1762 edition of the *Director*.

272. German(?) and John Bradburn (*fl.*1760–1781)

Cabinet-on-stand, late seventeenth century, and 1766

Tortoiseshell, pewter, ebony, oak, gilt and silvered bronze.
184.8 × 116.8 × 46.3 cm (6′ 0¾″ × 3′ 10″ × 1′ 6¼″)
RCIN 2587.2
PROVENANCE The cabinet undocumented until 1766; the stand made (to support the cabinet) for George III and Queen Charlotte, 1766 (PRO LC9/294, no. 27, qtr to 5 April 1766)
LITERATURE Roberts (H.) 2002, p. 7 and fig. 6

This elaborately inlaid cabinet, which is one of a pair, belongs to the tradition of *meubles d'apparat* or display furniture of the type first made in the seventeenth century for Louis XIV. The decoration consists principally of pewter, red-stained

271. Attributed to William Vile (*c*.1705–1767)

*Two hanging lanterns, c.*1765

Mahogany, glass, gilt bronze. 113.0 × diameter 63.0 cm (44½″ × 24¹³⁄₁₆″)
RCIN 36000.1–2
PROVENANCE Probably made for George III
LITERATURE Edwards 1964, p. 336 and fig. 4

In 1802 a description of the interior of Buckingham House noted in the Hall 'Three very large and superb lanterns, in the fashion of forty or fifty years since' hanging from the ceiling, and 'eight lamps in glasses . . . on carved pedestals' (*Gentleman's Magazine*, LXXII, p. 1184). The latter, which do not survive, are almost certainly to be identified with the '8 mohog. Hexogon Lanterns' on richly carved and painted term pedestals, made by William Vile in 1763 at a cost of £291 (PRO LC9/309, no. 35, qtr to Midsummer). The supply and fitting of the glass cost £52 and the '24 Brass Candlesticks' a further £3. The three hanging lanterns still in the Royal Collection (two of which are exhibited), for which no account has been discovered but which have often been incorrectly associated with the 1763 bill, seem likely to have been supplied by Vile at about the same period. An almost identical lantern, also undocumented, with scrolled mahogany base but lacking the crown, was recently on the

272

tortoiseshell and ebony, but also includes polychrome tortoiseshell flowers and (on the inside of the central door and the compartment within) polychrome figures and painted architectural devices. Although a Parisian origin cannot be ruled out, this style was widely imitated in other European centres of cabinet-making. The extensive use of pewter and polychrome tortoiseshell may indicate a German origin, perhaps in the workshop of Johann Daniel Sommer, active 1666–92 in Künzelsau am Kocher, Swabia, which produced furniture decorated in a comparable manner.

Nothing is known of the history of these cabinets until they were selected for George III and Queen Charlotte's bedroom at Richmond Lodge and thoroughly refurbished in 1766 at a cost of £30 10s by John Bradburn (see no. 273). His work included new brass balustrades for the interior of the central cupboards and the provision of '24 neat chased buttons' for each cabinet (of which only eleven survive). In addition, Bradburn provided two new stands with term legs of advanced neo-classical design at a cost of £24. The materials for the stands (pewter and ebony) were carefully matched to the cabinets in a consciously antiquarian spirit, and the drawer locks were adapted to Queen Charlotte's key, suggesting that the choice of the cabinets for Richmond was probably hers rather than the King's.

273. John Bradburn (fl.1760–1781)

Secretaire cabinet, 1774

Mahogany, mirror glass, gilt bronze. 211.0 × 79.5 × 58.0 cm (6′ 11¹/₁₆″ × 2′ 7⁵/₁₆″ × 1′ 10¹³/₁₆″)
RCIN 725
PROVENANCE Made for Charlotte, Princess Royal (£20; PRO LC9/322, no. 9, qtr to Christmas)
LITERATURE Smith 1931, p. 91 and pl. 71; Edwards and Jourdain 1955, p. 62 and pl. 88

John Bradburn succeeded his master William Vile as cabinet-maker to the Great Wardrobe in 1764, going into partnership with another of Vile's former employees William France (1734?–73) in the same year and with him undertaking the same range of duties formerly undertaken by Vile and his partner John Cobb (c.1715–78). In the 1760s and 1770s this consisted mainly of work at St James's Palace, Buckingham House, Richmond Lodge and (particularly after 1772) Kew. While fine carving may have been his speciality (see nos. 300, 306), he also provided a constant stream of well-made mahogany pieces for the King and Queen and their growing family.

273

No. 273 is entirely characteristic of this type of functional and unshowy furniture and was one of a number of secretaire cabinets, all with slight variations, supplied around this date for the elder children as they were established in their own apartments. Charlotte, the Princess Royal, although only 8, would have been considered old enough to make occasional use of this 'neat mahogany Secretary with drawers in front, and a writing drawer . . . a neat bookcase at top with looking glass doors . . . and a carved scrowl pediment top' which Bradburn provided at a cost of £20 for her apartment on the second floor of Buckingham House. He included in the cost the provision of two keys (not surviving), one for the Princess herself marked *PR*, the other for Lady Charlotte Finch, governess to the royal children, marked *LFC*.

274. Samuel Vaughan (*fl.*1751–1772) and Diederich Nicolaus Anderson (d. 1767)

Sedan chair, 1763

Oak, morocco leather, gilt metal, glass, silk.
188.0 × 100.0 × 78.0 cm (6′ 2″ × 3′ 3⅜″ × 2′ 6¹¹⁄₁₆″)
RCIN 31182
PROVENANCE Made for Queen Charlotte; from whom acquired (with a second, less elaborate, chair: RCIN 31181) by Prince Augustus, Duke of Sussex (d. 1843); his widow, the Duchess of Inverness (d. 1873); by whom given/bequeathed to the Duke of Teck; from whom purchased by Queen Victoria, 1883
LITERATURE Laking 1905, p. 51 and pl. 22

Queen Charlotte kept four chairmen for her sedan chair at an annual salary of £39 17s 6d, a figure which remained constant from the 1770s until her death (RA GEO/36838 and 36995). Her chair-maker was Samuel Vaughan of Coventry Street, Piccadilly, who succeeded to the business first established at this address by Edward and George Vaughan. In the 1780s the firm was known as Vaughan, Holmes and Griffin and later as Holmes and Griffin or Griffin & Co. (*DOEFM* 1986, pp. 373, 444, 920–21). No. 274 bears the label of Griffin, with an address at Whitcomb Street occupied by the firm from 1791: this label was probably applied to the chair during maintenance by Vaughan's successor.

On 1 January 1763 Samuel Vaughan was paid by Queen Charlotte's Treasurer £185 5s 4¾d for a new chair and on the same date the chaser and gilder D.N. Anderson was paid £250 'for decorating & Ornament^g a Sedan Chair' (BL Add. MS 17870, f. 5^r). These payments seem likely to be connected with no. 274, which is covered in red morocco and extravagantly decorated with gilt metal of extremely thin substance (for lightness of weight). The wide range of ornament includes the British lion and unicorn emerging from acanthus scrolls, swags of roses, laurel wreaths, oak and laurel sprays and the infant Mercury aboard a sailing boat, all framed by palm branches. The symbolic language of Victory employed here – similar in several respects to that of the state coach (see no. 88) – would certainly have been appropriate to the period immediately following the end of the Seven Years War in 1763. The author of this decorative scheme is not known, but James 'Athenian' Stuart, who designed a new throne for Queen Charlotte at St James's Palace (Percy and Jackson-Stops 1974, p. 251), has been proposed by Mr John Harris.

In 1771 Queen Charlotte ordered another new sedan chair which, according to Lady Mary Coke, was 'the prettiest thing of the kind ever seen' (*Coke Letters*, IV, p. 149, 22 November 1772). That chair, which was designed by Robert Adam, was no doubt also made by Vaughan, who had previously worked with Adam on a chair for Lady Coventry in 1764. The design of Adam's new chair for the Queen was published in 1771 (Bolton 1922, II, p. 302). Although Adam's chair has not survived, a second sedan chair associated with Queen Charlotte remains in the Royal Collection (RCIN 31181).

275. Matthew Boulton (1728–1809) and Sir William Chambers (1723–1796)

Pair of candle and perfume vases (King's vases), 1770–71

Blue john, gilt bronze, ebony.
57.1 × 55.2 × 17.8 cm (22½" × 21¾" × 7")
RCIN 21669.1–2
PROVENANCE Made for George III and Queen Charlotte
LITERATURE *Chambers* 1996, pp. 155–7; Goodison 2003, pp. 80–81, 165, 336–42 and pls. 42, 339–40

The support of English manufacturers by George III and Queen Charlotte can be seen as one of the most distinctive and significant aspects of their artistic patronage and Matthew Boulton was one of those who benefited most directly from this interest. Following a three-hour audience

with the King and Queen in late February 1770, Boulton received an order for a number of articles, chiefly a new chimney garniture to replace the existing garniture of porcelain vases in the Queen's Bedroom at Buckingham Palace. The order probably included two pairs of vases of the King's model (no. 275 and RCIN 21669.3–4) and a pair of sphinx vases (no. 276). All were to be manufactured from Boulton's 'or moulu' – rich gilt bronze of distinctive coppery colour – and from choice and highly polished specimens of Derbyshire fluorspar (blue john), the luxuriously coloured crystalline stone which Boulton made his speciality.

As the King's principal artistic adviser, Sir William Chambers was involved behind the scenes with this entire commission. A few days after Boulton's audience with the King and Queen, he was summoned to a breakfast meeting with Chambers to discuss the project, during the course of which Chambers gave him 'some valuable usefull and acceptable Modells' and promised an improved design for the foot of the candle vases which he was working up 'from a sketch of the King's' (Goodison 2003, p. 79). To underline his personal involvement, Chambers exhibited a drawing

275

of 'Various Vases, &c. to be executed in or moulu, by Mr Boulton, for their Majesties' in the Royal Academy exhibition of 1770 (*Chambers* 1996, fig. 231). In their finished appearance, the King's vases had become a more sophisticated and more thoroughly neo-classical version of the Caryatic vases of *c.*1770 (Goodison 2003, fig. 317): the 'Chambers' features include a pierced entrelac band at the neck, heavily looped laurel swags on the body, and coved fluting, lion-masks, paterae, key-pattern borders and spirally fluted feet for the bases.

276

276. Matthew Boulton (1728–1809) and Sir William Chambers (1723–1796)

Pair of perfume vases (sphinx vases), 1770–71

Blue john, gilt bronze, glass, tortoiseshell.
32.0 × 14.5 × 14.5 cm (12⅝″ × 5¹¹⁄₁₆″ × 5¹¹⁄₁₆″)
RCIN 21668.1–2
PROVENANCE Made for George III and Queen Charlotte
LITERATURE *Chambers* 1996, p. 158 and fig. 235; Goodison 2003, pp. 350–51 and pl. 355

These vases almost certainly formed part of the chimney garniture supplied by Boulton for Queen Charlotte's use at Buckingham House. Like no. 275, Boulton's first design was probably modified by Chambers, in this case to include features such as the grotesque masks on the body, the recumbent sphinxes and the *rinceaux* (scrolling foliage) on the bases. The use of sphinxes in this manner may have been influenced by James 'Athenian' Stuart's design for a plate-warmer at Kedleston Hall in Derbyshire of 1760 (*Chambers* 1996, p. 158), although Chambers himself drew sphinxes when in Paris and Rome in the 1750s (Goodison 1974, fig. 98).

That the visit to Buckingham House in February 1770 – for which, according to Josiah Wedgwood, Boulton had been 'scheming' for over a year – was a success can be judged by the fact that two years later Boulton sold the King 'a pair of cassoletts, a Titus, a Venus clock and some other things' (Goodison 1974, p. 38).

277. Matthew Boulton (1728–1809) and Sir William Chambers (1723–1796) and Thomas Wright (d. 1792)

Mantel clock (King's Clock), 1770–71

Blue john, gilt bronze, enamel, brass, steel. 48.7 × 28.3 × 21.4 cm (19³⁄₁₆″ × 11⅛″ × 8⁷⁄₁₆″)
RCIN 30028
PROVENANCE Made for George III
LITERATURE *Chambers* 1996, pp. 156–7; Goodison 2003, pp. 165, 207–15, pls. 160–61

This clock was probably ordered at the same time as the chimney garniture for the Queen's Bedroom at Buckingham House (see nos. 275, 276) and is the object from this commission for which there is the most direct evidence of William Chambers's involvement. A preliminary sketch for the clock by Chambers (RL 18366) incorporates elements from drawings made by him in France and Italy, including winged sphinxes

277

at either side of the base. The latter were eliminated in the finished drawing (not surviving), which Chambers provided for Boulton and which may also have incorporated some suggestions from the King. In the manufacture of the case, which was substantially finished by January 1771, Boulton's workmen apparently 'conformed to a hair breadth' with Chambers's design (Goodison 2003, p. 209). Thomas Wright's 8-day striking movement with verge escapement, subsequently altered to pin-wheel by B.L. Vulliamy, was only fitted to the case with difficulty and caused Boulton considerable frustration and delay in completing the order. The clock was finally ready for delivery to the King and Queen at Richmond in April 1771, but seems to have been kept thereafter at Buckingham House: by 1817 it was the centrepiece of a

chimney garniture (which included no. 276) in the Crimson Drawing Room (see no. 112). Although there are no payments to Boulton in George III's surviving accounts, a letter to Boulton from his partner John Fothergill in March 1772 indicates that the total cost to the firm of six vases (probably the two pairs of King's vases and the pair of sphinx vases; see nos. 275, 276) and the clock case was more than £412. Fothergill concluded, 'I don't imagine his Majesty will allow us much profit on that sum' (*Chambers* 1996, p. 157).

In spite of their designation as 'King's' clock and 'King's' vase, neither model was deemed by Boulton to be exclusive: he seems to have produced at least six clocks and an even larger number of vases for other clients without ever obtaining the King's authority.

278

278. Matthew Boulton (1728–1809)

Pair of candle vases, 1770–71

Blue john, gilt bronze. 20.5 × 7.7 × 7.7 cm
(8¹⁄₁₆″ × 3¹⁄₁₆″ × 3¹⁄₁₆″)
RCIN 6828.1–2
PROVENANCE Probably made for George III and Queen Charlotte
LITERATURE Goodison 2003, pp. 104–6, 331–3, pls. 70, 331

Known by Boulton as the 'Goat's head' vase, this elegant
object with reversible candle-nozzle was probably first made
in 1769 and remained one of the firm's most popular small
vases. Boulton used a wide variety of bodies for this model:
those with blue john bodies appear to have retailed at about
4 guineas (£4 4s) a pair. Some of the earlier versions, like
no. 278, are mounted with medallions of Alexander the Great,
the image perhaps derived by Boulton from a seal impression
produced by James Tassie. Although without documentation,
these vases may have been among the unspecified purchases
made by the King and Queen following Boulton's first visit
to Buckingham House in 1770.

279. Matthew Boulton (1728–1809)

*Tea-urn, c.*1770

Gilt bronze, ebony. 55.0 × 51.0 × 51.0 cm
(21⅝″ × 20¹⁄₁₆″ × 20¹⁄₁₆″)
RCIN 55429
PROVENANCE Bought by Queen Mary, 1938 (*QMB*, IV, p. 6, no. 10)
LITERATURE Goodison 2003, pp. 271–5, pl. 231

This imposing and elaborate tea-urn is likely to be of the
same model as the 'tripodic tea kitchen', designed by James
'Athenian' Stuart in 1769, that Matthew Boulton intended
to show George III and Queen Charlotte at his audience
in February 1770. The documentation for this category
of object is not as complete as it is for many of Boulton's
creations, but there are several features of the design and
construction of no. 279, notably the candle-branches and the
central bowl, which relate to other well-known examples of
his work. It is not known whether the King and Queen did
acquire a tea-urn of this model from Boulton: no. 279 was
purchased by Queen Mary in 1938.

280

280

280. John Carrack's Cabinet-maker (*fl.*1760–1780)

*Chest-of-drawers and pair of corner cupboards, c.*1770

Beech, pine, mahogany, walnut, gilt bronze.
RCIN 21220: 87.0 × 153.7 × 73.0 cm (2′ 10¼″ × 5′ 0½″ × 2′ 4¾″);
RCIN 21219: 87.0 × 73.0 × 50.8 cm (2′ 10¼″ × 2′ 4¾″ × 1′ 8″)
RCIN 21220 and 21219.1–2
PROVENANCE Acquired by Queen Charlotte
LITERATURE Wood 1994, pp. 82–6 and figs. 66–72; *Royal Treasures* 2002, no. 84

The acquisition by Queen Charlotte of this suite – a specifically French grouping of which relatively few examples are known in English furniture – is undocumented. The modified rococo style accords well with what is known of the Queen's taste, which was generally more adventurously continental than the King's, and the floral theme of the decoration reflects the Queen's known love of botany. The suite seems to have been placed in the Queen's State Bedchamber at Windsor Castle, where the chest-of-drawers is shown in a watercolour by James Stephanoff of 1818 (see no. 134). The furniture acquired by Queen Charlotte for this room, which lay in the north-west corner of Charles II's star building, included a new state bed with accompanying chairs and stools upholstered in flower-embroidered silk (no. 282).

Nothing is known about the maker of this suite except what can be inferred from its construction – which embodies features of both English and continental practice – and by

281

comparison with a very similar commode (also originally with a pair of corner cupboards), which was retailed by the otherwise unknown John Carrack, with the assistance of the former royal cabinet-maker John Cobb, to Sir John Hussey Delaval of Seaton Delaval, Northumberland (Wood 1994, no. 6). The precise roles of Carrack and Cobb remain mysterious and the picture is further complicated by the fact that certain features of the Delaval and royal suites, such as the angle mounts on the corner cupboards, are repeated on documented work by Cobb (e.g. the commode supplied to Paul Methuen in 1772; Wood 1994, figs. 75–7).

281. Thomas Chippendale (1718–1779)

Pair of armchairs and a sofa, c.1773

Gilded beechwood. RCIN 100201: 95.0 × 67.5 × 65.5 cm (3' 1⅜" × 2' 2⁹⁄₁₆" × 2' 1¹³⁄₁₆"); RCIN 100204: 104.5 × 213.4 × 89.0 cm (3' 5⅛" × 7' × 2' 11¹⁄₁₆")

RCIN 100201.1–2 (chairs), 100204.1 (sofa)

PROVENANCE (?)Made for William Henry, Duke of Gloucester

LITERATURE Gilbert 1978, I, pp. 82–3, 235 and figs. 185, 365

These three pieces, which form part of a suite consisting of eight armchairs and a pair of sofas (later enlarged by the addition of thirteen single chairs in two sizes and a pair of bergères), constitute the only physical evidence of a royal commission to the most celebrated cabinet-maker of the Georgian period. Chippendale was never attached to the

281

Great Wardrobe and though he boasted in 1768 to one of his most important clients, Sir Rowland Winn of Nostell Priory, that he had 'a great quantity of unexpected business . . . mostly for the Royal Family', the evidence for this was thought to be confined to the fact that some copies of the third edition of *The Gentleman and Cabinet-Maker's Director* (1762) bore a dedication to Prince William Henry, Duke of Gloucester, younger brother of George III.

While no evidence of a Chippendale commission has come to light in George III's or Queen Charlotte's accounts, payments to Chippendale totalling £134 15s 6d have been discovered since the publication of the suite in 1978 (see Literature) in the only surviving portion of the Duke of Gloucester's bank account, covering the years 1764–6 (RA GEO/54505b). These payments are too early to relate to this suite which, as has been pointed out, must date to the early 1770s. Assuming the suite was commissioned by the Duke, it was presumably intended for his London residence (Gloucester House, Park Lane) or for one of his country seats in the Windsor area – St Leonard's Hill (purchased by his wife in the year of their marriage, 1766), Cranbourne Lodge (the Duke's seat as Keeper of Cranbourne Chase, from 1767), or Bagshot Park, Surrey, which the Duke later gave to his son. The fact that the whole suite bears George IV's inventory brand, as used at Windsor, means that if the provenance is correct, it must have been given away by the Gloucesters' children William Frederick or Sophia Matilda, to whom the Duke on his death in 1805 had bequeathed his property 'share and share alike' (RA GEO/54397).

282. Attributed to Robert Campbell (*fl.*1754–1793) and Nancy Pawsey (*fl.*1778–1809)

*Two armchairs and two stools, c.*1780

Gilded beechwood, upholstered in silk and wool. RCIN 1141:
153.0 × 74.0 × 83.0 cm (5' 0¼" × 2' 5⅛" × 2' 8¹¹⁄₁₆"); RCIN 1142:
51.0 × 58.5 × 46.0 cm (1' 8¹⁄₁₆" × 1' 11¹¹⁄₁₆" × 1' 6⅛")
RCIN 1141.1–2 (armchairs); 1142.2 and .4 (stools)
PROVENANCE Made for Queen Charlotte
LITERATURE Hedley 1975, p. 130

The modernisation of the State Apartments at Windsor Castle c.1778–95 for George III and Queen Charlotte under the supervision of Sir William Chambers's assistant John Yenn is poorly documented and now largely forgotten. It was also short-lived, being overtaken first by James Wyatt's Gothic work in the first years of the nineteenth century and

282

282

then almost entirely obliterated by Sir Jeffry Wyatville in the remodelling of the 1820s and 1830s for George IV and William IV. Nevertheless, during this period significant changes to the decoration and furnishing of the King's and Queen's Apartments were introduced, notably in the King's Audience Chamber and in Queen Charlotte's State Bedroom (now part of the Royal Library). Unusually, Pyne records the names of some of the craftsmen involved in the Audience Chamber (Pyne 1819, I, *Windsor Castle*, p. 166). Robert Campbell was responsible for the King's throne, while the

283

remarkable flower-embroidered hangings of the throne canopy were designed by the celebrated flower painter and founder-member of the Royal Academy, Mary Moser; these hangings were still in place at the time of Wild's view of the room in 1818 (no. 128). They were worked by Mrs Pawsey of Great Newport Street, whose premises were adjacent to Campbell's and who had in 1778 taken over from her aunt Mrs Phoebe Wright the 'Royal school for embroidering females'. This establishment, which was actively supported by the Queen, was intended for the orphaned or impoverished daughters of professional men. After 1809 it transferred from London to Ampthill, Bedfordshire.

In the same year (1778), Queen Charlotte had installed in her State Bedchamber a magnificent new canopied bed in the neo-classical style, possibly designed by Yenn. The hangings, like those of the King's throne canopy, were decorated with richly coloured and botanically accurate floral needlework embroidered by the pupils of Mrs Wright's school in 1772–7 and very probably to her designs. Accompanying the bed, which is now at Hampton Court (RCIN 1470), were two armchairs and ten stools upholstered *en suite* (including no. 282), all originally finished in three colours of gold. This suite is similar in character – although more grandly detailed and expensively decorated – to the armchairs and stools supplied, perhaps later in the 1780s, for the King's State Apartments. All are likely to have been made by Campbell, who later described his firm as 'Upholsterers to Their Majesties' (but never held an official warrant). Campbell's association with this project continued until at least 1794–5, when he supplied the mirror glass for four new oval pier glasses for the King's State Apartments, designed by John

Yenn and carved by Richard Lawrence. One of the chairs is inscribed on the calico beneath the embroidered covers with the name of the workman responsible for the upholstery, James M. Brown(?) of Windsor, and the date 21 July 1780.

Floral embroideries by Mrs Pawsey's pupils, worked in the 1790s and 1800s, also adorned several rooms at Frogmore, including the Green Pavilion and the Red and Black Japan Rooms (nos. 137, 138; see Hedley 1975, p. 260).

283. English

Pair of pier tables, c.1780

Gilded pine, marble, stone. RCIN 57850.1: 90.0 × 173.5 × 69.0 cm (2' 11⁷⁄₁₆" × 5' 8⁵⁄₁₆" × 2' 3³⁄₁₆"); RCIN 57850.2: 90.5 × 174.0 × 68.8 cm (2' 11⁵⁄₈" × 5' 8½" × 2' 3¹⁄₁₆")
RCIN 57850.1–2
PROVENANCE Probably made for George III
LITERATURE Laking 1905, p. 49; Roberts (H.) 2001, pp. 418–19

These tables, like no. 282, may have formed part of the re-furnishing of the State Apartments at Windsor carried out for George III and Queen Charlotte c.1778–95. Although there is little supporting documentation, it seems possible that they were intended to accompany the refined neo-classical furniture attributed to Robert Campbell which was made for Queen Charlotte's State Bedchamber (no. 134), probably under the direction of Sir William Chambers's assistant John Yenn.

At a later date, tables of this description were at Hunter's House, Kew Green, a property purchased by the Prince Regent in 1819 and sold by him in 1823 (Desmond 1995, p. 417 and RA GEO/50454). They were subsequently refurbished by Morel and Seddon for Windsor, at which time the central panel of the frieze may have been altered.

284. William Gates (*fl*.1774–*c*.1800)
Pair of commodes, 1781

Oak, pine, satinwood, tulipwood, purplewood, sycamore, amboyna
and other woods. 89.5 × 114.3 × 53.3 cm (35¼″ × 45″ × 21″)
RCIN 2475.1–2
PROVENANCE Made for George IV when Prince of Wales
(PRO LC9/328, qtr to 5 April 1781, no. 25)
LITERATURE Smith 1931, p. 92 and pl. 86; Edwards and Jourdain
1955, p. 83 and pl. 183; Harris, De Bellaigue and Millar 1968,
p. 211; *QG Treasures* 1988, no. 95

In 1776–7 George III ordered the construction of a new
wing on the north side of Buckingham House to contain
a separate apartment for the Prince of Wales (the future
George IV), then in his sixteenth year. At the Prince's
coming of age in 1780, the tradesmen of the Great Wardrobe
were required to provide a splendid array of new furniture,
both for the new rooms in London and for the apartment
set aside for the Prince on the east front of Windsor Castle.
For London, the chair-maker John Russell (*fl*.1773–1822)
provided a suite of 'party colour'd Japan' chairs and sofa, and
the cabinet-maker William Gates made a substantial quantity
of expensive marquetry furniture including this pair of 'very
fine Sattin wood inlaid commode Tables', each with a writing
drawer in the frieze, priced at £80 with an additional charge
of £3 1s 6d for leather protective covers. Gates also supplied
a number of pieces of high quality carved giltwood furniture,
some of it made to designs chosen by the Prince.

Little is known about Gates beyond his royal commissions
(*DOEFM* 1986, pp. 332–3; and see no. 288). The evidence
suggests that he was as familiar with the repertoire of neo-
classical forms and ornament (made fashionable by Robert
Adam and others) as with the techniques of shaded and
engraved marquetry pioneered in the previous decade by
competitors such as Mayhew and Ince. However, by placing
each urn against a contrasting background on an apparently
receding plinth, Gates has created a degree of pictorial illusion not generally seen in the work of rival marqueteurs and
suggestive of continental, specifically French, influence.

285

285. English
*Reading stand, c.*1780

Tulipwood, kingwood, mahogany, box, ivory, tortoiseshell,
mother-of-pearl. Open 40.0 × 60.5 × 3.2 cm
(15¹¹⁄₁₆″ × 23¹³⁄₁₆″ × 1¼″)
RCIN 45115
PROVENANCE Made for or presented to Queen Charlotte
LITERATURE *Royal Miscellany* 1990, no. 5

The two hinged flaps of this stand enclose a panel of marquetry
of the highest quality, inlaid with the crowned cipher of Queen
Charlotte. Although no documentation has survived and no
directly comparable pieces are known, the function, materials
used and vocabulary of ornament (principally botanical), all
reflect the Queen's known tastes and interests.

286. English
Cabinet containing Lord Bute's Botanical tables, 1784

Painted satinwood and gilt bronze. 35.0 × 43.3 × 21.5 cm
(13¾″ × 17¹⁄₁₆″ × 8⁷⁄₁₆″)
RCIN 37017
PROVENANCE Presented by John Stuart, 3rd Earl of Bute,
to Queen Charlotte, 1784
LITERATURE Hedley 1975, pp. 137–9, 345 (n. 15)

John Stuart, 3rd Earl of Bute (1713–92), was George III's
mentor and chief adviser both before his accession and in
the early years of his reign. He was forced to resign in 1763.
Bute was active at Kew from 1747, assisting first Frederick,
Prince of Wales, and then his widow Augusta, with the
botanical and landscape gardens which they laid out there.

286

He was closely involved with the gardens at Kew until Augusta's death in 1772, at which point Joseph Banks assumed control. Bute was a serious and scholarly botanist and his *Botanical tables* (see no. 250), described as 'in the press' in 1761, were the result of many years' work. Their publication in 1784, with a dedication to Queen Charlotte, marked a milestone in the Queen's patronage of botanical studies and at the same time signalled her unequivocal support for botany as a subject suitable for feminine study. Bute's dedication described the work as 'composed solely for the Amusement of the Fair Sex under the Protection of your [i.e. the Queen's] Royal Name' and in her acceptance of the dedication, the Queen declared herself to be 'much flattered to be thought capable of so rational, beautiful, & enticing Amusement, & shall make it my endeavour not to forfeit this good opinion by pursuing this Study steadily, as I am persuaded this Botanical Book will more than encourage me in doing it' (Hedley 1975, p. 138).

The Queen hardly needed any encouragement to pursue the subject, which had occupied her consistently at Kew and then at Windsor where the presence of Mrs Delany (no. 165) – the Queen's friend, neighbour and fellow botanist – from 1785 until her death in 1788 must have provided a further incentive for this work. 'Botanising' was enjoyed by both the Queen and her daughters (see no. 64) and came to be concentrated from the early 1790s at the Queen's 'Little Paradise' at Frogmore where she assembled the major part of her botanical library, including the *Botanical tables*.

Bute's handsomely illustrated work, the result of more than twenty years' study, was privately printed. Only about a dozen copies were actually produced and among the recipients were Catherine the Great, Joseph Banks and the Queen's friend the dowager Duchess of Portland. The nine volumes of the specially bound dedication copy were housed in an elegant satinwood cabinet mounted with gilt bronze handles, painted with flowers and with the Queen's cipher on the top. It was reserved from the sale of Queen Charlotte's property after her death by the Prince Regent at £117.

287. Henry Emlyn (*c.*1729–1815)

*Two armchairs, c.*1785

Oak, beech, velvet. 109.5 × 68.5 × 64.5 cm
(43⅛″ × 26¹⁵⁄₁₆″ × 25⅜″)
St George's Chapel, Windsor Castle
PROVENANCE Made for George III and Queen Charlotte
LITERATURE Roberts (J.) 1976–7, pl. II

In 1782, following his decision to re-establish Windsor Castle as the principal residence of the royal family outside London, George III commissioned Henry Emlyn to undertake an extensive scheme of repair and embellishment to the interior

287

of St George's Chapel so that 'all [should be] made to accord, which, as it had been put up at different times, was not the case at present' (Papendiek 1887, II, p. 97). Emlyn was employed as carpenter, builder and architect at Windsor by the Office of Works (from 1761) and by the Dean and Chapter (1784–91). The King's work at St George's Chapel, which was funded from his Privy Purse (RA GEO/50447–8) and pre-dates by more than a decade his re-gothicising of the castle under James Wyatt, included the refurbishment of the Queen's Closet (on the north side of the Choir, overlooking the High Altar) for the use of Queen Charlotte and the younger members of the family. Mrs Papendiek records that Emlyn's work in the Closet began with 'Two chairs at the altar table', possibly to be identified with no. 287.

Emlyn's work at St George's, which continued until his retirement in 1792, included substantial additions to the choir stalls and the design of the Coade stone screen, achievements which both Horace Walpole and John Carter praised (see no. 135). Emlyn owed his reputation, as a contemporary in the *Gentleman's Magazine* pointed out (vol. LX, 1790, pp. 689–90 and 949), to the extraordinary skill with which he reproduced both the spirit and the quality of workmanship of the original Gothic fittings of the chapel. In the case of no. 287, where there was no relevant medieval precedent, Emlyn grafted the ornamental vocabulary of Perpendicular Gothic onto a modern chair. Although the results might be considered less convincingly Gothic than those achieved by Charles Elliott at Westminster some twenty years later (no. 290), the carving of the back, which incorporates the Garter badge, fleurs-de-lis and Tudor roses, is of the same exceptional quality that Emlyn achieved elsewhere in the chapel.

288. Josiah Wedgwood (1730–1795), and attributed to William Parker (*fl.*1756–1803)

*Pair of candelabra, c.*1790

Jasper ware, gilt bronze, glass. 88.0 × 51.0 × 37.0 cm
(34⅝″ × 20⅛″ × 14⁹⁄₁₆″)
RCIN 35291.1–2
PROVENANCE Possibly made for George III; possibly first recorded in the Collection in 1876 (WCCI, p. 187, no. 62)

A design for candelabra or 'girandoles', apparently of this form, was patented in 1781 by William Parker, the leading chandelier-maker of the last part of the eighteenth century (*Country House Lighting* 1992, no. 10). They were usually

288

supported on shaped four-sided plinths, made in a variety of materials including coloured and gilded glass and Wedgwood jasper ware. The more elaborate versions (such as no. 288) are fitted with chased ormolu mounts of elegant neo-classical design in the manner of Matthew Boulton. The figure subjects on the sides of the plinths are taken from designs provided to Wedgwood *c.*1785 by Elizabeth, Lady Templetown (1747–1823), one of a number of lady amateur artists on whose skill in rendering subjects of feminine interest Wedgwood was keen to capitalise (Reilly 1989, I, pp. 604–5). Three of the figures are taken from a design entitled *An Offering to Peace* (*ibid.*, I, fig. 892 and pl. C155) and one from a design entitled *Domestic Employment* (*ibid.*, fig. 1012). Although Lady Templetown's example was followed by the Princess Royal and Princess Elizabeth, no royal designs appear to have been used by Wedgwood. Some of Princess Elizabeth's 'engravings from silhouettes' were, however, used to decorate a Berlin porcelain tea and coffee service, c.1810 (see no. 83 and Sloan 2000, p. 237).

The tiered design of the candelabra utilises the prismatic, light-reflecting qualities of the glass spires and drops to make the most of the expensive beeswax candles with which they would have been lit. Evidence that this type of light was in use at Buckingham House is provided by a bill of 1782 from the cabinet-maker William Gates (see no. 284), acting as supplier rather than maker: as part of the furnishing of the Prince of Wales's Apartments he provided a pair of 'very superb Girandoles', each with three cut-glass branches, prisms and drops and mounted in gilt at a cost of £96 (PRO LC9/329, no. 7, qtr to 5 January). Parker's firm (from 1802–3 known as Parker and Perry) went on to supply the Prince of Wales with a spectacular series of light fittings (mainly chandeliers) at Carlton House in the first two decades of the nineteenth century.

No. 288, for which there is no contemporary documentation, is probably the pair referred to in the Windsor Castle Clocks Inventory, begun in 1876. Six other pairs with similar plinths, but with single candle-nozzles, are also recorded. These were adapted to match no. 288 by Queen Mary in 1914 and were placed in her Wedgwood Room at Windsor Castle.

289. Attributed to Robert Campbell (fl.1754–1793)
Pair of pier tables, c.1790

Gilded pine, marble. 91.0 × 132.0 × 49.5 cm
(2′ 11¹³⁄₁₆″ × 4′ 3¹⁵⁄₁₆″ × 1′ 7½″)
RCIN 33475.1–2
PROVENANCE Probably made for George III
LITERATURE Laking 1905, p. 48

In common with most of the neo-classical furniture associated with George III's modernisation of the State Apartments at Windsor, these tables have little or no documentation. The decoration of the frames is, however, sufficiently close to that of a surviving set of stools (RCIN 20463), almost certainly made by Robert Campbell as part of the refurnishing of the King's Audience Chamber, to support an attribution to this maker (see no. 282); and the inclusion of a Garter star and crossed sceptres on the friezes of the tables further strengthens the possibility that they were made for this important room.

The elaborate new scheme of decoration in the Audience Chamber was conceived principally as a glorification of the Order of the Garter and was personally supervised by the King, whose veneration for the Order provided one of the main-springs for his extensive and costly restoration of the castle.

289

The new furniture for the room included a spectacular throne made by Campbell, flower-embroidered hangings worked by Mrs Pawsey's school (see no. 282) and a set of stools. The tables may have stood in part of the room not shown in the view painted by Wild for Pyne (no. 128), either side of the door to the King's Guard Chamber at the opposite end from the throne.

290. John Russell (*fl.*1773–1822), Charles Elliott (1752–1832) and (?) James Wyatt (1746–1813)

Two armchairs, 1807

Gilded beech, gilt bronze, velvet. 99.5 × 67.0 × 61.0 cm
(39 3⁄16″ × 26 3⁄8″ × 24″)
RCIN 28728.1–2
PROVENANCE Made for Speaker's House, Palace of Westminster
(PRO LC9/368, ff. 108, 115)
LITERATURE Roberts (H.) 2003

In 1802 James Wyatt, Surveyor General and Comptroller of the Office of Works from 1796, began a controversial programme of modernisation of Speaker's House in the Palace of Westminster for Speaker Charles Abbot, a project in which George III took a personal interest both as sovereign and as Wyatt's employer in the re-gothicising of Windsor. The irregularly shaped house, parallel to Westminster Hall and at right angles to St Stephen's Chapel, was given a Tudor Gothic stuccoed façade, and within Wyatt constructed new state rooms including three fitted out entirely in the Gothic style. For the latter, which were probably situated on the first floor overlooking the river, the regular suppliers to the Royal Household – John Russell and Charles Elliott – were employed to make a large suite which originally consisted of 26 armchairs, 30 side chairs, 6 sofas, 5 tables, 6 screens and a pair of lantern tripods. Everything was japanned black, highly polished to look like ebony and partly gilt. The chairs and sofas were upholstered in scarlet morocco leather with protective covers of scarlet and black printed cotton. Elliott's bills make clear that the decorative parts of the tables and screens were modelled from 'ornaments selected from the Abbey'. The selection was no doubt overseen by Wyatt who, as Surveyor of the Abbey since 1782, was well qualified for the task, but as this furniture does not seem to have survived, the precise choice of ornaments is not known. In the case of the seat furniture, of which twenty-three armchairs and five sofas survive in the

290

Royal Collection, Russell's bills make no mention of the source of designs. However it is clear that here as well, direct quotations were taken from the Abbey. The battlemented string-courses which make up the frames and the diamond-pattern cylindrical shafts forming legs and arm-supports are borrowed from the elaborately carved late Gothic choir stalls in the Henry VII Chapel and skilfully incorporated into the conventional format of early nineteenth-century chair design. The bills from Elliott and Russell for the seat furniture amounted to £1,650 8s, the armchairs being charged by Russell at £25 5s each and the upholstery by Elliott at 6 guineas each with a further charge of £2 18s per case cover.

Speaker's House survived the fire at the Palace of Westminster in 1834, but was demolished in 1842. The chairs are recorded at Windsor later in the same decade.

291

291. Edward Wyatt (1757–1833)

Carved panel, 1807

Limewood. 43.5 × 182.5 × 10.0 cm
(1′ 5⅛″ × 5′ 11⅞″ × 3¹⁵/₁₆″)
RCIN 20701
PROVENANCE Made for George III (PRO WORK 5/97, qtr to
Midsummer 1808)
LITERATURE Laking 1905, pp. xi and 58; St John Hope 1913, I,
p. 351; Roberts (H.) 1990a

The ornamental carvings by Grinling Gibbons and others in
the State Apartments at Windsor Castle have been celebrated
since they were first installed for Charles II in the 1670s
and 1680s. During James Wyatt's extensive alterations for
George III at the beginning of the nineteenth century some
rearrangement of the carvings took place, probably supervised
by Wyatt's cousin Edward, who held the post of carver and
gilder to the Office of Works from 1798. At the same time as
the King's Dining Room was refurnished as the State Bedchamber, at George III's command, and the spectacular Gibbons
carvings there were removed to store, Wyatt carved for the
Queen's Audience Chamber a new overmantel panel of such
technical virtuosity and sophistication that it must be seen as
a direct challenge by Wyatt to the achievements of Gibbons:
it is shown in position in a watercolour by C. Wild (no. 131).

Wyatt's carefully worded account (amounting to £170)
for this exquisite carving reveals an iconographic programme
of great deliberation, suggesting at least the possibility of the
King's personal involvement in its creation. The elements of
earth and water are symbolised in the cornucopiae flanking
the royal coat of arms, which is surmounted by entwined
roses and shamrocks representing the Union and is supported
on the back of the British lion. The lion suppresses the force
of arms (the fasces and other militaria); the shield of the City
is bound to the anchor by laurels with emblems of Commerce
and Justice; the Order of the Garter is supported by branches
of oak for strength and the Order of the Bath by the laurels
of Victory. Finally Wyatt notes that the medals in the left
cornucopia 'are rewards His Majesty presents to his most
deserving Subjects'.

292. Attributed to Tatham, Bailey and Sanders
(*fl.*1809–1818)

Pair of torchères, *c.*1812

Gilded beechwood. 169.5 × 47.5 × 47.5 cm
(5′ 6¾″ × 1′ 6¹¹/₁₆″ × 1′ 6¹¹/₁₆″)
RCIN 45.1–2
PROVENANCE Made for Queen Charlotte
LITERATURE Roberts (H.) 2001, pp. 329, 331 and 333

The form and decoration of these torchères, notably the foliate
shaft and tripod base of the upper section and the bearded
ringleted masks on the triangular pedestal base, are derived

from classical sources. Similar features can be seen in the
published designs of Thomas Hope and of C.H. Tatham.
Some of the latter's designs were used by his brother's
cabinet-making partnership when supplying furniture for
the Prince Regent at Carlton House (e.g. the Council
Chairs of 1812; *Royal Treasures* 2002, no. 89).

No. 292, for which no documentation has been found,
were shown in the Crimson Drawing Room at Buckingham
House, flanking the door to the Saloon, in a view by James
Stephanoff published in 1817 (no. 112). They appear to have
been made with five-branch candelabra (which no longer
survive), and were almost certainly supplied as part of
the refurbishment of Queen Charlotte's apartments at
Buckingham House in *c*.1812. This work was undertaken
in order to provide a suitable and dignified setting for the
Queen to hold her Drawing Rooms and receptions after
the establishment of the Regency, St James's Palace being
by then in a dilapidated state as a result of the fire of 1809.

292

10. Time-keeping and science (nos. 293–308)

293. Thomas Mudge (1715–1794)

Queen Charlotte's lever watch and pedestal, 1770

Gold, tortoiseshell. 10.0 × 8.6 × 8.6 cm ($3^{15}/_{16}$″ × $3^3/_8$″ × $3^3/_8$″)
Backplate signed *Tho Mudge / London*. Gold case struck with
London hallmarks for 1769–70 and maker's mark *PM*, probably
for Philip Mounier
RCIN 63759
PROVENANCE Probably acquired by George III for
Queen Charlotte
LITERATURE Clutton and Daniels 1965, pp. 34–7

Because it incorporates the earliest known example of the
lever escapement this unique watch had been described
as 'perhaps the most historically important watch in the
world' (Baillie 1956, p. 288). With the exception of the
balance spring, this was the greatest single improvement
that has ever been applied to watches. As such, no. 293
is the forerunner of almost all modern wrist and pocket
watches. In addition this was the first pocket watch to
have an automatic device for compensating changes in
temperature.

Thomas Mudge invented the lever escapement in 1754
but no. 293, made in 1770, appears to have been the first
watch to incorporate this important innovation. It was
probably acquired by George III for Queen Charlotte: it was
referred to as the 'Queen's watch' in correspondence between
Mudge and his patron Count von Bruhl, Saxon Ambassador
to Great Britain, when it had been returned to Mudge's
Plymouth workshop for alterations and adjustment in the
early 1770s. Mudge subsequently described his invention as
'the most perfect watch that can be worn in the pocket, that
was ever made' (Mudge 1799, pp. 30–33).

It is not clear when the plinth was acquired. Signs of
alteration suggest that it may not have been made originally
for the watch. The first reference to the plinth is in 1825
when the watch was repaired and the plinth overhauled by
B.L. Vulliamy for George IV. The watch may have joined the

'twenty-five watches, all highly adorn'd with jewels' noticed
by Mrs Lybbe Powys in a case beside the Queen's bed at
Buckingham House in 1767 (*Lybbe Powys* 1899, p. 117).

293

294

294. George III (1738–1820)

Directions for mounting a watch, n.d.

Manuscript in pen and ink on paper. 31.6 × 44.4 cm
(12⁷⁄₁₆″ × 17½″)

RA GEO/15794–5

PROVENANCE Presumed to be part of the papers of George III
and George IV taken by the 1st Duke of Wellington (executor to
George IV) to Apsley House where they were rediscovered in
1912 and returned to Windsor Castle (see De Bellaigue (S.) 1998)

George III was fascinated by the complexities of clock and
watch movements and spent many hours taking them to
pieces and putting them together again. This two-page
manuscript in the King's hand lists the correct sequence of
operations for assembling a watch. It reads: 'Directions for
Mounting a Watch. On the Under Plate place the Barrel /
then the fusee or Great Wheel / then the Third Wheel / the
Contrate Wheel / the Center Wheel / fix the Upper plate /
place the third Wheel into the Upper plate / place the
Contrate Wheel / put in the pins of the Pillars that fasten
the two plates together / Hook the Chain into the Barrel /
Mount the Main Spring put your finger on the Barrel to
prevent the Chain from coiling among the Wheels / Fix the
Round Hook into the fusee / Wind up the Watch, be careful
the Chain goes into the Worm of the fusee, N.B. keep your
hand on the Contrate Wheel / let the Watch go down but at
times toutch [*sic*] the Contrate Wheel to prevent too great
velocity / Skrew [*sic*] on the Regulating plate of the Balance /
put on the Balance & fasten the Spring / then the Plate of the
Ballance / then the Minute Wheel / then the Hour Wheel /
put in the Pins that fasten the Dial Plate / put on the Hands'.

No. 294 is complemented by a second manuscript entitled
'Directions for unmounting a Watch' which also survives in
the Royal Archives (RA GEO/15794–7).

295. François-Justin Vulliamy (1712–1797)

Watch with cipher of Queen Charlotte, 1765–6

Gold, enamel. 6.1 × 4.8 × 2.0 cm (2⅜″ × 1⅞″ × ¾″)
Dial signed *Justin Vulliamy / London*. Gold case struck with London
hallmark for 1765–6 and maker's mark *PM*, probably for Philip
Mounier. Case inscribed *A present / to Sir John Pringle Bart. M.D. /
President of the Royal Society / of Great Britain / from / HER
MAJESTY QUEEN CHARLOTTE*

RCIN 4434

PROVENANCE Queen Charlotte; by whom presented to Sir John
Pringle; acquired by Queen Mary, 1931 (*QMB*, II, no. 435)

According to an inscription on the case this gold watch was a
present from Queen Charlotte to Sir John Pringle (1707–82),
President of the Royal Society. Pringle was an eminent

295

Scottish physician who had attended various members of the royal family since 1749. He studied medicine at the University of Leyden and served as Physician-General to the British army during the War of the Austrian Succession (1740–48). Drawing on his experiences of the appalling conditions of military hospitals, he published his great work *Observations on the Diseases of the Army* (1752) which proposed revolutionary changes in military medicine and sanitation. Although Pringle's speciality was the army, he was appointed Physician in Ordinary to Queen Charlotte in 1763 and later attended the birth of Princess Augusta. He was created a baronet by the King in 1766. Pringle was elected president of the Royal Society in 1772 and was appointed Physician to the King in the following year. He had been a staunch defender of the reputation of George III's mother, the Dowager Princess of Wales, at the time of the scandal surrounding her connection with Lord Bute and involvement in politics. In 1772 (the year of the Princess's death) he told James Boswell that 'his situation about the Royal Family gave him an opportunity of knowing circumstances that made it certain that the Princess was altogether free of both these concerns' (Hibbert 1998, p. 23).

The dial is signed by François-Justin Vulliamy, who supplied numerous clocks and watches to the King and Queen in the 1760s–80s (see no. 301).

296. Louis Recordon (*fl.*1778–1810)

Repeating watch with cipher of George III, 1802–3

Gold. 8.6 × 5.6 × 1.6 cm (3⅜″ × 2³⁄₁₆″ × ⅝″)
Struck with hallmarks for London, 1802–3 and maker's mark of Louis Comtesse, case and movement engraved with serial numbers; engraved inside case *This watch / was made in 1802 / and belonged to / King George III / To George, Duke of York on his marriage from his affectionate Uncle George, Duke of Cambridge, July 6ᵗʰ 1893*
RCIN 4712
PROVENANCE George III; Adolphus, Duke of Cambridge (d. 1850); by whom bequeathed to George, 2nd Duke of Cambridge; by whom given to his nephew, the future King George V, on his wedding day, 6 July 1893

George, 2nd Duke of Cambridge, gave this watch to his nephew the Duke of York (later King George V), on his wedding day in 1893. Like many other objects in the Cambridge collection it had formerly belonged to George III, the Duke's grandfather. A second watch, also made by Recordon in 1802–3, was included in the sale of the Cambridge collection in 1904.

296

297

The restrained simplicity of no. 296, a watch made for the King's personal use, is in marked contrast to the heavily jewelled and enamelled watches given by the King as presentation gifts (see no. 404). It incorporates a quarter-repeating mechanism, which strikes the last hour and divisions of the hour. This was a particularly useful function at night, at a time when illumination was not always readily available.

The movement is signed by the Swiss-born clock and watchmaker Louis Recordon whose first workshop was established in Greek Street, Soho. In 1805 Recordon took over the workshop of the eminent Swiss watchmaker Josiah Emery, the first watchmaker to use the lever escapement after Thomas Mudge.

Recordon is chiefly famous for his patent for a pedometer for winding watches in 1780. This was the world's first self-winding watch mechanism and the forerunner of modern self-winding watch mechanisms. He also acted as the London agent for the Parisian maker Abraham-Louis Breguet, the leading continental horologist of the time. Recordon retailed Breguet's movements, often signing them himself. No. 296 incorporates both French and English elements, a common practice at that time.

Recordon would have imported certain components, assembling the finished watch in his workshop.

297. Thomas Tompion (1639–1713) and Edward Banger (*fl.*1695–1707)

*Longcase equation clock, c.*1703

Walnut, oak, gilt bronze, brass, steel.
280.0 × 59.5 × 33.0 cm (9' 2¼" × 1' 11⁷⁄₁₆" × 1' 1")
RCIN 2754
PROVENANCE Made for Prince George of Denmark, consort of Queen Anne
LITERATURE Symonds 1951, pp. 269–70, 306–8 and figs. 28–9, 36, 66, 81–2; Jagger 1983, p. 64 and figs. 83–7

According to an anonymous description of *c.*1760, this 'most elegant & curious Piece of Workmanship' was made *c.*1703 for Queen Anne's husband, Prince George of Denmark (d. 1708) during the five-year period, ending *c.*1707, when Tompion was in partnership with his nephew Edward Banger. It was then in the 'State Bedchamber' at Kensington Palace. Not surprisingly – in view of its elaborate equation of time movement with perpetual calendar, which runs for 390 days on a single winding – this imposing creation was selected by George III (together with a second longcase equation clock by Tompion) for use at Buckingham House. As a dedicated and knowledgeable horologist, the King would have been well qualified to appreciate the mathematical skill and technical ingenuity of Tompion's workmanship. The principal dial records mean and solar time, the two subsidiary dials record the day of the week with the appropriate planet, day of the month (Old and New Style), month, sign of the Zodiac and the sun's place in the ecliptic as well as the number of years after a leap year.

No. 297 shares several features with Tompion's other royal commissions, notably the use of finely figured walnut and the well-chased and distinctive gilt bronze mounts, all probably provided by the same (unknown) subcontractor. The nearest comparison to no. 297 is probably the so-called 'Record' Tompion, now in Colonial Williamsburg, which was made for William III. Unlike no. 297, this still retains its original gilt bronze finials. Those on no. 297 were still *in situ* when it was drawn for the Pictorial Inventory (vol. B, no. 10), *c.*1827: it was then in store, having been at St James's Palace until the fire in 1809 and before that at Buckingham House.

According to the anonymous description of Buckingham House published in 1802, in 'every room the encouragement given by his Majesty to ingenious constructors of time-pieces is apparent' (*Gentleman's Magazine*, LXXII, 1802, p. 1184).

298. Ferdinand Berthoud (1727–1807); Charles Cressent (1685–1768); and Benjamin Lewis Vulliamy (1780–1854)

*Longcase equation clock, c.*1755

Oak, pine, purplewood, mahogany, gilt bronze, brass, steel.
236.2 × 70.5 × 35.0 cm (7' 9″ × 2' 3¾″ × 1' 1¾″)
RCIN 30035
PROVENANCE Possibly M. de Selle, sale Paris, 1761; probably acquired by George III, by 1765
LITERATURE Ronfort 1984, pp. 108–9; Pradère 1989, fig. 96; *Royal Treasures* 2002, no. 100; Roberts (H.) 2002, p. 8 and fig. 12

For a patron with the knowledge of clocks and clockmaking that George III certainly possessed, the appeal of a clock of this type lay in the equation of time movement constructed by one of the leading French horological theorists of the day, Ferdinand Berthoud. It may also be fair to say that the handsomely mounted case, one of the most felicitous creations of the cabinet-maker and sculptor Charles Cressent, would

298

also have aroused the King's admiration, but the fact that it appears in the background of Zoffany's celebrated portrait of Queen Charlotte with her two eldest sons (no. 4) strongly suggests that its acquisition was as much or perhaps more in deference to the Queen's taste for continental furniture as to the King's for horological invention. The date of acquisition is not known, but as it seems likely to have belonged (and to have been made for) the *Trésorier-général* of the French navy, M. de Selle, whose collection was sold in Paris in 1761, it had probably only recently arrived at the time Zoffany painted it (*c*.1765). At a later date it was in the Queen's Sitting Room at Kew.

Berthoud, who was awarded the rare distinction for a foreigner of election to a Fellowship of the Royal Society of London in 1764, became a *maître-horloger* in 1753. The case must therefore be a relatively late repetition of a model that Cressent first devised in the 1730s, but which remained popular late into the reign of Louis XV. The well-integrated and finely finished mounts show Cressent's skill as a sculptor to great advantage. The original movement was replaced by an eight-day equation movement made by B.L. Vulliamy in 1821 and numbered 783.

299. James Newton (*fl.*1760–1770)
*Bracket clock, c.*1765

Oak, tortoiseshell, brass, gilt bronze, enamel, silver.
38.0 × 23.0 × 17.5 cm (14¹⁵⁄₁₆″ × 9¹⁄₁₆″ × 6⅞″)
RCIN 2751
PROVENANCE Made for George III
LITERATURE Smith 1931, p. 253 and pl. 328; Jagger 1983, pp. 94–5

This elaborately mounted tortoiseshell-veneered clock is comparable in form and decoration – although on a greatly reduced, almost miniature scale – to the slightly later four-sided clock by Pinchbeck and others (no. 302); and while the striking and repeating movement (now with later anchor escapement) is relatively unsophisticated and by a maker of whom little is known, the domed, temple-like case is of the finest quality and, like nos. 300 and 302, is designed to be viewed in the round. The ormolu panels at the sides and back are very richly chased with trees in landscapes, foliage and *rocaille* ornament, suggestive of the work of one of the immigrant German craftsmen who dominated London chasing in the mid-eighteenth century, especially in the production of snuff boxes. The other mounts are of similarly refined quality.

Although direct evidence is lacking, it would seem likely that this clock was intended for the Queen's rather than the King's Apartments at Buckingham House: it was certainly in the Queen's Dressing Room at St James's Palace before the fire there in 1809 (William IV Clock Inventory, no. 175).

No payment has been discovered which could relate to this clock which, like no. 297, is known from the Pictorial Inventory (vol. B, no. 18) to have been originally at Buckingham House. It was moved to St James's Palace before being taken to Carlton House by George IV.

299

300

dials show the month and day and a third is for regulating the clock. The right dial functions as an orrery with six planets moving round the Zodiacal circle. The back dial shows the phases of the moon on a revolving half-silvered sphere, the age of the moon in arabic numerals and high and low water at thirty-two named seaports in roman numerals.

The *Gentleman's Magazine* for June 1765, which records (p. 299) that this clock had been installed at Buckingham House by Norton under the supervision of the King's clockmaker Christopher Pinchbeck, also notes that the calculations for the solar system were made by 'Dr. Bevis' and that the design for the dials and other calculations were made by 'Mr. Ferguson'. The latter was undoubtedly the natural philosopher and specialist in astronomical clocks James Ferguson (1713–85), who as a friend of Matthew Boulton advised on the movements of Boulton's celebrated 'Geographical' and 'Sidereal' clocks in the early 1770s (Goodison 2003, pp. 203–5, 226–7).

No. 300 cost the King's Privy Purse the very large sum of £1,042 (RA GEO/17137[r]). This payment probably included the charge for the exceptionally fine carved mahogany case, framed by palm-tree columns and mounted with silver plaques and lion and unicorn crestings. This is likely to have been

300. Eardley Norton (*fl*.1760–1794) and attributed to John Bradburn (*fl*.1760–1781)

Astronomical clock, 1765

Mahogany, silver, enamel and brass. 43.8 × 26.7 × 24.5 cm
(17¼" × 10½" × 9⅝")
RCIN 2870
PROVENANCE Made for George III
LITERATURE Harris, De Bellaigue and Millar 1968, p. 158;
Royal Miscellany 1990, no. 218

George III's consuming interest in horology and science is attractively encompassed in this clock. The complex and compact quarter-striking movement displays on the principal face the time of day on a 24-hour dial with hands for mean and solar time. In the centre a painted landscape with figures shows the passage of the sun across the sky and a small centre dial records the time at thirty locations around the world relative to mean time. A lunette at the top records the date and month. The left dial shows a year calendar on a spiral, indicated by a retracting vertical hand. Two further

FIG. 27 Robert Adam, *Design for a bracket for a clock*, 1766.
Pen and ink and watercolour (London, Soane Museum,
vol. 25, nos. 20–21)

made by John Bradburn, possibly using the specialist carver Sefferin Alken as a subcontractor. In the same year Bradburn supplied a glass cover for the clock to the King's direction costing £9 6s (PRO LC9/313, no. 8, qtr to Christmas).

The following year, 1766, Bradburn delivered 'a very rich Antique carved & burnish'd gilt Bracket' with a sliding and revolving top section designed to show all four sides of the clock, supported on a 'Demi Lyon & Unicorn' at a cost of £38 15s (PRO LC9/313, no. 64, qtr to Midsummer). The existence of the designs for this bracket among Robert Adam's drawings in the Soane Museum (fig. 27) implies that the clock case too may have been designed by Adam, whose involvement at Buckingham House (see no. 95) is generally somewhat overshadowed by that of Sir William Chambers. His bracket, which no longer survives, was presumably dispensed with when the clock was moved, probably c.1770, from the King's Dressing Room to the Octagon Library to stand on the central desk, where it is recorded in Stephanoff's view of 1818 (no. 117).

301. François-Justin Vulliamy (1712–1797)

Bracket clock, c.1765

Ebony, oak, gilt bronze, brass, enamel. 47.4 × 29.0 × 22.0 cm (18¹¹⁄₁₆″ × 11⁷⁄₁₆″ × 8¹¹⁄₁₆″)
RCIN 3011
PROVENANCE Probably made for George III
LITERATURE Smith 1931, p. 256 and pl. 332; Jagger 1983, pp. 89–90

The three-train and quarter-striking movement of this clock, constructed by the founder of the Vulliamy dynasty of royal clockmakers, is of characteristically high quality; but the lavishly mounted case, which is used as a vehicle for the display of the bronze-maker's and chaser's skill, is its most distinctive feature. The finely modelled and chased gilt bronze term angles and seated figure of a philosopher crowning the top reflect in miniature something of the rich sobriety seen in the Cumming barograph (no. 305), if on a greatly reduced scale and in a much more conventional and conservative format. No payment for the clock has been traced and it was first recorded at Buckingham House in the Pictorial Inventory (vol. B, no. 2).

Benjamin and Benjamin Lewis Vulliamy (see nos. 298, 304) were respectively the son and grandson of François-Justin, who was born in Switzerland. François-Justin received a large number of commissions from George III:

301

these included a watch for the King's use (RCIN 65350) and an almost identical watch which the King gave to Lord Harcourt. He certainly made the movement for the watch presented by the Queen to Sir John Pringle c.1772 (no. 295) and probably that in the chatelaine presented by the King to Lord Courtown a decade later (no. 404). He also signed the movement of the 'Andromache' bracket clock (no. 303).

302. Christopher Pinchbeck (1710–1783), Sir William Chambers (1723–1796) and others

Astronomical clock, 1768

Tortoiseshell, oak, gilt bronze, silver, brass, steel and enamel. 77.8 × diameter 51.4 cm (30⅝″ × 20¼″)
RCIN 2821
PROVENANCE Made for George III
LITERATURE Harris, De Bellaigue and Millar 1968, p. 159; Harris (J.) 1970, p. 219 and pls. 131–3; Goodison 2003, p. 33

Like the Eardley Norton clock of 1765 (no. 300), the mechanism of this clock is designed to impress with its comprehensiveness and complexity, and the case with its superb quality and glamorous materials. The four principal dials operate almost identically on both clocks, the main differences being that on the Pinchbeck clock the calendar dial incorporates a planisphere, the orrery dial includes a thermometer and the dials recording the time at locations round the world (relative to mean time and high and low water at seaports) vary in some of the places named. The enamelling of the dials on the two clocks compares very closely in style and may be by the same hand. The mechanism was constructed by Pinchbeck, the King's clockmaker, with the assistance of John Merigeot (apprenticed 1742) and John Monk (apprenticed 1762).

On a visit to Pinchbeck's workshop in London on 29 January 1768 to inspect the newly completed clock, the diarist Lady Mary Coke noted that the design was 'partly His Majesty's and partly Mr Chambers his Architect'. Although the extent of George III's contribution is difficult to judge, Chambers's involvement could be inferred from the temple-like appearance and laurel-draped urns of the clock case, resembling in miniature a building such as the Casino at Marino (begun in 1758, to Chambers's designs), and is confirmed by the existence in the Soane Museum of a highly finished design drawing by Chambers, varying in some details from the finished clock (Harris (J.) 1970, pl. 131; *Chambers* 1996, p. 155, fig. 229). No record of payment for the clock is recorded, nor is the name of Pinchbeck's case-maker known. Whoever was responsible had access to a metalsmith of distinction – possibly Diederich Nicolaus Anderson (see no. 274), as has been suggested (Goodison 2003, p. 33). The jewel-like gilt bronze and silver mounts are of outstanding quality and remarkable for the precision of their casting and chasing.

In George III's time the clock was kept in the Passage Room, which probably lay at the centre of his apartment at Buckingham House, on the west (garden) front. It was originally mounted on a circular tray resting on the head and upraised hands of a bearded herm pedestal of carved giltwood, perhaps also designed by Chambers. The pedestal, which was 167.6 cm (66 in.) high, is recorded in the Pictorial Inventory (fig. 28) but no longer survives in the Royal Collection.

302

FIG. 28 Page from the Pictorial Inventory showing the Pinchbeck clock on its original stand, designed by Sir William Chambers, c.1826. Watercolour (RCIN 933560: volume B, no. 3)

303

no. 304). The so-called 'Andromache' figure was probably modelled by the young sculptor John Deare, who left the Vulliamys' employ in 1785; it seems to be based on a composition by John Bacon, who also worked directly for Vulliamy on occasions.

According to Benjamin Lewis Vulliamy, grandson of François-Justin, George III's version of this clock (Pictorial Inventory, vol. B, no. 20), which varied in some small details from no. 303, was 'the first of this pattern . . . & was made expressly for His late Majesty King George the 3d' (William IV Clock Inventory, no. 47). No payment for this clock is identifiable in George III's accounts, but a second version, owned by George IV when Prince of Wales and recorded by B.L. Vulliamy at Brighton (*ibid.*, no. 137), may have been purchased from François-Justin Vulliamy in 1784 (£94 10s; RA GEO/25642). Neither of these clocks survives in the Royal Collection. No. 303, a third example of this model, was bequeathed to Queen Victoria by Lord Melbourne in 1848.

304. Benjamin Vulliamy (1747–1811) and J. J. W. Spängler (*fl.* late eighteenth century) for William (II) Duesbury's Derby Factory

Mantel clock, 1789–90

Marble, gilt bronze. 49.5 × 29.2 × 14.0 cm (19½″ × 11½″ × 5½″)
RCIN 30261
PROVENANCE Made for Queen Charlotte
LITERATURE Clifford 1978

Benjamin Vulliamy, Clockmaker to the King from 1773, was closely involved in the production and development of a new type of ornamental clock case in the 1780s, in which high quality gilt bronze was combined with finely modelled biscuit porcelain figures. In an attempt to surpass French biscuit porcelain production and to promote English manufacture, Vulliamy collaborated with William Duesbury of Derby in the employment of artists capable of producing small-scale sculpture of the finest quality in the most up-to-date neo-classical idiom. He engaged the interest of the royal family in pursuit of this aim, showing a Derby biscuit head from a clock case figure to Queen Charlotte, the Princesses and the Prince of Wales in February 1787. They were 'pleased to express great satisfaction at seeing it and were glad to see the improvement we were making in this Country', as he reported to Duesbury (Clifford 1990, p. 235). Possibly as a result of this demonstration, Vulliamy was commissioned to

303. François-Justin Vulliamy (1712–1797) and John Deare (1759–1798) (possibly after John Bacon) for William (II) Duesbury's Derby Factory

Mantel clock, c.1783

Gilt bronze, marble, enamel, porcelain. 43.0 × 25.9 × 19.9 cm (16¹⁵⁄₁₆″ × 10³⁄₁₆″ × 7¹³⁄₁₆″)
RCIN 2827
PROVENANCE 2nd Viscount Melbourne (1779–1848); by whom bequeathed to Queen Victoria
LITERATURE Clifford 1990, p. 230

Although the movement is signed by François-Justin Vulliamy, and is for that reason likely to be an early example of this popular model, the inspiration behind the development of these figural clock cases was certainly that of François-Justin's son Benjamin, and it was he who arranged with William Duesbury to improve the production of Derby biscuit porcelain by employing a series of well-trained sculptor-modellers (see

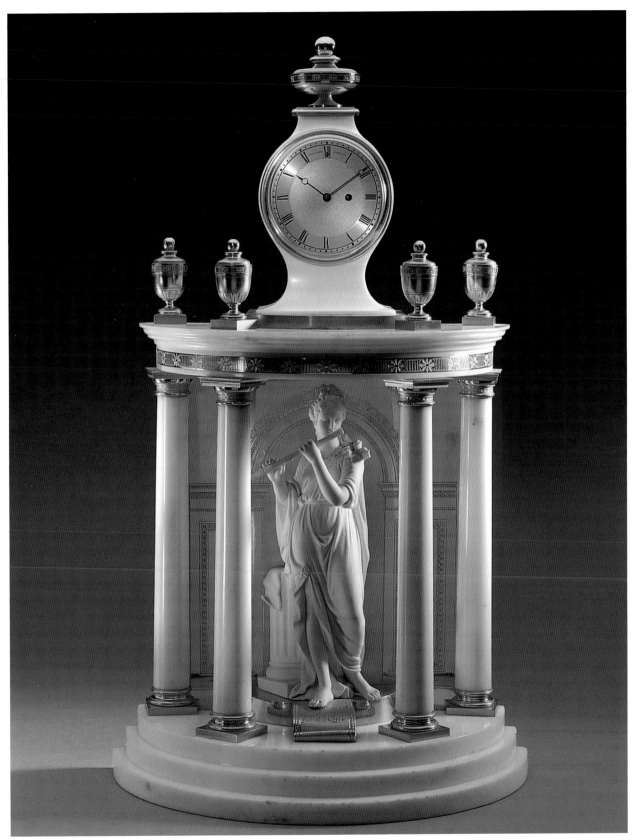

305

make this elegant neo-classical 'temple' clock for Queen Charlotte: the King and Prince of Wales already each possessed at least one Vulliamy clock with a Derby biscuit figure ornamenting the case (see no. 303). An earlier version of the 'temple' design, produced in 1787–8, included a Derby figure modelled by C.F. Rossi of a girl sacrificing. Rossi proved unsatisfactory and for the figure of Euterpe, the Muse of Lyric Poetry or Music, Duesbury and Vulliamy engaged the Swiss-born sculptor J.J.W. Spängler in 1790.

The clock was originally in Queen Charlotte's Dressing Room at Buckingham House (Pictorial Inventory, vol. B, no. 15). Its original watch movement was replaced in 1845 by Benjamin Lewis Vulliamy with an 8-day timepiece, numbered 1694 (William IV Clock Inventory, no. 179).

305. Alexander Cumming (*c.*1732–1814)
Barograph, 1763–5

Padouk, oak, ivory, gilt bronze, steel, enamel, parchment.
243.2 × 57.8 × 45.7 cm (7′ 11¾″ × 1′ 10¾″ × 1′ 6″)
RCIN 2752
PROVENANCE Made for George III
LITERATURE Harris, De Bellaigue and Millar 1968, pp. 148–9;
Royal Treasures 2002, no. 83

Among the substantial number of precision horological and scientific instruments that George III assembled at Buckingham House in the early part of the reign, this exceptional barograph is outstanding for both its mechanical complexity and the richness of its case. The movement was designed and made by the Scot Alexander Cumming and incorporates a month-going regulator clock with Cumming's own escapement and an Ellicott compensating pendulum. A siphon wheel barometer in the trunk, supported between ivory Corinthian columns, is mechanically connected to the concentric six- and twelve-month charts which surround the clock dial. No. 305 cost the King the large sum of £1,178 (RA GEO/17132ʳ), to which he added a payment of £150 and an annual retainer to Cumming of £37 10s for maintaining the barograph.

The identity of Cumming's cabinet-maker is unknown, but a likely candidate might be William Vile, with whose work (e.g. no. 266) the barograph case bears comparison, especially in the use of pierced gilt bronze angles (at the base) and pierced shell ornament (below the dial). The mount-maker (or makers, as more than one hand seems to have been involved) is equally unknown: the vividly modelled and finely chased drops of flower at the angles of the trunk are of remarkable quality, but quite different in character and finish to the martial trophies below. The origin of the gilt bronze group of Time(?) assisted by Cupid has not been identified but John Flaxman the Elder (1726–95) and the elder John Bacon (1740–99) are known to have supplied the bronze trade with models of this general type, some of which were certainly used on clock cases (Goodison 2003, pp. 97–8).

George III kept the Cumming barograph with the Pinchbeck clock (no. 302) in the Passage Room of his apartments at Buckingham House, where it was recorded for the Pictorial Inventory (vol. B, no. 9).

306. Attributed to François-Justin Vulliamy (1712–1797) and to John Bradburn (*fl.*1760–1781)

*Wheel barometer, c.*1770

Mahogany, brass, steel, glass. 123.2 × 32.7 × 11.6 cm
(48½″ × 12⅞″ × 4⁹⁄₁₆″)
RCIN 30808
PROVENANCE Made for George III
LITERATURE Goodison 1966

The earliest record of this very finely made but unsigned instrument, a scale drawing of 1826–7, is contained in George IV's Pictorial Inventory (vol. B, no. 8). This is annotated 'Made by Justin Vulliamy', apparently in the hand of Vulliamy's grandson, Benjamin Lewis Vulliamy. The probable accuracy of this inscription is supported by a comparison of no. 306 with the documented barometer by F.-J. Vulliamy, in a case by Thomas Chippendale, which was made for Nostell Priory (Goodison 1966, pl. XIII). The brass and steel mechanism, the weather dial with 3-inch scale, the hygrometer (for measuring moisture) and the thermometer on the lower door, are virtually identical on both barometers.

The inscription on the drawing in the Pictorial Inventory records that no. 306 was formerly in the late King's (i.e. George III's) Bedroom at Buckingham House and subsequently in the library. In either place it would have been in close proximity to George III's other scientific instruments and precision time-keepers, including the Eardley Norton four-sided clock (no. 300) with which it shares the same exquisite quality of carving. Although there is no record of payment for the barometer in the surviving part of George III's Privy Purse accounts (which run from Michaelmas 1763

306

to Christmas 1772), it is highly likely that John Bradburn was responsible for making the finely figured mahogany case, as he had (almost certainly) done for the Eardley Norton clock in 1765. Given that the specialist carver Sefferin Alken is known to have worked directly for Bradburn's master William Vile and for Bradburn himself, as well as for Sir William Chambers and Robert Adam (*DOEFM* 1986, p. 8), it is possible that Alken was subcontracted on this occasion for the distinctive and highly refined carved ornament.

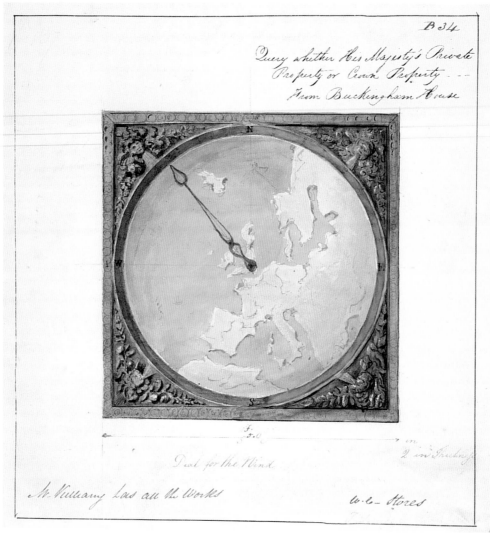

307

307. Francis Arundale (1807–1853)

*Wind-dial from the library at Buckingham House, c.*1826

Pencil and watercolour on paper.
25.1 × 15.6 cm (9⅞″ × 6⅛″)
RL 33560
PROVENANCE Drawn for George IV
LITERATURE Roberts (H.) 2001, p. 430, n. 176

The East Library (see no. 118) was the last of the four library rooms to be constructed for the King, in the new wing added immediately to the south of his own apartments at Buckingham House. The main library room was built in 1772–3; the Marine Gallery immediately above was added in 1774. By the time Sophie von la Roche visited Buckingham House in 1786, the wind-dial over the chimneypiece was *in situ* and was pointed out to her by her guide, the King's clockmaker François-Justin Vulliamy, as 'one of his eldest son's [i.e. Benjamin Vulliamy's] inventions'. Recognising

both the King's interest in science and his abiding concern for naval matters, she described the wind-dial as 'a large semi-sphere set in the wall [on which] he can follow which parts of the world are affected if a heavy gale is sweeping England; while the weather-vane on the house, with its eminent situation, calculates and records so accurately on this sphere that the king can conjecture how his fleet is faring' (*Sophie in London 1786*, p. 146). It is shown in position in James Stephanoff's view of the library (no. 118), published by W.H. Pyne in 1817. The mast attached to the wind-dial is clearly visible to the left of the main building in the exterior view of Buckingham House, also included in Pyne's series (no. 108).

All four libraries were altered beyond recognition in the remodelling of Buckingham House by John Nash in the 1820s. The wind-dial, drawn for George IV's Pictorial Inventory of works of art, was removed to store at this date but no longer survives in the Royal Collection.

308

308. William Walls (*fl.*1761–1765)

Door lock, 1761

Steel, brass, wood. 20.3 × 35.6 × 5.7 cm (8″ × 14″ × 2¼″)
Engraved *WILL^M WALLS / FECIT* and dated *1761*
RCIN 61078
PROVENANCE Presented by the maker to George III, 1765
LITERATURE *George III* 1974, no. 91

George III was presented with this somewhat macabre object
by its maker, William Walls, in 1765. It would certainly have
appealed to the King's interest in scientific instruments and
machinery. The mechanism incorporates two pistols and is
so designed that when an unwary intruder tampered with it,
alarm bells (now missing) would start ringing and the pistols
would fire. The drawbacks of such a mechanism however,

were pointed out when it was described in the *Gentleman's
Magazine* in 1765: 'honest inadvertent people might suffer
by it, who not being always recollected, might forget the
danger, tho' apprized of it and suffer for their want of
memory' (*Gentleman's Magazine*, XXXV, p. 295). William
Walls, about whom nothing else is known, was described
in the *Gentleman's Magazine* as a 'Birmingham manufacturer'.
The barrels of the flintlock guns, however, are stamped with
the mark used – from 1741 onwards – on the work of non-
members of the London Gunmakers' Company, proved in the
company's proof-house.

11. Ceramics (nos. 309–329)

309. Chelsea (Lawrence Street Factory)

Pieces from the 'Mecklenburg Service', c.1763

Soft-paste bone-ash porcelain. Centrepiece 42.5 × 66.7 × 59.0 cm (16¾″ × 26¼″ × 23¼″); large tureen 24.3 × 27.2 × 21.2 cm (9⁹⁄₁₆″ × 10¹¹⁄₁₆″ × 8⅜″); small tureen 14.2 × 27.2 × 21.2 cm (5⁹⁄₁₆″ × 10¹¹⁄₁₆″ × 8⅜″); cruet set (porcelain bottles) 31.8 × 21.9 × 22.7 cm (12½″ × 8⅝″ × 8¹⁵⁄₁₆″); cruet set (glass bottles) 30.0 × 28.0 × 15.3 cm (11¹³⁄₁₆″ × 11″ × 6″); sauceboat 17.2 × 21.7 × 11.6 cm (6¾″ × 8⁹⁄₁₆″ × 4⁹⁄₁₆″); salt 8.2 × 11.6 × 8.3 cm (3¼″ × 4⁹⁄₁₆″ × 3¼″); oval platter 41.0 × 51.0 cm (16⅛″ × 20¹⁄₁₆″); four plates diameter 23.5 cm (9¼″); two candelabra 19.0 × 38.5 × 32.5 cm (7⁷⁄₁₆″ × 15³⁄₁₆″ × 12¹³⁄₁₆″)
Marked on the underside of each piece with a gold anchor.
RCIN 57028 (centrepiece), 57012.2 (large tureen), 57012.3 (small tureen), 57014.2, 57023.1 (cruet sets), 57013.1 (sauceboat), 57024.6 (salt), 57022.1 (oval platter), 57024.8, .28, .44, .48 (plates), 57017.2a.2b, .3a.3b (candelabra)
PROVENANCE Commissioned by George III and Queen Charlotte; by whom presented to her brother Adolphus Frederick IV, Duke of Mecklenburg-Strelitz, 1764; by descent until 1919; Sir Joseph Duveen; James Oakes, by whom presented to HM Queen Elizabeth, 1947
LITERATURE *Royal Treasures* 2002, no. 108 (with further references)

In October 1766 the traveller Thomas Nugent noticed among the other 'curiosities' in the palace at Neustrelitz 'a complete service of Chelsea porcelane, rich and beautiful in fancy beyond expression. I really never saw any Dresden porcelane near so fine: her Majesty made a present of this choice collection to the duke her brother' (Nugent 1768, I, p. 338). This was the Queen's elder brother, Adolphus Frederick IV, Duke of Mecklenburg-Strelitz (1738–94), who was invested as a Knight of the Garter in April 1764 (see no. 443). This exceptionally grand service had been completed in March the previous year. It comprises pieces for the first course and dessert, and originally included tea and coffee wares. The inclusion of candelabra and the centrepiece which also holds candles shows that it was intended to furnish the Duke's table with every necessity, leaving him in no need of silver.

In this respect the service epitomises the intense competition for a place on the table that existed at this time between the makers and purveyors of silver and porcelain in England (see Mallet 1969). This is further indicated by the closeness in form between some of the shapes and their silver equivalents, which can clearly be seen by comparison of the cruet-stands, sauceboats and sugar vases with their counterparts in the Coronation Service (nos. 335, 339–41). The manager of the Chelsea porcelain factory from around 1745, the Liègeois Nicolas Sprimont (1716–71), was himself a successful and original goldsmith, working for Frederick, Prince of Wales, among others, but after only seven years transferred his energies to the medium of porcelain.

309

◁ No. 310 (detail)

309

Though it left the country in the year it was completed, the Mecklenburg Service was influential in England. The particularly intense blue enamel known as 'Mazarine blue', which was thinly applied and fused to the glaze, was clearly a response to the hugely successful dark blue enamels produced by the Sèvres factory, the underglaze *bleu lapis* in use from the early 1750s, and the more solid *bleu nouveau* which was introduced in December 1763, only a few months after the appearance of the Mecklenburg Service. An almost identical dinner service, with plates of a slightly different outline, seems to have been produced at Chelsea at around the same time.

310. Chelsea (Lawrence Street Factory), and Georg Philip Strigel (1718–1798)

Two clock case groups, c.1761–6

Soft-paste bone-ash porcelain. 42.2 × 31.7 × 22.8 cm
(16⁹⁄₁₆″ × 12½″ × 9″)
One (RCIN 2914) marked on the back with a gold anchor. Engraved on the backplate of the one surviving movement (in RCIN 2915) *Geo. Phi. Strigel / London* and *BBFF*. Both dials enamelled in black *STRIGEL / LONDON*.

RCIN 2914, 2915
PROVENANCE Queen Charlotte; her sale, Christie's, 7–11 May 1819, fourth day, lot 47; purchased by Loving on behalf of the Prince Regent (£73 10s)
LITERATURE *Rococo* 1984, pp. 260–61, no. O42

Porcelain clock cases or watch-stands were first produced by European factories in the 1720s, but do not appear in English porcelain until the late 1750s, when such objects were made at Bow and Chelsea. These are two examples of the same model, with minor differences and with variations in the decoration and gilding, suggesting that they are at least partly the work of different hands. They present something of a hybrid design, resembling the large-scale 'pastoral' groups of shepherds and shepherdesses which were made at Chelsea in the early 1760s, but surmounted by a small clock. They can be dated between 1761, when their strong crimson ground colour is first mentioned in the Chelsea sale catalogues; and 1766, when the factory's senior and most outstanding modeller Joseph Willems returned to his native Flanders. The figures of a shepherd awakening a sleeping shepherdess are characteristic of his style.

Georg Philip Strigel held the appointment of Watchmaker

310 (RCIN 2914)

310 (RCIN 2915)

to the Queen and may be identifiable with 'Stragael', the
'blunt, high-dried, honest German' who 'had the care of his
majesty's clocks' and was once interrupted by the King whilst
attending to a clock dial at Buckingham House, 'standing
upon a stool, placed upon a table, his hands extended above
his head' (Angelo 1828, I, pp. 205–6).

Only one of the movements survives. Originally 24-hour,
they had been altered to 8-day going by 1821, when Benjamin
Vulliamy refurbished them for George IV at Carlton House.

Duesbury & Co.
Three groups of the royal family (nos. 311–313)

311. George, Prince of Wales, Prince Frederick, Prince William and Prince Edward, c.1773

Biscuit porcelain. Height 22.0 cm (8¹¹⁄₁₆″)
RCIN 37021
PROVENANCE (?)Princess Sophia (d. 1848); Lady Carrington; by
descent to 3rd Lord Carrington, later Marquess of Lincolnshire;
Albert Amor Ltd; from whom purchased by Queen Mary, 1924

312. George III, c.1773

Biscuit porcelain. Height 30.0 cm (11¹³⁄₁₆″)
RCIN 37020
PROVENANCE Purchased by Queen Mary, 1920 (WCSI, p. 441)

313. Queen Charlotte with the Princess Royal and Princess Augusta, c.1773

Biscuit porcelain. Height 23.5 cm (9¼″)
RCIN 37022
PROVENANCE (?)Princess Sophia (d. 1848); Lady Carrington; by
descent to 3rd Lord Carrington, later Marquess of Lincolnshire;
Albert Amor Ltd; from whom purchased by Queen Mary, 1924
LITERATURE Hobson 1905, p. 61, no. II, 300; Clifford 1985,
pp. 12–15

These delicate groups of figures are extremely rare, not only
in themselves but as examples of the reproduction in porcelain
of an elaborate painted composition. Zoffany's group portrait
of the royal family in 'Van Dyck' costume (no. 7) was painted
early in 1770, and the porcelain groups were probably modelled
from the engraving by Richard Earlom published in October
of that year. The modeller, probably the sculptor John Bacon
(see no. 254), adapted the arrangement of the figures so
as to accommodate them within the bases, and focused the
attention of the group of four Princes more directly on the
cockatoo held by Prince William, which is now missing. The
figure of the King was intended to stand on a blue enamelled
and gilded base supported by crouching lions. (The only other
recorded example of the figure, in the British Museum,
preserves its stand.) The present base of the George III group
was made in 1924 to match the other two.

311 312 313

The royal groups are the first item in a list of 'the Principal Additions made this Year to the new Invented Groups, Vases . . . of Mr Duesbury's Derby and Chelsea Manufactory of Porcelaines' (Bemrose 1898, p. 54). This was probably issued shortly after June 1773, when William (II) Duesbury (1725–86), the proprietor of the Derby Porcelain Works, set up his new warehouse in London, having acquired the discontinued Chelsea manufactory in 1770. The groups of the royal family were clearly intended to promote the wares of the new company, and in particular its biscuit figures, modelled in a new body rich in bone ash and intended to rival the productions of Sèvres. Both George III and Queen Charlotte made numerous purchases of 'useful' wares from the London warehouse during the following decade (Bemrose 1898, pp. 89–93).

314. Wedgwood

*Vase, c.*1769–80

White terracotta stoneware, on black 'basalt' base.
Height 16.5 cm (6½")
Raised inscription within circular bands under base
WEDGWOOD & BENTLEY ETRURIA
RCIN 45759
PROVENANCE Acquired by Queen Mary, *c.*1920s
LITERATURE Dawson 1985, p. 640 and fig. 1

Josiah Wedgwood (1730–95) transformed the pottery industry of Staffordshire and established an international reputation for British ceramics. His success came from an exceptional understanding of the potential markets for useful and ornamental wares, combined with the business acumen of his partner, Thomas Bentley (1730–80). To these factors must be added Wedgwood's tireless pursuit of technical improvements, above all his invention of the so-called 'jasper' body (see no. 315).

Royal patronage was also critical to his early career. In 1765 he took over from another manufacturer an order from Queen Charlotte for a tea service in the glazed earthenware known as creamware, decorated in green with flowers and melons, and with the insides solidly gilt. The service does not survive, but from the following year Wedgwood was entitled to style himself on his bill heads 'Potter to Her Majesty', and his creamware body was renamed 'Queen's Ware'. The Queen remained a valuable customer, and in 1774 paid a private visit to Wedgwood's showroom in Greek Street to see the great creamware service (the 'Frog Service'), decorated with British topographical views, ordered by the Empress Catherine of Russia.

This ornamental vase, the 'pebble' glaze of which imitates a form of hardstone, would have been an ideal companion for mounted urns and vases made in Derbyshire spar or blue john (see nos. 275, 276, 278). The vase probably originally had a lid. Like many surviving pieces of this kind, the handles and swags have lost most of their gilding, which seems not to have been fired.

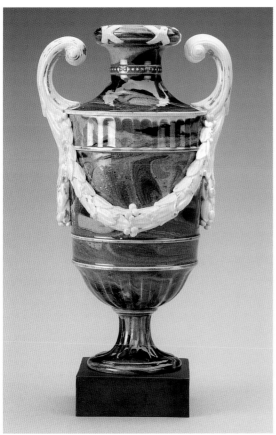

314

315. Wedgwood

Four busts on pedestals, c.1787

Jasper ware. Height maximum 15.0 cm (5⅞")
One (45780) impressed *Wedgwood* on the hollow of the bust.
Impressed *WEDGWOOD* underneath all four pedestals
RCIN 45780; 45778; 45779; 45777.1
PROVENANCE (?)Queen Charlotte
LITERATURE Dawson 1985, p. 640 and fig. 4; Reilly 1989, I, p. 633

Wedgwood's sole technical innovation, the coloured unglazed body known as 'jasper', enabled him to produce ornamental wares to harmonise with the colour schemes of neo-classical interiors. These rare miniature busts represent an unlikely quartet in which the French philosopher Denis Diderot is joined by Minerva, Endymion and Ariadne. They are probably what were described in Wedgwood's 1787 catalogue as 'small busts with emblematic terms', and may have been the 'female bust of biscuit, on china pedestal, and three smaller ones' in Queen Charlotte's posthumous sale (Christie's, 7–11 May 1819, third day, lot 3).

316. Wedgwood

Coffee can and saucer, late eighteenth century

Jasper ware. Can 6.2 × 9.0 cm (2⁷/₁₆" × 3⁹/₁₆"); saucer diameter 12.0 cm (4¾")
Impressed *WEDGWOOD* and *3* on the underside of both pieces, and *H* under the saucer
RCIN 36174.a–b
PROVENANCE Miss Hunter; by whom presented to Queen Mary, 1922
LITERATURE Dawson 1985, p. 640 and fig. 5

This particularly elaborately decorated can and saucer were made in white jasper, dipped in lilac jasper which was then partially removed on a lathe to create the 'chequered' effect before further green and white ornaments were added.

317. Wedgwood

Serving dish, c.1780

Creamware. 4.4 × 30.1 × 22.2 cm (1¾" × 11⅞" × 8¾")
Impressed *WEDGWOOD* on the underside
RCIN 39882.3
PROVENANCE Ordered for the Prince of Wales (later George IV)

This serving dish is from a service ordered for the Prince of Wales (the future George IV) of which thirty pieces survive in the Royal Collection. The Prince in his turn was to become an important customer for Wedgwood's firm in the years after the death of its founder in 1795.

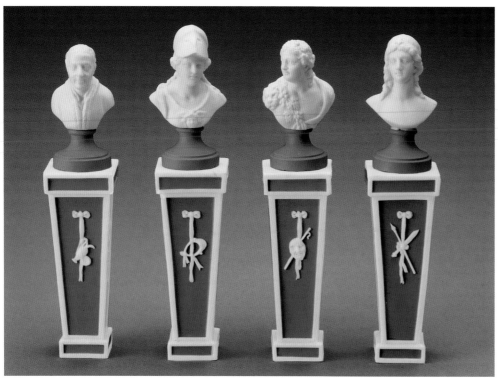

315

316

317

318. Wedgwood

Covered urn and centre dish, c.1795

Creamware. Urn diameter 32.2 cm (12¹¹⁄₁₆″); centre dish
13.2 × 29.5 × 19.3 cm (5⅜″ × 11⅝″ × 7⅝″)
Urn impressed *WEDGWOOD* and 7 on the underside; centre dish
impressed *WEDGWOOD* and 8 on underside
RCIN 53002.1; 53050.1
PROVENANCE Probably ordered by Queen Charlotte
LITERATURE Barnard (H.) 1924, p. 232

In November 1909 Queen Mary wrote from Frogmore House,
Windsor, to her friend Lady Mount Stephen, with whom
she shared many of her investigations into the collections of
Queen Charlotte from Frogmore: 'I believe I have here part
of what must have been Queen Charlotte's dairy set & I shall
have a piece taken to London to be identified by Mr Wedgwood'
(RA GV/CC 44/204). An entry in Wedgwood's Ledger G
under 'The Queen Windsor' included '12 Milk Pans'
supplied at a cost of £3 11s (information from Miss Gaye
Blake-Roberts). This urn and dish may have been intended
for the Queen's dairy in the grounds of Frogmore. The urn
corresponds with shape number 1110 ('Butterkit') in the
pattern book of Charles Gill, one of Wedgwood's 'travellers'
or salesmen (illus. Reilly 1989, I, fig. 395). The precise function
of the centre dish is unclear.

318

320 319

319. Worcester

Tea cup and saucer, c.1780

Porcelain. Cup 4.8 × 10.7 × 8.6 cm (1¹⁴/₁₆″ × 4³/₁₆″ × 3⅜″);
saucer diameter 13.8 cm (5⁷/₁₆″)
Underglaze crescent mark painted in blue on the base of both pieces
RCIN 73111.a–b
PROVENANCE (?)Queen Charlotte
LITERATURE Sandon 1996, pp. 214–15, 230

This and the following four pieces have royal associations,
but only nos. 322 and 323 post-date the visit of George III
and Queen Charlotte to the Worcester china manufacturers
in 1788, which was also a watershed year in the history of
porcelain-making in the city (see no. 323). The floral decoration of the tea cup and saucer conforms to a well-known design
known today as the 'marriage' pattern, but the addition of
the classical vase and the prominent word 'Kew' suggest that

they may have formed part of a tea service ordered for the
use of the royal family either at the Dutch House or possibly
at Queen Charlotte's Cottage at Kew.

320. Worcester

Mug with the cipher of George III, c.1780

Porcelain. 8.3 × 10.7 × 7.3 cm (3¼″ × 4³/₁₆″ × 2⅞″)
Underglaze crescent mark painted in blue on the base
RCIN 73113
PROVENANCE (?)George III

This is the sole example of this pattern in the Royal Collection.
It bears the floriated cipher of the King and since it does not
have the character of a commemorative piece it seems more
likely to have been ordered for his use.

321

322

321. Worcester

Saucer dish, sugar bowl and milk jug, c.1780

Porcelain. Saucer dish diameter 21.7 cm (8⁹⁄₁₆″); sugar bowl
11.3 × 12.3 cm (4⁷⁄₁₆″ × 4¹³⁄₁₆″); milk jug 9.5 × 12.2 cm
(3¾″ × 4¹³⁄₁₆″)
Underglaze painted hatched square mark (Sandon 1993, no. 19);
underglaze painted crescent mark (Sandon 1993, no. 7)
RCIN 73297 (saucer dish); 73294.a–b (sugar bowl and cover);
73295 (milk jug)
PROVENANCE Presented by Sir Arthur Penn to
Princess Elizabeth (HM The Queen), 1947
LITERATURE Sandon 1996, pp. 103, 105

These pieces are decorated in a pattern derived from
oriental porcelain which (for reasons that are not clear)
became known as the 'Queen Charlotte' pattern. Although
pieces in this pattern exist from the late 1750s the pattern
may have been renamed to commemorate the 1788 royal
visit to Worcester.

322. Worcester (Flight)

*Breakfast cup and saucer, sugar vase and cover,
and milk jug, c.1788–92*

Porcelain. Cup 6.6 × 12.8 × 10.5 cm (2⅝″ × 5¹⁄₁₆″ × 4⅛″);
saucer diameter 15.8 cm (6¼″); sugar vase 14.5 × 16.2 × 12.0 cm
(5¹¹⁄₁₆″ × 6⅜″ × 4¾″); milk jug 7.0 × 13.2 × 8.7 cm
(2¾″ × 5³⁄₁₆″ × 3⁷⁄₁₆″)
Sugar vase and milk jug painted on the underside with underglaze
crescent mark in blue
RCIN 11968.3a–b (cup and saucer); 11886 (sugar basin and cover);
11962 (milk jug)
PROVENANCE Presented by Mr N. Douglass to
HM The Queen, 1976
LITERATURE Binns 1877, p. 154; Sandon 1996, p. 294

The 'blue lily' pattern introduced at Worcester around
1780 was renamed 'royal lily' after the royal visit in 1788,
when the King and Queen ordered a breakfast service
decorated in this fashion.

323

323. Worcester (Barr, Flight and Barr)

Pieces from a breakfast service, c.1805

Porcelain. Coffee pot 22.0 × 24.5 × 10.0 cm (8¹¹⁄₁₆″ × 9⅝″ × 3¹⁵⁄₁₆″);
butter cooler 10.4 × 19.1 × 17.6 cm (4⅛″ × 7½″ × 6¹⁵⁄₁₆″),
stand diameter 24.4 cm (9⅝″); honey pot with attached stand
14.0 × diameter 14.4 cm (5½″ × 5¹¹⁄₁₆″)
The lid of the butter cooler incised with a capital 'B' (Sandon 1996,
Appendix 1, no. 32). Each piece marked in puce within a circle
(below a crown) *FLIGHT & BARR / Coventry Street / LONDON /
BARR FLIGHT & BARR / WORCESTER / Manufacturers to their /
MAJESTIES & / ROYAL FAMILY.*
RCIN 58469 (coffee pot); 58470.2 (butter cooler); 58461.1
(honey pot)
PROVENANCE Ordered by George III
LITERATURE Binns 1877, pp. 162–3; Sandon 1996, p. 174

George III and Queen Charlotte visited the city of Worcester
with their second son (Prince Frederick, Duke of York) and
three of their daughters in August 1788, to attend the Music
Meeting (subsequently known as the Three Choirs Festival).
They called at the retail premises of Joseph and John Flight
and placed several orders for china. The King then accepted
the Flights' invitation to visit their factory, gave the brothers
permission to style themselves 'Manufacturers to their

Majesties', and advised them to set up a shop in London.
Similar favours were bestowed on the rival firm of Robert
and Humphrey Chamberlain, which had recently opened
a shop in Flights' former premises in the High Street,
Worcester. An undated manuscript in the King's hand
headed simply 'to be made at Worcester', listing an 86-piece
dinner service (RA GEO/16841), may date from soon after
the visit.

This service was made in the old Worcester factory under
the management of Joseph Flight and Martin Barr. In 1804
the latter's son, also Martin, joined the partnership, known
thenceforth as Barr, Flight and Barr. The service is said to
have been ordered in 1805. It is decorated with the royal
arms with deep, cloudy blue borders very finely gilded with
berried laurel sprigs and oak garlands alternately enclosing
the crowned cipher of George III and sprigs of national
flowers tied with ribbons. Thirty-three pieces remain in
the Royal Collection.

324. German: (?)Meissen

*Transverse flute, c.*1760

Porcelain, gilt copper, leather. Length 63.5 cm (25″)

RCIN 72173

PROVENANCE (?)George III; Thomas Warner; by whom presented to Prince Alfred, Duke of Edinburgh, 1881; King George V

As well as the harpsichord and pianoforte, George III played the flute proficiently and clearly found it a consoling occupation; during his recovery at Kew in February 1789 he often played to himself. Frederick the Great of Prussia had earlier promoted the instrument and extended its repertoire with a number of his own compositions, and the 'transverse' flute, played horizontally rather than vertically, was known in the eighteenth century as the German flute. Around 1720, flutes began to be made in four sections, with interchangeable pieces known as *corps de rechange* which enabled the instrument to be played in a different key. Eighteenth-century flutes were almost invariably made of ebony, fruitwood or boxwood. In order to refine the tuning the maker could adjust the bore of the different sections (as is also possible with modern, metal instruments), whereas fired and glazed porcelain was not susceptible to such adjustment. This instrument must therefore have been made as something of a curiosity, although it produces a fine sound.

An apparently identical instrument which must be by the same maker is in the Metropolitan Museum of Art, New York (43.34; see Winternitz 1966, pp. 200–201). The porcelain and its decoration correspond with Meissen productions of around 1760, and the supposition that this instrument was made there is strengthened by a solitary reference in the work reports of the great Meissen modeller J.J. Kaendler (1706–75) to his having made a mould for a flute in February 1736 (information from Dr Hans Sonntag).

Among the 'Sundries' in an inventory of jewellery and snuff boxes at Windsor made by Sir Henry Wheatley and John Bridge in 1838 (RCIN 1114749, ff. 44–6) are three flutes which had formerly belonged to George III, one of which – 'a China Flute, belonged to his late Majesty, Geo. III' – may be no. 324. When presented to Alfred, Duke of Edinburgh (1844–1900), in 1881 by the Manchester collector Thomas Warner, it was described (impossibly) as having belonged to Charles II, and it may be that its former royal associations had simply been confused during its absence from the Royal Collection.

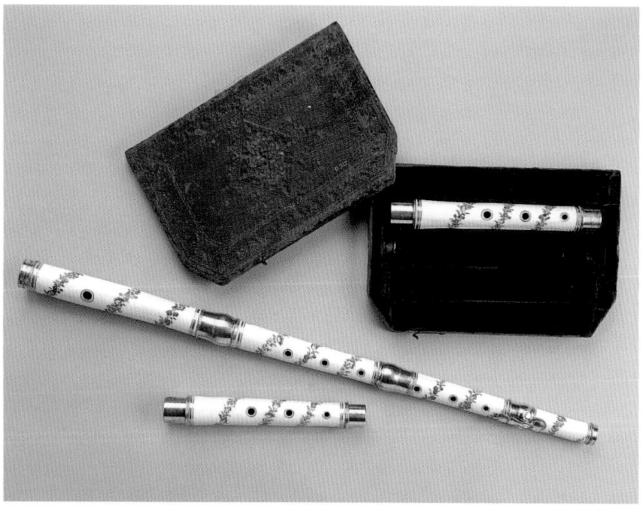

324

325. Fürstenberg

*Pieces from a dinner and dessert service, c.*1773

Porcelain. Large tureen and cover 28.0 × 37.8 × 26.0 cm (11″ × 14 7/8″ × 10 1/4″); large tureen stand 7.9 × 48.8 × 33.8 cm (3 1/8″ × 19 3/16″ × 13 5/16″); small tureen and cover 23.2 × 28.2 × 19.7 cm (9 1/8″ × 11 1/8″ × 7 3/4″); small tureen stand 6.7 × 40.9 × 28.6 cm (2 5/8″ × 16 1/8″ × 11 1/4″); large circular bowl 9.7 × diameter 44.7 cm (3 13/16″ × 17 5/8″); large circular dish 5.8 × diameter 30.7 cm (2 5/16″ × 12 1/16″); square dish 5.0 × 23.9 × 23.8 cm (1 15/16″ × 9 7/16″ × 9 3/8″); oval dish 4.8 × 24.4 × 19.0 cm (1 7/8″ × 9 5/8″ × 7 7/16″); three smaller oval dishes 3.6 × 18.4 × 14.1 cm (1 7/16″ × 7 1/4″ × 5 9/16″); two circular dishes 5.5 × diameter 26.2 cm (2 3/16″ × 10 5/16″); two plates 3.5 × diameter 24.5 cm (1 3/8″ × 9 5/8″); two soup plates 4.1 × diameter 24.4 cm (1 5/8″ × 9 5/8″); sauceboat 9.0 × 21.2 × 14.6 cm (3 9/16″ × 8 3/8″ × 5 3/4″); oval basket 10.5 × 24.0 × 16.3 cm (4 1/8″ × 9 7/16″ × 6 7/16″); round basket 8.0 × 18.7 × 16.7 cm (3 1/8″ × 7 3/8″ × 6 9/16″); three salts 6.0 × 11.3 × 6.1 cm (2 3/8″ × 4 7/16″ × 2 3/8″); three juice pots and covers 8.6 × 9.4 × 7.3 cm (3 3/8″ × 3 11/16″ × 2 7/8″)

All pieces marked on the underside with a cursive capital 'F' in underglaze blue. Some with incised marks. The larger pieces inscribed in maroon script with the location depicted

RCIN 58408.1 (large tureen and cover); 58415.1 (large tureen stand); 58409.1 (small tureen and cover); 58413.2 (small tureen stand); 58437.1 (large circular bowl); 58423.1 (large circular dish); 58421.1–2 (square dish); 58419.2 (oval dish); 58417.1, .3–4 (smaller oval dishes); 58422.1–2 (circular dishes); 58406.6, .13 (plates); 58407.17, .34 (soup plates); 58420.1 (sauceboat); 58433.1 (oval basket); 58432.3 (round basket); 58434.1, .5–6 (salts); 58435.1–2, .4 (juice pots and covers)

PROVENANCE Commissioned by Duke Charles I of Brunswick (d. 1780); (?)by whom presented to George III

LITERATURE *Fürstenberg* 1989, pp. 174–84, nos. 52–72 (entries by Annedore Müller-Hofstede)

325

Duke Charles I of Brunswick (1713–80) followed the example of many eighteenth-century German princes by establishing his own porcelain factory, at Fürstenberg on the River Weser, in 1747. (See no. 70 for the Ludwigsburg factory, founded in 1758.) The Fürstenberg factory was slow to develop but by the 1760s was capable of undertaking large commissions for table services as well as figures and vases.

In 1764 Duke Charles I's son, the future Duke Charles II (1735–1806), married George III's sister Augusta (1737–1813), and in 1795 their daughter Caroline was married to his eldest son, George, Prince of Wales, later George IV. This service, which represents the high point of eighteenth-century Fürstenberg production, seems to have been a gift from Duke Charles I to George III. The tureens, plates and dishes are all formed in the *graviertes muster* method by which hatched and scrolled ornament engraved into the mould is reproduced in relief. Most of the landscape paintings are by the master painter P.J.F. Weitsch (1723–1803), depicting views in the Harz mountains and Weserbergland, and prospects of the principal towns of the dukedom. Weitsch served in the Brunswick army and taught himself the art of landscape painting by copying the work of seventeenth-century Dutch painters such as Jan Both and Nicolas Berchem. Most of the views were probably worked up from Weitsch's own topographical drawings, but there are also scenes from Italy, France and Switzerland which may have been copied from prints. This is certainly true of the scene

on the large circular bowl, which is signed and dated 1773, and reproduces one of a set of engravings by Franz Edmund Weirotter (see Ducret 1965, II, p. 30, fig. 4).

The very distinctive outline of the landscapes, framed with rockwork and roots, was not unique to Weitsch (or indeed to the Fürstenberg factory) but he can be said to have perfected it. The decoration of some of the smaller pieces

325 (RCIN 58437.1)

326

such as the baskets and the juice-pots has been attributed by Dr Annedore Müller-Hofstede (in *Fürstenberg* 1989) to Weitsch's pupil A.A. Hartmann (1752–1818).

326. Sèvres

Pair of vases (vase à col cylindrique), 1768

Soft-paste porcelain. Height 31.0 cm (12⅜")
Painted with mauve interlaced *LL*s enclosing the date letter *P* for 1768
RCIN 31035.1–2
PROVENANCE Probably acquired by Queen Charlotte; delivered to Carlton House on 8 January 1819 (Jutsham II, f. 46)
LITERATURE *Sèvres* 1979, no. 109

327. Sèvres

Pair of vases and covers (?vase à étoiles), *c.*1770–75

Soft-paste porcelain. Height 32.5 cm (13⅞")
Painted with blue interlaced *LL*s and an unidentified artist's mark, *D.*
RCIN 2358.1–2
PROVENANCE Probably acquired by Queen Charlotte; delivered to Carlton House on 8 January 1819 (Jutsham II, f. 47)
LITERATURE *Sèvres* 1979, no. 104

Queen Charlotte was among the first significant collectors of Sèvres porcelain in Great Britain. Horace Walpole mentions Sèvres vases in his account of the Queen's Apartments at Buckingham House, probably in 1783 (Walpole 1928, p. 78), and the catalogues of the Queen's three posthumous sales in 1819 include twenty-one lots of (or including) Sèvres. In the illustrations of Buckingham House published for W.H. Pyne's *History of the Royal Residences*, ornamental vases corresponding with Sèvres shapes are seen in several rooms (see nos. 113, 114). Queen Charlotte's eldest son, who was to form his own outstanding collection of Sèvres porcelain, may have acquired something of his appetite in this direction from his mother. From the 1819 sales he purchased two *déjeuners* or tea sets, one with a purple ground and one with a 'grass green' ground.

Nos. 326 and 327 are probably two of the three pairs of vases delivered to the Prince Regent from Buckingham House in January 1819, a few months after Queen Charlotte's death. The pair with rising handles is one of the earliest known examples of a model (*vase à col cylindrique*) designed by J.-J. Bachelier, which dates from the mid-1760s. The shape may also have been called *vase à anses tortillés* in the factory records. The two scenes were probably painted by C.-N.

327

328

Dodin, reproducing engravings after paintings by François Boucher, *L'agréable Leçon* and *La Pipée*.

The second pair of vases is probably of the shape known as *vase à étoiles*. On the plaster model preserved at the factory and in other porcelain examples the lid is ornamented with a six-pointed star in place of the eight-petalled flower (see Savill 1988, I, pp. 412–16). They are painted by an unknown hand with bands of cherubs in grisaille, and the gilding is exceptionally finely tooled.

328. Sèvres

Pieces from a dessert, tea and coffee service, 1789

Hard- and soft-paste porcelain. Dessert service: six plates with cipher and motto diameter 24.1 cm (9½"); two plates with portrait medallions diameter 24.0 cm (9⁷⁄₁₆"); circular bowl 8.9 × 23.6 cm (3½" × 9⁵⁄₁₆"); shallow circular dish 4.2 × 21.0 cm (1⅝" × 8¼"); oval dish 4.4 × 27.7 × 21.1 cm (1¾" × 10⅞" × 8⁵⁄₁₆"); square dish 4.2 × 22.8 × 22.8 cm (1⅝" × 9" × 9"); shell-shaped dish 5.4 × 22.8 × 22.9 cm (2⅛" × 9" × 9"); monteith 13.0 × 29.7 × 20.7 cm (5⅛" × 11¹¹⁄₁₆" × 8⅛"); wine bottle cooler 18.5 × 26.5 × 20.4 cm (7⁵⁄₁₆" × 10⁷⁄₁₆" × 8¹⁄₁₆"); double liqueur bottle cooler 11.6 × 31.2 × 14.5 cm (4⁹⁄₁₆" × 12⁵⁄₁₆" × 5¹¹⁄₁₆"); ice pail and cover 20.8 × 23.1 × 20.5 cm (8³⁄₁₆" × 9⅛" × 8¹⁄₁₆"); sugar bowl and cover with attached stand 11.2 × 24.3 × 14.8 cm (4⁷⁄₁₆" × 9⁹⁄₁₆" × 5¹³⁄₁₆"); five ice-cream cups 6.3 × 6.9 × 5.9 cm (2½" × 2¹¹⁄₁₆" × 2⁵⁄₁₆"); shaped stand 2.9 × 21.1 × 21.1 cm (1⅛" × 8⁵⁄₁₆" × 8⁵⁄₁₆"); three preserve pots and covers on attached stand 20.8 × 23.1 × 20.5 cm (8³⁄₁₆" × 9⅛" × 8¹⁄₁₆"). Tea and coffee service: sugar bowl and cover 11.4 × 9.4 × 10.1 cm (4½" × 3¹¹⁄₁₆" × 4"); milk jug 12.0 × 12.5 × 9.5 cm (4¾" × 4¹⁵⁄₁₆" × 3¾"); basin 6.9 × 18.5 cm (2¹¹⁄₁₆" × 7⁵⁄₁₆"); two tea cups 4.7 × 7.5 × 5.6 cm (1⅞" × 2¹⁵⁄₁₆" × 2³⁄₁₆"); two tea saucers diameter 13.6 cm (5⅜"); two coffee cups 6.0 × 7.5 × 5.6 cm (2⅜" × 2¹⁵⁄₁₆" × 2³⁄₁₆"); two coffee saucers diameter 12.0 cm (4¾") Painted with interlaced *LL*s and three unidentified marks (*G*, *g*, and *L*) Dessert service: RCIN 95588.4, .5, .11, .18, .22, .28 (cipher plates);

95589.2, .9 (portrait plates); 95601.1 (circular bowl); 95602.1 (shallow circular dish); 95596.2 (oval dish); 95603.4 (square dish); 95593 (shell-shaped dish); 95599.1 (monteith); 95595.2 (wine bottle cooler); 95598.2 (liqueur bottle cooler); 95604.1 (ice pail); 95592.2a–b (sugar bowl); 95590.1–4, .7 (ice-cream cups); 95600.2 (stand); 95605 (preserve pots and stand). Tea and coffee service: RCIN 35552 (sugar bowl and cover); 35551 (milk jug); 35553 (basin); 35554.4, .6 (tea cups); 35555.2, .6 (tea saucers); 35556.2–3 (coffee cups); 35557.1–2 (coffee saucers)

PROVENANCE Commissioned by Bernardo del Campo y Pérez de la Serna, Marquis del Campo. Dessert service: presented by Del Campo to 2nd Earl Harcourt, 1796; by descent; purchased by HM The Queen, 2003. Tea and coffee service: (?)presented by Del Campo to Queen Charlotte, 1789; reputedly by descent from Princess Mary, Duchess of Gloucester (d. 1857); by whom bequeathed to George, 2nd Duke of Cambridge; Sir Augustus FitzGeorge; from whose estate purchased by Queen Mary, *c.*1934

LITERATURE De Bellaigue (G.) 1984

The King's recovery from his first serious bout of porphyria was announced on 26 February 1789, and the public mood of thanksgiving provided the English makers of commemorative medals (see no. 451), porcelain plaques and other items with an excellent opportunity. However, the pieces in this service, which are decorated with portrait medallions of the King, the cursive initial *G* and various inscriptions including *Huzza the King is well!*, *The Best of Kings*, *The Best of Fathers*, *The Patron of Arts*, *God Save the King* and *Viva el Rey*, were specially commissioned from the Sèvres porcelain factory. The dessert service numbers in total 100 pieces, and the tea and coffee service twenty-seven pieces.

The Spanish Ambassador in London, the Marquis del Campo, decided to celebrate the King's return to health with a magnificent gala in the Rotunda at Ranelagh Gardens in

329

Chelsea on 2 June. It was attended by Queen Charlotte and her daughters – but not by the King himself – and was reputed to have cost the Marquis £12,000. (For an account of the celebration at Windsor given by the Queen and the princesses a month earlier, see pp. 329–30.) Del Campo had already made a favourable impression on Queen Charlotte: in August 1786 after Margaret Nicholson had made an attempt on the King's life, it was Del Campo who had driven to Windsor to reassure the Queen that it had been unsuccessful. George III himself seems to have been unmoved either by this kindness or by the lengths and expense to which the Marquis had gone to commission the porcelain service. When Del Campo relinquished his post in London to be succeeded by Simón de las Casas, the King is said to have remarked that the *valet de chambre* had been replaced with the *maître d'hôtel* (Glenbervie 1928, I, p. 55). Del Campo's next appointment (from 1796) was Ambassador to the French Republic; he presented the dessert service to Earl Harcourt at around this time.

As rendered by the Sèvres grisaille artists the King's profile on the dessert plates tends to resemble more closely that of Louis XVI. Much of the historical interest of the service lies in the fact that it was commissioned from the French King's porcelain factory at precisely this time.

329. Naples

Pieces from the 'Etruscan Service', 1785–7

Soft-paste tin-glazed porcelain. Large soup tureen and stand 26.5 × 40.0 × 36.6 cm (10⁷⁄₁₆″ × 15¾″ × 14½″); krater-shaped bottle cooler 21.8 × 22.7 × 18.4 cm (8⁹⁄₁₆″ × 8¹⁵⁄₁₆″ × 7¼″); two ewer-shaped ice-cream coolers 38.0 × diameter 23.2 cm (14¹⁵⁄₁₆″ × 9⅛″); two round salad bowls 8.5 × diameter 26.7 cm (3⅜″ × 10½″); oval fruit basket 8.2 × 27.7 × 16.5 cm (3¼″ × 10¹⁵⁄₁₆″ × 6¾″); two wine-glass coolers 12.3 × 24.4 × 23.0 cm (4¹³⁄₁₆″ × 9⅝″ × 9¹⁄₁₆″); circular fruit basket 12.8 × diameter 18.0 cm (5¹⁄₁₆″ × 7¹⁄₁₆″); powdered sugar basin, cover and attached stand 11.1 × diameter 24.0 cm (4⅜″ × 9⁷⁄₁₆″); sugar basin and cover 15.0 × 18.6 × 13.0 cm (5⅞″ × 7⁵⁄₁₆″ × 5⅛″); cruet 17.5 × 20.6 × 10.7 cm (6⅞″ × 8⅛″ × 4³⁄₁₆″); two salts 5.4 × 13.2 × 9.7 cm (2⅛″ × 5⁵⁄₁₆″ × 3¹³⁄₁₆″); eight plates diameter 25.3 cm (9¹⁵⁄₁₆″)
Most of the pieces painted on the underside in red with the crowned cipher mark *FRF* (*Fabbrica Reale Ferdinandea*)
RCIN 58207.2 (large soup tureen and stand); 58211.1 (krater-shaped bottle cooler); 58218.1, .4 (ewer-shaped ice-cream coolers); 58208.1–2 (round salad bowls); 58210.2 (oval fruit basket); 58213.1, .4 (wine-glass coolers); 58216.3 (circular fruit basket); 35603.1a, .2b (powdered sugar basin, cover and attached stand); 58212.2 (sugar

basin and cover); 58215.1 (cruet); 58214.1, .4 (salts); 58204.10, .25, .41, .49, .57, .62, .78, .91 (plates)
PROVENANCE Commissioned by Ferdinand IV, King of Naples, 1783; by whom presented to George III, 1787
LITERATURE Venuti 1787; *Neo-classicism* 1972, pp. 688–9, no. 1464; *Porcellane di Napoli* 1986, pp. 346–75

These pieces are taken from the most ambitious service to have been produced in the royal porcelain factory established at Naples by the Bourbon King Ferdinand IV in 1771 and disbanded by the occupying French in 1807. It was ordered in 1783 as a diplomatic gift to George III, and was completed in 1787. Most of the 282 pieces survive but the very elaborate *surtout de table* – representing, in biscuit, King Tarchon of the Etruscans presiding over gladiatorial combats – does not. The director of the factory, Domenico Venuti (1745–1817), was also the Keeper of Antiquities, and the service was intended to show off the royal collection of ancient vases in the Museo Borbonico. Individual pieces were painted on each of the 143 plates, while some of the antique forms were ingeniously translated into modern ones, such as tureens and wine-bottle and glass coolers. Venuti prepared a book of engravings of all the designs on the plates and each of the shaped pieces; it is startlingly inaccurate in the interpretation of many of the paintings and even in the names of the modern shapes.

Antique vases were very highly sought after by collectors in the last decades of the eighteenth century. As a form of publication, the Etruscan service and Venuti's book compare unfavourably with the magnificent volumes prepared in the previous decade by the Baron d'Hancarville for the long-serving British Ambassador to the court of Naples, Sir William Hamilton. That work was partly aimed at the improvement of contemporary ceramic manufacture in England, and for the same reason the French King Louis XVI presented to the Sèvres factory a collection of antique ('Etruscan') vases formed in Naples by the French envoy Dominique Vivant-Denon. Surprisingly, some of these – rather than Neapolitan royal vases – are illustrated on the plates of the Etruscan Service.

The service was brought to England by the factory's chief modeller and painter in two naval vessels, whose officers had been charged with reporting on the English naval dockyards and shipbuilding industry to J.F.E. (later Sir John) Acton, the Anglo-Irish expatriate in charge of the reorganisation of the Neapolitan navy at this time. This part of the mission was less successful. One officer penetrated Woolwich and Deptford but was turned away at Portsmouth.

329

12. Silver-gilt (nos. 330–391)

DINING SILVER (nos. 330–377)

The 'Coronation Service', 1760–63
(nos. 330–352)

George III disliked magnificent public banquets and lavish dinners. He preferred to dine simply with his family. This aspect of the King's taste was often criticised by members of the court. Elizabeth, Duchess of Northumberland, Lady of the Bedchamber to Queen Charlotte, recalled that the King and Queen's table 'was neither sumptuous nor elegant & they always dined Tete a Tete' (Northumberland 1926, p. 79) while Paul Pindar quipped that 'a leg of mutton and his wife, were the chief pleasures' of the King's life (Glanville 1991, p. 107). Queen Charlotte herself was described as 'whimsically abstemious' who 'seldom eat [sic] more than two things at a meal' (Huish 1821, p. 360).

Despite their personal preferences, certain occasions still required the King and Queen to entertain on a grand scale. The young King had inherited a jewel house stocked with unexceptional and old-fashioned plate. This situation was rectified by a series of warrants issued between July 1761 (the month in which his betrothal was announced) and Lady Day 1762 for 9,918 ounces troy (308.45 kg) of new gilt plate and 6,036 ounces troy (187.7 kg) of white (ungilded) plate at a total cost of £8,783 6s 1d (PRO LC5/110, f. 356). In addition to the Queen's new toilet service (nos. 378–82), the gilt plate was to consist chiefly of a magnificent new dining service (including nos. 330–52). This huge service was the largest commission received by the Jewel House for many years. It included 8 dozen plates, 72 assorted serving dishes, 2 mazarines (fish strainers), 6 tureens, an epergne, 2 bread baskets, 16 sauceboats and ladles, 16 salts, 4 sugar vases, 2 cruets, 16 candlesticks, 12 waiters and 8 dozen knives, forks and spoons (PRO LC5/110, f. 339). The most expensive single item was the epergne (no. 333) at £241 19s, although the

eight dozen plates (see no. 349) cost £1,056 7s 6d (PRO LC9/48, ff. 203, 208). The cost of engraving the Royal Arms and King's ciphers was charged at an extra £232 19s 6d (PRO LC5/110, f. 356). Most pieces were subsequently re-engraved with the new Royal Arms as used after 1801.

The new service was supplied by Thomas Heming, appointed Principal Goldsmith to the King in 1760. It was Lord Bute, one of Heming's most important patrons, who encouraged this significant new appointment. Heming was the first working goldsmith to hold this post since the early seventeenth century and the majority of the pieces were in consequence made in his workshop. Exceptions include the cutlery made by Thomas and William Chawner (nos. 351, 352), and the candlesticks made by Louis Herne and Francis Butty (no. 348). Heming subsequently incorporated the design for the tureens from the royal service into his trade card, boldly headed by the Royal Arms and supporters. The style chosen for the service was a modified version of the French rococo, still fashionable in the early years of George III's reign (compare no. 309) and shows the strong influence of Pierre Germain's *Eléments d'orfèvrerie devisés*, published in Paris in 1748. Some of the King's new service appears to have been derived from examples supplied earlier to Bute; the epergne is a particularly close imitation (Lomax 1999, p. 138; sold Christie's, London, 3 July 1996, lot 79). The superb quality and refined delicacy of many of the pieces show the influence of the Huguenot Peter Archambo, to whom Heming had been apprenticed in 1738.

Most of this service survives in the Royal Collection, where it forms the core of the so-called 'Coronation Service' – a name used since at least the 1820s. Despite this title, the commission took nearly a year to complete and was therefore not finished in time for use at the King and Queen's coronation banquet on 22 September 1761. The service was however used at the 'extremely magnificent banquet' held on 19 September 1768 at the Queen's House in honour of Christian VII of

Denmark, who was George III's first cousin in addition to being his brother-in-law (following his marriage to Princess Caroline in 1766; see no. 6). The dinner was followed by a ball, with supper at 11 o'clock and further dancing until 4.30 a.m. (Glanville 1991, p. 116).

Modest additions were made to the service throughout the 1760s, although not all appear in the Jewel House records. The most significant was a set of thirty dish covers ordered in August 1762. The splendid pair of sauceboats with dragon handles (no. 340), made by John Swift in 1764–5, are now engraved with the badge of the Prince of Wales and perhaps entered the Collection at a later date. The magnificent pair of pierced mazarines (no. 332) engraved with various types of sea fish caught in a net bears the mark of George Hunter, 1762–3. The elegant dessert knives, forks and spoons (nos. 353–5), engraved with the Queen's cipher, were probably a private commission, paid for by the Privy Purse, and therefore would not have passed through the Jewel House books.

The King's usual daily routine consisted of a 'dish of tea' for breakfast, followed by dinner with the Queen at 4 o'clock and a simple supper later in the evening. However, by the early nineteenth century, the King was said often to dine alone at 2 o'clock, whilst the Queen preferred to eat with the princesses at 4 o'clock. The King's daily meals were remarkably consistent throughout his life. A typical dinner, on 27 September 1762, included 'Pottage Barley with Rhenish wine', veal pâté, smoked pork 'metwurst' and sauerkraut, roast lamb with mint sauce, roast ruffs, fried oysters with mushrooms, oysters 'a la braze', cold roast turkey, peas and lettuce and 'custard in cups' (PRO L59/179).

330

330. Thomas Heming (free 1746)

Four waiters, 1761–2

Silver-gilt. 4.5 × 36.0 × 36.7 cm (1¾″ × 14³⁄₁₆″ × 14⁷⁄₁₆″)
Struck with London hallmarks for 1761–2 and maker's mark of Thomas Heming
RCIN 51848.1–4
PROVENANCE Perhaps from a set of twelve waiters commissioned by George III, 24 July 1761 (PRO LC5/110, f. 339) and invoiced 27 October 1761 (£194 4s 2d; PRO LC9/48, f. 203)

331. Thomas Heming (free 1746)

Six waiters, 1760–62

Silver-gilt. 3.3 × 21.0 × 21.0 cm (1⁵⁄₁₆″ × 8¼″ × 8¼″)
Four struck with London hallmarks for 1760–61 and maker's mark of Thomas Heming; two struck with London hallmarks for 1761–2 and maker's mark of Thomas Heming
RCIN 51672.1–6
PROVENANCE Perhaps from a set of twelve waiters commissioned by George III, 24 July 1761 (PRO LC5/110, f. 339) and invoiced 27 October 1761 (£194 4s 2d; PRO LC9/48, f. 203)
LITERATURE Garrard 1914, no. 258

332. George Hunter (free 1748)

Pair of fish strainers (mazarines), 1762–3

Silver-gilt. 1.2 × 30.3 × 44.0 cm (½″ × 11¹⁵⁄₁₆″ × 17⁵⁄₁₆″)
Struck with London hallmarks for 1762–3 and maker's mark of George Hunter
RCIN 49161.1–2
PROVENANCE Supplied for George III (bill untraced)
LITERATURE Garrard 1914, no. 149

331

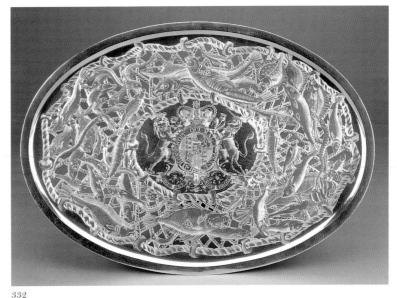

332

333

333. Thomas Heming (free 1746)

Centrepiece (epergne), 1762

Silver-gilt. 46.0 × 84.6 × 68.0 cm (18⅛″ × 33⁵⁄₁₆″ × 26¾″)
Struck with London hallmarks for 1762–3 and maker's mark of
Thomas Heming
RCIN 51487
PROVENANCE Commissioned by George III, 24 July 1761 (PRO
LC 5/110, f. 339) and invoiced April 1762 (£241 19s; PRO LC 9/48,
f. 208)
LITERATURE Garrard 1914, no. 166

334. Thomas Heming (free 1746)

Pair of bread baskets, 1761

Silver-gilt. 12.0 × 14.6 × 40.3 cm (4¾″ × 5¾″ × 15⅞″)
Struck with London hallmarks for 1761–2 and maker's mark of
Thomas Heming
RCIN 49148.1–2
PROVENANCE Commissioned by George III, 24 July 1761
(PRO LC 5/110, f. 339) and invoiced 27 October 1761 (£87 10s 7d;
PRO LC 9/48, f. 202)
LITERATURE Garrard 1914, no. 8

334

335

335. Thomas Heming (free 1746)

Two sugar vases, 1761

Silver-gilt. 21.7 × 13.7 cm (8⁹⁄₁₆″ × 5⅜″)
Struck with London hallmarks for 1761–2 and maker's mark of
Thomas Heming
RCIN 49181.1–2
PROVENANCE From a set of four commissioned by George III,
24 July 1761 (PRO LC5/110, f. 339) and invoiced 27 October 1761
(£58 3s 2d; PRO LC9/48, f. 202)
LITERATURE Garrard 1914, no. 132

336. Thomas Heming (free 1746)

Pair of tureens, 1761

Silver-gilt. 26.0 × 46.0 × 29.0 cm (10¼″ × 18⅛″ × 11⁷⁄₁₆″)
Struck with London hallmarks for 1761–2 and maker's mark of
Thomas Heming; engraved *Thomas Heming FECIT / 1761*
RCIN 50805.1–2
PROVENANCE Probably commissioned by George III, 24 July 1761
(PRO LC5/110, f. 339) and invoiced 27 October 1761 (£198 10s 7d;
PRO LC9/48, f. 203)
LITERATURE Garrard 1914, no. 236

337. Thomas Heming (free 1746)

Two tureens, 1761

Silver-gilt. 21.5 × 37.0 × 21.5 cm (8⁷⁄₁₆″ × 14⁹⁄₁₆″ × 8⁷⁄₁₆″)
Struck with London hallmarks for 1761–2 and maker's mark of
Thomas Heming; one (50804.3) engraved *Thomas Heming FECIT /
1761*
RCIN 50804.3–4
PROVENANCE From a set of four probably commissioned by
George III, 24 July 1761 (PRO LC5/110, f. 339) and invoiced
27 October 1761 (£520 18s 7d; PRO LC9/48, f. 202)
LITERATURE Garrard 1914, no. 237

338. Thomas Heming (free 1746)

Three salts, 1761

Silver-gilt. 6.8 × 10.6 × 10.6 cm (2¹¹⁄₁₆″ × 4³⁄₁₆″ × 4³⁄₁₆″)
Struck with London hallmarks for 1760–61 and maker's mark of
Thomas Heming
RCIN 51325.1–3
PROVENANCE From a set of twelve salts commissioned by
George III, 24 July 1761 (PRO LC5/110, f. 339) and invoiced
27 October 1761 (£58 3s 2d; PRO LC9/48, f. 202)
LITERATURE Garrard 1914, no. 203

339. Thomas Heming (free 1746)

Two sauceboats, 1762–3

Silver-gilt. 17.3 × 22.4 × 10.6 cm (6¹³⁄₁₆″ × 18¹³⁄₁₆″ × 4³⁄₁₆″)
Struck with London hallmarks for 1762–3 and maker's mark of
Thomas Heming
RCIN 51843.1–2
PROVENANCE From a set of sixteen sauceboats commissioned by
George III, 24 July 1761 (PRO LC5/110, f. 339; bill untraced)
LITERATURE Garrard 1914, no. 227

340. John Swift (free 1725)

Pair of sauceboats, 1764–5

Silver-gilt. 17.2 × 25.0 × 11.5 cm (6¾″ × 9¹³⁄₁₆″ × 4¾″)
Struck with London hallmarks for 1764–5 and maker's mark of
John Swift
RCIN 51677.1–2
PROVENANCE Bill untraced; engraved with the badge of the
Prince of Wales (later George IV)
LITERATURE Garrard 1914, no. 226

336
337 347 337
344 343

341. Edward Aldridge (free 1758)

Pair of cruet stands with the cipher of
Queen Charlotte, 1764–5

Silver-gilt. 21.0 × 16.9 × 17.0 cm (8¼″ × 6⅝″ × 6¹¹⁄₁₆″)
Struck with London hallmarks for 1764–5 and maker's mark of
Edward Aldridge
RCIN 51614.1–2
PROVENANCE Supplied for George III (bill untraced)
LITERATURE Garrard 1914, no. 35

342. English

Orange strainer, 1761

Silver-gilt. 3.0 × 28.3 × 11.0 cm (1³⁄₁₆″ × 11⅛″ × 4⁵⁄₁₆″)
Struck with London hallmarks for 1761–2 and maker's mark obscured
RCIN 51059
PROVENANCE One of two orange strainers commissioned by
George III (warrant untraced) and invoiced 27 October 1761
(£7 3s 1d; PRO LC9/48, f. 202)
LITERATURE Garrard 1914, no. 184

343. Thomas Heming (free 1746)

Ladle, 1761–2

Silver-gilt. 34.0 × 9.5 cm (13⅜″ × 3¾″)
Struck with London hallmarks for 1761–2 and maker's mark of
Thomas Heming
RCIN 51235.1
PROVENANCE Perhaps from a set of six ladles commissioned by
George III, 24 July 1761 (PRO LC5/110, f. 339; bill untraced)
LITERATURE Garrard 1914, no. 441

344. Thomas Heming (free 1746)

Two ladles, 1761–2

Silver-gilt. 28.6 × 8.3 × 5.3 cm (11¼″ × 3¼″ × 2¹⁄₁₆″)
Struck with London hallmarks for 1761–2 and maker's mark of
Thomas Heming
RCIN 50639.1–2
PROVENANCE As for no. 343
LITERATURE Garrard 1914, no. 442

345. Thomas Heming (free 1746)

Sifter spoon, 1760–61

Silver-gilt. 19.0 × 6.7 cm (7⁷⁄₁₆″ × 2⅝″)
Struck with London hallmarks for 1760–61 and maker's mark of
Thomas Heming
RCIN 51330.1
PROVENANCE Supplied to George III (bill untraced)

346. Thomas Heming (free 1746)

Four sauce ladles, c.1761–2

Silver-gilt. 18.0 × 5.0 × 6.0 cm (7¹⁄₁₆″ × 1¹⁵⁄₁₆″ × 2⅜″)
Struck with maker's mark of Thomas Heming only
RCIN 51261.1–4
PROVENANCE From a set of sixteen sauce ladles commissioned by
George III, 24 July 1761 (PRO LC5/110, f. 339; bill untraced)
LITERATURE Garrard 1914, no. 443

341 340 348 339 341
346 345
338 342 338

347. Thomas Heming (free 1746)

Ladle, c.1761–2

Silver-gilt. 33.0 × 7.5 × 6.0 cm (13″ × 2 ¹⁵⁄₁₆″ × 2 ⅜″)
Struck with maker's mark of Thomas Heming only
RCIN 50616.1
PROVENANCE As for no. 343
LITERATURE Garrard 1914, no. 463

348. Louis Herne and Francis Butty (*fl.*1757–1773)

Four candlesticks, 1761–2

Silver-gilt. 30.0 × 15.6 × 15.6 cm (11¹³⁄₁₆″ × 6⅛″ × 6⅛″)
Struck with London hallmarks for 1761–2 and maker's mark of
Louis Herne and Francis Butty
RCIN 50835.1–4
PROVENANCE From a set of twelve candlesticks commissioned by
George III, 10 December 1761 (PRO LC5/110, f. 356; bill untraced)
LITERATURE Garrard 1914, no. 26

349. Thomas Heming (free 1746)

Six dinner plates, 1761

Silver-gilt. 2.2 × diameter 24.6 cm (⅞″ × 9¹¹⁄₁₆″)
Struck with London hallmarks for 1761–2 and maker's mark of
Thomas Heming
RCIN 51683.1–6
PROVENANCE From a set of ninety-six plates commissioned by
George III, 24 July 1761 (PRO LC5/110, f. 339) and invoiced
27 October 1761 (£1,056 7s 6d; PRO LC9/48, f. 203)
LITERATURE Garrard 1914, no. 193

350. English

*Three table knives, c.*1761; blades later

Silver-gilt. 23.0 × 2.3 × 2.0 cm (9 ¹⁄₁₆″ × ⅞″ × ¾″)
Struck with maker's mark *M.B.* only. Blade stamped *PALMER*
RCIN 51722.1–3
PROVENANCE Perhaps from a canteen of forty-eight covers
(for two courses) commissioned by George III, 24 July 1761
(PRO LC5/110, f. 339) and invoiced 27 October 1761 (£103 10s 3d;
PRO LC9/48, f. 203)
LITERATURE Garrard 1914, no. 453

351 349 352 350

351. Thomas and William Chawner (*fl.*1758–1768)

Three table forks, 1761

Silver-gilt. 19.6 × 2.3 cm (7¹¹⁄₁₆″ × ⅞″)
Struck with London hallmarks for 1761–2 and makers' mark of
Thomas and William Chawner
RCIN 51918.1–3
PROVENANCE From a canteen of forty-eight covers (for two courses)
commissioned by George III, 24 July 1761 (PRO LC5/110, f. 339)
and invoiced 27 October 1761 (£294 4s 8d; PRO LC9/48, f. 203)
LITERATURE Garrard 1914, no. 430

352. Thomas and William Chawner (*fl.*1758–1768)

Three table spoons, 1761

Silver-gilt. 20.3 × 4.4 × 3.2 cm (8″ × 1¾″ × 1¼″)
Struck with London hallmarks for 1761–2 and makers' mark of
Thomas and William Chawner
RCIN 51908.1–3
PROVENANCE Perhaps from a canteen of forty-eight covers
(for two courses) commissioned by George III, 24 July 1761
(PRO LC5/110, f. 339) and invoiced 27 October 1761 (£294 4s 8d;
PRO LC9/48, f. 203)
LITERATURE Garrard 1914, no. 431

Pieces from Queen Charlotte's dessert canteen, 1767–1768 (nos. 353–356)

353. Thomas and William Chawner (*fl.*1758–1768)
Three dessert spoons with cipher of Queen Charlotte, 1767–8

Silver-gilt. Length 17.5 cm (6⅞″)
Struck with London hallmarks for 1767–8 and makers' mark of
Thomas and William Chawner
RCIN 100229.1–3
PROVENANCE From a dessert canteen for thirty-six covers
supplied to Queen Charlotte, *c.*1767–8 (bill untraced); Sotheby's,
London, 10 March 1949, lot 103; purchased by Queen Elizabeth, 1950

354. Attributed to William Portal (free 1761)
*Three dessert knives with cipher of Queen Charlotte, c.*1767–8

Silver-gilt. Length 21.5 cm (8⁷⁄₁₆″)
Struck with maker's mark attributed to William Portal
RCIN 100230.1–3
PROVENANCE As for no. 353

355. Attributed to William Portal (free 1761)
*Three dessert forks with cipher of Queen Charlotte, c.*1767–8

Silver-gilt. Length 18.5 cm (7⁵⁄₁₆″)
Struck with maker's mark attributed to William Portal
RCIN 100231.1–3
PROVENANCE As for no. 353

355 353 354

356. English
*Pepper mill with the cipher of George III, c.*1770

Steel, tortoiseshell, silver. 9.3 × diameter 4.9 cm
(3¹¹⁄₁₆″ × 1¹⁵⁄₁₆″)
Stamped inside *DOLLAND*
RCIN 9323
PROVENANCE Presumably made for George III

356

358 359 358
360 357 360

Pieces from a silver-gilt dining service, 1772–1774 (nos. 357–361)

357. Thomas Heming (free 1746)

Strawberry dish, 1772–3

Silver-gilt. 3.0 × 22.3 × 22.5 cm (1³⁄₁₆″ × 8¾″ × 8⅞″)
Struck with London hallmarks for 1772–3 and maker's mark of
Thomas Heming
RCIN 50582
PROVENANCE Supplied for George III (bill untraced)

358. Thomas Heming (free 1746)

Pair of cruet stands, 1773–4

Silver-gilt. 9.0 × 30.8 × 19.4 cm (3⁹⁄₁₆″ × 12⅛″ × 7⅝″)
Struck with London hallmarks for 1773–4 and maker's mark of
Thomas Heming
RCIN 51615.1–2
PROVENANCE Supplied for George III (bill untraced)
LITERATURE Garrard 1914, no. 35

359. Thomas Heming (free 1746)

Tureen, 1773–4

Silver-gilt. 28.8 × 37.6 × 22.3 cm (11⁵⁄₁₆″ × 14¹³⁄₁₆″ × 8¾″)
Struck with London hallmarks for 1773–4 and maker's mark of
Thomas Heming
RCIN 50632.1
PROVENANCE From a pair supplied for George III or the Prince
of Wales (bill untraced)
LITERATURE Garrard 1914, no. 240

360. Thomas Heming (free 1746)

Two scallop dishes, 1773–4

Silver-gilt. 3.0 × 11.5 × 11.7 cm (1⁹⁄₁₆″ × 4¾″ × 4⅝″)
Struck with London hallmarks for 1773–4 and maker's mark of
Thomas Heming
RCIN 51051.1–2
PROVENANCE From a set of six supplied for George III (bill untraced)
LITERATURE Garrard 1914, no. 211

361. Thomas Heming (free 1746)

Pair of waiters, 1773–4

Silver-gilt. 3.4 × 24.8 × 24.9 cm (1⁵⁄₁₆″ × 9¾″ × 9¹³⁄₁₆″)
Struck with London hallmarks for 1773–4 and maker's mark of
Thomas Heming
RCIN 51671.1–2
PROVENANCE Supplied for George III (bill untraced)

A small group of silver-gilt dining plate supplied by Thomas
Heming between 1772 and 1774 survives in the Collection.
The cruet frames in particular demonstrate Heming's ability
to work in the newly fashionable neo-classical style which
gradually replaced the rococo during the 1760s.

The pieces do not appear in the Jewel House records,
which suggests that they may have been a private commission paid for by the Privy Purse. The magnificent tureens
have finials in the form of the Prince of Wales's feathers,
similar to those surmounting the porringer given to the
Prince of Wales in his infancy (see no. 387). They are of the
same model as a pair supplied by George Wickes, c.1745 (Barr
1980, p. 87, fig. 46). They may therefore have been supplied
for the Prince's separate household. A large dining service
for their use was commissioned from the Jewel House in
April 1771, but it seems unlikely that it would have taken
over two years to complete (PRO LC5/111, f. 122).

361

362. Henri Auguste (1759–1816)

Tureen and stand, 1787

Silver-gilt. 40.0 × 48.0 × 48.0 cm (15¾″ × 18⅞″ × 18⅞″)
Struck with Paris hallmarks for 1787 and maker's mark of
Henri Auguste
RCIN 51694.1
PROVENANCE Made for Tommaso Somma, Marchese di Circello,
1787; sold Christie's, London, 11 November 1801, lot 38; purchased
by Rundell, Bridge and Rundell (£148 3s); by whom sold to
George III (Rundells 1832, p. 86)
LITERATURE Garrard 1914, no. 241; Hartop 1995

This magnificent French tureen and stand is one of a pair
acquired by George III in 1801. They originally formed part
of the ambassadorial plate of Tommaso Somma, Marchese di
Circello (1737–1826), who was appointed Ambassador to
the French Court by Ferdinand IV (d. 1825), King of Naples,
in 1787. It is tempting to suggest that the service may even
have been a gift from Louis XVI to the Marchese. In 1795
it was brought to London when Circello was appointed
Ambassador to the Court of St James. Described as a
'remarkable Elegant Sideboard of the most Fashionable
PLATE', the service was sold at Christie's on 11 November
1801, following the Marchese's return to Naples. No. 362
formed part of a set of four tureens acquired by Rundell,
Bridge and Rundell. Two of the set were subsequently sold
to George III when the applied arms of Queen Charlotte
were added. The two other tureens were purchased by
Lord MacDonald of Sleat, Lord Chief Baron of George III's
Exchequer (sold Christie's, New York, 11 April 1995, lot 155).

The tureens bear the mark of the Parisian goldsmith
Henri Auguste, goldsmith to Louis XVI and son of the
pre-eminent French goldsmith Robert-Joseph Auguste.
Robert-Joseph had been commissioned by George III to
supply a large neo-classical dining service for use in his
Hanoverian palaces; much of that service is now in the
Rothschild Collection, Waddesdon Manor. Henri Auguste
took over his father's workshop in 1785 and supplied large
quantities of plate to the French court in the years prior to
the French Revolution. Like his father, he was one of the chief
exponents of the neo-classical style in French silver. After
the Revolution he worked for Napoleon, although he was
declared bankrupt in 1806 and fled to England in 1809.
He died in Jamaica in 1816.

Pieces from a silver-gilt dining service, 1788–1790 (nos. 363–366)

PROVENANCE Probably from a service commissioned to celebrate the recovery of George III, 1789 (bill untraced)

363. John Wakelin and William Taylor
(1776–1792)

Tureen, 1789–90

Silver-gilt. 32.0 × 46.5 × 26.8 cm (12⅝″ × 18⁵⁄₁₆″ × 10⁹⁄₁₆″)
Struck with London hallmarks for 1789–90 and makers' mark of
John Wakelin and William Taylor
RCIN 50631.1
LITERATURE Garrard 1914, no. 238

364. John Wakelin and William Taylor
(1776–1792)

Pair of sugar vases, 1789–90

Silver-gilt. 17.8 × 12.0 × 7.5 cm (7¹⁄₁₆″ × 4¹¹⁄₁₆″ × 2⅞″)
Struck with London hallmarks for 1789–90 and makers' mark of
John Wakelin and William Taylor
RCIN 51687.1–2
LITERATURE Garrard 1914, no. 38

365. John Wakelin and William Taylor
(1776–1792)

Two sauceboats, 1789–90

Silver-gilt. 14.0 × 24.6 × 11.0 cm (5½″ × 9¹¹⁄₁₆″ × 4⁵⁄₁₆″)
Struck with London hallmarks for 1789–90 and makers' mark of
John Wakelin and William Taylor
RCIN 51841.1–2
LITERATURE Garrard 1914, no. 229

366. Richard Crossley (*fl.*1772–1815)

Two sauce ladles, 1788–9

Silver-gilt. 18.5 × 5.6 cm (7⁵⁄₁₆″ × 2³⁄₁₆″)
Struck with London hallmarks for 1788–9 and maker's mark of
Richard Crossley
RCIN 51833.1–2
LITERATURE Garrard 1914, no. 458

These pieces appear to be among the few surviving remnants of a magnificent neo-classical dining service commissioned to celebrate the recovery of the King from his first bout of illness in 1789. Mrs Papendiek records that 'the new gold service of plate' was used for the first time at Windsor Castle on 1 May 1789, at a ball and supper held by the Queen and princesses in honour of the King's recovery. She thought the salvers and cups 'particularly elegant. They were ornamented with serpents twisted round in a tasteful manner, and made in shining and mat gold, which raised the scales in relief, and made the reptiles look fearfully real' (Papendiek 1887, II, pp. 100–101).

A full account of this magnificent supper, 'which exceeded any thing of the kind ever given in this kingdom', was published in the *Annual Register*. The supper was held in St George's Hall, with the royal family's table across one end 'raised above the rest'. The guests were seated at two long tables which ran down the entire length of the hall: 'Her majesty's table was distinguished by gold plates, gold dishes, gold spoons, gold candle-branches, and gold knives and forks. On the ground-work of the royal table were the figures of Peace and Plenty, with the olive-branch and cornucopiae – the accompaniments various Genii weaving wreaths of flowers, – the pedestals presented vases of flowers. On one of the long tables, the platform was covered with dancing figures, – the other had emblematical figures, Hope, Charity, Peace, Plenty, Britannia . . . which being done on sand, glistened with the reflected light of the candles. That part of the supper which was hot, consisted of twenty tureens of different soups, roast ducks, turkey pouts, cygness [*sic*], green geese, land rails, chickens, asparagus, peas, and beans. The cold parts of the collation were the same kind of poultry boned, and swimming or standing in the centre of transparent jellies, which were supported by paste pillars . . . This with the lights playing from the candles, and reflected on by the polish of the plates and dishes, made a most beautiful appearance. Crayfish pies of all kinds were distributed with great taste; and the ham and brawn in masquerade, swimming on the surface of pedestals of jelly, seemingly supported but by the strength of an apparent liquid, called for admiration. The ornamental parts of the confectionery were numerous and splendid. There were temples four feet high, in which the different stories were sweetmeats. The various orders of architecture were also done with inimitable taste . . . The desert [*sic*] comprehended all the hothouse was competent to afford – and, indeed, more than it was thought art could produce at this time of year. There were a profusion of pine[apple]s, strawberries of every denomination, peaches, nectarines, apricots, cherries of each kind, from the Kentish to the

364 363 364
365 366 365

Morella, plums, and raspberries, with the best and richest preserved fruits, as well those that are dried as those that are in syrup. There were forty silver branches, each holding two large wax tapers, on the long tables, and six gold branches on the queen's table and at the side-boards were two magnificent candelabra, which gave out a great light' (*Annual Register*, 1789, pp. 252–3).

The restrained neo-classicism of the surviving pieces from the new service contrasts greatly with the fluid naturalism of the 'Coronation Service' made in the early 1760s (nos. 330–52) and admirably demonstrates the changes in taste which took place over the first thirty years of George III's reign.

The tureen, sugar vases and sauceboats are struck with the maker's mark of John Wakelin and William Taylor, who were among a number of goldsmiths who worked for the royal family following Burke's Economical Reform Act of 1782. Under the act, the duties of the Jewel House were taken over by the Lord Chamberlain in an attempt to save money following the costly war with America and the considerable cost of providing the Prince of Wales's new household with new plate. Thomas Heming, appointed Goldsmith to the King in 1760, was forced to tender for future work but was dismissed when his estimates were seen to be far higher than others (see Lomax 1999, pp. 138–9).

Pieces from Queen Charlotte's silver-gilt tea and coffee equipage, 1761–c.1770 (nos. 367–376)

367. Aymé Videau (free 1723/?4)

Hot water/milk jug with cipher of Queen Charlotte, 1762–3

Silver-gilt, fruitwood. 21.0 × 15.0 × 11.0 cm
(8¼" × 5⅞" × 4⁵⁄₁₆")
Struck with London hallmarks for 1762–3 and maker's mark of Aymé Videau
RCIN 47392
PROVENANCE Supplied for Queen Charlotte (bill untraced); Princess Mary, Duchess of Gloucester; by whom bequeathed to George, 2nd Duke of Cambridge; from whose estate sold Christie's, 7 June 1904, lot 24; bought by Stimpson (£49); by whose daughter sold to Queen Mary, 1942

368. Thomas Heming (free 1746)

Tea kettle and stand with cipher of Queen Charlotte, 1761–3

Silver-gilt, fruitwood. 37.5 × 16.5 × 25.0 cm (14¾" × 6¾" × 9¹³⁄₁₆")
Struck with London hallmarks for 1761–2 (tea kettle) and 1762–3 (stand), and maker's mark of Thomas Heming
RCIN 49128
PROVENANCE Supplied for Queen Charlotte (bill untraced)
LITERATURE Garrard 1914, no. 305

368 371 369
373 370 372 367

369. William Robertson (*fl.*1753–1773)

Coffee pot with cipher of Queen Charlotte, 1761–2

Silver-gilt, fruitwood. 25.4 × 16.9 × 11.5 cm (10″ × 6⅝″ × 4¾″)
Struck with London hallmarks for 1761–2 and maker's mark of
William Robertson
RCIN 51576
PROVENANCE Supplied for Queen Charlotte (bill untraced)
LITERATURE Garrard 1914, no. 308

370. Thomas Heming (free 1746)

Waiter with cipher of Queen Charlotte, 1761–2

Silver-gilt. 3.9 × 29.1 × 29.1 cm (1⁹⁄₁₆″ × 11⁷⁄₁₆″ × 11⁷⁄₁₆″)
Struck with London hallmarks for 1761–2 and maker's mark of
Thomas Heming
RCIN 100226
PROVENANCE Supplied for Queen Charlotte (bill untraced);
(?)Princess Augusta (see p. 387); her brother, King Ernest Augustus
of Hanover; by descent; acquired by HM Queen Elizabeth, 1950

371. Thomas Heming (free 1746)

Tea urn with cipher of Queen Charlotte, 1768–9

Silver-gilt, ivory. 51.0 × 24.0 × 26.0 cm (20¹⁄₁₆″ × 9⁷⁄₁₆″ × 10¼″)
Struck with London hallmarks for 1768–9 and maker's mark of
Thomas Heming
RCIN 49823
PROVENANCE Supplied for Queen Charlotte (bill untraced)
LITERATURE Garrard 1914, no. 306

372. John Langford II and John Sebille
(*fl.*1763–1770)

Pair of tea canisters, 1767–8

Silver-gilt. 11.2 × 6.2 × 4.8 cm (4⁷⁄₁₆″ × 2⁷⁄₁₆″ × 1⅞″)
Struck with London hallmarks for 1767–8 and makers' marks
of John Langford II and John Sebille
RCIN 51639.1–2
PROVENANCE Probably supplied for George III or
Queen Charlotte (bill untraced)
LITERATURE Garrard 1914, no. 317

373. John Langford II and John Sebille
(*fl.*1763–1770)

Pair of tea canisters, 1767–8

Silver-gilt. 12.1 × 6.2 × 4.8 cm (4¾″ × 2⁷⁄₁₆″ × 1⅞″)
Struck with London hallmarks for 1767–8 and makers' marks of
John Langford II and John Sebille
RCIN 51638.1–2
PROVENANCE Probably supplied for George III or Queen Charlotte
(bill untraced)
LITERATURE Garrard 1914, no. 318

374. English

Mote spoon with cipher of Queen Charlotte, c.1761–70

Silver-gilt. 14.4 × 2.4 × 1.2 cm (5¹¹/₁₆″ × ¹⁵/₁₆″ × ½″)
Unmarked
RCIN 50612
PROVENANCE Supplied for Queen Charlotte (bill untraced)
LITERATURE Garrard 1914, no. 445

375. English

Teaspoons with cipher of Queen Charlotte, c.1761–70

Silver-gilt. 11.6 × 2.3 cm (4⁹/₁₆″ × ⅞″)
Unmarked
RCIN 51345.1–3
PROVENANCE Supplied for Queen Charlotte (bill untraced)
LITERATURE Garrard 1914, no. 473

376. English

Sugar tongs with cipher of Queen Charlotte, c.1761–70

Silver-gilt. 13.4 × 5.1 × 1.5 cm (5¼″ × 2″ × ⁹/₁₆″)
Unmarked
RCIN 51741
PROVENANCE Supplied for Queen Charlotte (bill untraced)
LITERATURE Garrard 1914, no. 449

George III ordered a new tea and coffee equipage in December 1761. This included two dozen teaspoons, two pairs of 'tea tongs', two gilt coffee-pots, a gilt waiter, 'a Gilt vase Boiler and stand' and 'a Gilt Tea Kettle & Proviance' (PRO LC5/110, f. 356). The weights of the objects delivered (PRO LC9/48, f. 204) do not correspond with any surviving pieces in the Collection. It is likely therefore that the surviving pieces which are engraved with the ciphers of the Queen were commissioned privately and not through the Jewel House. This is probably also the case with the Queen's tea-urn, made in 1768–9, which is also absent from the Jewel House records.

The pierced bowl of the mote spoon would have been used to skim off stray tea leaves, while the pointed shaft was used to dislodge any leaves caught in the kettle spout.

Queen Charlotte normally dined at 4 o'clock, followed by coffee at 6 o'clock. Tea was taken during the evening entertainments (see nos. 407, 408). In the early years of the reign the tea was often made by the Queen, and was 'carried . . . about to the Ladies' by the King (Northumberland 1926, p. 195).

The Queen also attempted to grow her own tea in the gardens at Kew; on hearing that Dr John Fothergill had obtained several tea plants from the 'Indeas' she tried to

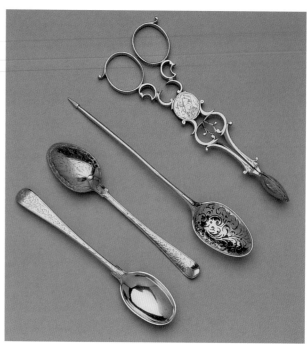

375 374 376

obtain one for herself (Hedley 1975, p. 114). Also at Kew the Queen built a picturesque thatched cottage, described in the *London Magazine* of 1774 as a 'pretty retreat'. Here the royal family would take tea, surrounded by their numerous pets, including kangaroos from Australia. To ease her terrible headaches the Queen drank a special tea made from the peel of bitter oranges and cardomom, which was served cold several times a day (Hedley 1975, p. 207).

377. John Edwards III (free 1782)

Egg boiler with ciphers of George III and his five youngest daughters, 1803–4

Silver-gilt. 36.0 × 21.0 × 12.0 cm (14³/₁₆″ × 8¼″ × 4¾″)
Struck with London hallmarks for 1803–4 and maker's mark of John Edwards III
RCIN 49122
PROVENANCE Part of a silver-gilt breakfast service presented to George III by the Princesses Augusta, Elizabeth, Mary, Sophia and Amelia, 4 June 1804 (bill untraced; Rundells 1832, pp. 97–8)

This ingenious object forms part of a silver-gilt breakfast service presented to George III by his five youngest daughters on his sixty-sixth birthday, 4 June 1804. The King would have boiled his own eggs at the breakfast table by opening the double lid of the boiler and placing the eggs in the frame

377

inside. Water inside was kept boiling by a lamp below, while the egg timer above ensured the perfect cooking time. The breakfast service was first recorded in the Collection in 1832 when it was described as 'presented to George the Third by the Princesses'; a manuscript addition to the inventory noted 'These things A Present from the Princesses to George the Third the 4 of June 1804' (Rundells 1832, pp. 97–8). The service also included a coffee pot, tea pot, sugar basin, cream ewer, two muffin dishes, an egg frame, china coffee cups, teaspoons, sugar tongs and waiter. A similar, though slightly heavier, silver-gilt egg boiler, also with serpent handles, was included in Queen Charlotte's sale in 1819 (19 May 1819, lot 84).

A unique description of the royal family's morning routine at Windsor at the time no. 377 was made was included in *The Public and Private Life of George the Third...*, published in 1821: 'When the King rises, which is generally about half-past seven o'clock, he proceeds immediately to the queen's saloon, where his majesty is met by one of the princesses; generally either Augusta, Sophia or Amelia; for each, in turn, attend their revered parent. From thence the sovereign and

his daughter, attended by the lady-in-waiting, proceed to the chapel in the castle, wherein divine service is performed by the dean, sub-dean: the ceremony occupies about an hour; when the king, instead of proceeding to his own apartment, and breakfasting alone, now takes that meal with the queen and the five princesses. The table is always set out in the queen's noble breakfasting-room, which has been recently decorated with very elegant modern hangings: and, since the late improvements by Mr Wyatt, commands a most delightful and extensive prospect of the Little-park. The breakfast does not occupy half an hour. The king and queen sit at the head of the table, and the princesses according to seniority. Etiquette in every other respect is strictly adhered to. On entering the room the usual forms are observed, agreeable to rank' (Huish 1821, p. 660).

DRESSING TABLE SILVER (nos. 378–384)

Pieces from a silver-gilt toilet service, engraved with the Royal Arms and cipher of George III, 1758–1759 (nos. 378–382)

378. Thomas Heming (free 1746)
Pair of candlesticks, 1758–9

Silver-gilt. 18.6 × 10.9 × 10.9 cm (7⁵/₁₆″ × 4⁵/₁₆″ × 4⁵/₁₆″)
Struck with London hallmarks for 1758–9 and maker's mark of Thomas Heming
RCIN 100232.1–2
PROVENANCE Probably supplied for George III, 1761; (?)Princess Augusta (see p. 387); acquired by Queen Mary, 1932 (*QMB*, III, no. 77)

379. Thomas Heming (free 1746)
Pair of large boxes, 1758–9

Silver-gilt. 7.0 × 12.5 × 12.7 cm (2³/₄″ × 4¹⁵/₁₆″ × 5″)
Struck with London hallmarks for 1758–9 and maker's mark of Thomas Heming
RCIN 100232.3–4
PROVENANCE Probably supplied for George III, 1761; (?)Princess Augusta (see p. 387); her brother, King Ernest Augustus of Hanover; by descent; acquired by Queen Mary, 1927 (*QMB*, II, no. 171)

378 382 378
380 381 379 379 381 380

380. Thomas Heming (free 1746)

Pair of tall boxes, 1758–9

Silver-gilt. 9.5 × 7.5 × 7.5 cm (3¾″ × 2¹⁵⁄₁₆″ × 2¹⁵⁄₁₆″)
Struck with London hallmarks for 1758–9 and maker's mark of
Thomas Heming. Engraved with the cipher of George Finch,
9th Earl of Winchilsea, inside lid
RCIN 100232.5–6
PROVENANCE Probably supplied for George III, 1761; Lady
Charlotte Finch; her son, George Finch, 9th Earl of Winchilsea;
thence by descent; acquired by the future King George V, 1907
(*QMB*, I, no. 78)

381. Thomas Heming (free 1746)

Pair of small boxes, 1758–9

Silver-gilt. 4.1 × 7.5 × 7.5 cm (1⅝″ × 2¹⁵⁄₁₆″ × 2¹⁵⁄₁₆″)
Struck with London hallmarks for 1758–9 and maker's mark of
Thomas Heming. Engraved with the cipher of George Finch,
9th Earl of Winchilsea, inside lid
RCIN 100232.7–8
PROVENANCE Probably supplied for George III, 1761; Lady
Charlotte Finch; her son, George Finch, 9th Earl of Winchilsea;
thence by descent; acquired by the future King George V, 1907
(*QMB*, I, no. 78)

382. Thomas Heming (free 1746)

Tray, 1758–9

Silver-gilt. 5.5 × 36.4 × 26.0 cm (2³⁄₁₆″ × 14⁵⁄₁₆″ × 10¼″)
Struck with London hallmarks for 1758–9 and maker's mark of
Thomas Heming
RCIN 100232.9
PROVENANCE Probably supplied for George III, 1761; (?)Princess
Augusta (see p. 387); her brother, King Ernest Augustus of Hanover;
by descent; acquired by Queen Mary, 1927 (*QMB*, II, no. 171)

On 10 December 1761 'a set of Gilt dressing plate for the
Queen's use' was ordered from the Jewel House. The warrant
added 'that you give order for new Gilding a set of Dressing
Plate in Being . . . for her Majesty to use whilst the other is
making' (PRO LC5/110, f. 339). Nos. 378–82 are perhaps
from this latter service. They were made in the workshop
of Thomas Heming in 1758–9, prior to his appointment as
Goldsmith to the King in 1760. It seems therefore that
Heming supplied a toilet service from old stock. It is possible
that it was the 'sett of Dressing plate', presumably intended
for George III's future bride, included in a warrant for
nearly 9,000 ounces (255.1 kg) of new gilt plate on 22 July
1761 (PRO LC5/110, f. 339). The King's betrothal had been
announced on 8 July and the couple were married two
months later.

384 383

It appears that a new service was ordered in December 1761 because the Queen found Heming's existing service unsuitable. The second, more elaborate, service was delivered the following February. It consisted of 2 comb boxes, 2 powder boxes, 2 essence boxes, 2 patch boxes, a comb tray, 4 brush handles, 2 plumets, a basin and ewer, a pair of candlesticks, 2 gilt porringers, 2 frankincense pots, a looking-glass frame, basin, mounts for a glass cup, jewel box and 2 waiters (PRO LC9/48, f. 204). A further set of dressing plate – probably made in Augsburg – was included in Zoffany's portrait of Queen Charlotte *c.*1765 (no. 4).

The toilet service shown here (nos. 378–82) appears to have been dispersed during Queen Charlotte's lifetime. The pieces included here were reassembled by King George V and Queen Mary between 1907 and 1932.

Pieces from a silver-gilt toilet service, 1771–1772 (nos. 383–384)

383. Thomas Heming (free 1746)
Toilet box with the cipher of Queen Charlotte, 1771–2

Silver-gilt. 11.4 × 19.0 × 11.6 cm (4½″ × 7⁷/₁₆″ × 4⁹/₁₆″)
Struck with London hallmarks and maker's mark of
Thomas Heming
RCIN 48656
PROVENANCE From a toilet service supplied for Queen Charlotte (bill untraced); (?)her sale, Christie's, London, 19 May 1819 (lot 66, see below); probably acquired by Queen Mary before 1904

384. Thomas Heming (free 1746)
Toilet tray with the cipher of Queen Charlotte, 1771–2

Silver-gilt. 3.0 × 30.0 × 20.0 cm (1³/₁₆″ × 11¹³/₁₆″ × 7⅞″)
Struck with London hallmarks and maker's mark of
Thomas Heming
RCIN 100234
PROVENANCE From a toilet service supplied for Queen Charlotte (bill untraced); (?)her sale, Christie's, London, 19 May 1819 (lot 68, see below); purchased by Queen Elizabeth, 1950

This beautifully chased box and tray belong to the 'SUPERB SERVICE OF SILVER GILT TOILET PLATE . . . enriched with roses and other flowers, richly chased in bold taste' included in the catalogue of Queen Charlotte's sale on 19 May 1819 (lots 63–74). Most of the service, including the 'noble large toilet glass', ewer and basin 'of elegant shape', candlesticks formed as 'figures of Flora' and a pair of large scalloped toilet boxes, was purchased from the sale by Earl Grosvenor and remains in the collection of the Dukes of Westminster. No. 383 may however be identifiable with 'A pair of small oval [scalloped toilet boxes] with handles' purchased by Goldney for £54 (lot 66) and no. 384 is perhaps the 'richly chased salver, with two handles' to 'a scalloped square box and pincushion' purchased by the Earl of Yarmouth for £73 15s 6d (lot 68). Although made by Thomas Heming in 1771–2, the service does not appear in the Jewel House records and was probably a private commission from the Queen. The pieces are very closely related to an earlier toilet service by Heming given by George III to his sister Caroline, on her marriage in

1766 to Christian VII of Denmark (Kunstindustrie Museum, Copenhagen). The tray from Queen Caroline's service has been described as having 'the vigour and movement . . . worthy of Lamerie twenty-five years earlier' (Grimwade 1974, p. 41). A third almost identical toilet service was supplied by Heming for the marriage of Sir Watkin Williams-Wynn (1749–89) to Lady Henrietta Somerset in 1769 (Cardiff, National Museum of Wales; see Hughes 1973).

SILVER FOR THE ROYAL NURSERY (nos. 385–387)

385. English(?)

Baby's rattle, c.1762

Silver filigree. 28.0 × 6.0 × 6.0 cm (11″ × 2⅜″ × 2⅜″)
Unmarked
RCIN 11944
PROVENANCE Presented to the royal nursery by Lady Charlotte Finch, 1763; her daughter; by whom bequeathed to Princess Augusta (d. 1840); passed to Princess Sophia (d. 1848); passed to Princess Mary, Duchess of Gloucester; by whom presented to Queen Victoria, 1848

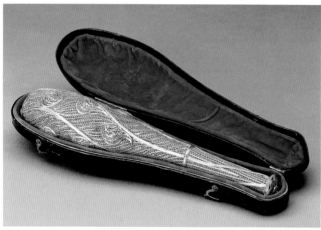

385

386. Thomas Heming (free 1746)

Covered child's mug, 1763

Silver-gilt. 9.8 × 8.6 × 6.9 cm (3⅞″ × 3⅜″ × 2¹¹⁄₁₆″)
Struck with London hallmarks for 1762–3 and maker's mark of Thomas Heming
RCIN 9322
PROVENANCE Supplied to the Prince of Wales, July 1763
(£2 16s 4d; PRO LC5/111, f. 30, LC9/48, f. 229)

387. Thomas Heming (free 1746)

Covered porringer, stand and two pap spoons, 1763

Silver-gilt. Porringer 10.2 × 25.4 × 16.2 cm (4″ × 10″ × 6⅜″);
stand 2.0 × 19.2 × 19.2 cm (¾″ × 7⁹⁄₁₆″ × 7⁹⁄₁₆″);
spoons 16.6 × 3.4 cm (6⁹⁄₁₆″ × 1⁵⁄₁₆″)
Struck with London hallmarks for 1763–4 and maker's mark of Thomas Heming, spoons unmarked
RCIN 51034.a–d
PROVENANCE Supplied to the Prince of Wales, July 1763
(£27 18s 7d; PRO LC5/111, f. 30, LC9/48, f. 229)
LITERATURE Garrard 1914, no. 169

The mug, engraved with the Prince of Wales's feathers, and the porringer topped with Prince of Wales's feathers finial, formed part of a set of plate supplied for the Prince of Wales when he was 11 months old. On 21 July 1763, a warrant entitled 'Plate for the Royal Nursery' contained an order for 'A Porringer and small Mug with cover, a plate for the Porringer, a pap boat and two pap spoons all Gilt. A warming pot and a saucepan with cover the inside Gilt with a lamp and Hand candlestick of White Plate' (PRO LC5/111, f. 30). The finished 'gilt porringer and cover and plate' and 'the small gilt mug and cover' were delivered to the Prince at the end of the month. The porringer cost £27 18s 7d and the mug £2 16s 4d (PRO LC9/48, f. 229). The young Prince had been given 'a gold coral with eight bells' the previous November, when 'one saucepan and cover gilt within, one Ranakin [*sic*], one flat Hand Candlestick' had also been delivered to the royal nursery (PRO LC9/45, f. 123). All fifteen of George III's children similarly received a gold-mounted coral shortly after their birth, followed by a gilt mug and porringer when they were around a year old.

The silver filigree rattle was a gift to the infant Prince of Wales from his governess, Lady Charlotte Finch (see no. 78). It was subsequently used by all of George III's children in the royal nursery. Following Lady Charlotte's death in 1813 the rattle passed to her daughter, who in turn bequeathed it to Princess Augusta (d. 1840), on whose death it passed to her sister, Princess Sophia. On Sophia's death in 1848 it passed to the last surviving daughter of George III, Princess Mary, Duchess of Gloucester, who presented it in the same year to Queen Victoria, for use in the royal nursery. This provenance is set out in an inscription on the case.

386 387

388. Thomas Cooke II and Richard Gurney
(*fl*.1721–1773)

Two-handled cup and cover, 1761

Silver-gilt. 40.0 × 34.7 × 19.0 cm (15¾″ × 13¹¹⁄₁₆″ × 7⁷⁄₁₆″)
Struck with London hallmarks for 1761–2 and makers' mark of
Thomas Cooke II and Richard Gurney. Inscribed *Presented to
Sir Thomas Munday knt. Mayor of the City of Oxford, as his Fee,
for performing in right of his Office, the Duty of under Butler, at the
Coronation of his Most Gracious Majesty King George the Third,
in the Year 1761*

RCIN 51088

PROVENANCE Presented by George III to Sir Thomas Munday,
1761; probably acquired by Queen Mary

Sir Thomas Munday, Mayor of Oxford, was presented with
this large two-handled cup and cover as part of his fee for
serving in the office of Under Butler at George III's coronation
banquet on 22 September 1761.

In accordance with ancient precedent, the Mayor and
eight burgesses of Oxford traditionally assisted the Lord
Mayor and twelve citizens of London as Assistant to the
Chief Butler of England at the coronation banquet. At the
end of the elaborate dinner in Westminster Hall, the Lord
Mayor of London, accompanied by the King's Cupbearer and

388

Assistant, offered the King wine held in a gold cup. The King afterwards returned the cup to the Lord Mayor who kept it as his fee. The Mayor and burgesses of Oxford, preceded by the King's Cupbearer, then offered the King three maplewood cups; the Mayor then received the cups as his fee. This fee however was traditionally augmented *ex gratia Regis* with a large silver-gilt bowl and cover.

No. 388 was one of a large number of perquisites traditionally claimed by various individuals and institutions for services performed at the coronation and coronation banquet. The gold and silver-gilt objects were supplied by the Jewel House. On 23 July 1761 a warrant was received to 'prepare & Deliver to the Mayor of Oxford against the Coronation a Gilt Bowl of the same Value and fashion as at the last coronation' (PRO LC5/110, f. 344). The finished cup and cover were delivered to Thomas Munday the following September 'for his claim at the Coronation as Assistant in the Butlership' (PRO LC9/45, f. 189).

When the royal couple entered Westminster Hall, lustres holding 3,000 candles were immediately lit using trains of flax. This, however, caused it to rain 'fire upon the heads of all spectators (the flax falling in large flakes) & and the Ladies (Queen and all) were in no small terrors'. The dinner comprised three services of a hundred dishes and the royal table was admired as a 'Triomfe of foliage and flowers'. The King and Queen ate venison from gilt plates, although Thomas Gray described them as 'eating like farmers'. No doubt he had forgotten that they had not eaten since the early morning (*Gray Correspondence*, II, p. 752). The 1761 coronation banquet was the last occasion on which a queen attended such an event. The banquet element of the ceremonial was abandoned by William IV and has never been reinstated.

389. Thomas Heming (free 1746)

Christening cup, 1762–3

Silver-gilt. 34.7 × 27.0 × 16.8 cm (13¹¹⁄₁₆″ × 10⅝″ × 6⅝″) Struck with London hallmarks for 1762–3 and maker's mark of Thomas Heming. Inscribed *This Cup was Given by George the 3rd. to George Visct St. Asaph. Born Decemr. 25 1760. Christen'd Jany. 29th. 1761 & was the first time that his Majesty stood Godfather in Person after his Accession to the Crown*
RCIN 51485
PROVENANCE A christening gift from George III to George, Viscount St Asaph, later 3rd Earl of Ashburnham (£67 14s 2d; PRO LC5/110, f. 357, LC5/111, f. 12, LC9/45, f. 174); probably acquired by Queen Mary

390. Thomas Heming (free 1746)

Christening cup, 1762–3

Silver-gilt. 36.0 × 26.0 × 16.6 cm (14³⁄₁₆″ × 10¼″ × 6⁹⁄₁₆″) Struck with London hallmarks for 1762–3 and maker's mark of Thomas Heming. Inscribed *The Gift of His Majesty King George the Third to his Godson The Honble. George Murray. Born 8th April 1780*
RCIN 49950
PROVENANCE A christening gift from George III to the Hon. George Murray (£62 5s 2d; PRO LC9/45, f. 236, LC9/49 2 June 1780); Queen Mary; by whom given as a christening present to Prince Charles, 1948

391. Thomas Heming (free 1746)

Christening cup, 1773–4

Silver-gilt. 34.7 × 27.0 × 16.0 cm (13¹¹⁄₁₆″ × 10⅝″ × 6⁵⁄₁₆″) Struck with London hallmarks for 1773–4 and maker's mark of Thomas Heming. Inscribed *This Cup was given by His Majesty King George The Third, to his Godson Augustus George Legge. Born April 21st 1773. Baptized The 21st of May*
RCIN 49568
PROVENANCE A christening gift from George III to the Hon. Augustus George Legge (£66 15s; PRO LC5/111, ff. 153–4, LC9/45, f. 270l); presented by the King and Queen of Greece, Duke and Duchess of Gloucester, Princess Royal and Lord Harewood to Queen Mary, Christmas 1942

George III stood as godparent to the children of a number of his friends and courtiers. The King was expected to present his godchild with a gift, the value of which was standardised in accordance with the rank of the child's parents. Silver-gilt two-handled cups and covers were a popular choice. The form had been introduced by Huguenot silversmiths and remained popular throughout the eighteenth century.

These three christening cups were supplied by the royal goldsmith Thomas Heming. Two bear the date letters for 1762–3 and one for 1773–4. The King presented one of the earlier cups to George, Viscount St Asaph (1760–1830), eldest surviving son of John, 2nd Earl of Ashburnham (1724–1812; Lord of the Bedchamber 1748–62; Master of the Great Wardrobe 1765–75; First Lord of the Bedchamber and Groom of the Stole, 1775–82). The King had attended the child's christening on 29 January 1761, the first time he had done so in person since his accession. However a warrant for the christening present was not received by the Jewel House until 18 February 1761. The warrant specified that 130 ounces troy (4.3 kg) of gilt plate were 'to be made into such vessels & after such fashion' as the Earl of Ashburnham

389 390 391

'shall direct'. The finished cup was finally delivered in March 1763, at a total cost of £67 14s 2d (PRO LC5/110, f. 357; LC5/111, f. 12; LC9/45, f. 174).

The second cup, although also marked for 1762–3, was presented in 1780. It was a gift from the King to the Hon. George Murray (1780–1848), second son of David, 7th Viscount Stormont (1727–96; he succeeded as 2nd Earl of Mansfield in 1793). In this instance it would appear that a cup of the prescribed weight was taken from old Jewel House stock. The cup was delivered to the boy's father, Viscount Stormont, on 29 June 1780 and cost £62 5s 2d (PRO LC9/45, f. 236; LC9/49 2 June 1780). The contrast between these two cups made at the same time by the same maker is remarkable. Viscount St Asaph's (no. 389) is closely based on a gold cup designed by William Kent and engraved by John Vardy in 1744 (Vardy 1744, p. 28); that cup had been presented by Frederick, Prince of Wales, to Colonel Pelham. George Murray's cup (no. 390) is an early example of the urn-shaped

neo-classical examples which became popular from the mid-1760s.

The third cup (no. 391) was presented to the Hon. Augustus George Legge (1773–1828), youngest son of William, 2nd Earl of Dartmouth (1731–1801); he was christened in May 1773 (Lichfield Parish Records). The Earl served as Secretary of State for the Colonies 1772–5 and Lord Privy Seal 1775–82. His surviving letters from George III indicate a close friendship; in November 1783 the King sent Dartmouth a 'model in wax of a much loved departed child [Prince Octavius, who had died in May] as a mark of my esteem and affection' (HMC, 11th Report, Appendix, pt V, 1887, p. 442). Like the Earl of Ashburnham, the Earl of Dartmouth was allowed 130 ounces troy (4.3 kg) of gilt plate 'made into such vessels and afterwards fashion' as he required. The finished cup however took only a short time to complete and was delivered in December 1773 at a cost of £66 15s (PRO LC5/111, ff. 153–4; LC9/45, f. 270).

13. *Objets de vertu* (nos. 392–420)

392. Attributed to Elisabeth Ziesenis (1744–1796) and Rundell, Bridge and Rundell

Snuff box incorporating a miniature of Queen Charlotte when Princess Sophie Charlotte of Mecklenburg-Strelitz, c.1761 and later

Tortoiseshell, gold, miniature on ivory. 2.8 × 8.1 × 6.0 cm
(1⅛″ × 3³⁄₁₆″ × 2⅜″)
RCIN 43892
PROVENANCE First recorded in May 1826 when mounted
as a snuff box by Rundell, Bridge and Rundell (£27 6s;
RA GEO/26114; Add. Cat., case 14, no. 26)
LITERATURE Walker 1992, no. 426

On 23 June 1826 Rundell, Bridge and Rundell were paid
£27 6s for setting this miniature 'of Her Late Majesty Queen
Charlotte' into the top of a tortoiseshell snuff box lined
with gold. The miniature is however much earlier. It depicts
Queen Charlotte when Princess of Mecklenburg-Strelitz.
Dressed in state robes, she gestures toward the ducal crown
of Mecklenburg-Strelitz. The portrait is derived from a
full-size three-quarter-length portrait in the Collection (RCIN
403562; fig. 5) by the Danish artist Johann Georg Ziesenis
(1716–76), perhaps painted to commemorate the Princess's
betrothal to George III in June 1761. No. 392 was probably
painted by Ziesenis's daughter Elisabeth, who is known to
have copied her father's work extensively; another miniature
of Charlotte, after the same source, is inscribed on the back
La Reine d'Angleterre peint par Elisabeth Ziesenis 1761 (Hanover,
Historisches Museum).

   At least two pictures of the Princess were sent to George III
prior to his marriage. It is tempting to suggest that no. 392
was one of them. Colonel Graeme, sent to Mecklenburg-
Strelitz to report on the suitability of the Princess, thought
the first picture 'a Daub'. He procured a second, 'done by
a young woman from Schwerin', from the Princess's great-
aunt. This he thought 'Like Her' although 'I cannot say
flattered, And the nose badly done' (Hedley 1975, pp. 28–9).

392

For other early portraits of Queen Charlotte, painted after
the marriage and coronation, see nos. 28 and 29.

393. French workmaster

Snuff box, c.1765

Vari-coloured gold, lid inset with glazed miniature painted on ivory.
4.2 × 8.2 × 6.1 cm (1⅝″ × 3¼″ × 2⅜″)
RCIN 100014
PROVENANCE Adolphus Frederick IV, Duke of Mecklenburg-
Strelitz; by whom given to Hugh Seton of Touch, 1769
(RA GEO/Add. 16/96–105); probably thence by descent to Col.
Sir Bruce Seton, 9th Baronet of Abercorn (1868–1932); Queen
Mary; by whom given to King George V on his sixty-eighth
birthday, 3 June 1933 (GV Boxes, IV, no. 349)
LITERATURE *Royal Treasures* 2002, no. 288

A remarkable group of letters, acquired by Queen Mary
with this box in 1933, provides a fascinating insight into its
history. It was a gift from Adolphus Frederick IV, Duke of
Mecklenburg-Strelitz, to Hugh Seton of Touch (Stirlingshire)
in April 1769. The Duke was Queen Charlotte's eldest brother.
The Queen corresponded regularly with 'le cher duc', although
she was constantly exasperated by her lack of success in
persuading him to marry. Seton, who like George III was a

◁ No. 398 (detail)

393 inside lid

393

394. German

*Snuff box, c.*1770

Amethystine quartz, gold, diamonds, rubies. 2.8 × 4.9 × 3.6 cm
(1⅛″ × 1¹⁵⁄₁₆″ × 1⁷⁄₁₆″)

RCIN 9162

PROVENANCE Possibly Queen Charlotte; Princess Sophia; passed
to Princess Mary, Duchess of Gloucester (d. 1857); by whom
bequeathed to Princess Mary Adelaide, Duchess of Teck; by whom
given/bequeathed to Queen Mary (*QMB*, I, no. 283)

Queen Charlotte was an enthusiastic taker of snuff, a finely
ground mixture of tobacco and aromatics popular from the
early eighteenth century. The sale of her possessions in 1819
included over 90 snuff boxes made of a wide variety of different
materials and 353 bottles of 'highly scented snuff from the
Royal Manufactory of Seville'.

The Queen perhaps used snuff to ease the terrible headaches
of which she often complained. Snuff-taking was a habit she
had adopted before her arrival in England and one which she
and the King did not share. To please his new bride, the King
had tried a pinch on the second day of their marriage, but
this was said to have 'made him sneeze prodigiously' (Hedley
1975, p. 46). The Queen's favoured blend of snuff was Violet
Strasbourg, a mixture of powdered rappee, bitter almonds,
ambergris and attarju, which she augmented with a spoonful
of green tea every morning (Snowman 1990, p. 20).

No. 394 belonged to Queen Charlotte's daughter Princess
Sophia, after whose death it passed to her sister the Duchess
of Gloucester. She in turn bequeathed it to her niece Princess
Mary Adelaide, Duchess of Teck, who passed it to her
daughter, Queen Mary. Queen Mary's passionate interest in
Queen Charlotte led her to identify no. 394, perhaps somewhat

keen agricultural reformer, had met the Duke the previous
September. He was entrusted with a number of letters from
the Duke to convey to his sister in England. On his arrival in
England Seton wrote to the Duke to confirm the safe delivery
of the letters to the Queen at the time of her confinement for
the birth of Princess Augusta; he added that he was sending
the Duke a gift of a post-chaise (four-wheeled carriage) as a
mark of friendship. The Duke was delighted with the present.
In his reply he thanked Seton for his generous gift, in which
he drove out daily, and begged him to accept no. 393, 'un petit
paquet', 'wrapped in brown paper', as a mark of his friendship.

The box was probably made in Germany by a French
workmaster. It is of superb quality and is elaborately chased
in vari-coloured gold with allegories of putti and cherubs,
emblematic of the arts and sciences. A miniature of the Duke,
by an unidentified German artist, is set into the underside
of the lid. It depicts the Duke wearing the star and collar of
the Garter, which he had received in 1764 (see no. 443).

394

optimistically, with the 'Snuff box of the rare and fine root of amethyst, the lid set with flowers formed of diamonds and coloured stones' sold in Queen Charlotte's sale on 18 May 1819 (lot 9).

395. German

Snuff box incorporating miniatures of Queen Charlotte and her family, c.1770

Gold, miniatures on ivory. 4.1 × 7.9 × 5.9 cm (1⅝″ × 3⅛″ × 2⁵⁄₁₆″)
RCIN 43884
PROVENANCE First recorded in the Royal Collection in 1914 (Add. Cat., case 14, no. 15)
LITERATURE Walker 1992, nos. 439–40

The early provenance of this gold snuff box is not recorded but it may have been a gift to Queen Charlotte from one of her brothers. A miniature set into the lid depicts the Queen seated with her four brothers, sister and sister-in-law supporting an infant niece. A second miniature inside the lid shows the Queen's parents with her elder brother and sister.

Both miniatures are clearly concoctions, derived from several existing portraits. The identifications of the individual sitters are based on details such as uniform and insignia rather than obvious likenesses. The miniatures depict groupings which could never have taken place, and include surprising juxtapositions. The Queen did not return to Mecklenburg-Strelitz after 1761 and she was destined never again to meet her beloved elder brother Adolphus Frederick IV (1738–94) and sister Christiane (1735–94), although they corresponded regularly (see no. 393). Nor did the Queen meet her sister-in-law Frederica of Hesse-Darmstadt (1752–82), who married the Queen's brother Charles (1741–1837) in 1768; Frederica was unable to accompany her husband to England in 1771.

The miniatures appear to have been painted around 1770. One might expect Queen Charlotte to be the seated figure with jewelled aigrette in her hair, seated left of centre, but she must instead be the figure seated further to the left, wearing the deep red ribbon of the Order of St Catherine which she had received from Empress Catherine II (the Great) in 1766. The figure with the aigrette would therefore be the unmarried sister, Christiane. Their eldest brother Adolphus Frederick stands to the right of centre, wearing the riband and star of the Garter, with which he was invested, at Strelitz, in 1764. The standing figure at left is the next brother, Charles

395 inside lid

395

– who succeeded Adolphus Frederick IV as Duke, becoming Grand Duke in 1815 – whose wife (Frederica) and infant daughter (Charlotte, 1769–1818) are seated at right. The standing figures behind are (at right) the third brother, Ernest (1742–1814) and (to the left of centre) the fourth brother, George (1745–85). Inside the lid, the portraits of the Queen's parents, Charles and Elisabeth Albertina, who died respectively in 1752 and 1761, must have been copied from earlier pictures, probably by Johann Georg Ziesenis, in the family collections (see no. 392).

396. Attributed to Benjamin Lucas (*fl*.1758–1784)

Snuff box incorporating miniature of George III, 1784

Gold, miniature on ivory. 3.2 × 9.8 × 6.0 cm (1¼″ × 3⅞″ × 2⅜″)
Struck with hallmarks for London, 1784–5 and maker's mark attributed to Benjamin Lucas; inscribed *The inestimable Gift of the best of Sovereigns His Majesty George the 3ʳᵈ, To his faithful and grateful subject John Caillaud, August 6ᵗʰ 1784*
RCIN 100233
PROVENANCE George III; by whom presented to Brigadier-General John Caillaud (d. 1810), 1784; bought by HM Queen Elizabeth, 1948

According to the inscription George III presented this gold navette-shaped snuff box to Brigadier-General John Caillaud in 1784. Caillaud (d. 1810) is said to have arrived in India from Europe in 1753 with a detachment of British soldiers. Described as a man of undaunted courage and great readiness of resource, Caillaud played a key role in the struggle against the French for military supremacy in India. In 1759 he was appointed, on Lord Clive's recommendation, commander of British troops in Bengal. He retired in 1775 and returned to England after being granted a pension from the East India Company. This handsome present from the King was perhaps given in recognition of Caillaud's contribution to the establishment of British power in India.

The ivory miniature of George III, inset into the lid, is taken from Gainsborough's full-length portrait of the King exhibited at the Royal Academy in 1781. This popular portrait was copied extensively by a number of different miniaturists for inclusion in presentation gifts from the King (see no. 405 and Walker 1992, pp. 83–4).

Very little is known of the goldsmith Benjamin Lucas. His mark was entered as a 'smallworker' at the Goldsmiths' Company in 1758.

397. Alexander James Strachan (*fl.*1799–*c.*1850)
Snuff box with cipher of George III, 1809–10

Gold, enamel, diamonds. 2.8 × diameter 9.3 cm (1⅛″ × 3¹¹⁄₁₆″)
RCIN 100227
PROVENANCE Bought by HM Queen Elizabeth, 1940

This large gold presentation box is patriotically chased with English oak leaves and embellished with the diamond cipher of George III. Although a particularly fine example, the original recipient is not recorded. It is hallmarked for the year 1809–10 and therefore may have been a Jubilee gift from the King.

Snuff boxes, like watches, were a favoured choice of presentation gift from the King. With its use of gold, rich blue enamel and diamonds, no. 397 repeats a scheme found on boxes and watches given throughout the reign (see no. 404)

The box is struck with the maker's mark of Alexander James Strachan, whose London workshop produced many gold boxes of high quality. This royal commission was almost certainly received through the royal goldsmiths Rundell, Bridge and Rundell, who retailed most of Strachan's boxes. Strachan has in consequence been called 'the Paul Storr of gold boxes' (Grimwade 1990, p. 673).

396

397

398. Emanuel Eichel I (1690–1752)
Jewel casket, 1737

Tortoiseshell, mother-of-pearl, gold, ivory, diamonds, rubies, enamel. 23.7 × 18.9 × 16.0 cm (9⁵⁄₁₆″ × 7⁷⁄₁₆″ × 6⁵⁄₁₆″)
Inscribed *VICTORIA AD PETRIVARAD · A · MDCCXVI · D · V · AVG / OCCVPATIO // TEMESVARIÆ · A · MDCCXVI · D · XII · OCT / VICTORIA AD // BELLOGRAD · A · MDCCXVII · D · XVI · AVG //* [4th side of base: original text missing] *// PRÆLVDIA PACIS INDVCIÆ / IVRATA FIDES PACIS FIRMAMENTVM A · MDCCXVIII · D* [·] *XXI* [·] *IVL / PRÆNVNTIA PACIS INDICIA / OBLATA MVNERA PACIS // MONVMENTVM · A · MDCCXIX* [· D ·] *IV · SEP / EMANUEL EICHELL* [sic] *Inven et fecit Augusti Vindeli 1737* (The victory at Peterswardein, 5 August 1716; The taking of Temesvar, 12 October 1716; The victory at Belgrade, 16 August 1717; [4th text missing]; The truce, the preliminaries of peace; The sworn faith, the support of peace, 21 July 1718; The tokens, the evidence of peace; The gifts offered, the memorial of peace, 4 September 1719; Emanuel Eichell effected and made [this] at Augsburg, 1737)
RCIN 9278
PROVENANCE (?)Commissioned by Emperor Charles VI; Queen Charlotte; her sale, Christie's, London, 18 May 1819, lot 30; bought by Gunn (£40 19s); re-entered Royal Collection by 1872 (Garrard 1872, p. 84)

No. 398 ▷

This extraordinary object was described as a 'UNIQUE and EXQUISITE SPECIMEN' when it was sold in Queen Charlotte's sale in 1819. It is lavishly decorated with panels of tortoiseshell inlaid with gold and mother-of-pearl – a technique known as *piqué*. The surmounting figure of Victory is made of gold and delicately tinted ivory set with diamonds and rubies.

The decorative scheme commemorates the military successes of the Habsburg general, Prince Eugene of Savoy (1663–1736), over the Ottoman Empire in the Austro-Turkish Wars of 1716–18. The sides of the box depict the Battles of Temesvar (now Timisoara, Romania), Belgrade and Peterswardein (now Petrovaradin, Serbia) with accompanying Latin inscriptions and maps of the battle sites below. Prince Eugene's campaigns were commemorated in a series of battle paintings by Jan van Huchtenburgh (1647–1733) and in numerous engraved maps and plans, which may have provided the models for the battle scenes and maps on this box.

Austria declared war on the Ottoman Empire in April 1716. Led by Prince Eugene, they defeated the Ottomans at Peterswardein in August 1716 and Temesvar (the last important Ottoman stronghold in Hungary) in October 1716. Prince Eugene finally took Belgrade in July 1718. The defeated Turks signed a peace treaty with Austria at Passarowitz (now Pozerevac, Serbia), an event depicted on the lid of no. 398. Substantial Turkish territories in the Balkans were ceded to the Austrian Emperor Charles VI (1685–1740) and Ottoman expansion westwards into Europe was halted.

The box is signed by Emanuel Eichel of Augsburg and dated 1737. A brief biography of Eichel was published in 1779 (Stetten 1779, pp. 38–9, 118). He was born in Danzig but moved to Augsburg where he specialised in making finely inlaid jewel caskets and boxes of tortoiseshell and ivory. However, as demand for elaborate *Schatzkammer* display pieces declined, Eichel was forced to make steel lettering and stamps for printers and bookbinders. He died in poverty in 1752. According to Stetten, Eichel's great masterpiece was a jewel casket commemorating Charles VI's victories over the Ottomans, inlaid with depictions of the conquered territories. This is almost certainly a reference to no. 398, which may have been one of the last pieces made by Eichel. It was probably commissioned to commemorate Prince Eugene of Savoy, who had died in the previous year, perhaps by Emperor Charles VI himself, although how it found its way into the collection of Queen Charlotte is not recorded.

399. French (Paris)

*Etui, c.*1740–50

Gold, ivory, hardstones, mother-of-pearl. 11.5 × 2.1 × 1.7 cm (4½″ × ¹³⁄₁₆″ × ¹¹⁄₁₆″)
Struck with obscured hallmarks and Paris census mark used in 1797 on articles bearing the marks of the previous regime
RCIN 9005
PROVENANCE In Paris in 1797; by repute belonged to Queen Charlotte; by whom given to Mrs Jacob de Budé; thence by descent to M.E. de Budé (d. 1889); acquired by Queen Mary, 1931 (*QMB*, II, no. 356)

A note inside the étui (a small case or container) reads: 'A gift to my Grand Mother from Queen Charlotte'. The note is signed M.E. de Budé, whose grandmother was presumably the wife of General Jacob de Budé (1737–1818), instructor (later Governor) to Prince William and his younger brothers. Originally from Geneva, de Budé served in the Hanoverian army and later became Private Secretary to the Duke of York. Fanny Burney described him as 'tall and showy, and his manners and appearance are fashionable. But he has a sneer in his smile that looks sarcastic, and a distance in his manner that seems haughty' (*Burney Diary*, II, p. 97). He died at Windsor in 1818.

The étui is struck with obscured hallmarks, but was probably made in Paris in the 1740s, although similarly decorated boxes and étuis – of gold inset with carved hardstones and mother-of-pearl – were also made in Dresden and Berlin. The étui was certainly in Paris in 1797, when it was struck with a census mark used on articles bearing hallmarks from the previous regime.

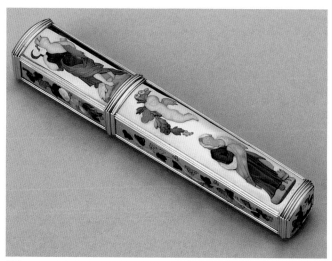

399

400

400. English

Notebook, case and pencil, with cipher of
Queen Charlotte, c.1765

Tortoiseshell, gold, diamonds. Case 11.0 × 8.3 × 2.5 cm
(4⁵⁄₁₆″ × 3¼″ × 1″); pencil length 11.1 cm (4⅜″)
RCIN 46707
PROVENANCE Queen Charlotte; Lady Mount Stephen; by whom
given to Queen Mary before 1920 (*QMB*, I, no. 510)
LITERATURE *Royal Treasures* 2002, no. 289

The elaborate *rocaille* gold mounts and crowned diamond
cipher of Queen Charlotte on the tortoiseshell case suggest
that this was made in the early years of her reign. The Queen
however appears never to have written in this sumptuous
object: the notebook inside, bound in red morocco, remains
unused. The small number of the Queen's historical and
religious notes which do survive, together with her diaries
of 1789 and 1793–4 (RA GEO/Add. 43), are all written in
simple paper-bound notebooks.

It is not known how no. 400 came to leave the Collection.
It is not identifiable in the catalogue of the 1819 sale of the
Queen's possessions. It re-entered the Collection in the early
twentieth century when it was given to Queen Mary by
Lady Mount Stephen, her lifelong friend and an enthusiastic
supporter of her passion for reacquiring royal relics.

401. German(?)

Vinaigrette and seal, 1761

Silver-gilt. 8.5 × 4.0 × 3.0 cm (3⅜″ × 1⁹⁄₁₆″ × 1³⁄₁₆″)
Struck with illegible hallmarks; inscribed *TO GEORGE THE III*
A.D. SEP. 8. 1761 / CHARLOTTE OF MECKLENBURG
STRELITZ / God Save the Queen [in reverse]
RCIN 65525
PROVENANCE Possibly given by Queen Charlotte to Mary Bertie,
Duchess of Ancaster, 1761; thence by descent to Lord Willoughby de
Eresby; by whom bequeathed to Princess Mary Adelaide, Duchess of
Teck; by whom given/bequeathed to Queen Mary (QMPP, X, no. 55)

Vinaigrettes were used to hold sponges soaked with scented
vinegars. They were popular in the eighteenth and nineteenth
centuries and were used by ladies to ward off attacks of
faintness. This vinaigrette is inscribed with the date of the
royal marriage, 8 September 1761, and the base is engraved
with the motto *God Save the Queen*, in reverse for use as a seal.
A nineteenth-century note inside the vinaigrette reads:
'. . . given by Queen Charlotte to George III Septr 8th 1761.
Afterwards came into the hands of the Duchess of Ancaster,
Mistress of the Robes . . .' The provenance as stated would
appear questionable: vinaigrettes were particularly feminine
objects and not usual gifts for a new husband or king (see
no. 402) and it is unlikely that such a personal gift would
have been given away.

Mary, Duchess of Ancaster, was appointed Mistress of
the Robes to the future Queen Charlotte on 1 August 1761.
She remained in this post, the most senior for a lady in the
household, until her death in 1793. The Duchess had, together
with the rest of the Queen's newly appointed household,
travelled to Mecklenburg-Strelitz in order to bring Princess
Charlotte back to England. The Duchess was expecting
her third child at the time and was said to be 'subject to
hysteric fits'. She must have found the stormy voyage back
particularly difficult, when she and the Duchess of Hamilton
were said to be 'very much out of order' (Hedley 1975,
pp. 20, 39). Her daughter, born a few months later, was named
Georgiana Charlotte in honour of the King and Queen.

No. 401 may therefore have been a gift to the Duchess
directly from the Queen. The misleading inscription was
perhaps added later, after the Duchess's death. During her
journey to England the future Queen is known to have
given presents to those who attended her. Many of these
had been supplied by the goldsmiths of Strelitz. No. 401,
with its continental crown finial, is almost certainly
German, although its hallmarks are now illegible.

403 401 402

402. English

Vinaigrette with cipher of Queen Charlotte, c.1780

Gold, enamel, diamond. 4.5 × 3.7 × 2.9 cm (1¾″ × 1⁷⁄₁₆″ × 1⅛″)
RCIN 23058
PROVENANCE Possibly George IV; Conyngham family; Jane,
Marchioness Conyngham (d. 1907); her sale, Christie's, London,
5 May 1908, lot 133; purchased by Queen Mary, 1927 (*QMB*, II,
p. 47, no. 161)

The sponges in vinaigrettes are held in place with internal
pierced grilles; in this example the grille incorporates the
crowned cipher of Queen Charlotte. The sale of the Queen's
possessions in 1819 included several vinaigrettes of various
forms, although no. 402 is not there identifiable.

No. 402 was included in the sale of the Conyngham
collection in 1908. The collection included many items
given to the first Marquess and Marchioness Conyngham
by George IV in the 1820s. The Conynghams were housed in
great luxury in George IV's private apartments at Windsor
Castle and the King's affection for Elizabeth, Marchioness
Conyngham (?1766–1861), scandalised society. George IV
showered the Marchioness with gifts of jewellery and works
of art and it is therefore tempting to suggest that no. 402
was also given to her, probably after the Queen's death.

403. English

Scent bottle with cipher of Queen Charlotte, c.1805

Silver-gilt, coloured paste, enamel. 5.0 × 3.5 × 1.6 cm
(1¹⁵⁄₁₆″ × 1⅜″ × ⅝″)
RCIN 9034
PROVENANCE Queen Charlotte; acquired by Queen Mary, 1934
(*QMB*, III, no. 224)

This richly jewelled scent bottle, encrusted with paste
'diamonds', 'rubies' and 'emeralds', was perhaps inspired by
the Indian jewellery sent to Queen Charlotte by the Nabob
of Arcot. It incorporates a plaque enamelled with the Royal
Arms and supporters as used after 1801 and the unusual
motto *PATENT PARATOUT*. The base is engraved with the
crowned cipher of Queen Charlotte.

A large number of scent bottles and boxes were included
in the sale of Queen Charlotte's possessions in 1819, many
no doubt used to hold the precious perfumes and essences
she was given by Indian rulers. The Nabob of Arcot was
particularly generous, sending attar of roses in addition
to jewels and luxurious Indian fabrics (Hedley 1975,
pp. 128–9, 304).

404. English

Watch case and chatelaine, c.1785

Gold, enamel, diamonds. 14.0 × 4.5 × 1.3 cm (5½″ × 1¾″ × ½″)
RCIN 43796 (watch case), 43797 (chatelaine)
PROVENANCE By repute presented by George III to George,
3rd Earl of Courtown; purchased by King George V and Queen
Mary, 1913 (Add. Cat., case 13, no. 18)
LITERATURE *Royal Treasures* 2002, no. 295

405. English

Locket and chatelaine, c.1785

Gold, enamel, diamonds, miniature on ivory. 14.0 × 4.7 × 1.3 cm
(5½″ × 1⅞″ × ¾″)
RCIN 43798 (locket); 43799 (chatelaine)
PROVENANCE By repute presented by George III to George,
3rd Earl of Courtown; purchased by King George V and Queen
Mary, 1913 (Add. Cat., case 13, no. 19)
LITERATURE Walker 1992, no. 321

These spectacular gold and enamel chatelaines incorporate
respectively a watch case and a locket decorated with the
crowned cipher of George III set with diamonds. They were
both acquired by King George V and Queen Mary in 1913,
when they were said to have been a gift from George III to
his godson James George, 3rd Earl of Courtown (1765–1835),
Treasurer of the Royal Household in 1793 and 1806–12. The
King had presented a watch and chatelaine of the same model
to his close friend Simon, 1st Earl Harcourt, before Harcourt's
death in 1777. Nos. 404 and 405 were however probably
made after 1781 since the locket contains a miniature of the
King taken from the full-length portrait by Gainsborough

exhibited at the Royal Academy in that year. This was an extremely popular image of the King and a number of presentation gifts incorporate miniatures copied from it (see no. 396). These chatelaines may have been gifts from the King to the Earl on his marriage in 1791: the watch a gift to the Earl and the locket, a particularly feminine object, a gift for his bride, Mary (1769–1823), daughter of the 3rd Duke of Buccleuch.

As the Earl's parents James, 2nd Earl of Courtown (1731–1810), and Mary (d. 1810), lived in Windsor Castle and had especially close links with the King and Queen, an alternative provenance is possible. The 2nd Earl had been Lord of the Bedchamber to the King when Prince of Wales, and was made Treasurer to the Royal Household in 1784. His wife Mary was 'the Queen's Lady in Waiting in the Country'. It may therefore be that nos. 404 and 405 were given to the 2nd Earl and his wife, probably in the early 1780s.

406

406. English

Three of George III's dress coat buttons, mounted as brooches, c.1780

Gold, enamel, pearls. Diameter 3.6 cm (1⁷⁄₁₆″)
RCIN 65734.1–3
PROVENANCE George III; George IV; given to Queen Adelaide (d. 1849), 1830; by whom bequeathed to her niece, Princess Augusta of Cambridge, Grand Duchess of Mecklenburg-Strelitz (d. 1916); by whom bequeathed to Queen Mary (*QMB*, II, no. 424)

Mrs Papendiek records that George III had a particular interest in buttons, 'for in his youth one of his favourite occupations had been turning and button-making. Of a German in Long Acre he had learned how to make the loop and attach it to the button.' And when in 1784 a Mr Clay showed him his newly perfected button, for gentlemen's mourning attire, the King is said to have exclaimed, 'Send me several sets of buttons, for as I am called George the button-maker, I must give a lift to our trade' (Papendiek 1887, I, pp. 212–13).

George III was renowned for his sobriety of dress. However, on festive occasions his appearance could be dazzling. According to *The Lady's Magazine*, the King wore at his Birthday Court of 1779 'an elegant set of mother of pearl buttons, set round with small brilliant diamonds . . . a garter, the george, and a star . . . His shoe and knee buckles were diamonds . . . a sword elegantly ornamented with jewels: likewise a brilliant diamond ring' (Scarisbrick 1994, pp. 228–9).

No. 406 are from a suite comprising two necklaces, five brooches and a pair of earrings made from twenty-two of George III's dress buttons. As men's fashions changed in the nineteenth century such elaborate jewelled buttons fell from favour. The set was presented to Queen Adelaide, who presumably had the buttons converted into jewellery. They are perhaps the 'fine set of pearl buttons, sent to the Queen' listed in the 'Inventory of Certain Valuable Jewel & Effects contained in Closets & Chests in Windsor Castle', compiled after the death of George IV in 1830 (copy made for Queen Mary, 1911, RCIN 1114749, f. 43).

404   405

407

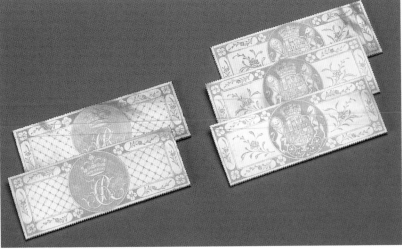

408

407. Chinese

Ten round gaming counters with cipher of
Queen Charlotte, c.1780

Mother-of-pearl. Diameter 3.95 cm (1⁹⁄₁₆″)
RCIN 55180.1–10
PROVENANCE As for no. 408

408. Chinese

Five rectangular gaming counters with cipher of
Queen Charlotte, c.1780

Mother-of-pearl. 7.1 × 2.7 cm (2¹³⁄₁₆″ × 1¹⁄₁₆″)
RCIN 55181.1–5
PROVENANCE Perhaps identifiable with the contents of the 'card
box of beautiful Japan lacquer, containing seven smaller boxes, with
thirty-six dozen and three mother of pearl counters', included in
Queen Charlotte's sale, 7 May 1819 (lot 117), or the box containing
124 mother-of-pearl counters bearing Queen Charlotte's cipher,
sold in the Duke of Sussex's sale, Christie's, London, 24 July 1845
(lot 177)

Queen Charlotte's evenings were often spent with the King
and members of the court listening to music and playing
cards, usually commerce or 'whisk', on which occasions the
Chinese mother-of-pearl gaming counters, engraved with the
Royal Arms and Queen Charlotte's cipher, were probably used.

409. Alexander James Strachan (*fl*.1799–*c*.1850)

Paper-knife with cipher of Queen Charlotte, 1815–16

Gold, citrine. 20.8 × 2.5 × 1.8 cm (8³⁄₁₆″ × 1″ × ¹¹⁄₁₆″)
Struck with London hallmarks for 1815–16
RCIN 4227
PROVENANCE George, 2nd Duke of Cambridge; his sale, Christie's,
14 June 1904 (part-lot 568); bought by Queen Mary (*QMB*, I, no. 323)

410. Alexander James Strachan (*fl*.1799–*c*.1850)

Pencil-case with cipher of Queen Charlotte, c.1815–16

Gold, citrine. 11.9 × 2.0 × 1.9 cm (4¹¹⁄₁₆″ × ¾″ × ¾″)
RCIN 4198
PROVENANCE George, 2nd Duke of Cambridge, not identifiable in
sale catalogue; acquired by Queen Mary before 1920 (*QMB*, I, no. 57)

Both the paper-knife and pencil-case appear to have come
from a desk set made for Queen Charlotte towards the end
of her life. The paper-knife is struck with gold hallmarks for
1815–16 and the maker's mark of Alexander James Strachan.
The handle is of faceted citrine and the blade is engraved
with the cipher used by Queen Charlotte throughout her life.
Although unmarked, the pencil-case is clearly by the same
maker and similarly incorporates Queen Charlotte's cipher,
engraved on a citrine seal set into the top of the case.

Strachan's large workshop, based in London, produced
considerable numbers of exceptionally fine boxes (see no.
397) and *objets de vertu*. He supplied the majority of boxes
retailed by the royal goldsmiths Rundell, Bridge and Rundell
and it is likely that nos. 409 and 410 were also commissioned
through Rundells.

410 409

411

412

411. James Tassie (1735–1799) and an unknown jeweller

Two double-sided pendants of George III and Queen Charlotte, c.1775

White glass, bloodstone, gold. 3.7 × 3.2 × 0.9 cm
(1⁷⁄₁₆″ × 1¼″ × ⅜″)

RCIN 10922, 33992

PROVENANCE RCIN 10922: given to Queen Mary by Lady Mount Stephen, Christmas 1931 (*QMB*, II, p. 91, no. 373). RCIN 33992: given to Queen Mary by Mr Harman-Oates, Christmas 1924 (*QMB*, II, p. 32, no. 104)

LITERATURE Gray 1894, p. 94, no. 76 and p. 109, no. 151

During the reign of George III the collecting of antique engraved cameos and intaglios reached a high point as a fashionable pursuit, and the King's acquisition of Consul Smith's collection in 1762 (see nos. 421–438) placed him in the first rank of collectors. Demand for ancient gems exceeded supply and the art of glyptics (gem-cutting) enjoyed a revival, especially in Rome, where artists such as Anton Pichler (1697–1779) made copies of antique cameos as well as portraits of contemporaries.

The Scottish modeller James Tassie pioneered the casting of imitation cameos and intaglios in a new form of fired vitreous paste of which the largest constituents were silica, lead oxide and potassium oxide. He produced small portrait medallions and reproductions of ancient gems in exceptionally large numbers (the number of different gems made in the course of his career exceeded 20,000). Although Tassie's paste formula was a closely guarded secret, the reproductive nature of the process led to widespread piracy of his models. The catalogue of Tassie's products published by R.E. Raspe in 1791 lists nine separate cameos and intaglios of George III and three of Queen Charlotte. For these two-sided pendants of the King and Queen, Tassie's profiles have been mounted by a jeweller on a background of bloodstone to imitate a carved cameo with two strata.

412. English

Pendant with Tassie cameos of George III and Queen Charlotte, c.1780

Gold, enamel, glass cameo, pearls. 6.3 × 4.1 × 0.8 cm
(2½″ × 1⅝″ × ⁵⁄₁₆″)

RCIN 33958

PROVENANCE By repute presented by George III and Queen Charlotte to the Hon. Georgiana Townsend; thence by descent to Robert Marsham Townsend (1834–1914); his sale, Knight, Frank and Rutley, Frognal, Chislehurst, Kent, 9 June 1915, lot 472; purchased by Queen Mary (QMPP, III, no. 211)

This pendant is said to have been presented by the King and Queen to the Hon. Georgiana Townsend (1761–1835), eldest daughter of Thomas, 1st Viscount Sydney, who had, as leader of the House of Commons, taken a prominent role in arranging terms of peace with America in 1783. It was his cousin Charles Townsend who had ignited unrest in the American Colonies by introducing the hated Stamp Act in 1765. Lord Sydney was twice Secretary of State; and in 1790 the newly discovered harbour of Sydney, Australia, was named after him.

Georgiana had known the royal family since she was a young girl and was friendly with the Queen and the princesses. In 1801 she was appointed to the sinecure of State Housekeeper at Windsor, a position she retained for the remainder of her life. Her residence was the Norman Tower, Windsor Castle. The pendant was among a number of objects acquired by Queen Mary from the sale of the Sydney collection in 1915. Other purchases at this sale included a gold musical box given to Lady Sydney by Queen Charlotte and two gold rings with cameo portraits of George III, given to Georgiana by the King.

413

414

413. G. Stephany and J. Dresch (*fl*.1791–1803) after Charles Rosenberg (1754–1844)

*George III, c.*1792–7

Ivory on backed glass. Modern frame. Unframed measurements
11.1 × 9.2 × 1.1 cm (4⁵⁄₁₆″ × 3¹¹⁄₁₆″ × ³⁄₈″)
Inscribed on reverse *George III* with arms and motto of
George Chetwynd
RCIN 37129
PROVENANCE George Chetwynd; acquired by Queen Mary
before 1920 (QMPP, I, p. 108, no. 1, *QMB*, I, no. 471)

414. G. Stephany and J. Dresch (*fl*.1791–1803) after Charles Rosenberg (1754–1844)

*Queen Charlotte, c.*1792–7

Ivory on backed glass. Modern frame. Unframed measurements
11.1 × 9.2 × 1.1 cm (4⁵⁄₁₆″ × 3¹¹⁄₁₆″ × ³⁄₈″)
Inscribed on reverse *Queen Charlotte / by Cousigner* with arms
and motto of George Chetwynd
RCIN 37120
PROVENANCE George Chetwynd; acquired by Queen Mary
before 1920 (QMPP, I, p. 108, no. 2; *QMB*, I, no. 472)

415. G. Stephany and J. Dresch (*fl*.1791–1803) after Charles Rosenberg (1754–1844)

*Charlotte, Princess Royal, c.*1792–7

Ivory on backed glass, ebonised wood. 15.0 × 12.2 × 1.5 cm
(5⁷⁄₈″ × 4¹³⁄₁₆″ × ⁹⁄₁₆″)
Inscribed on reverse *Princess Royal Queen of Wurtemburg carved
by Mr Stephana* [sic] *from a drawing by Mr Rosenberg born Sept. 29
1766 died Oct. 6 1828*
RCIN 90202
PROVENANCE Early history unknown; Mrs A.S. Howard; by

whom sold Christie's, London, 19 November 1946, lot 28; bought
by Marsh (15 gns.); bought by Queen Mary (£25)

These delicately carved ivory reliefs are a *tour de force* of
virtuoso ivory carving on a minute scale. The technique,
known as filigree or micro-carving, was popular in the late
eighteenth century and pieces were often incorporated into
jewellery or snuff boxes.

A nineteenth-century inscription on the back of the
portrait of the Princess Royal states that it was carved by a
'Mr Stephana [*sic*] from a drawing by Mr Rosenberg'. He is
identifiable with the German ivory carver G. Stephany, who
exhibited at the Royal Academy between 1792 and 1803.
Contemporary advertisements and trade labels show that
Stephany and his fellow countryman J. Dresch were business
partners with the silhouette painter Charles Rosenberg in
the fashionable spa town of Bath between 1792 and 1797.
They subsequently moved to their own premises in Bath but
by 1800 appear to have been permanently based in London
(see Stanton 1935, pp. 210–11; McKechnie 1978, pp. 559–60;
and Hartmann 1986, pp. 920–23). Little more is known about
Stephany, who is thought to have come from Augsburg,
a city renowned for its ivory carving, and appears to have
specialised in miniature carvings of breathtaking intricacy.

Stephany and Dresch were described as 'the most eminent
sculptors in ivory in Europe . . . who will execute any design
for Rings, Bracelets, Lockets, or for Cabinet pieces'. Their
work was 'so fine that a glass is necessary to discover its
beauties'. They soon attracted royal attention and by 1793
they were describing themselves as sculptors 'in ivory to Her
Majesty' and subsequently 'Sculptors in Miniature on Ivory

415

416

416. Attributed to G. Stephany and J. Dresch
(*fl*.1791–1803)
*Pendant with the cipher of Queen Charlotte, c.*1800

Ivory, mother-of-pearl, backed glass, gold, hair.
9.2 × 7.2 × 3.7 cm (3⅝″ × 2¹³⁄₁₆″ × 1⁷⁄₁₆″)
Inscribed *A LA MEILLEURE DES MERES*
RCIN 65531
PROVENANCE Probably acquired by Queen Mary

A LA MEILLEURE DES MERES written in gold across the
top of the pendant suggests that it was a gift to the Queen
from her children, although it is not clear which ones. It is
probably their hair (in seven different shades) which adorns
the back of the pendant. Jewellery which incorporated the
hair of loved ones was enormously popular during the second
half of the eighteenth century – for mourning pieces and,
as here, for sentimental keepsakes. Such trinkets appealed
greatly to the royal family. The King gave the Queen a pearl
bracelet with a clasp containing his hair and cipher prior to
their wedding in 1761 (Papendiek 1887, I, p. 12), and on her
marriage in 1816, Princess Mary put on a ring containing
her father's hair, declaring 'This I would not for the world
omit. I have a superstitious dread of misfortune if I did'
(Scarisbrick 1994, p. 339).

The minutely carved ivory and mother-of-pearl work can
be attributed with some confidence to the German carvers
G. Stephany and J. Dresch (see nos. 413–15). According to

to their Majesties' (see McKechnie 1978, pp. 559–60). As well
as portraits, much of their work consisted of miniature scenes,
characteristically set on blue 'Bristol' glass backgrounds. In
March 1798 Mrs Philip Lybbe Powys described Stephany and
Dresch's work as 'most exceedingly curious: Windsor Castle,
Greenwich Hospital, Eddystone Lighthouse &c., most ingen-
iously carved from solid pieces of ivory. Likenesses of their
Majesties astonishing well done' (*Lybbe Powys* 1899, p. 298).

Charles Rosenberg was a fashionable silhouette painter
on glass. Believed to be Austrian by birth, he is said to have
arrived in England in the entourage of Queen Charlotte as
a young page. His first advertisement appeared in the *Bath
Chronicle* in 1787; it described Rosenberg as 'having had the
honour of taking the Likenesses of most of the Princes of
Germany, as well as Their Majesties, the Prince of Wales,
Duke of York, and the Princesses at Windsor'. Works by
Rosenberg in the Royal Collection include silhouettes of the
Princess Royal, and of Princesses Augusta, Elizabeth and
Sophia painted during their stay at Cheltenham in 1788
(RCIN 452448). Other royal commissions followed and
Rosenberg used the title 'Profile Painter to their Majesties
and Royal Family' throughout the 1790s (McKechnie 1978,
pp. 558–66). Given this, it is probable that it was Rosenberg
who first brought the work of Stephany and Dresch to the
attention of the royal family. As with other silhouetted
likenesses (for instance, nos. 419, 420), the sitters' features
recorded in these portraits were not necessarily current.
Wedgwood produced an almost identical portrait of the
Princess Royal in jasper ware, thought to have been modelled
by John Charles Lochee *c.*1787 (Reilly and Savage 1973, p. 94).

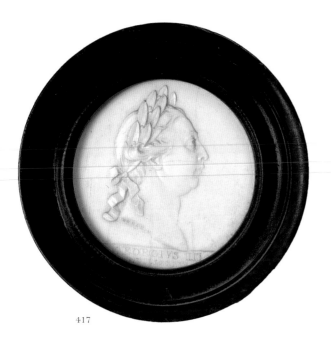

417

418

Mrs Lybbe Powys they were 'the only artists in this line' who would carve any device 'for lockets, bracelets, rings, or tooth-pick cases in as small pieces as I did the cherry-stone baskets' (*Lybbe Powys* 1899, p. 298). No other carvers capable of working ivory on such a scale appear to have worked in England at this time.

417. Edward Burch (1730–1814)

Profile head of George III, 1785

White vitreous paste. Sight size diameter 5.0 cm (1¹⁵⁄₁₆″)
Inscribed *BURCH F / GEORGIVS III / MDCCLXXXV*
RCIN 37085

In 1759 the Society for the Promotion of Arts and Manufactures sought to revive the art of gem-cutting in Britain by means of a competition, which was won by Nathaniel Marchant (1739–1816). The rising status of the art can be judged by the fact that in 1771 Marchant's teacher Edward Burch became the first member of the Royal Academy to be elected by the other members, all of whom had been appointed by the King. This portrait of George III appears with the same date on a prize medal to be awarded by the University of Göttingen in Hanover (Brown (L.) 1980, p. 63, no. 266), and again on a silver medal by Lewis Pingo celebrating the King's recovery from illness in 1789 (Brown (L.) 1980, p. 73, no. 312). Wedgwood produced a medallion bearing the same portrait on the latter occasion. The design may in fact be based on a drawing of the young King by Cipriani dated 1768 (Oppé 1950, no. 121), which was engraved as the head-piece to William Chambers's *Dissertation on Oriental Gardening* (1771).

418. Isaac Gosset (1713–1799)

George III when Prince of Wales, c.1759

Wax. Including ebonised wooden frame 14.7 × 12.1 × 2.4 cm (5¹³⁄₁₆″ × 4¾″ × ¹⁵⁄₁₆″)
RCIN 37108
PROVENANCE (?)George III
LITERATURE Gosset 1888–9; Murdoch 1985

During the last part of the eighteenth century portrait medallions in wax enjoyed a new popularity. Like those produced by Wedgwood in great numbers from the 1770s, most of these were not modelled from the life but reproduced existing images found on medals, or portraits in carved ivory, terracotta or bronze.

Although repetitions of his models were subsequently cast (he supplied them to Wedgwood, Tassie and others), the special ability of the Huguenot modeller Isaac Gosset was in the very rapid creation of wax portraits which were, unusually, made from sittings. His family had fled from Normandy to Jersey after the Revocation of the Edict of Nantes in 1685, and Isaac was born in St Helier. He came to work in London with his uncle Matthew Gosset, who also modelled in wax in addition to carving in marble as a 'statuary'.

It seems that Isaac was first trained as a carver of picture frames, and was in business with his brother Jacob in supplying giltwood frames for Hogarth, Amigoni and Ramsay among others. (Isaac Gosset and René Stone provided frames for the repetitions of Ramsay's State Portrait, no. 3.) As a modeller, Gosset was apparently capable of making a portrait in under

419   420

an hour, and was reported by George Vertue as 'universally approved of for likeness'. Vertue added that Gosset 'had the Honour of his Majestyes His setting to him. haveing done the Kings portrait in wax. extremely like him' (*Vertue Notebooks*, III, p. 160). When the designs for the coronation medal by the chief engraver of the Royal Mint were rejected in the spring of 1761, the German engraver Lorenz Natter was instructed to prepare new dies at very short notice (see no. 448); he was advised to take as a guide for the King's profile the wax model by 'Cossart' [i.e. Gosset] which was 'esteemed greatly like his Majesty' (PRO Mint I / XI, f. 136).

This portrait is one of a series of royal portraits that is known to have belonged to the King himself. He took delight in showing them in 1793 to Matthew Gosset, Vicomte of Jersey, when he was received in audience at Windsor.

419. James Lind (1736–1812) and Tiberius Cavallo (1749–1809)

George III, 1792

Monoprint. 11.5 × 7.8 cm (4½″ × 3¹⁄₁₆″)
Verso inscribed *(January 1792)*
RCIN 1047678.am

420. James Lind (1736–1812) and Tiberius Cavallo (1749–1809)

Queen Charlotte, 1792

Monoprint. 11.5 × 7.9 cm (4½″ × 3⅛″)
Verso inscribed *(January 1792)*
RCIN 1047678.al
PROVENANCE From the same album as nos. 79–82: Miss Sarah Sophia Banks (d. 1818); Lady Dorothy Nevill; bought by Queen Mary, 1930
LITERATURE McKechnie 1978, pp. 249–51

This pair of printed silhouettes belonged to Sir Joseph Banks's sister, to whom they were probably given by either Lind or Cavallo. Both were Fellows of the Royal Society, of which Miss Banks's brother was President from 1778. Other profiles by Lind and Cavallo are in the Banks collection in the British Museum (see McKechnie 1978, p. 251 and Griffiths and Williams 1987, p. 82). These portraits have been placed in frames for this exhibition.

Dr Lind, a physician to the royal family, settled in Windsor *c.*1777. In addition to his professional practice, he had a printing press at Windsor and his scientific experiments and 'tricks' were well known. (Among the miscellaneous tasks

entrusted to Lind by the King, in January 1782, was the planting of a cabbage garden at Windsor, in which hares – used for the royal sport – would be protected during snowy weather: see Roberts (J.) 1997, p. 64.) Cavallo, the son of a Neapolitan physician, was likewise a scientist with wide-ranging interests – including ballooning. Both Lind and Cavallo were present on the North Terrace, Windsor Castle, on the evening of 18 August 1783, with their friend Thomas Sandby who depicted the group witnessing a meteor flying overhead (Roberts (J.) 1995, no. 18). In the early 1790s Lind and Cavallo engaged in a lively (if somewhat surprising) correspondence on the subject of portrait silhouette-making. The two men worked as partners on their silhouettes: Lind would take the likeness at full scale, before sending it to Cavallo for reduction and recutting. The Royal Collection includes a number of other silhouettes which resulted from the partnership. These are contained in two volumes of silhouettes acquired in 1944 from Miss Violet Gosset, a descendant of Dr Lind (RCIN 1047658–9). The first two silhouettes in volume I are of the King and Queen and are identical to the present subjects. That of the King is inscribed *T. Cavallo* and that of the Queen *C.* The fact that they are dated respectively 1790 and 1788, while those from Miss Banks's album are both dated 1792, demonstrates that silhouette likenesses were reused over a number of years.

The portraits of the King and Queen recorded here would appear to date from the 1770s or early 1780s (compare no. 412). Monoprints were produced by dipping a silhouette – cut from stiff card – into oil-based ink, and then sandwiching the inked card between two pieces of paper; a pair of impressions from the card – one a mirror image of the other – would thus be obtained. The other silhouette portraits of the King in Miss Banks's album at Windsor, possibly also the work of Lind and Cavallo, are indeed an identical pair, and once formed a continuous piece of paper.

14. Gems, jewels and medals (nos. 421–456)

CAMEOS AND INTAGLIOS (nos. 421–438)

All illustrations are enlarged by 125 per cent.

421. Hellenistic

Cameo head of Zeus, second/first century BC

Onyx, gold mount. 6.0 × 4.9 cm (2⅜″ × 1¹⁵⁄₁₆″)
RCIN 65600
LITERATURE Gori 1767, I, pl. 1; *Royal Treasures* 2002, no. 139

421

422. Italian

Cameo head and bust of a young woman, sixteenth century

Agate, gold mount. 2.2 × 1.4 cm (⅞″ × ⁹⁄₁₆″)
RCIN 65817
LITERATURE Gori 1767, I, pl. LX

423. Italian(?)

Cameo bust of a man, second half sixteenth century

Agate, gold mount. 2.4 × 2.3 cm (¹⁵⁄₁₆″ × ⅞″)
RCIN 65177
LITERATURE Gori 1767, I, pl. XCIX

424. Italian(?)

Cameo bust of a woman, second half sixteenth century

Agate, gold mount. 3.4 × 2.7 cm (1⁵⁄₁₆″ × 1¹⁄₁₆″)
RCIN 65178
LITERATURE Gori 1767, I, pl. C

425. Italian

Cameo bust of a woman, second half sixteenth century

Agate, gold mount. 3.4 × 2.2 × 1.2 cm (1¹⁵⁄₁₆″ × ⅞″ × ½″)
RCIN 65858
LITERATURE Gori 1767, I, pl. XXXVI

426. Italian

Cameo bust of a man, second half sixteenth century

Rose agate, gold mount. 4.3 × 3.5 cm (1¹¹⁄₁₆″ × 1⅜″)
RCIN 65219
LITERATURE Gori 1767, I, pl. LXXIX

427. Italian

Cameo bust of a man, second half sixteenth century

Agate, gold mount. 4.1 × 3.1 cm (1⅝″ × 1¼″)
RCIN 65231
LITERATURE Gori 1767, I, pl. LVII

428. Italian

Cameo bust of a woman, second half sixteenth century

Agate, gold mount. 4.1 × 3.1 cm (1⅝″ × 1¼″)
RCIN 65235
LITERATURE Gori 1767, I, pl. LXXXV

422

423

424

425

426

427

428

429

430

431 recto

TITVS
AVGVSTVS
WESPASIANVS
IVDAEA
CAPTA

431 verso

432

433

434

435

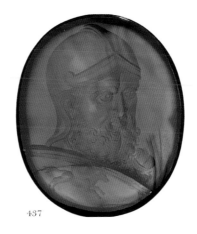

436

437

438

429. Italian

Cameo bust of a woman, second half sixteenth century

Agate, gold mount. 4.5 × 2.3 cm (1¾″ × ⅞″)
RCIN 65859
LITERATURE Gori 1767, I, pl. LXVI

430. Italian

Cameo bust of a man or woman, second half sixteenth century

Agate, gold mount. 3.4 × 2.4 cm (1⁵⁄₁₆″ × ¹⁵⁄₁₆″)
RCIN 65869
LITERATURE Gori 1767, I, pl. XIII

431. Italian

Cameo head of Titus, seventeenth century

Lapis lazuli, gold mount. 5.0 × 3.1 cm (1¹⁵⁄₁₆″ × 1¼″)
RCIN 65890
LITERATURE Gori 1767, I, pl. LXXIV

432. Italian

Cameo of Alexander in a chariot, late sixteenth century

Onyx, gold mount. 1.7 × 1.8 cm (¹¹⁄₁₆″ × ¹¹⁄₁₆″)
RCIN 43768
LITERATURE Gori 1767, I, pl. XII

433. Italian

Cameo of Neptune in a chariot, seventeenth century

Agate, gold mount. 2.4 × 2.6 cm (⁵⁄₁₆″ × 1″)
RCIN 43770
LITERATURE Gori 1767, I, pl. VI

434. Italian

Cameo head of a man, late sixteenth century

Agate, gold mount. 4.0 × 2.0 cm (1⁹⁄₁₆″ × ¾″)
RCIN 65838
LITERATURE Gori 1767, I, pl. LIV

435. Italian

Cameo of a sacrifice, seventeenth century

Agate, gold mount. 2.5 × 2.3 cm (1″ × ⅞″)
RCIN 43776
LITERATURE Gori 1767, I, pl. XI

436. Italian

Intaglio bust of a youth, eighteenth century

Cornelian, gold mount. 5.1 × 3.5 cm (2″ × 1⅜″)
RCIN 65828
LITERATURE Gori 1767, I, pl. LXXXII

437. Italian

Intaglio head of a warrior, eighteenth century

Cornelian, gold mount. 4.3 × 2.8 cm (1¹¹⁄₁₆″ × 1¹⁄₁₆″)
RCIN 65830
LITERATURE Gori 1767, I, pl. LI

438. Italian

Intaglio head of Medusa, eighteenth century

Cornelian, gold mount. 4.0 × 2.7 cm (1⁹⁄₁₆″ × 1¹⁄₁₆″)
RCIN 65829
LITERATURE Gori 1767, I, pl. XXI

The preceding eighteen gems are all from the collection of Consul Smith and were acquired by George III with the Consul's paintings, drawings, books, manuscripts and medals in 1762. The head of Zeus (no. 421), although fragmentary, is considered one of the finest surviving Hellenistic cameos, notable for the brilliant naturalism of the carving and elaborate undercutting, and it is by far the most important early gem from the Consul's collection. The majority of the remaining gems are north Italian sixteenth- and early seventeenth-century cameos. There are in addition a small number of eighteenth-century intaglios, probably of Roman origin. The publication in 1767 of Antonio Gori's catalogue, the *Dactyliotheca Smithiana*, dedicated by Smith to George III (fig. 29), ensured the lasting fame of the collection and placed it on a par with other celebrated collections catalogued by Gori. (All the antique and Renaissance gems and jewels in the Royal Collection, including those from the Smith collection, will be included in the forthcoming *catalogue raisonné* by Dr Kirsten Aschengreen Piacenti and Sir John Boardman.)

FIG. 29 Giovanni Volpato after P. A. Novelli, *Frontispiece to Gori's Dactyliotheca Smithiana, 1767, with profile portrait of George III, 1763.* Engraving (RCIN 1195717)

JEWELLED INSIGNIA (nos. 439, 440)

439. English

Garter star, second half eighteenth century(?), altered 1858

Diamonds, rubies, enamel, silver and gold. 13.0 × 13.0 cm (5⅛″ × 5⅛″)
RCIN 441147
PROVENANCE Possibly made for Queen Anne as a gift for her husband, Prince George of Denmark; belonged to George III, by 1788 (BL Add. 27543/item 3); altered for Queen Victoria, 1858 (Garrards list, RCIN 1116305)
LITERATURE *Royal Insignia* 1996, no. 63, pp. 102, 104, 201

George III was appointed to the Order of the Garter, the premier English order of chivalry, by his grandfather George II on 22 June 1749, at the age of 11. On his accession in 1760, he became Sovereign of the Order – along with the other British orders, the Thistle and the Bath (which was restructured in 1815). Later in the reign three new orders were instituted: the Orders of St Patrick (founded in 1783), of the Guelphs (founded in 1815) and of St Michael and St George (the Ionian Order, founded in 1818). However, the King's devotion to the Order of the Garter was paramount. In 1786 he appointed five of his sons to the Order; the eldest two sons were already members (since 1765 and 1771 respectively). These appointments preceded the King's 'Great Works' at St George's Chapel, Windsor Castle – the seat of the Order – in the 1780s and 1790s (see nos. 135, 287).

The King accepted no foreign orders and apart from Garter insignia appears to have owned only a diamond St Patrick badge and a diamond badge of the Bath. According to inventories of 1788 and 1819, the King's Garter insignia consisted of the diamond garter (worn around the left leg, below the knee), a diamond Garter badge 'belonging to the Collar', two other Georges (worn from a blue sash; including *Royal Treasures* 2002, no. 152) and a single diamond star, kept in a green case. The star was described as 'A very large Brilliant Star' in the inventory of the King's jewellery found at the Queen's House in 1819.

In 1844, John Bridge of Rundell and Bridge recorded that the star, which consisted of 838 brilliants and was valued at £2,500 (RA VIC/C 58/40), 'may have been made in Queen Anne's time'. It was described as 'a star which Queen Anne had provided for Prince George of Denmark, but which had never been worn by him'. In 1858 the centre was remade

439

440

with 18 brilliants, the Garter motto was reset in roses, the original 2-carat brilliant drop was replaced with a 1-carat stone and 398 brilliants were replaced. Possibly at the same time the rays, which were originally flexible, were reinforced with gold and fixed in place. It appears that Queen Victoria may have worn no. 439 on her Garter mantle.

440. (?)English

Garter badge (Great George), last quarter eighteenth century(?)

Diamonds, sapphires, rubies, amethysts, silver and gold.
15.0 × 6.7 × 3.5 cm (5⅞″ × 2⅝″ × 1⅜″)
RCIN 441144
PROVENANCE Probably converted into a Great George for George III, *c*.1800(?)
LITERATURE *Royal Insignia* 1996, no. 53, pp. 90, 200

The badge was one of those listed in Queen Charlotte's bedroom at Buckingham House in 1819 when an inventory was made of the King's jewels discovered there after the Queen's death. According to correspondence between Princess Augusta and Lord Liverpool in 1815, it appears that the King packed the pieces away in 1804. When preparing to wear the jewels for the Installation of the Knights of the

Garter on St George's Day (23 April) 1805, the King could not remember where he had stored them and became greatly distressed (Stuart 1939, p. 127). The 1819 inventory describes the badge as 'A very large Brilliant George with rubies, saphires [*sic*] in the drapery & Brilliant Fleur-de-lis at top'. There is no other provenance for the piece and it has been little worn, as later sovereigns have preferred other, lighter badges. The stone setting may be of the late eighteenth century and of continental, possibly Viennese, manufacture, while the reverse may be English. The use of the fleur-de-lis suspension is an interesting throwback to the suspensions of earlier Great Georges, most notably that depicted in Hollar's engraving of Garter Insignia for Ashmole's *History* of the Order, and the Marlborough George (see *Royal Insignia* 1996, p. 89). The piece is perhaps too large to have originally been intended as a Garter badge and it may be that the chased reverse, which is crudely held in place by a series of rivets and screws, was added at a later point with the fleur-de-lis suspension to convert it into a George. The sculptural qualities of the piece and the wide base mean that it is best viewed when it is standing upright rather than hanging from a collar, more evidence to suggest that the piece was converted into a pendant George at some point before 1819.

PERSONAL JEWELLERY (nos. 441–446)

All illustrations are enlarged by 200 per cent.

441. English; miniature by Jeremiah Meyer (1735–1789)

Finger ring with miniature of George III, 1761

Gold, diamonds, miniature on ivory. 1.8 × 2.2 × 2.2 cm
(¹¹⁄₁₆″ × ⅞″ × ⅞″)
RCIN 52211
PROVENANCE Presented to Queen Charlotte by George III, 8
September 1761; left the Collection; reacquired by the future King
George V and Queen Mary; by whom presented to King Edward VII,
9 November 1909 (Add. Cat., case 13, no. 11)
LITERATURE Scarisbrick 1981, p. 323; Walker 1992, no. 250

442. English

Diamond keeper ring, 1761

Gold, diamonds. 0.2 × diameter 2.0 cm (¹⁄₁₆″ × ¾″)
Inscribed inside band *Septr 8th 1761*
RCIN 65429
PROVENANCE Presented by George III to Queen Charlotte,
8 September 1761; passed to Charlotte, Princess Royal, Queen of
Württemberg; after whose death (1828) passed to Queen Victoria
(QVIJ, f. 359; R&S, case C, no. 37a)
LITERATURE Scarisbrick 1981, p. 323

These two rings formed part of a suite of jewels given
to Queen Charlotte by the King on their wedding day,
8 September 1761. Charlotte Papendiek records that part of
the King's 'particular present' to his bride was 'a diamond
hoop ring of a size not to stand higher than the wedding
ring, to which it was to serve as a guard'. She added, 'On that
finger the Queen never allowed herself to wear any other in
addition, although fashion at times almost demanded it.' A
second ring set with the 'likeness of the King in miniature,
done exquisitely beautiful for the coin, by our valued friend
Jeremiah Meyer' was 'given also to her Majesty to wear on
the little finger of the right hand on this auspicious day'
(Papendiek 1887, I, pp. 12–13). The Queen also received 'a
pair of bracelets, consisting of six rows of picked pearls as
large as a full pea; the clasps – one his picture, the other his
hair and cipher, both set round with diamonds [see no. 9];
necklace with diamond cross [see no. 28]; earrings, and the
additional ornaments of fashion of the day'.

These personal gifts from the King were additional to the
magnificent jewels formerly in the collection of George II (see

Appendix, p. 385). The young Queen Charlotte had at her
disposal a truly magnificent collection of jewels which made
her 'the first queen since the early seventeenth century to
possess jewels rivalling those of Continental royalty'
(Scarisbrick 1994, p. 227).

On her death the Queen's vast collection was dispersed;
her personal jewels, including the famous diamonds given
by the Nabob of Arcot, were left to her four youngest
daughters, who sold many pieces. The fate of the ring
containing the King's miniature (set under a large flat-cut
diamond) is unclear; it re-entered the collection in 1909.
The Queen's diamond hoop keeper ring passed to her
eldest daughter Charlotte, Princess Royal, Queen of
Württemberg, after whose death it passed to Queen
Victoria. Queen Charlotte's hereditary jewels, which
were bequeathed by her 'to the House of Hanover, or to
be settled upon it, and considered as an Heir Loom, in
the direct Line of Succession of that House' (Hedley 1975,
p. 303), passed to the Prince Regent. Most of these were
subsequently lost to the British crown under Queen
Victoria when the King of Hanover successfully claimed
them as part of his inheritance (see Bury 1988).

443. German

*Finger ring with miniature of Adolphus Frederick IV,
Grand Duke of Mecklenburg-Strelitz, c.*1764

Gold, paste diamonds, miniature on ivory.
2.2 × 2.1 × 2.0 cm (⅞″ × ¹³⁄₁₆″ × ¾″)
RCIN 422283
PROVENANCE Probably a gift from Adolphus Frederick IV to
Queen Charlotte; first certainly identifiable in the Collection, 1912
(R&S, case C, no. 12)
LITERATURE Walker 1992, no. 443

The ivory miniature, painted by an anonymous German
artist, depicts Queen Charlotte's eldest brother, Adolphus
Frederick IV, Duke of Mecklenburg-Strelitz. He is shown
wearing the riband and star of the Garter with which he
had been invested, at Strelitz, in 1764. Queen Charlotte
had hoped that her brother might be installed as a Knight
Companion at the same time as the King's installation as
Sovereign of the Order in 1762. However, the King had
already decided that his brother Prince William Henry and
Lord Bute would fill the vacancies on that occasion and the
Duke had to wait a further two years until the next vacancy
(Hedley 1975, p. 78).

The ring was probably made in Germany shortly after the Duke's investiture, and was perhaps a gift to the Queen from her brother. The pair corresponded regularly until the Duke's death in 1794 and the Duke had been the recipient of many valuable gifts from his sister (see no. 309). The Queen's seventh son, Prince Adolphus (later Duke of Cambridge), was named after his uncle.

The miniature is probably a copy after a portrait by Johann Georg Ziesenis (1716–76). A similar miniature, perhaps by the same hand, is incorporated into a snuff box given by the Duke to Hugh Seton of Touch in 1769 (see no. 393).

444. English; miniature by Jeremiah Meyer (1735–1789)

Finger ring with miniature of George III, c.1770

Enamel, gold, diamonds.
2.2 × 2.1 × 2.0 cm (⅞″ × ¹³⁄₁₆″ × ¾″)
RCIN 422280
PROVENANCE First recorded in the Royal Collection, 1912 (R&S, p. 17, no. 21)

This ring, which incorporates an enamel miniature of George III, was originally a stickpin; the pin has simply been bent around to convert it into a ring. Stickpins (or stockpins) were used to secure men's cravats and this example retains its twisted shaft, used to secure the pin in place in the fabric. Although the early provenance of this piece is not recorded, it was probably a gift from the King to a close friend or courtier.

Other versions of the enamel miniature by Meyer include those incorporated into the ring and bracelet given by the King to the Queen prior to their wedding in 1761 (see no. 441). For an enlarged version dated 1767 see no. 23.

445. English

Queen Charlotte's opal finger ring, c.1810

Gold, opal, pearls. 2.0 × diameter 1.7 cm (¾″ × ¹¹⁄₁₆″)
Inscribed inside band *From Duchess of Gloucester 1849 / belonged to / Queen Charlotte*
RCIN 52214
PROVENANCE Queen Charlotte; (?)Princess Sophia; Princess Mary, Duchess of Gloucester; by whom given to Queen Victoria, 1849 (QVIJ, ff. 362–3; Add. Cat., case 13, no. 14)

446. English

Queen Charlotte's finger ring, c.1810

Gold, diamond. 0.8 × 2.3 × 2.0 cm ($^{5}/_{16}$″ × $^{7}/_{8}$″ × $^{3}/_{4}$″)
Inscribed inside band *From Duchess of Gloucester 1849. Belonged to Queen Charlotte*
RCIN 52228
PROVENANCE Queen Charlotte; (?)Princess Sophia; passed to Princess Mary, Duchess of Gloucester; by whom given to Queen Victoria, 1849 (QVIJ, ff. 362–3; Add. Cat., case 13, no. 25)

Princess Mary, Duchess of Gloucester, gave these two rings to her niece Queen Victoria in 1849. The Duchess had been in constant attendance during Queen Charlotte's final illness at Kew in 1818 and it was perhaps during this difficult period that she was given the rings. The Duchess wrote that she had 'witnessed sufferings I can never describe, and I trust, we shall never forget, the Example she gave us of fortitude, & mildness, & every virtue, always trying to keep from us her anguish, & putting on a cheerful face when we came into her room, & receiving any little care & attention with pleasure' (Hedley 1975, p. 297). The rings may, alternatively, have passed into the collection of Princess Sophia, and thence to Princess Mary, who had presented certain items from her sister's estate to Queen Victoria in 1848 (including no. 385; see Appendix, p. 388.

MEDALS (nos. 447–456)

All coins and medals illustrated at actual size.

The collection of coins and medals from George III's library was presented in its entirety by George IV to the British Museum, where it arrived in June 1825. Numbering around 10,000 pieces, of which a sizeable proportion must have been in the collection before George III's time, this was – and remains – the most important single gift of medals in the museum's history.

A very complete picture of what it comprised is given in the manuscript 'Catalogue of the several Series of modern Medals & Coins in His Majesty's Collection' drawn up by Frederick Augusta Barnard in 1771 (MS, British Museum, Department of Coins and Medals). Like the book collection, it was formed on an encyclopaedic principle, with the individual pieces classified under the names of the kings, emperors, dukes or popes whose lives they chronicled, and a further category

of 1,100 pieces headed 'illustrious persons'. The English pieces form the longest list but the French, Flemish and Dutch holdings were almost as numerous. The catalogue was revised in 1814 when Charles Combe of the British Museum assisted Barnard in checking it against the collection.

The King kept his coins and medals in the library at Buckingham House (see p. 166, n. 32). Richard Dalton, George III's Librarian from 1755 to 1773, was 'Antiquarian and Keeper of the Medals, Drawings, etc.' from 1774 until his death in 1791, when he was succeeded by John Chamberlaine (see no. 215). After Chamberlaine's death in 1812, direct responsibility for this collection was returned to Barnard, the Librarian since 1774. It is unlikely that any of the pieces in the following selection belonged to the King or Queen. They are included to represent an important aspect of their collection.

447. Thomas Pingo the Younger (1714–1776)

Accession of George III, 1760

Silver. Diameter 5.5 cm (2$^{3}/_{16}$″)
RCIN 443290
LITERATURE Brown (L.) 1980, p. 3, no. 1; Eimer 1998, pp. 48–9, no. 16

No medal was struck by the Royal Mint to commemorate either the accession or the coronation of George III. In 1759 the independent medallist Thomas Pingo had issued a medal celebrating the majority of George, Prince of Wales (Eimer 1998, pp. 48–9, no. 13), which he reissued in the following year with a new inscription to mark the Prince's accession as George III. The portrait of the Prince was probably based on a wax model by Thomas's son Lewis Pingo (1743–1830), taken 'from the life', which was exhibited at the Royal Society of Arts in 1763.

448. Johann Lorenz Natter (1705–1763)

Coronation of George III, 1761

Gold. Diameter 3.42 cm (1$^{3}/_{8}$″)
RCIN 443291
LITERATURE Nau 1966, pp. 55–9, 120–22, nos. 151–3; Wollaston 1978, pp. 10, 74–6; Brown (L.) 1980, p. 7, no. 22

447

448

449

449. Johann Lorenz Natter (1705–1763)

Coronation of Queen Charlotte, 1761

Gold. Diameter 3.42 cm (1⅜")
RCIN 443292
LITERATURE Nau 1966, pp. 55–9, 121–2, nos. 155–7; Wollaston 1978, pp. 11, 75, 76; Brown (L.) 1980, p. 15, no. 66

Designs for a coronation medal by the chief engraver of the Mint, Johann Sigismund Tanner, were laid before the King in April 1761 by the Master of the Mint, but were rejected. The work was given instead to Lorenz Natter, who had been engraver of the Utrecht mint. In June he was reported as having been appointed 'medallist extraordinary to the King', and in view of the very short time available he was encouraged to use as a model a wax portrait by Isaac Gosset (see no. 418). The basis for the portrait of the Queen is not known. There are several versions of these medals, which were not struck by the Royal Mint; they may have been struck in different places, possibly including Germany. A total of 858 gold specimens of the King's medal were struck. The Queen's medal was made in smaller quantities. In accordance with custom the silver medals were thrown among the peers and peeresses by the Treasurer of the Household during the ceremony in the Abbey.

450. Thomas Pingo the Younger (1714–1776)

Birth of the Prince of Wales (later George IV), 1762

Silver. Diameter 4.0 cm (1⁹⁄₁₆")
RCIN 443316
PROVENANCE Presented by Lady Mount Stephen to Queen Mary, 1915
LITERATURE Brown (L.) 1980, p. 17, no. 77; Eimer 1998, p. 52, no. 26

Pingo's medal marking the birth of George III and Queen Charlotte's first child (the future George IV) was designed by the architect James 'Athenian' Stuart, who had earlier provided designs for the medals ordered by the Society for the Promotion of Arts and Manufactures to celebrate the victories of the Seven Years War. On the reverse of this medal, a seated Britannia receives the infant prince from Mercury in the guise of Commerce.

450

451

452

453

451. Unknown maker

George III: recovery from illness, 1789

Gold, enamelled in red, white and blue.
Diameter 3.5 cm (1⅜")
Lettered in gold *REGI · AMATO · REDVCI / MART · X / MDCCLXXXIX* and *VIVAT / G III R*
RCIN 65800
PROVENANCE Made for Queen Charlotte; Colonel Charles Swaine; Queen Mary (Add. Cat., p. 29, no. 13)
LITERATURE Brown (L.) 2002

The King's recovery in 1789 from a serious illness, which Dr Ida Macalpine and Dr Richard Hunter convincingly diagnosed as porphyria, was greeted with widespread celebrations. Parliament presented addresses of congratulation to the King on 10 March, the date inscribed on this uniface enamelled gold medallion. Much rarer than the many other commemorative objects arising from the King's recovery, it appears to have been commissioned by Queen Charlotte herself for presentation to individual courtiers; it includes a loop and ring, for suspension when worn. Fanny Burney, who served Queen Charlotte as Second Keeper of the Robes from 1786 to 1791, recorded in her diary for March 1789 that Lord Harcourt 'showed me a new medallion, just presented him by the Queen, with a Latin inscription in honour of the King's recovery' (*Burney Diary*, IV, p. 278). In the following month she herself was presented by Queen Charlotte with a medal of a different design: 'an extremely pretty medal of green and gold, and a motto, *Vive le Roi*' (*loc. cit.*, IV, p. 285).

452. Conrad Heinrich Küchler (*fl.*1763–1810)

George III preserved from assassination, 1800

Gilt copper. Diameter 4.8 cm (1⅞")
RCIN 440021
LITERATURE Pollard 1970, p. 293, no. 23; Brown (L.) 1980, p. 118, no. 483

On 15 May 1800 a discharged soldier, James Hadfield, fired a pistol from the stalls of the Drury Lane Theatre towards the King and Queen, who were in the royal box for a performance of Cibber's comedy *She Would and She Would Not* and the farce *The Humerist*. The royal couple were unharmed and the King's calm reaction was much praised and widely reported, creating a ready market for Küchler's medal, which was struck at Matthew Boulton's Soho Mint in Birmingham. A silver example was included in Queen Charlotte's sale (Christie's, 24–26 May 1819, second day, lot 9).

453. Thomas Webb (*fl.*1797–1830)

Foundation of Christ Church, Birmingham, 1805

Silver. Diameter 4.2 cm (1⅝")
RCIN 440035
LITERATURE Brown (L.) 1980, p. 148, no. 601

The foundation stone of Christ Church in Birmingham was laid on 22 July 1805 on the King's behalf by the Lord Chamberlain, the 3rd Earl of Dartmouth, in the presence of large crowds of spectators, many of whom wore Thomas Webb's medal suspended from ribbons. The King's gold example is in the British Museum, while the Queen's was sold in 1819 (Christie's, 24–26 May, second day, lot 32).

454

455

454. Lewis Pingo (1743–1830)

Captain Cook, 1784

Gold. Diameter 4.34 cm (1¹¹⁄₁₆″)
RCIN 443312
LITERATURE Brown (L.) 1980, p. 61, no. 258; Eimer 1998,
p. 65, no. 64

The commemoration of important national events by
means of medals became far more widespread in the reign
of George III than in earlier times. The Society for the
Promotion of Arts and Manufactures greatly encouraged
medallists through its distribution of monetary premiums
and annual prizes for 'Medallic Art'; the increase in the
number of independent medal-makers was at least partly a
result of this activity. It was customary for gold specimens
of the prize-winning medals to be presented to the King and
Queen, and in some cases to foreign sovereigns. The King
had taken a close interest in the voyages of Captain James
Cook (1728–79; see no. 485), endowing the Royal Society
with funds to sponsor the scientists who travelled with him
and offering some of his livestock for the establishment of
agriculture in Tahiti. After Cook's death at the hands of the
Sandwich Islanders in 1779, the Royal Society opened a
subscription for a memorial medal, of which thirteen gold
specimens were initially struck, including one each for the
King, the Queen and the Prince of Wales. The King's medal
is recorded in the manuscript catalogue of his medals (British
Museum, Department of Coins and Medals, f. 321, no. 242).

455. Conrad Heinrich Küchler (*fl.*1763–1810)

Battle of the First of June

Copper. Diameter 4.84 cm (1⅞″)
RCIN 443306
LITERATURE Pollard 1970, pp. 277–9, no. 8; Brown (L.) 1980,
p. 90, no. 383

Both George III and Queen Charlotte possessed medals
celebrating the naval victories of the Seven Years War, and

the victories during their own reign were similarly commemorated. At the Battle of the First of June 1794, Earl Howe
(1726–99) crowned a 50-year career at sea by capturing six
French ships off Ushant. His flagship, the *Queen Charlotte*, is
depicted in action on the reverse of the medal. Great attention
was paid by Küchler and by Matthew Boulton, who struck
the medal at Soho in Birmingham, to the accurate depiction
of the action.

456. G.F. Pidgeon (*fl.*1795–1819)

*Tribute to the 42nd Regiment from the London
Highland Society*, 1801

Gold. Diameter 4.48 cm (1¾″)
RCIN 443305
LITERATURE Brown (L.) 1980, p. 126, no. 512

The London Highland Society decided in 1801 to award a
medal to the officers and men of the 42nd Regiment who
had rescued Lord Abercromby at the Battle of Alexandria
in March of that year. The design of the reverse, in which a
Highlander captures a French standard, with a crocodile to
indicate the Egyptian setting, was commissioned by the Society
from Benjamin West. The medals were not in fact issued, since
it was determined that such honours could be conferred on
regiments only by the King; a small number of impressions
were presented 'to individuals who had served the Society'.

456

15. Textiles and fans (nos. 457–472)

457. Mary Knowles (1733–1807)

Needlework picture, 1779

Wool. 89.2 × 84.5 cm (35⅛″ × 33¼″)
RCIN 11912
PROVENANCE Probably commissioned by Queen Charlotte
LITERATURE Swain 1994, pp. 18–20

Mary Morris Knowles, born of a Quaker family in Rugely,
Staffordshire, was celebrated as much for her intellect,
religious conviction and unusual powers of conversation as
for her skill with the needle. A friend of the poetess Anna
Seward ('The Swan of Lichfield') and of Dr Johnson, she
is now regarded as an important early protagonist of the
feminist viewpoint in English cultural life. Her support
for the abolition of slavery, her investigation into mystical
science and her knowledge of garden design, in addition to
her accomplishment as a needlewoman, suggest the breadth
of her interests. In 1771 she was introduced by her fellow
Quaker Benjamin West to Queen Charlotte, who remained
on terms of friendship with her over the next thirty years
and whose interest in female accomplishments, notably
needlework, was well known (see no. 59). Mrs Knowles's
visits to Buckingham House included an occasion in 1778
on which she presented her 5-year-old son George to the
King and Queen.

Following the first visit in 1771, the Queen commissioned
Mrs Knowles to make a copy of Zoffany's portrait of George
III (no. 8) in needlework or 'needle painting' as it was also
known (RCIN 11913). This technique 'so highly finished, that
it has all the softness and Effect of painting' (*Birmingham
Gazette*, 3 June 1771, p. 3) was achieved with a combination
of irregular satin-stitch and long-and-short stitch, worked
on hand-woven tammy in an arbitrary pattern and at speed,
using fine wool dyed in a wide range of colours under her
own supervision. Eight years later Mrs Knowles embroidered the self portrait showing her at work on the Zoffany

457

which, like the earlier piece, she signed with initials and
dated. This appears always to have been in the Royal
Collection and was presumably also commissioned by
Queen Charlotte.

FANS (nos. 458–472)

458. Italian

*Fan painted with Blind Man's Buff, c.*1700

Paper leaf, painted in bodycolour; ivory, tortoiseshell,
mother-of-pearl. Guard length 26.0 cm (10¼″)
Verso: painted with a design based on acanthus leaves
RCIN 25063
PROVENANCE Queen Charlotte; The Hon. Lady Ward; by whom
presented to Queen Mary, 1927 (WC Fans, p. 10, no. 91)

458

459

459. French

Fan painted with trompe-l'oeil *lace, c.*1750

Double paper leaf painted in watercolour, bodycolour and gold;
tortoiseshell, garnet. Guard length 26.9 cm (10⁹⁄₁₆″)
Verso: painted with four peasants picking grapes watched by
two ladies
RCIN 25234
PROVENANCE Queen Charlotte; The Hon. Claude Yorke; by whom
presented to Queen Mary, 1939 (*QMB*, IV, p. 10, no. 19)

460. Italian; Giuseppe Trono (1739–1810), decorator

*Fan painted with Aurora and Apollo, c.*1780

Italian leaf (Giuseppe Trono after Guido Reni); English sticks
Double chickenskin leaf painted in watercolour and bodycolour,
signed *Trono F*; ivory, white paste. Guard length 29.9 cm (11¾″)
Verso: a lady seated with an anchor (?symbolic of Hope)
RCIN 25075

460

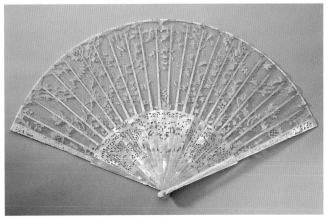

461

PROVENANCE Queen Charlotte; her sale, Christie's, London,
7 May 1819, second day, lot 38 (with two other fans); purchased
by Pophyman, 3 gns.; Anna Maria, Duchess of Bedford (wife of
the 7th Duke); by whom presented to Queen Victoria, c.1840
(WC Fans, p. 143, no. 1)

461. Belgian

*Brussels lace fan, c.*1780

Belgian lace; oriental sticks
Leaf cut from a flounce of Brussels needle lace; mother-of-pearl,
bamboo, white paste. Guard length 28.0 cm (11″)
RCIN 25098
PROVENANCE Queen Charlotte; (?)Princess Augusta; Prince
Augustus, Duke of Sussex; by whom given to Queen Victoria, 1841
(WC Fans, p. 7, no. 37)

462. English

*Brisé fan with Royal Arms, c.*1810

Tortoiseshell. Guard length 20.0 cm (7⅞″)
RCIN 25438
PROVENANCE (?)Queen Charlotte; Charlotte, Princess Royal,
Queen of Württemberg; by whom bequeathed to her step-daughter,
Princess Catherine of Württemberg; by whom given to Princess
Helen, Duchess of Albany; by whom bequeathed to Queen Mary,
1922 (QMB, II, p. 19, no. 59)

Fans were an essential – if ephemeral – part of female dress
in the eighteenth and nineteenth centuries and Queen
Charlotte is known to have patronised a number of different
fan-makers. In the 1780s and 1790s fans were supplied by
Ann Baylie, Joseph Clayton, Nicholas Mesureur, Ann Ward,
Margaret Williams, Thomas Williams and William Werndly
(RA GEO/36836–948). In addition, the Princesses are known
to have decorated fans (see no. 73). In January 1790 Lady
Mary Howe informed her sister 'Pss Royal is finishing a
beautiful Fan for the Queen with Feathers, Flowers, Insects,
Shells, Heads, Figures & Landscapes' (RA GEO/Add. 2.48).
After the Queen's death in 1818, her fans in London were

valued by Messrs Schneider & Hazell, and those at Frogmore
by Mr Bryan. Although no itemised list has survived, the
stated totals (£283 7s, and £272 16s) indicate the importance
of these pieces. Some of the Queen's fans (possibly including
nos. 461, 462) were taken by her daughters before the auction
sales in 1819 (see Appendix). These sales included 384 fans
(among them no. 460); nearly thirty of Queen Charlotte's
fans were purchased at auction by the Prince Regent.

The leaf of no. 461, cut from a piece of Brussels needle
lace, is a reminder of the important role played by lace in
the attire and furnishings of the Queen. At the start of her
reign many thousands of pounds were spent on lace for the
Queen's bedroom (see Walton 1975). Some of this is shown
in Zoffany's portrait of c.1765 (no. 4). According to the note
in Queen Mary's catalogue, Queen Charlotte 'had always
used [the fan] at the christening of her children'. It was
given by Prince Augustus, Duke of Sussex, to Queen Victoria
– who is shown holding it in her Golden Jubilee photographic
portrait. Prince Augustus was an executor of his sister,
Princess Augusta, who died in September 1840. It is possible
that the lace fan had previously belonged to Princess Augusta.

No. 462, made in England in imitation of oriental models,
bears an initial 'C' and the Royal Arms.

462

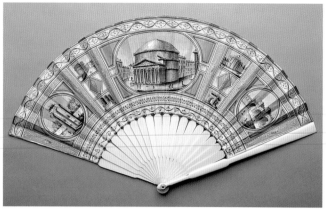

463

464

463. Italian

Grand Tour fan, c.1780

Double chickenskin leaf painted in bodycolour and watercolour;
ivory, metal, mother-of-pearl. Guard length 27.5 cm (10¹³⁄₁₆″)
RCIN 25073

PROVENANCE Princess Augusta; Queen Victoria (WC Fans,
p. 27, no. 36)

464. English

Fan painted with Catullus and the muse Lesbia, c.1790

Paper leaf mounted *à l'anglaise*, central oval printed and applied,
painted in bodycolour and watercolour; ivory, white paste. Guard
length 26.6 cm (10½″)
RCIN 25067

PROVENANCE Princess Augusta; Queen Victoria (WC Fans,
p. 26, no. 56)

465. English

Brisé fan with three painted fields, c.1790

Ivory painted in bodycolour; diamond, white paste.
Guard length 25.0 cm (9¹³⁄₁₆″)
RCIN 25086

PROVENANCE Princess Augusta; Queen Victoria (WC Fans,
p. 17, no. 81)

466. English

Brisé fan with Princess Augusta's monogram, c.1810

Tortoiseshell, red paste. Guard length 20.0 cm (7⅞″)
RCIN 25402

PROVENANCE (?)Princess Augusta; acquired by Queen Mary

The abstract inventory of Princess Augusta's possessions
made after her death in September 1840 included fans valued
at over £500. These, together with the rest of the Princess's
estate, appear to have been divided among her family, a group
of her fans being noted subsequently in Queen Victoria's
collection. There are six fans in the Royal Collection with a
traditional association with Princess Augusta; others described
as having belonged to 'one of the Queen's aunts' may also
have been hers. The majority of these are brisé fans, which
were extremely fashionable in England at the turn of the
eighteenth century. According to an old list, the medallions
in no. 465 were 'painted by one of George III's daughters'.

No. 463 is decorated with views of ancient buildings which
would have been seen by Englishmen travelling to Rome in
the late eighteenth century. Many thousands of fan leaves of
this type must have been made in Italy for the tourist trade.
The fan may possibly have been acquired by the Princess's

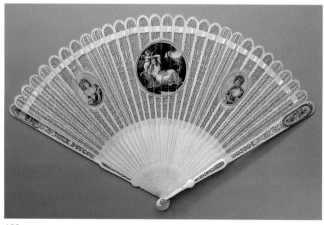

465

466

467

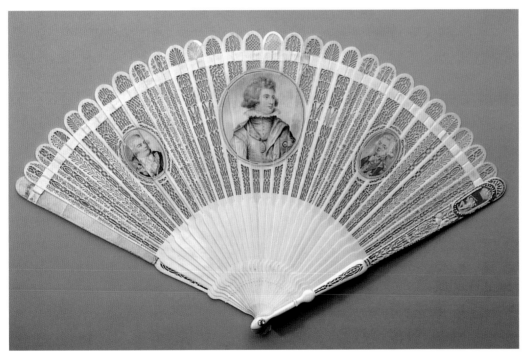

468

brother, Prince Augustus, who was in Rome in the early
1790s.

467. English

Brisé fan with Princess Sophia's monogram, c.1810

Ivory, mother-of-pearl. Guard length 16.5 cm (6½")
RCIN 25078
PROVENANCE (?)Princess Sophia; George, 2nd Duke of
Cambridge; his sale, Christie's, 14 June 1904, lot 695; bought by
Queen Mary (*QMB*, I, p. 146, no. 603; WC Fans, p. 16v, no. 92)

468. English

*Brisé fan with painted portraits of the three eldest sons
of George III, c.1790*

Ivory painted in bodycolour; jasper ware, pyrite, gold leaf, diamond.
Guard length 24.8 cm (9¾")
RCIN 25373
PROVENANCE Sir Henry Paulet St John-Mildmay, 6th Baronet
(d. 1916); Queen Mary (QMF, no. 28)

469

469 (holder)

469. Cantonese

Brisé cockade fan and holder with the arms and cipher of the Prince of Wales, c.1790

Ivory. Fan: diameter 38.0 cm (14¹⁵⁄₁₆″). Holder: 26.2 × 6.5 × 3.0 cm (10⁵⁄₁₆″ × 2⁹⁄₁₆″ × 1³⁄₁₆″)

RCIN 3683.1a–b

PROVENANCE Prince of Wales (later George IV)

470. English

Brisé fan with painted portrait of Frederick, Duke of York, c.1790

Ivory painted in watercolour and bodycolour; white paste. Guard length 24.6 cm (9¹¹⁄₁₆″)

RCIN 25375

PROVENANCE Augusta, Duchess of Cambridge (d. 1889); Queen Mary, by 1920 (*QMB*, I, p. 144, no. 591; QMF, no. 14)

471. English

Brisé fan celebrating the marriage of the Duke and Duchess of York, 1791

Ivory, steel, white paste. Guard length 25.7 cm (10⅛″)

RCIN 25094

PROVENANCE Queen Mary, by 1926 (WC Fans, p. 2, no. 88)

472. English

Fan commemorating the Garter Installation, 1805

Double silk leaf (stiffened ?with size), painted in bodycolour,
silver-coated paper binding strips, sequins; lacquer, mother-of-pearl.
Guard length 20.0 cm (7⅞")
RCIN 25156
PROVENANCE Queen Mary

A number of the fans or other small *objets de vertu* bearing
portraits or monograms of members of the royal family
would have been commissioned specifically to be given away
by the individuals concerned. That would certainly appear to
be the explanation for the 'I Rich Pierced and carved Ivory
Fan ornamented with the Portrait of H.R.H.' supplied to the
future George IV in 1795 by William Cook of 42 Pall Mall
(PRO HO 73/18). However, fans such as no. 468 may also have
been produced for sale, in the same way as portrait engravings
of royal sitters were the stock-in-trade of many print sellers.
As the fan with the painted portrait of the Duke of York
(no. 470) belonged to the sitter's sister-in-law, it may have
been a royal commission. The portraits on nos. 468 and 470
are copied from engravings published in the late 1780s. The
jasper ware Wedgwood plaques on no. 468, applied to the
carved ivory sticks, are a particular feature of this fan.

The unpainted ivory brisé fan (no. 471) was made to
commemorate the marriage of the Duke of York to Princess
Frederica of Prussia in 1791. The marriage was particularly
popular with fan-makers because of the Duchess's perceived
fondness for fans. Shortly after her arrival in England she
'displayed a pleated fan entirely of diamonds, with an ivory
stick pierced and set with diamonds in a mosaic pattern'
(Rhead 1910, p. 203).

The royal coats of arms and Prince of Wales's cipher on
the cockade fan and its carved ivory holder (no. 469) suggest
that it was either presented to, or made as a present from,
the Prince. The exceptionally fine workmanship indicates that
it must have been produced in the Far East rather than being
an English imitation.

The small silk fan (no. 472) was made to commemorate
the Garter Installation at Windsor on 23 April 1805. By
now all the King's sons had been appointed to the Order;
the ceremonial was also attended by their sisters (Hedley
1975, p. 222).

470

471

472

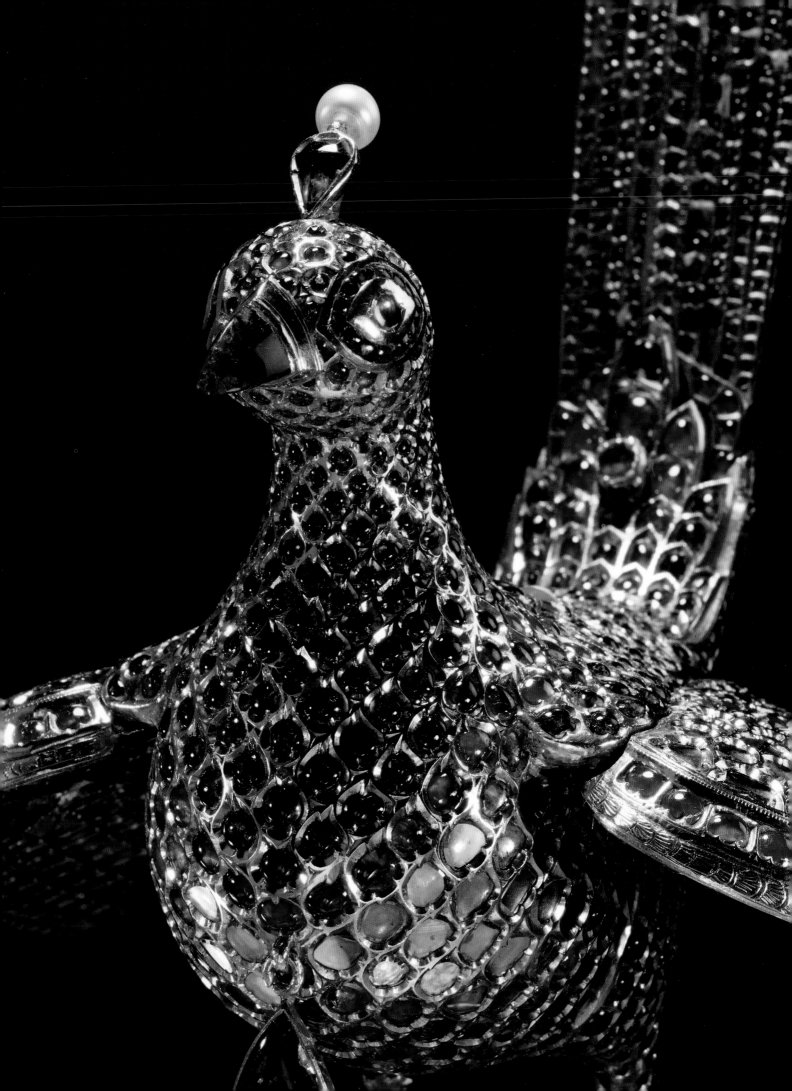

16. The wider world (nos. 473–485)

473. Mīr ʿAlī Şīr Nevā ʾī (1440–1501)

Hamse (Five poems), 1492

Open at folios 5v–6: (right) *The Last Judgement and Resurrection of the Dead* by Nānhā and Manohar, *c.*1605 and (left) *Seven couples in a garden* by Narsingh, *c.*1510

Bodycolour and gold on gold-flecked buff paper. Double spread 34.3 × 46.0 cm (13½" × 18⅛"); right image 33.0 × 14.8 cm (13" × 5¹³⁄₁₆"); left image 23.5 × 15.0 cm (9¼" × 5⅞")

RCIN 1005032

PROVENANCE Commissioned by Sultan Husayn Bayqara, ruler of Herat; transferred to Bukhara, in or after 1506; Emperor Jahangir (1605–6 mark of ownership); Emperor Shah Jahan (1628 mark of ownership); by descent; bought by Asafuddawla, Nawab of Oudh, by 1776; presented (via Lord Teignmouth, Governor-General of India) to George III, 1799

LITERATURE Losty 1982, no. 77; Skelton 1985; Waley 1992, p. 14

This is one of the six splendid oriental manuscripts presented to George III by the Nawab of Oudh in 1799, through Lord Teignmouth, the Governor-General of India. In addition to the Padshahnama (RCIN 1005025; see Beach and Koch 1997), there was also an Islamic album (RCIN 1005068), two volumes of Persian poetry (RCIN 1005015, 1005017) and one of Persian prose (RCIN 1005022).

Nevā'i was the greatest author to write in Chaghatay, the classical eastern Turkic language which was the forerunner of modern Uzbeq. He was a friend from boyhood of Sultan Husayn Bayqara (1468–1506), the ruler of Herat, where the manuscript was written. This copy of the manuscript, which is the earliest illustrated Islamic manuscript in the Royal Collection, was made in the author's lifetime by the great calligrapher Sultān ʿAlī of Mashhad (Mashhadī). The superb quality of both the calligraphy (see Waley 1992, pls. 9 and 10), and the illustrations, led the Emperor Jahangir (r. 1605–27) to value the manuscript – 'one of my most treasured books' – at 1,000 ashrafis, a valuation which Shah Jahan almost doubled, to 20,000 rupees (Seyller 1997, p. 270).

Miniatures appear to have been added to blank spaces in the manuscript after its transfer to Bukhara in the early sixteenth century. Each of the six pages with painted miniatures is within the 52-page section containing the first of the five poems, Hayret ul-ebrār. According to the note added by Jahangir to f. 1b of the manuscript, which entered his library in the first year of his reign (i.e. 1605), 'the paintings were completed in my workshop'. Jahangir's library is said to have contained 24,000 volumes when his father died. Whereas the painting of the Last Judgement and Resurrection dates entirely from the early seventeenth century, all but the faces and landscape in the facing painting on the left (which were reworked by Jahangir's artists) appears to be the work of a Bukhari artist of the early sixteenth century. These paintings are entirely unrelated to the text. The *Last Judgement* scene is based on a large print by Adrian Collaert after Stradanus; the print – published in the 1590s – had recently arrived in India, presumably via Jesuit missionaries, and had also inspired elements in the painting of the Deposition in the Large Clive Album (Victoria and Albert Museum), painted in Lahore – in the presence of the future Emperor Jahangir – in 1598.

474. Indian (Mysore), and Paul Storr (1771–1844)

Bird of paradise (huma) *from Tipu Sultan's throne,* *c.*1787–91; *stand,* 1815

Gold, rubies, emeralds, diamonds, pearls, silver-gilt.
42.0 × 20.0 × 28.0 cm (16⁹⁄₁₆" × 7⅞" × 11");
stand height 22.8 cm (9")

RCIN 48482

PROVENANCE Made for Tipu Sultan; acquired by Marquess Wellesley for the Directors of the East India Company, 1799; by whom presented to George III, March 1800 (BL, Indian and Colonial Collections, R. 3/98, p. 477); by whom given to Queen Charlotte; by whom bequeathed to four of her daughters, 1818; by whom given to the Prince Regent (later George IV), 1818

LITERATURE *Royal Treasures* 2002, no. 298

473

474

The defeat and death of Tipu, Sultan of Mysore, and the sack of his citadel of Seringapatam in 1799 put an end to more than a decade of conflict in southern India, and pre-empted a possible military alliance between Tipu and Napoleon Bonaparte. In the heat of the action the Sultan's magnificent treasury and library were ransacked by the British forces, and the gold coverings of his throne were cut up into small pieces for distribution as prize. The throne, which Tipu may never in fact have ascended in state, was an octagonal wooden platform raised 1.2 metres (4 feet) from the ground on eight supports in the shape of tiger legs. It was surrounded by a railing with a small jewelled tiger head above each support, and surmounted by a canopy raised on a post at the back. In the front was a life-size tiger head (later presented to William IV, RCIN 67212). Every element was overlaid with 2 mm (¹/₁₆ in.) gold sheet. Above the canopy hovered the *huma* or bird of paradise. In a letter of July 1799 to the Governor-General of India, Lord Mornington, Captain Macaulay (Private Secretary to the British Commander-in-Chief, General Harris) explained that the *huma* was 'supposed to fly constantly in the Air, and never to touch the ground. It is looked upon as a Bird of

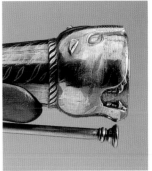

475

happy Omen, and that every Head it overshadows will in time wear a Crown' (BL, Indian and Colonial Collections). After the breaking up of the throne the *huma* had already been allocated when it was reacquired by Mornington, now Marquess Wellesley, for presentation to George III. The stand was made for it, by Paul Storr, after the King had passed the *huma* to the Queen.

475. Sayid Iqbal

Flintlock blunderbuss, 1793–4

Hardwood, steel, blued steel inlaid with gold, brass.
Length 93.9 cm (36 $^{15}/_{16}$")
RCIN 67239
PROVENANCE Presented by Marquess Wellesley, to George III, April 1800 (CHAC, no. 570)

Tipu's emblem was the tiger, whose slanted stripes were everywhere to be seen at Seringapatam, on the walls of the palace, on the uniforms of his soldiers and on his weapons, as on the hilt of no. 476. The muzzles of his cannon were formed as tiger's heads (see Archer, Rowell and Skelton 1987, p. 65, no. 68), but no. 475, which is signed by the general munition-maker Sayid Iqbal, is the only known firearm of this type with this feature.

476. Indian

Sabre, c.1790

Gilt copper, steel, moonstones. Length 88.0 cm (34 $^{5}/_{8}$")
Inscribed in six places on the blade in gold inlays with a Persian distich and Koranic verses
RCIN 67216
PROVENANCE Presented by Sir John Cradock to George III, May 1811 (CHAC, no. 2126)

Such was Tipu's infamy in England that collectors were eager to obtain personal relics, and many more swords survive in British country-house collections than can possibly have been found by the side of the Sultan's body where he fell in 1799. This sword, which bears an early nineteenth-century manuscript label inscribed 'Favourite sword of Tipoo', has a greater claim than most. The numerous inscriptions on no. 476 show beyond doubt that it was a fighting sword that belonged to Tipu. The hilt is covered with the *bubri* tiger-stripe emblem and two of the five tiger-head terminals have jewelled eyes. This refinement is not present on another sword which in other respects closely resembles this one, which was in the collection of the 2nd Baron Clive (Archer, Rowell and Skelton 1987, pp. 46–7, no. 33).

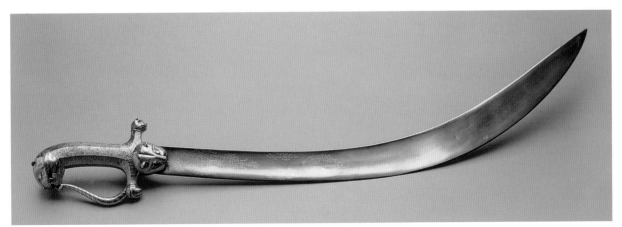

476

477. Indian (Vizagapatam)

*Settee, c.*1770

Sandalwood veneered with ivory, engraved and inlaid.
101.0 × 184.0 × 82.5 cm (3′ 3¾″ × 6′ 0⁷⁄₁₆″ × 32½″)
RCIN 489.1
PROVENANCE Alexander Wynch (d. 1781); his sale, Christie and
Ansell, Westhorpe House, 6 October 1781, lot 54; purchased by
George III (48 gns.) and presented to Queen Charlotte; her sale,
Christie's, London, 7–10 May 1819, lot 107; purchased by Loving
and Paten on behalf of the Prince Regent (£52 10s)
LITERATURE Jaffer 2001, pp. 197–200, no. 45

No fewer than fifty pieces of Indian furniture and boxes
appear in the catalogues of Queen Charlotte's posthumous
sales. A large proportion of what must have been the largest
concentration of such exotica in late eighteenth-century
Britain came in the form of gifts. While travelling in
Buckinghamshire in October 1781 the King stopped at
Westhorpe House near Marlow, the home of the recently
deceased Alexander Wynch (Governor of Madras 1773–5),
and was shown a quantity of ivory furniture by the
auctioneer James Christie (Whitley 1928, I, p. 364). The
King purchased a settee, ten chairs and two miniature
bureau-cabinets, all of the same type. The Queen subsequently added a further settee, six more chairs and two
corner chairs (see *Royal Treasures* 2002, no. 85). At the
sale of her effects in 1819 the Prince Regent purchased
the entire, augmented set for his use at Brighton Pavilion.
This type of furniture was made in some quantity in
Vizagapatam, on the eastern coast of India. The shapes
were probably copied from existing English-made furniture
rather than from the engraved designs in publications such
as Thomas Chippendale's *Gentleman and Cabinet-Maker's
Director*, which first appeared in 1754. The Royal Collection
chairs and others of the same type are usually dated around
1770; however, an ivory-veneered armchair of much the
same design but with far less engraved decoration and dated
1759 was sold anonymously in 1980 (Christie's, London,
19 June 1980, lot 26).

477

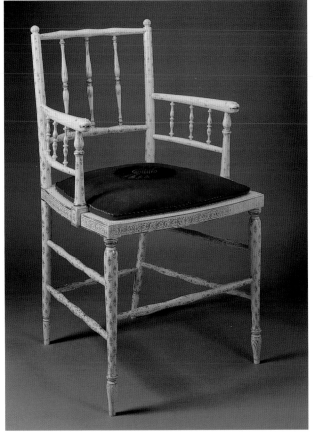

478

478. Indian (Murshidabad)

Two armchairs, c.1780

Ivory, partly painted and gilt, velvet with silver embroidery.
88.8 × 56.0 × 54.0 cm (34¹⁵⁄₁₆″ × 22¹⁄₁₆″ × 21¼″)
RCIN 11197.1–2
PROVENANCE Warren Hastings; (?)presented by Mrs Hastings to
Queen Charlotte, c.1784; (?)her sale, Christie's, 24–26 May 1819,
second day, lot 53; bought by Swabey (£17); Lord Gwydyr; his sale,
Christie's, London, 21 May 1829, lot 70; bought by E.H. Baldock
for George IV (£40; Jutsham II, p. 268)
LITERATURE Jaffer 1999; Jaffer 2001, pp. 244–5

These chairs were probably acquired by Warren Hastings
(1732–1818). This type of furniture, of which the Queen's
1819 sale catalogues include twenty pieces, was made in
Murshidabad from the third quarter of the eighteenth
century, in smaller quantities than the production of
Vizagapatam, and usually to a specific order (Jaffer 2001,
p. 238). The armchairs may have formed part of a large
group of pieces presented to Queen Charlotte in around
1784 by Hastings's wife Marian.

479. Chinese: Qianlong (1736–1795)

Circular covered box with dragons in clouds

Red, green and yellow lacquer on wood.
8.0 × diameter 20.0 cm (3⅛″ × 7⅞″)
Inscribed on the underside with the imperial reign mark
incised and filled with gold
RCIN 10806.1

480. Chinese: Qianlong (1736–1795)

Tiered covered box with dragon and phoenix

Red, green and yellow lacquer on wood.
20.7 × 15.3 cm (8⅛″ × 6″)
Inscribed on the underside with the imperial reign mark
incised and filled with gold
RCIN 10818

481. Chinese: Qianlong (1736–1795)

Covered rectangular box with dragon and phoenix

Red, green and yellow lacquer on wood.
8.2 × 25.8 × 15.7 cm (3¼″ × 10³⁄₁₆″ × 6³⁄₁₆″)
Inscribed on the underside with the imperial reign mark
incised and filled with gold
RCIN 10810.1

482. Chinese: Qianlong (1736–1795)

Rectangular tray with a collection of precious emblems

Red, green and yellow lacquer on wood.
3.0 × 13.2 × 21.9 cm (1³⁄₁₆″ × 5³⁄₁₆″ × 8⅝″)
Inscribed on the underside with the imperial reign mark
incised and filled with gold
RCIN 10809.1

482

482 480 481
484 479 483

483. Chinese: Qianlong (1736–1795)

Covered peach-shaped box with a Daoist immortal in a landscape

Red, green and yellow lacquer on wood.
10.4 × 16.3 × 16.5 cm (4⅛″ × 6⁷⁄₁₆″ × 6½″)
Inscribed on the underside with the imperial reign mark incised and filled with gold
RCIN 10821.2

484. Chinese: Qianlong (1736–1795)

Covered circular box

Red, green and yellow lacquer on wood.
6.9 × diameter 15.2 cm (2¹¹⁄₁₆″ × 6″)
Inscribed on the underside with the imperial reign mark incised and filled with gold
RCIN 10823
PROVENANCE (?)Presented to George III by the Emperor Qianlong, 1793
LITERATURE Singer 1992

By the end of the eighteenth century the East India Company had been trading with Chinese merchants for two hundred years, but in a strictly limited way. They were only allowed into Canton for five months in a year, and all trade had to be carried on through Chinese officials. The British Embassy of 1792–4, led by Earl Macartney of Lissanore (1737–1806), was charged with negotiating a treaty of friendship between George III and the Emperor Qianlong, establishing a permanent diplomatic post in Peking, and improving trading conditions in Canton. In these objectives it failed completely. In the eyes of the octogenarian Emperor, the British were coming to pay tribute to him rather than to establish diplomatic relations as understood in the West. In a lengthy edict addressed to the King, he refused to allow a permanent British mission to Peking, which was 'a request contrary to our dynastic usage'. When presented with the King's gifts, which included a Herschel telescope, a planetarium, artillery pieces, air pumps and carriages, as well as Wedgwood pottery, chandeliers, clocks and watches, he declared: 'I set no value on objects strange or ingenious, and have no use for your country's manufactures' (RA GEO/Add. 31/21; quoted in translation by Singer 1992, Appendix A).

Macartney's mission did not return empty handed. A list of the numerous gifts which the Emperor made to George III is preserved in the India Office Library (IOR G/12/92). The King was sent an agate *ruyi* sceptre and large quantities of porcelain, jade, carved lacquer and silk. Among them were 'caskets', some of them 'in the shape of a peach' and others decorated 'with clouds of Dragons' in 'red varnish' or lacquer. Aeneas Anderson, whose account of the Embassy was published in 1795, described them as 'a number of callibash boxes of exquisite workmanship, beautifully carved on the outside, and stained a scarlet colour, of the utmost softness and delicacy' (Anderson 1795, p. 149). The decoration, which is deeply carved into the many layers of vegetable lacquer, some of them in different colours, includes the five-clawed dragon reserved for use on imperial wares.

When Joseph Farington visited Frogmore in November 1797 he noticed 'some presents from the Emperor of China' (*Farington Diary*, III, p. 919), and carved boxes of this type can be seen in Pyne's view of the Green Closet (no. 141).

485. New Zealand (Maori)

Heitiki, (?)eighteenth century

Nephrite, flax, paua shell, bone.
10.0 × 5.0 × 5.5 cm (3¹⁵⁄₁₆″ × 1¹⁵⁄₁₆″ × 2³⁄₁₆″)
RCIN 69263
PROVENANCE Presented in New Zealand to James Cook, October 1769; by whom presented to George III, probably August 1771
LITERATURE *Cook's Endeavour* 1997, case 5

James Cook, FRS (1728–79), known to history simply as Captain Cook, was granted a one-hour audience by George III in August 1771 after his return from his second expedition to the Pacific. It was probably at this meeting that Cook presented the King with this precious ornament, which the explorer had received from the natives of Queen Charlotte Sound in South Island, New Zealand, in October 1769. In Maori culture, *tiki* was the name given to the first created man, and *hei* means suspended. Carved from the precious nephrite or greenstone known as Pounamu, the *heitiki* was worn round the neck close to the throat. Embodying the spirits of ancestors, it was a powerful mark of the status of the wearer. W. B. Monkhouse, a member of Cook's expedition, described one of the natives encountered by the crew of *Endeavour* as having 'a piece of green talk [*sic*] about two & half inches long, and an inch & half broad, flat, and carved into the figure of a most uncouth animal of fancy'.

James Cook's second voyage, sponsored by the Royal Society and with a substantial personal contribution from the King, had as its declared purpose the observation of the transit of Venus (see p. 162). The second, unspoken objective was the discovery of the 'Southern Continent', which was to be secured for British trade. The botanists Joseph Banks and Daniel Solander also took part in the expedition, which set sail from Plymouth in August 1768.

485

Among the objects that Cook took with him on his third and ultimately fatal voyage to the Pacific in 1772, as gifts for the natives he would encounter, were numerous ornaments – earrings, bracelets etc. – made by Boulton and Fothergill as facsimiles of those brought back on earlier voyages. They included '1 Green God w'ch is all we can send of them as 3 were done but crack'd in the cooling' (letter from Boulton and Fothergill to William Matthews, British Museum (Natural History), Banks Archive, URC 920328/020.037772). This may refer to a bronze *tiki*, probably cast from George III's example, which survives in a private collection in New Zealand.

The dispersal of Queen Charlotte's property

MATTHEW WINTERBOTTOM

QUEEN CHARLOTTE'S WILL

Queen Charlotte signed her final will on 16 November 1818, the day before her death at Kew Palace. (The main provisions of the will are given in Oulton 1819, pp. 470–72.)

JEWELS

The will divided Queen Charlotte's extensive and magnificent collection of jewels into three distinct groups.

1. *The hereditary jewels from the collection of George II.*
During the Jacobite uprising of 1745 George II had sent many important jewels to Hanover for safe keeping; in 1760 these were inherited by George III and were brought back to England. The jewels which had remained in England were bequeathed by George II to his second son, William, Duke of Cumberland, who sold them to his nephew, George III, for £54,900. The jewels suitable for female attire, from both sources, were presented to Queen Charlotte by George III prior to their wedding on 8 September 1761, as 'his gift to her and . . . her own to do whatever she pleased with'. According to Queen Charlotte's 1818 will, the jewels would pass to George III should he 'be restored to a sound state of mind', and if not 'to the House of Hanover, to be settled upon it, and considered as an Heir Loom, in the Direct Line of Succession of that House as established by the Laws and Constitution of the House of Hanover'. The collection thus passed to George IV. It included two brilliant (i.e. diamond) sleeve bows, a pair of three dropped brilliant earrings, a pair of single dropped brilliant earrings set with small brilliants at the back, a large necklace of brilliants with a brilliant cross, a large brilliant stomacher, a brilliant crown, pearl and brilliant bows to a large pearl necklace, pearl dropped earrings set round with brilliants, and a large brilliant nosegay. Most of the jewels were subsequently lost to the British crown in 1858 after the King of Hanover successfully claimed them as part of his inheritance (see Bury 1988). Queen Charlotte's nuptial crown remains in the collection of the princes of Hanover where it is used as the Hanoverian Royal Wedding Crown.

2. *The jewels 'Presented to me by the Nabob of Arcot'.*
Arcot, a city near Madras, had been captured and defended by Clive in 1751 during the war between rival claimants to the throne of the Carnatic. In 1767 its grateful ruler Nawab Azim-ud-daula presented George III and Queen Charlotte with a gift of arms and jewels which included seven large diamonds, subsequently known as the Arcot diamonds (*Crown Jewels* 1998, II, p. 91, n. 112). In her will Queen Charlotte specifically directed that they were to be sold and the money divided among her four youngest surviving daughters. George IV disregarded his mother's will and claimed the diamonds as his own personal property, apparently setting them into the new Imperial State Crown in 1821. After the coronation of William IV and Queen Adelaide in 1831 – when the diamonds were set in the Queen's crown – the diamonds were sold to Rundells, who auctioned them at Willis's Rooms, St James's, on 20 July 1837. There they were purchased by the Emanuel Brothers, who sold them to the 1st Marquess of Westminster for £11,000. In 1930 the two largest stones were set in the Westminster tiara, which was sold to Harry Winston of New York in June 1959. The Arcot diamonds were removed, recut and mounted as rings and are now thought to be in a private collection in Texas.

3. *The Queen's remaining jewels.*
The jewels 'purchased by Myself at various Periods or being Presents made to Me on Birthdays and other occasions' were bequeathed to the Queen's four youngest surviving daughters 'to be divided in equal shares between them according to a valuation to be made under the direction of my Executors'. These probably included certain jewels (such as nos. 441–2) presented to the Queen on her wedding day (see p. 362).

PICTURES, PRINTS, BOOKS AND WORKS OF ART

Queen Charlotte's 'Books, Plate, House Linen, China, Pictures, Drawings, Prints, all Articles of ornamental furniture and other Valuables and Personals' were also 'to be divided in equal shares according to a distribution and valuation to be made under the direction of my Executors among my four younger daughters'. Exceptions to this were various items 'brought from Mecklenburg' which the Queen instructed should revert to the House of Mecklenburg-Strelitz and be 'sent back to the Senior Branch of that House'; although Queen Charlotte intended to list these, she died before doing so.

LANDED PROPERTY

The Queen's house and grounds at Frogmore, with 'the fixtures and Articles of common Household furniture', were bequeathed to her second daughter, Princess Augusta. Princess Sophia was given Lower Lodge at Windsor 'with its Appendages and Appurtenances' but soon passed this on to her brother, the future George IV.

THE SALE OF QUEEN CHARLOTTE'S POSSESSIONS

In accordance with Queen Charlotte's will, her personal collection was valued and divided into equal lots to be shared among her four youngest surviving daughters. The executors, General Herbert Taylor and Lord Arden, decided that after the Princesses had chosen what they wanted to keep, the remainder should be sold by public auction – a decision described by Princess Mary as 'a sad pill to swallow' (Hedley 1975, p. 303).

FIG. 30 G.C. after Yedis, *Sales by Auction! – or provident children disposing of their deceased mother's effects for the benefit of the creditors*, 1819 (RCIN 1154695)

Thus on 23 December 1818 'the poor Queen's personals' were 'arranged and divided into four lots' at Frogmore (Hedley 1975, p. 303). The lots were drawn by the Princesses so 'no Preference can be supposed to have been shewn' (RA GEO/50387). No lists appear to survive of the contents of the different portions, nor of what was retained by each daughter. In total the Princesses retained £15,052 3s 2d of 'certain jewels & other specific articles'. Princess Augusta's share amounted to £6,897 9s, Princess Elizabeth's £1,513 5s, Princess Mary's £2,803 15s 11d and Princess Sophia's £3,837 13s 3d. The value of these reserved items was then deducted from each Princess's share of the proceeds from the public auction, and the balance redivided equally (RA VIC/Add. R 43).

George IV stipulated that any books in the Queen's extensive library 'which have any of her Majesty's writing or annotations upon them, or are otherwise particularly distinguished as objects of her Majesty's attention are to be reserved: and a special List made of them, so that the Princesses may have the option of selecting them-selves those which they wish to keep' (Stuart 1939, p. 126). Among the reserved books was no. 248, which they presented in 1829 to the Queen's executor, (by now) Sir Herbert Taylor. Other books were to be bought 'for the King's Library at a *reasonable* valuation' (Hedley 1975, p. 304). The Princesses decided that 'all the Tents that were Tippoo Saibs and others' were to be 'presented to the Prince Regent'. A bust of George III by Bacon (see no. 254) was to go to the King's Library and a cast was to be taken for each Princess. 'All the Portraits of the Mecklenburgh Family [were] to be deposited in Windsor Castle as Heir Looms' (RA GEO/50387).

The public – but ostensibly anonymous – auction of Queen Charlotte's possessions took place in thirty-five sales which ran from 4 January to 27 August 1819. In total just over £59,600 was raised in the sales of: Horses (£4,534); Carriages (£1,161: Tattersall's, London, 4 January); *Oriental Curiosities & Porcelain* (£6,439: Christie's, London, 7–10 May); *Jewels, Trinkets, Silver Fillagree Dessert, Silver Gilt dressing & Table Plate* (£35,055: Christie's, London, 17–19 May); *Carvings in Ivory, Trinkets, Coins, Porcelain, Furniture & Paintings* (£5,906: Christie's, London, 24–26 May); *Library of Books &c.* (£4,541: Christie's, London, 9 June–12 July); *Prints, Drawings & Books of Prints* (£1,235: Christie's, London, 13–16 July); *Miscellaneous*

Bookcases, Gobelin Tapestry, Needle Work, Carpets &c. (£729: Christie's, London, 26–27 August).

The future George IV bought many items from his mother's sales. From the Christie's sale of 7–10 May he purchased items amounting to £2,735 11s 10½d (RA GEO/Add. 2/88). These included 'an Ebony Cabinet . . . wth Gems of the old Florentine Mosaic' (no. 261) and 'a pair of Time pieces by Strigel' (no. 310) together with numerous mandarin dresses, silks, tassels, snuff, porcelain, sculpture, fans and curiosities. Among those acting for the Prince Regent at this sale were Messrs Loving and Paten, through whom the Prince acquired the suite of Indian ivory-veneered furniture (no. 477). The Prince Regent had also purchased items from his mother's estate prior to the public sales (RA GEO/50384): three pairs of Sèvres vases valued at £151 were delivered to Carlton House from Buckingham House on 8 January 1819 (nos. 326, 327).

The Queen's wardrobe was not auctioned. Mrs Charlotte Beckedorff, Keeper of the Queen's Wardrobe, 'reserved for especial Distribution a few Articles, which altho' not of much intrinsic value are very interesting as having been more particularly used by Her late Majesty; to be also divided into 4 lots' (RA GEO/50388). On 22 February 1819 Mrs Beckedorff 'commenced disposing of the silks, late property of the Queen, to various ladies who have called at the Queen's-Palace' (Hedley 1975, p. 304). Mrs Beckedorff was offered the Queen's unworn lace and the 'pieces of silk and satin, gold and silver, figured and plain, not made up, which were measured at the late Queen's house, amounting to 2,140 yards. They were either presents or purchases for the encouragement of manufacturers, and of various prices, from one guinea to five guineas per yard. This valuable collection the Princesses generously presented to Madame Beckedorff, as a mark of esteem for the favourite of their deceased Royal Parent. In another apartment was a large store of the most superb shawls (Oriental presents to her Majesty) but many of them nearly consumed by moths' (Oulton 1819, pp. 473–4). However, Mrs Beckedorff felt unable to accept such a generous and valuable gift. She wrote to General Taylor that 'He had taken a great burden from her mind by permitting Her to resign what she really never could have consented to keep – that the value of the unworn lace was beyond his conception' (Hedley 1975, p. 303). Among the gifts that she did accept was the Queen's landau 'to retire with it to Mecklenburg' (Oulton 1819, p. 474) and 'A picture of Queen Charlotte by Angelica Kauffmann, some lace and other things belonging to the Queen', which were subsequently bequeathed to Queen Charlotte's granddaughter, Princess Augusta of Cambridge, Dowager Grand Duchess of Mecklenburg-Strelitz (RA GV/O 2572/22).

Some of Queen Charlotte's 'Foreign Silks', 'selling in Germany' in April 1821 (RA VIC/Add. R 43) may have been those that were renounced by Mrs Beckedorff. The same document refers to 'the Cabinets of Botanical Plants; not sold'. This presumably refers to the celebrated herbarium of the Revd John Lightfoot, purchased for £100 by the King and presented to Queen Charlotte in 1788 (Hedley 1975, p. 179). The herbarium was presented to the Royal Botanic Gardens, Kew, by the Trustees of Saffron Walden Museum, Essex, in 1921.

QUEEN CHARLOTTE'S DAUGHTERS

Charlotte, Princess Royal, Queen of Württemberg (1766–1828)
In her will Queen Charlotte made no provision for her eldest daughter, 'having been so long established in Germany and being so amply provided for in all respects'. The Princess Royal, who had married Frederick I, Duke (later King) of Württemberg, in 1797, died at Ludwigsburg on 6 October 1828. There were no children of the marriage and most of the Princess's belongings were bequeathed to members of her husband's family. However, a small number of personal mementoes were left to members of her English family, including her mother and her brother Edward, Duke of Kent. Her final will was completed in 1816, the year of her husband's death; no additional provisions appear to have been made before her own death twelve years later.

Because the Princess's will pre-dates the death of her mother, no references are made to items which she might have acquired from her mother's estate. It is known that the Princess was given her mother's diamond hoop ring (no. 442) because Princess Victoria received it from her aunt's estate in 1829. This deeply personal object may have been given to the Princess by her younger sisters as a memento of their mother. Princess Victoria's inventory of jewels (RA VIC/Add. T 285d) states that the ring was 'Left by the Late Queen of Wurtemberg in Her Last Will' although this cannot have been the case. It may have been promised to Princess Victoria during the Princess Royal's final visit to England in 1828 and have been subsequently presented to the Princess by her aunt's executors.

Princess Elizabeth, Landgravine of Hesse-Homburg (1770–1840)
The Queen's third daughter, Princess Elizabeth, died at Homburg on 10 January 1840. She had married Frederick VI, Landgrave of Hesse-Homburg, in 1818; the marriage was childless and Frederick VI had died in 1829. The Princess bequeathed her jewels to Princess Louise of Hesse-Homburg, the wife of Gustav, her husband's younger brother (who succeeded as Landgrave in 1846). She left certain trinkets to members of her English family – to Princess Mary a bracelet with their father's picture, to the Queen of Hanover 'Ernest's picture as a child, worked with his hair' (almost certainly no. 45), to Princess Augusta a ring with a portrait of George III, and to Queen Victoria a gold toothpick which had belonged to the Duke of Kent (Stuart 1939, pp. 133, 200).

The Princess bequeathed most of her remaining possessions to Princess Caroline of Reuss, Gustav's daughter. Augusta, Grand Duchess of Mecklenburg-Strelitz (Princess Elizabeth's niece), recalled in a note to Queen Mary in 1915 that 'When Prussia took Homburg in 1866 they kept all the inside of half of the Schloss – Princess [Caroline of] Reuss sold her half, a few English family things were bought by me, and Alice (later Grand Duchess of Hesse [Queen Victoria's daughter]) bought others' (RA VIC/Add. R 95).

Princess Augusta (1768–1840)
The Queen's second daughter, Augusta, remained unmarried. She died intestate eight months after Princess Elizabeth, on 22 September 1840. Her brother, the Duke of Sussex, acted as one of her executors. Princess Augusta's estate included many items from Queen Charlotte's collection: in 1818 she had reserved items worth £6,897 9s – considerably more than the portions of her three sisters – within her share of her mother's estate (see above). Presumably the Princess had wanted to augment the fixtures and 'common Household furniture' she had inherited with Frogmore.

In March 1841 Frogmore House and its furnishings were purchased by the crown from Princess Augusta's executors for £12,500. An inventory made at that time indicates that the furnishings still included many of the fixtures and 'common furniture' inherited by the Princess, together with additional items allocated within the Princess's portion of her mother's estate (RA VIC/Add. Q 965). Many items which date from Queen Charlotte's time there remain at Frogmore: these include the pair of pier tables (no. 77) and framed drawings by the Princess Royal (including nos. 66–9). Some of Princess Augusta's 'bedchamber furniture and other effects removed from a Mansion' were sold at Christie's, London, on 6 April 1841. This may have included unwanted furniture from both Frogmore and Clarence House, the Princess's London home.

The Princess had sent tokens of remembrance to members of her family shortly before her death and her remaining possessions, of which no list survives, were divided among her surviving siblings (Stuart 1939, p. 135). Her books at Frogmore and Clarence House, valued by Christie's on 1 March 1841 at £1,327, were presumably similarly dispersed (RA VIC/Add. R 55). A number of fans associated with Princess Augusta entered the collection of Queen Victoria (see nos. 463–5); it is probable that the Duke of Sussex presented these to his niece from his late sister's collection. Queen Charlotte's lace fan (no. 461), given by the Duke of Sussex to Queen Victoria in 1841, may share this provenance.

Soon after Princess Augusta's death her brother, Ernest Augustus, King of Hanover, informed her executors that he was 'disposed to purchase the whole of the Jewels and Plate rather than that any part thereof should pass out of the Family' (RA VIC/Add. R 53). On 9 February 1841 the King wrote to Sir Francis Watson that he had 'had a long letter from the Duke of Sussex, who informs me . . . a certain Quantity of Diamonds, Guilt plate & Pictures she had bequeathed to me and my Son, which will be delivered to Your Care at St James's. That there was a small Service of Plate composed of that which we as Children had always eat off in the Nursery which Garards had offered 2000£, this I naturally cannot permit to be sold, and authorize You to purchase for me' (RA VIC/Add. A 31/847). The King was sent several boxes of the Princess's plate in April 1841 (RA VIC/Add. R 57). This may explain how plate from the collection of Queen Charlotte entered the Cumberland collection (see nos. 370, 378, 379, 382).

Princess Sophia (1777–1848)

Princess Sophia, the fifth daughter, died intestate in her house, Vicarage Place, Kensington, on 27 May 1848. The Princess, who never married, had amassed a considerable collection of jewels, plate, bibelots and furniture which included items selected in December 1818, together with other family pieces inherited from her deceased siblings.

The Princess's executors divided her possessions into three groups, each of which was valued separately: the diamonds, jewels, gold, silver and *objets de vertu* (valued by Garrard: £6,728 2s 6d); the 'Buhl Furniture, China etc.' (valued by Mr Owen: £7,188 12s); and the remaining household furniture, wine, pictures, prints and books (valued by Christie's: £1,998 15s. RA VIC/Add. R 77).

Garrard's twenty-page probate inventory of the Princess's jewels, gold, silver and *objets de vertu* was completed on 23 June 1848 (RA VIC/Add. R 74). Although the objects' provenances are not included, several pieces which subsequently re-entered the Royal Collection are clearly recognisable. These include the amethyst snuff box which may have belonged to Queen Charlotte (no. 394) and the silver filigree rattle given to George IV when a child, which Princess Sophia had inherited from Princess Augusta (no. 385). Garrard's bill for completing the inventory included the cost of dividing the contents into four portions (RA VIC/Add. R 75). This suggests that the objects were to be given to Princess Sophia's three surviving siblings: Princess Mary, the Duke of Cambridge, and the King of Hanover, and a fourth party – probably either Prince George (later 2nd Duke) of Cambridge or Queen Victoria. Princess Mary received in her portion the amethyst box and the filigree rattle, which she subsequently presented to Queen Victoria for use in her royal nursery (no. 385). The two rings which belonged to Queen Charlotte, presented to Queen Victoria by Princess Mary in 1849, may have been among the 210 finger rings listed in Princess Sophia's inventory (see nos. 445, 446). A selection of the Princess's household plate was 'divided among the family' and the remainder was sold by Garrard in November 1848 for £1,012 17s 6d (RA VIC/Add. R 81). The probate inventory compiled by Mr Owen of the Princess's 'Buhl furniture, China etc.' does not appear to survive; however it seems likely that these items were similarly shared out among the family.

Vicarage Place was sold on 12 December 1848 and its remaining household furnishings, together with a few paintings, drawings and 'a small parcel of port, sherry and Madeira', were sold by Christie's on 14 and 15 December 1848. Princess Sophia's library was sold at Christie's on 14–17 February and 26 March 1849.

Princess Mary, Duchess of Gloucester (1776–1857)

Princess Mary, the fourth daughter and last surviving child of George III and Queen Charlotte, died aged 81 on 30 April 1857. In 1816 she had married her first cousin, William, Duke of Gloucester; the marriage was childless. The Princess's nephew George, 2nd Duke of Cambridge, who 'loved her as a second mother', subsequently described her 'beautiful Will, not anybody forgotten, and her kindly feelings of charity expressed throughout all quite beautifully' (St Aubyn 1963, p. 124).

The 2nd Duke of Cambridge (whose father, the 1st Duke, had died in 1850) was named as the Princess's principal heir and therefore inherited the Princess's London home – Gloucester House – together with her extensive collection of pictures, jewels, bibelots, furniture and so on. This collection contained not only many of the items 'bought in' by the Princess from her mother's sale but also many other family things inherited from her deceased siblings (e.g. no. 269). Therefore a considerable number of Queen Charlotte's possessions which had passed to her daughters entered the Cambridge collection under the terms of Princess Mary's will.

Although the 2nd Duke of Cambridge was the Princess's chief heir, her detailed will made numerous specific bequests to other members of her family: Queen Victoria received a number of family paintings, jewels and miniatures. These included the full-length portraits of George III and Queen Charlotte by Gainsborough Dupont which had been given to the Princess by George IV, and the portraits of Princess Sophia and a dog by Reynolds, of Princess Sophia Matilda of Gloucester by Beechey, and of the Duke of York surrounded by his friends (Millar 1969, nos. 808–9, 1016, 662, 689), together with '6 Gilt Frames containing Miniature Pictures of most of the Royal Family' (including nos. 24, 28, 31).

Other beneficiaries included Prince Albert, the Duchess of Kent, Queen Victoria's children, the King of Hanover and his family, and the Hereditary Duke of Mecklenburg-Strelitz. Included in the Princess Royal's bequest were Princess Mary's pearl earrings 'which my father [George III] gave me'. Princess Louise received 'a bracelet of my brothers and sister's hair set in diamonds these diamonds are those which made my mother's hoop ring'. The King of Hanover received 'an ornamental Berlin China Vase . . . given to my mother by the late Queen of Prussia' and 'a box containing china which was given to my mother by her brother Charles Duke of Mecklenburg-Strelitz'.

Together with several items of jewellery, Princess Mary Adelaide of Cambridge (Princess Mary's niece) received the amethyst box which had been Princess Sophia's (no. 394). A number of paintings and works of art were specifically bequeathed to the Duke of Cambridge although as the residuary legatee he would have received the remainder of the Princess's estate not otherwise willed away. These included 'a black and gold trunk and stand belonging to my Mother . . . which stands in the front drawing room at Gloucester House . . . the gold Tooth pick case that belonged to my mother' and pictures by Batoni of Princess Sophia Matilda of Gloucester with a lion, and of Edward, Duke of York.

QUEEN CHARLOTTE'S SONS

With the exception of the hereditary jewels bequeathed to George IV (see above), Queen Charlotte made no provision for her sons in her will. However it is known that some of her possessions entered the collections of the Dukes of York and Sussex, because they appear in the posthumous sales of their effects. It is likely that the Queen's other sons similarly acquired mementoes from their mother's collection.

Frederick, Duke of York (1763–1827)

The Queen's second son, the Duke of York, died on 5 January 1827 leaving considerable debts. In 1791 he had married Princess Frederica of Prussia (died 1820); the marriage was childless. The Duke's extensive collection of plate, furniture, porcelain, jewels, trinkets and arms and armour, which in many ways paralleled his mother's, was sold at Christie's between February and May 1827. Two silver-gilt dishes bearing Queen Charlotte's cipher were sold on 22 March 1827 (lot 6). It is likely that other items in the Duke's collection had formerly been the Queen's. The dishes were purchased, together with other items, by the Duke of Sussex. Princess Sophia purchased several pieces of Boulle furniture from her brother's sale.

Augustus, Duke of Sussex (1773–1843)

The Queen's sixth son, the Duke of Sussex, died on 21 April 1843. He had married twice, both times in contravention of the Royal Marriages Act, and was survived by his second wife (the Duchess of Inverness) and by two children. He had amassed considerable debts and his vast collection was sold at Christie's in a series of sales in June and July 1843, July 1845 and April and May 1846. The residue was sold in 1853.

Various items from the collection of Queen Charlotte were included in the sales: a seal bearing her cipher (28 June 1843, lot 410); a satinstone and lapis lazuli box (29 June 1843, lot 535); an enamelled box (29 June 1843, lot 541); and a box containing 124 mother-of-pearl counters bearing the Queen's cipher (24 July 1845, lot 177; see nos. 407, 408). It is not known whether the Duke purchased these pieces from his mother's sale or inherited them from the estate of Princess Augusta (see above). The sales also included a number of pieces said to have belonged to George III, and pieces from the collections of the Dukes of Kent and York, who had died in 1820 and 1827 respectively.

Adolphus, Duke of Cambridge (1774–1850) and the Cambridge collection

Prince Adolphus, Duke of Cambridge, the Queen's seventh son, died on 8 July 1850. His estate passed to his wife Augusta and after her death in 1889 to their son George, 2nd Duke of Cambridge (1819–1904). Only a few items passed to their daughters Augusta (Grand Duchess of Mecklenburg-Strelitz) and Mary Adelaide (later Duchess of Teck; Queen Mary's mother). The 1st Duke's collection no doubt contained many family pieces inherited from his siblings. The Cambridge collection was certainly considerably enriched with such pieces in 1857 when the 2nd Duke became the principal legatee of the estate of his aunt, Princess Mary (see above).

Both Queen Victoria and Queen Mary recognised the importance of the Cambridge collection. In 1893, the future King George V and Queen Mary received the watch with George III's cipher (no. 296) as a wedding present from the Duke. But Queen Mary was frustrated by the lack of inventories and information about such an important collection of family things: 'Oh! Dear, Oh! Dear if only I could find the history of all of these things, how interesting it would be', she wrote to her Aunt Augusta (Pope-Hennessy 1959, p. 412). Despite promising Queen Victoria that he would leave his collection to the crown, the 2nd Duke of Cambridge's will directed, to Queen Mary's dismay, that it should be sold and the proceeds divided between his two youngest illegitimate sons. However, he did bequeath 'certain family pictures list of which I have made . . . to HRH The Princess of Wales [Queen Mary] and her three Brothers . . . to be equally divided between them'. He also directed that 'many other pictures, portraits and miniatures some of which may be of interest' should be offered to members of the family at a price agreed by his executors. Other family pieces passed to the Duke's sons: the second son, Rear-Admiral Sir Adolphus FitzGeorge (1846–1922), bequeathed no. 71 to Queen Mary; the Sèvres tea and coffee service (no. 328) was acquired after the death of the third son, Sir Augustus FitzGeorge (1847–1933).

But the majority of the Cambridge collection was sold at Christie's in June 1904, following the Duke's death three months

earlier: *Silver and silver-gilt plate*, 6 and 7 June; *Porcelain, old French furniture, miniatures, snuff boxes and other objects of vertu*, 8 and 13 June; *Pictures* 11 June. In addition to acquiring items (including no. 267) by private treaty, Queen Mary also purchased numerous items, many of which had been Queen Charlotte's (nos. 52, 409, 467), at these sales. Queen Mary continued to acquire items formerly in the Cambridge collection as they appeared thereafter (nos. 25, 59, 367, 410).

Ernest, Duke of Cumberland (1771–1851) and the Cumberland, Brunswick and Hanover princely collections

Following the accession of Queen Victoria in 1837, the British and Hanoverian thrones divided. Queen Charlotte's fifth son (Queen Victoria's uncle Ernest, Duke of Cumberland) became King Ernest Augustus of Hanover. As head of the House of Hanover he claimed the hereditary jewels of George II as his inheritance. Following the King's death in 1851 this claim was successfully continued by his son, King George V of Hanover (1819–78), who was awarded the jewels in 1858 (see above).

Ernest Augustus also appears to have retained all of the plate which remained in Hanover at the time of his accession in 1837. This included many English pieces dating from the late seventeenth and eighteenth centuries, and the extensive dining service made for George III by Auguste in the 1770s and 1780s (see p. 327). It is also known that he acquired much of the plate from the estate of his sister Princess Augusta; this almost certainly included pieces from the collection of Queen Charlotte (see above). The King subsequently denoted his ownership of all these pieces by engraving them with the initials *EAF* for *Ernesti Augusti Fideicommissum* (the entailed estate of Ernest Augustus). The King's collection also included other 'family pieces' inherited from his deceased siblings.

King George V of Hanover, 2nd Duke of Cumberland, was deposed when the Prussians annexed Hanover in 1866. His son Ernest Augustus, 3rd Duke of Cumberland (1845–1923), succeeded his kinsman as Duke of Brunswick in 1884 but was impeached from reigning in 1885. In 1913, when his son (also Ernest Augustus, 1887–1953) married the Kaiser's daughter, he renounced his rights to the Duchy in favour of his son, who was then allowed to rule. A catalogue of the Duke of Brunswick's miniatures published in 1913 included many English pieces relating to the family of George III. The Duke of Brunswick was deposed in 1918. His father, the Duke of Cumberland, was deprived of his English honours in 1919. Following the father's death, much of the historic collection was sold. Tapestries from the collection of the late Duke of Brunswick were sold at Christie's, London, on 3 April 1924. Paintings from the same collection were sold by Paul and Hugo Helbing in Berlin, on 27–28 April 1928. In November 1924 Crichton Brothers included the 'Old English Royal Plate . . . formerly the property of the Late Duke of Cumberland' at a selling exhibition in their London showrooms; they sold other pieces from the same source both before and after the exhibition. Further silver and *objets de vertu* were sold at Sotheby's, London, on 29 November 1931. Pieces of 'Cumberland plate' are now dispersed throughout collections in Europe and the United States. Several items associated with Queen Charlotte have subsequently re-entered the Royal Collection (nos. 370, 378, 379, 382). The contents of Schloss Cumberland, the Austrian home of the exiled Duke, were sold by Karl v.d. Portem, Hanover, on 22–24 June 1938. Many pieces from the Brunswick collection were exhibited at the Victoria and Albert Museum in 1952. The remnants of the collection of the Kings of Hanover remain with their descendants, the Princes of Hanover, at Marienburg Castle, near Hanover.

Bibliography and abbreviations

Add. Cat.
Catalogue of additions to the King's Audience
Room, 1914 (typescript; RCIN 1115976)

Anderson 1795
A. Anderson, *A Narrative of the British
Embassy to China*, London

Angelo 1828
Reminiscences of Henry Angelo, 2 vols., London

Arbuthnot Journal
Journal of Mrs Arbuthnot, ed. F. Bamford and
the Duke of Wellington, 2 vols., London, 1950

Archer, Rowell and Skelton 1987
*Treasures from India: The Clive Collection at
Powis Castle*, eds. M. Archer, C. Rowell and
R. Skelton, London

Aspinall 1962–70
A. Aspinall, ed., *The Later Correspondence of
George III*, 5 vols., Cambridge

Attar 2002
K.E. Attar, 'More than a Mythologist: Jacob
Bryant as Book Collector', *The Library*, 7th
series, III, pp. 351–66

Baillie 1956
Britten's Old Clocks and Watches, 7th edn, ed.
G.H. Baillie *et al.*, London

Banks Letters
*The Banks Letters. A Calendar of the Manuscript
Correspondence of Sir Joseph Banks preserved in
the British Museum (Natural History)*, ed. W.R.
Dawson, London

Barber 2000
P. Barber, 'Royal geography. The development
and destiny of King George III's geographical
collections', unpublished paper

Barnard (F.) 1820
F.A. Barnard, *Bibliothecae Regiae Catalogus*,
5 vols., London

Barnard (H.) 1924
H. Barnard, *Chats on Wedgwood Ware*, London

Barr 1980
E. Barr, *George Wickes, 1698–1761*, London

Baylis 1998
S. Baylis, '"Absolute Magic": a portrait of
George III on glass by James Pearson',
Journal of Stained Glass, XXII, pp. 16–30

Bayne-Powell 1985
R. Bayne-Powell, *Catalogue of Portrait Miniatures
in the Fitzwilliam Museum, Cambridge*, Cambridge

Beach and Koch 1997
M.C. Beach and E. Koch, *King of the World.
The Padshahnama, An Imperial Mughal
Manuscript from the Royal Library, Windsor
Castle*, London and Washington (exh. cat.)

Bellotto 1991
Bernardo Bellotto, Verona e le città europee, ed.
S. Marinelli, Milan (exh. cat.)

Bellotto 2001
Bernardo Bellotto and the Capitals of Europe,
ed. E.P. Bowron, New Haven and London
(exh. cat.)

Bemrose 1898
W. Bemrose, *Bow, Chelsea and Derby Porcelain*,
London

Binney 1989
M. Binney, 'Schloss Favorite, Ludwigsburg',
Country Life, 6 July, pp. 104–9

Binns 1877
R.W. Binns, *A Century of Potting in the City
of Worcester, being the History of the Royal
Porcelain Works from 1751 to 1851*, 2nd edn,
London and Worcester

BL
British Library, London

Blunt 1945
A. Blunt, *The French Drawings in the Collection
of His Majesty The King at Windsor Castle*,
London

Blunt 1954
A. Blunt, *The Drawings of G.B. Castiglione
and Stefano della Bella in the Collection of
Her Majesty The Queen at Windsor Castle*,
London

Blunt and Cooke 1960
A. Blunt and H.L. Cooke, *The Roman
Drawings of the XVII and XVIII Centuries in
the Collection of Her Majesty The Queen at
Windsor Castle*, London

Blunt and Croft-Murray 1957
A. Blunt and E. Croft-Murray, *The Venetian
Drawings of the XVII and XVIII Centuries in
the Collection of Her Majesty The Queen at
Windsor Castle*, London

Boalch 1995
D.H. Boalch, *Makers of the Harpsichord and
Clavichord 1440–1840*, 3rd edn, Oxford

Bolton 1922
A.T. Bolton, *The Architecture of Robert and
James Adam*, 2 vols., London

Boswell 1826
J. Boswell, *The Life of Samuel Johnson, LLD*,
4 vols., London

BP Inv. 1825
An inventory of the household furniture at
Buckingham Palace taken May 2nd 1825
(MS; RCIN 1114747)

Brewer 1997
J. Brewer, *The Pleasures of the Imagination.
English Culture in the Eighteenth Century*,
London

Brooke 1972
J. Brooke, *King George III*, London

Brooke 1977
John Brooke, 'The Library of King George
III', *Yale University Library Gazette*, LII, no. 1,
pp. 33–45

Brown (D.) 1982
D.B. Brown, *Ashmolean Museum, Oxford:
Catalogue of the Collection of Drawings, IV,
The Earlier British Drawings*, Oxford

Brown (I.G.) 1992
I.G. Brown, *Monumental Reputation: Robert
Adam and the Emperor's Palace*, Edinburgh

Brown (I.G.) 1993
I.G. Brown, '"With an Uncommon
Splendour . . .": the Bindings of Robert
Adam's Ruins at Spalatro', *Apollo*, CXXXVII,
pp. 6–11

Brown (L.) 1980
L.A. Brown, *A Catalogue of British Historical
Medals 1760–1960*, I, London

Brown (L.) 2002
L.A. Brown, 'Queen Charlotte's Medal
for the Recovery of George III', *British
Numismatic Journal*, LXXII, pp. 183–4

Burney Diary
*Diary and Letters of Madame D'Arblay
(1778–1840)*, ed. Charlotte Barrett and
A. Dobson, 6 vols., London, 1904–5

Bury 1988
S. Bury, 'Queen Victoria and the Hanoverian
Claim to the Crown Jewels', *The International
Silver and Jewellery Fair and Seminar:
Handbook*, London, pp. 9–16

Butterfield 1957
H. Butterfield, *George III and the Historians*,
London

Canaletto 1980
Canaletto, Paintings and Drawings, ed.
O. Millar, London (exh. cat., The Queen's
Gallery)

Carlton House Inventories, vol. E
A list of furniture &c at Carlton House,
supplied by the Lord Chamberlain's
Department (MS; RCIN 1114764)

Carlton House Inventories, vol. H1
A list of furniture &c. which did belong to
Carlton House in the Years [*sic*] 1826
(MS; RCIN 1114768)

Carlton House Inventories, vol. J
A list of furniture remaining in the
Riding House Stores which did belong
to Carlton House in the year 1826
(MS; RCIN 1114759)

Cassiano 1993
The Paper Museum of Cassiano dal Pozzo,
Milan (exh. cat., British Museum, London)

CDP
The Paper Museum of Cassiano dal Pozzo: a Catalogue Raisonné. Drawings and Prints in the Royal Library at Windsor Castle, the British Museum, the Institut de France and other Collections, ed. F. Haskell, J. Montagu and A. MacGregor, 5 vols., London, 1996– (continuing)

CHAC
A catalogue of arms. The property of HRH The Prince of Wales at Carlton House, compiled by Benjamin Jutsham, late eighteenth century–1827, 7 vols. (MS; RCIN 1113358–65)

Chaloner Smith
J. Chaloner Smith, British Mezzotint Portraits, 5 vols., London, 1878–83

Chambers 1763
W. Chambers, Plans, Elevations, Sections and Perspective Views of the Gardens and Buildings at Kew, London

Chambers 1996
Sir William Chambers, Architect to George III, ed. J. Harris and M. Snodin, New Haven and London (exh. cat.)

Clayton 1995
M. Clayton, Poussin: Works on Paper. Drawings from the Collection of Her Majesty Queen Elizabeth II, London (exh. cat.)

Clifford 1978
T. Clifford, 'J.J. Spängler: A Virtuoso Swiss Modeller at Derby', Connoisseur, June, pp. 146–55

Clifford 1985
T. Clifford, 'The Chelsea–Derby Royal Family Groups', Burlington Magazine, CXXVII (supplement, September 1985), pp. 12–15

Clifford 1990
T. Clifford, 'Vulliamy Clocks and British Sculpture', Apollo, October, pp. 226–37

Cloake 1996
J. Cloake, Palaces and Parks of Richmond and Kew: II Richmond Lodge and the Kew Palaces, Chichester

Clutton and Daniels 1965
C. Clutton and E. Daniels, Watches, London

Coke Letters
The Letters and Journals of Lady Mary Coke, 4 vols., Edinburgh, 1889–96

Colley 1984
L. Colley, 'The Apotheosis of George III: Loyalty, Royalty and the British Nation 1760–1820', Past and Present, 102, pp. 94–129

Colley 1992
L. Colley, Britons. Forging the Nation 1707–1837, New Haven and London

Colvin 1968
H. Colvin, Royal Buildings, London

Conroy 2002
T. Conroy, Bookbinders' finishing tool makers 1780–1965, New Castle (Delaware) and Nottingham

Constable and Links 1989
W.G. Constable and J.G. Links, Canaletto, 2nd edn (reprinted), 2 vols., Oxford

Cook's Endeavour 1997
Captain Cook's Endeavour, Whitby (exh. cat.)

Corboz 1985
A. Corboz, Canaletto: Una Venezia immaginaria, 2 vols., Milan

Cornforth 1990
J. Cornforth, 'Frogmore House, Berkshire', Country Life, 16 August, pp. 46–51 and 23 August, pp. 42–5

Country House Lighting 1992
Country House Lighting 1660–1890, Leeds (exh. cat.)

Coxe 1799
W. Coxe, Anecdotes of George Frederick Handel, and John Christopher Smith, London

Crown Jewels 1998
The Crown Jewels, ed. C. Blair, 2 vols., London

Cust 1893
L. Cust, Catalogue of the Collection of Fans presented to the British Museum by Lady Charlotte Schreiber, London

Dale 1913
W. Dale, Tschudi the Harpsichord Maker, London

Daniels 1976
J. Daniels, Sebastiano Ricci, Hove

Dawson 1985
A. Dawson, 'Creamware, Cameos and Coffee Cans', Country Life, 5 September, pp. 638–40

Dawson 1995
A. Dawson, British Museum. Masterpieces of Wedgwood, rev. edn, London

De Bellaigue (G.) 1984
G. de Bellaigue, 'Huzza the King is Well!', Burlington Magazine, CXXVI, pp. 325–31

De Bellaigue (S.) 1998
S. de Bellaigue, 'Courts and History I. The Royal Archives Windsor Castle', Court Historian, III, pp. 11–21

De Quincey 1863
T. de Quincey, Autobiographical Sketches 1790–1803 (De Quincey's Works, XIV), Edinburgh

Desmond 1995
R. Desmond, Kew: The History of the Royal Botanic Gardens, London

De Tolnay 1960
C. de Tolnay, Michelangelo V. The Final Period, Princeton

Dimond and Taylor 1987
F. Dimond and R. Taylor, Crown and Camera. The Royal Family and Photography 1842–1910, London (exh. cat.)

DOEFM 1986
Dictionary of English Furniture Makers 1660–1840, ed. C. Gilbert and G. Beard, Leeds

Domenichino 1996
Domenichino 1581–1641, Milan (exh. cat.)

Ducret 1965
S. Ducret, Fürstenberg Porzellan, Brunswick, 3 vols.

Dyson 1983
A. Dyson, 'The Engraving and Printing of the "Holbein Heads"', The Library, 6th series, V, no. 3, pp. 223–36

Edwards 1964
R. Edwards, The Shorter Dictionary of English Furniture, London

Edwards and Jourdain 1955
R. Edwards and M. Jourdain, Georgian Cabinet-makers, c.1700–1800, 3rd edn, London

Eimer 1998
C. Eimer, The Pingo Family and Medal Making in Eighteenth-century Britain, London

Elizabeth 1990
'Ich schreibe, lese und male ohne Unterlass.' Elizabeth, englische Prinzessin und Landgräfin von Hessen Homburg (1770–1840) als Künstlerin und Sammlerin, ed. R. Mattausch-Schirmbeck and G. Brandler, Bad Homburg and Greiz (exh. cat.)

Enlightenment 2003
Enlightenment. Discovering the World in the Eighteenth Century, ed. K. Sloan with A. Burnett, London

Esdaile 1928
K.A. Esdaile, The Life and Works of Louis François Roubiliac, London

Farington Diary
The Diaries of Joseph Farington, ed. K. Garlick, A. Macintyre and K. Cave, 16 vols., London and New Haven, 1978–84 (Index vol., 1998)

Fleming 1958
J. Fleming, 'Cardinal Albani's Drawings at Windsor: Their Purchase by James Adam for George III', Connoisseur, CXLII, pp. 164–9

Fleming 1962
J. Fleming, Robert Adam and his Circle in Edinburgh and in Rome, London

Foot 1993
M. Foot, Studies in the History of Bookbinding, Aldershot

Forrer 1902–30
L. Forrer, Biographical Dictionary of Medallists, 8 vols., London

Fraser 1883
W. Fraser, The Chiefs of Grant, 3 vols. Edinburgh

Fürstenberg 1989
Weisses Gold aus Fürstenberg, Brunswick (exh. cat.)

Fusco, Fogelman and Stock 2000
P. Fusco, P. Fogelman and S. Stock, 'John Deare (1759–1798): A British Neo-classical Sculptor in Rome', The Sculpture Journal, IV, pp. 85–126

Garrard 1872
Garrard & Co., Descriptive Inventory of the Various Services of Plate, &c belonging to the Crown (privately printed; RCIN 1114696)

Garrard 1914
Garrard & Co., Descriptive Inventory of the Various Services of Plate, etc., at Windsor Castle and Buckingham Palace, belonging to the Crown, 3 vols. (MS and printed; RCIN 1048090–2)

George III 1974
George III, Collector and Patron, London (exh. cat., The Queen's Gallery)

Gilbert 1978
C. Gilbert, The Life and Work of Thomas Chippendale, 2 vols., London

Gilbert and Murdoch 1993
C. Gilbert and T. Murdoch, *John Channon and Brass-inlaid Furniture 1730–1760*, New Haven and London

Glanville 1991
P. Glanville, *A King's Feast: The Goldsmith and Royal Banqueting in the Eighteenth Century*, London (exh. cat.)

Glanville 2003
P. Glanville, 'A George III Silver Service at Waddesdon Manor', *Apollo*, CLVII, p. 29

Glenbervie 1928
The Diaries of Sylvester Douglas (Lord Glenbervie), ed. F. Bickley, 2 vols., London

Goodison 1966
N. Goodison, 'Clockmaker and Cabinet-maker', *Furniture History*, II, pp. 18–22

Goodison 1974
N. Goodison, *Ormolu: The Work of Matthew Boulton*, London

Goodison 2003
N. Goodison, *Matthew Boulton: Ormolu*, London

Gori 1767
A.F. Gori, *Dactyliotheca Smithiana*, 2 vols., Venice

Gosset 1888–9
M.H. Gosset, 'A Family of Modellers in Wax', *Proceedings of the Huguenot Society of London*, III, pp. 540–68

Gray 1894
J.M. Gray, *James and William Tassie; A Biography and Critical Sketch with a Catalogue of their Portrait Medallions*, London

Gray Correspondence
Correspondence of Thomas Gray, ed. P. Toynbee and L. Whibley, 3 vols., Oxford, 1935

Greville 1930
R. Fulke Greville, *Diaries*, ed. F. Bladon, London

Greville 1938
The Greville Memoirs 1814–1860, ed. L. Strachey and R. Fulford, 8 vols., London

Griffiths 1989
A. Griffiths, 'The Print Collection of Cassiano dal Pozzo', *Print Quarterly*, VI, pp. 2–10

Griffiths and Williams 1987
A. Griffiths and R. Williams, *The Departments of Prints and Drawings in the British Museum. User's Guide*, London

Grimwade 1956
A. Grimwade, 'Royal Toilet Services in Scandinavia', *Connoisseur*, CXXXV, p. 175

Grimwade 1974
A. Grimwade, *Rococo Silver 1727–1765*, London

Grimwade 1990
A. Grimwade, *London Goldsmiths 1697–1837*, 3rd edn, London

Guercino in Britain 1991
Guercino in Britain. Paintings from British Collections, ed. Burlington Magazine, London

GV Boxes
Inventory of snuff, patch and other boxes in the collections of Queen Victoria, King Edward VII and King George V, 6 vols., 1929–35 (typescript; RCIN 1112523, 1114513, 1114515–18)

Hagedorn 2001
B. Hagedorn, 'Die Lacktafeln der Prinzessin Elizabeth, Landgräfin von Hessen-Homburg', *Froschkönige und Dornröschen. Einblicke in die Staatlichen Schlösser und Gärten Hessen 2000/01*, pp. 151–6

Harcourt Papers
The Harcourt Papers, ed. E.W. Harcourt, 14 vols., 1880–1905

Harris (E.) 2001
E. Harris, *The Genius of Robert Adam, His Interiors*, New Haven and London

Harris (E.) and Savage 1990
E. Harris and N. Savage, *British Architectural Books and Writers 1556–1785*, Cambridge

Harris (J.) 1970
J. Harris, *Sir William Chambers, Knight of the Polar Star*, London

Harris (J.) 1993
J. Harris, 'From Buckingham House to Palace. The Box within the Box within the Box', *Apollo*, CXXXVIII, pp. 28–36

Harris (J.) 1997
J. Harris, ed. *Masterpieces of the J. Paul Getty Museum. Decorative Arts*, Los Angeles

Harris, De Bellaigue and Millar 1968
J. Harris, G. de Bellaigue and O. Millar, *Buckingham Palace*, London

Hart and Taylor 1998
A. Hart and E. Taylor, *Fans*, London

Hartmann 1986
P.W. Hartmann, 'Meisterwerke filigraner Schnitzkunst', *Die Kunst*, 12, pp. 918–23

Hartop 1995
C. Hartop, 'Henri Auguste: Royal Silversmith', *Christie's International Magazine*, XII, no. 2, p. 18

Harwood 1806
T. Harwood, *The History and Antiquities of the Church and City of Lichfield*, London

Hayden 1992
R. Hayden, *Mrs Delany and her Flower Collages*, new edn, London

Hedley 1975
O. Hedley, *Queen Charlotte*, London

Heinzl 1966
B. Heinzl, 'The Luti Collection: Towards a Reconstruction of a Seventeenth-century Roman Collection of Master Drawings', *Connoisseur*, CLXI, pp. 17–22

Hibbert 1998
C. Hibbert, *George III. A Personal History*, London

Hirst 1981
M. Hirst, *Sebastiano del Piombo*, Oxford

HMC
Historic Manuscripts Commission

Hobson 1905
R.L. Hobson, *Catalogue of the Collection of English Porcelain in the . . . British Museum*, London

Hodson 1988
Y. Hodson, 'Prince William, Royal Map Collector', *Map Collector*, XLIV, pp. 2–12

Hodson (forthcoming)
Y. Hodson, 'Thomas Sandby's View of the Encampment on Warley Common, 1778'

Hogg 1963
O.F.G. Hogg, *The Royal Arsenal*, 2 vols., London

Honour 1961
H. Honour, review of Blunt and Cooke 1960, in *Connoisseur*, CXLVIII, pp. 240–41

Hughes 1973
P. Hughes, 'The Williams-Wynn Silver in the National Museum of Wales', *Connoisseur*, CXLVIII, pp. 33–8

Huish 1821
R. Huish, *The Public and Private Life of His Late Excellent and Most Gracious Majesty George the Third*, London

Il Guercino 1991
Giovanni Francesco Barbieri, Il Guercino 1591–1666, Bologna (exh. cat.)

Ingamells 1997
J. Ingamells, *A Dictionary of British and Irish Travellers in Italy 1701–1800 compiled from the Brinsley Ford Archive*, New Haven and London

Inventory A
A catalogue of the drawings and prints as they are arranged in book cases [a compilation, providing crucial information on the drawings in George III's collection], c.1770–1840 (MS; RCIN 1155585)

ISTC
Incunabula short-title catalogue. British Library database, 1980– (ongoing)

Jackson-Stops 1993
G. Jackson-Stops, '"A Noble Simplicity". Pyne's Views of Buckingham House', *Apollo*, CXXXVIII, pp. 44–56

Jaffer 1999
A. Jaffer, 'Tipu Sultan, Warren Hastings and Queen Charlotte: The Mythology and Typology of Anglo-Indian Ivory Furniture', *Burlington Magazine*, CXLI, pp. 271–81

Jaffer 2001
A. Jaffer, *Furniture from British India and Ceylon. A Catalogue of the Collections in the Victoria and Albert Museum and the Peabody Essex Museum*, London

Jagger 1983
C. Jagger, *Royal Clocks*, London

Jamison 1952
C. Jamison, *The History of the Royal Hospital of St Katharine by the Tower of London*, Oxford

Johnson 1976
E.M. Johnson, *Francis Cotes*, Oxford

Jones 1885
Mrs Herbert [C. Rachel] Jones, *The Princess Charlotte of Wales: An Illustrated Monograph*, London

Joopien 1973
R. Joopien, *Philippe Jacques de Loutherbourg*, London (exh. cat.)

Jutsham II
Ledger of furniture &c received by Benjamin Jutsham, 23 June 1816–7 December 1829 (MS; RCIN 1112775)

Kennedy Diary
The diary of Lucy Kennedy, October 1793–July 1816 (MS; RCIN 1180580)

Kent 1791
N. Kent, Plan submitted . . . to His Majesty, upon the present state and future improvement, of the Great Park at Windsor, 12th March 1791 (MS; RCIN 1047476)

Kerslake 1977
J. Kerslake, *National Portrait Gallery. Early Georgian Portraits*, 2 vols., London

Kew House Inventory
Catalogue of His Majesty's pictures at Kew House [i.e. the Dutch House], *c*.1800–1805 (MS; RCIN 1112543–4)

Kew Library Catalogue 1780
A catalogue of His Majesty's Library at Kew 1780 (MS; RCIN 1028954)

Kew Library Catalogue 1785
A catalogue of his Majesty's Library at Kew 1785 (MS; RCIN 1028953)

King's College Archives
Catalogue of books bequeathed by Bryant [1805] (MS; King's College, Cambridge, Archives LIB/8)

King's Purchase 1993
[J. Roberts,] *A King's Purchase: King George III and the Collection of Consul Smith*, London (exh. cat., The Queen's Gallery)

King's Works
The History of the King's Works, ed. H.M. Colvin, 6 vols., 1963–73, London

Knox 1994
G. Knox, 'The Large New Testament Subjects painted by Marco and Sebastiano Ricci for Consul Smith in the Royal Collection', *Apollo*, September, pp. 17–25

Knox 1996
G. Knox, 'Consul Smith's Villa at Mogliano. Antonio Visentini and Francesco Zuccarelli', *Apollo*, June, pp. 31–8

Kowalczyk 2001
B.A. Kowalczyk, *Canaletto Prima Maniera*, Venice (exh. cat.)

Kozakiewicz 1972
S. Kozakiewicz, *Bernardo Bellotto*, 2 vols., London

Kurz 1988
O. Kurz, *Bolognese Drawings of the XVII and XVIII Centuries in the Collection of Her Majesty The Queen at Windsor Castle*, London, 1955; reprinted, with appendix by H. McBurney, Bologna

Laking 1905
G.F. Laking, *The Furniture of Windsor Castle*, London

Lansdale 1965
R. Lansdale, *Dr Charles Burney: a Literary Biography*, Oxford

Levey 1991
M. Levey, *The Later Italian Pictures in the Collection of Her Majesty The Queen*, 2nd edn, Cambridge

Linley Sisters 1988
Dulwich Picture Gallery. Paintings and their Context: II. A Nest of Nightingales. Thomas Gainsborough – The Linley Sisters, London (exh. cat.)

Lloyd (C.) 1994
C. Lloyd, *Gainsborough and Reynolds. Contrasts in Royal Patronage*, London (exh. cat., The Queen's Gallery)

Lloyd (C.) 1998
C. Lloyd, *The Quest for Albion*, London (exh. cat., The Queen's Gallery)

Lloyd (C.) and Remington 1996
C. Lloyd and V. Remington, *Masterpieces in Little. Portrait Miniatures from the Collection of Her Majesty Queen Elizabeth II*, London (exh. cat.)

Lloyd (S.) 1995
S. Lloyd, *Richard and Maria Cosway. Regency Artists of Taste and Fashion*, Edinburgh (exh. cat.)

Loche and Roethlisberger 1978
R. Loche and M. Roethlisberger, *L'Opera completa di Liotard*, Milan

Lomax 1999
J. Lomax, 'Royalty and Silver: The Role of the Jewel House in the Eighteenth Century', *The Silver Society Journal*, no. 11, Autumn, pp. 133–9

Losty 1982
J. Losty, *The Art of the Book in India*, London (exh. cat.)

Lybbe Powys 1899
Passages from the Diary of Mrs Philip Lybbe Powys, 1756–1808, ed. E.J. Climenson, London (reference is also made to the original MS: BL Add. 42160, ff. 19–22)

Lysons 1792–6
D. Lysons, *Environs of London*, 4 vols. London

Lysons 1806
D. and S. Lysons, *Magna Britannia (Berkshire)*, London

Macalpine and Hunter 1969
I. Macalpine and R. Hunter, *George III and the Mad-Business*, London

McBurney 1997
H. McBurney, *Mark Catesby's Natural History of America: the Watercolours from the Royal Library Windsor Castle*, London (exh. cat.)

McKechnie 1978
S. McKechnie, *British Silhouette Artists and their Work, 1760–1860*, London

Mahon and Turner 1989
D. Mahon and N. Turner, *The Drawings of Guercino in the Collection of Her Majesty The Queen at Windsor Castle*, Cambridge

Mallet 1969
J.V.G. Mallet, 'Rococo English Porcelain, a Study in Style', *Apollo*, XC, pp. 100–13

Marsden and Hardy 2001
J. Marsden and J. Hardy, '"O Fair Britannia Hail!" The "Most Superb" State Coach', *Apollo*, CLIII, no. 468, February, pp. 3–12

Military Maps Catalogue
Catalogue of military maps and plans (MS; RCIN 1151052)

Millar 1963
O. Millar, *The Tudor, Stuart and Early Georgian Pictures in the Collection of Her Majesty The Queen*, 2 vols., London

Millar 1967
O. Millar, *Zoffany and his Tribuna*, London

Millar 1969
O. Millar, *The Later Georgian Pictures in the Collection of Her Majesty The Queen*, 2 vols., London

Millar 1972
O. Millar, *The Age of Charles I*, London (exh. cat.)

Millar 1986
O. Millar, 'Documents for the History of Collecting: 2. George IV when Prince of Wales: His Debts to Artists and Craftsmen', *Burlington Magazine*, CXXVIII, pp. 586–92

Millar 1992
O. Millar, *The Victorian Pictures in the Collection of Her Majesty The Queen*, 2 vols., Cambridge

Moore 1985
A. Moore, *Norfolk and the Grand Tour*, Fakenham

Morassi 1926
A. Morassi, 'Un libro di disegni e due quadri di Sebastiano Ricci', *Cronache d'Arte*, III, pp. 256–73

Morrison 1993/4
S.L. Morrison, 'Records of a Bibliophile. The Catalogues of Consul Joseph Smith and some Aspects of his Collecting', *Book Collector*, XLIII, no. 1, pp. 27–58

Morton and Wess 1993
A.Q. Morton and J.A. Wess, *Public and Private Science: The King George III Collection*, Oxford

Mozart Letters 1986
The Letters of Mozart and his Family, ed. E. Anderson, London

Mrs Harcourt's Diary
'Mrs Harcourt's Diary of the Court of King George III', *Miscellanies of the Philobiblon Society*, XIII, London, 1871–2

Mudge 1799
T. Mudge the Younger, *A Description . . . of the Timekeeper invented by the Later Mr Thomas Mudge*, London

Murdoch 1985
T. Murdoch, 'Counties and Classics: The Gosset Family', *Country Life*, 9 May, pp. 1282–3

Nau 1966
E. Nau, *Lorenz Natter 1705–1763, Gemmenschneider und Medailleur*, Biberach

Neff 1995
E.B. Neff, *John Singleton Copley in England*, London

Neo-classicism 1972
The Age of Neo-classicism, London (exh. cat.)

Nixon 1978
H.M. Nixon, *Five Centuries of English Bookbinding*, London

Nixon and Foot 1992
H.M. Nixon and M. Foot, *The History of Decorated Bookbinding in England*, London

Northumberland 1926
The Diaries of a Duchess. Extracts from the Diaries of the First Duchess of Northumberland (1716–1776), ed. James Greig, London

Nugent 1768
T. Nugent, *Travels through Germany . . . with a Particular Account of the County of Mecklenburg*, 2 vols., London

O'Connell 2003
S. O'Connell, *London 1753*, London (exh. cat.)

Oppé 1947
A.P. Oppé, *The Drawings of Paul and Thomas Sandby in the Collection of His Majesty The King at Windsor Castle*, London

Oppé 1950
A.P. Oppé, *English Drawings, Stuart and Georgian Periods, in the Collection of His Majesty The King at Windsor Castle*, London

Orr 2001
C.C. Orr, 'Queen Charlotte as Patron: Some Intellectual and Social Contexts', *The Court Historian*, VI, no. 3, pp. 183–212

Oulton 1819
W.C. Oulton, *Authentic and Impartial Memoirs of her Late Majesty Charlotte, Queen of Great Britain and Ireland*, London

Owen 1995
F. Owen, 'Joshua Kirby (1716–74): A Biographical Sketch', *Gainsborough's House Review*, pp. 61–75

Paintin 1989
E. Paintin, *The King's Library*, London

Papendiek 1887
C.L.H. Papendiek, *Court and Private Life in the Time of Queen Charlotte: Being the Journals of Mrs. Papendiek, Assistant-Keeper of the Wardrobe and Reader to Her Majesty*, ed. Mrs. Vernon Delves Broughton, 2 vols., London

Pares 1953
R. Pares, *King George III and the Politicians*, Oxford

Parker 1983
K. Parker, *The Drawings of Hans Holbein in the Collection of Her Majesty The Queen at Windsor Castle*, London, 1945; reprinted, with an appendix by S. Foister, New York and London

Parker 1990
K. Parker, *The Drawings of Antonio Canaletto in the Collection of His Majesty The King at Windsor Castle*, London, 1948; reprinted, with an appendix by C. Crawley, Bologna

Patterson 1996
S. Patterson, 'The Royal Library at Windsor Castle', *El Libro Antigua Espanol III: El libro en Palacio y otros estudios bibliograficos*, pp. 201–23

Paulson 1975
R. Paulson, *Emblem and Expression: Meaning in English Art of the Eighteenth Century*, London

Pennington 1809
A series of letters between Mrs Elizabeth Carter and Miss Catherine Talbot, ed. M. Pennington, 4 vols., London

Percy and Jackson-Stops 1974
V. Percy and G. Jackson-Stops, '"Exquisite taste and tawdry ornament". The Travel Journals of the 1st Duchess of Northumberland – II', *Country Life*, 7 February, pp. 250–52

Pictorial Inventory
George IV inventory of clocks etc [drawn and painted records of works of art in George IV's collection, particularly at Carlton House, made for the King in the late 1820s], 3 vols. (MS; RCIN 933559–61)

Plomp (forthcoming)
M. Plomp, 'Acquisitions for the English Royal Collection from the 1759 Abraham van Broyel Sale', forthcoming

Pointon 2001
M. Pointon, '"Surrounded with Brilliants": Miniature Portraits in Eighteenth-century England', *The Art Bulletin*, LXXXIII, pp. 48–71

Pollard 1970
G. Pollard, 'Matthew Boulton and Conrad Heinrich Küchler', *Numismatic Chronicle*, 7th series, X, pp. 259–318

Pope-Hennessy 1948
J. Pope-Hennessy, *The Drawings of Domenichino in the Collection of His Majesty The King at Windsor Castle*, London

Pope-Hennessy 1959
J. Pope-Hennessy, *Queen Mary*, London

Pope-Hennessy 1964
J. Pope-Hennessy, *Catalogue of Italian Sculpture in the Victoria and Albert Museum*, 2 vols., London

Popham and Wilde 1984
A.E. Popham and J. Wilde, *The Italian Drawings of the XV and XVI Centuries in the Collection of His Majesty The King at Windsor Castle*, London 1949; reprinted, with an appendix by R. Wood, New York and London

Porcellane di Napoli 1986
Le Porcellane dei Borbone di Napoli, Naples (exh. cat.)

Pradère 1989
A. Pradère, *Les Ebénistes Français de Louis XIV à la Révolution*, Paris

Princes as Patrons 1998
Princes as Patrons. The Art Collections of the Princes of Wales from the Renaissance to the Present Day, ed. M. Evans, London (exh. cat.)

PRO
Public Record Office, Kew

Prochaska 1995
F. Prochaska, *Royal Bounty. The Making of a Welfare Monarchy*, New Haven and London

Pyne 1819
W.H. Pyne, *The History of the Royal Residences of Windsor Castle, St James's Palace, Carlton House, Kensington Palace, Hampton Court, Buckingham House, and Frogmore*, 3 vols., London

QG Treasures 1988
Treasures from the Royal Collection, London (exh. cat., The Queen's Gallery)

QMB
Catalogue of Bibelots, Miniatures and other valuables, the property of H.M. Queen Mary, I, covering the period 1893–1920 (RCIN 1114504a); II, 1921–31 (RCIN 1114507); III, 1932–37 (RCIN 1114508a); IV, 1938–45 (RCIN 1114509). A series of four privately printed catalogues 'Printed and arranged specially for me [Queen Mary] at the Victoria and Albert Museum South Kensington under the direction of Sir Cecil Harcourt Smith', 1920, 1932, 1939 and 1946

QMF
Catalogue of Queen Mary's fans (in the fan screen) of historical interest, 1921, with later additions (illustrated typescript; RA GV/CC 74)

QMPP
Catalogue of miniatures, jewels and other valuables, the property of HM Queen Mary, illustrated typescript, 11 vols.: I, 1912 (RCIN 1114193); II, 1913 (RCIN 1114194); III, 1922 (RCIN 1114195); IV, 1925 (RCIN 1114196); V, 1929 (RCIN 1114197); VI, 1931 (RCIN 1114198); VII, 1933 (RCIN 1114199); VIII, 1936 (RCIN 1114500); IX, 1936–8 (RCIN 1114501); X, 1938–45 (RCIN 1114502); XI, 1946–8 (RCIN 1114503)

QVIJ
Inventory of jewels &c the property of Her Majesty The Queen [Victoria], 1896 (MS; RCIN 1114856)

R&S
Rings and seals, 1912 (illustrated typescript; RCIN 1114856)

RA
Royal Archives, Windsor Castle

Ramsden 1958
C. Ramsden, 'Bookbinders to George III and his Immediate Descendants and Collaterals', *The Library*, 5th series, XIII, pp. 186–93

RB Impressions
Volume of ink impressions of blocks, tools, rolls and pallets in the Royal Bindery, Windsor Castle, 1940 (RCIN 1101140.a)

RCIN
Royal Collection Inventory Number

Reilly 1989
R. Reilly, *Wedgwood*, 2 vols., London

Reilly and Savage 1973
R. Reilly and G. Savage, *Wedgwood: the Portrait Medallions*, London

Reynolds 1980
G. Reynolds, *Wallace Collection: Catalogue of Miniatures*, London

Reynolds 1988
G. Reynolds, *English Portrait Miniatures*, rev. edn, Cambridge

Rhead 1910
G.W. Woolliscroft Rhead, *The History of the Fan*, London

Ribeiro 1995
A. Ribeiro, *The Art of Dress. Fashion in England and France 1750 to 1820*, New Haven and London

RL
Royal Library Inventory Number (for drawings and watercolours in the Royal Collection)

Roberts (H.) 1990a
H. Roberts, 'Soe Thinn the Wood', *Furniture History*, XXVI, pp. 168–71

Roberts (H.) 1990b
H. Roberts, 'Metamorphoses in Wood. Royal Library Furniture in the Eighteenth and Nineteenth Centuries', *Apollo*, CXXXI, pp. 382–90

Roberts (H.) 1995
H. Roberts, 'So Beautiful a Style', *Country Life*, 23 November, pp. 58–9

Roberts (H.) 1997
H. Roberts, 'A Neo-classical Episode at Windsor', *Furniture History*, XXXIII, pp. 177–87

Roberts (H.) 2001
H. Roberts, *For the King's Pleasure: George IV's Apartments at Windsor Castle*, London

Roberts (H.) 2002
H. Roberts, 'Collecting French Furniture before George IV', *Apollo*, CLX, pp. 3–9

Roberts (H.) 2003
H. Roberts, 'James Wyatt's Furniture for the Palace of Westminster', *Furniture History*, XXXIX, pp. 98–108

Roberts (J.) 1976–7
J. Roberts, 'Henry Emlyn's Restoration of St George's Chapel', *Report of the Society of the Friends of St George's and the Descendants of the Knights of the Garter*, V, no. 8, pp. 331–8

Roberts (J.) 1987
J. Roberts, *Royal Artists from Mary Queen of Scots to the Present Day*, London

Roberts (J.) 1993
J. Roberts, *Holbein and the Court of Henry VIII. Drawings and Miniatures from the Royal Library, Windsor Castle*, Edinburgh (exh. cat.)

Roberts (J.) 1995
J. Roberts, *Views of Windsor. Watercolours by Thomas and Paul Sandby from the Collection of Her Majesty Queen Elizabeth II*, London (exh. cat.)

Roberts (J.) 1997
J. Roberts, *Royal Landscape. The Gardens and Parks of Windsor*, New Haven and London

Robertson 1897
A. Robertson, *Letters and Papers of Andrew Robertson*, ed. E. Robertson, 2nd edn, London

Rococo 1984
Rococo. Art and Design in Hogarth's England, ed. M. Snodin, London (exh. cat.)

Ronfort 1984
J.-N. Ronfort, 'Art et Horlogerie à l'époque de Ferdinand Berthoud: du rocaille au néo-classicisme', in *Ferdinand Berthoud 1727–1807, Horloger Mécanicien du Roi et de la Marine*, La Chaux-de-Fonds, pp. 103–24

Rorschach 1990
K. Rorschach, 'Frederick, Prince of Wales (1709–1751) as Collector and Patron', *Walpole Society*, LV (1989–90), pp. 1–76

Rosenberg and Prat 1994
P. Rosenberg and L.-A. Prat, *Nicolas Poussin 1594–1665. Catalogue raisonné des dessins*, 2 vols., Milan

Rowan 2003
A. Rowan, *'Bob the Roman'. Heroic Antiquity & the Architecture of Robert Adam*, London (exh. cat.)

Royal Insignia 1996
S. Patterson, *Royal Insignia. British and Foreign Orders of Chivalry from the Royal Collection*, London (exh. cat.)

Royal Miscellany 1990
A Royal Miscellany from the Royal Library, Windsor Castle, London (exh. cat., The Queen's Gallery)

Royal Treasures 2002
Royal Treasures: A Golden Jubilee Celebration, ed. J. Roberts, London (exh. cat., The Queen's Gallery)

Rücker and Stearn 1982
E. Rücker and W. Stearn, *Maria Sibylla Merian in Surinam*, London

Rundells 1832
Inventories of plate belonging to the crown, compiled by Rundells (printed and MS; RCIN 1114698)

Rundells 1837
An inventory of sundry articles of jewellery &c in the strong closet in Windsor Castle belonging to Her Majesty (MS; RCIN 1114746)

Russell 1987
F. Russell, 'King George III's Picture Hang at Buckingham House', *Burlington Magazine*, CXXIX, pp. 524–31

Russell (forthcoming)
F. Russell, *John, 3rd Earl of Bute: Patron and Collector*, London

Russett 2001
A. Russett, *Dominic Serres R.A. War Artist to the Navy*, Woodbridge

Rutgers 2002
J. Rutgers, 'Notes on Rembrandt in Venice. Paintings, Drawings and Prints in the Sagredo Collection', in *'Aux Quatre Vents'. A Festschrift for Bert W. Meijer*, ed. A. Boschloo et al., Florence

St Aubyn 1963
G. St Aubyn, *The Royal George*, London

St John Hope 1913
W.H. St John Hope, *Windsor Castle*, 2 vols., London

Sandby 1985
The Art of Paul Sandby, New Haven (exh. cat.)

Sandon 1978
H. Sandon, *Flight and Barr Worcester Porcelain 1783–1840*, Woodbridge

Sandon 1993
J. Sandon, *The Dictionary of Worcester Porcelain. Vol. I: 1751–1851*, Woodbridge

Sandon 1996
J. Sandon, *The Dictionary of Worcester Porcelain*, Woodbridge

Savill 1988
R. Savill, *The Wallace Collection. Catalogue of Sèvres Porcelain*, 3 vols., London

Scarisbrick 1981
D. Scarisbrick, 'With Heart and Hand: Royal Wedding Jewellery – I', *Country Life*, 30 July, pp. 321–3

Scarisbrick 1994
D. Scarisbrick, *Jewellery in Britain 1066–1837*, Norwich

Scarpa Sonino 1991
A. Scarpa Sonino, *Marco Ricci*, Milan

Schaffers-Bodenhausen and Tiethoff-Spliethoff 1993
K. Schaffers-Bodenhausen and M. Tiethoff-Spliethoff, *The Portrait Miniatures in the Collection of the House of Orange-Nassau*, Zwolle

Sèvres 1979
Sèvres Porcelaine from the Royal Collection, London (exh. cat., The Queen's Gallery)

Seyller 1997
J. Seyller, 'The Inspection and Valuation of Manuscripts in the Imperial Mughal Library', *Artibus Asiae*, LVII, pp. 243–349

Shearman 1972
J. Shearman, *Raphael's Cartoons in the Collection of Her Majesty the Queen and the Tapestries for the Sistine Chapel*, London

Shearman 1983
J. Shearman, *The Early Italian Pictures in the Collection of Her Majesty the Queen*, Cambridge

Shefrin 2003
J. Shefrin, *Such Constant Affectionate Care. Lady Charlotte Finch, Royal Governess, and the Children of George III*, Los Angeles

Shrub 1965
D. Shrub, 'The Vile Problem', *Victoria and Albert Museum Bulletin*, IV, pp. 26–35

Simon 1994
J. Simon, 'Frame Studies II: Allan Ramsay and Picture Frames', *Burlington Magazine*, CXXXVI, pp. 444–55

Singer 1992
A. Singer, *The Lion and the Dragon. The Story of the First British Embassy to the Emperor Qianlong in Peking, 1792–1794*, London

Skelton 1985
R. Skelton, 'Europe and India', in *Europa und die Kunst des Islam 15. bis 18, Jahrhundert*, ed. E. Liskar, Vienna, pp. 33–42

Sloan 2000
K. Sloan, *'A Noble Art': Amateur Artists and Drawing Masters c.1600–1800*, London (exh. cat.)

Smart 1992
A. Smart, *Allan Ramsay. Painter, Essayist and Man of Enlightenment*, New Haven and London

Smart and Ingamells 1999
A. Smart and J. Ingamells, *Allan Ramsay. A Complete Catalogue of his Paintings*, New Haven and London

Smith 1931
  H.C. Smith, *Buckingham Palace, its Furniture,
  Decoration and History*, London
Snowman 1990
  K. Snowman, *Eighteenth-century Gold Boxes
  of Europe*, 2nd edn, Woodbridge
Sophie in London 1786
  *Sophie in London 1786 being the Diary of Sophie
  v. la Roche*, ed. C. Williams, London, 1933
Spike 1986
  J.T. Spike, *Giuseppe Maria Crespi and the
  Emergence of Genre Painting in Italy*, Fort
  Worth (exh. cat.)
Stanton 1935
  G.R. Stanton, 'Ivory Miniature Sculpture',
  Connoisseur, LXXXVI, pp. 210–12
Stetten 1779
  P. von Geheimrath Stetten, *Kunst- Gewerb-
  und Handwerks Geschichte der Reichs-stadt
  Augsburg*, Augsburg
Stuart 1939
  D.M. Stuart, *The Daughters of George III*, London
Swain 1994
  M. Swain, *Embroidered Georgian Pictures*,
  Buckingham
Symonds 1951
  R.W. Symonds, *Thomas Tompion – His Life
  and Work*, London
Tait 1993
  A.Tait, *Robert Adam, Drawings and Imagination*,
  Cambridge
Thornton and Rieder 1972
  P. Thornton and W. Rieder, 'Pierre Langlois,
  Ebéniste: III', *Connoisseur*, March, pp. 176–87
Treasure Houses 1985
  *The Treasure Houses of Britain. Five Hundred
  Years of Private Patronage and Art Collecting*,
  ed. G. Jackson-Stops, Washington (exh. cat.)
Turner 1967
  G. L'E. Turner, 'The Auction Sales of the
  Earl of Bute's Instruments, 1793', *Annals of
  Science*, XXIII, no. 3, pp. 213–42
Turner 1992
  G. L'E. Turner, 'Queen Charlotte's
  Protractor and Joshua Kirby', *Bulletin of the
  Scientific Instrument Society*, no. 35, pp. 23–4
Vardy 1744
  J. Vardy, *Some Designs of Mr Inigo Jones and
  Mr William Kent*, London
Venuti 1787
  D. Venuti, *Interpretation des Peintures Dessinés
  sur un Service de Table Travaillé d'aprés la bosse
  dans la Royale Fabrique de Porcellaine par Order
  de sa Majesté le Roi des Deux Siciles*, Naples
Vertue Notebooks
  The Notebooks of George Vertue, I–VI, *Walpole
  Society*, XVIII, XX, XXII, XXIV, XXVI,
  XXX, 1930–55
Vivian 1971
  F. Vivian, *Il Console Smith mercante e
  collezionista*, Vicenza
Vivian 1989
  F. Vivian, *The Consul Smith Collection.
  Masterpieces of Italian Drawing from the Royal
  Library, Windsor Castle. Raphael to Canaletto*,
  Munich (exh. cat.)

Von Erffa and Staley 1986
  H. von Erffa and A. Staley, *The Paintings of
  Benjamin West*, New Haven and London
Waley 1992
  M.I. Waley, 'Islamic Manuscripts in the Royal
  Collection: A Concise Catalogue', *Manuscripts
  of the Middle East*, VI
Walker 1992
  R. Walker, *The Eighteenth and Early
  Nineteenth-century Miniatures in the Collection
  of Her Majesty The Queen*, Cambridge
Walker 1997
  R. Walker, *Miniatures. A Selection of Miniatures
  in the Ashmolean Museum, Oxford*, Oxford
Walker 1999
  R. Walker, 'Henry Bone's Pencil Drawings in
  the National Portrait Gallery', *Walpole Society*,
  LXI, pp. 305–67
Walpole 1928
  H. Walpole, 'Journal of Visits to Country Seats,
  &c.', ed. P. Toynbee, *Walpole Society*, XVI, pp. 9–80
Walpole Correspondence
  *The Yale Edition of Horace Walpole's Corre-
  spondence*, ed. W.S. Lewis, 48 vols., 1937–83
Walton 1975
  K.-M. Walton, 'Queen Charlotte's Dressing
  Table', *Furniture History*, XI, pp. 112–13
Waterfield 1991
  G. Waterfield, *Palaces of Art: Art Galleries in
  Britain 1790–1990*, London (exh. cat.)
Watkin 1984
  D. Watkin, *The Royal Interiors of Regency
  England*, London and Melbourne
Watson 1960
  J. Steven Watson, *The Reign of George III
  1760–1815*, Oxford
WCCI
  Windsor Castle inventory: clocks and
  candelabra, 1876–, 2 vols. (MS; RCIN
  1101200–1)
WC Fans
  Catalogue of fans in the Royal Collection,
  Windsor Castle, 1926 (RCIN 1126906)
WCSI
  Windsor Castle inventory: statuary, busts &c,
  1874– (MS; RCIN 1101202)
Webster 1976
  M. Webster, *Johan Zoffany 1733–1810*,
  London (exh. cat.)
Wedgwood 1995
  The Genius of Wedgwood, London (exh. cat.)
Wedgwood Letters 1965
  The Selected Letters of Josiah Wedgwood, ed.
  A. Finer and G. Savage, London
Welcker 1979
  C.J. Welcker, *Hendrick Avercamp en Barent
  Avercamp*, 2nd edn, Zwolle
White 1982
  C. White, *The Dutch Pictures in the Collection
  of Her Majesty The Queen*, Cambridge
White and Crawley 1994
  C. White and C. Crawley, *The Dutch and
  Flemish Drawings of the Fifteenth to the
  Early Nineteenth Centuries in the Collection of
  Her Majesty The Queen at Windsor Castle*,
  Cambridge

Whitley 1928
  W.T. Whitley, *Artists and their Friends in
  England*, 2 vols., London
Wiese 1988
  W. Wiese, *Johannes Klinckerfuss, Ein
  Württenbergischer Ebenist (1771–1831)*,
  Sigmaringen
William IV Clock Inventory
  List of clocks belonging to His Majesty taken
  by command of His Majesty William the 4th
  by B.L. Vulliamy, 1835 (MS; RCIN 1114929)
Williams 1971
  P. Williams, 'The Earl of Wemyss's
  Claviorgan and its Context in Eighteenth-
  century England', in *Keyboard Instruments:
  Studies in Keyboard organology 1500–1800*,
  ed. E. Ripin, New York, pp. 77–87
Williamson 1914
  G.C. Williamson, *Catalogue of a Collection of
  Miniatures. The Property of His Royal Highness
  Prince Ernest Augustus William Adolphus
  George Frederick, Duke of Cumberland, Duke of
  Brunswick-Lüneburg, K.G., G.C.H.*, London
Williamson and Engleheart 1902
  G.C. Williamson and H.L.D. Engleheart,
  *George Engleheart 1750–1829 Miniature
  Painter to George III*, London
Wilson 1992
  J.H. Wilson, The life and work of John
  Hoppner, Unpublished PhD Dissertation,
  Courtauld Institute of Art, London
Windsor Library Catalogue 1780
  A catalogue of His Majesty's library at
  Windsor 1780; revised 1812; by F.A. Barnard
  (MS; RCIN 1028949.a)
Winter 1948
  C. Winter, 'The British School of Miniature
  Portrait Painters', *Proceedings of the British
  Academy*, XXXIV, pp. 119–37
Winterbottom 2002
  M. Winterbottom, '"Such Massy Pieces of
  plate". Silver Furnishings in the English
  Royal Palaces 1660–1702', *Apollo*, CLX,
  pp. 19–26
Winternitz 1966
  E. Winternitz, *Musical Instruments of the
  Western World*, London
Wittkower 1952
  R. Wittkower, *The Drawings of the Carracci
  in the Collection of Her Majesty The Queen at
  Windsor Castle*, London
Wollaston 1978
  H. Wollaston, *British Official Medals for
  Coronations and Jubilees*, Long Eaton
Wood 1994
  L. Wood, *The Lady Lever Art Gallery:
  Catalogue of Commodes*, London
Worsley 1993
  G. Worsley, 'Out of Adam's Shadow',
  Country Life, 14 May, pp. 101–2
Young 1771
  A. Young, *The Farmer's Tour through the
  East of England*, 4 vols., London

Concordances

a) With Royal Collection Inventory Number (RCIN)

RCIN	NO.	RCIN	NO.	RCIN	NO.	RCIN	NO.	RCIN	NO.
		25067	464	43768	432	51843.1–2	339	61078	308
		25073	463	43770	433	51848.1–4	330	63759	293
45.1–2	292	25075	460	43776	435	51908.1–3	352	65177	423
148.7	265	25078	467	43796–7	404	51918.1–3	351	65178	424
252	267	25086	465	43798–9	405	52211	441	65219	426
489.1	477	25087	73	43884	395	52214	445	65231	427
725	273	25094	471	43892	392	52228	446	65235	428
1141.1–2	282	25098	461	45115	285	53002.1	318	65429	442
1142.2, .4	282	25156	472	45126	59	53050.1	318	65525	401
1366	264	25234	459	45759	314	53107.1	77	65531	416
1391	256	25373	468	45777.1	315	53333.1–2	70	65600	421
2358.1–2	327	25375	470	45778–80	315	54421	71	65734.1–3	406
2475.1–2	284	25402	466	46707	400	55180.1–10	407	65779	58
2571	268	25438	462	47392	367	55181.1–5	408	65800	451
2587.2	272	28728.1–2	290	48482	474	55429	279	65817	422
2751	299	30028	277	48656	383	57012.2–3	309	65828	436
2752	305	30035	298	49122	377	57013.1	309	65829	438
2754	297	30261	304	49128	368	57014.2	309	65830	437
2821	302	30808	306	49148.1–2	334	57017.2a–b,	309	65838	434
2827	303	31035.1–2	326	49161.1–2	332	.3a–b		65858	425
2870	300	31182	274	49181.1–2	335	57022.1	309	65859	429
2914–15	310	31610	254	49568	391	57023.1	309	65869	430
3011	301	31614	253	49823	371	57024.6, .8,	309	65890	431
3683.1a–b	469	33445	255	49950	390	.28, .44, .48		67216	476
4198	410	33475.1–2	289	50582	357	57028	309	67239	475
4227	409	33958	412	50612	374	57850.1–2	283	69263	485
4434	295	33992	411	50616.1	347	58204.10, .25,	329	72173	324
4712	296	35255	252	50631.1	363	.41, .49, .57,		73111.a–b	319
6828.1–2	278	35291.1–2	288	50632.1	359	.62, .78, .91		73113	320
9005	399	35298.1–2	257	50639.1–2	344	58207.2	329	73294.a–b	321
9034	403	35301	258	50804.3–4	337	58208.1–2	329	73295	321
9162	394	35474	259	50805.1–2	336	58210.2	329	73297	321
9278	398	35487	269	50835.1–4	348	58211.1	329	90202	415
9322	386	35489	260	51034.a–d	387	58212.2	329	95588.4–5,	328
9323	356	35551	328	51051.1–2	360	58213.1, .4	329	.11, .18, .22, .28	
10806.1	479	35552	328	51059	342	58214.1, .4	329	95589.2, .9	328
10809.1	482	35553	328	51088	388	58215.1	329	95590.1–4, .7	328
10810.1	481	35554.4, .6	328	51235.1	343	58216.3	329	95592.2a–b	328
10818	480	35555.2, .6	328	51261.1–4	346	58218.1, .4	329	95593	328
10821.2	483	35556.2–3	328	51325.1–3	338	58406.6, .13	325	95595.2	328
10823	484	35557.1–2	328	51330.1	345	58407.17, .34	325	95596.2	328
10922	411	35559	83	51345.1–3	375	58408.1	325	95598.2	328
11109	270	35560	83	51485	389	58409.1	325	95599.1	328
11197.1–2	478	35561	83	51487	333	58413.2	325	95600.2	328
11886	322	35563.1	83	51576	369	58415.1	325	95601.1	328
11894	261	35564.1	83	51614.1–2	341	58417.1, .3–4	325	95602.1	328
11896	262	35603.1a, .2b	329	51615.1–2	358	58419.2	325	95603.4	328
11912	457	36000.1–2	271	51638.1–2	373	58420.1	325	95604.1	328
11944	385	36174.a–b	316	51639.1–2	372	58421.1–2	325	95605	328
11962	322	37017	286	51671.1–2	361	58422.1–2	325	96001	195
11968.3a–b	322	37020	312	51672.1–6	331	58423.1	325	96002	196
20701	291	37021	311	51677.1–2	340	58432.3	325	96003–4	197
21219.1–2	280	37022	313	51683.1–6	349	58433.1	325	96005	198
21220	280	37085	417	51687.1–2	364	58434.1, .5–6	325	96006	199
21235.3–4	263	37108	418	51694.1	362	58435.1–2, .4	325	96007	200
21668.1–2	276	37120	414	51722.1–3	350	58437.1	325	96008	201
21669.1–2	275	37129	413	51741	376	58461.1	323	96009	202
23058	402	39228	266	51833.1–2	366	58469	323	96010	203
25063	458	39882.3	317	51841.1–2	365	58470.2	323	96011–12	204

100014	393	403029	148	420789	41	700895	142	1057400–3	236
100201.1–2	281	403030	149	420791	39	702947.a	121	1057904	213
100204.1	281	403525	157	420925	44	702947.s	122	1057923	214
100226	370	404334	6	420930	42	734032	211	1058008–9	235
100227	397	404405	155	420955	32	808991.a–c	243	1058010	229
100229.1–3	353	404434	160	420965	30	809364.a	215	1058715–16	221
100230.1–3	354	404558	162	420969	43	816785	61	1071086	208
100231.1–3	355	404762	156	420970	38	816786	62	1073037	223
100232.1–2	378	405071	9	420972	78	816795	63	1076265	245
100232.3–4	379	405072	8	421016	29	970323	170	1076266	246
100232.5–6	380	405073	145	421019	25	1005032	473	1076267	242
100232.7–8	381	405307	3	421024	52	1023360–2	237	1076269	220
100232.9	382	405340	154	421346	22	1023375	207	1079104	238
100233	396	405416	158	421851	23	1027838–9	239	1079266–8	226
100234	384	405743	143	421921	50	1027878	206	1079936–8	233
400146	4	406348	163	421947	34	1028731–40	230	1081256	247
400167	13	406983	161	421971	45	1029395–405	222	1082188–9	232
400168	12	420000	31	422280	444	1047478	219	1087907	210
400501	7	420001	49	422283	443	1047678.ar	82	1101143	205
400524	146	420003	53	440021	452	1047678.f,	81	1120175–7	249
400555	175	420004	35	440035	453	.o, .w, .ad, .aq		1121304	227
400582	174	420184	24	441144	440	1047678.h,	79	1121797–802	240
400685	152	420185	27	441147	439	.k, .ag, .ai, .aj,		1123772–80	250
400687	153	420220	54	443290	447	.ak, .as		1140706	248
400714	147	420647	48	443291	448	1047678.al	420	1141306	244
400747	159	420648	51	443292	449	1047678.am	419	1141308	241
400750	164	420649	37	443305	456	1047678.ap	80	1145267.a	212
400892	2	420650	40	443306	455	1047769–84	224	1150276	87
400897	1	420651	46	443312	454	1050566	217	1150780	209
400965	165	420652	55	443316	450	1051976	251		
401004	10	420656	26	452805	5	1052122	234		
401036	144	420657	33	503056	119	1055305–6	231		
401274	151	420785	47	604349	20	1055395	228		
401275	150	420786	28	604491	125	1055396–9	225		
401407	11	420788	36	604595	21	1057372	218		

b) With RL numbers (for drawings and watercolours)

RL	NO.								
		12922	190	22097	127	22141	111	30364	89
		13852	18	22099	130	22142	112	33560	307
0698	184	13861	16	22100	131	22143	114	K 93	57
01155	176	13864	14	22101	132	22144	116	K 206	56
01251	177	13865	15	22102	133	22145	113	K 299	60
357	182	14246	19	22103	134	22147	117	K 303	65
1798	181	14247	17	22105	129	22148	102	K 341	75
2515	186	14649	99	22109	128	22155	104	K 369	84
2762	187	14666	101	22115	135	22158	103	K 380	68
3461	169	14711	120	22118	136	22161	105	K 384	67
3894	171	14712	123	22119	139	23785	180	K 388	69
4091	185	14715	100	22120	140	24812	86	K 414	66
6084	188	14729	193	22121	137	24829	191	K 435	94
6470	189	17354	74	22122	138	26084	192	K 447	92
7098	172	17643a	95	22123	141	26331	115	K 515	72
7134	173	17942	88	22124	106	26527	97	K 613	76
7437	178	17948	124	22126	107	26530	98	K 1149	64
7539	179	18690	96	22137	108	27999	194	K 1419	93
7563	179	21156	166	22138	110	29705	90		
8249	183	21175	167	22139	109	30264	91		
12751	168	22096	126	22140	118	30311	85		

c) With miscellaneous references

St George's Chapel	287
RA GEO/15794–5	294
RA GEO/Add. 32/2020–21	216

Family Trees

TABLE I HANOVER

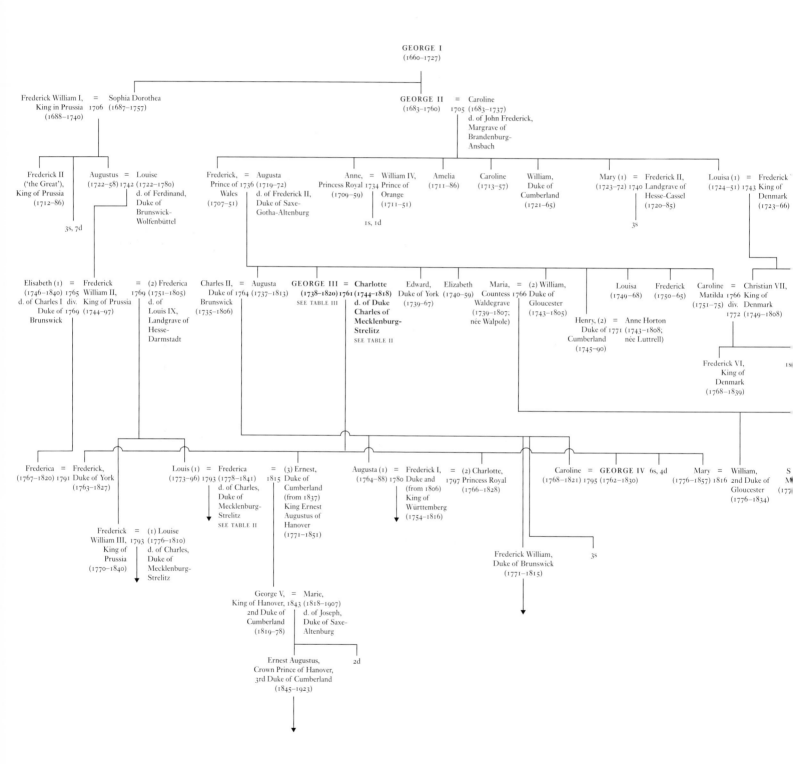

GEORGE I
(1660–1727)

Frederick William I, = Sophia Dorothea
King in Prussia 1706 (1687–1757)
(1688–1740)

GEORGE II = Caroline
(1683–1760) 1705 (1683–1737)
d. of John Frederick,
Margrave of
Brandenburg-
Ansbach

Frederick II = Augustus = Louise
('the Great'), (1722–58) 1742 (1722–1780)
King of Prussia d. of Ferdinand,
(1712–86) Duke of
Brunswick-
Wolfenbüttel

3s, 7d

Frederick, = Augusta
Prince of 1736 (1719–72)
Wales d. of Frederick II,
(1707–51) Duke of Saxe-
Gotha-Altenburg

Anne, = William IV,
Princess Royal 1734 Prince of
(1709–59) Orange
(1711–51)

1s, 1d

Amelia
(1711–86)

Caroline
(1713–57)

William,
Duke of
Cumberland
(1721–65)

Mary (1) = Frederick II,
(1723–72) 1740 Landgrave of
Hesse-Cassel
(1720–85)

3s

Louisa (1) = Frederick
(1724–51) 1743 King of
Denmark
(1723–66)

Elisabeth (1) = Frederick = (2) Frederica
(1746–1840) 1765 William II, d. of
d. of Charles I div. King of Prussia 1769 Louis IX,
Duke of 1769 (1744–97) Landgrave of
Brunswick Hesse-
Darmstadt

Charles II, = Augusta
Duke of 1764 (1737–1813)
Brunswick
(1735–1806)

GEORGE III = **Charlotte**
(1738–1820) 1761 (1744–1818)
SEE TABLE III **d. of Duke**
Charles of
Mecklenburg-
Strelitz
SEE TABLE II

Edward,
Duke of York
(1739–67)

Elizabeth
(1740–59)

Maria, = (2) William,
Countess 1766 Duke of
Waldegrave Gloucester
(1739–1807; (1743–1805)
née Walpole)

Henry, (2) = Anne Horton
Duke of 1771 (1743–1808;
Cumberland née Luttrell)
(1745–90)

Louisa
(1749–68)

Frederick
(1750–65)

Caroline = Christian VII
Matilda 1766 King of
(1751–75) div. Denmark
1772 (1749–1808)

Frederick VI,
King of
Denmark
(1768–1839)

Frederica = Frederick,
(1767–1820) 1791 Duke of York
(1763–1827)

Louis (1) = Frederica = (3) Ernest,
(1773–96) 1793 (1778–1841) 1815 Duke of
d. of Charles, Cumberland
Duke of (from 1837)
Mecklenburg- King Ernest
Strelitz Augustus of
SEE TABLE II Hanover
(1771–1851)

Augusta (1) = Frederick I, = (2) Charlotte,
(1764–88) 1780 Duke and 1797 Princess Royal
(from 1806) (1766–1828)
King of
Württemberg
(1754–1816)

Caroline = **GEORGE IV** 6s, 4d
(1768–1821) 1795 (1762–1830)

Mary = William,
(1776–1857) 1816 2nd Duke of
Gloucester
(1776–1834)

S
M
(177

Frederick = (1) Louise
William III, 1793 (1776–1810)
King of d. of Charles,
Prussia Duke of
(1770–1840) Mecklenburg-
Strelitz

Frederick William,
Duke of Brunswick
(1771–1815)

3s

George V, = Marie,
King of Hanover, 1843 (1818–1907)
2nd Duke of d. of Joseph,
Cumberland Duke of Saxe-
(1819–78) Altenburg

Ernest Augustus, 2d
Crown Prince of Hanover,
3rd Duke of Cumberland
(1845–1923)

TABLE II MECKLENBURG-STRELITZ

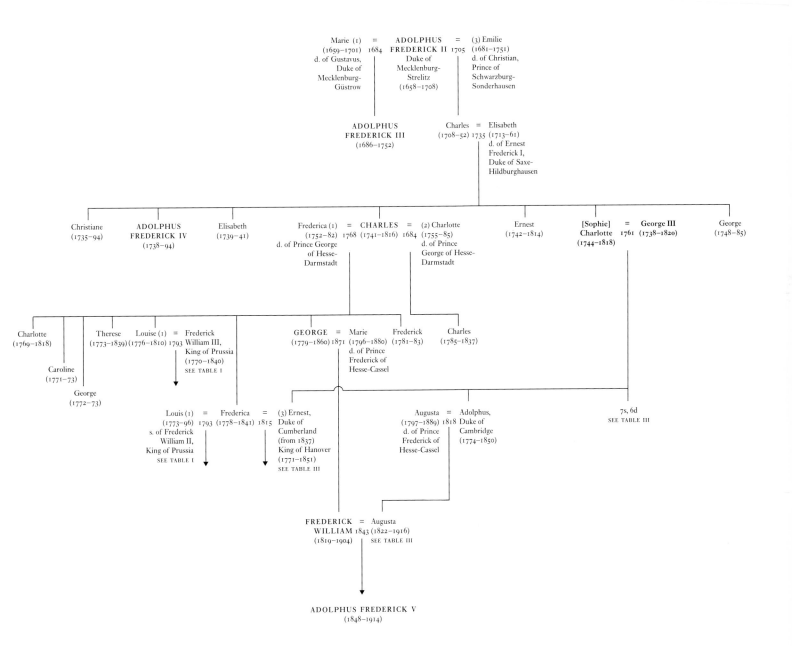

Marie (1) = **ADOLPHUS** = (3) Emilie
(1659–1701) 1684 **FREDERICK II** 1705 (1681–1751)
d. of Gustavus, Duke of d. of Christian,
Duke of Mecklenburg- Prince of
Mecklenburg- Strelitz Schwarzburg-
Güstrow (1658–1708) Sonderhausen

ADOLPHUS
FREDERICK III
(1686–1752)

Charles = Elisabeth
(1708–52) 1735 (1713–61)
d. of Ernest
Frederick I,
Duke of Saxe-
Hildburghausen

Christiane **ADOLPHUS** Elisabeth Frederica (1) = **CHARLES** = (2) Charlotte Ernest [Sophie] = **George III** George
(1735–94) **FREDERICK IV** (1739–41) (1752–82) 1768 (1741–1816) 1684 (1755–85) (1742–1814) **Charlotte** 1761 (1738–1820) (1748–85)
(1738–94) d. of Prince George d. of Prince (1744–1818)
of Hesse- George of Hesse-
Darmstadt Darmstadt

Charlotte Therese Louise (1) = Frederick **GEORGE** = Marie Frederick Charles 7s, 6d
(1769–1818) (1773–1839) (1776–1810) 1793 William III, (1779–1860) 1871 (1796–1880) (1781–83) (1785–1837) SEE TABLE III
King of Prussia d. of Prince
Caroline (1770–1840) Frederick of
(1771–73) SEE TABLE I Hesse-Cassel

George
(1772–73)

Louis (1) = Frederica = (3) Ernest, Augusta = Adolphus,
(1773–96) 1793 (1778–1841) 1815 Duke of (1797–1889) 1818 Duke of
s. of Frederick Cumberland d. of Prince Cambridge
William II, (from 1837) Frederick of (1774–1850)
King of Prussia King of Hanover Hesse-Cassel
SEE TABLE I (1771–1851)
SEE TABLE III

FREDERICK = Augusta
WILLIAM 1843 (1822–1916)
(1819–1904) SEE TABLE III

ADOLPHUS FREDERICK V
(1848–1914)

401

TABLE III GEORGE III AND QUEEN CHARLOTTE

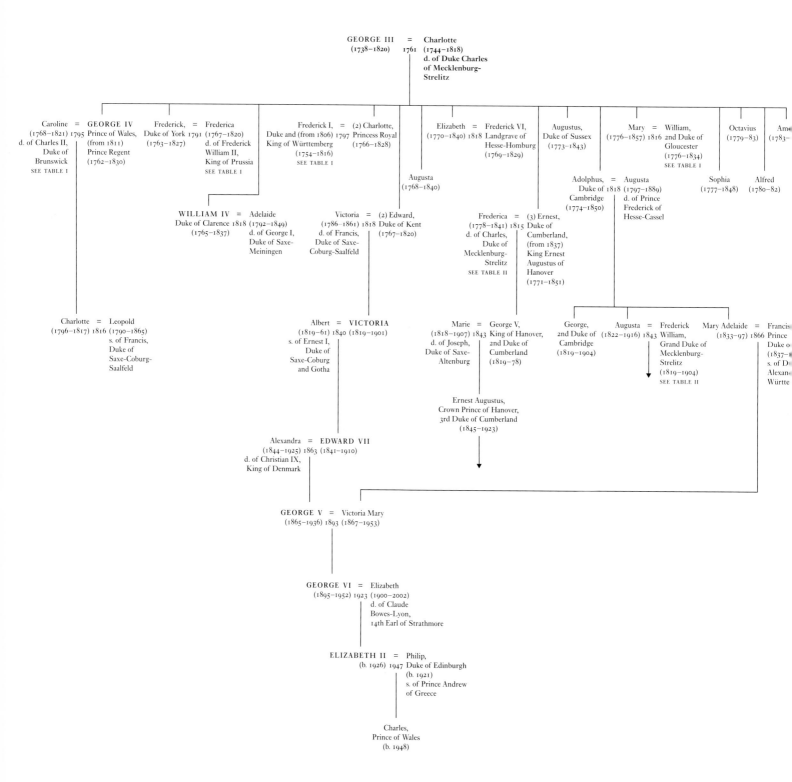

GEORGE III = Charlotte
(1738–1820) 1761 (1744–1818)
d. of Duke Charles
of Mecklenburg-
Strelitz

Caroline = GEORGE IV
(1768–1821) 1795 Prince of Wales,
d. of Charles II, (from 1811)
Duke of Prince Regent
Brunswick (1762–1830)
SEE TABLE I

Frederick, = Frederica
Duke of York 1791 (1767–1820)
(1763–1827) d. of Frederick
William II,
King of Prussia
SEE TABLE I

Frederick I, = (2) Charlotte,
Duke and (from 1806) 1797 Princess Royal
King of Württemberg (1766–1828)
(1754–1816)
SEE TABLE I

Augusta
(1768–1840)

Elizabeth = Frederick VI,
(1770–1840) 1818 Landgrave of
Hesse-Homburg
(1769–1829)

Augustus,
Duke of Sussex
(1773–1843)

Mary = William,
(1776–1857) 1816 2nd Duke of
Gloucester
(1776–1834)
SEE TABLE I

Octavius
(1779–83)

Ame
(1783–

WILLIAM IV = Adelaide
Duke of Clarence 1818 (1792–1849)
(1765–1837) d. of George I,
Duke of Saxe-
Meiningen

Victoria = (2) Edward,
(1786–1861) 1818 Duke of Kent
d. of Francis, (1767–1820)
Duke of Saxe-
Coburg-Saalfeld

Frederica = (3) Ernest,
(1778–1841) 1815 Duke of
d. of Charles, Cumberland,
Duke of (from 1837)
Mecklenburg- King Ernest
Strelitz Augustus of
SEE TABLE II Hanover
(1771–1851)

Adolphus, = Augusta
Duke of 1818 (1797–1889)
Cambridge d. of Prince
(1774–1850) Frederick of
Hesse-Cassel

Sophia
(1777–1848)

Alfred
(1780–82)

Charlotte = Leopold
(1796–1817) 1816 (1790–1865)
s. of Francis,
Duke of
Saxe-Coburg-
Saalfeld

Albert = VICTORIA
(1819–61) 1840 (1819–1901)
s. of Ernest I,
Duke of
Saxe-Coburg
and Gotha

Marie = George V,
(1818–1907) 1843 King of Hanover,
d. of Joseph, 2nd Duke of
Duke of Saxe- Cumberland
Altenburg (1819–78)

George,
2nd Duke of
Cambridge
(1819–1904)

Augusta = Frederick
(1822–1916) 1843 William,
Grand Duke of
Mecklenburg-
Strelitz
(1819–1904)
SEE TABLE II

Mary Adelaide = Francis
(1833–97) 1866 Prince
Duke o
(1837–
s. of D
Alexan
Württe

Ernest Augustus,
Crown Prince of Hanover,
3rd Duke of Cumberland
(1845–1923)

Alexandra = EDWARD VII
(1844–1925) 1863 (1841–1910)
d. of Christian IX,
King of Denmark

GEORGE V = Victoria Mary
(1865–1936) 1893 (1867–1953)

GEORGE VI = Elizabeth
(1895–1952) 1923 (1900–2002)
d. of Claude
Bowes-Lyon,
14th Earl of Strathmore

ELIZABETH II = Philip,
(b. 1926) 1947 Duke of Edinburgh
(b. 1921)
s. of Prince Andrew
of Greece

Charles,
Prince of Wales
(b. 1948)

Index

References are to page numbers. Italic references are to pages with illustrations – other than illustrations of catalogued items.

Acknowledgements and list of contributors

A large number of people have assisted in the preparation of this volume, which would not have been possible without the scholarly contributions – over many years – of Sir Geoffrey de Bellaigue and Sir Oliver Millar, now Royal Collection Surveyors Emeritus. Particular thanks are due to the authors of Royal Collection *catalogues raisonnés*, including those responsible for volumes which are currently in production (Dr Kirsten Aschengreen Piacenti and Sir John Boardman, Mr John Ayers, Dr Yolande Hodson, Mrs Henrietta Ryan).

The following have also provided valuable assistance: Reinier Baarsen, Peter Barber, Laurence Brown, Alec Cobbe, Claire Daly, Aileen Dawson, Scott Furlong, Dominic Gwynn, Eileen Harris, John Harris, Anthony Hobson, Nigel Israel, Jenny Knight, Véronique Lafage, Tony Littlechild, James Payne, Matthew Payne, Sue Pinel, Margaret Richardson, Alastair Rowan, Francis Russell, Robert Skelton, Hans Sonntag, Susan Stronge, Prudence Sutcliffe, David Watkin, Debbie Wayment, Friederike Weis, Annabel Westman, Rosamonde Williams.

And, within the Royal Household: Karen Ashworth, Julia Bagguley, Robert Ball, Anthony Barrett, Al Brewer, Paul Briggs, Jo Brooks, Dominic Brown, Perry Bruce-Mitford, Simona Brusa, Irene Campden, Juliet Carey, Heather Caven, Stephen Chapman, Claire Chorley, Julian Clare, Jacky Colliss Harvey, Siân Cooksey, Jean Cozens, Paul Cradock, Steven Davidson, Caroline de Guitaut, Allison Derrett, Alan Donnithorne, Frances Dunkels, Gemma Entwistle, Rupert Featherstone, Michael Field, Rhian Glover, Gay Hamilton, Henrietta Hudson, Adelaide Izat, Kathryn Jones, Jill Kelsey, Annaleigh Kennard, Roderick Lane, Karen Lawson, Marie Leahy, Simon Metcalf, Paul Miller, Theresa-Mary Morton, Stephen Murray, Elaine Pammenter, Daniel Partridge, Shruti Patel, David Rankin-Hunt, Janice Sacher, Rosanna de Sancha, Stephen Sheasby, Adrian Smith, James Smith, Stuart Stacey, Kate Stone, Nicola Swash, Richard Thompson, Shaun Turner, David Westwood, Margaret Westwood, David Wheeler, Paul Whybrew, Eva Zielinska-Millar.

We are most grateful to the Dean and Canons of Windsor for agreeing to the inclusion of Henry Emlyn's chairs (no. 287) in this exhibition.

Contributors

BW   BRIDGET WRIGHT (Bibliographer)

CL   CHRISTOPHER LLOYD (Surveyor of The Queen's Pictures)

ES   EMMA STUART (Assistant Bibliographer)

HR   HUGH ROBERTS (Director of the Royal Collection and Surveyor of The Queen's Works of Art)

JM   JONATHAN MARSDEN (Deputy Surveyor of The Queen's Works of Art)

JR   JANE ROBERTS (Librarian and Curator of the Print Room)

KB   KATHRYN BARRON (Assistant Curator, Paintings, and Loans Officer)

LW   LUCY WHITAKER (Assistant Surveyor of The Queen's Pictures)

MC   MARTIN CLAYTON (Deputy Curator of the Print Room)

MW   MATTHEW WINTERBOTTOM (Research Assistant, Works of Art)

PC   PAMELA CLARK (Registrar, Royal Archives)

SO   SUSAN OWENS (Assistant Curator of the Print Room)

SP   STEPHEN PATTERSON (Computer Systems Manager)

PORTRAITS: OILS, PASTELS, DRAWINGS AND PRINTS (nos. 1–21)
SO (nos. 1–2, 5, 14–21); LW (nos. 3–4, 7–11); KB (nos. 6, 12–13)

MINIATURES (nos. 22–55)
CL

ROYAL ART (nos. 56–84)
JR (nos. 56–7, 73, 82); MW (no. 58); HR (nos. 59, 71, 77); SO (nos. 60–69, 72, 74–6, 79–81, 84); JM (nos. 70, 83); CL (no. 78)

THE KING AND HIS ARCHITECTS (nos. 85–101)
JR

THE ROYAL RESIDENCES (nos. 102–42)
JR

PAINTINGS (nos. 143–65)
LW (nos. 143–7, 154, 156, 159–61, 164); KB (nos. 148–53, 155, 157–8, 162–3, 165)

DRAWINGS, WATERCOLOURS AND GOUACHES (nos. 166–94)
SO (nos. 166–7, 191–2); MC (Introduction and nos. 168–9, 171–90); ES (no. 170); JR (nos. 193, 194)

BOOKS AND BINDING (nos. 195–251)
ES (Introduction and nos. 195–208, 210, 212–15, 220–51); JR (nos. 209, 211, 215–16); PC (no. 216); BW (nos. 217–19)

SCULPTURE (nos. 252–6)
JM

FURNITURE (nos. 257–92)
MW (nos. 257–8); HR (nos. 259–61, 263–92); JM (no. 262)

TIME-KEEPING AND SCIENCE (nos. 293–308)
MW (nos. 293–6, 308); HR (nos. 297–307)

CERAMICS (nos. 309–29)
JM

SILVER-GILT (nos. 330–91)
MW

OBJETS DE VERTU (nos. 392–420)
MW (nos. 392–416); JM (nos. 417–18); JR (nos. 419–20)

GEMS, JEWELS AND MEDALS (nos. 421–56)
HR (nos. 421–38); SP (nos. 439–40); MW (nos. 441–6); JM (Medals Introduction and nos. 447–56)

TEXTILES AND FANS (nos. 457–72)
HR (no. 457); JR (nos. 458–72)

THE WIDER WORLD (nos. 473–85)
JR (no. 473); JM (nos. 474–85)